OXFORD LIBRARY OF PSYCHOLOGY

Editor in Chief PETER E. NATHAN
Area Editor STEVE W. J. KOZLOWSKI

The Oxford Handbook of Organizational Socialization

Edited by

Connie R. Wanberg

OXFORD
UNIVERSITY PRESS

OXFORD
UNIVERSITY PRESS

Oxford University Press, Inc., publishes works that further
Oxford University's objective of excellence in
research, scholarship, and education.

Oxford   New York
Auckland   Cape Town   Dar es Salaam   Hong Kong   Karachi
Kuala Lumpur   Madrid   Melbourne   Mexico City   Nairobi
New Delhi   Shanghai   Taipei   Toronto

With offices in
Argentina   Austria   Brazil   Chile   Czech Republic   France   Greece
Guatemala   Hungary   Italy   Japan   Poland   Portugal   Singapore
South Korea   Switzerland   Thailand   Turkey   Ukraine   Vietnam

Published by Oxford University Press, Inc.
198 Madison Avenue, New York, New York 10016
www.oup.com

Oxford is a registered trademark of Oxford University Press

Library of Congress Cataloging-in-Publication Data
The Oxford handbook of organizational socialization/edited by Connie R. Wanberg.
    p. cm. — (Oxford library of psychology)
  ISBN-13: 978–0–19–976367–2
  ISBN-10: 0–19–976367–4
  1. Adjustment (Psychology)   2. Socialization.   3. Organizational behavior.   I. Wanberg, Connie.
BF335.O94 2012
302.3'5—dc23
2011047728

9 8 7 6 5 4 3 2
Printed in the United States of America
on acid-free paper

The Oxford Handbook of
Organizational Socialization

OXFORD LIBRARY OF PSYCHOLOGY

SHORT CONTENTS

The *Oxford Library of Psychology,* a landmark series of handbooks, is published by Oxford University Press, one of the world's oldest and most highly respected publishers, with a tradition of publishing significant books in psychology. The ambitious goal of the *Oxford Library of Psychology* is nothing less than to span a vibrant, wide-ranging field and, in so doing, to fill a clear market need.

Encompassing a comprehensive set of handbooks, organized hierarchically, the *Library* incorporates volumes at different levels, each designed to meet a distinct need. At one level are a set of handbooks designed broadly to survey the major subfields of psychology; at another are numerous handbooks that cover important current focal research and scholarly areas of psychology in depth and detail. Planned as a reflection of the dynamism of psychology, the *Library* will grow and expand as psychology itself develops, thereby highlighting significant new research that will impact on the field. Adding to its accessibility and ease of use, the *Library* will be published in print and, later on, electronically.

The *Library* surveys psychology's principal subfields with a set of handbooks that capture the current status and future prospects of those major subdisciplines. This initial set includes handbooks of social and personality psychology, clinical psychology, counseling psychology, school psychology, educational psychology, industrial and organizational psychology, cognitive psychology, cognitive neuroscience, methods and measurements, history, neuropsychology, personality assessment, developmental psychology, and more. Each handbook undertakes to review one of psychology's major subdisciplines with breadth, comprehensiveness, and exemplary scholarship. In addition to these broadly conceived volumes, the *Library* also includes a large number of handbooks designed to explore in depth more specialized areas of scholarship and research, such as stress, health and coping, anxiety and related disorders, cognitive development, or child and adolescent assessment. In contrast to the broad coverage of the subfield handbooks, each of these latter volumes focuses on an especially productive, more highly focused line of scholarship and research. Whether at the broadest or most specific level, however, all of the *Library* handbooks offer synthetic coverage that reviews and evaluates the relevant past and present research and anticipates research in the future. Each handbook in the *Library* includes introductory and concluding chapters written by its editor to provide a roadmap to the handbook's table of contents and to offer informed anticipations of significant future developments in that field.

An undertaking of this scope calls for handbook editors and chapter authors who are established scholars in the areas about which they write. Many of the nation's and world's most productive and best-respected psychologists have agreed to edit *Library* handbooks or write authoritative chapters in their areas of expertise.

For whom has the *Oxford Library of Psychology* been written? Because of its breadth, depth, and accessibility, the *Library* serves a diverse audience, including graduate students in psychology and their faculty mentors, scholars, researchers, and practitioners in psychology and related fields. Each will find in the *Library* the information they seek on the subfield or focal area of psychology in which they work or are interested.

Befitting its commitment to accessibility, each handbook includes a comprehensive index, as well as extensive references to help guide research. And because the *Library* was designed from its inception as an online as well as a print resource, its structure and contents will be readily and rationally searchable online. Further, once the *Library* is released online, the handbooks will be regularly and thoroughly updated.

In summary, the *Oxford Library of Psychology* will grow organically to provide a thoroughly informed perspective on the field of psychology, one that reflects both psychology's dynamism and its increasing interdisciplinarity. Once published electronically, the *Library* is also destined to become a uniquely valuable interactive tool, with extended search and browsing capabilities. As you begin to consult this handbook, we sincerely hope you will share our enthusiasm for the more than 500-year tradition of Oxford University Press for excellence, innovation, and quality, as exemplified by the *Oxford Library of Psychology.*

Peter E. Nathan
Editor-in-Chief
Oxford Library of Psychology

ABOUT THE EDITOR

Connie R. Wanberg

Connie R. Wanberg is the Industrial Relations Faculty Excellence Chair and Associate Dean of Undergraduate Programs at the Carlson School of Management at the University of Minnesota. She received her PhD in Industrial/Organizational Psychology from Iowa State University. Her research has been focused on the individual experience of unemployment, job-search behavior, organizational change, employee socialization, and employee development.

CONTRIBUTORS

Sue Ashford
Ross School of Business
University of Michigan
Ann Arbor, MI

Blake E. Ashforth
Department of Management
W.P. Carey School of Business
Arizona State University
Tempe, AZ

Talya N. Bauer
School of Business Administration
Portland State University
Portland, OR

George B. Bradt
PrimeGenesis Executive Onboarding and
    Transition Acceleration
Stamford, CT

Sarah E. Burke
OPRA Consulting Group and Victoria
    University at Wellington
Wellington, New Zealand

Yongjun Choi
Carlson School of Management
University of Minnesota
Minneapolis, MN

Jay A. Conger
Kravis Leadership Institute
Claremont McKenna College
Claremont, CA

Helena D. Cooper-Thomas
Department of Psychology
The University of Auckland
Auckland, New Zealand

Angelo S. DeNisi
A. B. Freeman School of Business
Tulane University
New Orleans, LA

Irene E. De Pater
University of Amsterdam
Department of Work and Organizational
    Psychology

Amsterdam, The Netherlands

Pamela M. Dixon
Director of Research and Assessment
Menttium Corporation
Richfield, MN

Stacy Doepner-Hove
Carlson School of Management
University of Minnesota
Minneapolis, MN

Berrin Erdogan
School of Business Administration
Portland State University
Portland, OR

Daniel C. Feldman
Terry College of Business
The University of Georgia
Athens, GA

Jamie A. Gruman
Department of Business
University of Guelph
Guelph, Ontario, Canada

Charlice Hurst
Ivey School of Business
University of Western Ontario
London, Ontario, Canada

Markku Jokisaari
Employment and Economic Development
    Office
Kotka, Finland

John Kammeyer-Mueller
Warrington College of Business
    Administration
University of Florida
Gainesville, FL

Howard J. Klein
Department of Management and Human
    Resources
Fisher College of Business
The Ohio State University
Columbus, OH

Geoffrey J. Leonardelli
Rotman School of Management
University of Toronto
Toronto, Ontario, Canada

Beth Livingston
School of Labor and Industrial Relations
Cornell University
Ithaca, NY

Jari-Erik Nurmi
Department of Psychology
University of Jyväskylä
Jyväskylä, Finland

Samir Nurmohamed
Ross School of Business
University of Michigan
Ann Arbor, MI

Beth Polin
Department of Management and Human
Resources
Fisher College of Business
The Ohio State University
Columbus, OH

Keith Rollag
Management Division
Babson College
Babson Park, MA

Alan M. Saks
Centre for Industrial Relations and Human
Resources
University of Toronto
Toronto, Ontario, Canada

Lynn P. Sontag
Chief Mentoring Officer and President
Menttium Corporation
Richfield, MN

Soo Min Toh
Rotman School of Management
University of Toronto
Toronto, Ontario, Canada

Jeffrey B. Vancouver
Department of Psychology
Ohio University
Athens, OH

Annelies E. M. van Vianen
University of Amsterdam
Department of Work and Organizational
Psychology
Amsterdam, The Netherlands

Kimberly Vappie
Chief Executive Officer
Menttium Corporation
Richfield, MN

Connie R. Wanberg
Industrial Relations Faculty Excellence
Chair
University of Minnesota
Minneapolis, MN

Michael A. Warren
Department of Psychology
Ohio University
Athens, OH

CONTENTS

PART 1

Introduction and Foundations

Facilitating Organizational Socialization: An Introduction

Connie R. Wanberg

Abstract

This handbook focuses on organizational socialization, or the process through which individuals acquire the knowledge, skills, attitudes, and behaviors required to adapt to a new work role. This chapter launches the handbook by defining *organizational socialization*, differentiating this term from the related concept of onboarding. The importance of organizational socialization is discussed, and the major sections and contributions of this handbook are outlined.

Key Words: organizational socialization, onboarding, new employees, employee adjustment, learning new jobs, expatriation, proactivity, work transitions, diversity

Organizational socialization is about new beginnings—individuals starting new jobs within an organizational context. This handbook comprehensively examines the organizational socialization process from a number of angles: why does it matter, what types of employees adapt most quickly, and what organizations, coworkers, and the new employees themselves can do to promote successful adjustment in a new job. There are two main purposes of this handbook: *(1)* to take stock of where the field is with respect to the knowledge and practice of new employee socialization, and *(2)* to stimulate ideas for future research and excellent practice in this area. Several thought leaders in the area of new socialization were invited to write chapters. The resulting volume takes an expansive view of organizational socialization, discussing a wide array of topics including organizational, individual, and coworker-related factors that facilitate new employee success, current socialization practices in companies today, and future research and practice needs.

Defining Organizational Socialization

For purposes of this handbook, organizational socialization is defined as the process through which individuals acquire the knowledge, skills, attitudes, and behaviors required to adapt to a new work role. Organizational socialization may pertain to a new employee beginning work at an organization (i.e., an organizational newcomer), or to an individual moving into a new role within the organization (i.e., a promotion, lateral transfer, expatriate assignment, etc.). Over the last decade, a new term, *onboarding*, has also entered the scene. The term *onboarding* has been particularly popular in practice-oriented outlets and organizations, such as the American Society for Training and Development and the Society for Human Resource Management (e.g., Derven, 2008; Skrzypinski, 2011). The emerging view is that the terms *onboarding* and *socialization* should be differentiated and that care should be taken that the two terms are not used interchangeably (e.g., see Klein & Polin, Chapter 14 of this volume).

A primary differentiation between onboarding and socialization is that onboarding is a narrower term. According to Klein and Polin, onboarding refers to the specific practices initiated by an organization or its agents to facilitate employee adjustment to new roles. These practices might include doing something to make the first day on the job feel special to the employee, providing a mentor for the newcomer, or clarifying roles and responsibilities (Bauer, 2010). Organizational socialization may also include onboarding, but furthermore more broadly encompasses the information seeking, learning, and other adaptation processes involved in socialization on the part of the newcomer. Socialization occurs *within* the newcomer and numerous factors, onboarding included, can influence that socialization. Hypothetically speaking, socialization could occur without any onboarding activities and onboarding activities could fail to assist socialization (Klein and Polin, this volume). Agreeing with this differentiation, Chao (in press) states that in contrast to the term *onboarding*, the term *organizational socialization* (a) captures the broader learning and adjustment processes that individuals go through when they adapt to a new role, and (b) includes efforts on the part of both the organization and the individual.

Organizational Socialization is Important

Do those first days on the job really matter? If so, how do they matter? Chapter 15 of this handbook begins with a story about a young woman on her first day of work. It is only midmorning before this young woman begins to question whether or not she made the right choice about taking her new job. From time to time, when I see these stories on newcomer socialization, I admit to thinking the socialization literature may be guilty of making much ado about nothing. To the new employee that is questioning her choice so quickly, I want to say: "Deal with it!" "Adapt and move on!" Yet, the empirical research (and practical experience) that we have at our disposal suggests that socialization, and first impressions, *do* matter.

First, from the newcomer's perspective, beginnings are not easy. Individuals face a great deal of uncertainty in their first few weeks and months in an organization. They may want to prove themselves and their worth, or they may merely want to make sure they keep their job. Individuals also have a high need to belong. It is sometimes difficult for a newcomer to break into existing employee networks and to feel at home in a new work group. Meta-analytic evidence suggests that the tactics that

an organization uses, as well as efforts on the part of the newcomers themselves, are related to higher levels of role clarity, social acceptance, and self-efficacy (Bauer, Bodner, Erdogan, Truxillo, & Tucker, 2007; Saks, Uggerslev, & Fassina, 2007). Higher role clarity, social acceptance, and self-efficacy are also related to higher job satisfaction, commitment, and intention on the part of the newcomer to remain with the organization (Bauer et al., 2007).

Effective socialization is also critical to the organization in a number of ways. The socialization tactics used by organizations, as well as proactivity on the part of the newcomer, have been associated with important organizational outcomes including job performance and turnover (Bauer et al., 2007; Saks et al., 2007). We are also learning more about how the first few weeks of an individual's experience with an organization shape newcomer attitudes and behaviors. Good experiences may result in good outcomes, which may lead to additional good experiences. For example, positive interactions with others in the work group, as well as receiving challenging assignments and information about one's job, foster "learning, confidence, and credibility, thereby paving the way for further growth opportunities and additional learning, confidence, and credibility" (Ashforth, Sluss, & Harrison, 2007, p.2).

Overall, research to date suggests that what organizations and individuals do in the organizational socialization process can make a big difference with respect to a variety of important outcomes including employee satisfaction, commitment, retention, and performance. This handbook will explore more deeply what we know about the socialization process, what current companies do well and might do better, and where we need more research.

Overview of this Handbook

Part One of this handbook (Introduction and Foundations) highlights a chapter by Sue Ashford and Samir Nurmohamed, titled "From Past to Present and Into the Future: A Hitchhiker's Guide to the Socialization Literature." This chapter is meant to be a fun "jump start" into the socialization literature. The chapter describes the progression of the socialization literature over time, major theoretical perspectives that have been used in socialization research, primary research questions in this area, and necessary next directions. Their hitchhiker's guide includes fun facts about the socialization literature (such as the most cited socialization article) and ends with a list of "Top Ten Socialization Reads."

Part Two of the handbook reviews what we know (based on previous literature) and still need to know (future research needs) about the antecedents and outcomes of successful newcomer adjustment. The practices that organizations use to socialize newcomers are reviewed by Saks and Gruman (Chapter 3). These authors conclude that the literature on organizational socialization practices is fragmented and underdeveloped, and introduce a valuable new framework (titled Socialization Resources Theory) to organize 17 resources that organizations should provide to enhance newcomer adjustment. A variety of proactive behaviors used by newcomers as they adapt to a new job are summarized by Cooper-Thomas and Burke in Chapter 4. Their extensive review covers positive and negative consequences of proactive behavior, characteristics of newcomers likely to engage in proactive behavior, patterns of change over time in proactive behavior, and future research needs in this area.

The importance of newcomers' social networks to the socialization experience is covered by Jokisaari and Nurmi in Chapter 5. Jokisaari and Nurmi make a compelling argument that socialization research has not sufficiently addressed the role of social networks. They propose a framework for examining how newcomer networks have significance for an array of important socialization outcomes including learning, sensemaking, and success in the organization. Finally, Bauer and Erdogan (Chapter 6) provide a comprehensive discussion of socialization outcomes, reviewing research that has shown how effective socialization, as indexed by acceptance by insiders, role clarity, and self-efficacy, is related to a wide array of important outcomes including job attitudes, job performance, and retention. Collectively, the authors contributing to this section put forth several new and stimulating ideas.

Part Three of the handbook addresses issues of person–organizational fit. In Chapter 7, Hurst, Kammeyer-Mueller, and Livingston address issues faced by new employees who are different from their coworkers with respect to three forms of diversity: separation (e.g., differences in opinion), variety (e.g., difference in knowledge), and disparity (e.g., differences in a socially valued asset such as being a member of a majority group). The authors integrate research from a variety of literatures to propose relationships between these forms of diversity and important socialization outcomes, including work group cohesion and newcomer retention. Their proposed model portrays individual (e.g., identity formation, proactivity) and interpersonal (e.g., support,

conflict, and exclusion) processes that are likely to mediate diversity/outcome relationships, as well as individual and organizational variables that may act as moderators. The authors of Chapter 8 (van Vianen and DePater) discuss person–organization fit from the perspective of congruence between the newcomer and the organization's culture. This chapter discusses what we know about changes in person–organization fit during the socialization process, and to what extent changes are due to changes in the person, the workplace, or both. The two chapters in this section provide excellent fodder for future research.

Part Four of the handbook includes two chapters focused on socialization dynamics, methods, and measurement. In Chapter 9, Ashforth makes a compelling argument that researchers need to better integrate the examination of time into socialization work. Within the chapter, a framework for explicating the various ways in which time plays a role in socialization is provided. The chapter is thought provoking, and creates a long list of research opportunities and prescriptions for improving our understanding of how newcomer learning and adjustment unfolds across time. Chapter 10, by Vancouver and Warren, is a valuable "go back to the basics" chapter. The chapter includes discussions of specific methodologies, as well as threats to validity associated with these methodologies. But rather than being a dull treatment of these issues, the chapter stimulates reflection on the limitations that are characteristic in socialization research and ways in which research designs can be improved or triangulated to counter these limitations.

Part Five of the handbook examines socialization "beyond the organizational newcomer." In Chapter 11, Daniel Feldman explores a myriad of ways in which the socialization process affects veteran (i.e., existing) employees. He argues, for example, that following the arrival of newcomers, current employees may be prompted to evaluate their own levels of career success and external marketability, as well as to contemplate whether their current employer has treated them fairly. Newcomers can also influence current employees' global views of the organization as well as the organization's values and priorities. Feldman describes how newcomers can influence current employees' receptivity to change and work group conflict levels, for the good or bad. In conclusion, he suggests that "understanding the impact of socialization on insiders is the next frontier for socialization research."

In Chapter 12, Toh, DeNisi, and Leonardelli address the socialization experience of employees who are assigned to do work for their companies overseas (expatriates). These authors pay particular attention to the role of host country nationals in facilitating the adjustment of expatriates to their new work environments. Their detailed review provides several excellent suggestions for facilitating expatriate socialization through paying more attention to the role of host country nationals, and delineates several opportunities for research in this area. Keith Rollag (Chapter 13) provides a fresh and new extension of socialization theory to the sphere of new customers. He argues that although several trends have amplified the extent to which companies must socialize newcomers, most organizations pay little attention to customer socialization. Rollag outlines several issues relevant to customer socialization, ranging from the layout of products, how signs and counters are used, and whether customers should be socialized as a group or individually. Finally, he provides case examples of how new customer socialization occurs in four companies, and suggests several directions for research in this area.

Part Six of the handbook, "Socialization in Practice," begins with a chapter by Howard Klein and Beth Polin. This chapter summarizes what we know, from an academic standpoint, about practices that (a) inform, (b) welcome, and (c) guide new hires. The authors then discuss the practitioner literature, identifying seven prevalent recommendations for best practices in socialization in this literature. Because these literatures do not sufficiently inform us about what practices companies are currently using to socialize employees, the authors also provide the results of a survey of 482 human resource professionals about their companies' socialization practices. The authors illustrate gaps in the academic literature and between what we know from research findings and what is recommended in the practice-based literature.

In Chapter 15, Stacy Doepner-Hove provides a clear and interesting account of the development of an onboarding program for the University of Minnesota. Her chapter begins with a committee's conclusion that the university's socialization practices were not up to par, and describes the creative and comprehensive recommendations and steps that were taken to develop an onboarding program at the university. The chapter is a valuable read for someone who must create an onboarding program, or for students wanting insight into one organization's approach to creating such a program. Chapter 16, by Jay Conger, discusses the socialization of individuals moving into higher level jobs within the same organization. This chapter notes that organizations tend to overlook the importance of socializing promoted individuals into their new roles. Two in-depth case studies are provided as examples of how organizations can use socialization programs for newly promoted individuals as a means of preempting leadership failures.

Chapters 17 and 18 are written by practitioners that consult with organizations to improve their onboarding practices. Chapter 17 is written by George Bradt, Managing Director of Prime Genesis, an executive onboarding and transition acceleration group. George is also author of *The New Leader's 100-Day Action Plan* (2009) and *Onboarding: How to Get Your New Employees Up to Speed in Half the Time* (2009). In this chapter, George points out mistakes that he has seen companies make with respect to socializing new employees, and stresses the need for hiring managers to take a proactive approach to new employee socialization. Bradt provides several suggestions for hiring managers to help new employees adjust, such as introducing new employees to important stakeholders (up, across, down; internal, external; cross-function, cross-region; etc.). Chapter 18 is authored by Dixon, Sontag, and Vappie of Menttium Corporation, a consulting group that provides cross-company and internal mentoring programs. This chapter describes what mentoring programs can contribute to the socialization experience of new employees and delineates how Menttium structures mentoring programs for newcomers.

Finally, Part Seven of this handbook includes a closing chapter by me and a colleague, Yongjun Choi. We provide a summary of necessary next directions for this field of research and also delineate general recommendations to researchers doing work in this area. Enjoy the handbook and good luck with your research and practice of employee socialization and onboarding!

References

Ashforth, B. E., Sluss, D. M., & Harrison, S. H. (2007). Socialization in organizational contexts. In G. P. Hodgkinson & J. K. Ford (Eds.), *International Review of Industrial and Organizational Psychology, 22,* 1–70. England, UK: John Wiley & Sons Ltd.

Bradt, G. B. and Vonnegut, M. G. (2009) *Onboarding: How to Get Your New Employees Up to Speed in Half the Time.* Hoboken, NJ: John Wiley & Sons.

Bradt, G. B., Check, J. A. and Pedraza, J. E. (2009) *The New Leader's 100-Day Action Plan.* Hoboken, NJ: John Wiley & Sons, Second Edition.

Bauer, T. N. (2010). Onboarding new employees: Maximizing success. *SHRM Foundation's Effective Practice Guideline Series.* SHRM. The report can be downloaded at http://www.shrm.org/about/foundation/products/Pages/OnboardingEPG.aspx.

Bauer, T. N., Bodner, T., Erdogan, B., Truxillo, D. M., & Tucker, J. S. (2007). Newcomer adjustment during organizational socialization: A meta-analytic review of antecedents, outcomes, and methods. *Journal of Applied Psychology, 92*, 707–721.

Chao, G. T. (in press). Organizational socialization: Background, basics, and a blueprint for adjustment and work. In S. W. J. Kozlowski (Ed.), *The Oxford Handbook of Organizational Psychology.* New York: Oxford University Press.

Derven, M. (2008, April). Management Onboarding: Obtain early allegiance to gain a strategic advantage in the war for talent. *American Society for Training & Development,* 48–52.

Klein, H. J., & Heuser, A. E. (2008). The learning of socialization content: A framework for researching orientating practices. In J. J. Martocchio (Ed.), *Research in Personnel and Human Resources Management, 27,* 279–336. Bingley, United Kingdom: Emerald Group.

Saks, A. M., Uggerslev, K. L., & Fassina, N. E. (2007). Socialization tactics and newcomer adjustment: A meta-analytic review and test of a model. *Journal of Vocational Behavior, 70,* 413–446.

Skrzypinski, C. (2011, April 13). *SHRM study: Most organizations provide orientation to new hires.* Retrieved from www.shrm.org/hrdisciplines/orgempdev/articles/Pages/OnboardingSurvey.aspx.

From Past to Present and Into the Future: A Hitchhiker's Guide to the Socialization Literature

Sue Ashford *and* Samir Nurmohamed

Abstract

To navigate any universe, it helps to have a guide. This chapter takes readers on a lightning-fast journey through a nearly 40-year-old socialization literature that has generated many theoretical and empirical articles and become a core area of study in organizational behavior and human resource management. We visit the numerous theoretical perspectives and major questions (and answers) in the literature, comment on the different methodological approaches used to study socialization, and present ideas about future galaxies to be explored in subsequent research on socialization. We end our tour with our list of the "top 10" must reads in the socialization literature and some thoughts from an early explorer of this domain. We hope that our chapter provides a useful overview of research on socialization not only for individuals who are familiar with some of this work, but also for readers who are encountering it for the first time.

Key Words: socialization, proactivity, newcomers, adjustment, learning, identity, uncertainty

Forty Two. In the original, *The Hitchhiker's Guide to the Galaxy*, this simple, two-digit response from the supercomputer "deep thought" answered a group of "hyper-intelligent, pan-dimensional beings" seeking the ultimate answer to "The Ultimate Question of Life, the Universe and Everything" (Adams, 2002, p. 181). In our Hitchhiker's Guide to the Socialization Literature, the questions are a bit more modest and the answers, fortunately or unfortunately, far more complex and nuanced. Our intent is to provide an overview to those encountering the socialization literature for the first time, highlighting the theoretical perspectives that have been applied to socialization research, major questions raised, areas of emphasis in the literature, and opportunities for the future. We also provide a "Top 10" list of "must reads" in this literature for those starting their own galactic exploration and hoping to get up to speed quickly.

There is something inherently interesting about the socialization process. Perhaps it is because we all have gone through it at various times throughout our lives and can vividly remember the feelings of anxiety, hope, expectation, and joy that accompanied it. Perhaps it is because the importance of the process for organizations is so readily apparent. If people struggle to get started in new organizational roles, time is lost; if the process yields molded, committed employees who fit well with the organization and stay, efficiencies are gained. Or, perhaps it is the tensions inherent in the process that make it so intriguing. The contrast between the organization's desire to mold and shape individuals to gain efficiencies and organizational performance pressures that draw mentors' time and attention away from the effort; between the individual's desire to fit in and succeed, but also to maintain freedom and self-expression; or between the organization's desire for increased conformity to gain efficiency and its simultaneous need for innovation and flexibility. Whatever it is, the socialization literature has attracted scholars and research since the mid-1960s. Many theoretical ideas have been expressed, much data collected, and reviews and meta-analyses conducted. So strap on your seatbelts; our explorative overview of the galaxy of socialization now begins.

Boundaries of the Socialization Universe

First, a few definitional matters and boundary issues. The most cited definition of socialization describes it as the "process by which an individual acquires the social knowledge and skills necessary to assume an organizational role"(Van Maanen & Schein, 1979, p. 211). Their definition generalizes from an earlier definition that specified more clearly the social knowledge to be acquired as "the value system, the norms, and the required behavior patterns of an organization or group" (Schein, 1968, p. 2). Socialization occurs throughout an individual's career whenever boundaries are crossed, whether it be the boundary between the outside and inside of an organization (e.g., the boundary crossed by newcomers into a company), that defining a particular group within an organization (e.g., the boundary crossed when an employee is transferred into a new group within a company), or that between two levels within an organization (e.g., the boundary crossed when one is promoted Van Maanen & Schein, 1979). Thus, socialization is an ongoing issue for individuals, with greater and lesser intensity, throughout their work lives and an ongoing management problem for organizations as people are hired, moved from functional area to functional area, and promoted. Despite this thesis, Van Maanen and Schein's influential theory-based articulation of the tactics organizations use to socialize newcomers helped shape a literature that has clearly emphasized newcomer socialization over that associated with other transitions, and organizational activity over individuals' experiences in the process. Indeed, our frequent use of the label "newcomers" to indicate people being socialized or undergoing socialization keeps our focus on the entry period to the detriment of other transitions. Our emphasis on outcomes of importance to the organization, such as organizational commitment and performance, place other outcomes that may be of more importance to individuals, such as their anxiety and other affective experiences, in the background.

An important boundary question for our socialization literature pertains to socialization's beginning and end. When does socialization begin? Early stage models of socialization (e.g., Feldman, 1976, 1981) describe individuals' experiences as starting with an anticipatory stage that begins when an individual first connects to an organization (e.g., in an interview). Other writers refer back to the long-term socialization of a person entering an occupation or profession (Ashforth, Sluss, & Harrison, 2007). These authors would be concerned with all that happens in medical school, for example, whereas the former authors date the process's start to be when one is preparing for a specific organization or job (e.g., the doctor joining a specific medical practice). While occupational and professional socialization is clearly relevant, it expands the field dramatically. Parental and childhood socialization (whether one was raised in a high-income versus low-income household, for example) would also matter.

The end point is even trickier. Estimates regarding the duration of organizational socialization range from a matter of weeks (Bauer & Green, 1994), to 3–6 months (Feldman, 1977), 12 to 18 months (Bauer, Morrison, & Callister, 1998), and even as long as neverending, as employees are continually learning about how to contribute to their organizations (Harvey, Wheeler, Halbesleben, & Buckley, 2010). Though these estimates sometimes are based on the findings of individual studies, this point is far from established empirically—when can we say that someone has truly "learned the ropes"? However, construing organizational socialization as something that begins in childhood and continues throughout a person's entire tenure in an organization is a bit problematic. It also probably takes us beyond what most people would consider the bounds of what might appropriately be called *organizational behavior* (e.g., to the psychology of early childhood behavior). Some boundaries are needed. It makes sense to bound organizational socialization by the period in which a person anticipates a specific transition (of any of the types identified by Van Maanen and Schein in 1979) to a set period following. The continual learning that would occur after that point is probably more appropriately studied under the heading of "job performance or advancement predictors" or "learning" more generally, rather than socialization per se. If socialization becomes the study of learning over a lifetime, we lose something of the essence of the term.

This endpoint issue is inextricably linked to an additional boundary issue, that pertaining to the outcomes of socialization. Van Maanen and Schein's (1979) definition suggests that the outcomes of interest would be knowledge and skill acquisition. And yet, many influential models of socialization also include job satisfaction, organizational commitment, and intent to remain, as relevant, though more distal, outcomes (Bauer, Bodner, Erdogan, Truxillo, & Tucker, 2007; Bauer et al., 1998; Goethals, 1986; Wanberg & Kammeyer-Mueller, 2000). While clearly organizations hope for these outcomes as well, socialization as typically defined (i.e., as knowledge and skill acquisition), doesn't require them. For example, it is possible to find out all there is to know about a specific lousy job and to acquire sufficient skills to do it while also being very dissatisfied with the job and developing an intention to leave the organization. For now, the relevant point is that depending on which outcomes researchers have in mind, what would be considered the endpoint varies.

A Brief Timeline of the Socialization Galaxy

Despite the lexical emphasis in prominent definitions of socialization on the individual as the star of the process, early work had a decidedly organizational focus. Early socialization stage models (e.g., Feldman, 1976, 1981) describing individuals' experiences during anticipatory, encounter, and change/acquisition stages of socialization gave way to an emphasis on what organizations might do to bring about the outcomes organizations wished to see in the individuals they hired. Indeed, beyond the definition quoted above, the most lasting remnant of Van Maanen and Schein's (1979) early theoretical work in this area is their articulation of six tactics that organizations can use to socialize newcomers and longer-term employees to new positions. These tactics, as refined by Jones (1986), studied extensively (Allen & Meyer, 1990b; Ashforth et al., 2007; Cable & Parsons, 2001; Kim, Cable, & Kim, 2005), and subjected to meta-analyses (Bauer et al., 2007; Saks, Uggerslev, & Fassina, 2007) are a well-known and well-developed "planet" in the socialization galaxy. Findings suggest that organizations will enjoy different employee outcomes if they socialize their newcomers formally and collectively as opposed to informally and individually; in a fixed, specified sequence as opposed to more randomly; and when experienced members of the organization communicate, "we like you just as you are" versus providing no mentors and communicating that the newcomer must change to be acceptable (Ashforth et al., 2007; Saks et al., 2007). The first pattern (formal, collective, fixed, specified, serial, and investiture) is explicitly oriented to the newcomer's integration into the organization, whereas the opposite pattern leaves the newcomer essentially on his or her own. Institutionalized tactics have been associated with many positive outcomes (see Ashforth, et al., 2007

for a review); the individualized pattern is associated with greater role innovation (Allen & Meyer, 1990a; Baker, 1995).

Although the literature on organizational socialization tactics added much to our understanding of newcomer adjustment, it implicitly portrayed newcomers and job transitioners as somewhat passive and reactive in the process, when they actually can be agentic and proactive (Ashforth & Saks, 1996; Jones, 1983). It is not organizations alone that hold goals in the socialization process. Individuals too hope to get on board successfully, establish themselves relationally, create a positive image, and assess their fit with the new job setting. The second wave to go through the socialization galaxy (to mix metaphors horribly) was an increased emphasis on what individuals were experiencing and doing in the socialization process. This emphasis prompted interest in individuals' information and feedback seeking, relationship building, perspective framing, and network building (Ashforth & Saks, 1996; Morrison, 1993; Wanberg & Kammeyer-Mueller, 2000). More on findings here later.

More recently, a third wave of socialization research has taken shape that integrates organizational tactics and individual proactivity together. These studies take a person-by-situation approach to understanding the socialization process, by highlighting the importance of both the organization and individual. Many of these studies show how both individual dispositions and behaviors and broader organizational tactics are crucial to successful adjustment via their influence on more proximal outcomes such as task mastery, role clarity, and social acceptance (Bauer et al., 2007; Kammeyer-Mueller & Wanberg, 2003). We will discuss this integrated perspective in greater detail below.

Prominent Planets: Theoretical Perspectives

The socialization literature has "done theory" in a variety of ways. First, scholars have imported established theories or theoretical tenets from other topic areas in organizational behavior and other disciplines to gain insight into this specific process and context. Second, theories have been developed that pertain specifically to socialization. Van Maanen and Schein (1979), cited earlier, is a prominent exemplar of socialization-specific theorizing. Finally, this literature has also grown inductively with scholars developing logics for various hypotheses that are then tested with data from newcomers or job changers and incorporated as established theory in subsequent studies.

Fact Box 1 The Hitchhiker's Guide to the Galaxy (HHGTTG)

Author: Douglas Adams

Published in 1979

Sold 250,000 copies in its first 3 months

The book tells the story of hapless Englishman Arthur Dent, who travels the galaxy after being grabbed from Earth just before a galactic construction team annihilated the planet to build a freeway. After leaving Earth, Arthur, along with his new friends Ford Prefect (named after the Ford Prefect car after he arrived on Earth), President of the Galaxy Zaphod Beeblebrox, Trillian, and chronically depressed robot Marvin, travel the galaxy while discovering more about the nature of their universe, and about the supercomputer called *Deep Thought* that was programmed to calculate the Answer to the Ultimate Question of Life, the Universe, and Everything.

> **Interesting Fact #1**: Although the HHGTTG is promoted as a trilogy, it is actually a set of five books.
>
> **Interesting Fact #2**: It was originally a comedy on BBC Radio 4, first run in 1978, before being converted into a set of novels, computer game, comic books, and movie.
>
> **Interesting Fact #3**: The theme music used for the radio, television, LP, and film versions of HHGTTG, "Journey of the Sorcerer," was also recorded by The Eagles on their album *One of These Nights*.

Given that socialization is most often construed as a learning task (e.g., learning the ropes), and the situation as ambiguous, new, and often complex, it is not surprising that the theories invoked to gain leverage into socialization have been decidedly cognitive. For instance, uncertainty reduction and desire for control are frequently invoked theoretical perspectives. Entering a new setting is thought to involve a great deal of uncertainty regarding task, roles, the group, the organization, and culture (Chao, O'Leary-Kelly, Wolf, Klein, & Gardner, 1994; Kammeyer-Mueller & Wanberg, 2003). The anxiety associated with that uncertainty (Berger, 1979; Greenberger & Strasser, 1986) motivates individuals to reduce it to gain a sense of control. For example, Ashford and Black (1996) looked at individual differences in desire for control as predictors of individuals' tendencies to engage in tactics thought to bring about control (e.g., seeking information and feedback and building relationships). Morrison (1993) also invokes uncertainty reduction in her predictions regarding newcomers' information-seeking tendencies, proposing uncertainty as an aversive state and arguing that by reducing it, newcomers become more satisfied, perform more effectively, and are less likely to leave the organization.

A second prominent import to the socialization literature is person–environment fit theory.

This theory proposes that misfit or lack of fit experienced on the job is associated with numerous negative outcomes (Edwards, 1996; Kristof-Brown, Zimmerman, & Johnson, 2005). As such, both individuals and organizations are motivated to bring about a good fit for newcomers and job changers. The fit literature suggests that fit/misfit can occur between individuals' abilities and the job's demands, their needs and the rewards they receive (e.g., pay, training), and between their values and organization's values (Cable & DeRue, 2002). Empirical findings indicate that fit is higher when the individual goes through an institutionalized socialization process (Cable & Parsons, 2001). The fit literature posits that misfit is stressful (Edwards, 1996), suggesting that it might motivate individuals to take steps to bring about a better fit or, failing that, to withdraw from the situation. The suggestion that poor fit leads to increased proactivity and/or role change has yet to be tested.

The final prominent theory imported to explain socialization and its processes is social identity theory. This theory portrays individuals as wanting to develop a "situated identity" (Ashforth et al., 2007, p. 38) in their new setting. Ibarra and Barbulescu (2010) suggest that building a situated identity requires identity work on the part of the individual undertaking the transition. Identity work involves creating a narrative that makes sense to the person and others. Such an identity narrative articulates a provisional self that is relevant to the new setting (Ibarra, 1999), one that links the past and future into a harmonious sense of self for the individual transitioning, and serves to enlist others in lending credibility to the desired changes (Ibarra & Barbulescu, 2010). Narratives in this way form a bridge across the gaps that arise between the new and old roles. Morgan Roberts (2005) also describes the identity work involved in creating a professional image during periods of transition. She highlights individuals' attempts to downplay or emphasize particular group affiliations (e.g., racial or gender groups) to create a desired professional image. These more recent arguments embellish and deepen Reichers' (1987) early treatise, the first that really drew socialization scholars' attention to the very real social interactionist forces at work in periods of transition. In such periods, transitioning individuals and "oldtimers" in the new environment interact together to create a defined reality. While older treatments put the individual more in the role of "learner" and others in the environment as teachers, these more recent treatments also foreground the transitioners' active attempts to portray and manage their identities in the new setting. Through their identity work, they are also actively selling or "teaching" others in the environment about who they are.

Theoretical perspectives developed specifically to address organizational socialization go beyond Van Maanen and Schein's (1979) propositions about organizational socialization tactics cited earlier. A second prominent example is Nicholson's (1984) model of newcomer adjustment. He theorizes that transitions stimulate two kinds of outcomes: personal development as transitioning individuals try to absorb the new demands of the role, and role development as people redesign situational demands to suit their preferences. While Ashforth et al. (2007) remind us that these outcomes are not ends of a continuum, but rather that high levels of development is possible in each domain, this theory opened up new questions for the literature. When might individuals be nonconformists and push the organization to change rather than simply trying to fit in? This question is addressed in Bell and Staw's (1989) evocatively titled chapter on "People as Sculptors Versus Sculpture" and in Ashford and Taylor's (1990) model of individual adaptation after transitions. This work laid out the individual and contextual predictors of when people entering a new

organization will try to fit in versus try to change things to better suit them, clearly foreshadowing later work on job crafting in organizations in general (Wrzesniewski & Dutton, 2001).

Theorizing about the situation (as opposed to what the person might do in socialization) also has addressed characteristics of the transition itself. Ashford and Taylor (1990) suggest that the magnitude of the transition (number of factors changing), its onset (sudden versus gradual), its source (chosen versus not), and its affective charge (a perceived gain versus loss) all will matter. Ibarra and Barbulescu (2010) echo Ashford and Taylor's magnitude and desirability dimensions and add that it might also matter whether the transition is part of an institutionalized progression, a "typical path" versus one that is novel or idiosyncratic. Finally, Ashforth et al. (2007) posit two underlying dimensions that also might help us characterize and sort transition types. These are the intensity of the transition (the number of hurdles and socialization agents involved) and its length, with a relatively complicated transition being one that involves a protracted set of experiences to feel completely on board. Crossing those two dimensions, or empirically examining those mentioned by Ashford and Taylor (1990) and by Ibarra and Barbulescu (2010), would give us a strong start on Harvey et al.'s (2010) call for more theorizing on important differences between various transitions.

The Ultimate Questions of the Socialization Literature (and Everything): Frequently Posed Queries by Inter-Galactic Travelers
How do newcomers and the organizational context interact to facilitate newcomers' adjustment?

As is clear in the preceding discussion, the question should not be whether the organization *or* newcomers themselves facilitate adjustment, but rather how both are crucial to the socialization process. Recent studies have begun to investigate empirically how the organization and newcomers simultaneously facilitate adjustment. For instance, a newcomer's pre-entry knowledge of the role and proactive personality, along with socialization tactics by the newcomer's subsequent workgroup, leaders, and the organization itself, have been found to facilitate adjustment via proximal outcomes such as task mastery, role clarity, and workgroup integration (Kammeyer-Mueller & Wanberg, 2003). Similarly, newcomer information-seeking—one form of newcomer proactivity—and organizational socialization tactics both contribute to higher role clarity, self-efficacy, and social acceptance for newcomers (Bauer et al., 2007). Furthermore, while institutionalized socialization tactics are positively related to newcomers' perceptions of fit with their organization, proactive behaviors by newcomers also further strengthen this relationship (Kim et al., 2005). These studies and theory present a clear portrait of both the organization and newcomers themselves contributing to the socialization process, suggesting that a prominent focus for future research will be on how these interactions occur and what predicts their unfolding throughout the process.

Does socialization follow a sequence?

Some of the earliest research on socialization articulated a sequence of stages that newcomers go through to become capable organizational members. Much of this research is focused around three stages (Ashforth et al., 2007; Feldman, 1981). *Anticipatory* relates to the period before a newcomer joins the organization. At this stage, the newcomer may develop expectations and learn about his/her job. *Encounter* describes the stage at which the newcomer first experiences life in the organization. At this stage, newcomers may begin to experience some changes around their skills, attitudes, and behaviors, as they begin to find out what life in the organization and job is actually like and what is required to be successful. *Adjustment* relates to the period during which the newcomer becomes an ever-increasing insider as he/she adapts to the job and organization. Lastly, *stabilization* signals the period during which newcomers become fully-blown insiders as they are fully integrated into the job and organization. While stage models provide insights into the challenges that newcomers and their organizations experience, they have been criticized for several reasons (Ashforth et al., 2007). For example, these models suggest that newcomers transition from one stage to the next, but often neglect *how* newcomers transition through these stages (Bauer et al., 1998). Furthermore, they portray a linear socialization process in which newcomers are passive participants, neglecting the proactive role that newcomers may take in facilitating this process (Morrison, 1993). Finally, it is interesting to note that stage models have been invoked almost exclusively with respect to newcomers. If there are stages related to other transitions (e.g., crossing levels or entering new groups), these have not been specifically articulated. Nevertheless, these models do provide an insight into understanding the rate at which newcomers are socialized and the events that newcomers experience as they transition into their new jobs.

Fact Box 2 Socialization Literature

Over 400 journal articles have been published on "organizational socialization" over a period of 48 years. The phrase yields 155,000 results in a Google Scholar search.

"Organizational Socialization" first appears in the title of a journal article: William M. Evan—"Peer-Group Interaction and Organizational Socialization: A Study of Employee Turnover," *American Sociological Review*, 1963.

Most Cited Article: John Van Maanen and Edward Schein—"Toward a theory of organizational socialization"—*Research in Organizational Behavior*, 1979 (1615 citations).

Interesting Fact #1: Adams' *Hitchhiker's Guide to the Galaxy* and Van Maanen and Schein's seminal article were both published in 1979…coincidence?

Interesting Fact #2: Following John Van Maanen's full-on qualitative immersion study of the police force in 1970, he became a victim of his own socialization theory—he has not been able since to sit at a table in a restaurant without a clear view of the front door and his back to the wall.

Interesting Fact #3: Of the three indicators of newcomer adjustment studied in Bauer et al.'s (2007) meta-analysis of the socialization literature, only "gaining social acceptance" was significantly related to all five of the outcomes studied: job performance, job satisfaction, organizational commitment, turnover, and intentions to remain.

What do newcomers learn about?

If the heart of socialization is acquiring the social knowledge and skills to assume an organizational role, then an important question is, "What do newcomers learn about?" The literature notes that learning can span across the job or role, dyadic or group relationships, and the organization (Ashforth et al., 2007). For example, during socialization newcomers learn about whether they are proficient at their jobs, the language used on the job and in the organization, the politics in the organization, the people in the organization, organizational goals/values, and history (Chao et al., 1994). However, it is not clear whether these are the only six content dimensions that newcomers learn about, as it may depend on the field in which newcomers join and the line of work in which they are involved (Chao et al., 1994). Indeed, future work needs to investigate whether these content areas are valid across jobs and organizations. Furthermore, Chao (in press) notes that the socialization literature has yet to study the tacit knowledge—that is, the personal knowledge acquired from implicit learning—that newcomers gain during the process of entry. For example, she indicates that learning can be less conscious, and knowledge acquisition may occur for newcomers, regardless of whether it was intended or not. Prior work has demonstrated that tacit knowledge is an antecedent of creativity and innovation (Leonard & Sensiper, 1998; Osterloh & Frey, 2000), and the tacit knowledge gained in the entry process may play an important role in shaping these outcomes.

How do newcomers learn?

Much of this learning is likely to take place during the encounter stage of socialization, as it is during this period that newcomers seek to resolve uncertainty about their new roles and the organization (Morrison, 1995). To facilitate learning at this stage or later, newcomers may rely on both social/interpersonal and nonsocial sources (Ostroff & Kozlowski, 1992). Interpersonal sources include coworkers, supervisors, and mentors, while nonsocial sources include official organizational documents, experimenting with new behaviors, and observation (Morrison, 1993). As previously discussed, newcomers may learn about their new roles by engaging in proactive behaviors (Ashford, 1986; Morrison, 1993). One form of proactive behaviors is inquiry, which includes seeking direct information and feedback by asking questions and testing limits (Ashford & Cummings, 1983). At the same time, proactive behaviors to foster learning can be less overt. Newcomers may obtain needed information via monitoring, which involves observing others, asking indirect questions, and/or engaging in what Miller and Jablin label "disguising conversations" (e.g., joking, self-disclosure; Miller & Jablin, 1991, p. 108). For example, newcomers may use humor to disguise questions that may be too embarrassing to ask, or they may disclose personal information to see whether others respond favorably to their ideas about how a task should be performed. These tactics may constitute the micro moves by which transitioners enact the provisional selves hypothesized by Ibarra and Barbulescu (2010). The reasons for engaging in inquiry, monitoring, or the even more indirect disguising conversations may depend on several factors, including the social costs involved. For example, if newcomers engage in inquiry to obtain information or feedback, they may be perceived as bothersome or uninformed (Ashford & Cummings, 1983); if a high-status entry to the organization does so, he or she may be considered weak or an ineffective leader.

Furthermore, newcomers may learn by building networks with organizational members to help them learn the ropes of their new role (Morrison, 2002). Depending on the type of information that newcomers need, they may have different patterns of relationships. For instance, if they require information about their specific role, they are more likely to have a dense network with local, task-related peers, whereas if they require information about the organization at large, they are likely to have a broader information network (Morrison, 2002). Fang, Duffy, and Shaw (2011) similarly propose that newcomers' access to social capital via the configuration and structural characteristics of their relationships with organizational insiders and the social resources embedded in their network play a crucial role in facilitating newcomer learning and social integration. Indeed, the relationships that newcomers have with peers seem to be fundamental to their learning, but are relatively understudied.

How do we study socialization?

Similar to other topics in organizational behavior, many empirical studies on socialization have been driven by convenience. Easy access to graduating MBA and undergraduate samples has meant that field studies have tended to focus on newcomers to an organization as opposed to those who are changing jobs within the organization. Moreover, empirical research has often sampled those who are holding jobs for the first time as opposed to those who have prior experience, along with restricting samples to university, if not MBA business school, graduates. These sample characteristics are clearly relevant (many who take jobs for the first time are university graduates) but increasingly cited as limiting (Ashforth, et al., 2007). We learn little about the socialization processes of the more experienced, those entering jobs in organizations and/or professions where a university degree is not required, and about transitions other than organizational entry.

Socialization has typically been studied via survey methodology, following samples over time. Thus, socialization research has been effective at temporally separating antecedents, mediators, and outcomes, thereby reducing common method biases (Podsakoff, MacKenzie, Lee, & Podsakoff, 2003). Many studies have gathered data at 3-month intervals throughout the entry process. The most frequent intervals used for data collection are at entry, 3 months, and 6 months following the entry transition (Bauer et al., 2007). Socialization studies also typically have measured newcomer behaviors multiple times during the entry period, which allows us to understand how newcomers' behavior may change over time as they adapt to their new roles (Boswell, Shipp, Payne, & Culbertson, 2009; Chen, 2005). Studies that ask others (e.g., the transitioner's supervisor) to report on socialization outcomes are rare in the socialization literature, but will also strengthen findings methodologically.

What represents successful socialization?

When is a person fully socialized? Successful newcomer adjustment has been conceptualized according to both distal and proximal outcomes. Indicators of successful newcomer adjustment include higher job performance, more positive job attitudes (e.g., job satisfaction, organizational commitment, intentions to remain) and lower turnover (Bauer et al., 2007b). While these distal outcomes are informative of adjustment, research has noted that they do not capture the process of adjustment and whether socialization has occurred successfully (as opposed to a person just being satisfied with the job due to pay or working conditions, for example; Bauer et al., 2007b; Saks & Ashforth, 1997). If socialization is appropriately conceptualized as a process of learning and uncertainty reduction, then a variety of more proximal outcomes appear to be relevant (Bauer et al, 2007). More proximal indicators such as task mastery, role clarity, and work group integration can be viewed as more direct indicators of the quality of newcomer adjustment,

as they reflect "the acquisition of requisite knowledge and skill for the organizational role as well as the development of social relationships that will help to bind the newcomer to the organization and its goals" (Kammeyer-Mueller & Wanberg, 2003, p. 781). Scholars are now more frequently calling for research to examine these more proximal indicators of socialization that directly relate to antecedents of socialization, such as organizational tactics and newcomer proactivity. Whether these proximal outcomes result in the more distal outcomes typically invoked will likely be the result of several additional moderator variables. For example, if one achieves role clarity, but the role is awful, job satisfaction may suffer; if one becomes integrated into the group, but the group has anti-management norms, performance may suffer. Keeping the distinction of proximal and more distal outcomes clear opens up new research questions on the interesting and nuanced ties between them.

In addition, organizations are actually interested in more than newcomers just gaining the requisite knowledge and skills for their jobs—they care whether individuals become committed and stay longer in the organization. While less noted by researchers, socialization also is, in part, a process of cooptation or seduction (Lewicki, 1981)—a process by which individuals come to see their goals as aligned with the organization, to believe in the meanings leaders work hard to convey (Podolny, Khurana, & Hill-Popper, 2005), and in the mission organizations espouse and live by. Indeed, when we think of individuals as being socialized we not only think of them as being knowledgeable and skilled, but also as people who have bought into the prevailing norms, who feel part of the organization and who are excited about its goals. This broader sense of outcomes suggests a needed expansion of our definition of socialization, from one simply about acquiring knowledge and skills to one also referencing a growing identification with the organization and internalization of its values. It also suggests an emphasis on different mediating processes than those that have dominated the literature to date. For example, the literature to date has focused on what organizations do to teach and what individuals do to learn during a transition. The perspective we are developing here suggests that we also might focus on what organizations do to engage and seduce people into the mission of the organization, and how individuals come to identify and internalize those messages—essentially, how organizations win hearts, not just minds. This distinction also suggests, as referenced by Ashforth et al. (2007), that the timing of the process may vary depending on which outcome is considered. It may take mere minutes for some newcomers to learn that their peers are untrustworthy, longer to learn the norms of the place, and quite a while to internalize the values of the organization. Our expectations regarding timing may vary depending on the outcome in question. Kammeyer-Mueller and Wanberg's (2003) work on differentiating proximal and distal outcomes is a helpful first step in sorting out this issue.

The Newcomer at the End of the Universe: Future Destinations for Inter-Galactic Explorers
Examining "Local" Factors in Facilitating Adjustment

While organizations use tactics and newcomers engage in proactive behaviors to facilitate socialization, researchers have noted that much of socialization occurs through interactions between organizational incumbents (e.g., coworkers and leaders) and newcomers (Reichers, 1987). For example, by asking questions, stopping by people's offices to talk, and initiating social opportunities, newcomers are better able to understand their roles and identity in the organization. When newcomers think of fitting in, it is often with the local context in mind (e.g., Will my group like me? How do I best work with my new boss? What does it feel like to have my desk where it is?). In other words, some of the most important socialization is decidedly local.

Despite the recognition of interpersonal and group interactions as being heavily responsible for successful socialization, there is still much to be learned in this area. First, much of the literature remains too broad by focusing on organizational tactics of socialization but neglecting more proximal and immediate sources of socialization, such as coworkers and leaders. On the other hand, the literature remains too narrow by focusing only on the proactive behaviors of newcomers while neglecting the local context in which they are embedded. Indeed, coworkers, leaders, and teams are the likely "face" of the organization; they are likely the most frequently encountered by newcomers, and to have a large impact on socialization outcomes (Moreland & Levine, 1982). As Ashforth and colleagues (2007) point out, supervisors and coworkers are the ones who bring organizational values to life through their actions. For example, an organization may proclaim that it values employee development but it is the supervisor and members of the work group that bring this value to life via the sharing of feedback and social support (or they don't, creating a disconnect). Recent research shows that a newcomer's teammates and supervisor influence newcomer outcomes via a variant of the Pygmalion effect (Chen & Klimoski, 2003). When these folks have high expectations of the newcomer, these prompt more positive social exchanges with the newcomer and thereby positively influence his or her adjustment. Similarly, the local team's effectiveness prior to the newcomer entering has an effect on newcomers' initial and subsequent performance, as team members are likely to attract and select members similar to them (Chen, 2005). Additional theorizing about the local context has the potential to open up new questions and generate new insights for the socialization literature.

There is additional value to moving beyond investigating only transitioning individuals to also engaging in a more careful study of the motivations and actions of those they encounter in their local context. Let's study the socializers, as well as the socialized. By investigating coworkers and supervisors, we can learn more about what individuals in the immediate context are doing to facilitate successful socialization. These agents do much more than provide information to newcomers about the task and social environment, for example. In her study of investment bankers and consultants, Ibarra (1999) found that more senior organizational members served as role models for provisional identities. They also shaped newcomers through their reactions to the identities newcomers were testing out, thereby assisting newcomers to learn more about themselves and what they aspired to be. Similarly, organizational members facilitate meaning for newcomers undergoing role transitions, as they may affirm or disaffirm the narratives that newcomers' enact (Ibarra & Barbulescu, 2010). Furthermore, studying other organizational members would inform us about the expectations newcomers face, for example, in regard to how long the period of socialization is expected to last. Rollag (2004) reminds us that the labels of "newcomers" and "veterans" are socially constructed. The transition from newcomer to veteran is likely to depend, in part, on how organizational members perceive the appropriate timing of this change. Such expectations are important to the individual entering the organization or into a new role, as these expectations identify the likely time span of the important "honeymoon period" and suggest when certain image costs might kick in for the transitioner. Therefore, the organization and the newcomers or job transitioners themselves should not be the only focus of socialization research. More local socialization agents such as leaders, coworkers, and teams should be investigated as well.

Taking Into Account the Affective and Cognitive Experiences of Newcomers

Although research has linked both organizational tactics and newcomer proactivity to newcomer adjustment, many of the constructs we use to represent successful adjustment overlook the affective and cognitive experiences of newcomers when they enter a new role. Proximal outcomes, such as task mastery and role clarity, along with more distal outcomes, such as job satisfaction and organizational commitment, capture some degree of newcomer adjustment but they do not capture the range of emotions that newcomers experience when they enter a new role, nor how they cope with those emotions effectively. For instance, newcomers may experience disappointment and doubt during the socialization process (Bullis & Bach, 1989). In addition to being prompts for sensemaking (Louis, 1980), such emotions may require attention in their own right. After experiencing these emotions, newcomers may engage in a range of self-regulatory tactics, including cognitive ones such as the positive framing studied by Ashford and Black (1996). To prevent themselves from ruminating on negative events, individuals use positive framing to recast emotional experiences from problems to opportunities. Stronger, more troubling emotions such as alienation, anxiety, and stress may require more considered responses. The literatures on stress and coping (Edwards, 1992; Nelson & Sutton, 1990), individual and relational resources (Feldman, 2004; Spreitzer, Sutcliffe, Dutton, Sonenshein, & Grant, 2005), resilience (Carver, 1998; Sutcliffe & Vogus, 2003), and emotion regulation (Gross, 1998), all suggest questions that might be asked of the affective experiences of transitioners—and give insights into their answers. The emotions people feel during socialization, and individual responses for dealing with them, may be crucial to successful adjustment—and yet, they are a relatively understudied area of research. An examination of the emotional realities of socialization would also extend to the explicit manipulation of emotions as an impression-management tactic available to transitioners. Individuals may engage in surface or deep acting (Ashforth & Humphrey, 1993; Coté, 2005; Grandey, 2003) to display emotions that will help

them better fit into the group or stand out among their peers.

Given the socialization literature's emphasis on socialization as a learning process, cognitive processes have enjoyed much more emphasis than have affective ones. However, the extensive literature on cognitive heuristics and biases has not been brought to bear, and may serve as an additional source of insight. Newcomers especially may fall prey to biases such as the availability heuristic, for example, whereby a few prominent instances of a phenomenon (e.g., the first few encountered) create inappropriate beliefs regarding its importance. As an additional example, newcomers who are especially concerned about image issues may be susceptible to escalation of commitment pressures as they justify their first actions in a setting with the investment of more resources (even if just their own time and effort) in an attempt to make it look good. Examining the ways in which both cognitive and affective processes influence newcomers may shed additional light on how newcomers actively manage their adjustment. Essentially, we are arguing that individuals are not just proactive behaviorally during the entry period, as the literature has documented (Ashford & Black, 1996), but they are also likely to be cognitively and emotionally proactive.

In addition to a new focus on heuristics and biases in the socialization process, there are likely new things to discover about the literature's dominant emphasis: how people learn within the socialization process. The focus to date has (reasonably) been on information and feedback seeking, proposing that individuals who do more of both will learn more. Recent literature in the leadership area, however, has focused on how people learn leadership from experience—through how they engage with and process various experiences. Given that much of what we hope newcomers will learn during socialization has a nuanced and intangible element similar to leadership, this perspective may be suggestive of future research questions for the socialization literature as well. Specifically, DeRue and Ashford (2010) articulate a process of "mindful engagement" to understand how people learn from experience. They suggest that to learn from an experience, individuals must approach and frame the experience in a way that facilitates development. Within the experience, individuals need to actively experiment with their behavior and responses, seek and receive feedback from others, and regulate their cognitions and emotions. Lastly, they need to reflect periodically to understand what enabled or prevented their success (DeRue & Ashford, 2010). This perspective suggests that we might focus on individuals' tendencies to frame transitions as learning opportunities (as opposed to primarily or solely about performance and proving themselves; Dweck, 1986; Dweck, Chiu, & Hong, 1995); to experiment within them in the manner suggested by Ibarra and Barbulescu (2010) in their discussion of trying on provisional selves; to seek feedback on their experiments and to reflect on them periodically to extract learning as documented by Anseel, Lievens, & Schollaert (2009) as a way to enhance learning. Future research can evaluate whether newcomers or transitioners who are mindfully engaged in this way learn more than those who are not.

One way to also capture the richness of affective and cognitive processes is to turn to alternative methodologies. Advances in quantitative methods, such as experience sampling methods (Beal & Weiss, 2003), can provide insights into the affective and cognitive fluctuations of newcomer entry by capturing what newcomers experience on a day-to-day basis and can help us understand the trajectories of newcomers over time. Similarly, qualitative methods can portray the diverse range of emotions and feelings that newcomers have by examining the narratives that newcomers provide. Organizational socialization researchers would benefit from examining the work in occupational socialization, which includes rich ethnographies detailing how individuals become doctors, lawyers, firefighters, and engineers, among others (Barley, 1989; Kunda, 2006; Van Maanen, 2009). This work has done a tremendous job in documenting the experiences of those becoming members of an occupation as they learned the ropes of their respective occupations. There are likely to be parallels between how individuals get socialized into occupations and how they get socialized into organizations, and qualitative treatments have the potential to portray this process in rich detail. The use of alternative methodologies in the socialization literature has the potential to capture the temporal dynamics of cognitive and affective experiences of newcomers.

All Newcomers are Not Created Equal

There is often a tendency to assume that all newcomers are identical when, in fact, they have very different backgrounds, experiences, and identities. Indeed, the ways in which newcomers deal with uncertainty often depends on their past experiences and what they have previously learned (Jones, 1983).

These prior experiences also influence the identities they enact, their ability to enact them, and therefore their level and quality of adjustment within an organization (Beyer & Hannah, 2002). So, for different groups of newcomers different questions are likely to be pertinent. Indeed, the type of transition taking place and the background of the individual should play a role in the outcomes we decide to study. For those who come to a job with no prior work experience, questions about how they fit into the job and organization are likely to be less salient, as they are likely to trying to make sense of what working in any capacity for the first time really entails. On the other hand, those who are changing jobs within the same organization are more likely to already understand their fit with the broader organization, so they should be more focused on their fit with the demands of the new job and how their skills, abilities, and interests fulfill these new responsibilities.

Newcomers also come to organizations with different goals. While we often portray newcomers as having joined organizations to fit in and learn, some newcomers may know they are staying in organizations for only a short period of time, so fitting in is not of primary importance. Others may be less interested in learning as they may already be experts; instead, they may be more interested in expanding their networks and making contacts with others in the organization (Beyer & Hannah, 2002). Thus, our typical measures of successful socialization, such as social acceptance or self-efficacy, may not apply to these different groups of newcomers.

One prominent goal difference reflects a bias in the literature to date. That is, we often presume that newcomers engage in proactive behaviors during the entry process to reduce uncertainty and fit in. However, they may do so for other motives, such as managing impressions and standing out. For example, newcomers may ask questions not just to reduce their uncertainty about how to perform tasks, but also to create favorable impressions in the minds of their coworkers and supervisors. Surely image enhancement is likely to be a strong motive for newcomers as they try to gain social acceptance from others in the organization.

Taking an impression management perspective on newcomer proactivity may enrich our understanding of why newcomers choose to engage in some behaviors and seek information from specific people over others. For instance, the impression-management literature suggests that behaviors

Fact Box 3 Reflections of an Original Hitchhiker: John Van Maanen on Van Maanen & Schein (1979)

#1: According to John, the chapter was a lesson in "working the binaries"—Schein studying "up" the organization to the high ranks and Van Maanen studying "down" the organization to the low ranks; Schein looking to those undergoing socialization and Van Maanen to those acting as socialization agents; Schein with a psychological take on the process and Van Maanen with a sociological take.

#2: The piece was perhaps the least touched up by editors of any that John can recall. The first draft sailed through with nary a comment. John speculates that this was perhaps because 1979 was the first volume of Staw's *Research in Organizational Behavior* series and Barry was desperate for submissions.

#3: Both John and Ed shifted emphasis from "process" in the 1970s to "content" in the 1980s—What is it that socialization agents deliver and recruits absorb? And that took us both to organizational and occupational culture.

#4: Of coincidental interest, many socialization researchers including Bill Evan, Dave Berlew, Tim Hall, Edward Schein, and John himself were at MIT at the same time writing various pieces related to the topic.

#5: John characterizes his Disneyland work as in some way a reaction to doing what some might regard as the most unpleasant work on the planet (police work) to doing what is (purportedly) rather pleasant work—from being in the rather grim places on earth to being in the (purportedly) happiest places on earth.

consistent with the values of the organization are more image enhancing (Bolino, 1999). For example, if an organization values initiative then it is likely that newcomers will engage in direct proactive behaviors over ones that are less overt, since this will enhance their image. Likewise, the impression management literature also places importance on the "target" of behaviors, suggesting that proactivity may be strategically aimed at some individuals in the organization over others. Extending the previous example, if the supervisor also believes that taking initiative is important then a newcomer may ask his or her supervisor questions as opposed to discussing questions with coworkers.

Furthermore, the desire to stand out from others may be more salient in some contexts versus others. In organizations where there are a large group of newcomers, proactive behaviors may be a way for newcomers to stand out and differentiate themselves from the rest, while in organizations with only a handful of newcomers this may be less of a concern. This example is suggestive of the possible motives besides uncertainty reduction and adaptation to a setting that might underlie the proactive behaviors of newcomers. Considering the variety of

goals individuals bring to transitions allows us to expand the questions asked about what they will do within those situations.

Socializing in New Organizational Forms

It is interesting to note that while there are a wide variety of theories invoked or created to explain individuals' actions and reactions within the socialization process, fewer theories explain the same for organizations. Efficiency is the presumed motive for organizations, with organizations investing just enough resources to bring about the ends it needs. Are completely socialized individuals necessary to our organization? Then we'll create expensive, formal systems to bring about integration (conformity). If not, then fewer resources will be devoted to it. If innovation is what we're after as a firm, then we'll go about socializing newcomers in more of an individualized way. However, the prominent theorizing on the organizational side, the now oft-mentioned Van Maanen and Schein (1979), has a decidedly "large organization" feel to it. Are there outcomes of interest to the organization besides efficiency and innovation? What does organizational socialization look like in small start-ups? Virtual-based Internet firms? Hyper-growth firms? What does it look like in firms where the expectation is that people will only stay awhile and move on? Where people come in sporadically, as opposed to in a group? When a large percentage of workers will do their work from home and come in only occasionally? Where temporary and/or contract workers need to be brought into a setting with permanent employees? Are there variables beyond innovation and conformity that are of importance to organizations? Perhaps the speed of socialization mentioned by Reichers (1987) and studied by Pinder and Schroeder (1987) will become more important in many of these contexts. Perhaps it is not conformity versus innovation that is important, but rather socializing for flexibility so that individuals can be used in a variety of positions with little subsequent adaptation. These "distant planets" of small, virtual, and/or transitory organizations that are becoming more prominent in today's organizational solar system are attractive ones for future research.

When we start thinking about different contexts for socialization, it also opens the literature up to different dependent variables of interest. For instance, small start-up companies in the high-tech industry are likely to be especially interested in socializing for creativity, as the development of new ideas is essential in such organizations. In these organizations newcomers are likely to be a source for new ideas right away, so they may be expected to contribute quickly and spend less time "learning the ropes" (Gino, Bauer, Cable, & Erdogan, 2010). In fact, these newcomers may spend just as much time teaching as learning from more senior employees, as the group may look to them to improve group processes and routines. These examples start us on a path of looking at how the transition from organizational outsider to insider may look very different from our current theoretical models in these contexts. As more and more new organizational forms spring up, the outcomes and processes of interest for socialization may fundamentally change.

DON'T PANIC: Conclusions to Guide Us

On the cover of *The Hitchhiker's Guide to the Galaxy*, the phrase "DON'T PANIC" served to keep intergalactic travelers from extreme anxiety. Arthur C. Clarke, author of *2001, A Space Odyssey* characterized this phrase as perhaps the best advice that could be given to humanity. We offer it here as well. At the beginning of this chapter, we cautioned that, unlike Douglas Adams' *Hitchhiker's Guide to the Galaxy*, the answers to the questions posed in the socialization literature would be more complex and nuanced. Our ending words of wisdom to

those currently studying socialization, along with those who are encountering it for the first time, are the same as Douglas Adams' slogan to his readers: "DON'T PANIC."

Over the past 40 years, both theoretical and empirical research on socialization has advanced significantly. The literature has evolved from simply examining the tactics that organizations use to socialize newcomers, to also taking into account the proactive role that newcomers play in this process and what they do to get adjusted to the organization, to considering both actors' motives and actions simultaneously. Insights have been gained from applying a relevant but limited set of theoretical perspectives, including theories of uncertainty reduction, person–environment fit, and social identity. These different theoretical perspectives have helped address numerous questions pertinent to socialization, such as how both the organization and newcomers themselves facilitate adjustment, socialization's sequence, what and how newcomers learn, and what it means to be successfully socialized. But exploration continues in this active galaxy. To support that exploration we offered several potential destinations for researchers to visit, and travel itineraries to follow, as the study of socialization continues into the future. The many questions that still remain should be encouraging for individuals interested in this topic, as it offers numerous opportunities for future research.

According to the *Hitchhiker's Guide* (1979, p. 215), "The history of every major galactic civilization tends to pass through three distinct and recognizable phases, those of survival, inquiry and sophistication." Just as the universe we live in started from a single point ("the big bang"?) and has expanded in size as time passes, the socialization galaxy continues to grow from its starting points, the seminal articles by Schein (1968) and Van Maanen and Schein (1979), into a full blown inquiry stage and moving toward sophistication. Fortunately, just as more researchers have gravitated toward studying the universe and their methods for doing so have improved, we now find more people studying socialization and using a wider array of methods to understand it. At the end of the original *Hitchhiker's Guide*, the novel's protagonists went to The Restaurant at the End of the Universe, where they could watch the entire universe come to an end while eating lunch. Socialization researchers are far from this destination of a relaxing meal at an endpoint for all knowledge. Rather, we are on a journey with many subsequent stops to come. And besides, the *Hitchhiker's Guide* was a "trilogy," so we have a ways to go....

The Hitchhikers Guide—Top 10 Socialization Reads

Van Maanen & Schein (*Research in Organizational Behavior*, 1979)—Toward a Theory of Organizational Socialization

The seminal article on organizational socialization theorizes about the process and inspired interest in the topic. The article highlighted six tactics that organizations can use to socialize employees.

Louis (*Administrative Science Quarterly*, 1980)—Surprise and Sense Making: What Newcomers Experience in Entering Unfamiliar Organizational Settings

First to really highlight what individuals experience when entering new organizations. Discusses the types of "surprises" that transitions trigger and how individuals cope with them.

Jones (*Academy of Management Review*, 1983)—Psychological Orientation and the Process of Organizational Socialization: An Interactionist Perspective

Takes into account the role of the individuals in the socialization process as it theorizes about different types of newcomer orientations (e.g., naïve, competent and dominant).

Nicholson (*Academy of Management Review*, 1984)—A Theory of Work Role Transitions

Offers a theory for understanding work role transitions, and for when people will adapt to versus attempt to change the roles they encounter.

Reichers (*Academy of Management Review*, 1987)—An Interactionist Perspective on Newcomer Socialization Rates

Underscores the importance of seeking out interaction opportunities by both transitioning individuals and organizational insiders as crucial to the rate at which newcomers are successfully socialized.

Ashford & Black (*Journal of Applied Psychology*, 1996)—Proactivity During Organizational Entry: The Role of Desire for Control

Portrays individuals as agentic as opposed to passive in socialization and depicts how newcomers' desire for control drives proactive behaviors (e.g., feedback-seeking, relationship building, job change negotiating) during socialization.

Morrison (*Academy of Management Journal*, 2002)—Newcomers' Relationships: The Role of Social Network Ties during Socialization

Examines how the network structures of newcomers, and the configuration of relationships with individuals across levels and departments in organizations, influence their learning and assimilation during socialization.

Kammeyer-Mueller & Wanberg (*Journal of Applied Psychology*, 2003)—Unwrapping the Organizational Entry Process: Disentangling Multiple Antecedents and Their Pathways to Adjustment

Integrates the organizational context and individual as integral to successful socialization—both in terms of distal and proximal outcomes.

Ashforth, Sluss & Harrison (*International Review of Industrial and Organizational Psychology*, 2007)—Socialization in Organizational Contexts

A comprehensive, in-depth review of the socialization literature, which details the many theoretical and empirical articles on the topic and suggests directions for future research.

Ibarra & Barbulescu (*Academy of Management Review*, 2010)—Identity as Narrative: Prevalence, Effectiveness, and Consequences of Narrative Identity Work in Macro Work Role Transitions

Investigates how individuals use self-narratives during work role transitions to revise and reconstruct their identities. Introduces the concept of provisional selves as something transitioners offer up to the context to test out their acceptability and self-relevance.

References

Adams, D. (2002). *The Hitchhiker's Guide to the Galaxy*. New York: Pocket Books.

Allen, N. J., & Meyer, J. P. (1990a). The measurement and antecedents of affective, continuance and normative commitment to the organization. *Journal of Occupational Psychology*, *63*(1), 1–18.

Allen, N. J., & Meyer, J. P. (1990b). Organizational socialization tactics: A longitudinal analysis of links to newcomers' commitment and role orientation. *The Academy of Management Journal*, *33*(4), 847–858.

Anseel, F., Lievens, F., & Schollaert, E. (2009). Reflection as a strategy to enhance task performance after feedback. *Organizational Behavior and Human Decision Processes*, *110*(1), 23–35.

Ashford, S. J., & Black, J. (1996). Proactivity during organizational entry: The role of desire for control. *Journal Of Applied Psychology*, *81*(2), 199–214.

Ashford, S. J., & Cummings, L. L. (1983). Feedback as an individual resource: Personal strategies of creating information. *Organizational Behavior and Human Performance*, *32*(3), 370–398.

Ashford, S. J. (1986). Feedback-seeking in individual adaptation: A resource perspective. *The Academy of Management Journal*, *29*(3), 465–487.

Ashford, S. J., & Taylor, M. S. (1990). Adaptation to work transitions: An integrative approach. *Research in personnel and human resources management*, *8*, 1–39.

Ashforth, B., & Saks, A. (1996). Socialization tactics: Longitudinal effects on newcomer adjustment. *The Academy of Management Journal*, *39*(1), 149–178.

Ashforth, B. E., & Humphrey, R. H. (1993). Emotional labor in service roles: The influence of identity. *The Academy of Management Review*, *18*(1), 88–115.

Ashforth, B. E., Sluss, D. M., & Harrison, S. H. (2007). Socialization in organizational contexts. In G. P. Hodgkinson & J. K. Ford (Eds.), *International Review of Industrial and Organizational Psychology*, Vol. 22, 1–70. Chichester: Wiley.

Baker, W. K. (1995). Allen and Meyer's 1990 longitudinal study: A reanalysis and reinterpretation using structural equation modeling. *Human Relations*, *48*(2), 169.

Barley, S. R. (1989). Careers, identities, and institutions: the legacy of the Chicago School of Sociology. In M. B. Arthur, D. T. Hall & B. S. Lawrence (Eds.), *Handbook of Career Theory*, (pp. 41–65). New York: Cambridge University Press.

Bauer, T. N., & Green, S. G. (1994). Effect of newcomer involvement in work-related activities: A longitudinal study of socialization. *Journal of Applied Psychology*, *79*(2), 211.

Bauer T. N., Morrison, E. W,. & Callister, R. R. (1998). Organizational socialization: A review and directions for future research. *Research in Personnel and Human Resources Management*, *16*, 149–214. Bauer, T. N., Bodner, T., Erdogan, B., Truxillo, D. M., & Tucker, J. S. (2007). Newcomer adjustment during organizational socialization: A meta-analytic review of antecedents, outcomes, and methods. *Journal of Applied Psychology*, *92*(3), 707.

Beal, D. J., & Weiss, H. M. (2003). Methods of ecological momentary assessment in organizational research. *Organizational Research Methods*, *6*(4), 440.

Bell, N., & Staw, B. (1989). People as sculptors versus sculpture: The roles of personality and personal control in organizations. In Arthur, M.B., Hall, D.T. and Lawrence, B.S. (Eds.), *Handbook of Career Theory* (pp. 232–274). Cambridge: Cambridge University Press.

Berger, C. R. (1979). Beyond initial interaction: Uncertainty, understanding, and the development of interpersonal relationships. *Language and Social Psychology17*, 122–144.

Beyer, J. M., & Hannah, D. R. (2002). Building on the past: Enacting established personal identities in a new work setting. *Organization Science*, *12*(6), 636–652.

Bolino, M. C. (1999). Citizenship and impression management: Good soldiers or good actors? *The Academy of Management Review*, *24*(1), 82–98.

Boswell, W. R., Shipp, A. J., Payne, S. C., & Culbertson, S. S. (2009). Changes in newcomer job satisfaction over time: Examining the pattern of honeymoons and hangovers. *Journal of Applied Psychology*, *94*(4), 844.

Bullis, C., & Bach, B. W. (1989). Socialization turning points: An examination of change in organizational identification. *Western Journal of Communication*, *53*(3), 273–293.

Cable, D. M., & Parsons, C. K. (2001). Socialization tactics and person-organization fit. *Personnel Psychology*, *54*(1), 1–24.

Cable, D. M., & DeRue, D. S. (2002). The convergent and discriminant validity of subjective fit perceptions. *Journal of Applied Psychology*, *87*(5), 875.

Carver, C. S. (1998). Resilience and thriving: Issues, models, and linkages. *Journal of Social Issues*, *54*(2), 245–266.

Chao, G. T., O'Leary-Kelly, A. M., Wolf, S., Klein, H. J., & Gardner, P. D. (1994). Organizational socialization: Its content and consequences. *Journal of Applied Psychology*, *79*(5), 730.

Chao, G. T. (in press). Organizational socialization: Background, basics, and a blueprint for adjustment at work. In S. W. J. Kozlowski (Ed.), *The Oxford Handbook of Organizational Psychology*. New York: Oxford University Press.

Chen, G., & Klimoski, R. (2003). The impact of expectations on newcomer performance in teams as mediated by work characteristics, social exchanges, and empowerment. *The Academy of Management Journal*, *46*(5), 591–607.

Chen, G. (2005). Newcomer adaptation in teams: Multilevel antecedents and outcomes. *The Academy of Management Journal*, *48*(1), 101–116.

Coté, S. (2005). A social interaction model of the effects of emotion regulation on work strain. *The Academy of Management Review*, *30*(3), 509–530.

DeRue, D. S., & Ashford, S. (2010). Power to people: Where has personal agency gone in leadership development. *Industrial and Organizational Psychology: Perspectives on Science and Practice*, *3*, 24–27.

Dweck, C. (1986). Motivational processes affecting learning. *American Psychologist*, *41*(10), 1040–1048.

Dweck, C., Chiu, C., & Hong, Y. (1995). Implicit theories and their role in judgments and reactions: A world from two perspectives. *Psychological Inquiry*, *6*(4), 267–285.

Edwards, J. (1996). An examination of competing versions of the person-environment fit approach to stress. *The Academy of Management Journal*, *39*(2), 292–339.

Edwards, J. R. (1992). A cybernetic theory of stress, coping, and well-being in organizations. *The Academy of Management Review*, *17*(2), 238–274.

Fang, R., Duffy, M. K., & Shaw, J. D. 2011. The organizational socialization process: Review and development of a social capital model. *Journal of Management*, *37*(1), 127.

Feldman, D. C. (1976). A contingency theory of socialization. *Administrative Science Quarterly*, *21*(3), 433–452.

Feldman, D. C. (1977). The role of initiation activities in socialization. *Human Relations*, *30*(11), 977.

Feldman, D. C. (1981). The multiple socialization of organization members. *The Academy of Management Review*, *6*(2), 309–318.

Feldman, M. S. (2004). Resources in emerging structures and processes of change. *Organization Science*, *15*(3), 295–309.

Gino, F., Bauer, T. N., Cable, D. M., & Erdogan, B. (2010). When good apples spoil the barrel: Predicting the impact and acceptance of newcomers' ideas. Paper presented at the Academy of Management, Montreal, Quebec.

Goethals, G. (1986). Social comparison theory: Psychology from the lost and found. *Personality and Social Psychology Bulletin*, *12*(3), 261.

Grandey, A. A. (2003). When "the show must go on": Surface acting and deep acting as determinants of emotional exhaustion and peer-rated service delivery. *Academy of Management Journal*, *46*(1), 86–96.

Greenberger, D. B., & Strasser, S. (1986). Development and application of a model of personal control in organizations. *The Academy of Management Review*, *11*(1), 164–177.

Gross, J. J. 1998. The emerging field of emotion regulation: An integrative review. *Review of General psychology*, *2*(3), 271.

Harvey, J., Wheeler, A., Halbesleben, J. R. B., & Buckley, M. R. (2010). How did you figure that out? Employee learning during socialization. In J. Martocchio & H. Liao & A. Joshi (Eds.), *Research in Personnel and Human Resources Management*, Vol. 29, 167–200. Bingley, UK: Emerald Group Publishing Limited.

Ibarra, H. (1999). Provisional selves: Experimenting with image and identity in professional adaptation. *Administrative Science Quarterly*, *44*(4), 764–791.

Ibarra, H., & Barbulescu, R. (2010). Identity as narrative: Prevalence, effectiveness, and consequences of narrative identity work in macro work role transitions. *The Academy of Management Review*, *35*(1), 135–154.

Jones, G. R. (1983). Psychological orientation and the process of organizational socialization: An interactionist perspective. *The Academy of Management Review*, *8*(3), 464–474.

Jones, G. R. (1986). Socialization tactics, self-efficacy, and newcomers' adjustments to organizations. *The Academy of Management Journal*, *29*(2), 262–279.

Kammeyer-Mueller, J. D., & Wanberg, C. R. (2003). Unwrapping the organizational entry process: Disentangling multiple antecedents and their pathways to adjustment. *Journal of Applied Psychology*, *88*(5), 779.

Kim, T. Y., Cable, D. M., & Kim, S. P. (2005). Socialization tactics, employee proactivity, and person-organization fit. *Journal of Applied Psychology*, *90*(2), 232.

Kristof-Brown, A. L., Zimmerman, R. D., & Johnson, E. C. (2005). Consequences of individuals' fit at work: A meta-analysis of person-job, person-organization, person-group, and person-supervisor fit. *Personnel Psychology*, *58*(2), 281–342.

Kunda, G. 2006. *Engineering culture: Control and commitment in a high-tech corporation*. Philadelphia: Temple University Press.

Leonard, D., & Sensiper, S. (1998). The role of tacit knowledge in group innovation. *California Management Review*, *40*(3), 112–132.

Lewicki, R. J. (1981). Organizational seduction: Building commitment to organizations. *Organizational Dynamics*, *10*(2), 5–21.

Louis, M. R. (1980). Surprise and sense making: What newcomers experience in entering unfamiliar organizational settings. *Administrative Science Quarterly*, *25*(2), 226–251.

Miller, V. D., & Jablin, F. M. (1991). Information seeking during organizational entry: Influences, tactics, and a model of the process. *The Academy of Management Review*, *16*(1), 92–120.

Moreland, R. L., & Levine, J. M. (1982). Socialization in small groups: Temporal changes in individual-group relations. *Advances in experimental social psychology*, *15*, 137–192.

Morrison, E. W. (1993). Newcomer information seeking: Exploring types, modes, sources, and outcomes. *The Academy of Management Journal*, *36*(3), 557–589.

Morrison, E. W. (1995). Information usefulness and acquisition during organizational encounter. *Management Communication Quarterly*, *9*(2), 131.

Morrison, E. W. (2002). Newcomers' relationships: The role of social network ties during socialization. *The Academy of Management Journal*, *45*(6), 1149–1160.

Nelson, D. L., & Sutton, C. (1990). Chronic work stress and coping: A longitudinal study and suggested new directions. *The Academy of Management Journal*, *33*(4), 859–869.

Nicholson, N. (1984). A theory of work role transitions. *Administrative Science Quarterly*, *29*(2), 172–191.

Osterloh, M., & Frey, B. S. (2000). Motivation, knowledge transfer, and organizational forms. *Organization Science*, *11*(5), 538–550.

Ostroff, C., & Kozlowski, S. W. (1992). Organizational socialization as a learning process: The role of information acquisition. *Personnel Psychology*, *45*(4), 849–874.

Pinder, C. C., & Schroeder, K. G. (1987). Time to proficiency following job transfers. *The Academy of Management Journal*, *30*(2), 336–353.

Podolny, J. M., Khurana, R., & Hill-Popper, M. (2005). Revisiting the meaning of leadership. *Research in Organizational Behavior: An Annual Series of Analytical Essays and Critical Reviews*, *26*, 1–36.

Podsakoff, P. M., MacKenzie, S. B., Lee, J. Y., & Podsakoff, N. P. (2003). Common method biases in behavioral research: a critical review of the literature and recommended remedies. *Journal of Applied Psychology*, *88*(5), 879.

Reichers, A. E. (1987). An interactionist perspective on newcomer socialization rates. *The Academy of Management Review*, *12*(2), 278–287.

Roberts, L. M. (2005). Changing faces: Professional image construction in diverse organizational settings. *The Academy of Management Review*, *30*(4), 685–711.

Rollag, K. (2004). The impact of relative tenure on newcomer socialization dynamics. *Journal of Organizational Behavior*, *25*(7), 853–872.

Saks, A. M., & Ashforth, B. E. (1997). Organizational Socialization: Making Sense of the Past and Present as a Prologue for the Future. *Journal of Vocational Behavior*, *51*,(2), 234–279.

Saks, A. M., Uggerslev, K. L., & Fassina, N. E. (2007). Socialization tactics and newcomer adjustment: A meta-analytic review and test of a model. *Journal of Vocational Behavior*, *70*(3), 413–446.

Schein, E. H. (1968). Organizational socialization and the profession of management. *Industrial Management Review, 9,* 1–16.

Spreitzer, G., Sutcliffe, K., Dutton, J., Sonenshein, S., & Grant, A. M. (2005). A socially embedded model of thriving at work. *Organization Science, 16*(5), 537–549.

Sutcliffe, K., & Vogus, T. (2003). Organizing for resilience. *Positive organizational scholarship: Foundations of a new discipline* (pp. 94–110). San Francisco: Berrett-Koehler.

Van Maanen, J., & Schein, E. H. (1979). Toward a theory of organizational socialization. *Research in Organizational Behavior, 1,* 209–264.

Van Maanen, J. (2009). Identity work and control in occupational communities. In S. B. Sitkin & L. B. Cardinal & K. M. Bijlsman-Frankema (Eds.), *Control in organizations: New directions in theory and research* (pp. 111–166). New York: Cambridge University Press.

Wanberg, C., & Kammeyer-Mueller, J. (2000). Predictors and outcomes of proactivity in the socialization process. *Journal of Applied Psychology, 85*(3), 373–338.

Wrzesniewski, A., & Dutton, J. E. (2001). Crafting a job: Revisioning employees as active crafters of their work. *The Academy of Management Review, 26*(2), 179–201.

PART 2

Conceptualizations of Socialization, Antecedents, and Outcomes

Getting Newcomers On Board: A Review of Socialization Practices and Introduction to Socialization Resources Theory

Alan M. Saks *and* Jamie A. Gruman

Abstract

There are many practices and methods that organizations can employ to socialize new hires and get them on board. In this chapter, we review five socialization practices that have received the most attention in the socialization literature: orientation programs, training programs, socialization tactics, job characteristics, and socialization agents. We conclude that as a whole, the socialization literature remains fragmented, undeveloped, and incomplete, as it has failed to adequately identify and study the socialization practices used by organizations today. In an effort to address these limitations, we review the practitioner literature and provide examples of what several organizations do to socialize their new hires. Based on this information in combination with the research literature, we then introduce a new, more complete and integrated approach to organizational socialization called *Socialization Resources Theory* (SRT). Socialization Resources Theory focuses on the resources that newcomers require for a successful adjustment and socialization. We describe 17 socialization resources that organizations can provide before entry, immediately after entry, during the first 6 months of the socialization process, and after the formal socialization period. The chapter concludes with a discussion of the implications of SRT for socialization theory, research, and practice.

Key Words: Socialization Resources Theory, socialization tactics, orientation programs, training programs, job characteristics, socialization agents

When individuals join and enter organizations, they find themselves in a state of unfamiliarity and uncertainty in many respects. They are unsure of their role and how well they will perform their job. They are unaware of the appropriate and acceptable ways of behaving in the organization. In effect, they are like strangers in a strange land who must learn how to think, behave, and interact with other members of the organization if they are to become accepted and effective members themselves. Thus, they not only need to learn the technical requirements of the job to become proficient and effective in the performance of their work, they must also learn the social behaviors and attitudes that are acceptable and required for becoming a functioning member of the organization (Katz, 1980). The period and process

in which this transformation occurs is known as *organizational socialization.*

As described by Van Maanen and Schein (1979), socialization is the process through which one "learns the ropes" of a particular organizational role. More specifically, it is "the process by which an individual acquires the social knowledge and skills necessary to assume an organizational role" (p. 211). Katz (1980) defines the socialization period as the "introductory events and activities by which individuals come to know and make sense out of their newfound work experiences" (p.88). The type of events and activities provided by organizations for this purpose is the focus of this chapter.

In this chapter we review the socialization antecedents or organization-initiated practices and programs directed toward the socialization and adjustment of newcomers. The chapter is organized in four sections. First, we discuss the experience of organizational entry from the newcomers' perspective and what socialization programs must try to accomplish if they are to be effective for newcomers. Second, we provide a comprehensive review of five of the most studied organization-initiated antecedents in the socialization literature (orientation programs, training programs, socialization tactics, job characteristics, and socialization agents). Third, we briefly review the professional and practitioner literature on the socialization and onboarding practices of organizations to learn what organizations are doing today to socialize their new hires and to identify the gaps in the research literature. Fourth, we introduce a new approach to organizational socialization called *Socialization Resources Theory* and discuss its implications for socialization theory, research, and practice.

The Organizational Entry Socialization Experience

Before we review socialization practices, it is important to first understand what newcomers experience during organizational entry. This sets the stage for understanding newcomers' needs during socialization and how socialization practices should be designed to meet those needs and confront the challenges newcomers face during organizational entry.

Entry into an organization has been described as a transition that "thrusts one from a state of certainty to uncertainty; from knowing to not knowing; from the familiar to the unfamiliar" (Van Maanen, 1977, p.16). As described by Katz (1980), newcomers enter "a somewhat alien and stressful territory" in which they must find order in unfamiliar and vague surroundings. Thus, newcomers are motivated to reduce uncertainty and build an acceptable identity.

Socialization has been described as primarily a learning process in which newcomers need to acquire a variety of types of information and knowledge to become adjusted and effective members of the organization (Klein & Weaver, 2000). The theoretical and conceptual underpinning of socialization research is uncertainty reduction theory (Lester, 1987). According to Miller and Jablin (1991),

> ...during the encounter phase of organizational assimilation newcomers depend upon information from others for developing role clarity. Although newcomers receive role-related information, the

information they receive is frequently perceived as inadequate; hence, they usually experience fairly high levels of uncertainty. This uncertainty is reflected in the levels of role ambiguity and role conflict which newcomers experience and is of importance because it may have an impact on employees' job satisfaction, productivity, and, ultimately, job tenure (p. 93).

Thus, based on the newcomer experience during organizational entry, one can determine what it is that newcomers are most in need of during their socialization. First and foremost, they need *information* to reduce their uncertainty and to learn to perform their jobs and adjust to life in the organization. Second, newcomers need to have their *anxiety* reduced so that they can begin to perform their jobs and function effectively as a member of the organization. Third, newcomers need to feel *confident* about themselves and their ability to perform their jobs and become an effective member of the organization. Fourth, newcomers require *feedback* so that they know how they are doing and what they need to do to correct inappropriate behaviors and improve. Finally, newcomers require *social support* to help them deal with the pressures of a new job and to cope with new job demands, as well as the many changes, contrasts, and surprises they will experience during their socialization (Louis, 1980). With this in mind we now turn to a review of the socialization practices that have been the focus of socialization research.

Research on Organizational Socialization Practices

What are organizational socialization practices? In general, socialization practices refer to the techniques that organizations use to orient and socialize new employees (Louis, Posner, & Powell, 1983). Klein and Heuser (2008) used the term *orientation practices* to refer to "all formal and informal practices, programs, and policies enacted or engaged in by the organization or its agents to help socialize new members" (p.317–318). Thus, socialization practices can be both formal and informal and, as described by Klein and Heuser (2008), include actions to facilitate and encourage newcomer proactivity and the assistance of social agents. For the purpose of this chapter, we define organizational socialization practices as *organization-initiated activities, programs, events, and experiences that are specifically designed to facilitate newcomers' learning, adjustment, and socialization into a job, role, work group, and organization so that they can become effective members of the organization.* To be clear, this definition includes interactions and activities that are initiated by organizational members (socialization agents) even though they might not be formalized or sanctioned by the organization. Thus, any practice, activity, event, or experience that is initiated by somebody in the organization other than the newcomer him/herself and has the goal of promoting newcomer adjustment is considered to be an organization-initiated socialization practice. This is in contrast to those practices that are initiated by newcomers themselves, such as information seeking or other proactive behaviors.

Several studies have taken a broad approach to this topic to find out what socialization practices newcomers find most helpful and effective. For example, Louis et al. (1983) conducted a study to compare the availability and helpfulness of alternative socialization practices and the effect they have on newcomer attitudes. Business students were contacted 6–9 months after graduation and asked to indicate if various socialization practices were available to them when they entered their organizations and how helpful the practices were for "learning the ropes" and becoming effective organizational members. It was found that the three most available socialization practices were interactions with peers, supervisors, and buddy relationships with senior coworkers, followed by social/recreational activities with people from work and formal onsite orientation. The most helpful practices were interactions with peers, buddy relationships with senior coworkers, and supervisor interactions, followed by having a mentor/sponsor and interactions with other new recruits. As a set, the availability of the socialization practices was positively related to job satisfaction, organizational commitment, and tenure intention. As well, the helpfulness of many of the practices was positively related to job satisfaction, organizational commitment, and tenure intention. Louis et al. (1983) concluded that the most important factor for making newcomers feel effective was daily interactions with peers while working. It was the most available practice and it was significantly related to job satisfaction, commitment, and tenure intention.

Nelson and Quick (1991) examined the availability and helpfulness of the same 10 socialization practices examined by Louis et al. (1983). They found that daily interactions with peers were the most available practice followed by formal orientation and interactions with secretary/support staff. Offsite training sessions, business trips, and having a mentor/sponsor were the least available practices.

As for the helpfulness of the practices, daily interactions with peers, one's supervisor, and having a buddy/senior worker were rated as the most helpful practices, while business trips and training sessions were rated as the least helpful. The availability and helpfulness of the practices were also found to predict several indicators of adjustment. The availability of offsite training sessions and business trips was associated with lower psychological distress symptoms. Somewhat surprisingly, they found that newcomers who did not have mentors/sponsors reported higher job satisfaction compared to those who did. The helpfulness of one's supervisor and other newcomers was related to fewer psychological distress symptoms, and the helpfulness of the secretary/support staff and daily interactions with peers was positively related to job satisfaction. The helpfulness of the mentor was negatively related to job satisfaction and positively related to intentions to leave the organization. Daily interactions with peers were negatively related to intentions to leave the organization. In addition, the helpfulness of several of the practices (buddy/senior workers, daily interactions with peers, mentor, other newcomers) was negatively related to job performance. According to Nelson and Quick (1991), this might be because newcomers who are having performance problems are more likely to seek out help from others.

Finally, in a study that used the critical incidents technique to find out what incidents and events were most important for newcomers, Lundberg and Young (1997) found that, contrary to expectations, orientation and training were not the most important. The types of events that were mentioned most frequently as important for newcomers were supportiveness and being shown concern, interest, and caring from others or lack of it; being appreciated, recognized, and praised or blamed; being made to feel welcome or unwelcomed; and being made to feel part of the family/team or experiencing conflict and separation between workers. The events that had the least impact on newcomers included task assignment, politics/trust, and job security. They also found that more than half of all the incidents reported were interpreted as negative, including 71% on the first day.

Most studies in the socialization literature have focused on one particular socialization practice. In the remainder of this section, we review the following socialization practices that have received the most research attention: *(1)* orientation programs, *(2)* training programs, *(3)* socialization tactics, *(4)* job characteristics, and *(5)* socialization agents.

When considering these practices, an important first question to ask is: *What makes an organizational socialization practice effective?* The answer, of course, depends on what is meant by *effective*. If reducing uncertainty and anxiety is a major goal of newcomers, then socialization practices that accomplish this would be considered effective. This, however, primarily reflects the newcomer's perspective. The major goal of organizations might be positive attitudes, high job performance, and retention. Therefore, the extent to which a socialization practice is effective depends on the criteria that one is most concerned about. The main point is that socialization practices will be differentially effective in terms of the extent to which they relate to socialization outcomes. This means that it is not only important to identify effective socialization practices but also to identify practices that are most effective for particular socialization outcomes, as well as those practices that lead to outcomes that are of most concern to newcomers and organizations.

Recent approaches to organizational socialization have tended to distinguish between proximal outcomes, or what has also been referred to as *newcomer adjustment* (e.g., role clarity), as well as distal outcomes, which refer to traditional socialization outcomes such as job satisfaction and organizational commitment. In general, it has been suggested that socialization practices lead to proximal outcomes, such as role clarity, which then lead to distal socialization outcomes such as organizational commitment (Bauer & Green, 1998; Kammeyer-Mueller & Wanberg, 2003). Several studies have shown that socialization antecedents are related to proximal and distal socialization outcomes, and proximal outcomes (e.g., self-efficacy, role clarity, learning, fit perceptions) at least partially mediate the relationship between socialization antecedents and distal outcomes (Ashforth, Sluss, & Saks, 2007; Bauer, Bodner, Erdogan, Truxillo, & Tucker, 2007; Kammeyer-Mueller & Wanberg, 2003; Saks, Uggerslev, & Fassina, 2007). Therefore, when considering the effectiveness of socialization practices, one should keep in mind the extent to which a practice has been shown to be related to proximal outcomes, or newcomer adjustment, and distal socialization outcomes. This then leads to a second, related question that is fundamental for socialization research and practice: *What organizational socialization practices are most effective?*

Figure 3.1 shows the linkages between the five socialization practices described in this section, as well as the proximal and distal socialization outcomes that have been studied in the socialization literature. The model shows that socialization practices have direct effects on the distal outcomes, as well as indirect or mediated effects through the proximal outcomes. Although learning is generally considered to precede proximal outcomes (Klein & Heuser, 2008; Saks & Ashforth, 1997a), we include it as a proximal outcome simply because most of the studies to be reviewed have not treated it as a precursor of proximal outcomes. Nonetheless, it is important to recognize that learning is a precondition for at least some of the proximal outcomes (e.g., task mastery, role clarity).

Orientation Programs

For most newcomers, socialization begins with an orientation program during the first day or week on the job in which they are introduced to the job, the people they will be working with, and the larger organization (Klein & Weaver, 2000). In addition to introducing newcomers to the organization, a main purpose of orientation is to begin communicating the psychological contract (Wanous & Reichers, 2000).

Orientation is considered to be part of the socialization process but distinct and different from socialization. According to Wanous and Reichers (2000), orientation differs from socialization in several respects. First, the orientation period is relatively short and usually lasts from the first day to the end of the first week. Second, fewer organizational members are involved in the orientation of new hires compared to socialization. Third, orientation covers far fewer areas compared to socialization, which covers all work-related facets of one's life and involves broad-based changes in newcomers. A final difference is that orientation is a program or event, while socialization is more of a process, making the former a much more focused topic. Thus, "orientation can be thought of as a combination of events occurring early after entry that can be studied separately from socialization" (Wanous & Reichers, 2000, p.438). Although they are different, orientation programs play an important role in facilitating the process of socialization (Wesson & Gogus, 2005).

Anderson, Cunningham-Snell, and Haigh (1996) found that an overwhelming majority of 100 major British organizations provided new hires with formal orientation programs within 4 weeks of entry. Most of the organizations provided standardized programs that were designed and conducted by in-house personnel practitioners. The content was general in nature and pertained mostly to health

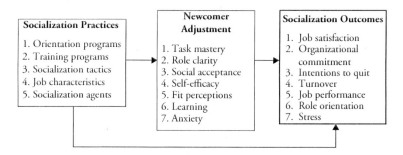

Socialization Practices	Newcomer Adjustment	Socialization Outcomes
1. Orientation programs 2. Training programs 3. Socialization tactics 4. Job characteristics 5. Socialization agents	1. Task mastery 2. Role clarity 3. Social acceptance 4. Self-efficacy 5. Fit perceptions 6. Learning 7. Anxiety	1. Job satisfaction 2. Organizational commitment 3. Intentions to quit 4. Turnover 5. Job performance 6. Role orientation 7. Stress

Figure 3.1. Socialization Practices, Newcomer Adjustment, and Socialization Outcomes

and safety, terms and conditions of employment, organizational history and structure, specific training provisions, and human resource management policies and procedures. As indicated earlier, Louis et al. (1983) found that onsite orientation sessions were among the most formal and planned socialization practices used by organizations, although they were found to be only modestly helpful.

There have been surprisingly few studies on orientation programs in the academic literature. One of the first, and now classic, was an experiment conducted by Gomersall and Myers (1966) at Texas Instruments. The study was based on evidence that employees were experiencing anxiety and this was having a negative effect on their work performance. As a result, a 1-day program was designed to help new employees overcome anxieties. The anxiety-reduction session followed the standard 2-hour orientation, which involved information on hours of work, insurance, parking, work rules, and employee services. The anxiety-reduction session emphasized that most employees will be successful, described facts about the good and bad aspects of the job and what was expected, encouraged employees to take initiative in communication and ask questions, and offered detailed descriptions of the personalities of supervisors. When compared to a control group that only received the standard 2-hour orientation, the experimental group was more productive, had better job attendance, and reached higher levels of competence much sooner. Similar results were found when other groups of employees received the anxiety-reduction session. The program is also credited with reducing costs and improving quality and profitability.

Saks (1994a) studied the information that seasonal employees of a large amusement park received from the organization's orientation program. He found that the accuracy and completeness of the information employees received from the orientation program was positively related to having met expectations, organizational commitment and

ability to cope, which were subsequently related to job satisfaction, intention to quit, and job survival.

Klein and Weaver (2000) tested the effectiveness of an organizational-level orientation program on new hire socialization and organizational commitment. Newly hired employees at a large educational institution were invited to attend a voluntary 3-hour orientation program for all full-time employees who had been employed less than six months. All new hires were asked to complete a survey and invited to attend the orientation program. They were also asked to complete a survey 10 weeks after the first survey, which was 1 to 2 months following the orientation program. The results indicated that employees who attended the orientation program had higher scores on several socialization content dimensions (i.e., history, goals/values, people) and also reported higher affective organizational commitment. Further, the effect of the orientation program on organizational commitment was mediated by the socialization content dimensions (i.e., goals/values, history).

A study by Wesson and Gogus (2005) compared a traditional (social-based) orientation program to a multimedia, computer-based orientation program in a sample of 261 newcomers from a large technology-based consulting firm. New hires were assigned to conditions based on orientation availability dates (new hires were placed in the computer-based orientation program because their employment began during off-cycle hiring periods). The traditional social-based orientation program was a 1-week program to familiarize new hires with the organization and its practices and procedures, and to create a sense of community and belonging between newcomers and the organization. Newcomers were flown to a central location in the United States and secluded with a group of new hires, orientation instructors, and guest speakers from various parts of the organization. The orientation program consisted of presentations, videos, reading assignments, team-building activities, and question-and-answer sessions. The computer-based orientation program was a self-guided program that covered the same material as the traditional program through the use of a multimedia orientation that included written, audio, and video-based sessions. The program was designed to take 2 to 3 days to complete.

A comparison between the two groups on socialization content dimensions after 2 months on the job indicated that newcomers who attended the computer-based orientation program had lower scores on the more social-related content dimensions of socialization (i.e., people, politics, and organizational goals and values) but not for the more information-based content areas of socialization (i.e., knowledge of the organization's history, language, and performance proficiency). In addition, newcomers in the computer-based orientation program had lower levels of job satisfaction and organizational commitment after 4 months on the job and their supervisors rated them lower on organizational goals and values socialization and role understanding. Further, the socialization content dimensions (i.e., organization goals and values, politics, and people) mediated the effects of the computer-based orientation program on job satisfaction and organizational commitment. These results suggest that the computer-based orientation program hindered the socialization of newcomers on socially oriented content areas of socialization but not information-based content areas.

Wanous and Reichers (2000) have argued that most orientation programs are too narrow in focus, in that they primarily involve imparting information. They suggest that orientation programs should be designed to lower the stress of newcomers and should therefore teach newcomers coping skills for the most important stressors they will face, as well as interpersonal skills. They refer to this kind of orientation program as *ROPES*, or Realistic Orientation Programs for New Employee Stress.

ROPES programs should be designed to teach both emotion-focused and problem-focused coping skills. The basic principles for the design of ROPES are: *(1)* provide realistic information that forewarns newcomers about typical disappointments to expect and possible adjustment problems, as well as how to cope by setting goals and taking action; *(2)* provide general support and reassurance; *(3)* use behavior modeling training to show coping skills and give newcomers the opportunity to rehearse and receive feedback; *(4)* teach self-control of thoughts and feelings; and *(5)* target specific stressors for specific newcomers.

In one of the few studies to investigate a ROPES type orientation program, Waung (1995) compared an experimental group of new hires in entry-level service jobs at a quick-service food chain and local hospital. The orientation programs were administered before the first day of work. Participants in the experimental condition received self-regulatory training that included cognitive restructuring, positive self-talk, and statements to bolster self-efficacy, as well as information about common affective reactions to unpleasant situations. A comparison group received realistic information about the negative aspects of the job and suggested coping behaviors. Immediately after the orientation program, the experimental group reported higher levels of organizational supportiveness but there were no differences in self-efficacy. Four weeks after the orientation, the experimental group had higher job satisfaction and higher turnover; however, there were no differences for organizational supportiveness, self-efficacy, organizational commitment, anxiety, or intentions to quit. Although there was not a significant difference between the groups for intention to quit, the experimental group participants did indicate that they were more likely to remain on the job for a year or longer.

More recently, Fan and Wanous (2008) conducted a study in which they compared a ROPES intervention to a more traditional orientation program on a sample of 72 new graduate students from Asia attending a large university in the United States. The study focused on graduate students from Asia because their adjustment was worse than students from other regions. Based on interviews with international students as well as several pilot tests, a ROPES intervention was designed to teach international students how to cope with three major entry stressors: *(1)* the fast pace of the academic quarter system (the university has three quarters vs. two semesters), *(2)* language difficulties, and *(3)* social interaction difficulties. Students were randomly assigned to receive the ROPES intervention or a more traditional 3-hour orientation session that focused mostly on students' immediate concerns, such as how to keep legal status in the United States, personal safety issues, how to connect a home phone, and so forth. Students in the experimental condition received a shorter version of the traditional orientation program plus ROPES. The results indicated that the ROPES participants reported significantly lower expectations (at the end of the orientation program—i.e., the intervention lowered inflated pre-entry expectations), lower stress, and higher academic and interaction adjustment 6 and 9 months after the program. The results also indicated that the positive effects of ROPES became stronger over time, and stress mediated the effect of the ROPES intervention on academic and interaction adjustment. Thus, stress reduction was a key factor for the effectiveness of the ROPES intervention.

SUMMARY

Orientation programs play an important role in the socialization process and have been found to be effective for imparting socialization content (i.e., learning), lowering anxiety and stress, and for having a positive effect on traditional socialization outcomes (e.g., organizational commitment). Unfortunately, relatively little is known about the effects of orientation programs on other indicators of newcomer adjustment or how best to design and implement them. In fact, we really don't know much more than the simple fact that attending an orientation program is more effective than not attending one. The research on ROPES does provide some guidance as to how to design effective orientation programs; however, only two studies have been conducted on ROPES type interventions and one of them involved students. The use of technology and e-learning programs for orientation programs is likely to increase, although the one study conducted to date suggests that they may have some limitations (Wesson & Gogus, 2005) and should probably be used in combination with more traditional methods. This is an area where there clearly is a need for more research.

In summary, there is still a great deal to learn about how to design orientation programs and the effect they have on other indicators of newcomer adjustment and socialization outcomes. They do, however, seem to be an effective means of providing newcomers with information for learning socialization content and for reducing entry anxiety, and they seem to have a positive effect on job satisfaction and organizational commitment.

Training Programs

Training is one of the most formal and planned socialization practices and is often one of the first experiences a newcomer has with an organization (Saks, 1996). While orientation programs focus on organizational issues that are of concern and relevance to all newcomers, formal training programs focus on the knowledge and skills that are required to perform particular tasks or jobs. Training can

therefore help to get newcomers up to speed as quickly as possible (Saks, 1996).

Formal training represents an important socialization practice. As described by Feldman (1989), most newcomers attend some type of formal training when they enter an organization. The training that newcomers receive have a major influence on norm development, learning the boundaries of acceptable behavior, and attitudes toward the job and organization (Feldman, 1989; Louis et al., 1983; Tannenbaum, Mathieu, Salas, & Cannon-Bowers, 1991). According to Feldman (1989), training "plays a major role in how individuals make sense of and adjust to their new job settings" (p. 399):

> More and more, training has become the setting where perceptions and expectations about the organization are formed, where norms about social behavior are developed, where corporate values and ideology are communicated, and where individuals formulate their career paths. Indeed, in many cases, training has gone beyond being part of the socialization process and has become synonymous with it (pp. 398–399).

Relatively few studies in the socialization literature have focused on training as a socialization practice. As indicated earlier, Louis et al. (1983) found that offsite residential training programs were positively correlated with job satisfaction, organizational commitment, and tenure intentions. In one of the few studies to focus on training as a socialization practice, Tannenbaum et al. (1991) examined the effects of military recruit socialization training on the post-training attitudes of military trainees. The focus of the study was *training fulfillment*, which is defined as "the extent to which training meets or fulfills a trainee's expectations and desires" (p.760). Tannenbaum et al. (1991) found that training fulfillment was positively related to organizational commitment, training motivation, and academic and physical self-efficacy. Trainee satisfaction with training was also positively related to organizational commitment, training motivation, and physical self-efficacy. The results suggest that "fulfilling trainees' expectations and desires can play an important role in the development of post-training attitudes" (p.765).

Saks (1994b) compared the effects of formal training and tutorial (self-study) training on the anxiety and stress reactions of newly hired entry-level accountants in their first month on the job. The results indicated that self-efficacy moderated the relationship between training method and anxiety. Formal training was related to lower anxiety for newcomers with low technical self-efficacy, while tutorial training resulted in higher anxiety for newcomers who had lower academic self-efficacy. In other words, the method of training mattered most to newcomers with low self-efficacy and formal training was most helpful for reducing the anxiety of low self-efficacy newcomers. The anxiety of newcomers with high self-efficacy did not vary as a function of the training method. Thus, the training method made more of a difference for low self-efficacy newcomers who benefited from the structure and guidance of formal training.

In a study on the role of self-efficacy in the relationship between training and newcomer adjustment, Saks (1995a) found that the amount of training received by newly hired entry-level accountants in their first 6 months was positively related to post-training self-efficacy, ability to cope, job satisfaction, and organizational and professional commitment, and negatively related to intention to quit the organization and profession. In addition, newcomers' self-efficacy at entry moderated the relationship between training and adjustment such that training was more strongly related to several indicators of adjustment for newcomers who had lower levels of self-efficacy at entry. Saks (1995) also found that post-training self-efficacy partially mediated the relationship between training and newcomer adjustment. These results not only indicate that training was related to the adjustment of newcomers, but that it was especially beneficial to those newcomers who had lower self-efficacy at entry. Thus, as noted by Saks (1995), socialization practices are not only differentially available to newcomers (Louis et al., 1983), but they are also differentially effective for newcomers.

In a related study, Saks (1996) found that newcomers' ratings of the amount of training they received during the first 6 months were significantly related to their ratings of the helpfulness of the training. In other words, the more training newcomers received the more helpful they believed it to be. In addition, both the amount and helpfulness of training were related to a number of indicators of work adjustment (job satisfaction, organizational commitment, intention to quit, ability to cope, and job performance), and anxiety partially mediated the relationship between training and newcomer adjustment. Thus, the relationship between training and newcomer adjustment was due in part to a reduction in newcomers' anxiety.

SUMMARY

Although training is considered to be an important socialization practice, there has been relatively little research on training and socialization. In fact, as is the case with research on orientation programs, we really do not know much more than simply that more training is better. Further, a relatively small number of proximal and distal outcomes have been included in socialization training research. As a result, we only know that training can strengthen newcomers' self-efficacy, lower anxiety, and lead to more positive job attitudes. There is also some indication that training will be more effective for some newcomers, particularly those who have lower self-efficacy. What we do not know is what kind of training in terms of content and what training methods (e.g., traditional training versus e-learning) are most effective for newcomers and the extent to which they are related to various proximal and distal outcomes.

In summary, much more research is needed on training as a socialization practice that focuses on the content, methods, timing, and kinds of training that are most effective for newcomer adjustment and socialization. This research should draw upon the general training literature (see Brown & Sitzmann, 2011) as well as the full array of findings about what matters to newcomers. Although several authors have made linkages between the training and socialization literature (e.g., Feldman, 1989; Klein & Heuser, 2008), there remains a vast literature that has implications for socialization training programs (e.g., program design, the importance of the work environment, conditions of learning, and instructional theory; Goldstein, 1991) that have all but been ignored in socialization research. Experimental or quasi-experimental designs similar to those that have been used in research on orientation programs are also needed, as they have also been absent in the socialization training literature even though experimental designs are common in the training literature.

Socialization Tactics

By far the most research conducted to date on organization-initiated socialization practices has been on socialization tactics. Van Maanen and Schein (1979) define socialization tactics (or what they also refer to as *people processing* techniques) as "the ways in which the experiences of individuals in transition from one role to another are structured for them by others in the organization" (p. 230). These dimensions of socialization can be used by managers when socializing new recruits into the organization or at various boundary passages. According to Van Maanen and Schein (1979),

> ... any given tactic represents a distinguishable set of events which influence the individual in transition and which may make innovative responses from that individual more likely than custodial (or vice-versa). It is possible, therefore, to denote the various tactics used by organizations and then to explore the differential results of their own use upon the people to whom they are directed (p.230).

Van Maanen and Schein (1979) identified six tactical dimensions and described how they influence newcomers' custodial, content-innovative, or role-innovative responses. Each tactical dimension is said to exist on a bipolar continuum with considerable range between the two poles. *Collective* socialization refers to grouping newcomers and putting them through a common set of experiences together, while *individual* socialization involves isolating newcomers from one another and putting them through more or less unique sets of experiences. *Formal* socialization is the practice of segregating a newcomer from regular organizational members during a defined socialization period and putting them through a set of experiences tailored for newcomers, as opposed to *informal* socialization, which does not clearly distinguish a newcomer from more experienced members and learning occurs on the job through trial and error. *Sequential* socialization involves a fixed sequence of discrete and identifiable steps leading to the assumption of the role, as compared to *random* socialization in which the sequence of steps is ambiguous, unknown, or continually changing. *Fixed* socialization provides a timetable for the steps involved in the assumption of the role and precise knowledge of the time it will take to complete a given passage that is communicated to newcomers, whereas *variable* socialization does not provide information about the time it will take to assume the new role. *Serial* socialization means that the newcomer is socialized by experienced members of the organization, who groom the newcomer and serve as role models, as compared to a *disjunctive* socialization process, where role models are not available to inform newcomers how to proceed in a new role. Finally, *investiture* socialization confirms the incoming identity and personal characteristics of the newcomer, compared to *divestiture* socialization which seeks to disconfirm, deny, and strip away newcomers' identity and personal characteristics.

In the first empirical study on socialization tactics, Jones (1986) investigated the relationship between socialization tactics and newcomer adjustment in a sample of recent graduates from an MBA program. He suggested that Van Maanen and Schein's (1979) six tactics form a gestalt called *institutionalized socialization*. According to Jones (1986), the collective, formal, sequential, fixed, serial, and investiture tactics encourage newcomers to passively accept preset roles, thus reproducing the organizational status quo. Institutionalized tactics provide newcomers with information that reduces the uncertainty inherent in early work experiences and reflects a more structured and formalized socialization process. At the opposite end of the socialization continuum, the individual, informal, random, variable, disjunctive, and divestiture tactics encourage newcomers to question the status quo and to develop their own unique approach to their roles. Thus, individualized socialization reflects an absence of structure such that newcomers are socialized more by default than by design (Ashforth, Saks, & Lee, 1997), which may increase the uncertainty as well as anxiety of early work experiences (Jones, 1986).

Jones (1986) also suggested that the six tactics represent three broad factors. The *social* tactics consist of the investiture and serial dimensions and are considered to be the most important "because they provide the social cues and facilitation necessary during learning processes" (Jones, 1986, p. 266). The *content* tactics consist of the sequential and fixed dimensions and have to do with the content of the information given to newcomers. The *context* tactics consist of the collective and formal dimensions and have to do with the way in which organizations provide information to newcomers.

It is worth noting that Jones' (1986) classification scheme deviates from Van Maanen and Schein (1979) in two respects. Contrary to Van Maanen and Schein (1979), Jones (1986) argued that the fixed and investiture tactics will lead to a custodial response, while the variable and divestiture tactics will lead to an innovative response. Thus, in his classification scheme the placement of the fixed–variable dimension and the investiture–divestiture dimensions is opposite to what Van Maaen and Schein (1979) proposed. This is noteworthy because most studies have adhered to Jones' (1986) classification scheme with respect to what are considered to be institutionalized and individualized socialization tactics.

In addition to role orientation, Jones (1986) argued that tactics will also be related to a number of indicators of newcomer adjustment. In support, he found that institutionalized socialization tactics were negatively related to role ambiguity, role conflict, and intention to quit, and positively related to job satisfaction, organizational commitment, and a custodial role orientation. Jones (1986) also found that self-efficacy moderated the relationship between socialization tactics and role orientation such that institutionalized socialization tactics were more strongly related to a custodial role orientation for newcomers with low self-efficacy. He also found that the social tactics were the most strongly related to the outcomes, followed by the content tactics and then the context tactics.

Since the Jones (1986) study, there have been over two dozen studies on socialization tactics. The results of two recent meta-analyses found that institutionalized socialization tactics are negatively related to role ambiguity, role conflict, and intentions to quit, and positively related to fit perceptions, self-efficacy, social acceptance, job satisfaction, organizational commitment, job performance, and a custodial role orientation (Bauer et al., 2007; Saks et al., 2007). In addition, the social tactics were most strongly related to socialization outcomes, while the weakest relationships were found for the context tactics (Bauer et al., 2007; Saks et al., 2007).

According to both meta-analyses, socialization tactics lead to traditional socialization outcomes (e.g., job satisfaction) through more proximal outcomes (e.g., fit perceptions). For example, Bauer et al. (2007) found that role clarity, self-efficacy, and social acceptance mediated the relationship between socialization tactics and socialization outcomes, and Saks et al. (2007) found that role conflict, role ambiguity, and fit perceptions mediated the relationship between socialization tactics and socialization outcomes. It is also worth noting that the type of newcomer (recent graduate or other newcomers) as well as the type of study design (cross-sectional versus longitudinal) was found to moderate the relationships between the tactics and various outcomes such that the relationships tend to be stronger for recent graduates (school-to-work transition) and cross-sectional designs (Bauer et al., 2007; Saks et al., 2007). Saks et al. (2007) also found stronger relationships between the tactics and outcomes for newcomers who were on the job for less than 6 months, suggesting that the structure, guidance, and formality associated with institutionalized socialization tactics is especially beneficial to newcomers during the first 6 months.

Besides the main findings from the two meta-analyses linking socialization tactics to newcomer adjustment and socialization outcomes, there are a number of other findings that are worth noting. For example, socialization tactics have been shown to be related to newcomer proactive behaviors. In particular, newcomers are more likely to engage in proactive behaviors when the socialization tactics are institutionalized (Gruman, Saks, & Zweig, 2006). In addition, institutionalized socialization tactics have been found to be related to newcomer learning (Ashforth et al., 2007) and on-the-job embeddedness (Allen, 2006).

SUMMARY

Research on socialization tactics has almost defined the socialization literature over the last several decades, as it has come to represent the primary example of organization-initiated socialization practices. Indeed, socialization tactics have been found to predict most of the indicators of newcomer adjustment and socialization outcomes shown in Figure 3.1. However, research on socialization tactics is not without its problems. Researchers have continually noted the limitations of Jones' (1986) scales and questioned their reliability and validity (Ashforth & Saks, 1996; Saks et al., 2007). Some have used shortened versions of the scales and continue to do so, even though this is ill-advised (Ashforth & Saks, 1996) and Saks et al. (2007) found differences in the strength of relationships between tactics and outcomes for studies that used the complete versus modified versions of Jones' (1986) scales. Studies that used the complete scale found stronger relationships between the tactics and outcomes.

In addition, Ashforth and Saks (1996) have argued that the Jones (1986) measure of the investiture tactic is more like a measure of social support than identity affirmation, which is how it was defined by Van Maanen and Schein (1979). According to Van Maanen and Schein (1979), investiture and divestiture socialization processes concern "the degree to which a socialization process is constructed to either confirm or disconfirm the entering identity of the recruit" (p.250). As a result, Ashforth and Saks (1996) developed a new measure of the investiture tactic that is more consistent with Van Maanen and Schein's (1979) identity affirmation conceptualization, and Ashforth et al. (2007) recently adapted the Ashforth and Saks (1996) investiture measure.

Some concern has also been expressed over Jones' (1986) classification scheme with respect to the investiture–divestiture dimension. In particular, some studies have found that the investiture tactic does not operate in the same manner as the other institutionalized socialization tactics, and its role as such has been contested (Ashforth & Saks, 1996; Ashforth et al., 2007). In fact, depending on what an organization is trying to achieve and the sample, the investiture tactic can be either an institutionalized tactic or an individualized tactic (Ashforth et al., 2007). As described by Van Maanen and Schein (1979), whether or not socialization is divestiture or investiture is a function of the newcomer's characteristics. Thus, if an organization carefully selects new hires with certain characteristics, then they will probably choose the investiture tactic regardless of whether the other tactics are institutionalized or individualized.

Perhaps most problematic in research on socialization tactics is that it says very little about what organizations actually do or should do when they socialize newcomers. As noted by Ashforth et al. (2007), socialization tactics are a "black box" when it comes to the specific activities that they involve. For example, when socialization is collective we do not know what newcomers are doing; we only know that whatever they are doing, they are doing it together. This is because socialization tactics measure the structure of the socialization process or what Van Maanen and Schein (1979) refer to as the "structural side" of organizational socialization—not the actual activities, events, or content of socialization. As a result, there is very little to offer organizations in the way of guidance other than to tell them, for example, to make sure newcomers know when their socialization will end, what will happen throughout the process, and to make it as formal and structured as possible. In this regard, the overwhelming emphasis on socialization tactics over the last 20 years has not resulted in very meaningful practical or theoretical advancements. In fact, we really do not know much more today than we did 25 years ago: *institutionalized socialization tactics result in more positive socialization outcomes than individualized socialization tactics.*

In summary, future research on socialization tactics needs to focus more on what happens and the specific activities and events that occur within each particular tactic. For example, what are senior coworkers doing when the socialization tactic is serial? In addition, future research might investigate the conditions when individualized tactics might be more effective than institutionalized tactics, and whether or not there is a time period during the socialization process when institutionalized tactics are no longer necessary and individualized tactics

become more important. Finally, although other tactics have been suggested (e.g., tournament versus contest and open versus closed; Van Maanen, 1982), as far as we can tell they have never been measured or included in research on socialization tactics. These and other tactics should also be considered in future research.

Job Characteristics

Although the emphasis in the socialization literature has been on socialization tactics, also important is the nature of the work that newcomers are required to perform during their socialization. The most comprehensive research in this area is Katz's (1980) work on job characteristics and his transitional stage model of job longevity. According to Katz (1980), the importance of job characteristics (skill variety, task identity, task significance, autonomy, and job feedback) and the extent to which they will be related to employee attitudes and behaviors will vary throughout an employee's time in a job and tenure in an organization. In other words, job or organization longevity affects the importance of job characteristics and employees' responses to them. This is because "different sets of common issues and concerns are particularly important and influential in each of the separate job tenure periods" (Katz, 1980, p. 115).

Katz (1980) argues that during the socialization period, newcomers are primarily concerned with reducing uncertainty and establishing their own situational identity during the first few months, as well as learning the social and technical aspects of their new jobs and roles. Because newcomers are focused on building their situational identity during the first 3 or 4 months, some of the job characteristics, such as skill variety and autonomy, are not important to them. Katz (1980) argues that because newcomers are primarily concerned about psychological safety, security, integration, and identity (rather than achievement, accomplishment, and challenge, which come at later stages), they will be most receptive to task significance, task identity, and feedback. In fact, he argues that what is most important to newcomers during the initial months of socialization is the amount of task significance, not the amount of challenging work per se. He further notes that positive feedback is especially important because "it helps establish a sense of contribution and worth in addition to providing a more secure and acceptable feeling" (p.98). In addition, interpersonal feedback might be more important than feedback from the job itself.

In support of these predictions, Katz (1978) found that for employees who were new to an organization (3 months or less), task significance was positively related to job satisfaction and autonomy was negatively related. However, all the job characteristics were positively related to job satisfaction for newcomers who had been in the organization for 4 months or more. In other words, all of the job characteristics were important for newcomers by 4 months. With respect to the negative relationship between autonomy and job satisfaction for newcomers with less than 3 months of organization tenure, Katz (1978) suggests that "it may be more rational to confer autonomy gradually, carefully, and with considerable support during the first job months" (p.220).

Only a handful of other studies have focused on the characteristics of the job in the socialization literature. For example, Colarelli, Dean, and Konstans (1987) studied the effects of personal and situational factors on job outcomes of newly hired entry-level accountants. They found that among the situational factors that included autonomy, feedback, and context factors (satisfaction with supervision, coworkers, job security, and compensation), autonomy was positively related to performance, promotability, job satisfaction, and organizational commitment, and feedback was positively related to job satisfaction and organizational commitment. It should be noted that the situational factors were measured 1 year following entry, which would explain the positive relationship between autonomy and the work outcomes. In a related study on accountants in a large industrial firm and in accounting firms, Dean, Ferris, and Konstans (1988) found that expectations for several of the job characteristics at the start of employment were not met one year later. In other words, expectations for the five core job characteristics were not met on the job. Furthermore, those with greater unmet expectations had lower organizational commitment and higher intentions to quit. Thus, it would appear that the participants in this study wanted more of the job characteristics than they actually experienced and this had a negative effect on their job attitudes and intentions.

Feldman and Weitz (1990) investigated the work experiences and outcomes of business students on a summer internship. Among the job characteristics, they found that autonomy was significantly related to four job attitude variables (i.e., job satisfaction, organizational commitment, job involvement, internal motivation), and dealing with others, task identity, and skill variety were related to three of the

outcomes. Task significance was positively related to job involvement, and feedback from agents and the work itself were not related to any of the outcomes. Thus, the design of the work was a key factor for a successful summer internship.

In a study on entry-level accountants in public accounting firms, Saks (1995b) found that feedback from coworkers, senior coworkers, and one's manager was positively related to organizational commitment. In addition, feedback from senior coworkers and the manager was negatively related to intention to quit the organization and positively related to job performance, and feedback from the manager was also positively related to commitment to the profession. The strongest correlations with the outcomes were for feedback from the manager followed by feedback from senior coworkers. Saks (1995b) also found that newcomers who reported higher job challenge had more positive job attitudes and higher overall job performance.

Finally, Ashforth, Saks, and Lee (1998) examined the relationships between work context, socialization tactics, and newcomer adjustment in a sample of recent university graduates. They found that a motivating potential score (MPS) based on the five core job characteristics was positively related to newcomer adjustment (i.e., organizational identification, job satisfaction, and intentions to quit) after 4 and after 10 months on the job. Furthermore, MPS was a stronger predictor of work adjustment than socialization tactics.

SUMMARY

While the nature of a newcomer's new job is of primary importance to newcomers, very few studies in the socialization literature have studied newcomers' work tasks and assignments. However, the few studies that have been conducted suggest that the job itself, and job characteristics in particular, are important factors for newcomer socialization. In general, all five of the core job characteristics have been linked to socialization outcomes. However, most studies have focused on traditional socialization outcomes (e.g., organizational commitment) rather than proximal indicators of newcomer adjustment.

Unfortunately, except for Katz (1978) little attention has been given to the role of time with respect to the design of newcomers' work. In addition, little attention has been given to the type of work or its complexity. Too much autonomy might be especially harmful for jobs that are more complex and might have an effect on newcomers similar to that of individualized socialization tactics. In terms of practice, it would seem that all of the job characteristics are important for newcomer adjustment and socialization, especially after the first few months. Based on Katz's (1978) theory, it would seem that feedback, especially interpersonal feedback, and task significance are most important, and too much autonomy during the first few months might be more harmful than good.

Overall, research on the work that newcomers perform during their socialization has been limited and scattered and has not really advanced beyond simply testing relationships between the core job characteristics and socialization outcomes. Besides knowing what job characteristics are most important at different times during the socialization process, it would also be helpful to know what job characteristics are most important for certain proximal and distal outcomes. It would also be worthwhile to investigate how newcomers' work assignments change during the first year in terms of the job characteristics and the amount of challenge and responsibility. Such changes are likely to have an effect on newcomer adjustment (Jokisaari & Nurmi, 2009).

In addition, there is a need to study other aspects of newcomers' work that might be important for their socialization. For example, Rollag, Parise, and Cross (2005) suggested the notion of *network assignments,* which are assignments that require a newcomer to interact with other members of the organization. Rollag et al. (2005) found that newcomers adjust more quickly if their first assignment requires them to build relationships with a wide variety of people. Newcomers who were given standalone assignments remained isolated and failed to build relationships. As a result, they felt less connected to the organization and were more likely to quit. Thus, future research should look more closely at the nature of network assignments and how best to design them.

As for work design characteristics, Humphrey, Nahrgang, and Morgeson (2007) identified several other dimensions of work design that they refer to as *social characteristics* (e.g., social support) and *work context characteristics* (e.g., work conditions) besides the core job characteristics, which they refer to as *motivational characteristics* and that include several additional characteristics (e.g., information processing, job complexity, specialization, problem solving) besides the five core job characteristics. They conducted a meta-analysis on these work design characteristics and found that social characteristics explained incremental variance in several work

outcomes (e.g., job satisfaction, turnover intentions, organizational commitment), and work context characteristics explained incremental variance in job satisfaction and stress beyond the motivational and social characteristics. The social characteristics would seem to be especially important for newcomer adjustment and socialization, given the important role played by socialization agents.

Socialization Agents

Members of the organization, or *socialization agents* as they are known, play an extremely important and integral role in the socialization of newcomers (Bauer, Morrison, & Callister, 1998). Socialization agents are individuals who help to facilitate the adjustment of newcomers through various actions such as providing information, feedback, resources, and so on (Klein & Heuser, 2008). According to Reichers (1987), "co-workers, supervisors, subordinates, clients, and/or customers act as agents of socialization through which newcomers learn their appropriate work roles, engage in sensemaking activities, and establish situational identity" (p.285).

Although some members of the organization might be given formal roles to facilitate the socialization of newcomers (e.g., mentor), the role of socialization agents is often informal. As noted by Feldman (1989), "A great deal of what new recruits learn is learned through informal interactions with peers, supervisors, and mentors outside the context of formal training" and these informal interactions "play an important role in filling the gaps left by formal training and orientation" (p.386). In fact, the frequency of interactions with insiders has been described as the primary mechanism through which socialization occurs and newcomers are transformed into insiders (Reichers, 1987). As indicated earlier, Louis et al. (1983) found that interactions with peers, supervisors, and senior coworkers were rated as the three most helpful socialization practices. In a study on newly hired engineers in a large manufacturing organization, Korte (2010) found that developing relationships with coworkers and managers, and the quality of interactions, was the primary mechanism for learning and a successful socialization.

Thus, while orientation and training represent highly formal socialization practices, socialization agents represent an important informal socialization practice. In fact, there is some evidence that they are even more important for newcomer adjustment than formal practices. Nelson and Quick (1991) found that the helpfulness of relational attachments with peers, secretaries, and staff were of greater importance for newcomer adjustment than formal practices such as orientation sessions, training, and business trips. Similarly, Lundberg and Young (1997) found that relational attachments were more important for newcomers than orientation and training programs. In a study that compared the coping strategies used by job changers and new hires, Feldman and Brett (1983) found that new hires were more likely to cope by seeking out information about job duties, and performance appraisal, social support, and help. Thus, newcomers cope primarily by getting help and support from insiders.

Socialization agents perform several functions that facilitate newcomer adjustment and socialization. First, they are an important source of information for newcomer learning (Major, Kozlowski, Chao, & Gardner, 1995). As described by Fisher (1986), "in virtually all cases, most learning relies in some way upon other people—agents of socialization" (p.132). Ostroff and Kozlowksi (1992) investigated newcomers' acquisition of information in several different content domains and sources. They found that newcomers relied primarily on observation of others followed by interpersonal sources (i.e., supervisors and coworkers) to acquire information. Supervisors and coworkers provided task and organization information to an equal extent; however, supervisors provided more role information and coworkers provided more group information. Obtaining more information from supervisors was positively related to job satisfaction and organizational commitment, and negatively related to turnover intentions. Obtaining more information from coworkers was positively related to job satisfaction and organizational commitment, and negatively related to stress and turnover intentions. Ostroff and Kozlowksi (1992) also found that newcomers who increased the amount of information they obtained from supervisors over time was associated with a positive change in their job satisfaction, organizational commitment, and adjustment. These results suggest that newcomers rely primarily on observation of others, supervisors, and coworkers for information, and the acquisition of information is associated with positive adjustment and socialization outcomes.

A second important function of socialization agents is to provide newcomers with social support (Bauer et al., 1998). The importance of social support has long been considered a critical factor in the socialization of newcomers (Fisher, 1985; Katz,

1980). As indicated earlier, Lundberg and Young (1997) found that the critical events newcomers reported most frequently involved supportiveness and caring from coworkers and managers. Fisher (1985) investigated the role played by social support from coworkers and the supervisor in facilitating the adjustment of newly graduated nurses working in hospitals during the first 6 months. She conceptualized social support as "the number and quality of friendships or caring relationships which provide either emotional reassurance, needed information, or instrumental aid in dealing with stressful situations" (p.40). She found that social support from coworkers and the immediate supervisor was negatively related to unmet expectations stress. Social support from both coworkers and the immediate supervisor was also positively related to several socialization outcomes (job satisfaction, performance, organizational commitment) and negatively related to turnover and intentions to leave the organization and profession. Fisher (1985) concluded that support from coworkers was of equal importance to support from superiors. However, social support did not lessen the negative effects of unmet expectations stress on adjustment as predicted.

Although Fisher (1985) did not find a difference in the support provided by supervisors or coworkers, it is generally believed that support from a newcomer's immediate supervisor is of primary importance given the supervisor's formal authority and power to provide rewards and allocate resources and work assignments, in addition to providing information and feedback (Jokisaari & Nurmi, 2009). In a novel study that focused on supervisor support during the first two years of employment, Jokisaari and Nurmi (2009) found that newcomers' perceived supervisor support declined 6–21 months following organizational entry, and this decline was related to a decrease in role clarity and job satisfaction and a slower increase in salary. Although perceived supervisor support was positively related to initial work mastery, a decline in perceived supervisor support was not related to a decrease in work mastery. These results highlight the importance of continuous supervisor support beyond the first 6 months of the socialization period and into the second year of employment.

The nature or quality of the relationship between a newcomer and his/her supervisor and coworkers is also important and has been found to predict socialization outcomes (Bauer et al., 1998; Fisher, 1986). For example, Major et al. (1995) found that leader–member exchange (LMX) and team–member exchange (TMX) predicted socialization outcomes (organizational commitment, job satisfaction, turnover intention). In addition, the negative effects of unmet expectations on socialization outcomes were ameliorated for newcomers who had favorable (high quality) role development relationships with their supervisor or workgroup. In a study on manager behavior and socialization, Bauer and Green (1998) found that manager behavior was positively related to newcomer accommodation and socialization outcomes (performance, job satisfaction, organizational commitment). In particular, manager clarifying behavior was positively related to role clarity and performance efficacy, and manager supporting behavior was positively related to feelings of acceptance by the manager. Newcomer accommodation mediated the relationship between manager behavior and socialization outcomes. Further, the effects of manager behavior on accommodation and socialization outcomes were much greater than newcomer information-seeking behavior.

Kammeyer-Mueller and Wanberg (2003) investigated the influence of the organization (e.g., orientation, training), supervisors, and coworkers on proximal and distal socialization outcomes. They found that each source of influence was related to different outcomes. For example, organization influence was positively related to role clarity and negatively related to work withdrawal (behaviors that reflect an attempt to psychologically disengage from work tasks); leader influence was positively related to political knowledge and negatively related to turnover; and coworker influence was positively related to group integration.

There is also some evidence that the size of a newcomer's information and friendship networks are important for newcomer adjustment. Morrison (2002) found that structural characteristics of newcomers' informational networks (i.e., size, density, strength, range, status) were related to organizational knowledge, task mastery, and role clarity, and structural characteristics of friendship networks were related to organizational knowledge, role clarity, social integration, and organizational commitment. For example, newcomers whose friendship networks included individuals from different subunits and levels reported higher organizational commitment, while those with larger networks reported greater social integration. Rollag et al. (2005) found that newcomers who were most quickly adjusted had developed a broad network of relationships with coworkers. They suggested that what matters most for successful adjustment and socialization is

how quickly newcomers develop relationships with a variety of coworkers.

Finally, several studies have found that having a mentor can facilitate the adjustment and socialization of newcomers. For example, Blau (1988) conducted a study on intern apprentices in an insurance company where assignment managers volunteer to serve as mentors, in what Blau (1988) referred to as an *apprenticeship organizational socialization* strategy. Blau (1988) found that the quality of interns' relationships with their assignment managers (mentors) was positively related to interns' met expectations, role clarity, organizational commitment, and performance, and moderated the relationship between role clarity and performance.

In a study on entry-level auditors in public accounting firms, Chatman (1991) found that spending time with a mentor was positively related to the newcomer's person–organization fit. Ostroff and Kozlowski (1993) investigated the role of mentoring for newcomers' information acquisition and found that newcomers who had mentors used them to learn about the organization and their role, rather than about their task and workgroup. Those with mentors also learned more about organizational issues and practices than those without a mentor, suggesting that mentors are an especially important source for learning about the organization. Furthermore, compared to newcomers with mentors, newcomers without mentors used coworkers more as a source of information. Thus, newcomers with mentors relied on their mentors for information, while those without mentors relied on their coworkers for information.

In a study on formal peer mentoring, in which first-year MBA students were formally assigned a second-year MBA peer mentor, Allen, McManus, and Russell (1999) found that both the psychosocial and career-related mentoring functions were positively related to learning socialization content (e.g., politics, organization goals, and values). Psychosocial mentoring was related to politics and performance proficiency, and career-related mentoring was related to people socialization content. In addition, both of the mentoring functions were positively related to protégé beliefs that their mentors helped them reduce and cope with their work-related stress. Allen et al. (1999) concluded that "formal group peer mentoring relationships can contribute to the successful socialization of newcomers" (p.463).

SUMMARY

Although the role of insiders or socialization agents has often been noted as critical for newcomer adjustment and socialization, there have actually been very few studies on the role of socialization agents. Those that have been conducted tend to focus on a specific dimension or role of socialization agents, such as providing information or social support. As a result, we do not know very much about what socialization agents actually do or should do, and the effect they have on the various proximal and distal socialization outcomes.

What we do know is that they provide newcomers with information that can facilitate learning and they are an important source of support that can lower newcomer stress and result in positive job attitudes. We also know that socialization agents might vary in terms of their roles, the information they provide, and the effect they have on different proximal and distal socialization outcomes (Kammeyer-Mueller & Wanberg, 2003). For example, supervisors have been found to provide more role information, while coworkers have been found to provide more group information (Ostroff & Kozlowksi, 1992). Morrison (1993) also found that newcomers prefer coworkers (e.g., social information) for certain types of information and supervisors (e.g., performance feedback) for other types. Thus, overall various aspects of socialization agents (e.g., information provided, social support, LMX, TMX, manager behavior, influence, social network ties) have been found to be related to both proximal (e.g., knowledge, learning, task mastery, role clarity, performance efficacy, social integration) and distal socialization outcomes (e.g., job satisfaction, organizational commitment, turnover intentions, performance, stress).

What is lacking, however, is a comprehensive model or framework that clearly outlines the specific behaviors of different socialization agents and links them to various proximal and distal outcomes. Rather, what we have is a handful of disparate studies that essentially look at different aspects or roles of socialization agents. There has been no attempt to integrate the various roles and behaviors or to build on existing research. In effect, each study seems to go off in its own direction. Furthermore, although different types of socialization agents have been identified in the literature, the emphasis has been on coworkers and supervisors, with relatively little attention given to other possible socialization agents (e.g., members in other departments, subordinates, customers, clients, etc.). One study, however, has looked at extraorganizational referents (i.e., family and friends) as a source of information and found that newcomers used them less frequently than coworkers and supervisors (Settoon & Adkins, 1997).

In addition, other than a few studies on mentoring, there have not been any studies that examine formally assigned socialization agents or so-called "buddies." Furthermore, although a common recommendation has been to develop programs to train insiders on how to facilitate newcomer adjustment and socialization (Ostroff & Kozlowski, 1992), we are not aware of any research that has either gathered data from insiders on how they have helped newcomers, or programs that have trained insiders on how to be effective socialization agents. This is an area that remains in need of research. Future research should gather data from insiders so we can learn more about the behaviors they engage in to assist newcomers, as well as the reasons why they do or do not participate in the socialization of newcomers.

Research on Organizational Socialization Practices: Summary

When one considers what we have learned from the research literature on socialization practices in organizations, it is easy to understand the long-standing criticism that the socialization literature is fragmented (Bauer et al., 2007; Fisher, 1986; Saks & Ashforth, 1997a). In fact, not only is it fragmented, it is undeveloped and incomplete. Each of the socialization practices are in effect standalone, independent, and isolated socialization topics. There has been little attempt to understand how they might be integrated and combined with each other into a complete, coherent framework of socialization practices. In fact, the only integration across topics in the socialization literature seems to have been a handful of studies that investigated newcomer proactive behaviors in combination with socialization tactics (Ashforth et al., 2007; Gruman et al., 2006; Saks & Ashforth, 1997b) and manager behaviors (Bauer & Green, 1998).

Furthermore, even within each area of research there has been little attempt to build upon existing research and to advance the area. For example, we really do not know much more today about socialization tactics or job characteristics then we did decades ago. As for research on orientation and training programs, we really don't know much more than that more of each (i.e., more orientation and more training) is better. And although there have been numerous studies on socialization agents, each study seems to focus on a specific role or behavior of socialization agents rather than build on previous studies.

As a result, it is difficult to answer the second question that we asked earlier in the chapter: *What organizational socialization practices are most effective*? We know relatively little about what practices work best for particular outcomes. Only the research on socialization tactics has studied a host of proximal and distal socialization outcomes. What we can say is that orientation programs seem to be effective for learning, anxiety and stress reduction, and creating positive attitudes; training programs seem to be effective for improving self-efficacy, lowering anxiety, and creating positive job attitudes; institutionalized socialization tactics are effective when it comes to most indicators of adjustment and distal socialization outcomes; job characteristics are effective for developing positive attitudes; and socialization agents are effective for a number of proximal (e.g., learning) and distal (organizational commitment) outcomes.

It is also difficult to know when certain socialization practices should be provided to newcomers, other than the need to provide orientation immediately after entry. It makes sense that during the initial socialization period, socialization should be institutionalized given newcomers' need for structure, guidance, and information, and given the motivation to lower entry uncertainty and anxiety. As described by Ashforth and Saks (1996), "the institutionalized practices help combat the initial reality shock and uncertainty that newcomers often encounter" (p.172). However, once newcomers begin to feel secure and comfortable in their new roles, they are likely to become less receptive to institutionalized socialization practices and more receptive to other stimuli, such as opportunities for challenge and growth (Ashforth & Saks, 1996).

Ideally, it would be nice to be able to say that certain socialization practices are particularly effective at certain times during the socialization process and for certain outcomes. However, this is not possible because not all of the proximal and distal outcomes have been studied within each area and, more importantly, because each area has been studied independent of the others, so we do not know which practice is most predictive of specific outcomes at different times throughout the socialization process.

Perhaps the greatest limitation of the existing research on organizational socialization practices is that so few practices have actually been studied—and those that have been studied are not very revealing in terms of what actually happens to newcomers throughout the socialization process. Klein and Heuser (2008) have also noted how surprising it is that there has been little research on specific socialization practices. Thus, there appears to be a huge gap in the socialization literature when it comes to socialization practices, thereby leading to the conclusion that the literature on organizational socialization practices is incomplete.

In an attempt to close this gap, Klein and Heuser (2008) identified three categories of socialization practices based on a review of the academic and practitioner literature: *inform* (providing newcomers with information through communication efforts, providing resources, and training); *welcome* (celebrating the arrival of the newcomer and/or providing opportunities for newcomers to meet and socialize with other members of the organization); and *guide* (providing a "hands-on" personal guide to help new hires navigate the transition). Klein and Heuser (2008) linked these practices to different socialization content dimensions using an instructional system approach. Their intent was to identify socialization practices that are most effective for learning different socialization content dimensions.

Our intent is to develop a more comprehensive framework of socialization practices that can be linked not only to learning outcomes, but to various proximal and distal socialization outcomes that can form the basis for future socialization research and practice. To begin this process, we need to go beyond the socialization practices that have been investigated in the academic literature to find out what practices organizations are using to socialize their new hires. Therefore, in the next section we provide a brief review of socialization and onboarding practices that have been described in the professional and practitioner literature.

Socialization Practices in Organizations

The professional and practitioner literature often publishes detailed descriptions of what organizations do to socialize their new hires. While some of the practices and activities overlap with the research on socialization, many of the practices have never been studied in the academic literature. Therefore, in this section we provide a brief review of the practices and programs that organizations use to socialize newcomers (see also Klein and Polin, Chapter 14). This helps set the stage for the kinds of practices that might be studied in future research on organizational socialization.

For starters, consider what the accounting firm PricewaterhouseCoopers (PwC) does for new hires as part of their Connectivity Program, which was designed to make sure employees have experienced peers to go to when they have questions:

> When new hires arrive, they are immediately assigned a Connectivity partner who contacts them, arranging to meet for lunch, or in some other informal setting, to establish a relationship that will be ongoing as long as the new employee is with the company...Connectivity partners pinpoint areas new hires need to develop, sometimes recommending them for specific corporate learning programs, supporting the new recruits throughout the programs. They can also act as career counselors (Weinstein, 2007, p.24).

In 2007, PwC implemented a new comprehensive onboarding program that was "designed to more fully indoctrinate workers into the firm and reduce first-year staff turnover" (Boehle, 2008, p.36). The idea was to create an end-to-end onboarding program that begins as soon as new hires accept a job offer with the firm. They are immediately given access to the "PwC Inside" portal which is a web-based interface with information about PwC's business, culture, and values. The portal also includes videos that showcase PwC people and experiences, as well as e-learning and other resources. The onboarding program then proceeds as follows:

> Next up, a new hire's first week involves networking, learning, and celebrating—beginning with a welcome day covering logistics and setup in each office. For experienced hires, days two and three bring PwC Inside Culture and Values, an experiential learning opportunity designed to help new hires better understand the firm's cultural foundation. Days four and five focus on PwC's business through e-learning; small group instruction; and meetings with coaches, peer hosts, and supervisors. Additionally, each service line and internal function runs follow-up sessions, with a special focus on campus and intern hires (Boehle, 2008, p.39).

To teach teamwork skills and the importance of investing in the communities where it does business, the onboarding program includes a team-based bicycle-building exercise, in which new hires work in groups to build bikes for children and adults. The bikes are then donated to youth organizations, senior-care facilities, and other nonprofit organizations (Boehle, 2008).

At Fairmont Hotels and Resorts, the largest luxury hotel company in North America, new hires receive an invitation to the hotel prior to their first day on the job. Newcomers are told to come to the front door of the hotel, where they are greeted by senior hotel management. They are then taken to a dining room for breakfast, where they have an informal discussion about the hotel. A short video is shown in which members of the corporate executive team welcome them and tell them where they can get assistance (Schettler & Johnson, 2002).

On the second day of orientation, newcomers listen to presentations and participate in role-playing exercises that simulate encounters with guests. Each hotel has its own unique way of showing newcomers the property. For example, some hotels have scavenger hunts in which teams of new hires compete with each other. Some hotels have celebrity tours, such as The Queen Elizabeth Hotel in Montreal where John Lennon and Yoko Ono had their "Bed-in for Peace" (Schettler & Johnson, 2002).

Between the second and third month, newcomers are paired with a mentor of their choice. Supervisors conduct a personal development interview in which they discuss goals and provide feedback. Employees are also reminded about what they were told during their first couple of days and asked to talk about their work experiences. Any issues or problems that an employee has experienced are addressed (Schettler & Johnson, 2002).

The Ritz-Carlton has a 2-day orientation program that is designed to immerse employees in the company's culture. A key part of the orientation program is personalization. To personalize the experience, interpreters are available for newcomers who need one and a favorite snack is waiting for each new hire at break time. Orientation takes place in the same meeting rooms that guests use, and they eat in the hotel's finest restaurant. Following the 2 days of orientation, newcomers work for 3 weeks with a departmental trainer who can also become their mentor. On day 21 there is a follow-up to make sure that the company is delivering what it promised. After one year, there is a pin ceremony to mark the new hires' first year at the company (Durett, 2006).

Finally, Eddie Bauer developed a standardized orientation program called "Bauer Beginnings" that begins with a 4-hour session that includes a review of the associate resource guide, 2 hours of training to learn desktop skills, and a campus tour. The resource guide includes a 90-day performance plan that newcomers must follow and an introduction to a portal that provides online access to information. During the first 3 months, newcomers attend four seminars that cover corporate history, product, and brand overview. A seminar on performance management provides information on performance appraisals and succession planning. Supplemental components cover topics that are specific to each new hire, such as an in-store program which is for designers, merchandisers, and planners (Schettler & Johnson, 2002).

After the 3-month orientation period is complete, newcomers complete a survey that asks about the support they received from their supervisor during their orientation. The results of the survey are then reported to corporate officers, directors, and managers. To help newcomers stay in contact and to ask questions, they are sent targeted emails every 6 months to make sure they have the information they need and to remind them that help is available (Schettler & Johnson, 2002).

These examples highlight a number of important points about organizational socialization practices. First, all of the main areas of socialization research are key parts of the socialization/onboarding at these organizations. They all have orientation programs, training programs, and make extensive use of socialization agents and provide newcomers with a variety of work experiences. Furthermore, the socialization process in all of these organizations is, structurally speaking, institutionalized. That is, newcomers are socialized together in formal programs; there is a timetable for when events will occur, often by day, week, and month; and the order or sequence of the various programs, events, and activities is clearly marked. Furthermore, experienced members of the organization are involved in the socialization of new hires and provide support throughout the process.

Second, there is much more detail about what happens during the orientation and training programs in terms of content (e.g., teamwork skills), methods (e.g., role playing), and participation of insiders (e.g., senior management) than what has been studied in socialization research. Third, there are many activities and events that organizations use that have seldom been the focus of socialization research or even described in the socialization literature (e.g., survey newcomers about their socialization experiences, maintain contact with newcomers following orientation, etc.). Fourth, there is a clear ordering or sequence of socialization events that occur before entry, immediately after entry, throughout the initial socialization period, and at the end of the formal socialization period. And finally, socialization is treated as a constant, continuous, ongoing process rather than a single event (e.g., orientation or training program) or time limited (e.g., first week or month). In some cases, it lasts up to one year

and involves a series of orientation sessions, training programs, follow-ups, and so on.

Thus, when compared to the socialization research literature, there is a clear a gap between socialization research and socialization practice. As described by Klein and Heuser (2008), "the absence of systematic research assessing the effectiveness of different socializing activities, both formal and informal, that occur during the socialization process is a major gap in the literature" (p.326). What this means is that socialization research is incomplete and needs to begin to incorporate and study the practices that are being used by organizations. This will not only help close the gap in the research literature, it will also aid in the development of a more complete and integrated theory of organizational socialization. In the next section, we begin this process by introducing a new approach to organizational socialization that we call *Socialization Resources Theory* (SRT).

Socialization Resources Theory

Successfully adjusting to new situations and dealing with the stressors they can present is facilitated by the presence of resources, which can be defined as entities that are inherently valued (e.g., self-esteem) or serve to facilitate the acquisition of valued ends (e.g., social support) (Hobfoll, 2002). For example, the availability of resources is central to effectively adjusting to the changing circumstances generated by health problems (Elizur & Hirsh, 1999; Pakenham, & Rinaldis, 2001), divorce (Wang & Amato, 2000), expatriate assignments (Farh, Bartol, Shapiro, & Shin, 2010), and the transition to retirement (Wang, Henkens, & van Solinge, 2011).

Resources are particularly important in the context of novel and stressful circumstances that tax people's ability to cope (Bakker, van Veldhoven, & Xanthopoulou, 2010; Hobfoll, 2002). Among the different benefits of resources, Hobfoll (2002) notes that the availability of resources makes people less likely to experience stress, more capable of solving problems, suffer less drain on their existing resources, and more likely to cultivate further resources.

Socialization Resources Theory (SRT) is an approach to organizational socialization and onboarding that focuses on the resources newcomers require for successful adjustment to their jobs, roles, workgroup, and the organization. It consists of a comprehensive set of resources that newcomers can draw on to manage the transition to work or changes in work roles. The basic premise of SRT is that the transition to a new job or role is inherently challenging and stressful, and that presenting newcomers with the resources they need to cope with this challenge is the most effective and efficient way to foster their adjustment and successful socialization. As described by Lundberg and Young (1997), newcomers have expectations and needs, such as feeling welcomed, receiving appropriate training, being assigned relevant tasks, and receiving adequate support, and these needs are often not met. Earlier in the chapter we noted that newcomers need information, anxiety reduction, confidence, feedback, and social support. Providing newcomers with the resources they need to promote and hasten their adjustment should have salutary effects on both proximal (e.g., task mastery) and distal (e.g., job satisfaction) socialization outcomes. Furthermore, certain resources will be more or less effective in their influence on various proximal and distal socialization outcomes and at different times during the socialization/onboarding process.

The conceptual basis for Socialization Resources Theory is the Job Demands–Resources Model (JD-R model: Bakker & Demerouti, 2007). According to the JD-R model, the work environment can be divided into demands and resources. *Job demands* refers to the physical, psychological, social, or organizational features of a job that require sustained physical and/or psychological effort from an employee that can result in physiological and/or psychological costs. Common job demands include work overload, job insecurity, role ambiguity, and role conflict. *Job resources* refers to the physical, psychological, social, or organizational features of a job that are functional, in that they help achieve work goals, reduce job demands, and stimulate personal growth, learning, and development. Job resources can come from the organization (e.g., pay, career opportunities, job security), interpersonal and social relations (supervisor and coworker support, team climate), the organization of work (e.g., role clarity, participation in decision making), and from the task itself (e.g., skill variety, task identity, task significance, autonomy, performance feedback; Bakker & Demerouti, 2007).

The basic principle of the JD-R model is that high job demands exhaust employees' physical and mental resources and lead to a depletion of energy and health problems. Job resources are motivational and can lead to positive attitudes, behavior, and well-being (Bakker & Demerouti, 2007). The motivational potential of job resources can be extrinsic because they are instrumental for achieving work goals, or intrinsic because they facilitate growth, learning, and development (Bakker & Demerouti,

2007), and satisfy basic human needs such as the needs for autonomy, relatedness, and competence (Deci & Ryan, 1985). Job resources are also important because they help individuals cope with job demands and have been found to buffer the negative effect of job demands on job strain (Bakker & Demerouti, 2007, 2008). As noted by Bakker and Demerouti (2007),

> . . . work environments that offer many resources foster the willingness to dedicate one's efforts and abilities to the work task. In that case it is likely that the task will be completed successfully and that the work goal will be attained. For instance, supportive colleagues and proper feedback from one's superior increase the likelihood of being successful in achieving one's work goals (p.314).

Research on the JD-R model has found support for the links between job resources and positive outcomes, and job demands and negative outcomes. In particular, job demands have been found to be related to burnout, disengagement, and health problems. Job resources have been found to predict work engagement, extra-role performance, and organizational commitment (Bakker & Demerouti, 2007). Additionally, although job resources may be inherently valuable to employees, such resources acquire their saliency in the face of situations with high job demands (Bakker et al., 2010), such as those experienced by organizational newcomers. In fact, job demands such as role conflict, role ambiguity, role overload, and unmet expectations have been found to be negatively related to newcomer adjustment and socialization outcomes (Nelson, Quick, & Eakin, 1988; Saks & Ashforth, 2000).

Socialization Resources Theory is built on both the academic and practitioner literatures and consists of 17 dimensions that address specific socialization/onboarding resources that can facilitate newcomer adjustment and socialization. These dimensions represent the most common resources that have been shown to benefit organizational newcomers from the academic and practitioner literature. Each dimension pertains to specific socialization events (as opposed to general experiences or learning content) and involves concrete socialization behaviors (as opposed to a subjective accounts). Thus, SRT is diagnostic and actionable; it can be used to assess an organization's current socialization efforts and serve as the basis for the development and improvement of existing onboarding programs.

One particularly valuable aspect of SRT is that its multiple dimensions allow organizations to tailor their socialization programs to the specific needs faced by newcomers in different roles (e.g., Xanthopoulou, Bakker, Dollard, Demerouti, Schaufeli, Taris, & Schreurs, 2007). For example, adjustment difficulties associated with the stress newcomers experience handling the emotional demands of customers might be best mitigated by increasing supervisor support, whereas adjustment problems stemming from complicated work procedures may be best addressed through information and regular feedback. Earlier it was noted that specific socialization practices are differentially related to socialization outcomes. SRT allows researchers and practitioners to tailor socialization resources to the specific needs and outcomes associated with onboarding into particular jobs and roles.

Table 3.1 presents the 17 SRT dimensions along with sample questions that can be used as a socialization resources audit. Following is a brief description of each of the socialization resources dimensions and the time period that we believe they should occur during the socialization/onboarding process.

Prior to Entry

Newcomers should be provided with resources prior to the first day of work. As Feldman (1976) has noted, "the socialization process begins even before employees enter the organization" (p. 65). We refer to this dimension as *anticipatory socialization*.

Anticipatory Socialization

Anticipatory socialization refers to the extent to which the organization contacts new hires before their first day on the job (e.g., early welcome, sent materials). This might involve a social event to introduce new hires to members of the organization, or contact from members of the organization. As indicated earlier, Lundberg and Young (1997) found that being made to feel welcome and part of the family/team was one of the most important experiences reported by newcomers. At Randstad North America, new hires receive a phone call from their manager to offer a welcome before the first day of work (Gustafson, 2005).

Immediately After Entry

Newcomers should be provided with a number of resources as soon as they begin their job. The resources that newcomers should receive at entry include formal orientation, proactive encouragement, and formal assistance.

FORMAL ORIENTATION

As noted earlier, orientation programs play an important role in the socialization of newcomers and can facilitate learning socialization content and positive job attitudes (Gomersall & Myers, 1966; Klein & Weaver, 2000). *Formal orientation* refers to the nature of the orientation received by the new hire; for example, how long it lasted, what it involved in terms of methods (classroom, online); what it involved in terms of exercises, fun activities, games, competition, and so on; and who was involved in the orientation (HR, senior management, etc.).

PROACTIVE ENCOURAGEMENT

A substantial body of research demonstrates the value of proactive behavior during the socialization process (e.g., Ashford, 1986; Morrison, 1993; Wanberg & Kammeyer-Mueller, 2000). For example, Ashford and Black (1996) found that newcomers who take the initiative to increase social interactions and build relationships have higher job satisfaction. Furthermore, research on proactive socialization behavior has found that various forms of newcomer proactivity (e.g., information seeking, general socializing) result in proactive outcomes such as obtaining information and feedback (Saks, Gruman, & Cooper-Thomas, 2011), as well as proximal and distal socialization outcomes (Ashforth et al, 2007; Gruman et al., 2006).

The SRT dimension of *proactive encouragement* refers to the extent to which the new hire has been encouraged to be proactive during his or her socialization (e.g., told to introduce him/herself to others, to ask for help, etc.). In other words, newcomers should be encouraged to be proactive and to ask for information, to socialize, develop relationships, and so on.

Klein and Heuser (2008) also consider organization actions to promote, facilitate, and encourage newcomer proactivity and to maximize its effectiveness to be an *organization orienting* practice. Cooper-Thomas and Anderson (2006) also suggest that organizations should encourage newcomers to use information seeking and other proactive strategies.

FORMAL ASSISTANCE

This dimension involves the extent to which the new hire is assigned a buddy or mentor to offer help and assistance. Recall how PricewaterhouseCoopers immediately assigns all new hires a Connectivity partner who will establish a relationship with the new hire as long as the newcomer is with the company. It was also noted that newcomers are paired with a mentor of their choice at Fairmont Hotels and Resorts between the second and third month, and newcomers at The Ritz-Carlton work for 3 weeks with a departmental trainer who can

Table 3.1 Socialization Resources Theory Dimensions and Sample Questions

SRT Dimension	Sample Question
Period: Prior to Entry	
1. Anticipatory Socialization	My boss got in touch with me before my first day on the job.
Period: Immediately After Entry	
2. Formal Orientation	The orientation program for new hires covered many issues and topics.
3. Proactive Encouragement	I have been encouraged to meet other members of my department and the organization.
4. Formal Assistance	I have been assigned a mentor.
Period: Following Orientation—Social Capital Resources	
5. Social Events	Social events have been held for new hires in this organization.
6. Socialization Agents	My coworkers frequently offer me help and assistance.
7. Supervisor Support	My supervisor makes him/herself available to me if I need assistance.
8. Relationship Development	Time was made for me to meet other people in my department/this organization.
Period: Following Orientation—Work-related Resources	
9. Job Resources	I was provided with everything I need (e.g., tools, materials, etc.) to do my job as soon as I arrived for work.
10. Personal Planning	My boss has discussed goals and expectations with me.
11. Training	The organization has provided the training I need to perform my job.
12. Assignments	I have been assigned tasks that are challenging.
13. Information	My coworkers often provide me with helpful information about how to perform my job.
14. Feedback	My boss lets me know how well I am doing my job.
15. Recognition and Appreciation	My coworkers compliment me for good work.
Period: Following Formal Socialization/Onboarding Period	
16. Follow-up	Every once in a while the organization checks to see how well I am adjusting.
17. Program Evaluation	I have been asked to provide feedback about the helpfulness of my orientation.

become their mentor. As noted earlier, having a mentor has been found to be related to distal and proximal socialization outcomes (Allen et al., 1999; Chatman, 1991; Ostroff & Kozlowski, 1993). In addition, Rollag et al. (2005) found that newcomers who had a "buddy" were more quickly adjusted compared to those who did not.

Following Orientation (First 6 Months): Social Capital Resources

The time frame or temporality of socialization has not been clearly determined in the socialization literature (Klein & Heuser, 2008). As a result, we really don't know the best time to provide newcomers with various resources. Klein and Heuser (2008) offer an optimal time for learning various socialization content dimensions that consists of eight time lines. However, because there is no research evidence on which to base the timing of many of the socialization resources, we suggest that they be provided at various times during the first 6 months. The optimal time is likely to vary as a function of a number of factors, such as nature of the job, the newcomer, the organization, and so on.

We distinguish between two types of resources during the first 6 months: social capital resources and work-related resources. Fang, Duffy and Shaw (2011) suggest that effective socialization requires that newcomers access and use the social capital contained within the social relationships they develop with organizational insiders. Further, Korte (2010) found that becoming a full member of a workgroup "requires the deliberate effort of co-workers in the group to reach out to newcomers and include them into the relational structure or social system of the group" (p.40). In this section, we describe *social capital resources*, which include social events, socialization agents, supervisor support, and relationship development.

SOCIAL EVENTS

This dimension involves *social events,* which refer to the extent to which the organization holds formal events (e.g., office parties, lunches, etc.) for new hires to meet and become acquainted with other members of the organization. Such events promote social interaction and enable newcomers to develop relationships. As such, they should help facilitate social acceptance, fit perceptions, and positive job attitudes. Chatman (1991) found that newcomers who attended more firm-sponsored social and recreational events during their socialization had higher person–organization fit.

SOCIALIZATION AGENTS

As suggested by Louis et al. (1983), interactions with other organizational insiders are particularly valuable during the socialization process. Given the value of social interaction during socialization, targeted efforts by organizational insiders to assist newcomers should have a positive effect on socialization outcomes. Indeed, relationship building has been suggested as the primary driver of socialization (Korte, 2009).

Socialization agents refers to the extent to which insiders have gone out of their way to help the new hire (e.g., coworkers have offered help, assistance, or gone out of their way to introduce themselves and get to know the new hire). As indicated earlier, coworkers are an important source of support and provider of information that facilitates newcomers' adjustment and socialization.

SUPERVISOR SUPPORT

Supervisor support refers to the extent to which immediate supervisors exhibit behaviors that demonstrate they care about and value the newcomer and take action to assist newcomers and help them adjust. Support from one's supervisor is especially important for successful socialization, given the supervisor's formal authority to provide rewards, resources, work assignments, development opportunities, and to provide information and feedback.

In support of the importance of supervisor support, Jokisaari and Nurmi (2009) showed that a decrease in perceived supervisor support was associated with decreases in newcomers' role clarity and job satisfaction and a slower increase in salary. Thus, while general social support is important for the successful adjustment of newcomers, support from one's supervisor is especially valuable. Perceived supervisor support has been shown to have stronger associations with positive attitudinal outcomes than perceived support from one's coworkers (Ng & Sorensen, 2008).

RELATIONSHIP DEVELOPMENT

This dimension refers to the extent to which time is made for the new hire to meet and get to know members of the organization (e.g., get introduced to coworkers and key people, be told about others in the organization and who to contact if they require certain expertise or resources, etc.). This is distinct from formal and planned social events that are sanctioned by the organization and were described earlier. This refers to any actions by insiders to help newcomers develop relationships, such as introductions, brief chats, invitations for lunch or drinks after work, and so on. Time devoted to the development of relationships will promote social capital and help newcomers cope with job demands they face when occupying a new role. As indicated earlier, Korte (2010) found that building good relationships with coworkers and managers was a key factor for the successful socialization of newly hired engineers.

Following Orientation (First 6 Months): Work-Related Resources

In addition to resources that are associated with social capital, newcomers also require resources that are directly tied to the performance of their job. These are resources that newcomers require in order to learn to perform their jobs and roles effectively, and will hasten their adjustment and socialization. Work-related resources include job resources, personal planning, training, assignments, information, feedback, and recognition and appreciation.

JOB RESOURCES

Fundamental to adjusting effectively to a new job is having the equipment necessary to perform one's job. The SRT dimension of *job resources* refers to the extent to which the office space, physical resources, materials, tools, and so on, are ready and available for new hires when they arrive. Lundberg and Young (1997) found that almost half of the newcomers in their study reported at least one critical incident on their first day and most of them were negative, such as a lack of appropriate tools or work space.

PERSONAL PLANNING

Personal planning refers to the extent to which the new hire's manager or organization has communicated expectations, made plans for the new hire, and discussed work goals. Previous research has shown that career plans and work goals are related to work and career outcomes (Gould, 1979). A study by Maier and Brunstein (2001) found that newcomers with personal work goals reported higher affective job attitudes, suggesting that "personal work goals are integral to newcomers' sense of organizational commitment and job satisfaction" (p.1040). A study by Chen and Klimoski (2003) found that team expectations were positively related to newcomers' role performance. As indicated earlier, supervisors at Fairmont Hotels and Resorts conduct personal development interviews with newcomers to discuss goals and provide feedback, and at Eddie Bauer newcomers are given a 90-day performance plan to follow.

TRAINING

Training refers to formal programs that provide newcomers with the knowledge and skills that are required to effectively perform their jobs. In addition to the amount of training provided, it also refers to the content of training and the use of different methods of training (e-learning, classroom, on the job). As indicated earlier in the chapter, training is an important and common socialization practice that is related to proximal outcomes such as self-efficacy, as well as distal outcomes such as job satisfaction and turnover intentions. Training is also used by a number of the organizations featured in the previous section on socialization practices in organizations.

ASSIGNMENTS

Assignments refer to newcomers' early assignments and tasks in terms of the job characteristics, as well as other characteristics of work (e.g., degree of challenge versus routine; working with others on group assignments or working alone, etc.). As noted earlier, job characteristics are important for newcomer adjustment and socialization and have been found to be related to socialization outcomes. The initial assignment is believed to be especially important for newcomers and a significant factor in the overall socialization process (Katz, 1980).

INFORMATION

Information refers to the extent to which organizational members provide new hires with information about their job, role, and the organization. As indicated earlier, socialization agents are an important source of information for newcomer learning. Newcomers have been found to rely on observation of others, followed by interpersonal sources (i.e., supervisors and coworkers) to acquire information; obtaining more information from coworkers has been found to be positively related to job satisfaction and organizational commitment, and negatively related to stress and turnover intentions (Ostroff & Kozlowksi,1992).

FEEDBACK

Feedback refers to the extent to which newcomers are provided with accurate and timely feedback on their job performance and work-related behaviors. As noted earlier, newcomers require feedback to assess their performance and adjust to their jobs and the organization. It allows newcomers to know if their behavior and performance is inappropriate and needs to be changed (Morrison, 1993). Additionally, as previously discussed, feedback is one of the job characteristics that Katz (1978) noted was especially important during the first 3 months of socialization. Receiving feedback from coworkers and one's supervisor has been found to be related to a number of distal socialization outcomes (Saks, 1995b).

RECOGNITION AND APPRECIATION

Recognition and appreciation refers to the extent to which newcomers receive acknowledgement and praise for their effort and performance. The organization reward system is a key mechanism by which newcomers are assimilated into the organization (Jokisaari & Nurmi, 2009). Praise has been shown to be associated with increased job performance (Crowell, Anderson, Abel, & Sergio, 1988; Rice, Austin, & Gravina, 2009). Although praise, recognition, and appreciation are valuable at any stage of an employee's tenure, they are particularly beneficial during the early entry period when newcomers are trying to make sense of their new environments and develop new or modified identities. As indicated earlier, Lundberg and Young (1997) found that appreciation by being recognized and praised or blamed and punished were among the most important events experienced by newcomers.

Following the Formal Socialization/Onboarding Period

Several of the organizations described earlier continued the socialization process even after the formal orientation period had ended. They continued to stay in touch with newcomers to see how they were doing and to gather data from newcomers about their onboarding experiences. Thus, two practices following the formal socialization/onboarding period are follow-up and program evaluation.

FOLLOW-UP

Follow-up involves the extent to which the organization follows up with new hires after the formal orientation period has ended (e.g., checking in to see how they are doing, if they need help, etc.). The practitioner literature suggests that following up with new hires eases their transition and helps them succeed in their new jobs (Shelat, 2004). As indicated earlier, Ritz-Carlton conducts a follow-up to make sure that the company is delivering what it promised, and Eddie Bauer sends targeted emails every 6 months to make sure newcomers have the information they need and to remind them that help is available in the HR department.

PROGRAM EVALUATION

Program evaluation refers to the extent to which the organization evaluates its orientation and socialization practices (e.g., new hires are asked to provide feedback, complete surveys, etc.). Such evaluations can focus on the costs of orientation and socialization programs, but should also address their impact on helping newcomers adjust (Fitz-enz & Davidson, 2002). As indicated earlier, Eddie Bauer has newcomers complete a survey that asks about the support they received from their supervisor during their orientation. Randstad North America has a 16-week orientation program that is monitored and evaluated throughout the program. Managers are also assessed on a monthly basis and incentives are linked to the performance of their new hires (Gustafson, 2005).

Socialization Resources Theory: Implications for Theory, Research, and Practice

Socialization Resources Theory has a number of implications for socialization theory, research, and practice. First, it focuses on socialization resources rather than just practices. This shifts the focus of socialization to newcomers' needs, and then on the practices required to fulfill those needs. This serves a number of advantages for newcomers and organizations. For newcomers, it means that the organization is providing them with resources that will facilitate their adjustment and help them become effective in their new job and role. For organizations, it means that they can identify the kinds of practices that will be most effective for providing particular resources that newcomers require that will lead to positive socialization outcomes. Organizations can also choose socialization practices (e.g., events, exercises, methods, technology, etc.) that best suit their culture.

Second, SRT offers a more complete list of socialization resources than currently exists in the socialization literature and brings them together in a coherent framework, thereby addressing the long-standing criticism that the socialization literature is fragmented (Fisher, 1986; Saks & Ashforth, 1997a). SRT also indicates when each resource should be provided during the socialization process.

SRT offers many new avenues for future socialization research. First, and perhaps most importantly, is the need to develop and validate scales to measure each of the socialization resources. Sample questions for each socialization resource are provided in Table 3.1. Second, SRT provides researchers with a framework to conduct research on socialization and for examining the most effective resources for different jobs, job families, organizational levels, and socialization periods. For example, the resources most needed during the socialization process may differ for neophyte and veteran newcomers.

Third, each of the resources is expected to be differentially related to proximal and distal socialization outcomes. For example, information is likely to be strongly related to learning, while feedback and training will be most strongly related to task mastery and performance. Thus, future research can test these and other relationships to determine what socialization resources are most important for achieving particular socialization outcomes, and what combination of resources produce the strongest effect on proximal and distal outcomes. A related issue concerns the timing of these relationships. That is, some socialization resources might be more strongly related to certain outcomes during the first few months (e.g., orientation program), while other resources might be more strongly related to outcomes following the initial socialization period (e.g., assignments, socialization agents). Thus, future research is needed to identify the extent to which the resources are related to different outcomes and at what point during the first year they are most strongly related.

Future research might also identify the kinds of organizations that are more or less likely to provide the various socialization resources, given that there is some evidence that organizational context influences socialization practices (Ashforth et al., 1998). That is, some organizations—perhaps those in certain industries, professions, or occupations—might be more or less likely to provide each of the socialization resources. In addition, future research across organizations might investigate the extent to which organizations that use more of the socialization resources, and/or use particular sets of resources, predict organizational-level outcomes such as firm turnover and performance. Thus, SRT has implications for socialization research at the individual, group, and organization level.

In terms of practice, SRT provides managers and organizations with a framework to develop, monitor, and evaluate their onboarding and socialization programs. For example, the sample questions in Table 3.1 can be used to conduct a socialization resources audit of an organization's existing socialization/onboarding practices by assessing the extent to which each resource is provided to newcomers (yes/no or to what extent, 1 = very little, 5 = very much). The results of the audit can then be used to further investigate areas that appear to be weak, and identify resources that newcomers are not receiving. Organizations can then develop and implement practices that will provide the resources that newcomers require. After improvements have been made, the audit questions can be used to evaluate each dimension in terms of effectiveness (How effective are the following, 1 = not very effective, 5 = very effective).

In summary, SRT forces organizations to think about the socialization and onboarding process in terms of the resources that newcomers need, when they need them, and how best to provide them. Thus, the focus is not on what organizations need to do, or what practices they need to adopt, but rather what resources new hires need and what is the best way to provide them in terms of practices and programs.

Conclusion

Organizational socialization is a critical process for organizations that have invested a great deal of time and resources to attract and hire employees. The time and resources that organizations invest in recruitment and selection will be wasted if the socialization process fails to get newcomers quickly adjusted to their job, roles, and organization, and to become effective members of their organizations.

Although there has been a great deal of socialization research over the last several decades, most of the advances have been made in the areas of socialization content-learning and newcomer proactive behavior. Much less attention has been given to socialization practices. Furthermore, most of the research on socialization practices has been on socialization tactics, which has failed to provide concrete and tangible information about the effectiveness of specific socialization practices. In fact, the overemphasis on socialization tactics is perhaps one of the reasons that the literature on socialization practices has remained undeveloped and stagnant for so long.

Although the five socialization practices described in this chapter are important for newcomer adjustment and socialization, the research in each area has been limited. For example, in the case of job characteristics, there has not been any new development since Katz's (1980) work in the area over 30 years ago. Research on socialization tactics has not advanced much since Jones' (1986) first study, other than the addition of dependent variables. There are relatively few studies on orientation and training programs for newcomers. And although there have been several studies on socialization agents, each study exists as a separate entity having paid little attention to previous studies. Thus, each area remains limited, narrow, and undeveloped.

As a whole, there has actually been little theory development in the socialization literature (Cooper-Thomas & Anderson, 2006). In fact, the closest thing to a theory of organizational socialization is Van Maanen and Schein's (1979) work on socialization tactics. However, it remains limited to just six very broad and abstract structural dimensions of socialization, and in its original conception the focus of the theory was to link each tactic to the role orientation that an individual would be most likely to adopt during a role transition. Thus, the literature on organizational socialization practices remains fragmented, undeveloped, and not very practical. This is all the more clear in light of the very practical and tangible things that organizations are doing to socialize their new hires.

In this chapter we have attempted to begin the process of developing a more complete and integrated theory of organizational socialization in several respects. First, we have tried to include many of the socialization resources that have been identified in both the academic and practitioner literature. This is an attempt to address the longstanding criticism that the socialization literature is fragmented and lacks a coherent theory that integrates various socialization processes (Saks & Ashforth, 1997a). SRT is an attempt to be comprehensive and integrative in its inclusion of many socialization resources.

Second, SRT incorporates the notion of temporality, which has largely been absent in the socialization literature (Klein & Heuser, 2008). In this respect, SRT indicates when the resources should occur at different times during the socialization process.

Third, the focus of SRT is on the resources that newcomers require to successfully adjust to their new surroundings and the practices that are necessary to provide those resources. The hope is that research on SRT will help to determine the extent to which each resource, or perhaps "bundles" of resources, predicts proximal and distal socialization outcomes and therefore helps us answer the question we posed at the beginning of the chapter: *What organizational socialization practices are most effective?* Before we can answer this question, however, we need research on the relationships between each of the socialization resources and the various proximal and distal outcomes shown in Figure 3.1, as well as research on when to provide particular resources, the best way to provide each resource, and research on bundles or packages of resources and how they relate to the different socialization outcomes.

In conclusion, research on organizational socialization has the potential to provide organizations with important information on how to transform new hires into well-adjusted and effective members of the organization. A successful socialization program is a necessary and vital component of an effective talent management strategy. Without a successful socialization program, new hires will remain strangers in their organizations wandering aimlessly in an unknown and strange place that remains uncertain and unfamiliar. The eventual result will be poorly adjusted employees who choose to leave the organization. We believe that SRT provides a framework for the development of a more complete and integrated theory of organizational socialization that will also provide organizations with information on how to design and improve their socialization/onboarding programs.

References

Allen, D. G. (2006). Do organizational socialization tactics influence newcomer embeddedness and turnover? *Journal of Management, 32,* 237–256.

Allen, T. D., McManus, S. E., & Russell, J. E. A. (1999). Newcomer socialization and stress: Formal peer relationships as a source of support. *Journal of Vocational Behavior, 54,* 453–470.

Anderson, N. R., Cunningham-Snell, N. A., & Haigh, J. (1996). Induction training as socialization: Current practice and attitudes to evaluation in British organizations. *International Journal of Selection and Assessment, 4,* 169–183.

Ashford, S. J. (1986). Feedback seeking in individual adaptation: A resource perspective. *Academy of Management Journal, 29*(3), 465–487.

Ashford, S. J., & Black, J. S. (1996). Proactivity during organizational entry: The role of desire for control. *Journal of Applied Psychology, 81*(2), 199–214.

Ashforth, B. E., & Saks, A. M. (1996). Socialization tactics: Longitudinal effects on newcomer adjustment. *Academy of Management Journal, 39,* 149–178.

Ashforth, B. E., Saks, A. M., & Lee, R. T. (1997). On the dimensionality of Jones' (1986) measures of organizational socialization tactics. *International Journal of Selection and Assessment, 5,* 200–214.

Ashforth, B. E., Saks, A. M., & Lee, R. T. (1998). Socialization and newcomer adjustment: The role of organizational context. *Human Relations, 51,* 897–926.

Ashforth, B. E., Sluss, D. M., & Saks, A. M. (2007). Socialization tactics, proactive behavior, and newcomer learning: Integrating socialization models. *Journal of Vocational Behavior, 70,* 447–462.

Bakker, A. B., & Demerouti, E. (2007). The job demands-resources model: State of the art. *Journal of Managerial Psychology, 22,* 309–328.

Bakker, A. B., & Demerouti, E. (2008). Toward a model of work engagement. Career Development International, 13, 209–223.

Bakker, A. B., van Veldhoven, M., & Xanthopoulou, D. (2010). Beyond the demand-control model: Thriving on high job demands and resources. *Journal of Personnel Psychology, 9,* 3–16.

Bauer, T. N., Bodner, T., Erdogan, B., Truxillo, D. M., & Tucker, J. S. (2007). Newcomer adjustment during organizational socialization: A meta-analytic review of antecedents, outcomes, and methods. *Journal of Applied Psychology, 92,* 707–721.

Bauer, T. N., & Green, S. G. (1998). Testing the combined effects of newcomer information seeking and manager behavior on socialization. *Journal of Applied Psychology, 83,* 72–83.

Bauer, T. N., Morrison, E. W., & Callister, R. R. (1998). Organizational socialization: A review and directions for future research. In G. R. Ferris (Ed.), *Research in personnel and human resources management* (Vol. 16, pp. 149–214). Greenwich CT: JAI Press.

Blau, G. (1988). An investigation of the apprenticeship organizational socialization strategy. *Journal of Vocational Behavior, 32,* 176–195.

Boehle, S. (2008, February). True vision. *Training, 45*(2), 32–39.

Brown, K. G., & Sitzmann, T. (2011). Training and employee development for improved performance. In S. Zedeck (Ed.), *Handbook of industrial and organizational psychology* (vol. 2, pp. 469–503). Washington, DC: American Psychological Association.

Chatman, J. A. (1991). Matching people and organizations: Selection and socialization in public accounting firms. *Administrative Science Quarterly, 36,* 459–484.

Chen, G., & Klimoski, R. J. (2003). The impact of expectations on newcomer performance in teams as mediated by work characteristics, social exchanges, and empowerment. *Academy of Management Journal, 46,* 591–607.

Colarelli, S. M., Dean, R. A., & Konstans, C. (1987). Comparative effects of personal and situational influences on job outcomes of new professionals. *Journal of Applied Psychology, 72,* 558–566.

Cooper-Thomas, H., & Anderson, N. (2006). Organizational socialization: A new theoretical model and recommendations for future research and HRM practices in organizations. *Journal of Managerial Psychology, 21,* 492–516.

Crowell, C. R., Anderson, D. C., Abel, D. M., & Sergio, J. P. (1988). Task clarification, performance feedback, and social praise: Procedures for improving the customer service of bank tellers. *Journal of Applied Behavior Analysis, 21,* 65–71.

Dean, R. A., Ferris, K. R., & Konstans, C. (1988). Occupational reality shock and organizational commitment: Evidence from the accounting profession. *Accounting, Organizations and Society, 13,* 235–250.

Deci, E. L. & Ryan, R. M. (1985). *Intrinsic motivation and self-determination in human behavior.* New York: Plenum Press.

Durett, J. (2006, March). Plug in and perform. *Training, 43(3),* 30–34.

Elizur, Y., & Hirsh, E. (1999). Psychosocial adjustment and mental health two months after coronary artery bypass surgery: A multisystemic analysis of patients' resources. *Journal of Behavioral Medicine, 22,* 157–177.

Fan, J., & Wanous, J. P. (2008). Organizational and cultural entry: A new type of orientation program for multiple boundary crossings. *Journal of Applied Psychology, 93,* 1390–1400.

Fang, R., Duffy, M. K., & Shaw, J. D. (2011). The organizational socialization process: Review and development of a social capital model. *Journal of Management, 37,* 127–152.

Farh, C. I. C., Bartol, K. M., Shapiro, D. L., & Shin, J. (2010). Networking abroad: a process model of how expatriates form support ties to facilitate adjustment. *Academy of Management Review, 35,* 434–454.

Feldman, D. C. (1976). A practical program for employee socialization. *Organizational Dynamics, 5,* 64–80

Feldman, D.C. (1989). Socialization, resocialization, and training: Reframing the research agenda. In I. L. Goldstein (Ed.), *Training and development in organizations* (pp.376–416). San Francisco: Jossey-Bass.

Feldman, D. C., & Brett, J. M. (1983). Coping with new jobs: A comparative study of new hires and job changers. *Academy of Management Journal, 26,* 258–272.

Feldman, D. C., & Weitz, B. A. (1990). Summer interns: Factors contributing to positive developmental experiences. *Journal of Vocational Behavior, 37,* 267–284.

Fisher, C. D. (1985). Social support and adjustment to work: A longitudinal study. *Journal of Management, 11,* 39–53.

Fisher, C. D. (1986). Organizational socialization: An integrative review. In K.M. Rowland & G.R. Ferris (Eds.), *Research in personnel and human resources management* (Vol. 4, pp.101–145). Greenwich, CT: JAI Press.

Fitz-enz, J., & Davidson, B. (2002). *How to Measure Human Resources Management (3rd ed.).* New York: McGraw Hill.

Goldstein, I. L. (1991). Training in work organizations. In M. D. Dunnette & L. M. Hough (Eds.), *Handbook of industrial and organizational psychology* (2nd ed., Vol.2, pp.507–620). Palo Alto, CA: Consulting Psychologists Press.

Gomersall, E. R., & Myers, M. S. (1966). Breakthrough in on-the-job training. *Harvard Business Review, 44,* 62–72.

Gould, S. (1979). Characteristics of career planners in upwardly mobile occupations. *Academy of Management Journal, 22,* 539–550.

Gruman, J. A., Saks, A. M., & Zweig, D. I. (2006). Organizational socialization tactics and newcomer proactive behaviors: An integrative study. *Journal of Vocational Behavior, 69,* 90–104.

Gustafson, K. (2005, June). A better welcome mat. *Training, 42(6),* 34–41.

Hobfoll, S. E. (2002). Social and psychological resources and adaptation. *Review of General Psychology, 6,* 307–324.

Humphrey, S. E., Nahrgang, J. D., & Morgeson, F. P. (2007). Integrating motivational, social, and contextual work design features: A meta-analytic summary and theoretical extension of the work design literature. *Journal of Applied Psychology, 92,* 1332–1356.

Jokisaari, M., & Nurmi, J-E. (2009). Change in newcomers' supervisor support and socialization outcomes after organizational entry. *Academy of Management Journal, 52,* 527–544.

Jones, G. R. (1986). Socialization tactics, self-efficacy, and newcomers' adjustments to organizations. *Academy of Management Journal, 29,* 262–279.

Kammeyer-Mueller, J. D., & Wanberg, C. R. (2003). Unwrapping the organizational entry process: Disentangling multiple antecedents and their pathways to adjustment. *Journal of Applied Psychology, 88,* 779–794.

Katz, R. (1978). Job longevity as a situational factor in job satisfaction. *Administrative Science Quarterly, 23,* 204–223.

Katz, R. (1980). Time and work: Toward an integrative perspective. In B. Staw & L. L. Cummings (Eds.), *Research in organizational behavior* (Vol. 2, pp. 81–127). Greenwich CT: JAI Press.

Klein, H. J., & Heuser, A. E. (2008). The learning of socialization content: A framework for researching orientating practices. *Research in Personnel and Human Resources Management, 27,* 279–336. Emerald Group.

Klein, H. J., & Weaver, N. A. (2000). The effectiveness of an organizational-level orientation training program in the socialization of new hires. *Personnel Psychology, 53,* 47–66.

Korte, R. F. (2009). How newcomers learn the social norms of an organization: A case study of the socialization of newly hired engineers. *Human Resource Development Quarterly, 20,* 285–306.

Korte, R. (2010). "First get to know them": A relational view of organizational socialization. *Human Resource Development International, 13,* 27–43.

Lester, R. E. (1987). Organizational culture, uncertainty reduction, and the socialization of new organizational members. In S. Thomas (Ed.), *Culture and communication: Methodology, behavior, artifacts, and institutions* (pp. 105–113). Norwood, NJ: Ablex.

Louis, M. R. (1980). Surprise and sense making: What newcomers experience in entering unfamiliar organizational settings. *Administrative Science Quarterly, 64,* 226–251.

Louis, M. R., Posner, B. Z., & Powell, G. N. (1983). The availability and helpfulness of socialization practices. *Personnel Psychology, 36,* 857–866.

Lundberg, C. C., & Young, C. A. (1997). Newcomer socialization: Critical incidents in hospitality organizations. *Journal of Hospitality & Tourism Research, 21,* 58–74.

Maier, G. W., & Brunstein, J. C. (2001). The role of personal work goals in newcomers' job satisfaction and organizational commitment: A longitudinal analysis. *Journal of Applied Psychology, 86,* 1034–1042.

Major, D. A., Kozlowski, S. W. J., Chao, G. T., & Gardner, P. D. (1995). A longitudinal investigation of newcomer expectations, early socialization outcomes, and the moderating effects of role development factors. *Journal of Applied Psychology, 80,* 418–431.

Miller, V. D., & Jablin, F. M. (1991). Information seeking during organizational entry: Influences, tactics, and a model of the process. *Academy of Management Review, 16,* 92–120.

Morrison, E. W. (1993). Newcomer information seeking: Exploring types, modes, sources, and outcomes. *Academy of Management Journal, 36,* 557–589.

Morrison, E. W. (2002). Newcomers' relationships: The role of social network ties during socialization. *Academy of Management Journal, 45,* 1149–1160.

Nelson, D. L., & Quick, J. C., & Eakin, M. E. (1988). A longitudinal study of newcomer role adjustment in U. S. organizations. *Work and Stress, 2,* 239–253.

Nelson, D. L., & Quick, J. C. (1991). Social support and newcomer adjustment in organizations: Attachment theory at work? *Journal of Organizational Behavior, 12,* 543–554.

Ng, T. W. H., & Sorensen, K. L. (2008). Toward a fuller understanding of the relationship between perceptions of support and work attitudes. *Group and Organization Management, 33,* 243–268.

Ostroff, C., & Kozlowski, S. W. J. (1992). Organizational socialization as a learning process: The role of information acquisition. *Personnel Psychology, 45,* 849–874.

Ostroff, C., & Kozlowski, S. W. J. (1993). The role of mentoring in the information gathering processes of newcomers during early organizational socialization. *Journal of Vocational Behavior, 42,* 170–183.

Pakenham, K., & Rinaldis, M. (2001). The role of illness, resources, appraisal, and coping strategies in adjustment to HIV/AIDS: The direct and buffering effects. *Journal of Behavioral Medicine, 24,* 259–279.

Reichers, A. E. (1987). An interactionist perspective on newcomer socialization rates. *Academy of Management Review, 12,* 278–287.

Rice, A., Austin, J., & Gravina, N. (2009). Increasing customer service behaviors using manager-delivered task clarification and social praise. *Journal of Applied Behavior Analysis, 42,* 665–669.

Rollag, K., Parise, S., & Cross, R. (2005). Getting new hires up to speed quickly. *MIT Sloan Management Review, 46,* 35–41.

Saks, A. M. (1994a). A psychological process investigation for the effects of recruitment source and organization information on job survival. *Journal of Organizational Behavior, 15,* 225–244.

Saks, A. M. (1994b). Moderating effects of self-efficacy for the relationship between training method and anxiety and stress reactions of newcomers. *Journal of Organizational Behavior, 15,* 639–654.

Saks, A. M. (1995a). Longitudinal field investigation of the moderating and mediating effects of self-efficacy on the relationship between training and newcomer adjustment. *Journal of Applied Psychology, 80,* 211–225.

Saks, A. M. (1995b). The relationship between job content and work outcomes for entry-level staff in public accounting firms. *Journal of Accounting & Business Research, 3,* 15–38.

Saks, A. M. (1996). The relationship between the amount and helpfulness of entry training and work outcomes. *Human Relations, 49,* 429–451.

Saks, A. M., & Ashforth, B. E. (1997a). Organizational socialization: Making sense of the past and present as a prologue for the future. *Journal of Vocational Behavior, 51,* 234–279.

Saks, A. M., & Ashforth, B. E. (1997b). Socialization tactics and newcomer information acquisition. *International Journal of Selection and Assessment, 5,* 48–61.

Saks, A. M., & Ashforth, B. E. (2000). The role of dispositions, entry stressors, and behavioral plasticity theory in predicting newcomers' adjustment to work. *Journal of Organizational Behavior, 21,* 43–62.

Saks, A, M., Gruman, J. A., & Cooper-Thomas, H. (2011). The neglected role of proactive behavior and outcomes in newcomer socialization. *Journal of Vocational Behavior, 79,* 36–46.

Saks, A. M., Uggerslev, K. L., & Fassina, N. E. (2007). Socialization tactics and newcomer adjustment: A meta-analytic review and test of a model. *Journal of Vocational Behavior, 70,* 413–446.

Schettler, J., & Johnson, H. (2002, August). Welcome to ACME Inc. *Training, 39(8),* 36–43.

Settoon, R. P., & Adkins, C. L. (1997). Newcomer socialization: The role of supervisors, coworkers, friends and family members. *Journal of Business and Psychology, 11,* 507–516.

Shelat, L. (2004, May 3). First impressions matter—a lot. *Canadian HR Reporter, 17(9),* 11–13.

Tannenbaum, S. I., Mathieu, J. E., Salas, E., & Cannon-Bowers, J. A. (1991). Meeting trainees' expectations: The influence of training fulfillment on the development of commitment, self-efficacy, and motivation. *Journal of Applied Psychology, 76,* 759–769.

Van Maanen, J. (1977). Experiencing organizations: Notes on the meaning of careers and socialization. In J. Van Maanen (Ed.), *Organizational careers: Some new perspectives* (pp. 15–48). New York, NY: Wiley International.

Van Maanen, J. (1982). Boundary crossings: Major strategies of organizational socialization and their consequences. In R. Katz (Ed.), *Career issues in human resource management* (pp. 85–115). Englewood Cliffs, NJ: Prentice-Hall, Inc.

Van Maanen, J., & Schein, E. H. (1979). Toward a theory of organizational socialization, In B. M. Staw (Ed.), *Research in Organizational Behavior,* (Vol. 1, pp. 209–264). Greenwich, CT: JAI Press.

Wanberg, C. R., & Kammeyer-Mueller, J. D. (2000). Predictors and outcomes of proactivity in the socialization process. *Journal of Applied Psychology, 85(3).* 373–385.

Wang, H., & Amato, P. R. (2000). Predictors of divorce adjustment: Stressors, resources, and definitions. *Journal of Marriage and the Family, 62,* 655–668

Wang, M., Henkens, K., & van Solinge, H. (2011). Retirement adjustment: A review of theoretical and empirical advancements. *American Psychologist, 66,* 204–213.

Wanous, J. P., & Reichers, A. E. (2000). New employee orientation programs. *Human Resource Management Review, 10,* 435–451.

Waung, M. (1995). The effects of self-regulatory coping orientation on newcomer adjustment and job survival. *Personnel Psychology, 48,* 633–650.

Weinstein, M. (2007, March). Balancing act. *Training, 44(2),* 22–28.

Wesson, M. J. & Gogus, C. I. (2005). Shaking hands with a computer: An examination of two methods of organizational newcomer orientation. *Journal of Applied Psychology, 90,* 1018–1026.

Xanthopoulou, D., Bakker, A. B., Dollard, M. F., Demerouti, E., Schaufeli, W. B., Taris, T. W., & Schreurs, P. J. G. (2007). When do job demands particularly predict burnout? *Journal of Managerial Psychology, 22,* 766–786.

Newcomer Proactive Behavior: Can There Be Too Much of a Good Thing?

Helena D. Cooper-Thomas *and* Sarah E. Burke

The aim of this chapter is to provide a comprehensive review of research on newcomer proactive behavior. We start by outlining why proactive behavior is important for new employees today and situating this within the broader proactive behavior literature. Following this, the chapter has six main sections. First, we outline the range of proactive behaviors that newcomers use, under the three categories of changing the role or environment (e.g., changing work procedures), self-change (e.g., feedback seeking), and mutual development (e.g., networking). Second, we discuss the consequences of each proactive behavior by newcomers that has been studied in detail and third, we examine the antecedents of newcomer proactive behaviors. Fourth, we outline longitudinal patterns of change in newcomer proactive behavior. Fifth, we present ideas around the potential for proactive behavior to be maladaptive for organizations and also for newcomers themselves. This is followed with a sixth section on practical implications, comprising a review of the sparse research to date on interventions to increase newcomer proactive behavior. We finish with ideas for future research and concluding thoughts.

organizational socialization, newcomer, newcomer adjustment, proactive behavior, proactivity

Research on newcomer proactive behavior has developed rapidly in recent years (Ashford & Black, 1996; Kammeyer-Mueller & Wanberg, 2003) and provides an important contribution to the literature on organizational socialization, also known as *newcomer adjustment* or *onboarding*. The process of organizational socialization is concerned with getting new employees up to speed in an organization as quickly as possible. This benefits all parties: The newcomer spends less time experiencing anxious uncertainty, and can more quickly learn, adapt, and achieve effective performance and concomitant improvements in well-being (Kammeyer-Mueller & Wanberg, 2003); colleagues can more quickly shift from providing task help to the newcomer toward exchanging assistance and resources for mutual benefit (Anderson & Thomas, 1996; Feldman, 1994); and the organization gains a performing organizational member more quickly (Rollag, 2007).

The increased focus on newcomer proactive behavior has occurred in tandem with broader workplace changes occurring over the past few decades (Howard, 1995; Finkelstein, Kulas, & Dages, 2003). Previously, when jobs were for life and employees rarely switched employers, there was an understandable focus on how organizations shaped newcomers through providing specific types of experience which molded them to fit specific roles (Van Maanen & Schein, 1979; also see Saks and Gruman, Chapter 3 of this volume). Moreover, for organizations it was worth investing in intensive, lengthy, off-site socialization programs because employees would remain with and contribute to the organization for a long period of time, possibly their whole working lives (Berlew & Hall, 1966; Van Maanen, 1973; Van Maanen & Schein, 1979). However all this has changed in recent years. Globalization, increased competition, and technological developments are key factors that have led to workplace flexibility and, coupled with this, instability (Arnold & Cohen, 2008). Employees in organizations frequently experience restructuring, delayering, downsizing, mergers and acquisitions, as well as redundancies either for themselves or colleagues (Datta, Guthrie, Basuil, & Pandey, 2010). All of these changes cause employees to be in modified roles or to need socialization into completely new roles. Data from the United States illustrates that an increasing number of people are experiencing socialization, with a predicted 51 million job openings between 2008 and 2018 (Bureau of Labor Statistics, 2009). Further, of a predicted 167 million people in the US civilian labor force for the same time period, less than 20 million positions were expected to offer some short-term on-the-job training. These figures confirm the need for newcomers to be self-starting if they wish to be successful in their careers (Seibert, Crant, & Kraimer, 1999) and for the hiring organization to remain flexible and actively compete in the global economy (Sonnentag, 2003).

Newcomer Proactive Behavior

We follow the work of Parker and colleagues to define proactive behavior as being anticipatory or future oriented, self-initiated, and about taking control to make things happen (Parker & Collins, 2010). These behaviors may aim to change the situation, oneself, or both (Parker, Bindl, & Strauss, 2010; Parker & Collins, 2010). Among the categories of proactive behavior proposed in the last several years (Grant & Ashford, 2008; Parker et al., 2010), proactive person–environment (PE) fit behaviors are the most relevant to the context of new

employees (see also Kim, Cable, & Kim, 2005; and van Vianen and De Pater, Chapter 8 in this volume). Parker and Collins (2010) note that proactive PE fit behaviors are distinctive in that they focus more on the self, compared to other types of proactive behaviors that may aim to change the organization's internal environment or the organization's fit with the external environment. As examples of proactive PE fit behaviors relevant to newcomers, job change negotiation reflects new employees attempting to change their immediate work environment to better fit their skills or abilities (Ashford & Black, 1996; Nicholson, 1984), whereas feedback seeking reveals the new employee's intention of using feedback to achieve positive self-change (Ashford & Black, 1996; Wanberg & Kammeyer-Mueller, 2000).

Types of Newcomer Proactive Behavior

Recent empirical work by Cooper-Thomas, Anderson, and Cash (2011) provides a useful way of approaching proactive PE fit behaviors. They proposed three categories for newcomer adjustment strategies: change role or environment, change self, and mutual development. Whereas Cooper-Thomas and colleagues aimed to include the widest range of strategies identified to date, we have taken a narrower approach. Specifically, we reviewed the strategies that they identified and have kept only those which fit with the definition above; that is, that such behaviors are self-started, future focused, and change oriented. The resultant behaviors are shown in Table 4.1.

The first column contains proactive behaviors which the new employee uses to change her role or her work environment. These include the new employee changing work procedures and, in some

Table 4.1 A Categorization of Newcomer Proactive Behaviors

Change Role or Environment	Change Self	Mutual Development
Change work procedures/minimize	Direct inquiry/information-seeking	Boss relationship building
Redefine the job	Feedback seeking	Exchanging resources
Experimenting/testing limits/action & feedback	Indirect inquiry	Job change negotiation
Delegate responsibilities	Inquiry of third parties	Networking
Persuasive attempts/presentation	Monitoring	General socializing
Gain credibility/give information & advice	Positive framing	
	Listening	
	Role modeling	

cases, minimizing new role requirements to achieve a better fit to his or her current skills and abilities (Feldman & Brett, 1983, Cooper-Thomas et al., 2011), or redefining the job (Feldman & Brett, 1983). The new employee may experiment or test limits by carrying out work in his/her preferred way and seeing if it works (Kramer, 1993; Ostroff & Kozlowski, 1992). The new employee may also try to change his/her role by delegating responsibilities (Feldman & Brett, 1983) or attempting to persuade others to change work factors (Kramer, 1993). Finally, the newcomer may try to gain credibility in order to have more influence, which may be achieved through giving information and advice to insider colleagues and proving competence (Cooper-Thomas et al., 2011; Kramer, 1993).

The second column comprises proactive behaviors by which the new employee tries to change herself; for example role modeling, which involves trying to emulate the ways others behave in order to achieve better outcomes (Cooper-Thomas et al., 2011). A number of information-seeking or sense-making behaviors are also included within change self, including direct inquiry, feedback seeking, indirect inquiry, and inquiry of third parties (Ashford & Cummings, 1983; Feldman & Brett, 1983; Miller & Jablin, 1991; Ostroff & Kozlowski, 1992). These comprise different behaviors that newcomers may use to learn about their new roles and the broader work environment. An interesting issue this raises is that proactive behavior can be furtive, with indirect inquiry and inquiry of third parties fulfilling the criteria of being self-started, future focused, and change oriented. This contrasts with overt proactive behaviors such as voice (LePine & Van Dyne, 1998) and issue selling (Dutton & Ashford, 1993), which might come to mind more easily when considering proactive behaviors. An additional interesting issue is raised by the final behaviors within change self, in that monitoring, positive framing, and listening (Ashford & Black, 1996; Burke, 2009; Ostroff & Kozlowski, 1992) may be seen as passive and cognitive. However, they require the new employee to initiate such behaviors (self-started); they are aimed at enabling the new employee to acquire a better understanding of the role and situation (change oriented) and to achieve more rapid and positive socialization so as to become an insider (future focused). Hence, they fit the criteria for proactive behaviors (Ashford & Black, 1996; Burke, 2009; Kim et al., 2005).

The final column of Table 4.1 consists of behaviors that involve mutual development of the new employee and his or her work environment. The first three behaviors—relationship building with boss, exchanging resources, and role negotiation (Ashford & Black, 1996; Cooper-Thomas et al., 2011; Kramer, 1993)—are about a mutual give and take to find a good fit between what the individual offers and what the environment affords (Gibson, 1977). Networking is akin to these previous behaviors, although the future focus is arguably longer term and uncertain in nature yet likely to be work-related (Ashford & Black, 1996; Cooper-Thomas et al., 2011). Similarly, general socializing depends on the new employee (self-starting) as well as the organization in order to occur, is change oriented in that it aims to build work relationships, and is future focused because these relationships are anticipated as having forthcoming benefits (Ashford & Black, 1996; Cooper-Thomas et al., 2011). While networking has task-related aims, general socializing may bring task or social future rewards.

Looking at research on newcomer proactive behaviors at a broad level, most research has investigated multiple proactive behaviors in the same study. Interestingly, there is a consistent finding that newcomers who use one kind of proactive behavior tend also to use other proactive behaviors. While this fits with a view of proactive behavior stemming from personality factors (Crant, 2000; Wanberg & Kammeyer-Mueller, 2000), it may also be that environmental factors in those settings allow for proactive behaviors in general. Ashford and Black (1996), in their seminal research with practicing managers graduating from a US business school, identified seven proactive behaviors. These seven behaviors show mostly moderate to strong correlations with each other—particularly building relationship with boss and job change negotiation, which have the most positive associations (five of a possible six) with the other behaviors. Similarly, Gruman, Saks, and Zweig (2006) found mostly moderate to strong positive correlations between six common proactive behaviors in a sample of Canadian cooperative placement students, as did Kim et al. (2005) with newcomers at seven large organizations in South Korea and Wanberg and Kammeyer-Mueller (2000) in research with job seekers across one US state's employment service centers. Indeed, in some research these behaviors have been aggregated, with Ashforth, Sluss, and Saks (2007) showing that an aggregated proactive behavior scale was positively associated with learning, role innovation, performance, job satisfaction, and organizational identity, and negatively associated with intentions to quit. Also using an aggregated measure, Burke (2009) showed that proactive behavior was trainable in newcomers with the resultant shift in behavior observable to managers. Furthermore, research by Brown, Ganesan, and Challagalla (2001) has shown that employees may use proactive behaviors synergistically, with employees who have high self-efficacy being able to use a combination of inquiry and monitoring to achieve greater role clarity, whereas employees with low self-efficacy showed no such interactive effect. The potential complementary and interactive relationships of newcomer proactive behaviors provide an interesting avenue for further research.

The Consequences of Newcomer Proactive Behaviors

The increased focus on employee proactive behavior in general, and newcomer proactive behavior in particular, is due both to the necessity of being adaptable in a shifting and unpredictable work environment and also the perceived benefits that proactivity brings. At a more general level, proactive behavior has been associated with higher levels of innovation (Scott & Bruce, 1994; Seibert, Kraimer, & Crant, 2001), leadership effectiveness (Bateman & Crant, 1993), task performance (Fuller & Marler, 2009; Thompson, 2005), and greater career success (Seibert et al., 2001). For newcomers, proactive personality—which leads to more proactive behaviors (Crant, 2000)—is positively associated with motivation to learn (Major, Turner, & Fletcher, 2006) and creativity (Kim, Hon & Crant, 2009), as well as task mastery, group integration, political knowledge, organizational commitment, and intent to remain (Kammeyer-Mueller & Wanberg, 2003). For newcomer proactive behavior, the picture is more mixed (Saks, Gruman, & Cooper-Thomas, 2011) and therefore we explore it in greater detail, looking at each category of proactive behavior in turn along with each of the behaviors within those categories. We present the proactive behaviors in the same order as above; that is, those which concern trying to change the role or environment, changing the self, and mutual development. Note that there is insufficient evidence for some of the behaviors we reviewed above and summarized in Table 4.1, and hence these are excluded from further analysis.

The Consequences of Newcomer Proactive Behaviors Aimed at Changing the Role or Environment

EXPERIMENTING

While there has been a body of research that confirms experimenting as a strategy (Cooper-Thomas et al., 2011; Feldman & Brett, 1983; Ostroff & Kozlowski, 1992), there is only one study that looks at experimenting in relation to newcomer adjustment indicators. Ostroff and Kozlowski (1992) found that experimenting was positively associated with task, role, group, and organizational learning, yet also with psychological and physical stress and intent to turnover. Thus, experimenting seems to work well in facilitating newcomer learning but has a significant downside in that newcomers who experiment report higher stress. It remains an empirical question as to whether the stress leads to more experimenting behavior by newcomers or whether the experimenting itself results in stress.

It is notable that a range of more self-reliant newcomer proactive behaviors have been identified (see Table 4.1), yet their consequences have been neglected by researchers. This may reflect the difficulty attached to enacting behaviors that are self-initiated (Cooper-Thomas & Wilson, 2011). A more pragmatic explanation is that most researchers have used Ashford and Black's (1996) measures of newcomer proactive behaviors, and none of these are within the change role or environment category.

The Consequences of Newcomer Proactive Behaviors Aimed at Self-Change

INFORMATION SEEKING

Newcomer information seeking has been one of the most explored research areas, with studies investigating the types of information that new employees seek (Morrison, 1993a, b; Ostroff & Kozlowski, 1992), learn (Chao, O'Leary-Kelly, Wolf, Klein, & Gardner, 1994; Haueter, Macan, & Winter, 2003; Cooper-Thomas & Anderson 2002, 2005) and find most useful (Morrison, 1995). Here we look more broadly at information seeking as a proactive behavior, and focus on active seeking in the form of direct inquiry.

Direct inquiry of supervisors is associated with political and language learning, whereas direct inquiry of experienced coworkers is associated with broader learning across performance, history, goals and values, and organizational politics (van der Velde, Ardts, & Jansen, 2005). Following on from learning, there is some evidence that information seeking through direct inquiry is associated with role clarity (Bauer, Bodner, Erdogan, Truxillo, & Tucker, 2007; Gruman et al., 2006; Holder, 1996;

Saks et al., 2011) although null results have been found (Wanberg & Kammeyer-Mueller, 2000). Moreover, as for learning, research has shown different results for coworkers versus supervisors. Thus, Callister, Kramer, and Turban (1999) found that transferees over their first year showed no association between coworker inquiry and role clarity, and only weak relations at 3 and 12 months post-transition between supervisor inquiry and role clarity. A similarly mixed pattern exists for the role of direct inquiry with task mastery and job performance, with some evidence confirming a relationship (Ashford & Black, 1996; Bauer et al., 2007; Saks et al., 2011), some findings of no relationship (Fedor, Rensvold, & Adams, 1992; Gruman et al., 2006), and other research showing a negative relationship (Settoon & Adkins, 1997).

A weak positive relationship has been found between direct inquiry and person–organization fit in one study (Kim et al., 2005) yet not in another (Gruman et al., 2006), and there is initial evidence for a relationship of direct inquiry with person–job fit (Gruman et al., 2006). More consistent results have been found for the relationship of direct inquiry with social integration, confirming that this is positive (Bauer et al., 2007; Gruman et al., 2006; Morrison, 1993a; Saks et al., 2011).

Positive relationships have been found between direct inquiry and job satisfaction (Bauer et al., 2007; Gruman et al., 2006; Morrison, 1993b; Saks et al., 2011; Wanberg & Kammeyer-Mueller, 2000). The relationships of direct inquiry with organizational commitment have sometimes been positive (Bauer et al., 2007; Saks et al., 2011; van der Velde et al., 2005), yet in other studies nonsignificant (Gruman et al., 2006). Direct inquiry has been positively associated in some studies with intention to remain (Bauer et al., 2007; Morrison, 1993b), yet no significant associations have been found in other research for either intent to remain or actual retention (Saks et al., 2011; Wanberg & Kammeyer-Mueller, 2000).

FEEDBACK SEEKING

Feedback seeking has received a lot of attention in research in general (Ashford & Cummings, 1983; Ashford, Blatt, & VandeWalle, 2003), as well as for newcomers specifically (Gruman et al., 2006; Kammeyer-Mueller, Livingston, & Liao, 2011). There is mixed but largely supportive evidence that feedback seeking is associated with superior job performance for newcomers. Saks and Ashforth (1997) found that feedback-seeking behaviors toward other newcomers, senior coworkers, and supervisors were positively associated with criteria of task mastery, role orientation, and job performance. Similarly, there is evidence that feedback seeking is positively correlated with role clarity (Saks et al., 2011; Wanberg & Kammeyer-Mueller, 2000), job performance (Ashford & Black, 1996), and person–job fit (Gruman et al., 2006). Kammeyer-Mueller et al. (2011) found a positive relationship of feedback seeking with creative performance but not with role clarity. In line with the latter finding, Morrison (1993a) found that performance feedback inquiry was largely unrelated to task mastery or role clarity, yet Saks et al. (2011) found a positive relationship of feedback seeking with task mastery.

In terms of social outcomes, feedback seeking has been positively associated with social integration (Gruman et al., 2006; Saks et al., 2011; Wanberg & Kammeyer-Mueller, 2000), person–organization fit (Gruman et al., 2006), and organizational citizenship behavior (Kammeyer-Mueller et al., 2011). Mostly positive associations have been found between feedback seeking from various sources and distal adjustment attitudinal outcomes, including job satisfaction, commitment, and intent to remain or, in the case of cooperative placement students, intent to return (Gruman et al., 2006; Saks & Ashforth, 1997; Wanberg & Kammeyer-Mueller, 2000). However, Wanberg and Kammeyer-Mueller (2000) found that feedback seeking was not associated with actual retention.

Overall, while the evidence mostly shows a positive relationship between newcomers seeking feedback and their understanding and performance of their jobs, there are occasions when this is not the case. It is possible that differences in the consequences of feedback seeking are due to the quality of feedback received (Adams, 2005; Ashford et al., 2003), and it is the responsibility of newcomers and insiders to drive this. More straightforwardly, greater feedback seeking is consistently associated with better integration into the social fabric of the organization and, for the most part, is related to more positive attitudes of the newcomer toward the new job and organization.

MONITORING

Monitoring behavior is well established in the general literature on employee information seeking (Anseel, Lievens, & Levy, 2007; Ashford & Cummings, 1983), as well as the newcomer literature (Filstad, 2004; Miller & Jablin, 1991; Morrison, 1993a, b; Saks & Ashforth, 1997). Monitoring refers to observing the work environment to see what others are doing and learn from this. This is distinct from role modeling, in which a specific high-performing colleague is identified and emulated. Research has shown newcomer monitoring behavior to be associated with higher levels of learning in task, role, group, and organizational domains (Ostroff & Kozlowski, 1992), as well history, goals and values, language, performance, and political areas (van der Velde et al., 2005). In research with transferees, Callister et al. (1999) found that greater levels of peer and supervisor monitoring were associated with greater role clarity, and this pattern was consistent at 1, 3, and 12 months post-transition. Other research has shown positive correlations between monitoring and task mastery (Saks & Ashforth, 1997) and performance (Morrison, 1993b), although one study found no relationship of monitoring with performance (Fedor et al., 1992). Barring this one study, then, monitoring is positively associated with understanding, role clarity, task mastery, and performance.

Turning to measures of social integration and attitudes toward work that are distal indicators of socialization, monitoring behaviors by newcomers are positively associated with social integration and acculturation (Morrison, 1993a), adjustment (Ostroff & Kozlowski, 1992), job satisfaction (Morrison, 1993b; Saks & Ashforth, 1997), organizational commitment (Saks & Ashforth, 1997; van der Velde et al., 2005), and intention to remain (Morrison, 1993b; Saks & Ashforth, 1997). Intriguingly, monitoring has been positively associated with psychological and physical stress (Ostroff & Kozlowski, 1992), yet negatively with anxiety (Saks & Ashforth, 1997). While these results seem paradoxical, it may be that anxiety reduces the likelihood of newcomers engaging in monitoring behavior, but that when newcomers do monitor others this results in greater stress . Regardless of the direction of the relationships between monitoring, anxiety, and stress, monitoring has consistent rewards. Moderating this, though, we note that successful monitoring may often depend on the selection of multiple coworkers and adopting the best from each (Filstad, 2004; Gibson, 2004).

POSITIVE FRAMING

Positive framing is a positive self-management behavior whereby the newcomer tries to see challenges as opportunities and not obstacles (Ashford & Black, 1996). For example, the newcomer is given a tight deadline for delivering a project. Instead of seeing this as an impossible task, the newcomer

using positive framing would purposely perceive the situation in a positive manner, such as seeing the tight deadline as reflecting the supervisor's belief in the newcomer's abilities to deliver under pressure. Positive framing has shown positive relationships with role learning (Owens, 2010) and job performance (Ashford & Black, 1996), a negative relationship with PO fit (Kim et al., 2005), and no relationship with role clarity (Wanberg & Kammeyer-Mueller, 2000). In terms of attitudes, higher levels of positive framing are associated with greater social integration and job satisfaction, and lower intention to quit (Ashford & Black, 1996; Wanberg & Kammeyer-Mueller, 2000), although no significant association with actual turnover has been found (Wanberg & Kammeyer-Mueller, 2000). Positive framing shows promise as a useful newcomer proactive behavior, but clearly more research is needed.

The Consequences of Newcomer Proactive Behaviors Aimed at Mutual Development
BOSS RELATIONSHIP BUILDING

The relationship between the new employee and his or her supervisor is critical to the new employee, given that an adequate performance appraisal from the supervisor is necessary for continued employment (Cooper-Thomas & Anderson, 2006). In line with this, there is consistent evidence of positive correlations between relationship building with one's boss and socialization adjustment outcomes. Boss relationship building is positively associated with performance indicators, including task mastery and role clarity (Gruman et al., 2006; Kammeyer-Mueller et al., 2011; Saks et al., 2011), job and creative performance (Ashford & Black, 1996; Kammeyer-Mueller et al., 2011), and organizational citizenship behavior (Kammeyer-Mueller et al., 2011). Boss relationship building is also positively correlated with social integration, job satisfaction, commitment, intent to return, person–job fit, and person–organization fit (Gruman et al., 2006; Saks et al., 2011). Intriguingly, one study found a negative relationship between the quality of one's boss relationship and the volume of corrective feedback given (Adams, 2005). It is unclear whether having a good relationship requires less feedback to be given, since perhaps this is given in other, less direct ways, or whether the supervisor would refrain from feedback for fear of damaging the relationship (Levy & Williams, 2004).

JOB CHANGE NEGOTIATION

Job change negotiation is a potentially risky behavior for newcomers given that it requires going against the ways things are currently done, even though the newcomer may be trying to achieve a better fit for her skills and potentially a better outcome for the organization as well. Looking at the evidence for newcomers using this behavior, Ashford and Black (1996) found no significant associations between newcomer job change negotiation and either job satisfaction or performance. However, Gruman et al. (2006) found that job change negotiation was positively correlated with task mastery, role clarity, social integration, and commitment, but was not associated with job satisfaction, intent to return, person–job fit, or person–organization fit, with similar results found by Saks et al. (2011). The initial evidence suggests that newcomers who use this strategy do have a clear idea of their assigned job and have established some level of competence in it, although given that relationships are shown from cross-sectional data, this may occur prior to effective negotiation to alter the job. Interestingly, job change negotiation is not associated with particularly high or low levels of job satisfaction or person–job or person–organization fit, so it appears that using this strategy does not seem to bring about these kinds of benefits, or at least not in the short term.

NETWORKING

Networking has been a growing area of interest in organizational psychology and organizational behavior literature in general (Chiaburu & Harrison, 2008; Ibarra, Kilduff, & Tsai, 2005), with a smaller amount of research investigating this for newcomers (Miller & Jablin, 1991; Morrison, 2002b; Settoon & Adkins, 1997). Research has shown that networking is positively associated with learning across role, social, and organizational domains (Owens, 2010), and also that networking is positively correlated with social integration, job satisfaction, commitment, intent to return, person–job fit, and person–organization fit (Ashford & Black, 1996; Gruman et al., 2006). Whereas Gruman et al. (2006) report no relationship between networking and task mastery or role clarity, Saks et al. (2011) report positive relationships. Morrison (2002b) provides insights as to how the overall size and diversity of one's relational networks matter. Whereas a strong, dense network is linked to task mastery and role clarity, a large network is linked to greater organizational knowledge among newcomers. Overall, networking seems to be effective for learning and fitting in to the organization at a personal and social level, as well as offering direct task benefits.

GENERAL SOCIALIZING

Alongside networking, establishing social relationships with colleagues can help in learning norms that influence levels of organizational citizenship behaviors (Bommer, Miles, & Grover, 2003; Chiaburu & Harrison, 2008), as well as influencing role perceptions, work attitudes, effectiveness, and withdrawal (Chiaburu & Harrison, 2008). Looking specifically at newcomers, there is evidence that socializing with colleagues is positively associated with task-specific and general work performance (Adkins, 1995), role clarity (Gruman et al., 2006; Kammeyer-Mueller et al., 2011; Saks et al., 2011; Wanberg & Kammeyer-Mueller, 2000), task mastery (Saks et al., 2011), person–job fit (Gruman et al., 2006), and organizational citizenship behavior (Kammeyer-Mueller et al., 2011). However, other research has found no relationship of general socializing with task mastery (Gruman et al., 2006) or performance (Ashford & Black, 1996; Kammeyer-Mueller et al., 2011). There is more consistent evidence that general socializing is positively associated with social integration (Gruman et al., 2006; Saks et al., 2011; Wanberg & Kammeyer-Mueller, 2000), job satisfaction (Ashford & Black, 1996; Gruman et al., 2006; Saks et al., 2011; Wanberg & Kammeyer-Mueller, 2000), organizational commitment (Saks et al., 2011), and both person–organization fit and intent to remain (Gruman et al., 2006; Saks et al., 2011; Wanberg & Kammeyer-Mueller, 2000), although not actual turnover (Wanberg & Kammeyer-Mueller, 2000). Overall, from these results it seems that general socializing is related more to understanding and perceiving a fit with the role and with colleagues, and only in some cases does this facilitate understanding and performance of both task and role elements.

NEW PERSPECTIVES ON THE CONSEQUENCES OF PROACTIVE BEHAVIOR: THE NEGLECTED ROLE OF PROACTIVE OUTCOMES AND OTHER MODERATORS

It is intriguing that mixed evidence is found for the effects of some proactive behaviors. For example, direct inquiry has shown a positive relationship with performance (Ashford & Black, 1996), no relationship (Gruman et al., 2006), and a negative relationship (Settoon & Adkins, 1997). Similarly, for feedback seeking, Saks et al. (2011) found a positive relationship with task mastery yet

Kammeyer-Mueller et al. (2011) found a negative relationship with the similar construct of role clarity and Morrison (1993a) found negative relationships of performance feedback inquiry with task mastery and role clarity. Discrepant findings such as these were noted by Saks et al. (2011). They proposed that the missing element was proactive outcomes; that is, the extent to which proactive behaviors had been successful in attaining their intended aims. For example, the discrepant results for feedback seeking could be because feedback seeking primarily has a positive relationship with outcomes such as role clarity, and task mastery through the attainment of feedback. While proactive outcomes had not been measured prior to Saks et al.'s (2011) research, it is plausible that the positive relationships of proactive behaviors with socialization outcomes occurred when outcomes were achieved—even though the mediation of proactive outcomes was not measured—and null relationships occurred when the outcomes were not attained.

In addition to these mediating effects of proactive outcomes, Saks et al. (2011) also proposed that proactive outcomes have moderating effects. That is, while a relationship between a proactive behavior and socialization outcome might be positive (or negative), the strength of this relationship is influenced by the degree to which the proactive outcome is attained. Taking networking as an example, this is positively associated with social integration and job satisfaction, among other outcomes (Ashford & Black, 1996; Gruman et al., 2006). With moderation occurring, these relationships will be stronger to the extent that networks—the proactive outcome—have been established. Saks and colleagues found some support for their mediation and moderation hypotheses. Investigating six socialization outcomes, they found full or partial mediation for five of these and moderation for three. These initial results confirm proactive outcomes as an important theoretical development and support their inclusion in future research to better qualify their contribution.

Moderating effects are not new in newcomer research. Earlier research showed that the accessibility of supervisors and colleagues (Major & Kozlowski, 1997; Major, Kozlowski, Chao, & Gardner, 1995) influenced information seeking, job satisfaction, and intention to turnover. There is also interesting research showing that team expectations of newcomers influence social exchanges (Chen, 2005; Chen & Klimoski, 2003). Both anticipated and actual newcomer performance, as well as other newcomer behaviors, may influence insiders'

reactions and receptivity to newcomer proactivity. Thus, in addition to proactive outcomes other newcomer and environmental influences, such as colleague accessibility and perceptions of performance, should be considered in future research. We return to the discussion of future research at the end of the chapter.

The Antecedents of Newcomer Proactive Behaviors

Having looked at the consequences of proactive behaviors, we turn now to consider antecedents. We divide these into three sources: those that exist in the environment to influence the availability of and necessity for proactive behavior; those that stem from insider norms, availability, or proximity to influence what proactive behaviors are feasible; and newcomer individual factors that influence whether such employees have the personal resources and desire to enact proactive behaviors.

Environment

The main environmental factor that organizational socialization research has considered in relation to newcomer proactive behaviors is organizational socialization tactics (Jones, 1986; Saks & Ashforth, 1997; Van Maanen & Schein, 1979; see also Saks and Gruman, Chapter 3 of this volume). Organizations may either design carefully structured "institutionalized" socialization activities, or use unstructured "individualized" tactics (Jones, 1986; Ashforth, Saks, & Lee, 1997). Institutionalized tactics comprise socialization occurring for newcomers as a group, mostly segregated from insiders (collective and formal tactics), progressing through a stepped program in accordance with a timetable (sequential and fixed tactics), relying on insiders as role models and valuing the contribution of newcomers (serial and investiture tactics; Jones, 1986). Individualized tactics are the opposite of institutionalized tactics (keeping the order as above, these are: individual, informal, random, variable, disjunctive, and divestiture).

In a theoretical model integrating organizational socialization tactics with newcomer proactive behaviors, Griffin, Colella, and Goparaju (2000) propose that organizational tactics influence newcomer behaviors in two ways. First, the tactics provide a context for proactive behaviors, inhibiting some while enabling others, and can therefore be considered antecedent. For example, a newcomer cannot monitor coworkers if none are readily observable. More specifically, Griffin et al. (2000)

propose that newcomer proactive behaviors will be more important when the organization provides a less structured individualized experience, because the newcomer has to figure things out for himself or herself. Second, Griffin et al. (2000) suggest that organizational socialization tactics moderate the relationships between proactive behaviors and socialization outcomes, either increasing or limiting the success of such behaviors. For example, they suggest that when the organization uses random and variable tactics, the relationship between socially oriented proactive behaviors, such as relationship building, networking, and general socializing, will be more strongly associated with socialization outcomes. This is because the lack of guidance from the organization will make these informal social sources more important. Effectively, Griffin et al. (2000) argue that some proactive behaviors can replace the lack of structure from individualized organizational socialization tactics.

Several studies have used an aggregated measure of organizational tactics, providing a broad view of the relationship of tactics with proactive behaviors. Institutionalized socialization tactics by the organization have been associated with higher levels of proactive behavior in aggregate (Ashforth et al., 2007). Further, institutionalized tactics are positively associated with feedback seeking and general socializing, as well as job change negotiation, boss relationship building, and information seeking, but not networking (Gruman et al., 2006; Kim et al., 2005). Evidence has also been found for a mediating effect, with institutionalized tactics predicting proactive behaviors and these in turn predicting outcomes. Thus, Gruman and colleagues (2006) found that, beyond the variance predicted by institutionalized tactics, the proactive behaviors of feedback seeking, general socializing, boss relationship building, information seeking, and job change negotiation (negative) predicted additional variance in a range of socialization outcomes, such as social integration and job satisfaction. Hence, proactive behaviors remain important for newcomers to achieve positive adjustment even when organizations provide a structured socialization program. In research investigating the independent effects of newcomer information seeking and institutionalized socialization on proximal adjustment outcomes, both information seeking and institutionalized tactics predicted role clarity and social acceptance (Bauer et al., 2007).

In contrast to the antecedent approach, Kim et al. (2005) investigated the potential moderating effects of organizational socialization tactics on

newcomer proactive behaviors in the prediction of PO fit. Of six interactions they examined, three were significant. Specifically, when the organization used institutionalized tactics, and newcomers used higher levels of general socializing and positive framing, these behaviors increased the positive relationship between institutionalized socialization tactics and PO fit. That is, the two behaviors of general socializing and positive framing both served to reinforce the positive associations of institutionalized socialization tactics with PO fit. However, there was a negative interaction for a third behavior of boss relationship building. For newcomers who worked to build a good relationship with their bosses, the organization's socialization tactics had no impact, whereas institutionalized socialization tactics were a significant predictor of PO fit for those newcomers who did not try to build a good relationship with their bosses.

Other researchers have investigated organizational tactics at a more detailed level, with mixed results. Looking first at the collective tactic, some researchers have found that this tactic is associated with greater use of monitoring (Miller, 1996; Saks & Ashforth, 1997), as well as indirect questions and questions to third parties (Miller, 1996). In one study, collective socialization has been associated with greater feedback seeking (Saks & Ashforth, 1997), although another study found no such relationship (Morrison, Chen, & Salgado, 2004). Serial and investiture tactics were positively associated with both feedback and monitoring across a range of sources in one study (Saks & Ashforth, 1997), although other research has found only minimal relationships of serial and investiture tactics with newcomer proactive behaviors (Miller, 1996). Formal tactics have also not shown significant relationships with newcomer proactive behaviors (Morrison et al., 2004). One possible reason for the more mixed evidence when looking at individual tactics is that some of these have examined more covert proactive behaviors, such as indirect questions and asking third parties. It is plausible that such behaviors stem more from individual differences than from environmental factors.

Overall, the evidence for positive association of organizational socialization tactics with newcomer proactive behavior is stronger at the aggregate, institutionalized level. It may be that, in general, structured socialization programs are associated with greater proactive behavior. It is logical that structured programs provide greater opportunities for the proactive behaviors that we define in the mutual development category (see Table 4.1), such as relationship building or seeking feedback, because there are sources for these behaviors. Moreover, by providing clear performance standards and a timetable for achieving these, institutionalized tactics may motivate self-change proactive behaviors such as information seeking and feedback seeking. In contrast, institutionalized tactics may inhibit proactive behaviors aimed at changing the role or environment, since these could violate norms.

A small number of other environmental factors have been considered in research on newcomer proactive behaviors. Kim et al. (2005) found that organizational size was positively associated with five of six proactive behaviors they measured: feedback seeking, information seeking, general socializing, boss relationship building, and networking. Thus, newcomers entering large organizations were more likely to behave proactively. Size was correlated at .29 with institutionalized tactics, and became nonsignificant in predicting PO fit when these tactics were entered. Moreover, size and institutionalized tactics showed fairly similar relationships with proactive behaviors with the exception of networking, which was only significantly correlated with size. It makes sense that larger organizations are more likely to use institutionalized socialization tactics, as they have the resources to make structured programs cost-effective. However, given the result for networking, it may be that organizational size also offers additional opportunities for proactive behaviors.

One other environmental factor that has been little considered is the riskiness of the environment for the newcomer and his or her colleagues. Holder (1996) cites an interviewee who noted that if she was uncertain, then she needed to ask questions directly and immediately because, "if I don't have the right information, someone might be electrocuted!" (p. 20). It may be that newcomers use proactive behaviors more when the newcomer's performance is vital to a safe working environment or another critical outcome for the organization (Cooper-Thomas & Wilson, 2011).

Insiders

The seminal work of Louis, Posner, and Powell (1983) introduced the idea that organizational insiders might be differentially useful to newcomers. They found that newcomers rated peers, senior coworkers, and supervisors as the most available and helpful sources for adjustment. Subsequent research has investigated the relative use and benefits of different information sources for newcomers (Cooper-Thomas, 2009).

Comparing different sources, some research has found that supervisors and coworkers are approximately equally used by newcomers when monitoring or experimenting for task and role information, although coworkers are preferred for information about the work group (Ostroff & Kozlowski, 1992) and technical information with respect to newcomers' jobs (Chan & Schmitt, 2000). Other research has shown that newcomers use direct inquiry of supervisors more for task and performance information, yet use direct inquiry of peers for social and normative information (Morrison, 1993b). Looking only at newcomer behaviors and not their goals, Teboul (1994) found a slight preference among newcomers to behave proactively toward coworkers rather than supervisors for strategies including direct inquiry, testing, and monitoring, although both sources were preferred to subordinates. The evidence is mixed, but suggests a slight preference for newcomers to behave proactively toward supervisors for role and performance information, and toward coworkers for social, technical, and cultural information. This suggests that newcomers are strategic in their patterns of information seeking: on the one hand, they may seek to maximize the benefits of gaining information in terms of both their own learning and other potential upsides, such as positive impression management. Equally, they may aim to minimize costs, such as the effort and time required, and potential personal embarrassment (Morrison, 2002a; Morrison & Vancouver, 2000).

The costs of proactive behaviors provide a useful lens for examining the role of insiders in newcomer proactive behavior. The potential costs of proactive behaviors have been investigated in two ways. First, costs have been examined indirectly through variables such as task interdependence and availability. Insider sources vary in their task interdependence with, and availability to, newcomers, in turn making the appropriate context for a proactive behavior more or less accessible, which in turn incurs greater costs for behaving proactively. Second, costs have been explored directly through asking newcomers about the social and personal—or ego—costs of different behaviors. In such research, newcomers are asked to rate whether a certain behavior might be viewed negatively by colleagues or be personally embarrassing.

Looking first at what we suggest are variables that indirectly reflect costs, few meaningful differences have been found for availability. Neither the availability of different insider sources (Louis et al., 1983; Miller, 1996) nor accessibility have been associated with information seeking behaviors (Major & Kozlowski, 1997). However, task interdependence and opportunity to interact have been consistently associated with newcomer proactive behaviors. Task interdependence has been positively associated with information seeking (Major & Kozlowski, 1997), feedback seeking, and boss relationship building, but not general socializing (Kammeyer-Mueller et al., 2011). Opportunity to interact has been positively associated with information seeking, feedback seeking, and relationship building behaviors (Wanberg & Kammeyer-Mueller, 2000). We suggest that the difference is between passive availability and active opportunities to interact, in that when the work context affords or supports interaction this reduces the costs to the newcomer of behaving proactively. They do not have to engineer the context or initiate an interaction because these are already naturally occurring.

Turning to research that measures the costs of proactive behaviors directly, in his experimental study with newcomers Miller (1996) found little evidence for different costs across insider sources. Note that Miller's (1996) measure of social costs also includes ego costs such as personal embarrassment. Newcomers who were more aware of social and ego costs were less likely to use direct inquiry and more likely to use covert behaviors such as monitoring, asking indirect questions, and asking third parties. Similar results were found by Holder (1996) in an investigation of newcomer women in nontraditional blue collar jobs. She found that newcomers who reported higher levels of social costs at a general level were more likely to ask indirect questions or ask a third party, and were less likely to directly inquire for information. A similar pattern was found for uncertainty and, in addition, these female newcomers showed greater use of monitoring, a covert strategy. Finally, Fedor and colleagues (1992) found that perceived costs of seeking feedback were negatively associated with actively inquiring for feedback and monitoring for feedback. Overall, the more newcomers perceive that being proactive will incur social and ego costs, the more they choose less obvious, lower-cost proactive behaviors.

Some research has also looked at attributes and behaviors of insiders and the associations of these with newcomer proactive behavior. Bauer and Green (1998) investigated the behaviors of newcomers' managers and found that neither manager clarifying nor manager supportive behaviors interacted with

newcomer information seeking (task or social) to predict socialization adjustment. Taking a broader approach, Kammeyer-Mueller et al. (2011) investigated the similarities between newcomers and their workgroups. They found that newcomers who were similar to their workgroup in education showed greater relationship building, while newcomers who were similar in gender showed greater boss relationship building. Intriguingly, newcomers more similar to the workgroup in age showed less feedback seeking and boss relationship building. Kammeyer-Mueller and colleagues (2011) explain this negative relationship by suggesting that age may act as a proxy for experience or different skills, and therefore newcomers may consider they will gain more from coworkers of dissimilar age. Overall, then, demographic similarities and behavioral support from insiders do not necessarily act to promote newcomer proactive behavior.

A related experimental study is worth mentioning here because it offers interesting possibilities for reciprocal effects. In a study investigating reactions to various scenarios outlining protégé proactive behavior, Thomas, Hu, Gewin, Bingham, and Yanchus (2005) found that respondents were more willing to peer mentor students who were portrayed as proactive. A similar result could occur for newcomers, with newcomers who demonstrate proactive behavior receiving more support from insiders in return. This is an interesting avenue for future research. Furthermore, it may be that newcomer proactive behavior is reciprocated in different ways, according to insiders' individual and collective attributes, and does not always garner support. Three possibilities are first, that newcomer proactive behaviors might be reciprocated in kind by insiders; for example, both parties work at facilitating direct inquiry. Second, it is possible that newcomer behaviors are viewed as sufficient and hence lead to less activity from insiders; so for instance, newcomers' direct inquiry is viewed as sufficient to establish a good understanding of the role, and insiders consider that no further action is needed. A third scenario is that insiders take a negative view of newcomer proactivity as either unnecessary or disruptive, and work to negate its effects. In this scenario, we would anticipate that insiders show a low level of proactive behavior regardless of newcomers' proactivity. An example of this would be the newcomer asking direct questions and insiders reciprocating with incorrect information. While this third scenario does not fit with Thomas et al.'s (2005) finding that potential mentors prefer proactive protégés, there is evidence that not all proactive behavior is beneficial (Bateman & Crant, 1993). Drawing on this, it seems plausible that not all newcomer proactive behavior will be met with a positive response. Indeed, Grant and Ashford (2008) offer the interesting idea that insiders evaluate the perceived individual or organizational benefit of a newcomer's proactive efforts, and offer reward or punishment reinforcers accordingly.

Newcomers

A number of newcomer demographic variables have been investigated in relation to proactive behavior. In the main, no relationships have been found for age (Ashforth et al., 2007; Kammeyer-Mueller et al., 2011), gender (Ashforth et al., 2007; Bauer & Green, 1998; Kammeyer-Mueller et al., 2011), ethnicity (Ashforth et al., 2007), academic major (Ashforth et al., 2007), type of job (Bauer & Green, 1998), salary (Bauer & Green, 1998), or work experience (Adkins, 1995; Ashforth et al., 2007; Bauer & Green, 1998; Wanberg & Kammeyer-Mueller, 2000). The few results that contrast with these are for work experience, tenure, and gender. In qualitative research, Beyer and Hannah (2002) found that there was a benefit of having work experience. Specifically, experienced new employees drew on a wider variety of personal tactics, including information seeking, goal setting, learning by doing or experimenting, and avoiding conflict. Notably, some of the experienced new employees in Beyer and Hannah's (2002) interviews talked of these behaviors as being ones that they had used before to adjust to new settings, suggesting that these are particularly successful strategies. Similarly, Major and Kozlowski (1997) found that for cooperative students, the number of previous internships was positively related to a broad information seeking measure. For tenure, Smith (1993, as cited in Chan & Schmitt, 2000) found a negative relationship between tenure and technical information seeking, although other research has found no effect of tenure on task or social information seeking (Bauer & Green, 1998). For gender and age, Kim et al. (2005) found that these were positively associated with some proactive behaviors. Newcomers who were male or older were more likely to use general socializing and networking, although Morrison et al. (2004) found that women were more likely to seek feedback, while Wanberg and Kammeyer-Mueller (2000) found that newcomers' age was related to positive framing only.

A final demographic variable worth mentioning is job skill level, which may be a proxy for education.

Wanberg and Kammeyer-Mueller (2000) found that the skill level of newcomers' new jobs was positively associated with all four proactive behaviors investigated (relationship building, information seeking, feedback seeking, and positive framing). Assuming that skill level is positively correlated with cognitive ability, Wanberg and Kammeyer-Mueller's (2000) finding fits with Parker et al.'s (2010) suggestion that those with greater cognitive ability will set more proactive goals and find various ways to work toward them.

Various personality variables have also been considered. Ashford and Black (1996) proposed that desire for control would be associated with newcomers aiming to reduce their uncertainty through greater use of proactive behaviors. In line with this, they found that desire for control was positively associated with job change negotiation, information seeking, positive framing, general socializing, and networking. Other researchers have directly measured uncertainty, anxiety, or tolerance for ambiguity as predictors of proactive behavior. They have found negative relationships between tolerance for ambiguity with inquiring and monitoring for feedback (Fedor et al., 1992); positive relationships between uncertainty and more covert proactive behaviors of monitoring, asking indirect and third party questions (Holder, 1996); a negative relationship of uncertainty with direct inquiry (Holder, 1996); and negative relationships of anxiety with feedback seeking and monitoring (Saks & Ashforth, 1997). From these varying results, it seems that newcomers who have a strong motivation to understand the situation, because of their individual differences, are more likely to behave proactively to get their needs met. However, newcomers who are anxious or uncertain will be more cautious in choosing which proactive behaviors to engage in.

A number of studies have investigated the role of self-efficacy in predicting newcomer proactive behavior (Gruman et al., 2006; Major & Kozlowski, 1997), which mirrors research on this relationship for employees in general (Brown, Ganesan, & Challagalla, 2001; Morrison & Phelps, 1999; Parker, Williams, & Turner, 2006). Parker (1998, 2000) developed the notion of role breadth self-efficacy as an indicator of proactive motivation, on the basis that employees need to feel capable of enacting behaviors that go beyond the narrow technical requirements of their jobs. These ideas fit well for new employees, where the initial period of adjustment may require both quantitatively and qualitatively more proactive behavior than is necessary once employees have become insiders. Hence, we would expect self-efficacy to predict proactive behavior for newcomers. This has been confirmed, with Gruman and colleagues (2006) finding a positive relationship of self-efficacy with feedback seeking, general socializing, networking, boss relationship building, and information seeking, but not job change negotiation (see also Filstad, 2004). Ohly and Fritz (2007) found that role-based self-efficacy was the only motivational variable to contribute to team ratings of proactive behavior, while Major and Kozlowski (1997) found that self-efficacy was not directly related with a broad measure of information seeking, but anticipated moderating effects were found. Specifically, they found a three-way interaction of self-efficacy with accessibility and task interdependence, such that low self-efficacy newcomers reported greater information seeking when they had high task interdependence and high accessibility, and to a lesser extent when they had high task interdependence and low accessibility. Major and Kozlowski (1997) propose that this is because high task interdependence and accessibility reduced the perceived costs of information seeking. Practically, it means that newcomers with low self-efficacy may benefit most from environmental factors that reduce costs and support proactive behavior. It is also worth noting that the limited research to date suggests that the benefit to newcomers is specifically around self-efficacy rather than core self-evaluations more broadly (Judge, Bono, Erez, & Locke, 2005). Specifically, Fedor et al. (1992) found that self-esteem was not associated with either inquiring or monitoring for feedback.

Several studies have confirmed the role of certain "Big Five" personality factors and the proactive behaviors of newcomers, with extroversion and openness to experience the more important predictors of such behaviors (Kammeyer-Mueller et al., 2011; Wanberg & Kammeyer-Mueller, 2000). The results of these two studies are reasonably similar. Openness to experience and extroversion were associated with greater feedback seeking, general socializing, and positive framing, with extroversion also associated with greater boss relationship building (Kammeyer-Mueller et al., 2011; Wanberg & Kammeyer-Mueller, 2000). In addition, neuroticism was associated with lower levels of—and conscientiousness with higher levels of—relationship building and positive framing (Kammeyer-Mueller et al., 2011; Wanberg & Kammeyer-Mueller, 2000). Together, these results confirm that Big Five personality factors are important in influencing how newcomers will attempt to direct their own adjustment.

The remaining studies investigating the role of personality in predicting proactive behavior have chosen a range of different predictors. While these results initially seem quite piecemeal, there are some underlying common threads that we come to shortly. Considering both positive and negative affectivity, Ashforth et al. (2007) showed that positive affectivity was associated with higher levels of proactive behavior and negative affectivity associated with lower levels of proactive behavior. This fits with Parker et al.'s (2010) research suggesting that activated positive affect is a necessary antecedent of proactive behavior. Parker and colleagues (2010) suggest that positive affect drives intrinsic motivation and consequently causes people to feel more driven to achieve their goals. For newcomers, many of these goals relate to fitting in and performing in the new work context, hence intrinsic motivation will stimulate proactive behaviors toward these goals. In research comparing US and Hong Kong Chinese employees, Morrison et al. (2004) found that women, US employees, and those higher in self-assertiveness and lower in power-distance were more likely to seek feedback. Morrison and Vancouver (2000) found that newcomers with a higher need for achievement adapted their proactive behaviors according to expertise source. Finally, drawing from her qualitative research with real estate agents, Filstad (2004) deduced that newcomer individual differences of expectations, experience, self-confidence, and competitive instinct are important in determining how well newcomers are able to interact with and observe role models, and use these to develop their own ways of behaving.

Reviewing newcomer individual factors as antecedents of proactive behavior, there are surprisingly few relationships supporting the role of sociodemographic variables in predicting proactive behaviors. The most promising to follow up on are age, work experience, and tenure. Age and work experience often correlate; there is evidence that older workers are happier at work (Clark, Oswald, & Warr, 1996), which fits with their greater positive framing (Wanberg & Kammeyer-Mueller, 2000). This may be due to the greater satisfaction they experience from personal relationships, hence older workers' higher use of networking and general socializing (Kim et al., 2005). Given the aging of the workforce in many developed countries (OECD, 2006; Statistics New Zealand, 2010), it is good news that older workers are more willing to use some proactive behaviors that can help them adjust into new roles. For work experience, Beyer and Hannah (2002) found that experienced workers used a wider variety of strategies. It is also possible that new employees with more work experience will be able to use proactive behaviors more effectively. For example, they may not network more than newcomers with less work experience, but they may make more useful network links (Morrison, 2002b). It is equally plausible that the seasoned newcomer may actually be less motivated to engage in proactive effort. For example, they may have used their prior experience to move to an organization where they have a high degree of natural fit (Carr, Pearson, Vest, & Boyar, 2006). The relative merit of both arguments is fertile ground for future research. We suggest, also, that there may be an interesting difference between work experience in general and transition experience in particular, with the latter conferring greater benefits for the newcomer in providing knowledge as to which proactive behaviors are most effective. In contrast to research on sociodemographic factors, there is more consistent evidence for the role of personality variables as antecedents of newcomer proactive behavior. Newcomers are more likely to behave proactively if they have greater confidence in their abilities (i.e., higher self-efficacy); lower tolerance for uncertainty or ambiguity; greater need for achievement, need for control, competitiveness, or goal-focus (e.g., conscientiousness); and if they are open to experience and extroverted. Conversely, newcomers are less likely to behave proactively when they have higher anxiety or neuroticism, negative affect, or have a higher power-distance.

Longitudinal Patterns of Change in Newcomer Proactive Behavior

Newcomers may vary their proactive behaviors over time, using specific behavior at appropriate times toward achieving certain outcomes. For example, a newcomer might use general socializing early on to develop a broad set of social contacts and later on might use networking to target specific relationships. Early research by Ashford (1986) showed intriguing results. She found that employees sought less feedback information by inquiry and monitoring as their tenure increased, yet continued to place a similar value on feedback. Thus, even though feedback was seen as equally valuable by "less new" newcomers, they sought it less. Ashford (1986) suggested that with greater tenure the social costs of seeking feedback are greater, and this deters employees from seeking it. There are various interesting avenues of

research that may follow from this—such as what factors influence newcomers to be more or less sensitive to the costs of proactive behaviors, including individual and environmental factors; and which behaviors themselves are, in general, viewed as more or less costly. Subsequent research has not investigated these issues, but instead has allowed an accumulation of evidence on how proactive behaviors vary over the entry period.

In a detailed longitudinal study, Morrison (1993b) investigated newcomer information seeking for five types of information. In general, she found that newcomers' levels of information seeking were relatively stable, although over time, newcomers sought technical (i.e., task) information less but referent (i.e., role) information more. Morrison (1993b) suggested that the 6-month time frame she used might be too short. Callister, Kramer, and Turban (1999) also found relative stability in information seeking over a 1-year period post-entry, with supervisor inquiry, supervisor monitoring, and peer monitoring showing no change and peer inquiry reducing. Building on Morrison's (1993b) findings, Chan and Schmitt (2000) found that newcomers continued to seek technical information from their supervisors at a stable rate, yet sought referent information from supervisors at an increasing rate. Newcomers sought technical information from coworkers less over time, yet reference information at a constant level. Intriguingly, whereas Morrison (1993b) had proposed that technical information seeking decreased due to task mastery, Chan and Schmitt (2000) were able to negate this suggestion. Specifically, they looked at rates of change for technical information seeking and task mastery and found that only the former showed individual change over time. Thus, the reduction in technical information seeking from coworkers must be due to reasons other than task mastery. This fits with Ashford's (1986) suggestion regarding costs; in particular, social and performance costs should be considered here as potential mechanisms affecting information seeking (Ashford, 1986; Cooper-Thomas & Wilson, 2007, 2011; Miller & Jablin, 1991).

Looking at tenure, Wanberg and Kammeyer-Mueller (2000) found a positive association between days employed and general socializing, showing that as newcomers had longer tenure they engaged in more general socializing. Interestingly, days employed was not associated with three other proactive behaviors of information seeking, feedback seeking, and positive framing, indicating relative stability in these. Wanberg and Kammeyer-Mueller

(2000) suggest that the result for general socializing may be because newcomers initially can rely on others to perform introductions and help them in building networks, but subsequently insiders feel they have done their duty and leave newcomers to take over responsibility for building relationships themselves.

At a more immediate level, daily changes in the amount of proactive effort an employee engages in may also be due to simply not having enough mental resources available, particularly if the employee is still recovering from the work stressors and work demands of the previous day. To perceive opportunities for, and to persist in, proactive effort requires the employee to be working at an optimal mental state (Sonnentag, 2003).

In summary, it seems that newcomer behaviors relating to role or performance information may be more sensitive to cost concerns, as well as dispositional factors. Hence, newcomers may either decrease these behaviors over time or switch to more covert proactive behaviors, such as monitoring or indirect questions, which have lower social costs and require less emotional effort.

Can Proactive Behaviors be Maladaptive for Newcomers or Their Organizations?

In research that has investigated proactive behaviors broadly (as opposed to focusing solely on organizational socialization), such behaviors have been depicted as useful, supporting important and positive individual and organizational outcomes (Grant & Ashford, 2008), including career success (Erdogan & Bauer, 2005; Seibert et al., 1999), creativity and innovation (Kim et al., 2009; Seibert et al., 2001), and performance (Chan, 2006; Crant, 1995; Thomas, Whitman, & Viswesvaran, 2010). To a large extent, similar positive associations of proactive behaviors with important outcomes are found in the organizational socialization literature (Ashford & Black, 1996; Gruman et al., 2006; Saks et al., 2011). Yet, not all proactive behavior to outcome relationships have been positive; some findings have been mixed and, more occasionally, proactive behaviors have been associated with negative outcomes (see above section, "The Consequences of Newcomer Proactive Behaviors"). We delve into possible explanations for the mixed findings in the section below (see "Future Research Directions"). Here, we examine the potential downsides of this enthusiasm for greater employee proactivity. In particular, the risks of proactive behavior have been outlined by Campbell (2000), who suggests that the evolution of the employee role toward a more proactive stance blurs the boundary between manager and employee. Campbell notes that employees are being encouraged to take risks and to even defy superiors (Stewart, 1996, as cited in Campbell, 2000). While this sounds bold, irreverent, and possibly fun, it poses risks for organizations (Campbell, 2000) and newcomers, and we explore the perils for each of these next.

Risks of Newcomer Proactive Behavior for Organizations

First, looking at the three categories of proactive behaviors for newcomers outlined in Table 4.1 (see above), behaviors in the first column of change role or environment pose the most risk for organizations. Specifically, newcomers may try to influence the organization to provide a role that allows them a better fit or gives greater credence to their abilities, enabling newcomers to take on an expert role or delegate aspects of their role to others. Such behavior may in some cases be highly adaptive, allowing new employees to adjust their roles in ways that enable them to better use their skills for the benefit of the organization. Yet, we argue that there may be situations where newcomers are focused on self-interested ends, using strategies such as minimizing new tasks to boost performance (Cooper-Thomas et al., 2011) or proactive self-handicapping in order to set low expectations (Grant & Ashford, 2008), regardless of the organization's needs. A more minor risk is posed by the behaviors in the second column, where new employees may try to change themselves in ways they think are appropriate, but which actually reduce their contribution to the organization. For example, newcomers who rely too much on information and feedback from insiders may change themselves from having complementary to supplementary fit with colleagues, reducing their value to the organization (Jansen & Kristof-Brown, 2005). Behaviors in the third column of mutual development are the least risky, as organizational insiders will provide norms to newcomers to help ensure that newcomers stay on track; and since it is more a two-way process, newcomers are less likely to change themselves radically.

Second, research consistently shows that institutionalized socialization tactics reduce the need for some types of proactive behavior (Griffin et al., 2000) and yield positive outcomes such as learning, social integration, job satisfaction, organizational commitment, performance, and intention to remain (Bauer et al., 2007; Saks & Ashforth,

1997). In contrast, individualized socialization tactics are associated with greater role conflict and role ambiguity, anxiety, and intent to quit (Jones, 1986; Saks & Ashforth, 1997). This shows that neglecting to provide a structured socialization experience, and expecting newcomers to behave proactively to fill the void, is a risky strategy. Indeed, Kim et al.'s (2005) research intriguingly shows that some proactive behaviors can complement institutionalized organizational socialization practices in achieving positive outcomes (i.e., positive framing and general socializing), whereas others appeared to substitute for institutionalized tactics (i.e., relationship building with boss). Early research by Van Maanen (1973) with rookie police officers hints at similar substitution results, where new employees were encouraged by their buddies to ignore their extensive training and take a more individualized approach to their work. However, Burke (2009) found that an institutionalized environment might actually propel newcomers into self-directed activity, and signal to newcomers that they are valued organizational members who have an "important, meaningful, effectual and worthwhile" role to play (Pierce, Gardner, Cummings, & Dunham, 1989, p. 625). Thus, while the relationships between institutionalized socialization tactics and newcomer proactive behaviors need to be explored further, it is risky to assume that either reducing structured organizational socialization tactics or leaving newcomers to figure things out for themselves will encourage greater proactive behavior and help achieve positive outcomes. Newcomer proactivity may come at the expense of organizational tactics (Kim et al., 2005). We suggest that, at a minimum, organizations should consider which structured elements are most important for socializing new employees in their specific context, and continue to provide those resources. Practically, it also suggests that employers need to design the right mix of socializing elements to retain high-performing employees at different stages in their careers, but to guard against employees becoming so fully embedded into an organization that it stifles innovation (Ng & Feldman, 2007).

Related to this, Bolino, Valcea, and Harvey (2010) raise the issue that organizations may come to depend on new employee proactivity. As new employees successfully manage their own socialization, the organization may happily reduce investment in organizational socialization, orientation, or onboarding programs. Yet, given that greater proactivity is associated with career initiative (Seibert

et al., 2001), it may be that these new employees, while productive for the time that they stay with the organization, are more likely to leave. This could become a vicious cycle for organizations, in that the very behaviors that they find useful in improving individual performance and, in turn, organizational performance, are also those attributes that make their employees more marketable and could contribute to increased turnover. As well as the ongoing loss of organizational knowledge, it may be that the organization is unable to replace these employees with newcomers who are either inclined or can be trained to be proactive. Hence, it may be risky to rely on employee proactivity in general, and new employee proactivity in particular.

Risks of Proactive Behavior for Newcomers

Turning to look at the risks of proactive behavior for newcomers, the feedback seeking literature notes a range of costs for behaving proactively, including social, performance, and personal (ego) costs (Ashford, 1986; Ashford & Cummings, 1983; Ashford et al., 2003; Morrison & Bies, 1991). These costs have been picked up in the newcomer literature, also (Cooper-Thomas & Wilson, 2007, 2011; Fedor et al., 1992; Miller & Jablin, 1991). Social costs refer to the impression-management risks of behaving proactively: new colleagues may view the proactive newcomer in negative ways, such as being pushy or else weak and uncertain. Performance costs refer to the time and effort required to behave proactively and interpret any results or information discovered. Personal costs comprise any embarrassment or loss of face. Thus, newcomers who do decide to behave proactively may incur a range of social, performance, and personal costs that may offset or even result in a negative return on their efforts. For example, a newcomer who works hard to establish a network may achieve his or her desired outcome of making a range of useful contacts, but inevitably this behavior will incur some costs. For example, if the newcomer is seen by her new contacts as pushy, those contacts may make no attempts to provide useful information to the newcomer. Even worse, these new contacts may badmouth the newcomer to others as being pushy or overly ambitious. These examples show neutral or even negative returns on the initial behavioral investments (costs) of the newcomer. Bolino et al. (2010) also note that proactive behavior may result in more work for colleagues. In the case of newcomers, this may be viewed as rocking the boat and disrupting accepted performance standards such as average productivity (Bolino et al., 2010; Jansen & Kristof-Brown, 2005). Beyond this, insiders may structure the environment to try and restrict proactive behavior, which in turn may be stressful for proactive newcomers (Bolino et al., 2010).

A second issue is the uncertainty that newcomers face, whereby being proactive in a relatively unknown environment adds extra strain at a time when new employees already have to overcome the stress of the adjustment period (Bolino et al., 2010; Fisher, 1985; Saks & Ashforth, 1996; Wanous, 1992). Bolino et al. (2010) suggest that this stress is due to the depletion of resources incurred by behaving proactively, which relates to the costs literature referenced above. Such resources may include individual skills, traits, or ability to judge situations (Bolino et al., 2010; Chan, 2006), or job characteristics such as autonomy and challenge (Grant & Ashford, 2008; Parker et al., 2006). Bolino and colleagues (2010) suggest that employees who lack the resources to be proactive will find the requirement to behave proactively more stressful. For new employees in the already stressful situation of having to learn their new roles and figure out how they fit in to their new organization, any additional requirements to behave proactively may cause unnecessary strain.

Can the Risks of Proactive Behaviors be Mitigated?

For organizations, Campbell (2000) suggests four approaches that may help resolve what he calls the *initiative paradox*, whereby organizations want their employees to be proactive yet need to ensure that this benefits the organization. The first solution is goal alignment, which he suggests can be achieved through communicating the organization's core values consistently, and especially during selection and socialization. This fits with socialization being integrated with the selection process (Anderson, 2001), such that employees coming into the organization know up front what kinds of proactive behaviors are valued. The second solution is clear communication of boundaries, to ensure that employees are clear as to the circumstances when initiative is welcomed. A good example here would be the newcomer's supervisor discussing the newcomer's role, and clarifying those elements of the role that are fixed versus elements where there is flexibility to allow a proactive approach. Third, good information sharing and trust help to establish shared interpretations of situations, and hence similar judgments. Information sharing and trust rely on the establishment of

positive relationships and this may be an outcome of socially oriented proactive behaviors, such as general socializing and boss relationship building. Given the importance of developing shared interpretations, in this solution the onus is equally on the organization and the newcomer to develop constructive working relationships. The fourth solution, of dynamic accountability, is effectively leaving the risk with employees and merely making it clear that independent action is welcome but mistakes are made at the employee's own peril. This fits with proactive behaviors in the change role or environment category (see Table 4.1), such as experimenting, testing limits, and action and feedback. As we noted above, there is research showing that newcomers use such behaviors but there is minimal investigation as to their effects. It is plausible that newcomers recognize the greater risks of these experimenting behaviors and therefore use them more judiciously (Cooper-Thomas & Wilson, 2011).

Overall, the solutions suggested by Campbell (2000) have a negative tone that is discordant with the predominantly positive findings associated with proactive behavior. Thus, while it is useful to identify and manage potential risks, this should not discourage organizations or employees from aiming to increase the use of appropriate proactive behaviors. In line with this, there is evidence from a study by Saks and Ashforth (1996) that new employees who are proactive through a range of self-management behaviors (e.g., self-goal setting, self-observation) can benefit both the newcomers and the organization. Relationships with these self-management behaviors include lower anxiety and greater ability to cope, and greater internal motivation. Taking this further, one solution that seems to hold considerable promise is that of organizations providing support to newcomers to help them become more proactive, and we discuss this emerging research area next.

Practical Implications: Training Newcomers to Be Proactive

Training is an important instrument in the socialization of new employees (Feldman, 1989) and "plays a major role in how individuals make sense of, and adjust to, their new job settings" (Feldman, 1989, p. 399). In the last several years, there has been an increasing move toward the integration of both training and socialization research streams. This research has emphasized both the availability and helpfulness of various training approaches (Nelson & Quick, 1991), the amount of training (Saks, 1996), the benefits of individual versus group training (Moreland & Myaskovsky, 2000), and the effectiveness of training (Axtell & Parker, 2003; Kirby, Kirby, & Lewis, 2002; Waung, 1995). To date, there is only a very small, albeit important body of research that links the training and proactive socialization literature (Axtell & Parker, 2003; Kirby et al., 2002). The scarcity of research exploring the training–proaction link is understandable. Not only is this an expensive organizational investment, but if there is limited opportunity to practice newly learned proactive behaviors then any gains associated with training could be lost (Parker, 1998). Axtell and Parker (2003) suggest that it is via enhancing employees' level of self-efficacy that organizational interventions—such as training—can develop employees' potential and ultimately enhance proactivity.

In an innovative test of this theory, Burke (2009) coached two groups of police newcomers in a repertoire of four proactive behaviors over 8 weeks and found that among the group who participated in training, proactive behavior was the most pronounced for newcomers who had higher role-based self-efficacy prior to training. Without training, role breadth self-efficacy had a nonsignificant relationship with future proaction. Providing proactive behavior training to the group signaled that they had the opportunity to take the initiative and to exercise autonomy, and that this was not only acceptable but expected.

Going forward, there is scope to tailor socialization training programs to better reflect the pre-training self-efficacy level of new employees. For example, behavioral modeling (Gist, Schwoerer, & Rosen, 1989) and formal orientation programs (Saks, 1994) have been found to be particularly effective for trainees with low self-efficacy. Thus, an important direction for future research might be to investigate the development of self-efficacy as a deliberate training intervention to build newcomer proactivity.

Future Research Directions

The process of reviewing past research on newcomer proactive behavior opened up many exciting avenues for future research. We list a number of questions below that we hope will stimulate readers to take up the challenge of trying to find answers. We suggest that researchers include a range of proactive behaviors from across the three categories presented here (see Table 4.1), as this provides a theoretical framework to investigate differences and ensures that the effects of specific proactive behaviors are not overstated (Ashford & Black, 1996).

To what extent are newcomer proactive behaviors interactive? For example, one behavior may increase the effectiveness of another, such as boss relationship building behavior increasing the benefits of feedback seeking behavior (from the boss). Alternatively, one behavior may decrease the effectiveness of another by making it redundant. An example of this would be direct inquiry reducing the benefits of monitoring.

Why have studies been inconsistent in findings regarding proactive behavior to outcome relationships? What moderators may be playing a role in these relationships?

Are there distinct patterns of relationships between institutionalized tactics and the different categories of newcomer proactive behaviors? **We propose that institutionalized tactics would be positively related to change-self and mutual development behaviors, and negatively related to change role or environment behaviors.**

What other environmental factors, beyond organizational socialization tactics, are important predictors of proactive behavior? **To what extent do work design features, such as job enjoyment, drive proactive behavior?**

In what ways are newcomer proactive behaviors reciprocated by insiders? **We suggest three possibilities for investigation: (i) insiders reciprocate in kind, by being more proactive themselves; (ii) insiders reciprocate in the negative, by behaving successively less proactively as newcomers behave more proactively; (iii) insiders show a steady level of proactive behavior regardless of newcomer proactivity.**

Do interventions to increase proactive behavior have most effect for newcomers with low self-efficacy? **Initial research suggests this may be the case.** An interesting additional conundrum, if the answer to this is affirmative, is what alternative interventions provide benefits to newcomers with high self-efficacy?

Do more experienced workers use a greater breadth of proactive behaviors (i.e., range), or use proactive behaviors more (i.e., frequency), or use similar proactive behaviors but more successfully (i.e., quality)? Related to this, does transition experience offer greater benefits than work experience for effective proactive behavior use?

What individual and environmental factors influence newcomers to be more or less sensitive to the costs of proactive behaviors? **Related to this, what are the relative costs of different proactive behaviors? Do newcomers switch to lower-cost proactive behaviors with increasing tenure?**

Is there evidence of newcomer proactive behaviors being maladaptive, and what other variables are involved? **Is there a cultural or ethnic difference in terms of what behaviors are considered maladaptive? For example, might some proactive behaviors be considered too direct or even rude in some countries or cultures?**

What individual and environmental factors maximize the effectiveness of proactive behavior training interventions? **What variables, in addition to role breadth self-efficacy, moderate the relationship between training and proactive behavior?**

Conclusion

As organizations shift from production economies to knowledge economies, proactive behavior is becoming more important than ever before for employees in general (Grant & Ashford, 2008), and this holds true for new employees also (Ashford & Black, 1996). Drawing on the work of Cooper-Thomas et al. (2011), we have presented proactive behaviors under three categories of change role or environment, change self, and mutual development, and we anticipate that these categories will prove useful for future theorizing. We then discussed the consequences and antecedents associated with newcomer proactive behavior. The consequences are mostly positive, such as greater learning, social integration, job performance, and job satisfaction (Kammeyer-Mueller & Wanberg, 2003; Saks et al., 2011), although our detailed analysis shows considerable underlying complexity and variation. A relatively small range of antecedents have been studied, and we consider that insiders' behaviors may be a particularly rich vein for future research. In line with the title of our chapter, we then discussed the potential for newcomer proactivity to be maladaptive both for organizations and for newcomers, as well as presenting suggestions for keeping proactive behaviors on track. Finally, we have discussed nascent work on proactive behavior interventions. Given the positive potential of newcomer proactive behavior, this is also a highly promising direction.

References

Adams, S. M. (2005). Positive affect and feedback-giving behavior. *Journal of Managerial Psychology, 20*(1), 24–42.

Adkins, C. L. (1995). Previous work experience and organizational socialization: A longitudinal examination. *Academy of Management Journal, 38*(3), 839–862.

Anderson, N. (2001). Towards a theory of socialization impact: Selection as pre-entry socialization. *International Journal of Selection and Assessment, 9*(1/2), 84–91.

Anderson, N., & Thomas, H. D. C. (1996). Work group socialization. In M. A. West (Ed.), *Handbook of work groups* (pp. 423–450). Chichester: Wiley.

Anseel, F., Lievens, F., & Levy, P. E. (2007). A self-motives perspective on feedback-seeking behavior: Linking organizational behavior and social psychology research. *International Journal of Management Reviews, 9*(3), 211–236.

Arnold, J., & Cohen, L. (2008). The psychology of careers in industrial and organizational settings: A critical but appreciative analysis. In G. P. Hodgkinson & J. K. Ford (Eds.), *International Review of Industrial and Organizational Psychology* (Vol. 23, pp. 1–44). Chichester: Wiley.

Ashford, S. J. (1986). Feedback-seeking in individual adaptation: A resource perspective. *Academy of Management Journal, 29*(3), 465–487.

Ashford, S. J., & Black, J. S. (1996). Proactivity during organizational entry: The role of desire for control. *Journal of Applied Psychology, 81*(2), 199–214.

Ashford, S. J., Blatt, R., & VandeWalle, D. (2003). Reflections on the looking glass: A review of research on feedback-seeking behavior in organizations. *Journal of Management, 29*(6), 773–799.

Ashford, S. J., & Cummings, L. L. (1983). Feedback as an individual resource: Personal strategies of creating information. *Organizational Behavior and Human Performance, 32*, 370–398.

Ashforth, B. E., Saks, A. M., & Lee, R. T. (1997). On the dimensionality of Jones' (1986) measures of organizational socialization tactics. *International Journal of Selection and Assessment, 5*(4), 200–214.

Ashforth, B. E., Sluss, D. M., & Saks, A. M. (2007). Socialization tactics, proactive behavior, and newcomer learning: Integrating socialization models. *Journal of Vocational Behavior, 70*(3), 447–462.

Axtell, C. M., & Parker, S. K. (2003). Promoting role breadth self-efficacy through involvement, work design, and training. *Human Relations, 56*(1), 112–131.

Bateman, T. S., & Crant, J. M. (1993). The proactive component of organizational behavior: A measure and correlates. *Journal of Organizational Behavior, 14*(2), 103–118.

Bauer, T. N., Bodner, T., Erdogan, B., Truxillo, D. M., & Tucker, J. S. (2007). Newcomer adjustment during organizational socialization: A meta-analytic review of antecedents, outcomes, and methods. *Journal of Applied Psychology, 92*(3), 707–721.

Bauer, T. N., & Green, S. G. (1998). Testing the combined effects of newcomer information seeking and manager behavior on socialization. *Journal of Applied Psychology, 83*(1), 72–83.

Berlew, D. E., & Hall, D. T. (1966). The socialization of managers: Effects of expectations on performance. *Administrative Science Quarterly, 11*, 207–223.

Beyer, J. M., & Hannah, D. R. (2002). Building on the past: Enacting established personal identities in a new work setting. *Organization Science, 13*(6), 636–652.

Bolino, M., Valcea, S., & Harvey, J. (2010). Employee, manage thyself: The potentially negative implications of expecting employees to behave proactively. *Journal of Occupational and Organizational Psychology, 83*, 325–345.

Bommer, W. H., Miles, E. W., & Grover, S. L. (2003). Does one good turn deserve another? Coworker influences on employee citizenship. *Journal of Organizational Behavior, 24*(2), 181–196.

Brown, S. P., Ganesan, S., & Challagalla, G. (2001). Self-efficacy as a moderator of information-seeking effectiveness. *Journal of Applied Psychology, 86*(5), 1043–1051.

Bureau of Labor Statistics (2009). *Employment Projections: 2008–2018 Summary.* Retrieved from http://www.bls.gov/news.release/ecopro.nr0.htm.

Burke, S. E. (2009). *Proactive socialisation: A longitudinal investigation of newcomer adjustment inside both an institutionalised and individualised workplace.* Unpublished PhD thesis, Victoria University of Wellington, Wellington, NZ.

Callister, R. R., Kramer, M. W., & Turban, D. B. (1999). Feedback seeking following career transitions. *Academy of Management Journal, 42*(4), 429–438.

Campbell, D. J. (2000). The proactive employee: managing workplace initiative. *The Academy of Management Executive (1993–2005), 14*(3), 52–66.

Carr, J. C., Pearson, A. W., Vest, M. J., & Boyar, S. L. (2006). Prior occupational experience, anticipatory socialization, and employee retention. *Journal of Management, 32*(3), 343–359.

Chan, D. (2006). Interactive effects of situational judgment effectiveness and proactive personality on work perceptions and work outcomes. *Journal of Applied Psychology, 91*(2), 475–481.

Chan, D., & Schmitt, N. (2000). Interindividual differences in intraindividual changes in proactivity during organizational entry: A latent growth modeling approach to understanding newcomer adaptation. *Journal of Applied Psychology, 85*(2), 190–210.

Chao, G. T., O'Leary-Kelly, A. M., Wolf, S., Klein, H. J., & Gardner, P. D. (1994). Organizational socialization: Its content and consequences. *Journal of Applied Psychology, 79*(5), 730–743.

Chen, G. (2005). Newcomer adaptation in teams: Multilevel antecedents and outcomes. *Academy of Management Journal, 48*(1), 101–116.

Chen, G., & Klimoski, R. J. (2003). The impact of expectations on newcomer performance in teams as mediated by work characteristics, social exchanges, and empowerment. *Academy of Management Journal, 46*(5), 591–607.

Chiaburu, D. S., & Harrison, D. A. (2008). Do peers make the place? Conceptual synthesis and meta-analysis of coworkers effects on perceptions, attitudes, OCBs, and Performance. *Journal of Applied Psychology, 93*(5), 1082–1103.

Clark, A., Oswald, A., & Warr, P. (1996). Is job satisfaction U-shaped in age? *Journal of Occupational & Organizational Psychology, 69*, 57–81.

Cooper-Thomas, H. D. (2009). The role of newcomer–insider relationships during organizational socialization. In R. Morrison & S. Wright (Eds.), *Friends and enemies in organizations: A work psychology perspective* (pp. 32–56). Basingstoke, UK: Palgrave Macmillan.

Cooper-Thomas, H. D., & Anderson, N. (2002). Newcomer adjustment: The relationship between organizational socialization tactics, information acquisition and attitudes. *Journal of Occupational & Organizational Psychology, 75*(4), 423–437.

Cooper-Thomas, H. D., & Anderson, N. (2005). Organizational socialization: A field study into socialization success and rate. *International Journal of Selection and Assessment, 13*(2), 116–128.

Cooper-Thomas, H. D., & Anderson, N. (2006). Organizational socialization: A new theoretical model and recommendations for future research and HRM practices in organizations. *Journal of Managerial Psychology, 21*(5), 492–516.

Cooper-Thomas, H. D., Anderson, N., & Cash, M. L. (2011). Investigating organizational socialization: A fresh look at newcomer adjustment strategies. *Personnel Review, 41*(1), 51–55.

Cooper-Thomas, H. D., & Wilson, M. G. (2007, August). *Newcomer adjustment strategies: A cost-benefit model.* Paper presented at the Academy of Management Conference, Philadelphia, PA.

Cooper-Thomas, H. D., & Wilson, M. G. (2011). Influences on newcomers' adjustment tactic use. *International Journal of Selection and Assessment, 19*(4), 388–404.

Crant, J. M. (1995). The proactive personality scale and objective job performance among real estate agents. *Journal of Applied Psychology, 80*(4), 532–537.

Crant, J. M. (2000). Proactive behavior in organizations. *Journal of Management, 26*(3), 435–462.

Datta, D. K., Guthrie, J. P., Basuil, D., & Pandey, A. (2010). Causes and effects of employee downsizing: A review and synthesis. *Journal of Management, 36*(1), 281–348.

Dutton, J. E., & Ashford, S. J. (1993). Selling issues to top management. *Academy of Management Review, 18*, 397–428.

Erdogan, B., & Bauer, T. N. (2005). Enhancing career benefits of employee proactive personality: The role of fit with jobs and organizations. *Personnel Psychology, 58*(4), 859–891.

Fedor, D. B., Rensvold, R. R., & Adams, S. M. (1992). An investigation of factors expected to affect feedback seeking: A longitudinal field study. *Personnel Psychology, 45*, 779–805.

Feldman, D. C. (1989). Careers in organizations: Recent trends and future directions. *Journal of Management, 15*(2), 135–156.

Feldman, D. C. (1994). Who's socializing whom? The impact of socializing newcomers on insiders, work groups, and organizations. *Human Resource Management Review, 4*(3), 213–233.

Feldman, D. C., & Brett, J. M. (1983). Coping with new jobs: A comparative study of new hires and job changers. *Academy of Management Journal, 26*, 258–272.

Filstad, C. (2004). How newcomers use role models in organizational socialization. *Journal of Workplace Learning, 16*(7), 396–409.

Finkelstein, L. M., Kulas, J. T., & Dages, K. D. (2003). Age differences in proactive newcomer socialization strategies in two populations. *Journal of Business & Psychology, 17*(4), 473–502.

Fisher, C. D. (1985). Social support and adjustment to work: A longitudinal study. *Journal of Management, 11*(3), 39–53.

Fuller, J. B., & Marler, L. E. (2009). Change driven by nature: a meta-analytic review of the proactive personality literature. *Journal of Vocational Behavior, 75*(3), 329–345. Gibson, D. E. (2004). Role models in career development: New directions for theory and research. *Journal of Vocational Behavior, 65*(1), 134–156.

Gibson, J. J. (1977). The theory of affordances. In R. Shaw & J. Bransford (Eds.), *Perceiving, acting, and knowing: Toward an Ecological Psychology* (pp. 67–82). Hillsdale, NJ: Lawrence Erlbaum.

Gist, M. E., Schwoerer, C., & Rosen, B. (1989). Effects of alternative training methods on self-efficacy and performance in computer software training. *Journal of Applied Psychology, 74*(6), 884–891.

Grant, A. M., & Ashford, S. J. (2008). The dynamics of proactivity at work. *Research in Organizational Behavior, 28*, 3–34.

Griffin, A. E., Colella, A., & Goparaju, S. (2000). Newcomer and organizational socialization tactics: An interactionist perspective. *Human Resource Management Review, 10*(4), 453–474.

Gruman, J. A., Saks, A. M., & Zweig, D. I. (2006). Organizational socialization tactics and newcomer proactive behaviors: An integrative study. *Journal of Vocational Behavior, 69*(1), 90–104.

Haueter, J. A., Macan, T. H., & Winter, J. (2003). Measurement of newcomer socialization: Construct validation of a multidimensional scale. *Journal of Vocational Behavior, 63*(1), 20–39.

Holder, T. (1996). Women in nontraditional occupations: Information-seeking during organizational entry. *The Journal of Business Communication, 33*(1), 9–26.

Howard, A. (1995). A framework for work change. In A. Howard (Ed.), *The changing nature of work* (pp. 3–44). San Francisco, CA: Jossey-Bass.

Ibarra, H., Kilduff, M., & Tsai, W. (2005). Zooming in and out: Connecting individuals and collectivities at the frontiers of organizational network research. *Organization Science, 16*(4), 359–371.

Jansen, K. J., & Kristof-Brown, A. L. (2005). Marching to the beat of a different drummer: Examining the impact of pacing congruence. *Organizational Behavior and Human Decision Processes, 97*(2), 93–105.

Jones, G. R. (1986). Socialization tactics, self-efficacy, and newcomers' adjustments to organizations. *Academy of Management Journal, 29*(2), 262–279.

Judge, T. A., Bono, J. E., Erez, A., & Locke, E. A. (2005). Core self-evaluations and job and life satisfaction: The role of self-concordance and goal attainment. *Journal of Applied Psychology, 90*(2), 257–268.

Kammeyer-Mueller, J. D., Livingston, B. A., & Liao, H. (2011). Perceived similarity, proactive adjustment, and organizational socialization. *Journal of Vocational Behavior, 78*(2), 225–236.

Kammeyer-Mueller, J. D., & Wanberg, C. R. (2003). Unwrapping the organizational entry process: Disentangling multiple antecedents and their pathways to adjustment. *Journal of Applied Psychology, 88*(5), 779–794.

Kim, T.-Y., Cable, D. M., & Kim, S.-P. (2005). Socialization tactics, employee proactivity, and person-organization fit. *Journal of Applied Psychology, 90*(2), 232–241.

Kim, T.-Y., Hon, A. H. Y., & Crant, J. M. (2009). Proactive personality, employee creativity, and newcomer outcomes: A longitudinal study. *Journal of Business and Psychology, 24*, 93–103.

Kirby, E. G., Kirby, S. L., & Lewis, M. A. (2002). A study of the effectiveness of training proactive thinking. *Journal of Applied Social Psychology, 32*(7), 1538–1549. Kramer, M. W. (1993). Communication after job transfers—social-exchange processes in learning new roles. *Human Communication Research, 20*(2), 147–174.

LePine, J. A., & Van Dyne, L. (1998). Predicting voice behavior in work groups. *Journal of Applied Psychology, 83*, 853–868.

Levy, P. E., & Williams, J. R. (2004). The social context of performance appraisal: A review and framework for the future. *Journal of Management, 30*(6), 881–905. Louis, M. R., Posner, B. Z., & Powell, G. N. (1983). The availability and helpfulness of socialization practices. *Personnel Psychology, 36*(4), 857–866.

Major, D. A., Kozlowski, S. W. J., Chao, G. T., & Gardner, P. D. (1995). A longitudinal investigation of Newcomer expectations, early socialization outcomes, and the moderating effects of role development factors. *Journal of Applied Psychology, 80*(3), 418–431.

Major, D. A., & Kozlowski, S. W. J. (1997). Newcomer information seeking: Individual and contextual influences. *International Journal of Selection and Assessment, 5*(1), 16–28.

Major, D. A., Turner, J. E., & Fletcher, T. D. (2006). Linking proactive personality and the big five to motivation to learn and development activity. *Journal of Applied Psychology, 91*(4), 927–935.

Miller, V. D. (1996). An experimental study of newcomers' information seeking behaviors during organizational entry. *Communication Studies, 47*, 1–24.

Miller, V. D., & Jablin, F. M. (1991). Information seeking during organizational entry—influences, tactics, and a model of the process. *Academy of Management Review, 16*(1), 92–120.

Moreland, R. L., & Myaskovsky, L. (2000). Exploring the performance benefits of group training: Transactive memory or improved communication? *Organizational Behavior and Human Decision Processes, 82*(1), 117–133.

Morrison, E. W. (1993a). Longitudinal-study of the effects of information seeking on newcomer socialization. *Journal of Applied Psychology, 78*(2), 173–183.

Morrison, E. W. (1993b). Newcomer information-seeking—exploring types, modes, sources, and outcomes. *Academy of Management Journal, 36*(3), 557–589.

Morrison, E. W. (1995). Information usefulness and acquisition during organizational encounter. *Management Communication Quarterly, 9*, 131–155.

Morrison, E. W. (2002a). Information seeking within organizations. *Human Communication Research, 28*(2), 229–242.

Morrison, E. W. (2002b). Newcomers' relationships: The role of social network ties during socialization. *Academy of Management Journal, 45*(6), 1149–1160.

Morrison, E. W., & Bies, R. J. (1991). Impression management in the feedback-seeking process: A literature review and research agenda. *Academy of Management Review, 16*(3), 522–541.

Morrison, E. W., Chen, Y.-R., & Salgado, S. R. (2004). Cultural differences in newcomer feedback seeking: A comparison of the United States and Hong Kong. *Applied Psychology: An International Review, 53*(1), 1–22.

Morrison, E. W., & Phelps, C. C. (1999). Taking charge at work: extra-role efforts to initiate workplace change. *The Academy of Management Journal, 42*(4), 403–419.

Morrison, E. W., & Vancouver, J. B. (2000). Within-person analysis of information seeking: The effects of perceived costs and benefits. *Journal of Management, 26*(1), 119–137.

Nelson, D. L., & Quick, J. C. (1991). Social support and newcomer adjustment in organizations: Attachment theory at work? *Journal of Organizational Behavior, 12*(6), 543–554.

Ng, T. W. H., & Feldman, D. C. (2007). Organizational embeddedness and occupational embeddedness across career stages. *Journal of Vocational Behavior, 70*(2), 336–351.

Nicholson, N. (1984). A theory of work role transitions. *Administrative Science Quarterly, 29*, 172–191.

OECD (2006). *Live longer, work longer: A synthesis report.* Retrieved from http://www.oecd-ilibrary.org/docserver/download/fulltext/8106021e.pdf?expires=1328661242&id=id&accname=ocid177592&checksum=71D03719BAF9E7F3D89117AE2E04ACF1

Ohly, S., & Fritz, D. (2007). Challenging the status quo: What motivates proactive behaviour? *Journal of Occupational and Organizational Psychology, 80*(4), 623–629.

Ostroff, C., & Kozlowski, S. W. (1992). Organizational socialization as a learning process: The role of information acquisition. *Personnel Psychology, 45*(4), 849–874.

Owens, F. K. (2010). *Can we help newcomers adjust at work by seeing things differently? Assessing a positive framing intervention.* Master of Science, The University of Auckland, Auckland.

Parker, S. K. (1998). Enhancing role breadth self-efficacy: The roles of job enrichment and other organizational interventions. *Journal of Applied Psychology, 83*, 835–852.

Parker, S. (2000). From passive to proactive motivation: the importance of flexible role orientations and role breadth self-efficacy. *Applied Psychology, 49*(3), 447–469. Parker, S. K., Bindl, U. K., & Strauss, K. (2010). Making things happen: a model of proactive motivation. *Journal of Management, 36*(4), 827–856.

Parker, S. K., & Collins, C. G. (2010). Taking stock: integrating and differentiating multiple proactive behaviors. *Journal of Management, 36*(3), 633–662. Parker, S. K., Williams, H. M., & Turner, N. (2006). Modeling the Antecedents of Proactive Behavior at Work. *Journal of Applied Psychology, 91*(3), 636–652.

Pierce, J. L., Gardner, D. G., Cummings, L. L., & Dunham, R. B. (1989). Organization-based self-esteem: Construct definition, measurement, and validation. *Academy of Management Journal, 32*(3), 622–648.

Rollag, K. (2007). Defining the term 'new' in new employee research. *Journal of Occupational and Organizational Psychology, 80*, 63–75.

Saks, A. M. (1994). Moderating effects of self-efficacy for the relationship between training method and anxiety and stress reactions of newcomers. *Journal of Organizational Behavior, 15*(7), 639–654.

Saks, A. M. (1996). The relationship between the amount and helpfulness of entry training and work outcomes. *Human Relations, 49*(4), 429–451.

Saks, A. M., & Ashforth, B. E. (1996). Proactive socialization and behavioral self-management. *Journal of Vocational Behavior, 48*(3), 301–323.

Saks, A. M., & Ashforth, B. E. (1997). Socialization tactics and newcomer information acquisition. *International Journal of Selection and Assessment, 5*(1), 48–61.

Saks, A. M., Gruman, J. A., & Cooper-Thomas, H. D. (2011). The neglected role of proactive behavior and outcomes in newcomer socialization. *Journal of Vocational Behavior, 79*(1), 36–46.

Saks, A. M., Uggerslev, K. L., & Fassina, N. E. (2007). Socialization tactics and newcomer adjustment: A meta-analytic review and test of a model. *Journal of Vocational Behavior, 70*(3), 413–446.

Scott, S. G., & Bruce, R. A. (1994). Determinants of innovative behavior: A path model of individual innovation in the workplace. *Academy of Management Journal, 37*, 580–607.

Seibert, S. E., Crant, J. M., & Kraimer, M. L. (1999). Proactive personality and career success. *Journal of Applied Psychology, 84*(3), 416–427.

Seibert, S. E., Kraimer, M. L., & Crant, J. M. (2001). What do proactive people do? A longitudinal model linking proactive personality and career success. *Personnel Psychology, 54*(4), 845–874.

Settoon, R. P., & Adkins, C. L. (1997). Newcomer socialization: The role of supervisors, coworkers, friends and family members. *Journal of Business and Psychology, 11*(4), 507–516.

Sonnentag, S. (2003). Recovery, work engagement, and proactive behavior: a new look at the interface between nonwork and work. *Journal of Applied Psychology, 88*(3), 518–528.

Statistics New Zealand (2010). *National Labour Force Projections 06–61 update HOTP.* Retrieved from http://www.stats.govt.nz/~/media/Statistics/Browse%20for%20stats/NationalLabourForceProjections/HOTP06-61/NationalLabourForceProjections06-61HOTP.pdf

Teboul, J. B. (1994). Facing and coping with uncertainty during organizational encounter. *Management Communication Quarterly, 8*(2), 190–224.

Thomas, J. P., Whitman, D. S., & Viswesvaran, C. (2010). Employee proactivity in organizations: A comparative meta-analysis of emergent proactive constructs. *Journal of Occupational and Organizational Psychology, 83*, 275–300. Thomas, K. M., Hu, C., Gewin, A. G., Bingham, K., & Yanchus, N. (2005). The roles of protégé race, gender, and proactive socialization attempts on peer mentoring. *Advances in Developing Human Resources, 7*(4), 540–555.

Thompson, J. A. (2005). Proactive personality and job performance: A social capital perspective. *Journal of Applied Psychology, 90*(5), 1011–1017.

Van der Velde, M. E. G., Ardts, J. C. A., & Jansen, P. G. W. (2005). The longitudinal effect of information seeking on socialisation and development in three organisations: Filling the research gaps. *Canadian Journal of Career Development, 4*(2), 32–42.

Van Maanen, J. (1973). Observations on the making of policemen. *Human Organizations, 32*, 407–418.

Van Maanen, J., & Schein, E. H. (1979). Toward a theory of organizational socialization. In B. M. Staw (Ed.), *Research in Organizational Behavior* (Vol. 1, pp. 209–264). Greenwich, CT: JAI Press.

Wanberg, C. R., & Kammeyer-Mueller, J. D. (2000). Predictors and outcomes of proactivity in the socialization process. *Journal of Applied Psychology, 85*(3), 373–385.

Wanous, J. P. (1992). *Organizational Entry: Recruitment, Selection, Orientation, and Socialization* (2nd ed.). Reading, MA: Addison-Wesley.

Waung, M. (1995). The effect of self-regulatory coping orientation on newcomer adjustment and job survival. *Personnel Psychology, 48*, 633–650.

Getting the Right Connections? The Consequences and Antecedents of Social Networks in Newcomer Socialization

Markku Jokisaari *and* Jari-Erik Nurmi

Abstract

The interaction between newcomers and more experienced members of the organization is assumed to be a main contributor to newcomers' success in their transition into an organization. Previous studies have, however, mainly examined newcomers' interactions with formal organizational members, such as supervisors and coworkers, and little is known about how the characteristics of the newcomers' social networks might contribute to their socialization over time. The social network approach is a framework that provides a theoretical and methodological background to better understand the role of social environment in organizational socialization. This chapter will introduce a theoretical framework for understanding how the structural and relational characteristics of newcomers' networks are related to their learning, sensemaking, success in the organization, and adjustment to work. Moreover, the role of newcomers' learning, success in the organization, and related organizational feedback will be discussed as the antecedents of their evolving networks in the organization.

Key Words: social networks, socialization, newcomers, new employees, job performance

Introduction

Many scholars of organizational socialization have argued that in order to understand how newcomers enter a new organization, one needs to know not only formal organizational practices such as training but, more importantly, the informal practices and interactions among personnel in the workplace (e.g., Graen, 1976; Reichers, 1987). For example, ethnographic studies suggest that "the ways people actually work usually differ fundamentally from the ways organizations describe that work in manuals, training programs, organizational charts, and job descriptions" (Brown & Duguid, 1991, p. 40). Thus it is reasonable to argue that new employees acquire the knowledge and skills to perform their jobs and to participate in the organization by working with their supervisors, coworkers, colleagues, and customers (e.g., Van Maanen & Schein, 1979). For example, new workers perceive relationships with

their supervisors and coworkers as the most valuable source of support in adjusting to a new organization (e.g., Louis et al., 1983).

The social network approach proposes that employees learn about their jobs and organizations through social relations and interactions in the workplace (e.g., Burt, 1992; Tichy, Tushman & Fombrun, 1979). Through their position in the social networks, individuals are able to attain information and advice and identify opportunities and resources that enable them to progress in their jobs and to integrate into the workplace. In order to understand people's behavior in the job and success in the organization, one has to focus on their social relations in the workplace and the kinds of positions they hold in the social networks (e.g., Burt, 1992). The social network approach shares the notion that "one can learn most about other people's behavior by studying the...social environment within which that behavior occurs and to which it adapts" (Salancik & Pfeffer, 1978, p. 226). Unfortunately, research on organizational socialization and social networks has so far, to a large extent, proceeded without paying attention to the reciprocal exchange between newcomer socialization and social networks (see Fang, Duffy, & Shaw, 2011; Jablin & Krone, 1987; Morrison, 2002; Rollag, 2004).

In this chapter we will first present a model describing the role of social networks in newcomer socialization and the role of socialization in newcomers' network development in the workplace. We also present the social network approach and its central concepts and premises. We then review earlier theories and findings on social networks and what they propose for newcomer socialization, as indicated by the newcomer's learning, sensemaking, success in the organization, and adjustment to work. Next, we examine how newcomer socialization and related learning and success in the organization might contribute to the evolvement of the newcomers' networks. Finally, we suggest that focusing on the interaction between newcomers' social networks and socialization over time is of great importance for understanding newcomer socialization into an organization.

Framework for Social Networks in Newcomer Socialization

Figure 5.1 presents a framework for describing the role of social networks in newcomer socialization. In this model, newcomers' socialization is characterized by their learning, sensemaking, success in the organization and related organizational feedback, and adjustment to work. First, socialization is a learning process during which newcomers face many different tasks that are critical to success in their transition into an organization (e.g., Feldman, 1981; Ostroff & Kozlowski, 1992). For example, one critical task for newcomers is to learn the skills and routines required to perform their jobs. This learning is then reflected in job performance. Another critical task for newcomers is to develop relationships with their coworkers and to be included in a variety of social groups. Such learning is reflected in employees' social integration in the workplace. Second, newcomers' sensemaking is an important part of organizational socialization because it helps them to achieve understanding in a new and often uncertain situation (Katz, 1980; Louis 1980). Newcomers are motivated to seek information and feedback about their roles as a way to obtain understanding and a sense of mastery in the new situation (e.g., Louis, 1980; Miller & Jablin, 1991). Third, organizational feedback, such as new job assignments, promotion, and remuneration, is essential in newcomer socialization (e.g., Schein, 1978). This organizational feedback is an important sign to newcomers of how they are succeeding in the organization and plays a key role in how they are assimilated to the organization (Fisher,

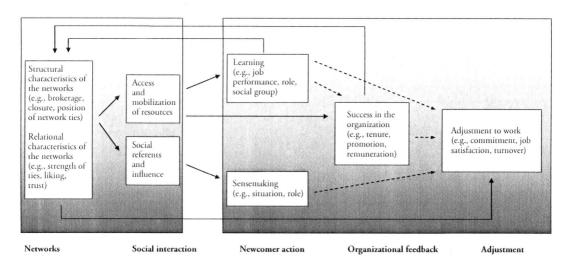

Note. *The main focus of this model, the relation between social networks and newcomer socialization, is represented by straight lines in the figure.*

Figure 5.1 Model of Social Networks and Newcomer Socialization, and Focus of the Review.

1986; Graen, 1976; Schein, 1978). Finally, scholars of socialization have argued that newcomers' learning, sensemaking, and success in the organization should be related to newcomers' adjustment to work (e.g., Schein, 1978). This adjustment to work is an important part of socialization and has been indicated by attitudinal and behavioral indicators such as organizational commitment, job satisfaction, and turnover (e.g., Feldman, 1981).

Newcomers' networks also contribute in important ways to their socialization (i.e., sensemaking, learning, success in the organization, and adjustment to work) because they offer access to resources and are a source of social referents and influence. For example, the characteristics of the newcomer's networks influence the kind of resources—such as knowledge, advice, and sponsorship—a newcomer has access to, and the kind of resources they can mobilize in the workplace (e.g., Burt, 1992; Lin, 1982; Tichy, Tushman & Fombrun, 1979). These resources are also related to newcomers' learning on the job and success in the organization. In addition, the characteristics of the newcomers' networks define the social informants and influential others for newcomers' sensemaking in the organization. As Van Maanen and Schein (1979) suggested: "Any person crossing into a new organizational region is vulnerable to clues on how to proceed that originate within the *interactional zone* [emphasis added] that immediately surrounds him. Colleagues, superiors, subordinates, clients, and other associates support and guide the individual in learning the new role" (p. 215). The characteristics of newcomers' networks, such as the quality of the relationships, are also related to their adjustment to work.

Finally, organizational socialization may also contribute to newcomers' network development. First, success in the organization and related organizational feedback, such as tenure and promotion, may relate to how newcomers' networks develop later on, since formal roles and job assignments define the people with whom one shares activities and the related opportunities for network development in the organization (Feld, 1981; Kossinets & Watts, 2009). Second, the way in which a newcomer learns to perform his or her job and become attached to social groups in the workplace is related to network development. For example, when a newcomer is perceived as a competent performer by others, this should also increase his or her centrality in the advice network in the workplace; in other words, others will seek information or advice from the newcomer. Third, the initial characteristics of the newcomers'

networks may also either enable or constrain the development of their networks later on.

We propose this framework for social networks and newcomer socialization with the aim of increasing our understanding of the relation between social networks and newcomer socialization, since previous research has three major limitations. First, research on organizational socialization has mainly focused on the formal ties between a newcomer and his or her coworkers and supervisors. In many cases, however, employees' interaction and communication ties do not form according to only formal organizational roles and work group boundaries; network ties evolve based on shared activities, work projects, and personal sentiments, among others, since "... work has become a collaborative endeavor accomplished less through standardized processes and formal structures than through informal networks of relationships" (Cross et al., 2005, p. 125). Second, in examining the interaction between a newcomer and organizational insiders, most of the theories and research on newcomer socialization has focused on the relational level, specifically dyadic pairs such as newcomer–supervisor, and the quality of social exchange in these relations (e.g., Graen, 1976; Reichers, 1987). However, the ways in which newcomers' supervisors, coworkers, and other "socialization agents" are connected to each other and to other people in the organization (i.e., structural level of the networks), may also have important consequences for newcomer socialization. Finally, earlier socialization research has not focused on how organizational socialization is related to the development of newcomers' social networks and related resources.

As Figure 5.1 shows, the first aim of this chapter is to focus on both the relational and structural characteristics of the newcomers' social networks and how they are related to newcomers socialization at individual (learning, sensemaking, and adjustment) and organizational (success in the organization and related organizational feedback) levels. The second aim is to examine how newcomer socialization at both individual and organizational levels is related to the development of newcomers' social networks.

Social Network Approach: Importance of the Relationships

The social network approach argues that people's actions are *embedded* in their social environment (Granovetter, 1985). In other words, exchange or interaction between people is rarely independent of the wider social context and related networks. In the organizational context, the social network approach also aims to understand how people's behavior, adjustment, and success in the organization is dependent on how they are located in the networks of social relations (for reviews on networks in the organizational context, see Brass, Galaskiewicz, Greve & Tsai, 2004; Burt, 2005; Kilduff & Brass, 2010; for a practical review on the role of networks in organizations, see Cross & Parker, 2004; for a general review of theories related to networks, see Monge & Contractor, 2003). Social embeddedness can be further divided into structural and relational levels (Granovetter 1992). Structural embeddedness refers to impersonal characteristics of the networks, such as the extent to which people have ties with each other. The relational level concerns the quality of a relationship between people, such as how close they are to each other.

STRUCTURAL EMBEDDEDNESS

Most network concepts and measures concern structural embeddedness, or network structure and composition. These structural characteristics of networks have been typically measured as "whole" and "personal" networks (e.g., Marsden, 2005). A whole network refers to a bounded social environment, such as a work unit, in which all or most of the people report their connections to each other (Scott, 2000; Wasserman & Faust, 1994). That is, a researcher usually asks participants to indicate their relations with people in a focal unit concerning different exchange or interaction contents, such as advice-seeking ("who are the people you ask for advice?"), advice-giving ("who are the people that turn to you for advice?"), and friendship ("who do you count as your friends?"). This procedure enables a researcher to map patterns of relationships in different social domains in the workplace and use network analysis as a statistical analysis method (Scott, 2000; Wasserman & Faust, 1994). Social network analysis as a statistical method offers a different kind of index for the properties of a network and a focal person's position in the network. "Network centrality" and its variations, such as "betweenness centrality," are among the most often used measures in network studies. *Network centrality* indicates how many times a person is named as someone to whom people turn to for advice (centrality in advice network), for example, or as a friend (centrality in friendship network). *Betweenness centrality* refers to the extent to which a person is an intermediary between people who don't have a direct tie between

them (for measures of network see Scott, 2000; Wasserman & Faust, 1994).

A *personal network* typically refers to a focal individual's direct ties and his or her perceptions of the relations among these ties in the network. These networks are often called *ego networks* and the named network person is an "alter." In this procedure, research participants are first asked, with specific "name-generators," to name, say, "with whom you discuss important personal matters" (for examples of name-generators, see, e.g., Burt 1992; Podolny & Baron, 1997). Typically, additional questions on the nature of the relations between a respondent and the named network persons are also posed, such as "How close are you to this person?"… "What is this person in relation to you (e.g., coworker, supervisor)?" Finally, participants are asked to evaluate the extent to which these named network persons interact with each other or know each other. Indices of network structure can be measured by asking participants to rate the extent to which network persons or alters are connected to each other. For example, *network density* refers to how well people in a focal individual's network are connected to each other. The more they are connected to each other, the higher the network density. The important concept of *network closure* refers to a network that is characterized by high density (e.g., Burt, 2005).

RELATIONAL EMBEDDEDNESS

Relational embeddedness indicates the quality of personal relationships between people that have developed over time. Often an indicator of this is *tie strength*, which typically refers to the closeness or intimacy of a relationship between persons. On the one hand, the social network approach emphasized the importance of "weak ties" in knowledge transfer. In his seminal paper, Granovetter (1973) presented his "strength of weak ties" thesis: networks characterized by weak ties, such as acquaintances, offer more new information than networks with strong ties, such as one's spouse and friends. Unlike strong ties, which bind interconnected individuals who then often share the same information, weak ties are often a bridge between different social groups and consequently enable access to new information.[1] Weak ties appear to be related to making contacts in higher hierarchical positions (Lin, Ensel & Vaughn, 1981; Seibert, Kraimer & Liden, 2001) and in diverse functions (Seibert et al., 2001); in other words, they are a bridge to different social groups. However, strong ties enhance social exchange and resource sharing among people, or mobilization of resources, since they are characterized by liking, reciprocation, and trust (Burt, 2005; Granovetter, 1982; Krackhardt, 1992). For example, people with strong ties are likely to provide social support (e.g., Wellman & Frank, 2001).

Most of the earlier theories and research on newcomer socialization have focused on the relational level: examining the interaction between a newcomer and organizational insiders. For example, Reichers' (1987) interactionist perspective argues that the activity between newcomers and organizational insiders such as supervisors plays an important role in newcomer socialization. However, the social network approach argues that both the structural and the relational characteristics of the networks influence how a focal person is able to access and mobilize resources, and affect who the person's social referents are (e.g., Granovetter, 1992). For example, earlier research has shown that the structural and relational characteristics of the networks are related to adjustment to work (Morrison, 2002), different aspects of job performance (Moran, 2005), and that network structure enhances the knowledge transfer beyond the relational or dyadic characteristics of network ties (e.g., Reagans & McEvily, 2003).

Role of Networks in Organizational Socialization

Social capital theory argues that social networks and related resources, such as knowledge, advice, social credentials, and influence, play an important role in how a focal person learns to perform in his or her job, and how his or her career in the organization proceeds (for reviews see Burt, 2005; Lin, 2001). We next examine how structural and relational characteristics of the networks can function as a channel for important resources in respect to learning on the job and success in the organization.

Role of Networks in Newcomers' Learning
STRUCTURAL LEVEL OF NETWORKS

Burt's (1992) concept of *structural holes* is based on resource benefits through network structure. When a person's network includes people who don't share a relationship with each other, there are "structural holes" in it. In other words, a structural hole reflects a missing connection or an absence of a tie between the people in one's network. When there are structural holes in a person's network, he or she is in a brokerage position between the people who are not themselves connected to each other, in other words, who are nonredundant contacts. A brokerage position, therefore, presumably connects

a person to different people and social units and to more heterogeneous information, since different social groups typically have different kinds of knowledge and points of view (e.g., Granovetter, 1973). Earlier research has shown that a brokerage role in the network and a related sparse (i.e., non-dense) network structure generates knowledge-related benefits for learning after organizational entry.

Morrison (2002) examined new auditors' networks and their self-reported socialization outcomes. She found that newcomers' network range (connections to different industry professions) was related to increased organizational knowledge and role clarity. Zhou and others (2009) found that the number of weak ties in employees' networks (i.e., a proxy for brokerage) showed a curvilinear relation with supervisor-rated creativity (see also Perry-Smith, 2006). Jokisaari (2011) found that newcomers' network density was related to supervisor-rated job performance: the lower the newcomer's network density (i.e., the more brokerage opportunities), the better was his or her job performance. In an ethnographic study, Hill (1992) examined the socialization of new managers. All of the interviewed managers emphasized the importance of relationships when learning their jobs as managers; they particularly appreciated relations to different social groups and organizational levels. All these findings support the argument that sparse networks offer brokerage opportunities, which increase the likelihood of a newcomer quickly getting information and feedback about "how work really gets done here."

Other findings among more experienced employees also support the argument that network brokerage is related to learning and related job performance (for a review, see Burt 2005). People who have sparse networks, which offer brokerage opportunities, report more innovative ideas in work projects (Burt, 2004) and show higher job performance as rated by their supervisors (e.g., Sparrowe et al., 2001) or in performance evaluations, based on company records (e.g., Burt, 2007), compared to people with networks offering no brokerage opportunities. However, it is important to note that earlier research has shown that the relation between network structure and job performance is contingent on various factors. These contingency factors, or factors that moderate the relation between performance and networks, include job characteristics (Brass, 1981), individual or group level (Sparrowe, Liden, Wayne & Kraimer, 2001), and formal positions within the organization (Gargiulo, Ertug & Galunic, 2009). For example, Sparrowe et al. (2001)

found that advice network centrality was related to individual job performance, whereas at the group level, network centralization (i.e., network relations that are concentrated among a few individuals) was negatively related to group performance. Authors further reasoned that at the group level, network ties that are concentrated among a few individuals hinder cooperation among people in the group because information is not equally shared. Group performance suffers.

RELATIONAL LEVEL OF NETWORKS

Relational-level characteristics of the networks also seem to play an important role in how a focal person can access, and more specifically *mobilize,* resources such as knowledge and advice. Earlier research on socialization suggests that newcomers do not get all the essential information from coworkers until they are trusted by them (Feldman, 1976). Along similar lines, research on social networks and citizenship behavior in organizations suggests that people who are in need of others' informal support do not usually receive it (Bowler & Brass, 2006). Consequently, it is important to focus on the relational or dyadic level in networks as a source of important leverage for resource mobilization. The social network approach argues that strong ties enhance social exchange and resource sharing among people, since they are characterized by liking, reciprocation, and trust (Burt, 2005; Granovetter, 1982; Krackhardt, 1992). In line with this argument are findings indicating that the relational-level characteristics of the newcomers' networks enhance their socialization. It has been found that newcomers' networks characterized by strong ties are related to task mastery, role clarity (Morrison, 2002), and supervisor-rated work group performance (Jokisaari, 2011). One reason for these findings might be that strong ties are likely to provide a focal person with support (e.g., Wellman & Frank, 2001) and facilitate the sharing of tacit knowledge (Hansen, Mors & Løvås, 2005). Furthermore, a focal person is more likely to ask for advice and information from a social tie when he or she likes that person (Casciaro & Lobo, 2008) or has a strong tie to them (McDonald & Westphal, 2003). Earlier research has also found that the threshold for actual transfer of knowledge between actors is lower among those with a history of collaboration (Hansen, 1999).

Social Networks and Success in the Organization

The social network approach also argues that networks and related resources are related to focal individuals' reputations and foster career success in the organization (e.g., Burt, 1992, 2005). Through network ties, a focal person can obtain credentials and referrals, which endorse his or her reputation (Burt, 1992). This "reputational endorsement" (Nahapiet & Ghoshal, 1998, p. 252) may be particularly important among newcomers, since they may not yet have their own credibility or visibility to stand out from others in the workplace in order to get higher remuneration or promotions. Interestingly, earlier research on cognitive networks (i.e., people's perceptions of others' networks) has shown that others' perceptions that a focal person has powerful connections affects his or her reputation in the organization, even when that focal person does not actually have these connections (Kilduff & Krackhardt, 1994).

The brokerage role in the network, and related heterogeneous and sparse network structure, are also related to reputational benefits for a focal person. A broker has contacts in different social units or groups and these contacts may often be a source of recommendations or legitimacy within a group (e.g., Burt, 1992). An outsider gains credibility and trust within a new group through recommendations and third party information. For example, third party information is more influential in group admission than direct information from the focal individual (e.g., Stiff & Van Vugt, 2008). Furthermore, Burt (1992) reported that recently hired managers with networks that provided brokerage opportunities showed a higher promotion rate than managers with more dense networks (see also Podolny & Baron, 1997). Interestingly, applicants and new employees benefit already in the recruitment phase from their network ties as bridges to the new organization. Namely, those applicants who have a social tie to the organization or who are recommended by a current employee (employee referral) in the organization attain higher initial salary (Seidel, Polzer, & Stewart, 2000), present more appropriate résumés, and apply during better market conditions (Fernandez & Weinberg, 1997) compared to those applicants who do not have a social tie to or employee referral from the organization (see also Barley & Kunda, 2004).

However, it should be noted that earlier research has also shown contingency factors in the relation between network structure and career success, such as number of peers in the job (Burt, 1997), network content (Podolny & Baron, 1997), and culture (Xiao & Tsui, 2007). For example, Podolny and Baron (1997) examined the relation between networks and mobility in a high-technology corporation. They found that sparse (i.e., many structural holes) advice networks were related to upward mobility within the organization. However, sparse authority networks (i.e., people who delineate expectations and goals of the job in question) were negatively related to mobility. The authors argued that (p. 689) "the effects of structural holes on promotion are positive for ties that convey resources and information and negative for ties that transmit identity and expectations."

Another network mechanism focuses on with whom the social tie exists. Social capital theory emphasizes that the resources available through social ties depend on the people with whom a person has a connection (Lin, 1982; 2001). A social contact's position in the organizational hierarchy is important because it enables access to organization-related resources, such as information, credentials, and social influence (Lin, 1982; 2001). For example, a manager typically has more control over the resources of an organization than an employee. Consequently, a newcomer who has the opportunity to connect to a manager through his or her ties has more network-based resources available than a person who has a connection to an employee. In line with the social capital theory, Seibert and others (2001) showed that for a focal employee, the sponsorship of senior colleagues', through such mechanisms as enhancing visibility in the organization and offering challenging job assignments, is related to his or her current salary and career promotions.

In socialization research, the supervisor is most often the person who typically has positional power and related resources. Earlier research has also shown the importance of supervisors in newcomer socialization (Bauer & Green, 1998; Jokisaari & Nurmi, 2009; Major et al., 1995; Ostroff & Kozlowski, 1992). For example, Jablin (2001) concluded in his review on organizational socialization: "Research has shown that a newcomer's communication relationship with his or her initial supervisor is a crucial factor in the newcomer's assimilation" (p. 778). Supervisors may contribute to newcomer's socialization in many ways. First, they typically have formal authority and power to influence the formation of new employees' roles in their jobs, job assignments, and the projects in which they participate. Second, supervisors play a central role in providing knowledge and feedback through which job and role behaviors are learned (e.g., Ostroff & Kozlowski, 1992). Finally, supervisors typically have the formal authority to influence subordinates' advancement in the organization, such as recommendation for a promotion, remuneration, or new job assignments (e.g., Seibert et al., 2001). Some research exists on how supervisors' positions in the networks influence their subordinates' job performance and success in the organization. More specifically, earlier research has shown that employees whose supervisors were in brokerage positions in the network, both within and outside the organization, were more likely to be promoted over time (Katz & Tushman, 1983). Similarly, recent meta-analysis showed that teams in which the formal leader was central in the communication network performed better than teams in which the formal leader was not in a central network position (Balkundi & Harrison, 2006).

To conclude, the social network approach and related earlier findings support the claim that social networks are a source of important resources that enhance a focal person's learning on the job and related outcomes, such as job performance. In addition, network-based resources play an important role in a person's success in the organization, as indicated in organizational feedback such as promotion and remuneration.

Role of Networks in Newcomers' Sensemaking

Organizational entry is often a situation of uncertainty for a newcomer. In order to reduce this uncertainty, newcomers have to make an effort to interpret and explain their new environment as a way to obtain meaning and a sense of mastery in the new situation (Louis, 1980; Miller & Jablin, 1991). This kind of sensemaking is a cognitive process which fosters understanding and clarifies the meaning of the new situation "through reformulating cognitive schemas, scripts, and behavioral models…and related methods of interpreting and constructing social reality." (Jablin, 2001, p. 758) In contrast to newcomer learning, which is characterized by acquisition of accurate knowledge, skills, and abilities to perform well and be successful in the job, sensemaking is a more personal way to construct meaning and understanding in the new situation; in other words, to gain "…ongoing retrospective development of plausible images that rationalize what people are doing." (Weick et al., 2005, p. 409).

Other people play an important role in how a focal person interprets and understands a new situation such as transition into an organization (Salancik & Pfeffer, 1978). For example, "social relationships…are particularly important in shaping one's interpretive scheme of reality and in formulating a perspective about what is expected and acceptable in a given role." (Katz, 1980, p. 95) In the same way, social comparison theory (Festinger, 1954) emphasizes the importance of others when people need to evaluate themselves and acquire comparison standards. Along similar lines, the social network approach argues that "in a situation involving ambiguity, people obtain normative guidance by comparing their attitudes with those of a reference group of similar others" (Marsden & Friedkin, 1994, p. 5). In addition, both the relational and structural-level characteristics of the networks define the social referents and influential others for people's sensemaking in the new situation.

RELATIONAL LEVEL OF NETWORKS

People's attitudes and opinions are often influenced by others with whom they have close and direct interpersonal ties, or cohesive ties (e.g., Marsden & Friedkin, 1994). It has been argued that close ties enhance direct interaction among people, which in turn increases information sharing and shared understanding (e.g., Burt, 2005). For example, mutual exploration of a new environment among cohesive relations is a central channel through which to acquire knowledge and experience of the new situation (e.g., Denrell & Le Mens, 2007). Furthermore, increased interaction among people with close relations presumably leads to similarity in attitudes and opinions over time, since "...direct interaction with others results in socially constructed perceptions" (Shah, 1998, p. 250). Finally, this kind of shared understanding helps to reduce the uncertainty and ambiguity of the new situation (e.g., Shah, 1998). For example, in an uncertain situation people tend to ask for advice from direct and strong ties (McDonald & Westphal, 2003).

STRUCTURAL LEVEL OF NETWORKS

An additional channel for social referents and influence is *structural equivalence* among people in the network (Burt 1987, 2005; Marsden & Friedkin 1994). Two people are structurally equivalent when they have similar relations to the same people, such as two newcomers who have the same supervisor. People are motivated to observe others who have a similar position in the network (i.e., structural equivalence) since such people are often dependent on the same resources and network ties (e.g., Marsden & Friedkin, 1994). Furthermore, in competitive environments people are motivated to observe others in the same position in order to maintain their status and prospects in the focal organization (Burt, 1987). For example, newcomers working for the same supervisor may monitor each other in order to secure their position and attraction to the supervisor. Finally, people in a similar network position may also face similar kinds of role demands and expectations from others (e.g., Shah, 1998). It is also important to note that a structurally equivalent position does not imply a direct relation between people. Consequently, among structurally equivalent actors, information gathering often happens by observation and monitoring. Earlier socialization research has found that newcomers obtain much of their knowledge by observing others (Ostroff & Kozlowski, 1992), perhaps because direct solicitation of information may include social costs, such as signaling a need for reassurance (e.g., Ashford & Tsui, 1991). Furthermore, newcomers may have limited knowledge of the networks, as they do not yet know who knows what and who is willing to share their knowledge (see, Cross & Sproull, 2004). Thus, they prefer observation as a method to obtain information. In other words, structurally equivalent actors may be an important reference group for sensemaking among newcomers.

Ho and Levesque (2005) studied newcomers' social ties and sensemaking in a research organization. They found that when newcomers evaluated the fulfillment of organization-related promises, their social referents were coworkers with whom they had direct ties. When evaluating job-related promises, newcomers' referents were coworkers to whom they had a multiplex tie, such as both a friend and advice-giver. In addition, Shah (1998) found that more experienced employees monitored structurally equivalent network ties and compared themselves to these ties in respect of job performance. Cohesive network ties were also referents for organizational information and a comparison point for job performance.

Earlier research among more experienced employees has also shown that cohesive and structurally equivalent ties affect social influence among people (e.g., Burt, 1987). For example, people tend to make decisions in choice situations (Kilduff, 1990), have organizational justice perceptions (Umphress et al., 2003), and change their values (Gibbons, 2004) according to their cohesive network ties. In addition, emotions and job attitudes are contagious among employees and their networks influence how emotion and job attitudes spread among them (Pollock et al., 2000; Totterdell et al., 2004). Social networks also affect people's attitudes toward new technology and whether they personally use it in the workplace (Burkhardt, 1994; Rice & Aydin, 1991; cf. Denrell & Le Mens 2007). For example, employees' attitudes and use of new technology are influenced by their structurally equivalent coworkers (Burkhardt, 1994). In other words, the use of new technology by coworkers with similar network positions increases the likelihood that a focal person also adopts it later on. However, other findings also suggest that structurally equivalent people have nonsimilar attitudes toward their work tasks (Meyer, 1994) or new technology (Rice & Aydin, 1991). Some scholars have argued that social proximity does not require convergence in attitudes and behavior, and instead may produce differentiation (Goel, Mason, & Watts, 2010).

In summary, earlier research suggests that newcomers' network ties and people in similar network positions are important sources of information and targets of observation for newcomers' sensemaking. Since newcomers are often uncertain about their role in the workplace and related adequate action, others in a similar position provide sources of information and vicarious learning that supports newcomers' understanding and sensemaking in the new situation (e.g., Louis, 1980).

Role of Networks in Newcomers' Adjustment to Work

It has been argued that newcomer socialization is a process by which newcomers' adjustment to work changes as a consequence of learning to perform in the job and being accepted as a member of an organization (e.g., Feldman, 1981; Schein, 1978). Earlier socialization research has shown the importance of supervisors and coworkers in newcomers' adjustment to work, since they are important sources of information and feedback for newcomers' learning and of social support (e.g., Bauer & Green, 1998; Jokisaari & Nurmi, 2009; Ostroff & Kozlowski, 1992).

Some research exists which indicates that both the structural and relational characteristics of newcomers' networks are related to their adjustment to work. Results concerning relational level characteristics indicate that newcomers who have strong ties in the workplace are better adjusted than newcomers with weaker ties. For example, Kramer (1996), in his examinations of employees who faced geographical job transfer found that a high number of informational ties with whom transferees discussed only impersonal task-related matters (i.e., weak ties) was related to low adjustment to work 1 month

after entry. However, the effect weakened over time. Morrison (2002) reported that strong friendship ties in the workplace were related to newcomers' organizational commitment.

It has been found that among the structural level characteristics of the newcomers' networks informational ties with high-status persons, typically a supervisor, are related to newcomers' organizational commitment (Morrison, 2002), perhaps because the supervisor is a central representative of the organization to a newcomer (e.g., Jablin, 2001). In addition, in four entrepreneurial organizations, newcomers with higher centrality in the workplace network were perceived by their coworkers to be "less new" in the organization than newcomers with a less central position in the network (Rollag, 2007). Conversely, a peripheral position (i.e., social isolation) in the networks was related to lower job satisfaction among employees 3 months after employees' new units were organized in military organizations (Roberts & O'Reilly, 1979).

It has been suggested that a central indicator of social inclusion in the workplace is newcomers' perceptions of their social integration with coworkers, meaning their perceptions of how coworkers accept them as a member of the group and how they feel about the other employees (e.g., Feldman, 1981). For example, social integration in the workplace is related to newcomers' general adjustment to work as indicated by job attitudes such as job satisfaction and organizational commitment (e.g., Kammeyer-Mueller & Wanberg, 2003). In addition, social inclusion gives a person a sense of attachment and belonging (Baumeister & Leary, 1995), collegiality (Gersick, Bartunek & Dutton, 2000), and confirms his/her identity (e.g., Milton & Westphal, 2005). Newcomers also mention social relationships as a source of critical experiences at work (Gundry & Rousseau, 1994). For example, the critical issue most often reported by newcomers after organizational entry was conflict between themselves and their supervisor (Gundry & Rousseau, 1994).

Finally, an important indicator of newcomer adjustment to work has been voluntary turnover from the organization (e.g., Feldman, 1981). In other words, a new employee leaving an organization has been seen as a central indicator of unsuccessful socialization into the workplace. A network effect on turnover starts as early as during the recruitment of new employees. When a new employee is recruited through the informal channel— for example, they find the job through a personal relation such as a friend—they are less likely to quit the job after organizational entry, as compared to employees who were recruited through formal channels such as newspaper ads (Weller et al., 2009; see also, Fernandez, Castilla & Moore 2000). This finding indicates that "...those entering a work situation through contacts have automatic entrée into the cliques and friendship circles of the workplace. Besides making daily work more pleasant, this access is likely to yield fringe benefits on 'learning the ropes,' finding out how to really get things done—information not contained in the company's personnel booklets" (Granovetter 1995, p. 135).

Earlier research on networks among more experienced employees has shown that the characteristics of employees' networks are related to turnover (e.g., Burt, 2005; Feeley & Barnett, 1997; Krackhardt & Porter, 1986). For example, findings from a sample of healthcare employees showed that employees who were high in network centrality were less likely to quit during a 5-year period than employees with a less central position in the network. Interestingly, employees' own perceptions of attachment to coworkers and perceived coworker support were not related to turnover (Mossholder, Settoon & Henagan, 2005). Another study showed that bankers embedded in networks in which their coworkers were highly connected with each other (i.e., network closure) were less likely to leave than bankers with more open networks (Burt, 2005).

Organizational Socialization and Network Development

One critical aspect in organizational socialization is how newcomers' networks develop over time in the workplace and which antecedents contribute to that development. Earlier research has shown that newcomers report more social ties outside the organization than more experienced employees, whose social ties are located more within the organization (Lee & Allen 1982; Burt 1992). Unfortunately, little is known about how newcomers' positions in the networks of the workplace and their personal ties develop after organizational entry. Similarly, the dynamics of networks have not received much attention, since most theory and research has focused on the consequences of networks (e.g., Brass et al., 2004). As shown in Figure 5.1, we propose that organizational socialization might contribute to newcomers' network development. First, success in the organization and related organizational feedback, such as tenure and promotion, may relate to how newcomers' networks develop later on. Second, the way in which newcomers learn to perform their

job and become attached to social groups in the workplace may also contribute to network development. People's personal attributes and actions have also been researched to some extent as antecedents of network development. Finally, the initial characteristic of newcomers' networks may either enable or constrain tie development later on.

Success in the Organization, Organizational Feedback, and Network Development

Organizational feedback, such as tenure, new job assignments, and promotions, is a mechanism by which newcomers are assimilated into the organization (e.g., Fisher, 1986). This organizational feedback is an important sign for newcomers, informing them about how they are succeeding in the organization (e.g., Graen, 1976; Schein, 1978). This kind of feedback typically brings changes to newcomers' positions in the horizontal or vertical structure of the organization, and such changes in formal positions presumably are also reflected in newcomers' networks. Namely, people's social networks in the workplace are formed to a very large extent according to their formal position and location in the organization (Han, 1996; Kleinbaum, Stuart & Tushman, 2008; Kossinets & Watts, 2009). First, people's rank in the formal hierarchy affects their network position and with whom they communicate (Han, 1996; Kleinbaum, Stuart & Tushman, 2008). For example, people communicate most often with the people within their own level of hierarchy (Kleinbaum et al., 2008; Stevenson, 1990), and people ask for advice from those within their rank level or higher than their own status (Lazega & Duijn, 1997). Furthermore, there is an association between people's rank and their centrality in instrumental networks, such as advice networks (e.g., Burt, 2005, Ibarra & Andrews, 1993; Lincoln & Miller, 1979). Similarly, newcomers at the managerial level are more often asked for advice (i.e., they show higher network centrality) compared to newcomers with lower ranks (Rollag, 2004). Second, formal units influence with whom people communicate and develop ties. For example, people communicate with those within their formal work units (e.g., Kleinbaum et al., 2008) and teams (Baldwin et al 1997). Furthermore, employees' physical proximity in the workplace is related to friendship development over time (Sias & Cahill, 1998).

The ways in which people's network ties generally develop in the workplace are, to a large extent, based on formal job assignments, tasks, and roles. In other words, formal job assignments and roles define recurring social interaction and shared activities between people in the workplace. In turn, these shared activities offer possibilities for social exchange between newcomers and organizational insiders, and this interaction enables them to further get to know each other over time (Feld, 1981). Consequently, we argue that newcomers' success in the organization as indicated in the form of new job assignments, tenure, or promotion is likely to produce change in newcomers' networks because formal organization and job assignments can either constrain or enable the emergence of networks.

Newcomer Learning, Social Integration, and Network Development

The ways in which newcomers learn to perform their jobs and become integrated as members in social groups during organizational entry may also contribute to their network development. First, a newcomer learning to perform well in his or her job might bring reputational benefits. When a newcomer is perceived as a competent performer, this should also increase his or her centrality in the advice network of the workplace, such that others will seek information or advice from the newcomer. Earlier research on networks has found that perceived competence of a person increases the likelihood that he or she is asked for advice by others (Cross & Sproull, 2004), is selected as a group member (Hinds et al., 2000), and is related to the development of working relationships (Gabarro, 1987). In addition, the likelihood of a person seeking information from a network tie increases when others value this person's knowledge and skills (Borgatti & Cross, 2003). Moreover, an individual's brokerage position in the network depends on his or her performance history (Lee, 2010). Employees who are the first to adopt new technology have a central position in the network later on (Burkhardt & Brass, 1990). Newcomers' initial job performance is related to the quality of their working relationship with their supervisor later on (Bauer & Green, 1996). In all, these findings suggest that the way in which newcomers learn to perform in their jobs, and the related visibility, may in part have significant consequences for how their personal networks develop later on and for the kind of position they will have in the workplace networks.

The second important task for newcomers is to be integrated as a member in social groups in the workplace (e.g., Feldman, 1981). Although many network scholars have argued that the development of networks is more an unintentional consequence of shared activities rather than intentional "networking" (e.g., Burt, 2005, Granovetter, 1995, see also, Cross & Parker, 2004; Nebus, 2006), some research has examined whether individual attributes and social activity are related to people's positions in the networks or their network structure. Newcomer's personal attributes and social activity may relate to how they are perceived by others and are accepted in social networks. For example, newcomers' social activity is related to their perception of acceptance by their coworkers as a member of the work group (Wanberg & Kammeyer-Mueller, 2000). One personal attribute that may contribute to their position in the networks is *self-monitoring*. This refers to an individual's tendency to change his or her attitudes and views according to the opportunities and demands of the situation (e.g., Day & Schleicher, 2006). Earlier cross-sectional research provides mixed evidence on the role of self-monitoring in people's networks. It has shown that high self-monitors are more likely to have a central position in informal networks, such as friendship (Mehra et al., 2001) and acquaintance (Oh & Kilduff, 2008) networks, but not in more formal networks such as workflow networks (Mehra et al., 2001). In addition, Mehra and others (2001) found that among employees in a high-tech company, tenure moderated the effect of self-monitoring on network centrality: among employees with shorter tenure in the company, self-monitoring was not related to centrality in the friendship network as it was among employees with longer tenure. Similarly, among first year psychology students, self-monitoring was not related to a brokerage role in the network (Kalish & Robins, 2006). However, a recent study conducted in a Dutch radiology department showed that people with a high tendency to self-monitor were more likely to have a brokerage role in the network over time than people with a low tendency to self-monitor (Sasovova, Mehra, Borgatti, & Schippers, 2010).

Some research exists on the 5-factor model of personality (i.e., personality as five general traits [the "Big Five"]: neuroticism, extraversion, agreeableness, conscientiousness, openness to experience; e.g., John, 1990) as an antecedent of network position and structure. Klein and others (2004) examined the 5-factor model of personality as an antecedent of network centrality in the advice network, friendship network, and adversary network (i.e., a difficult person to work with) among MBA (master of business administration) students. The results showed that among personality traits, openness to experience was positively related and neuroticism was negatively related to advice centrality in the network. Moreover, the higher the neuroticism, openness to experience, and extraversion, the higher the centrality in the adversary network. In addition, neuroticism seems to be related positively to the brokerage role, and extraversion related to network closure among students (Kalish & Robin, 2006). Among other trait-like constructs another study found that core self-evaluations (self-esteem, self-efficacy, locus of control, emotional stability) as a general trait are not related to network centrality among healthcare employees (Scott & Judge, 2009; for the role of other individual propensity constructs, see Obstfeld, 2005; Totterdell et al., 2008; see also, Marrone et al., 2007).

Initial Network Characteristics and Network Development

Newcomers' initial network characteristics may also influence their tie formation and dissolution later on. Both initial structural and relational characteristics of the networks may contribute to network development. Network persons and their actions may also relate to network development, as they provide sponsorship for a newcomer.

STRUCTURAL LEVEL OF NETWORKS

Earlier research suggests that initial network structure has an effect on how ties form and dissolve over time (Burt, 2005). Gibbons and Olk (2003) examined initially unacquainted MBA students and how their relations developed over time. They found that students who initially had a similar network position—that is, who were related to similar others (structural equivalence)—were more likely to become friends over time. According to the authors, this result is in line with the transitivity principle in the networks. Given that there is a relationship between persons A and B, and a relationship between person A and person C, it is also likely that there is a relationship between persons B and C. According to the balance theory (Heider, 1958) if two people are friends, they should share similar sentiments toward a third person, otherwise they would feel uneasy.

Burt (2000, 2002) examined the development of bankers' relations in a financial organization over a period of 4 years and suggested that there is a "liability of newness" in the relationship development over time. This means that relationships that begin due to exogenous factors, such as work relations, tend to weaken over time and that this dissolution is more likely among new relationships than old ones.

After the "honeymoon period," which protects the initial relationship development from conflict and negative outcomes (Fichman & Levinthal, 1991), there is an increased risk of relations dissolving during the initial few years. However, network closure (i.e., a network in which people are highly interconnected) around a focal relationship decreased the likelihood that new relationships would dissolve over time (Burt, 2000).

It has been further argued that network closure facilitates the development of ties, since interconnections among people in the group help maintain social norms and facilitate monitoring of each other's behavior and reputation (e.g., Coleman, 1988). For example, research findings show that network closure enhances tie formation among similar people over time (Kossinets & Watts, 2009). Network closure also enhances trust between people (Chua, Ingram & Morris, 2008). In other words, two people have not only their personal relationship but are also tied through third parties in a closed network, and these third parties can enhance the trustworthiness of a focal relationship.

RELATIONAL LEVEL OF NETWORKS

The "homophily principle" is perhaps the most often used argument in network development when one focuses on the relational or dyadic level characteristics of networks (review, McPherson et al., 2001). According to this principle, people have a tendency to form ties with those who are like themselves in attributes such as age (Zenger & Lawrence, 1989), ethnicity (Mehra et al. 1998), gender (Ibarra 1992), and values (Burkhardt, 1994). This similarity between people then eases communication and the development of trust, which in turn enhance the development of the relationship. For example, the more similar work group members are in the form of tenure, the more they interact with each other (Reagans, Zuckerman & McEvily, 2004). Conversely, interaction between people who have different social characteristics, such as status and role, requires more effort than interaction between people whose social characteristics are similar (e.g., McPherson et al., 2001). For example, people report more negative emotions when interacting with formal ties such as supervisors compared to interaction with friends (Kahneman et al., 2004). In addition, among newcomers, namely people forming new groups, the effects of homophily influence tie formation over time. For example, ethnicity is related to friendship formation over time (Gibbons & Olk, 2003; Mollica, Gray, Treviño, 2003).

It is also important to note that, as well as individual's preferences to attach themselves to similar kinds of people, organizational structures strongly influence tie formation within focal organizations and reinforce interaction between similar people. As Kossinets and Watts (2009, p. 436) discussed in their findings on network development over time: "the vast majority of new ties are formed between individuals who already share a friend or a group..." In other words, the social environment around the people affects with whom they share activities, and thus affects the opportunities for tie formation and development.

Newcomers may also benefit from sponsorship or "borrowed social capital" (e.g., Burt, 1998) provided by their network ties, which enables them to further develop their networks. This sponsorship refers to a process in which a network person enables a focal person to develop his or her network ties by offering opportunities, recommendations, or other signals of trustworthiness or legitimacy on behalf of a person (e.g., Sparrowe & Liden, 2005). Among newcomers in particular, trustworthiness or the legitimacy to develop new ties is typically limited, as they do not have familiar ties in the workplace or a related history of interaction, which are antecedents for the development of trust (e.g., Burt, 2005). In other words, it takes time for newcomers to pass the "inclusionary boundary" to become an integrated insider in the organization and its networks (Schein, 1978). Indeed, earlier research suggests that before people are accepted as members, they might find it difficult to obtain help and support from influential others (Bowler & Brass, 2006). Furthermore, a third-party contact to a group, such as an acquaintance among strangers, greatly enhances the possibility that people will try to make contact with these others they don't know (Ingram & Morris, 2007).

Unfortunately, there is no research among newcomers on sponsorship and network development (see, Sparrowe & Liden, 1997). Some indirect evidence comes from studies examining the role of supervisor sponsorship using samples of more experienced employees. Sparrowe and Liden (2005) showed that employees' social influence in the organization was related to their supervisors' sponsorship. When supervisors were central in advice networks and shared their ties with their employees (i.e., sponsorship), employees' social influence in the workplace was higher. Similarly, employees trusted fellow workers more when these were also trusted by their supervisors compared to fellow workers who were less trusted by supervisors (Lau & Liden,

2008). The other side of the coin is that a supervisor's sponsorship may also isolate a protégé from his or her coworkers if they see him or her the as supervisor's "favorite" (Sias & Jablin, 1995). Conversely, a conflict with the supervisor relates to increased cohesion with coworkers (Sias & Cahill, 1998).

Finally, models on workgroup socialization suggest that newcomers' immediate work groups influence their tie formation during organizational entry (Anderson & Thomas, 1996; Moreland & Levine, 2001). There are two-way relations between a group and a new individual and their characteristics, expectations, and beliefs affect how relationship development proceeds. Furthermore, group socialization has been seen as a process which consists of different stages: anticipatory, socialization, and adjustment stages, with stage-specific challenges. Chen and Klimoski (2003) examined two-way interaction between newcomers and their workgroups or teams. They found that newcomers' work experience was related to team members' expectations of newcomer performance, and team expectations were related to newcomer empowerment and social exchange between a newcomer and his or her team.

However, one limitation of these group socialization models is that there is no empirical research concerning how groups influence newcomers' relationship development over time. In addition, workgroups in these models are typically constructed in isolation from other organizational units. For example, organization-level practices and resources may influence the group's opportunities to socialize new members (cf., Gersick, 1988). Similarly, formal group leaders may play a central role in how the assimilation between a new member and group unfolds over time (Kozlowski et al., 1996).

To conclude, we suggest different antecedents for the development of the newcomers' networks after organizational entry. First, success in the organization and related organizational feedback may change a newcomer's position in the organization, which in turn brings changes in the network. As many network scholars have argued that the development of networks is more an unintentional consequence of shared activities rather than intentional "networking" (e.g., Burt, 2005; Granovetter, 1995), the findings reviewed suggest that formal positions influence shared activities, which in turn shape people's networks. Second, a newcomer's learning of his or her job may also change his or her networks such that his or her reputation spreads in the work group and others increasingly ask her or him for advice or information. Earlier research has also found that personal attributes, such as self-monitoring, are related to network development. Finally, the initial characteristics of the newcomers' networks may either enable or constrain network development.

Conclusions and Future Directions

In this chapter we have focused on the role of social networks in newcomers' socialization. We first argued that the structural and relational characteristics of the newcomers' networks contribute to their socialization because they offer access to resources such as information, advice, and credentials, which relate to newcomers learning on the job and becoming successful in the organization. In addition, the characteristics of the newcomers' networks define the social informants and influential others for newcomers' sensemaking in order to acquire understanding in the new situation. However, only few earlier studies have examined the relation between the structural and relational characteristics of the newcomers' networks and socialization-specific outcomes such as learning. Second, we proposed that organizational socialization contributes to newcomers' network development. For example, success in the organization and related organizational feedback, such as tenure and promotion, may relate to how newcomers' networks develop later on, since formal roles, ranks, and job assignments define with whom people have network ties and shared activities in the organization. In addition, how a newcomer learns to perform his or her job and becomes attached to social groups in the workplace may also contribute to network development. However, little is known about the reciprocal exchange between newcomer socialization and development of the newcomers' networks and related resources.

In the future, modeling change in newcomers' networks, network-based resources, and their socialization over time is of high importance in order to more fully understand newcomer socialization. First, little is known about how social networks and related resources change after organizational entry and what kind of antecedents contribute to that change, particularly when compared to research on the consequences of networks. It has even been stated that "without a corresponding theory of behavior—of dynamics—a theory of network structure is essentially uninterpretable and, therefore, of little practical use" (Watts, 2003, p. 51). The few earlier findings on network development indicate that the benefits of network positions like brokerage are temporary, since networks evolve over time and network positions change (Burt, 2005, Kossinets

& Watts, 2006). Further research is also needed to more fully understand the reciprocal exchange between newcomers' action and their networks; for example, what kind of joint activities a focal newcomer and his or her network ties share concerning the mobilization of resources, and how these joint activities change over time.

Second, in socialization literature a newcomer has been seen as a person who is in need of information and feedback in order to reduce his or her uncertainty in the new situation. However, it would be important to examine how a newcomer's role changes over time to that of a provider of advice and information to others in the workplace networks. This change to information and advice provider to others would also show that a newcomer is an insider in the organization (Louis, 1980; cf., Rollag, 2004). Advice and information giving may reflect the fact that a newcomer is competent in his or her work and coworkers are also aware of his or her skills and knowledge. Indeed, research on social networks has found that the likelihood of a person seeking information from a network tie increases when they value this person's knowledge and skills (Borgatti & Cross, 2003). In addition, as others perceive a newcomer as a source of valuable knowledge and advice they may increase their interaction with him or her, and this increased interaction is then reflected in the newcomer's increased feeling of acceptance among coworkers.

Third, the social network approach argues, on the one hand, that networks and related resources contribute to an individual's learning on the job, performance, and success in the organization. On the other hand, some earlier findings suggest that a focal individual's network position may be a consequence of his or her earlier performance and success in the job (e.g., Lee, 2010). Consequently, there is a need to more fully examine the reciprocal exchange between social networks and newcomer learning. For example, if a newcomer learns to perform well, this may bring reputational benefits and success in the organization such as promotion and new job assignments. As a consequence of this success, others are more likely to ask for advice and information from a focal individual, thus giving him or her a more central position in the network. Alternatively, the networks may cause a snowball effect in the focal individual's performance and career in the organization. An individual's initial network and related resources may contribute to his or her learning of the job and visibility within the organization. For example, network ties provide opportunities for challenging initial job assignments in which the focal individual is able to develop his or her performance and visibility (see, De Pater et al., 2009). As a result of this, an individual's enhanced visibility and performance might contribute to success in the organization, such as promotion, which in turn fosters change in his or her networks and related resources.

Finally, to better understand organizational practices that foster newcomers' networks and related resources, it seems warranted to examine how the training of supervisors might evolve to support the development of newcomers' networks in organizations. This training might include providing supervisors with knowledge about the importance of sponsorship and initial job assignments in the development of newcomers' networks in the workplace. First, as suggested previously, "the relationships with leaders are pivotal in facilitating the development of members' network. Because, under sponsorship, members 'borrow' leaders' networks, it follows that member' outcomes dependent on relationships are derived primarily from leaders' networks rather than from members' own networks" (Sparrowe & Liden, 1997, p. 538). This sponsorship requires that the supervisor himself or herself has a network position that enables him or her to legitimately lend "social capital" to a newcomer (Sparrowe & Liden, 2005); in other words, "legitimacy is keyed to the social situation of a person, not to the person's attributes" (Burt, 1998, p. 16). Second, supervisors should have the organizational resources and authority to be able to define new workers' job assignments in order to support newcomer learning to perform in the job and enhance newcomers' visibility in the organization. This will presumably lead to the enhanced performance and reputation of the newcomer, which further contributes to his or her own network development. Consequently, future research is needed to better understand the antecedents and consequences of supervisor sponsorship for newcomers' network development: for example, how supervisors' organizational resources, their network characteristics, and the quality of the working relationship between supervisor and newcomer contribute to sponsorship and provide a basis for newcomers' evolving networks.

Acknowledgment

The work of the first author was supported by The Finnish Work Environment Fund (#108067).

Note

1. It should be noted that Granovetter (1973) based the strength of the weak tie argument on network structure, although a weak tie is a relational characteristic between two people (i.e. a relationship defined as infrequent interaction, low emotional intensity and intimacy, and limited reciprocity). Specifically, he argued that weak ties increase the opportunity for indirect contacts in the network, i.e. a weak tie is a bridge or channel between otherwise disconnected people or groups ("bridging weak ties"; Granovetter, 1973, p. 1371). However, "ties may be weak in terms of relationship quality without fulfilling the critical advantage of bridging to distant social locales." (Liden & Sparrowe, 1997, p. 528). In other words, one should measure network structure in more detail in order to define bridging network ties (e.g., Burt, 1992).

References

Anderson, N., & Thomas, H. D. (1996). Work group socialization. In M. A. West. (Ed.), *Handbook of work group psychology* (pp. 423–450). Chichester, UK: Wiley.

Ashford, S. J., & Tsui A. S. (1991). Self-regulation for managerial effectiveness: The role of active feedback seeking. *Academy of Management Journal, 34,* 251–280.

Baldwin, T. T., Bedell, M. D., & Johnson, J. L. (1997). The social fabric of a team-based M.B.A. program: Network effects on student satisfaction and performance. *Academy of Management Journal, 40,* 1369–1397.

Balkundi, P., & Harrison, D. A. (2006). Ties, leaders, and time in teams: Strong inference about network structure's effects on team viability and performance. *Academy of Management Journal, 49,* 49–68.

Barley, S. R., & Kunda, G. (2004). *Gurus, hired guns, and warm bodies: Itinerant experts in a knowledge economy.* Princeton, NJ: Princeton University Press.

Bauer, T. N., & Green, S. G. (1996). Development of leader-member exchange: A longitudinal test. *Academy of Management Journal, 39,* 1538–1567.

Bauer, T. N., & Green, S. G. (1998). Testing the combined effects of newcomer information seeking and manager behavior on socialization. *Journal of Applied Psychology, 83,* 72–83.

Baumeister, R. F., & Leary, M.R. (1995). The need to belong: Desire for interpersonal attachments as a fundamental human motivation. *Psychological Bulletin, 117,* 497–529.

Borgatti, S. P., & Cross, R. (2003). A relational view of information seeking and learning in social networks. *Management Science, 49,* 432–445.

Bowler, . M., & Brass, D. J. (2006). Relational correlates of interpersonal citizenship behavior: A social network perspective. *Journal of Applied Psychology, 91,* 70–82.

Brass, D. J. (1981). Structural relationships, job characteristics, and worker satisfaction and performance. *Administrative Science Quarterly, 26,* 331–348.

Brass, D. J., Galaskiewicz, J., Greve, H. R., & Tsai, W. (2004). Taking stock of networks and organizations: A multilevel perspective. *Academy of Management Journal, 47,* 795–817.

Brown, J. S., & Duguid, P. (1991). Organizational learning and communities of practice: Toward a unified view working, learning, and innovating. *Organization Science, 2,* 40–57.

Burkhardt, M. (1994). Social interaction effects following a technological change: A longitudinal investigation. *Academy of Management Journal, 37,* 869–898.

Burkhardt, M., & Brass, D. J. (1990). Changing patterns or patterns of change: The effect of a change in technology on social network structure and power. *Administrative Science Quarterly, 35,* 104–127.

Burt, R. S. (1987). Social contagion and innovation: Cohesion versus structural equivalence. *American Journal of Sociology, 92,* 1287–1335.

Burt, R. S. (1992). *Structural holes: The social structure of competition.* Cambridge, MA: Harvard University Press.

Burt, R. S. (1997). The contingent value of social capital. *Administrative Science Quarterly, 42,* 339–365

Burt, R. S. (1998). The gender of social capital. *Rationality and Society, 10,* 5–46.

Burt, R. S. (2000). Decay functions. *Social Networks, 22,* 1–28.

Burt, R. S. (2002). Bridge decay. *Social Networks, 24,* 333–363.

Burt, R. S. (2004). Structural holes and good ideas. *American Journal of Sociology, 110,* 349–399.

Burt, R. S. (2005). *Brokerage and closure: An introduction to social capital.* Oxford, UK: Oxford University Press.

Burt, R. S. (2007). Second-hand brokerage: Evidence on the importance of local structure for managers, bankers, and analysts. *Academy of Management Journal, 50,* 119–146.

Casciaro, T., & Lobo, M. S. (2008). When competence is irrelevant: The role of interpersonal affect in task-related ties. *Administrative Science Quarterly, 53,* 655–684.

Chen, G., & Klimoski, R. J. 2003. The impact of expectations on newcomer performance in teams as mediated by work characteristics, social exchanges, and empowerment. *Academy of Management Journal, 46,* 591–607.

Chua, R. Y. J., Ingram, P., & Morris, M. (2008). From the head and the heart: Locating cognition- and affect-based trust in managers' professional networks. *Academy of Management Journal, 51,* 436–452.

Coleman, J. (1988). Social capital in the creation of human capital. *American Journal of Sociology, 94*(Suppl.), 95–120.

Cross, R., Liedtka, J., & Weiss, L. (2005). A practical guide to social networks. *Harvard Business Review, 83,* 124–132.

Cross, R., & Parker, A. (2004). *The hidden power of social networks: Understanding how things really get done in organizations.* Boston, MA: Harvard Business School Press.

Cross, R., & Sproull, L. (2004). More than an answer: Information relationships for actionable knowledge. *Organization Science, 15,* 446–462.

Day, D. V., & Schleicher, D. J. (2006). Self-monitoring at work: A motive-based perspective. *Journal of Personality, 74,* 685–713.

Denrell, J., & Le Mens, G. (2007). Interdependent sampling and social influence. *Psychological Review, 114,* 398–422.

De Pater I. E., Van Vianen, A. E., Bechtoldt, M. N., & Klehe, U.-E. (2009). Employees' challenging job experiences and supervisors' evaluations of promotability. *Personnel Psychology, 62,* 297–325.

Fang, R., Duffy, M. K., & Shaw, J. D. (2011). The organizational socialization process: Review and development of a social capital model. *Journal of Management, 37,* 127–152.

Feeley, T. H., & Barnett, G. A. (1997). Predicting employee turnover from communication networks. *Human Communication Research, 23,* 370–387.

Feld, S. L. (1981). The focused organization of social ties. *American Journal of Sociology, 86,* 1015–1035.

Feldman, D. C. (1976). A contingency theory of socialization. *Administrative Science Quarterly, 21,* 433–452.

Feldman, D. C. (1981). The multiple socialization of organization members. *Academy of Management Review, 6,* 309–318.

Fernandez, R. M., Castilla, E. J., & Moore, P. (2000). Social capital at work: Networks and employment at a phone center. *American Journal of Sociology, 105,* 1288–1356.

Fernandez, R. M., & Weinberg, N. (1997). Sifting and sorting: Personal contacts and hiring in a retail bank. *American Sociological Review, 62,* 883–902.

Festinger, L. (1954). A theory of social comparison processes. *Human Relations, 1,* 117–140.

Fichman, M., & Levinthal, D. A. (1991). Honeymoons and the liability of adolescence: A new perspective on duration dependence in social and organizational relationships. *Academy of Management Review, 16,* 442–468.

Fisher, C. D. (1986). Organizational socialization: An integrative review. *Research in Personnel and Human Resource Management, 4,* 101–145.

Gabarro, J. J. (1987). The development of working relationships. In J. W. Lorsch (Ed.), *Handbook of organizational behavior* (pp. 172–189). Englewood Cliffs, NJ: Prentice-Hall.

Gargiulo M., Ertug G., & Galunic, C. (2009). The two faces of control: Network closure and individual performance among knowledge workers. *Administrative Science Quarterly, 54,* 299–333.

Gersick, C. J. (1988). Time and transitions in work teams: Toward a new model of group development. *Academy of Management Journal, 31,* 9–41.

Gersick, C. J., Bartunek, J. M., & Dutton, J. E. (2000). Learning from academia: The importance of relationships in professional life. *Academy of Management Journal, 43,* 1026–1044.

Gibbons, D. E. (2004). Friendship and advice networks in the context of changing professional values. *Administrative Science Quarterly, 49,* 238–262.

Gibbons, D. E., & Olk, P. M. (2003). Individual and structural origins of friendship and social position among professionals. *Journal of Personality and Social Psychology, 84,* 340–351.

Goel, S., Mason, W., & Watts, D. J. (2010). Real and perceived attitude agreement in social networks. *Journal of Personality and Social Psychology, 99,* 611–621.

Graen, G. B. (1976). Role-making process within complex organizations. In M. Dunnete (Ed.), *Handbook of industrial and organizational psychology* (pp. 1201–1245). Chicago: McNally.

Granovetter, M. S. (1973). The strength of weak ties. *American Journal of Sociology, 78,* 1360–1380.

Granovetter, M. S. (1982). The strength of weak ties: A network theory revisited. In P. Marsden, N. Lin (Eds.), *Social Structure and Network Analysis* (pp. 105–130). Beverly Hills, CA: Sage.

Granovetter, M. S. (1985). Economic action and social structure: The problem of embeddedness. *American Journal of Sociology, 91,* 481–510.

Granovetter, M. S. (1992). Problems of explanation in economic sociology. In N. Nohria & R. Eccles, (Eds.), *Networks and organizations* (pp. 25–56). Boston: Harvard University Press.

Granovetter, M. S. (1995). *Getting a job: A study of contacts and careers.* (2nd ed.). Chicago: University of Chicago Press.

Gundry, L. K., & Rousseau, D. M. (1994). Critical incidents in communicating culture to newcomers: The meaning is the message. *Human Relations, 47,* 1063–1087.

Han S.-K. (1996). Structuring relations in on-the-job networks. *Social Networks, 18,* 47–67.

Hansen, M. T. (1999). The search-transfer problem: The role of weak ties in sharing knowledge across organization subunits. *Administrative Science Quarterly, 44,* 82–111.

Hansen, M. T., Mors, M. L., & Løvås, B. (2005). Knowledge sharing in organizations: Multiple networks, multiple phases. *Academy of Management Journal, 48,* 776–793.

Heider, F. (1958). *The psychology of interpersonal relations*. New York, NY: John Wiley & Sons.

Hill, L. A. (1992). *Becoming a manager: Mastery of a new identity*. Boston, MA: Harvard Business School Press.

Hinds, P. J., Carley, K. M., Krackhardt, D., & Wholey, D. (2000). Choosing work group members: Balancing similarity, competence, and familiarity. *Organizational Behavior and Human Decision Processes, 81,* 226–251.

Ho, V. T., & Levesque, L. L. (2005). With a little help from my friends (and substitutes): Social referents and influence in psychological contract fulfillment. *Organization Science, 16,* 275–289.

Ibarra, H. (1992). Homophily and differential returns: Sex differences in network structure and access in an advertising firm. *Administrative Science Quarterly, 37,* 422–447.

Ibarra H., & Andrews, S. B. (1993). Power, social influence, and sensemaking: Effects of network centrality and proximity on employee perceptions. *Administrative Science Quarterly, 38,* 277–303.

Ingram P., & Morris, M. W. (2007). Do people mix at mixers? Structure, homophily, and the "life of the party." *Administrative Science Quarterly, 52,* 558–585.

Jablin, F. M. (2001). Organizational entry, assimilation, and disengagement/exit. In F. M. Jablin & L. L. Putnam (Eds.), *The new handbook of organizational communication: Advances in theory, research, and methods* (pp. 732–818). Thousand Oaks, CA: Sage.

Jablin, F. M., & Krone, K. J. (1987). Organizational assimilation. In C. R. Berger & S. H. Chaffee (Eds.), *Handbook of communication science* (pp. 711–746). Newbury Park, CA: Sage.

John, O. P. (1990). The "Big Five" factor taxonomy: Dimensions of personality in the natural language and in questionnaires. In L. Pervin, (Ed.), *Handbook of Personality: Theory and Research* (pp. 66–100). New York: Guilford.

Jokisaari, M. (2011). The role of supervisor and network ties in newcomers' in-role and extra-role performance. Paper presented at the annual meeting of the Academy of Management, San Antonio, TX.

Jokisaari, M., & Nurmi, J.-E. (2009). Change in newcomers' supervisor support and socialization outcomes after organizational entry. *Academy of Management Journal, 52,* 527–544.

Kahneman, D., Krueger, A. B., Schkade, D. A., Schwarz, N., & Stone, A. A. (2004). A survey method for characterizing daily life experience: The day reconstruction method. *Science, 306,* 1776–1780.

Kalish, Y., & Robins, G. (2006). Psychological predispositions and network structure: The relationship between individual predispositions, structural holes and network closure. *Social Networks, 28,* 56–84.

Kammeyer-Mueller, J. D., & Wanberg, C. R. (2003). Unwrapping the organizational entry process: Disentangling multiple antecedents and their pathways to adjustment. *Journal of Applied Psychology, 88,* 779–794.

Katz, R. (1980). Time and work: Toward an integrative perspective. In B. M. Staw & L. L. Cummings (Eds.), *Research in Organizational Behavior, 2,* 81–127. Greenwich, CT: Jai.

Katz, R., & Tushman, M. (1983). A longitudinal study of the effects of boundary spanning supervision on turnover and promotion in research and development. *Academy of Management Journal, 26,* 437–456.

Kilduff, M. (1990). The interpersonal structure of decision making: A social comparison approach to organizational choice. *Organizational Behavior and Human Decision Making, 47,* 270–288.

Kilduff, M., & Brass, D. J. (2010). Organizational social network research: Core ideas and key debates. *Academy of Management Annals, 4,* 317–357.

Kilduff, M., & Krackhardt, D. (1994). Bringing the individual back in: A structural analysis of the internal market for reputation in organizations. *Academy of Management Journal, 37,* 87–108.

Klein, K. J., Lim, B.-C., Saltz, J. L., & Mayer, D. M. (2004). How do they get there? An examination of the antecedents of centrality in team networks. *Academy of Management Journal, 47,* 952–963.

Kleinbaum, A., M., Stuart, T. E., & Tushman, M. L. (2008). *Communication (and Coordination?) in a Modern, Complex Organization*. Working papers 09–004, Harvard Business School.

Kossinets, G., & Watts, D. J. (2006). Empirical analysis of an evolving social network. *Science, 311,* 88–90.

Kossinets, G., & Watts, D. J. (2009). Origins of homophily in an evolving social network. *American Journal of Sociology, 115,* 405–450.

Kozlowski, S. W., Gully S. M., Salas, E., & Cannon-Bowers, A. (1996). Team leadership and development: Theory, principles, and guidelines for training leaders and teams. *Advances in Interdisciplinary Studies of Work Teams, 3,* 253–291.

Krackhardt, D. (1992). The strength of strong ties: The importance of philos in organizations. In N. Nohria & R. Eccles (Eds.), *Networks and organizations: Structure, form, and action.* (pp. 216–239). Boston, MA: Harvard Business School Press.

Krackhardt, D., & Porter, L. W. (1986). The snowball effect: Turnover embedded in communication networks. *Journal of Applied Psychology, 71,* 50–55.

Kramer, M. (1996). A longitudinal study of peer communication during job transfers: The impact of frequency, quality, and network multiplexity on adjustment. *Human Communication Research, 23,* 59–86.

Lau, D. C., & Liden R. C. (2008). Antecedents of coworker trust: Leaders' blessings. *Journal of Applied Psychology, 93,* 1130–38.

Lazega, E., & van Duijn, M. (1997). Position in formal structure, personal characteristics and choice of advisors in a law firm: A logistic regression model for dyadic network data. *Social Networks, 19,* 375–397.

Lee, J. J. (2010). Heterogeneity, brokerage, and innovative performance: Endogenous formation of collaborative inventor networks. *Organization Science, 21,* 804–822.

Lee, D. M., & Allen, T. J. (1982). Integrating new technical staff: Implications for acquiring new technology. *Management Science, 28,* 1405–1420.

Lin, N. (1982). Social resources and instrumental action. In P. Marsden & N. Lin (Eds.) *Social structure and network analysis* (pp. 131–145). Beverly Hills, CA: Sage.

Lin, N. (2001). *Social capital: A theory of social structure and action.* New York: Cambridge University Press.

Lin, N., Ensel, W, M., & Vaughn, J. C. (1981). Social resources and strength of ties: Structural factors in occupational status attainment. *American Sociological Review, 46,* 393–405.

Lincoln, J. R., & Miller, J. (1979). Work and friendship ties in organizations: A comparative analysis of relational networks. *Administrative Science Quarterly, 24,* 181–199.

Louis, M. R. (1980). Surprise and sense-making: What newcomers experience in entering unfamiliar organizational settings. *Administrative Science Quarterly, 25,* 226–251.

Louis, M. R., Posner, B. Z., & Powell, G. N. (1983). The availability and helpfulness of socialization practices. *Personnel Psychology, 36,* 857–866.

Major, D. A., Kozlowski, S. W., Chao, G. T., & Gardner, P. D. (1995). A longitudinal investigation of newcomer expectations, early socialization outcomes and moderating effects of role development factors. *Journal of Applied Psychology, 80,* 418–431.

Marrone, J. A., Tesluk, P. E., & Carson, J. B. (2007). A multilevel investigation of antecedents and consequences of team member boundary-spanning behavior. *Academy of Management Journal, 50,* 1423–1439.

Marsden, P. (2005). Recent developments in network measurement. In P. J. Carrington, J. Scott, & S. Wasserman (Eds.), *Models and methods in social network analysis* (pp. 8–30). New York: Cambridge University Press.

Marsden, P., & Friedkin, N. (1994). Network studies of social influence. In S. Wasserman & J. Galaskiewicz (Eds.), *Advances in social network analysis: Research in the social and behavioral sciences (pp.* 3–25). London: Sage Publications.

McDonald, M. L., & Westphal, J. D. (2003). Getting by with the advice of their friends: CEOs' advice networks and firms' strategic response to poor performance. *Administrative Science Quarterly, 48,* 1–32.

McPherson, M., Smith-Lovin, L., & Cook, J. M. (2001). Birds of a feather: Homophily in social networks. *Annual Review of Sociology, 27,* 415–444.

Mehra, A., Kilduff, M., & Brass, D. J. (1998). At the margins: A distinctiveness approach to the social identity and social networks of underrepresented groups. *Academy of Management Journal, 41,* 441–452.

Mehra, A., Kilduff, N., & Brass, D. J. (2001). The social networks of high and low self-monitors: Implications for workplace performance. *Administrative Science Quarterly, 46,* 121–146.

Meyer, G. W. (1994). Social information processing and social networks: A test of social influence mechanisms. *Human Relations, 47,* 1013–1047.

Miller, V. D., & Jablin, F. M. (1991). Information seeking during organizational entry: Influences, tactics, and a model of the process. *Academy of Management Review, 16,* 92–120.

Milton, L. P., & Westphal, J. D. (2005). Identity confirmation networks and cooperation in work groups. *Academy of Management Journal, 48,* 191–212.

Mollica, K. A., Gray, B., & Treviño. L. K. (2003). Racial homophily and its persistence in newcomers' social networks. *Organization Science, 14,* 123–136.

Monge, P., & Contractor, N. 2003. *Theories of communication networks.* New York: Oxford University Press.

Moran, P. (2005). Structural vs. relational embeddedness: Social capital and managerial performance. *Strategic Management Journal, 26,* 1129–1151.

Moreland, R. L., & Levine, J. M. (2001). Socialization in organizations and work groups. In M. E. Turner (Ed.), *Groups at work: Theory and research* (pp. 69–112). Mahwah, NJ: Lawrence Erlbaum.

Morrison, E. W. (2002). Newcomers' relationships: The role of social network ties during socialization. *Academy of Management Journal, 45,* 1149–1160.

Mossholder, K. W., Settoon, R. P., & Henagan, S. C. (2005). A relational perspective on turnover: Examining structural, attitudinal, behavioral predictors. *Academy of Management Journal, 48,* 607–618.

Nahapiet, J., & Ghoshal, S. (1998). Social capital, intellectual capital, and the organizational advantage. *Academy of Management Review, 23,* 242–266

Nebus, J. (2006). Building collegial information networks: A theory of advice network generation. *Academy of Management Review, 31,* 615–637.

Obstfeld, D. (2005). Social networks, the tertius iungens orientation, and involvement in innovation. *Administrative Science Quarterly, 50,* 100–130.

Oh, H., & Kilduff, M. (2008). The ripple effect of personality on social structure: Self-monitoring origins of network brokerage. *Journal of Applied Psychology, 93,* 1155–1164.

Ostroff, C., & Kozlowski S. W. (1992). Organizational socialization as a learning process: The role of information acquisition. *Personnel Psychology, 45,* 849–874.

Podolny, J. M., & Baron, J. N. (1997). Resources and relationships: Social networks and mobility in the workplace. *American Sociological Review, 62,* 673–693.

Pollock, T. G., Whitbred, R. C., & Contractor N. (2000). Social information processing and job characteristics: A simultaneous test of two theories with implications for job satisfaction. *Human Communication Research, 26,* 292–330.

Reagans R., & McEvily, B. (2003). Network structure and knowledge transfer: The effects of cohesion and range. *Administrative Science Quarterly, 48,* 240–267.

Reagans, R, Zuckerman, E., & McEvily, B. (2004). How to make the team: Social networks vs. demography as criteria for designing effective teams. *Administrative Science Quarterly, 49,* 101–133.

Reichers, A. E. (1987). An interactionist perspective on newcomer socialization rates. *Academy of Management Review, 12,* 278–287.

Rice, R. E., & Aydin, C. (1991). Attitudes toward new organizational technology: Network proximity as a mechanism for social information processing. *Administrative Science Quarterly, 36,* 219–244.

Roberts, K. H., & O'Reilly, C. A. (1979). Some correlations of communication roles in organizations. *Academy of Management Journal, 22,* 42–57.

Rollag, K. (2004). The impact of relative tenure on newcomer socialization dynamics. *Journal of Organizational Behavior, 25,* 853–872

Rollag K. (2007). Defining the term 'new' in new employee research. *Journal of Occupational and Organizational Psychology, 80,* 63–75

Salancik, G. R., & Pfeffer, J. (1978). A social information processing approach to job attitudes and task design. *Administrative Science Quarterly, 40,* 224–253.

Sasovova, Z., Mehra, A., Borgatti, S. P., & Schippers, M. C. (2010). Network churn: The effects of self-monitoring personality on brokerage dynamics. *Administrative Science Quarterly, 55,* 639–670.

Schein, E. H. (1978). *Career dynamics: Matching individuals and organizational needs.* Reading, MA: Addison-Wesley.

Scott, B. A., & Judge, T. A. (2009). The popularity contest at work: Who wins, why, and what they receive. *Journal of Applied Psychology, 94,* 20–33.

Scott, J. (2000). *Social network analysis: A handbook* (2nd ed.). Thousand Oaks, CA: Sage.

Seibert, S. E., Kraimer, M. L., & Liden, R. C. (2001). A social capital theory of career success. *Academy of Management Journal, 44,* 219–237.

Seidel, M.-C. L., Polzer, J. T., & Stewart, K. J. (2000). Friends in high places: The effects of social networks in discrimination in salary negotiations. *Administrative Science Quarterly, 45,* 1–24.

Shah, P. P. (1998). Who are employees' social referents? Using a network perspective to determine referent others. *Academy of Management Journal, 41,* 249–268.

Sias, P. M., & Cahill, D. J. (1998). From coworkers to friends: The development of peer friendships in the workplace. *Western Journal of Communication, 62,* 273–299.

Sias, P. M., & Jablin, F. M. (1995). Differential superior-subordinate relations, perceptions of fairness, and coworker communication. *Human Communication Research, 22,* 5–38

Sparrowe, R. T., & Liden, R. C. (1997). Process and structure in leader-member exchange. *Academy of Management Review, 22,* 522–552.

Sparrowe, R. T., & Liden, R. C. (2005). Two routes to influence: Integrating leader-member exchange and social network perspectives. *Administrative Science Quarterly, 50,* 505–535.

Sparrowe, R. T., Liden, R. C., Wayne, S. J., & Kraimer, M. L. (2001). Social networks and the performance of individuals and groups. *Academy of Management Journal, 44,* 316–325.

Stevenson, W. B. (1990). Formal structure and networks of interaction within organization. *Social Science Research, 19,* 113–131.

Stiff, C., & Van Vugt, M. (2008). The power of reputations: The role of third party information in the admission of new group members. *Group Dynamics: Theory, Research, and Practice, 12,* 155–166.

Tichy, N. M., Tushman, M. L., & Fombrun, C. (1979). Social network analysis for organizations. *Academy of Management Review, 4,* 507–519.

Totterdell, P., Holman, D., & Hukin, A. (2008). Social networkers: Measuring and examining individual differences in propensity to connect with others. *Social Networks, 30,* 283–296.

Totterdell, P., Wall, T., Holman, D. Epitropaki, O., & Diamond, H. (2004). Affect networks: A structural analysis of the relationship between work ties and job-related affect. *Journal of Applied Psychology, 89,* 854–867.

Umphress, E. E., Labianca, G., Brass, D. J., Kass, E., & Scholten, L. (2003). The role of instrumental and expressive social ties in employees' perceptions of organizational justice. *Organization Science, 14,* 738–753.

Van Maanen, J., & Schein, E. H. (1979). Toward of theory of organizational socialization. *Research in Organizational Behavior, 1,* 209–264.

Wanberg, C. R., & Kammeyer-Mueller, J. D. (2000). Predictors and outcomes of proactivity in the socialization process. *Journal of Applied Psychology, 85,* 373–385.

Wasserman, S., & Faust, K. (1994). *Social network analysis: Methods and applications.* Cambridge, UK: Cambridge University Press.

Watts, D. J. (2003). *Six degrees: The science of connected age.* London, UK: Vintage.

Weick, K. E., Sutcliffe, K. M., & Obstfeld, D. (2005). Organizing and the process of sensemaking. *Organization Science, 16,* 409–421.

Weller, I., Holtom, B. C., Matiaske, W., & Mellewigt, T. (2009). Level and time effects of recruitment sources on early voluntary turnover. *Journal of Applied Psychology, 94,* 1146–1162.

Wellman, B., & Frank, K. A. (2001). Network capital in the multilevel world: Getting support from personal communities. In N. Lin, K. Cook & R. Burt (Eds.). *Social capital: Theory and research* (pp. 233–273). New York: Aldine de Gruyter.

Xiao, Z., & Tsui, A. S. (2007). When brokers may not work: The cultural contingency of social capital in Chinese high-tech firms. *Administrative Science Quarterly, 52,* 1–31.

Zenger, T. R., & Lawrence, B. S. (1989). Organizational demography: The differential effects of age and tenure on technical communication. *Academy of Management Journal, 32,* 353–376.

Zhou, J., Shin, S. J., Brass, D. J., Choi, J., & Zhang, Z.-X. (2009). Social networks, personal values, and creativity: Evidence for curvilinear and interaction effects. *Journal of Applied Psychology, 94,* 1544–1552.

Organizational Socialization Outcomes: Now and Into the Future

Talya N. Bauer *and* Berrin Erdogan

Abstract

After decades of research on organizational socialization, much is now known about the important process of adjustment into a new organization and new organizational role. This chapter will focus on an overview of what organizations and newcomers do to help facilitate socialization. We will also review indicators of socialization, identify established outcomes of socialization as well as areas deserving of more attention, and will outline some potential new avenues for research.

Key Words: organizational socialization, new employees, onboarding, newcomers, adjustment, socialization outcomes

Introduction

Organizational socialization is the process of moving from being an organizational outsider who is unfamiliar with the norms, procedures, and culture of a new organization to becoming an organizational insider who has working mastery of the internal working norms, procedures, and culture of the organization (Louis, 1980). Socialization has also been called the process of learning the ropes (Schein, 1968). Work on organizational socialization has evolved over the years. Over time, it has moved from the realm of understanding adjustment into a given occupation, such as how to be a nurse, police officer, or teacher, toward a more individual-focused interactionist process where new employees (often termed *newcomers*) respond to organizations and organizational insiders as they adjust, and how organizational insiders respond to newcomers (Reichers, 1987). This interactionist perspective means that researchers studying the adjustment process are challenged to understand organizational socialization from both the individual newcomer's perspective as well as the perspective of organizational factors such as the way in which on-the-job

training, orientation, and inculcation takes place. Practitioners have recently begun to use the term *onboarding* to describe the formalized process within an organization that is designed to help facilitate newcomer success (Bauer, 2010).

To date, several reviews of the organizational socialization literature exist and include summarizing socialization outcomes (Bauer & Erdogan, 2010; Bauer, Morrison, & Callister, 1998; Fisher, 1986; Saks & Ashforth, 1997b; Wanous & Collela, 1989) as well as targeted reviews of the literature (e.g., Anderson & Ostroff, 1997; Ashforth, Sluss, & Harrison, 2007; Cooper-Thomas, van Vianen, & Anderson, 2004; Fang, Duffy, & Shaw, 2011; Feldman, 1997) and meta-analyses (Bauer, Bodner, Erdogan, Truxillo, & Tucker, 2007; Saks, Uggerslev, & Fassina, 2007). Therefore, the focus of this chapter will be to qualitatively review key studies of the proximal and distal outcomes that have traditionally and most recently been studied and those that we believe deserve more attention.

Chapter Outline

Figure 6.1 serves as a visual summary of the chapter and how outcomes fit into the socialization

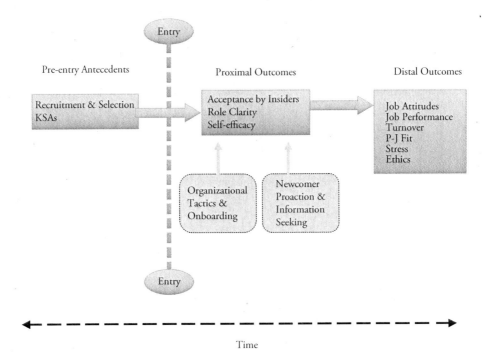

Pre-entry Antecedents

Proximal Outcomes

Distal Outcomes

Entry

Recruitment & Selection
KSAs

Acceptance by Insiders
Role Clarity
Self-efficacy

Job Attitudes
Job Performance
Turnover
P-J Fit
Stress
Ethics

Organizational
Tactics &
Onboarding

Newcomer
Proaction &
Information
Seeking

Entry

Time

Figure 6.1. S Response: summary model of socialization over time.

process. We will start our review by summarizing two key groups of antecedents (i.e., organizational and individual) in the socialization process. As the goal of this chapter is to review the outcomes, these are summarized with an eye toward further understanding socialization outcomes. Next, key research findings regarding proximal outcomes of the socialization process will be discussed. After this, we will review measures of organizational socialization. This will be followed by a review of research on distal outcomes where both the traditionally studied and newly emerging socialization outcomes will be covered. Finally, we will suggest areas for future research in terms of potential new outcomes for organizational socialization. Our hope is that this review of the outcomes of organizational socialization will serve as a mechanism that allows researchers and practitioners alike to take stock of where we have been and where we may be headed, as well as stimulating additional research and better practices in the area of organizational socialization.

What Organizations Do During Socialization
Organizational Socialization Tactics

Organizational tactics have been studied for decades and continue to be an effective way to characterize differences in how organizations engage in socializing newcomers (see Bauer et al., 2007 and

Saks et al., 2007 for meta-analytic summaries of this work). Van Maanen and Schein (1979) originally conceptualized a set of tactics that ranged from highly individualized tactics to highly institutionalized tactics. Using key indicators from six factors, Van Maanen and Schein theorized that newcomers who encountered individualized socialization would be likely to encounter one-on-one socialization, informal training, on-the-job learning, a variable time to complete learning about aspects of the job, a supportive insider to help facilitate their adjustment, and receive feedback that helps to affirm their identity. Top level managers are often socialized in an individualized way (Watkins, 2003). Conversely, newcomers in organizations with institutionalized tactics are likely to encounter collective socialization in a large group, formal training, segregation from insiders while in training, a fixed time to complete learning milestones, and receive feedback that disconfirms their current identity. New accountants at big firms are often socialized in this manner.

Socialization tactics are perhaps one of the most studied constructs in the socialization literature, as noted by Saks et al. (1997). Several researchers have examined tactics in conjunction with key socialization relationships and outcomes (for example see Allen, 2006; Ashforth & Saks, 1996; Ashforth, Sluss, & Saks, 2007; Cable & Parsons, 2001; Gruman, Saks, & Zweig, 2006; Hart & Miller, 2005; Jones,

1986; Kim, Cable, Kim, 2005; Laker & Steffy, 1995; Saks & Ashforth, 1997a). Given this, we know a great deal about the relationship between tactics and socialization. However, relatively less is known about the actual programs and mechanisms organizations utilize to help new employees adjust to their jobs.

Onboarding Programs

Organizations differ dramatically in the degree to which they engage in formal onboarding of new employees. Research has found that around 30% of organizations spend little time thinking about their onboarding process, 50% spend time and effort on their onboarding process but do not see it as a strategic initiative, while the remaining 20% of firms engage in proactive onboarding (Bauer, 2010). Bauer (2010) also reports that best practices for onboarding include implementing the basic paperwork before the first day, making the first day on the job feel special to the newcomer, having formal orientation programs, developing a written onboarding plan, making onboarding participatory, running the program consistently, monitoring onboarding over time, using technology to help facilitate the process, engaging stakeholders, and being clear on objectives, timelines, roles, and responsibilities.

Overall, while organizational socialization tactics have been one of the most heavily studied constructs in the organizational socialization literature, what is actually done in terms of onboarding strategy and implementation has been one of the least studied aspects of socialization. Klein and Heuser (2008) argue that a key component of newcomer socialization is actualizing learning across key organizational levels such as the job, workgroup, and organization. Payne, Culbertson, Boswell, and Barger (2008) found that newcomers' behaviors differed depending on how much attention they received from a key stakeholder—a mentor—and the time they spent in training. They engaged in more socialization activities when they felt the need to rebalance relationships with their organization. Bauer and Green (1994) found that new doctoral students who engaged in more social activities at work had better outcomes. This was also found by Slaughter and Zickar (2006) in a subsequent study of doctoral student adjustment.

Louis, Posner, and Powell (1983) found that the helpfulness of various socialization practices was related to post-entry job satisfaction and organizational commitment for newcomers. They found that the orientation programs varied in their

effectiveness. Klein and Weaver (2000) studied 116 newcomers and found that those new employees who attended a new employee orientation were more highly socialized several months later than those who did not. Part of this finding may be related to the social aspect of the orientation. For example, Wesson and Gogus (2005) found that newcomers who attended an online orientation rather than one in person had less favorable socialization as reported by their supervisors.

What Newcomers Do During Socialization
Newcomer Proaction and Information Seeking

Newcomer proaction encompasses a wider net than information seeking. It includes information seeking, feedback seeking, relationship building, and positive framing (Wanberg & Kammeyer-Mueller, 2000). Ashford and Black (1996) studied MBA students while they joined new organizations. They found that sensemaking, relationship building, positive framing, and negotiation of job changes mattered and that newcomer desire for control was related to all four of these proactive newcomer behaviors. Saks and Ashforth (1996) studied new accountants and found that new employee proaction was related to positive socialization outcomes. Saks, Gruman, and Cooper-Thomas (2011) found that proaction mattered to new coop student socialization.

In addition, proactive personality has begun to be studied as an important part of understanding newcomer proaction (Kammeyer-Mueller & Wanberg, 2003). Crant (2000) defines proactive personality as "taking initiative in improving current circumstances or creating new ones" (p. 436). Parker and Collins (2010) point out that proactive personality may take a number of different forms. While not a study of newcomers, Major, Turner, and Fletcher (2006) studied employees in the financial services and found that proactive personality was related to developmental activity, which is relevant to newcomer socialization as well as predicting motivation to learn.

Newcomers need information to learn about their new organizations, colleagues, roles, and job duties. While organizational members continue to learn new things throughout their careers, organizational entry is a special boundary shift that intensifies the need for information (Ashford, 1986). Ashford and Tsui (1991) found that for managers, seeking feedback on what they needed to improve upon served to increase their understanding and increased ratings of perceived effectiveness. Conversely, managers seeking positive feedback about themselves were perceived as less effective. Ultimately, newcomers are also signaling to insiders about their personality and abilities when they seek information. Therefore, choices regarding what information to seek and how to seek it are relevant for impression management (Ashford & Northcraft, 1992; Morrison & Bies, 1991). Finkelstein, Kulas, and Dages (2003) found that older workers in both academic and retail positions were more likely to engage in covert information seeking than their younger counterparts.

Morrison (1993a) found that new accountants who sought information during their first six months on the job did better at learning their new jobs and fit in better than their colleagues who did not. She also found that different patterns emerged in terms of the type of information being sought (Morrison, 1993b). For example, she reports that newcomers tended to seek technical information by proactively asking questions, while they sought specific types of information from supervisors such as technical, role, and performance feedback. However, they sought normative and socialization information primarily from other coworkers who were more at their peer level. In a recent study, Saks, Gruman, and Cooper-Thomas (2011) set out to understand why proaction is sometimes effective for newcomers while sometimes it is not. They theorized that the emphasis on frequency in interaction has masked the importance of the effectiveness of proaction. Their study of coop university students found a strong relationship between information seeking and obtaining information.

Researchers have studied a variety of factors relating to information seeking for a variety of occupations (e.g., Major & Kozlowski, 1997; Morrison, 1993a; 1993b; Ostroff & Kozlowski, 1992, 1993). Further, several studies have examined both organizational socialization tactics and/or newcomer proactive and information-seeking behaviors in a single study (e.g., Ashforth et al., 2007; Bauer & Green, 1998; Griffin, Colella, & Goparaju, 2000; Gruman, Saks, & Zweig, 2006; Kim, Cable, & Kim, 2005), which has built our understanding of the various interrelationships among these variables and socialization outcomes. Meta-analytically, information seeking was related to socialization tactics at .22 (Bauer et al., 2007).

Proximal Outcomes

Proximal outcomes are those that indicate how well a newcomer is adjusting to his or her new position within the new organization. These outcomes tend to be measured early on in the adjustment process, such as at entry, and then potentially in 3-month intervals until the newcomer has been with the organization for a year (Bauer et al., 1998). Proximal indicators (also called *adjustment indicators* or *accommodation*) are often captured by understanding how accepted the newcomer feels by organizational insiders such as coworkers and supervisors, how much role clarity they have, and how high their performance self-efficacy is (Bauer et al., 2007). We now review the extensive research on adjustment indicators during organizational socialization.

Adjustment Indicators

As mentioned in the previous section, adjustment indicators include the degree to which new employees are integrated into the social fabric of the organization, termed *acceptance by insiders*. This is often measured by Fey's (1955) 5-item scale, which has demonstrated a strong alpha. A sample item includes "My coworkers seem to respect my opinion about things." To illustrate the importance of feeling accepted, 60% of managers who failed to socialize effectively noted that their inability to establish effective working relationships with insiders was an integral aspect of their failure to effectively adjust (Fisher, 1985).

Research shows that feelings of acceptance by insiders (or the social dimension of socialization tactics) is significantly related to distal measures of socialization. For example, it is positively related to organizational commitment (Bauer & Green, 1998; Kammeyer-Mueller & Wanberg, 2003; Saks et al., 2007) and job satisfaction (Ashford & Black, 1996; Saks et al., 2007). In addition, acceptance has also been shown to be positively related to performance (Bauer, Erdogan, Liden, & Wayne, 2006) and negatively related to actual turnover (Bauer et al., 2006; Kammeyer-Mueller & Wanberg, 2003).

The second adjustment indicator is *role clarity*. Role clarity is a concern that is of importance to researchers and practitioners alike. In fact, Bauer (2010) notes that confusion regarding job duties costs US and UK organizations up to $37 billion dollars each year (Cordin, Rowan, Odgers, Barnes, & Redgate, 2008). Role clarity is well known in the stress and strain literature. Researchers have often utilized Rizzo, House, and Lirtzman's (1970) 6-item measure to assess how much a newcomer understands his or her role. A sample item is "Clear, planned goals and objectives exist for my work."

Role clarity is an important predictor of distal socialization outcomes. In fact, it has been consistently related to job satisfaction and organizational commitment (Adkins, 1995; Bauer & Green, 1998; Menguc, Han, & Auh, 2007) and positive adjustment outcomes (e.g., Bauer et al., 2007; Kammeyer-Mueller & Wanberg, 2003). Adkins (1995) found that role clarity was the most prominent predictor of nurses' socialization success in terms of understanding their job satisfaction and commitment levels over time. Role clarity is also related to performance, with greater clarity being associated with higher levels of newcomer performance. In the realm of new graduate students, Slaughter and Zickar (2006) found that engagement in research and departmental activities was related to lower role conflict and role ambiguity. Bauer and Green (1994) studied new doctoral students in the hard sciences and found that those who engaged in their programs had less role conflict, felt more accepted, and were more productive in terms of research presentations and publications than those who were less engaged in departmental functions.

Finally, *performance self-efficacy* is based on Bandura's (1986) self-efficacy concept which predicts that increased confidence in one's ability to do one's job should relate to positive organizational outcomes such as performance. Research has often utilized measures modeled after Bandura's 0 to 10 confidence scale. A sample performance self-efficacy item is "I am confident that I can effectively perform my job." The literature has established that self-efficacy is related to performance (Bandura, 1997).

In terms of distal outcomes, self-efficacy is related to both attitudinal and behavioral outcomes such as job satisfaction, organizational commitment, performance, and turnover (Bauer et al., 2007; Gruman et al., 2006; Kammeyer-Mueller & Wanberg, 2003), but especially related to performance (Bauer & Green, 1998). In addition to these studies of newcomers, McNatt and Judge (2008) conducted an actual self-efficacy intervention with 71 first- and second-year auditors at a Big Four accounting firm. They found that those who were randomly assigned to the experimental group were more likely to remain with the firm and to have higher ratings on job attitude surveys. Saks (1995) conducted a longitudinal field examination of new accountants and found that self-efficacy partially mediated the relationships among new employee training and job satisfaction, organizational commitment, and intentions to quit.

The inter-correlations between these adjustment variables are not modest, but are also not so high as to cause concern about whether they are actually measuring the same thing. Based on meta-analytic findings (Bauer et al., 2007), social acceptance is related to role clarity at .23 and with self-efficacy at .28. Role clarity is related to self-efficacy at .45. Overall, understanding newcomer adjustment is an important aspect to predicting and maximizing newcomers' socialization success. Adjustment is a key mediator between individual and organizational antecedents and more distal socialization outcomes.

Finally, newcomer proaction (e.g., Wanberg & Kammeyer-Mueller, 2000; Chan & Schmitt, 2000) and information seeking (Morrison, 1993a; Morrison, 1993b) have been consistently shown to relate to adjustment. Meta-analysis reveals that information seeking is significantly related to social acceptance at .16, role clarity at .17, and self-efficacy at .14 (Bauer et al., 2007). Similarly, organizational socialization tactics have been found to be related social acceptance (.19), role clarity (.27), and self-efficacy (.42).

Other Measures of Socialization

In addition to adjustment indicators, several organizational socialization studies have conceptualized organizational socialization as the understanding of the way in which the organization functions. For example, does the newcomer understand the organization's culture and organizational politics? If so, they are seen as better adjusted than a newcomer who does not. The next section will outline the different measures of organizational socialization that exist to date.

Chao et al. Socialization Scale

The Chao, O'Leary-Kelly, Wolf, Klein, and Gardner (1994) scale was developed to measure what they determined were the key different content areas that must be learned during organizational socialization. The authors reviewed the literature, engaged in scale development, and concluded that six socialization dimensions captured the socialization process. These include performance proficiency, politics, language, people, organizational goals and values, and history. Sample items of this scale include "I know the organization's long-held traditions" (history) and "I know how things 'really work' on the inside of this organization" (politics).

Of the six dimensions, the dimension of performance proficiency refers to the degree an individual has mastered the required knowledge, skills, and abilities of his or her job. Further, the politics dimension refers to the individual's success in gaining information regarding formal and informal work relationships and power structures within the organization. The language dimension is the degree to which newcomers have knowledge of technical language such as acronyms, slang, and jargon that is unique to the organization. The dimension of people involves the degree to which newcomers have established successful and satisfying working relationships with organizational members. The dimension of organizational goals and values refers to the degree to which individuals understand the goals of their workgroups and organization. And finally, history refers to the degree to which newcomers know an organization's traditions, customs, myths, and rituals.

Research has shown that newcomers who understand organizational politics, understand the goals and values of an organization, and learn the language unique to the organization will have higher levels of commitment, satisfaction, and lower levels of turnover (Chao et al., 1994; Klein & Weaver, 2000; Wesson & Gogus, 2005). Understanding politics was also related to higher personal income across 3 years, and history and goals/values were related to job satisfaction across this same time period (Chao et al., 1994). Wesson and Gogus (2005) conducted a quasi-experimental design with newcomers at a consulting firm in terms of whether or not they took an in-person orientation or a self-paced online orientation covering similar material. They found that the people, politics, and organizational goals and values were higher for the in-person orientation groups, indicating that computer-based orientation may hinder socialization—especially in terms of potentially more subtle social aspects of a new organization.

Socialization Content Scales

As Klein and Heuser (2008) note, the learning of the content of socialization is a critical component of understanding orientation practices during newcomer adjustment. Klein, Polin, and Sutton (2010) did extensive work to revise and expand the Chao et al. (1994) scale. They created items to tap 12 socialization content dimensions. Work on the dimensions is preliminary but to date, 44 items capture language, history, task proficiency, working relationships, social relationships, structure, politics, goals and strategy, culture and values, rules and policies, navigation, and inducements. Sample items include "I know the meaning of jargon used in my

organization" (language item) and "I am aware of the unwritten procedures for getting things done in my organization" (navigation item).

Newcomer Socialization Questionnaire

Haueter, Macan, and Winter's (2003) 35-item scale was designed to capture organizational socialization by focusing on three dimensions including task (11 items), group (12 items), and organizational (12 items) socialization. Each dimension includes items that tap both factual information and comprehension of expected role behaviors. A sample task item for task is "I understand how to perform the tasks that make up my job." A sample item for group socialization is "I understand how to behave in a manner consistent with my work group's values and ideals." A sample item for organizational socialization is "I understand this organization's objectives and goals." In their initial validation work, Haueter et al. (2003) found that their scale was related to job satisfaction and organizational commitment but not necessarily to actual performance. Boswell, Shipp, Payne, and Culbertson (2009) used this scale to study the relationship of the extent of socialization to changes in job satisfaction over time. They found that socialization was related to job satisfaction and that the scale had an alpha of .94.

Organizational Socialization Inventory

Taormina (1994, 2004) developed and validated his 20-item socialization scale to address four socialization dimensions. These include training received, coworker support, understanding the job and organization, and future prospects in the employing organization. A sample item from this scale is "This organization has provided excellent job training for me" (training received). In his subsequent work on the organizational socialization inventory (OSI), Taormina (2004) gathered data from 193 employees from different industries in Hong Kong. He then conducted confirmatory factor analyses on the OSI and the Chao et al. (1994) scale with job satisfaction and commitment. He reports that the OSI had greater dimensional integrity, with the OSI covering one more dimension than the other scale. However, both scales were related to the job attitudes studied.

Distal Outcomes

Distal outcomes are key to studying the ultimate outcomes of organizational socialization, as they indicate the degree to which newcomer organizational socialization matters to organizational outcomes such as job attitudes and actual newcomer behavior. When surveyed, organizations perceive effective socialization as improving retention rates (52%), time to productivity (60%), and overall customer satisfaction (53%; Bauer, 2010). To date, in the literature, the most common outcomes are attitudinal. Given this, we begin our review of distal outcomes with job attitudes before turning our attention toward behavioral outcomes.

Job Attitudes

Job attitudes include job satisfaction, organizational commitment, and turnover intentions. Job satisfaction and organizational commitment have been consistently studied in the socialization context. This makes sense, as job attitudes are variable and understanding how socialization affects this can help to understand a newcomer's performance and likelihood to leave their new organization. Research has shown that some factors influence all three attitudinal outcomes. For example, Chang, Chang, and Jacobs (2009) studied the degree to which new IT (information technology) employees in South Korea engaged in communities of practice that were supported by their new organization. They found that engagement was related to all three attitudinal socialization outcomes.

Maier and Brunstein (2001) studied newcomers in 14 companies in Germany. They found that personal goals were related to changes in job satisfaction and organizational commitment over the first months while being relatively stable across their three data collection periods. In addition, attainment and commitment to goals moderated this relationship such that those who were committed and felt that they were attaining their goals had more positive job attitudes than those who did not. In their study of 132 newcomers at entry on their first day, 3 months post-entry, 6 months post-entry, and 1 year post-entry, Boswell et al. (2009) found a curvilinear pattern of job satisfaction over time, such that job satisfaction was high upon entry (the honeymoon phase) later decreased (the hangover phase) and finally leveled out at the 1-year point. This study went beyond the earlier work of Boswell, Boudreau, and Tichy (2005), which initially established these effects utilizing an executive sample of job changers. O'Reilly and Caldwell (1981) examined how alternatives to taking a given job affected organizational commitment in the first 6 months of new graduates' work experiences. They found that for the 108 MBAs they studied, those who felt they had options and had chosen to take a job because they wanted to—not just because they felt they had to—were more satisfied and committed 6 months later. Major, Kozlowski, Chao, and Gardner (1995) studied 248 new hires and found that met expectations and insider exchanges were related to job satisfaction, organizational commitment, and turnover intentions. Chen (2005) found that initial newcomer performance levels predicted later newcomer intentions to quit.

In their meta-analysis of the socialization literature, Bauer et al. (2007) found that socialization acceptance was correlated to job satisfaction at .33, organizational commitment at .35, and intentions to quit at .24. They also found that role clarity was related to job satisfaction at .32, organizational commitment at .29, and intentions to quit at .23. Finally, they found that self-efficacy was related to job satisfaction at .28, organizational commitment at .20, and intentions to quit at .15.

In terms of other organizational antecedents, information seeking was related to job satisfaction (.20), organizational commitment (.21), and turnover (-.08), while organizational socialization tactics were related to job satisfaction even more strongly at .43, organizational commitment at .15, and turnover at -.14 (Bauer et al., 2007).

Newcomer Behavior
JOB PERFORMANCE

Research in socialization has often utilized performance as an important outcome. For example, Chen and Klimoski (2003) found that newcomers within three large high-tech organizations had general self-efficacy, which was subsequently related to newcomer role performance indirectly through newcomer performance expectations and newcomer empowerment. Work has begun that examines the role that competencies play in predicting newcomer performance. Molleman and Van der Vegt (2007) studied 68 new nurses over 18 months and found that 6 weeks post-entry their confidence in their ability to give good nursing care was more highly related to a positive performance evaluation than for non–care related competence. However, 18 months after entry the pattern reverses and non–care related competence becomes more important than care related competence. While this effect may be most salient for nurses who deal with life or death issues each day, competence is an important dimension of job performance. Successful socialization must facilitate appropriate job related knowledge if newcomers are to be successful in their jobs. Bauer et al. (2007) found that performance was consistently related to adjustment, with a correlation of .21 with socialization acceptance, .29 with role clarity, and .35 with self-efficacy. Finally, they found that information seeking was related to performance at .08 and tactics were related at .15.

TURNOVER

Inadequate socialization has been cited as a primary reason for unwanted turnover (Bauer et al., 1998). Losing an employee who is a poor fit or not performing well may be a desirable outcome. However, losing employees because they feel alienated from their coworkers, are confused regarding their job tasks, and/or lack confidence in their ability to perform well, indicates inadequate onboarding. Allen (2006) studied 256 new employees at a large financial services firm that included employees across 18 states. He found that on-the-job embeddedness was negatively related to turnover for these new employees. Fu, Shaffer, and Harrison (2005) examined the role of adjustment on turnover for foreign employees. They found that across four data collection points, increased organizational and community fit was predicted by proactive socialization tactics and increased fit decreased intent to quit and turnover. O'Reilly and Caldwell (1981) found that feeling confident in job choice at entry was related to lowered turnover for new employees 2 years later. Realistic job previews (RJPs) can also serve to influence new employee turnover behavior. For example, Waung (1995) conducted an experiment with new hires in service jobs. The group that received RJP information was more likely to remain with the organization for a year or longer when compared to the group that did not receive this type of information. This is consistent with work on RJP and newcomers (Wanous, 1992).

Kammeyer-Mueller, Wanberg, Glomb, and Ahlburg (2005) demonstrated that turnover within the first 2 years of employment is related to a series of critical events and attitudes that unfold for newcomers over time. Turnover is an interesting outcome to study because it is so costly to organizations and has the potential to be greatly affected by the socialization process.

Finally, meta-analytically, Bauer et al. (2007) found that actual new employee turnover was consistently related to adjustment, with a correlation of −.16 with socialization acceptance, −.11 with role clarity, and -.16 with self-efficacy. Further, information seeking was related to turnover at -.08, while tactics were −.14.

Additional Distal Outcomes of Organizational Socialization

In addition to these four key distal outcomes, researchers have also focused on other distal outcomes such as person–organization fit, stress, and ethics. The burgeoning literature on these topics will now be reviewed.

Person–Job and Person–Organization Fit

Fit can be seen as an antecedent as well as an outcome. For example, Wang, Zhan, McCune, and Truxillo (2011) found, in their longitudinal sample of over 600 Chinese newcomers, that person–environment fit was related to job performance, job satisfaction, and turnover intentions. Ferris, Youngblood, and Yates (1985) found that fit was related to airline flight attendant turnover. Kim et al. (2005) examined the relationship between organizational socialization tactics and person–organization fit for 279 new Korean employees in 7 diverse organizations including hospitals, manufacturing organizations, and financial services companies. They found that the type of tactics experienced did affect perceptions of person–organization fit. This work extended and replicated the earlier work of Cable and Parsons (2001). The idea is that highly structured socialization serves to reduce ambiguity and allows new employees to accept their new roles and become accepted within those roles. Kim et al. (2005) also argue that proactive personality might also moderate this relationship and Gruman et al. (2006) subsequently examined this relationship. They found partial moderation for relationship building. In another study examining the role of prior occupational experience on new employee adjustment, Carr, Pearson, Vest, and Boyar (2006) studied 274 new transportation employees over 8 months and found that the relationship was mediated. It is interesting to note that Cooper-Thomas, van Vianen, and Anderson (2004) studied newcomer fit over time and found that socialization tactics influenced perceived fit but not actual fit. Clearly there is room for additional work regarding the role of fit as both a predictor and outcome of the socialization process (Chatman, 1991; see also van Vianen and De Pater, Chapter 8). Given that fit has been shown to be such an important factor in fostering important organizational outcomes (Kristof, 1996; Kristof, Zimmerman, & Johnson, 2005), this can only serve to strengthen the organizational socialization literature further.

Stress

Newcomers often experience a type of "reality shock" upon organizational entry (Louis, 1980). This can be especially pronounced for recent graduates embarking upon new careers. Researchers have studied stress in relation to socialization from time to time over the last 25 years. Some researchers have examined stress and/or stressors as antecedents, and others as outcomes of the socialization process. For example, Ostroff and Kozlowski (1992) studied 151 graduating seniors in engineering and management and found that psychological stress was negatively related to task knowledge for new employees. In addition, watching and trying were related to higher stress in their early tenure. Fisher (1985) studied new nurses and found that social support helped to buffer the effects of unmet expectation stress. Saks (1994) found that for the 198 new entry-level accountants he studied, self-efficacy was related to anxiety but not stress. Conversely, Saks and Ashforth (2000) found that for the recent college graduates they studied, entry stressors predicted all the outcomes covered in their study including job attitudes, stress outcomes, and job performance. So, while stress has not been studied nearly as often as other socialization outcomes, it appears that a great deal of potential exists to further refine its role as both a predictor and outcome of successful socialization. Fan and Wanous (2008) conducted a longitudinal field experiment for newcomers to both a new organization and culture. They conducted a training focused on stress management. The newcomers were 72 Asian students who were new to the United States. Across their first 9 months, those in the experimental group reported less stress and were better adjusted than those who received the traditional orientation.

Ethics

As Brown, Treviño, and Harrison (2005) note, most employees are not solely guided by an internal compass. Instead, most look outside of themselves and to significant others within their organizations for ethical guidance. In other words, ethical behavior is deeply influenced by social learning theory. As occupational and organizational entry are major times of shock and upheaval, it makes sense that they would also be periods where ethical questions arise and ethical conduct could be greatly influenced either positively or negatively. Hannah (2007) interviewed 111 high-tech employees starting new jobs. The main question was if and under what circumstances new employees would share

trade secrets for the benefit of their new employers. A major finding was that the level of identification with the previous and present employer was a major factor in their decision to share or not to share. In their study of 371 early career lawyers, Kammeyer-Mueller, Simon, and Rich (in press) found that the type of socialization tactics used (in this case divestiture) was related to emotional exhaustion (i.e., mental weariness and emotional depletion). However, this relationship was partially mediated by ethical conflict. So, the greater the misfit in ethical orientation between the new lawyer and his or her firm, the more burnout he or she experienced. Clearly, ethics are a potentially rich avenue to continue studying in the socialization context. To be especially relevant for the socialization literature, such studies should clearly link to the socialization context, making them particularly focused on how being new in an organization matters in terms of ethics.

We see these areas of research as promising as a set, and encourage further research on the roles that fit, stress, and ethics play in the socialization process and the associated outcomes. In the following section we move forward to ideas for future research directions. This includes several proposed new outcomes of organizational socialization. These are surely not the only potential new outcomes, but rather a representative sample of ideas we had while reviewing the organizational socialization outcomes literature.

Future Directions: New Outcomes of Organizational Socialization
Organizational Change

The entry of newcomers into existing work groups can serve to stimulate change in operational procedures, structure, or even a group or organization's culture. Of course, not all newcomers will have the ability to enact culture change and there will also be newcomers who are expected to adapt to the existing conditions without attempting to modify them. However, particularly at higher levels in organizations new employees are often hired with the expectation that their coming on board will stimulate new values and new practices to be adopted, resulting in a change in group, business unit, or even organizational culture. What is the role of the organizational socialization process in bringing about culture change? Can new hires act as change agents and does their ability to serve as change agents depend on successful socialization?

It is our expectation that proximal outcomes of socialization will play an important role in the ability of a newcomer to initiate change that will be supported by company insiders and key stakeholders. An understanding of the company's history, language, politics, and people, or what we termed earlier as socialization *content*, will serve an essential role in helping newcomers introduce change as well as increasing the newcomer's credibility. This seems tied to social integration but has not yet been studied. In contrast, new hires who do not understand the politics, people, language, and history of the business may be regarded as naive by organizational insiders, their ideas and proposals will meet with greater skepticism, and eventually will be ignored or even sabotaged. Therefore, we predict that socialization content dimensions will be related to one's ability to initiate successful change.

Moreover, role clarity, social acceptance, and self-efficacy will be critical in a new hire's ability to initiate change effectively by giving them the required credibility and social support they would need in enacting the change effort. Therefore, we view successful socialization as a prerequisite for new hire–initiated change efforts and the degree to which new hires can successfully act as change agents.

To date, only a few studies examined the extent to which new hires may act as initiators of change. For example, Hansen and Levine (2009) showed in an experimental setting that new hires' ability to have their ideas adopted by the group depended on their communication style. Kane, Argote, and Levine (2005) showed in an experimental situation context that existing employees of a group were less likely to adopt a superior production routine presented by a newcomer if they did not share an identity with the newcomer. These results suggest that newcomers may initiate successful change in the degree to which they have insider status or have been successfully socialized into the organization. While successful socialization will not alone predict organizational change, it will likely interact with behaviors and personality traits that have been related to organizational change efforts, such as transformational leadership style (Herold, Fedor, Caldwell, & Liu, 2008) and proactive personality (Fuller, Marler, & Hester, 2006).

Work–Life Conflict

Being a newcomer to an organization is a stressful event for many individuals. During their early tenure, newcomers are in the process of maintaining positive impressions in the eyes of leaders and coworkers, aiming to establish clarity with respect to their roles, and to become confident in performing their jobs. This may often entail working long hours, not taking advantage of any flexibility offered by the organization in terms of working times, and taking advantage of any opportunities to get to know one's coworkers and manager in nonwork settings. All of these actions on the part of newcomers may result in a high level of time-based role stress, with the ultimate outcome of work–family as well as work–life conflict. Impression-management concerns may also unnecessarily increase the amount of stress newcomers experience. Oftentimes newcomers avoid asking questions to those around them for fear of looking ignorant or incompetent, further creating stress for them even though asking for feedback and information could ease their pace of adjustment.

For example, research has found that newcomers experience social stressors, overload, and cooperation problems at work (Grebner, Elfering, Semmer, Kaiser-Probst, & Schlapbach, 2004). It is reasonable to expect that the employee's stressful experiences in the new job will have implications for his or her family life. In other words, successful socialization of newcomers may result in reduced work–family conflict. Difficulties in the socialization process are likely to yield higher levels of work–family conflict by taking away time and resources available for the employee's family role. Research has shown that work demands are positively related to work–family conflict (Bakker, Demerouti, & Dollard, 2008). There is reason to expect that for new hires, proximal socialization outcomes will be a significant predictor of work–family conflict.

We also expect that the extent to which new hire socialization is related to work–family conflict will depend on the organization as well as the person. For example, given that dual career employees who have childrearing responsibilities will more likely be subjected to work–family conflict, the effects of new employee socialization for work–family conflict of these employee groups will be stronger. The degree to which the newcomer assigns high importance to his/her work role compared to the family role is also a predictor of work–family conflict (Adams, King, & King, 1996) and will likely raise the importance of successful socialization to the organization for the outcome of experienced work–family conflict.

While proximal socialization outcomes will likely affect the degree to which an employee experiences work-family conflict, the amount of family support the newcomer receives from his/her family during the early stages of the new job may alleviate the relationship between socialization and work–family conflict. Finally, we expect that work–family conflict is likely to be an outcome of the socialization process for employees who do not change jobs very often, as well as for employees higher up in the organization who perform complex and challenging work. For individuals who work in high turnover industries and who change jobs frequently, the degree to which one's family life is affected as a result of one's adjustment to work may be more limited.

Finally, an interesting possible outcome of newcomer socialization relating to the work–family interface relates to outcomes experienced by the family. For example, in dual career couples, we may expect that as one member of the couple goes through the socialization process the other member will have to pick up the slack at home, resulting in family-to-work interference for the individual who has not changed jobs. In other words, studying the effects of workplace socialization beyond its effects on organizational outcomes is an interesting research avenue.

Life Satisfaction

Life satisfaction is an indicator of subjective well-being and it is an outcome of interest not only because it relates to outcomes such as one's health, but because it is a desirable end state in itself (Diener, Sapyta, & Suh, 1998; Erdogan, Bauer, Truxillo, & Mansfield, in press). While the socialization literature focused on the effects of socialization process on an employee's job attitudes, its potential relation to an individual's well-being has not yet been studied. There is reason to expect that newcomer life satisfaction and subjective well-being will be a function of successful socialization. Studies have shown that work satisfaction is an important correlate of life satisfaction (Tait, Padgett, & Baldwin, 1989). Moreover, many of the proximal outcomes of socialization, such as role clarity (Carlson, Kacmar, & Williams, 2000), self-efficacy (Yan, Kwok, Tang, & Ho, 2007), and social acceptance (Simon, Judge, & Halvorsen-Ganepola, 2010) have been shown to be related to life satisfaction.

While these studies were not conducted on newcomers to an organization, we expect that they are suggestive of an even stronger relationship for new hires. New hires are less likely than existing employees of an organization to take their jobs for granted, and they are more likely to spend cognitive and emotional energy on their work until they feel that they have adjusted to their new positions. Therefore, new hires are more likely to pay attention to their adjustment to their new position in their

assessments of life satisfaction, leading to a relationship between proximal outcomes of socialization and life satisfaction.

Perceived Overqualification

Is there a downside to employees socializing into a new workplace too quickly? Is it possible that an individual who achieves role clarity, social acceptance, and self-efficacy may feel bored and unchallenged by his or her job? It is plausible that one of the potential outcomes of socialization process is perceived overqualification. Perceived overqualification refers to the degree to which the person believes that he or she possesses skills, experience, and education that is not required by or utilized on the job (Erdogan & Bauer, 2009). Little is known about antecedents of overqualification, but factors such as psychological contract violations have been related to perceptions of overqualification (Lee, 2005).

It is plausible that an employee may feel overqualified to the degree to which he/she masters the job easily and therefore starts feeling that the job is beneath his/her skill levels. In this case, the employee is likely to experience *emergent overqualification* as defined by Erdogan, Bauer, Peiro, and Truxillo (2011). In other words, even though the employee may not feel overqualified at the time the job offer is accepted, the employee will perceive that he/she is overqualified after organizational entry.

We predict that perceptions of overqualification are more likely when employees adjust to their new jobs faster than they expect. If the job is perceived as low in complexity and if employees develop high levels of role clarity and self-efficacy in a short amount of time, they may start feeling that they are overqualified for their position. In other words, the possibility that there may be an optimal time of adjustment in each job—and that significantly faster adjustment to the job compared to the employee's own expectations and to other newcomers to the organization may result in perceived overqualification—is worth exploring.

Another related idea is to understand how socialization is similar or different for newcomers who have recently undergone a prolonged period of unemployment. Past research shows that unemployment affects the self-efficacy of job searchers over time (Wanberg, Glomb, Song, & Sorenson, 2005) as well as their networking activity (Wanberg, Kanfer, & Banas, 2000). It would be interesting to see if these differences carried over into the organizational entry and adjustment phases as well.

Changes in Organizational Relationships

While newcomers move from being outsiders to insiders, they are also likely to change the organizational fabric within the organization. The new relationships they form with their coworkers and managers may affect the nature of the relationships among coworkers as well. For example, when a highly competent new employee joins the organization and builds relationships with the leader, the new relationship may reduce the quality of the relationship between the leader and other coworkers. The leader's time, attention, and other resources may be divided. By comparison, some existing employees may lose their privileges. The work ethic and commitment of the newcomer may change the images of some existing employees in the eyes of management. In other words, one of the outcomes of socialization process may be changes in the quality of the relationships among existing members and leaders and cause disruptions in the status quo. We expect that a newcomer who brings more knowledge, skills, and abilities to a team compared to the existing members of a team may attract the envy or jealousy of coworkers if the newcomer is perceived as a threat to the status quo and particularly coworkers' own standing in the eyes of management.

Similarly, a newcomer's socialization into the new job and organization may improve the relationships among other coworkers to the degree to which the newcomer acts as a bridge between employees who had low communication and interaction frequency in the past. According to balance theory, the relationships between three people will converge. To the degree to which the new hire develops high-quality exchanges with two members who did not previously have much interaction, the two previously unconnected coworkers may get closer to each other.

These possibilities indicate that while changing their behaviors, adapting and adjusting to their new jobs, newcomers may prove to be the catalysts of changes in the social network of their group. These changes are more likely to follow a successful socialization process, where the new employee masters his/her job, and achieves role clarity and a certain degree of social acceptance. We consider the structure of the organizations' social network a potentially interesting outcome of the socialization process.

Additional research on job changers is also an area that is likely to prove beneficial to understanding the similarities and differences between those entering new organizations and those finding themselves in new roles with new demands and stakeholders but within the same organization. Work on job changers has established some interesting findings (e.g., Feldman & Brett, 1983; Jablin & Kramer, 1998; Pinder & Schroeder, 1987) but additional work seems warranted.

Leader Stress and Well-being

To date, the outcomes of organizational socialization tended to focus on newcomers themselves and their organizationally relevant behaviors. It is plausible, however, that successful socialization of newcomers into the workplace may serve as a factor which reduces stress and increases the well-being of immediate supervisors. Introducing newcomers into the workplace is likely a stressful event for leaders as well as newcomers, and their new coworkers. Leaders would have reason to worry that the new hire will not be a good fit for the organization, will not be a positive addition to the group's culture, and will disrupt work relationships. Therefore, when newcomers adjust to their jobs with ease, connect to others, and start taking on some of the load for which they were hired, leaders would realize that their work unit is closer to meeting its goals and objectives, they have to devote less time to training and answering the questions of the new hire as the newcomer matures, and in general will feel that the hiring decision they have made was successful and resulted in positive outcomes. Therefore, new hire socialization may result in outcomes such as increased self-efficacy, reduced stress, and increased enjoyment of work on the part of managers. We feel that conducting longitudinal research examining changes in leader perceptions and attitudes and their relation to the newcomer's adjustment to the organization would be an interesting direction for future researchers to take.

The Role of Time in Socialization Outcomes

While time is an explicitly integral aspect of the socialization process, to date researchers have not come up with overly compelling ways to understand the role of time in socialization. As Ashforth et al. (2007) note, tenure has been the default way that researchers have conceptualized and controlled for time differences among newcomers and their progression toward becoming fully socialized organizational insiders. It is refreshing to see an entire chapter in this *Handbook* devoted to the role of time (Ashforth, Chapter 9). Hopefully, this chapter and more sophisticated research and statistical methods for dealing with time will help to stimulate research into the role of time in socialization outcomes.

Conclusion

As Klein and Heuser (2008) note, it makes sense to conceptualize the outcomes of newcomer socialization as including the newcomer, the job, the work group, the unit, and the organization. Doing so will allow the constellation of socialization outcomes to continue to expand. In this chapter we have reviewed what organizations and newcomers do during newcomer socialization, the proximal and distal outcomes of organizational socialization, as well as outlining potential new outcomes deserving of additional attention. We hope that this chapter has served to inform readers about these important outcomes as well as stimulating thinking about future research in the area of socialization.

References

Adams, G. A., King, L. A., & King, D. W. (1996). Relationships of job and family involvement, family social support, and work-family conflict with job and life satisfaction. *Journal of Applied Psychology, 81,* 411–420.

Adkins, C. L. (1995). Previous work experience and organizational socialization: A longitudinal examination. *Academy of Management Journal, 38,* 839–862.

Allen, D. G. (2006). Do organizational socialization tactics influence newcomer embeddedness and turnover? *Journal of Management, 32,* 237–256.

Anderson, N., & Ostroff, C. (1997). Selection as socialization. In N. Anderson & P. Herriot (Eds.), *International handbook of selection and assessment* (pp. 413–440). New York: John Wiley & Sons, Inc.

Ashford, S. J. (1986). Feedback-seeking in individual adaptation: A resource perspective. *Academy of Management Journal, 29,* 465–487.

Ashford, S. J. & Black, J. S. (1996). Proactivity during organizational entry: The role of desire for control. *Journal of Applied Psychology, 81,* 199–214.

Ashford, S. J., & Northcraft, G. B. (1992). Conveying more (or less) than we realize: The role of impression management in feedback seeking. *Organizational Behavior and Human Decision Processes, 53,* 310–334.

Ashford, S. J., & Tsui, A. S. (1991). Self-regulation for managerial effectiveness: The role of active feedback seeking. *Academy of Management Journal, 34,* 251–280.

Ashforth, B. E., & Saks, A. M. (1996). Socialization tactics: Longitudinal effects on newcomer adjustment. *Academy of Management Journal, 39,* 149–178.

Ashforth, B. E., Sluss, D. M., & Harrison, S. H. (2007). Socialization in organizational contexts. G. P. Hodgkinson & J. K. Ford (Eds.), *International Review of Industrial and Organizational Psychology, 22,* 1–70. Sussex, England: Wiley Press.

Ashforth, B. E., Sluss, D. M., & Saks, A. M. (2007). Socialization tactics, proactive behavior, and newcomer learning: Integrating socialization models. *Journal of Vocational Behavior, 70,* 447–462.

Bakker, A. B., Demerouti, E., & Dollard, M. F. (2008). How job demands affect partner's experience of exhaustion: Integrating work-family conflict and crossover theory. *Journal of Applied Psychology, 93,* 901–911.

Bandura, A. (1997). *Self-efficacy: The exercise of control.* New York, NY: Worth Publishers.

Bandura, A. (1986). *Social foundations of thought and action: A social-cognitive view.* Englewood Cliffs, NJ: Prentice Hall.

Bauer, T. N. (2010). Onboarding new employees: Maximizing success. *SHRM Foundation's Effective Practice Guideline Series.* Society for Human Resource Management. The report can be downloaded at http://www.shrm.org/about/foundation/products/Pages/OnboardingEPG.aspx.

Bauer, T. N., Bodner, T., Erdogan, B., Truxillo, D. M., & Tucker, J. S. (2007). Newcomer adjustment during organizational socialization: A meta-analytic review of antecedents, outcomes, and methods. *Journal of Applied Psychology, 92,* 707–721.

Bauer, T. N., & Erdogan, B. (2010). Organizational socialization: The effective onboarding of new employees. In S. Zedeck, H. Aguinis, W. Cascio, M. Gelfand, K. Leung, S. Parker, & J. Zhou (Eds.). *APA Handbook of I/O Psychology,* Volume III, pp. 51–64. Washington, DC: American Psychological Association.

Bauer, T. N., Erdogan, B., Liden, R. C., & Wayne, S. J. (2006). A longitudinal study of the moderating role of extraversion: Leader-member exchange, performance, and turnover during new executive development. *Journal of Applied Psychology, 91,* 298–310.

Bauer, T. N., & Green, S. G. (1994). The effect of newcomer involvement in work-related activities: A longitudinal study of socialization. *Journal of Applied Psychology, 79,* 211–223.

Bauer, T. N., & Green, S. G. (1998). Testing the combined effects of newcomer information seeking and manager behavior on socialization. *Journal of Applied Psychology, 83,* 72–83.

Bauer, T. N., Morrison, E. W., & Callister, R. R. (1998). Organizational socialization: A review and directions for future research. In G. R. Ferris (Ed.), *Research in personnel and human resource management*: Vol. 16 (pp. 149–214). Greenwich, CT: JAI Press.

Boswell, W. R., Boudreau, J. W., & Tichy, J. (2005). The relationship between employee job change and job satisfaction: The honeymoon-hangover effect. *Journal of Applied Psychology, 90,* 882–892.

Boswell, W. R., Shipp, A. J., Payne, S. C., & Culbertson, S. S. (2009). Changes in newcomer job satisfaction over time: Examining the pattern of honeymoons and hangovers. *Journal of Applied Psychology, 94,* 844–858.

Brown, M. E., Treviño, L. K., & Harrison, D. A. (2005). Ethical leadership: A social learning perspective for construct development and testing. *Organizational Behavior and Human Decision Processes, 97,* 117–134.

Cable, D. M., & Parsons, C. K. (2001). Socialization tactics and person-organization fit. *Personnel Psychology, 54,* 1–23.

Carlson, D. S., Kacmar, K. M., & Williams, L. J. (2000). Construction and initial validation of a multidimensional measure of work-family conflict. *Journal of Vocational Behavior, 56,* 249–276.

Carr, J. C., Pearson, A. W., Vest, M. J., & Boyar, S. L. (2006). Prior occupational experience, anticipatory socialization, and employee retention. *Journal of Management, 32,* 343–359.

Chan, D., & Schmitt, N. (2000). Interindividual differences in intraindividual changes in proactivity during organizational entry: A latent growth modeling approach to understanding newcomer adaptation. *Journal of Applied Psychology, 85,* 190–210.

Chang, J., Chang, W., & Jacobs, R. (2009). Relationship between participation in communities of practice and organizational socialization in the early careers of South Korean IT employees. *Human Resource Development International, 12,* 407–427.

Chao, G. T., O'Leary-Kelly, A. M., Wolf, S., Klein, H. J., & Gardner, P. D. (1994). Organizational socialization: Its content and consequences. *Journal of Applied Psychology, 79,* 730–743.

Chatman, J. A. (1991). Matching people and organizations: Selection and socialization in public accounting firms. *Administrative Science Quarterly, 36,* 459–484.

Chen, G. (2005). Newcomer adaptation in teams: Multilevel antecedents and outcomes. *Academy of Management Journal, 48,* 101–116.

Chen, G., & Klimoski, R. J. (2003). The impact of expectations on newcomer performance in teams as mediated by work characteristics, social exchanges, and empowerment. *Academy of Management Journal, 46,* 591–607.

Cooper-Thomas, H. D., van Vianen, A., & Anderson, N. (2004). Changes in person-organization fit: The impact of socialization tactics on perceived and actual P-O fit. *European Journal of Work and Organizational Psychology, 13,* 52–78.

Cordin, E., Rowan, L., Odgers, P., Barnes, A., & Redgate, R. (2008). $37 billion: Counting the cost of employee misunderstanding. *A white paper commissioned by Cognisco.* London: IDC.

Crant, J. M. (2000). Proactive behavior in organizations. *Journal of Management, 26,* 435–462.

Diener, E., Sapyta, J. J., & Suh, E. (1998). Subjective well-being is essential to well-being. *Psychological Inquiry, 9,* 33–37.

Erdogan, B., & Bauer, T. N. (2009). Perceived overqualification and its outcomes: The moderating role of empowerment. *Journal of Applied Psychology, 94,* 557–565.

Erdogan, B., Bauer, T. N., Peiro, J. M., & Truxillo, D. M. (2011). Overqualified employees: Making the best of a potentially bad situation for individuals and organizations. *Industrial and Organizational Psychology: Perspectives on Science and Practice, 4,* 215–232.

Erdogan, B., Bauer, T. N., Truxillo, D. M., & Mansfield, L. R. (in press). Whistle while you work: A review of the life satisfaction literature. *Journal of Management.*

Fan, J., & Wanous, J. P. (2008). Organizational and cultural entry: A new type of orientation program for multiple boundary crossings. *Journal of Applied Psychology, 93,* 1390–1400.

Fang, R., Duffy, M. K., & Shaw, J. D. (2011). The organizational socialization process: Review and development of a social capital model. *Journal of Management, 37,* 127–152.

Feldman, D. C. (1997). Socialization in an international context. *International Journal of Selection and Assessment, 5,* 1–8.

Feldman, D. C., & Brett, J. M. (1983). Coping with new jobs: A comparative study of new hires and job changers. *Academy of Management Journal, 26,* 258–272.

Ferris, G. R., Youngblood, S. A., & Yates, V. L. (1985). Personality, training performance, and withdrawal: A test of the person-group fit hypothesis for organizational newcomers. *Journal of Vocational Behavior, 27,* 377–388.

Fey, W. F. (1955). Acceptance by others and its relation to acceptance of self and others: A re-evaluation. *Journal of Abnormal and Social Psychology, 50,* 274–276.

Finkelstein, L. M., Kulas, J. T., & Dages, K. D. (2003). Age differences in proactive newcomer socialization strategies in two populations. *Journal of Business and Psychology, 17,* 473–502.

Fisher, C. D. (1985). Social support and adjustment to work: A longitudinal study. *Journal of Management, 11,* 39–53.

Fisher, C. D. (1986). Organizational socialization: An integrative review. In K. M. Rowland & G. R. Ferris (Eds.), *Research in personnel and human resources management: Vol. 4* (pp. 101–145). Greenwich, CT: JAI Press.

Fu, C. F., Shaffer, M. A., & Harrison, D. A. (2005). Proactive socialization, adjustment, and turnover: A study of self-initiated foreign employees. Paper presented at the Annual Meeting of the Academy of Management.

Fullar, J. B., Marler, L. E., & Hester, K. (2006). Promoting felt responsibility for constructive change and proactive behavior: Exploring aspects of and elaborated model of work design. *Journal of Organizational Behavior, 27,* 1089–1120.

Grebner, S., Elfering, A., Semmer, N. K., Kaiser-Probst, C., & Schlapbach, M. L. (2004). Stressful situations at work and private life among young workers: An event sampling approach. *Social Indicators Research, 67,* 11–49.

Griffin, A. E. C., Colella, A., & Goparaju, S. (2000). Newcomer and organizational socialization tactics: An interactionist perspective. *Human Resource Management Review, 10,* 453–474.

Gruman, J. A., Saks, A. M., & Zweig, D. L. (2006). Organizational socialization tactics and newcomer proactive behaviors: An integrative study. *Journal of Vocational Behavior, 69,* 90–104.

Hannah, D. R. (2007). An examination of the factors that influence whether newcomers protect or share secrets of their former employers. *Journal of Management Studies, 44,* 465–487.

Hansen, T., & Levine, J. M. (2009). Newcomers as change agents: Effects of newcomers' behavioral style and teams' performance optimism. *Social Influence, 4,* 46–61.

Hart, Z., & Miller, V. D. (2005). Context and message content during organizational socialization. *Human Communication Research, 31,* 295–309.

Haueter, J. A., Macan, T. H., & Winter, J. (2003). Measurement of newcomer socialization: Construct validation of a multidimensional scale. *Journal of Vocational Behavior, 63,* 20–39.

Herold, D. M., Fedor, D. B., Caldwell, S., & Liu, Y. (2008). The effects of transformational and change leadership on employees' commitment to a change: A multilevel study. *Journal of Applied Psychology, 93,* 346–357.

Jablin, F. M., & Kramer, M. W. (1998). Communication-related sense-making and adjustment during job transfers. *Management Communication Quarterly, 12,* 155–182.

Jones, G. R. (1986). Socialization tactics, self-efficacy, and newcomers' adjustments to organizations. *Academy of Management Journal, 29,* 262–279.

Kammeyer-Mueller, J. D., & Wanberg, C. R. (2003). Unwrapping the organizational entry process: Disentangling multiple antecedents and their pathways to adjustment. *Journal of Applied Psychology, 88,* 779–794.

Kammeyer-Mueller, J. D., Wanberg, C. R., Glomb, T. M., & Ahlburg, D. (2005). The role of temporal shifts in turnover processes: It's about time. *Journal of Applied Psychology, 90,* 644–658.

Kammeyer-Mueller, J. D., Simon, L. S., & Rich, B. L. (2012). The psychic cost of doing wrong: Ethical conflict, divestiture socialization, and emotional exhaustion. *Journal of Management, 38,* 784–808.

Kane, A. A., Argote, L., & Levine, J. M. (2005). Knowledge transfer between groups via personnel rotation: Effects of social identity and knowledge quality. *Organizational Behavior and Human Decision Processes, 96,* 56–71.

Kim, T.-Y., Cable, D. M., & Kim, S.-P. (2005). Socialization tactics, employee proactivity, and person-organization fit. *Journal of Applied Psychology, 90*, 232–241.

Klein, H. J., & Heuser, A. E. (2008). The learning of socialization content: A framework for researching orientating practices. *Research in Personnel and Human Resources Management* (Vol. 27, pp. 279–336). Greenwich, CT: JAI Press.

Klein, H. J., Polin, B., & Sutton, K. L. (2010). Effectively onboarding new employees. Annual Meeting of the Academy of Management. Montreal, Quebec.

Klein, H. J., & Weaver, N. A. (2000). The effectiveness of an organizational-level orientation training program in the socialization of new hires. *Personnel Psychology, 53*, 47–66.

Kristof, A. L. (1996). Person-organization fit: An integrative review of its conceptualizations, measurement, and implications. *Personnel Psychology, 49*, 1–49.

Kristof, A. K., Zimmerman, R. D., & Johnson, E. C. (2005). Consequences of individuals' fit at work: A meta-analysis of person-job, person-organization, and person-group, and person-supervisor fit. *Personnel Psychology, 58*, 281–342.

Laker, D. R., & Steffy, B. D. (1995). The impact of alternative socialization tactics on self-managing behavior and organizational commitment. *Journal of Social Behavior and Personality, 10*, 645–660.

Lee, C. H. (2005). A study of underemployment among self-initiated expatriates. *Journal of World Business, 40*, 172–187.

Louis, M. R. (1980). Surprise and sense making: What newcomers experience in entering unfamiliar organizational settings. *Administrative Science Quarterly, 25*, 226–251.

Louis, M. R., Posner, B. Z., & Powell, G. (1983). The availability and helpfulness of socialization practices. *Personnel Psychology, 36*, 857–866.

Maier, G. W., & Brunstein, J. C. (2001). The role of personal work goals in newcomers' job satisfaction and organizational commitment: A longitudinal analysis. *Journal of Applied Psychology, 86*, 1034–1042.

Major, D. A., & Kozlowski, S. W. J. (1997). Newcomer information seeking: Individual and contextual influences. *International Journal of Selection and Assessment, 5*, 16–28.

Major, D. A., Kozlowski, S. W. J., Chao, G. T., & Gardner, P. D. (1995). A longitudinal investigation of newcomer expectations, early socialization outcomes, and the moderating effects of role development factors. *Journal of Applied Psychology, 80*, 418–431.

Major, D. A., Turner, J. E., & Fletcher, T. D. (2006). Linking proactive personality and the Big Five to motivation to learn and developmental activity. *Journal of Applied Psychology, 91*, 927–935.

McNatt, D. B., & Judge, T. A. (2008). Self-efficacy intervention, job attitudes, and turnover: A field experiment with employees in role transition. *Human Relations, 61*, 783–810.

Menguc, B., Han, S. L., & Auh, S. (2007). A test of a model of new salespeople's socialization and adjustment in a collectivist culture. *Journal of Personal Selling and Sales Management, 27*, 149–167.

Molleman, E., & Van der Vegt, G. S. (2007). The performance evaluation of novices: The importance of competence in special work activity clusters. *Journal of Occupational and Organizational Psychology, 80*, 459–478.

Morrison, E. W. (1993a). Longitudinal study of the effects of information seeking on newcomer socialization. *Journal of Applied Psychology, 78*, 173–183.

Morrison, E. W. (1993b). Newcomer information seeking: Exploring types, modes, sources, and outcomes. *Academy of Management Journal, 36*, 557–589.

Morrison, E. W., & Bies, R. J. (1991). Impression management in the feedback-seeking process: A literature review and research agenda. *Academy of Management Review, 16*, 522–541.

O'Reilly, C. A., & Caldwell, D. F. (1981). The commitment and job tenure of new employees: Some evidence of postdecisional justification. *Administrative Science Quarterly, 26*, 597–616.

Ostroff, C., & Kozlowski, S. W. J. (1992). Organizational socialization as a learning process: The role of information acquisition. *Personnel Psychology, 45*, 849–874.

Ostroff, C., & Kozlowski, S. W. J. (1993). The role of mentoring in the information gathering processes of newcomers during early organizational socialization. *Journal of Vocational Behavior, 42*, 170–183.

Parker, S. K., & Collins, C. G. (2010). Taking stock: Integrating and differentiating multiple proactive behaviors. *Journal of Management, 36*, 633–662.

Payne, S. C., Culbertson, S. S., Boswell, W. R., & Barger, E. J. (2008). Newcomer psychological contracts and employee socialization activities: Does perceived balance in obligations matter? *Journal of Vocational Behavior, 73*, 465–472.

Pinder, C. C., & Schroeder, K. G. (1987). Time to proficiency following job transfers. *Academy of Management Journal, 30*, 336–353.

Reichers, A. E. (1987). An interactionist perspective on newcomer socialization rates. *Academy of Management Review, 12*, 278–287.

Rizzo, J. R., House, R. J., & Lirtzman, S. I. (1970). Role conflict and ambiguity in complex organizations. *Administrative Science Quarterly, 15*, 150–163.

Saks, A. M. (1994). Moderating effects of self-efficacy for the relationship between training method and anxiety and stress reactions of newcomers. *Journal of Organizational Behavior, 15*, 639–654.

Saks, A. M. (1995). Longitudinal field investigation of the moderating and mediating effects of self-efficacy on the relationship between training and newcomer adjustment. *Journal of Applied Psychology, 80*, 211–225.

Saks, A. M., & Ashforth, B. E. (1996). Proactive socialization and behavioral self-management. *Journal of Vocational Behavior, 48*, 301–323.

Saks, A. M., & Ashforth, B. E. (1997a). Socialization tactics and newcomer information acquisition. *International Journal of Selection and Assessment, 5*, 48–61.

Saks, A. M., & Ashforth, B. E. (1997b). Organizational socialization: Making sense of past and present as a prologue for the future. *Journal of Vocational Behavior, 51*, 234–279.

Saks, A. M., & Ashforth, B. E. (2000). The role of dispositions, entry stressors, and behavioral plasticity theory in predicting newcomers' adjustment to work. *Journal of Organizational Behavior, 21*, 43–62.

Saks, A. M., Gruman, J. A., & Cooper-Thomas, H. (2011). The neglected role of proactive behavior and outcomes in newcomer socialization. *Journal of Vocational Behavior, 79*, 36–46.

Saks, A. M., Uggerslev, K. L., & Fassina, N. E. (2007). Socialization tactics and newcomer adjustment: A meta-analytic review and test of a model. *Journal of Vocational Behavior, 70*, 413–446.

Schein, E. H. (1968). Organizational socialization and the profession of management. *Industrial Management Review, 9*, 1–16.

Simon, L. S., Judge, T. A., & Halvorsen-Ganepola, M. D. K. (2010). In good company? A multi-study, multi-level investigation of the effects of coworker relationships on employee well-being. *Journal of Vocational Behavior, 76*, 534–546.

Slaughter, J. E., & Zickar, M. J. (2006). A new look at the role of insiders in the newcomer socialization process. *Group & Organization Management, 31*, 264–290.

Tait, M., Padgett, M. Y., & Baldwin, T. T. (1989). Job and life satisfaction: A reevaluation of the strength of the relationship and gender effects as a function of the date of the study. *Journal of Applied Psychology, 74*, 502–507.

Taormina, R. J. (1994). The organizational socialization inventory. *International Journal of Selection and Assessment, 2*, 133–145.

Taormina, R. J. (2004). Convergent validation of two measures of organizational socialization. *International Journal of Human Resource Management, 15*, 76–94.

Van Maanen, J., & Schein, E. H. (1979). Toward a theory of organizational socialization. In B. M. Staw (Ed.), *Research in Organizational Behavior*, (Vol. 1, pp. 209–264). Greenwich, CT: JAI Press.

Wanberg, C. R., Glomb, T. M., Song, Z., & Sorenson, S. (2005). Job search persistence during unemployment: A 10-wave longitudinal study. *Journal of Applied Psychology, 90*, 411–430.

Wanberg, C. R., & Kammeyer-Mueller, J. D. (2000). Predictors and outcomes of proactivity in the socialization process. *Journal of Applied Psychology, 85*, 373–385.

Wanberg, C. R., Kanfer, R., & Banas, J. T. (2000). Predictors and outcomes of networking intensity among unemployed job seekers. *Journal of Applied Psychology, 85*, 491–503.

Wang, M., Zhan, Y., McCune, E. A., & Truxillo, D. M. (2011). Understanding newcomers' adaptability and work-related outcomes: Testing the mediating roles of perceived P-E fit variables. *Personnel Psychology*, 64, 163–189.

Wanous, J. P. (1992). *Organizational entry: Recruitment, selection, orientation, and socialization of newcomers*. Reading, MA: Addison-Wesley.

Watkins, M. (2003). *The first 90 days: Critical success strategies for new leaders at all levels*. Boston, MA: Harvard Business Press.

Waung, M. (1995). The effects of self-regulatory coping orientation on newcomer adjustment and job survival. *Personnel Psychology, 48*, 633–650.

Wesson, M. J., & Gogus, C. I. (2005). Shaking hands with a computer: An examination of two methods of organizational newcomer orientation. *Journal of Applied Psychology, 90*, 1018–1026.

Yan, E., Kwok, T., Tang, C., & Ho, F. (2007). Factors associated with life satisfaction of personal care workers delivering dementia care in day care centers. *Social Work in Health Care, 46*, 37–45.

Zimmerman, R. D. (2008). Understanding the impact of personality traits on individuals' turnover decisions: A meta-analytic path model. *Personnel Psychology, 61*, 309–348.

PART 3

Organizational Context, Systems, and Tactics

The Odd One Out: How Newcomers Who Are Different Become Adjusted

Charlice Hurst, John Kammeyer-Mueller, *and* Beth Livingston

Abstract

Contemporary work groups and organizations are diverse in many ways, but comparatively little research has examined how diversity will impact the process of socialization for newcomers. In this chapter we consider how theory and research on socialization, newcomer adjustment, relational demography, and diversity can be integrated to arrive at a model of how newcomers who are "different" in some way from their coworkers either will or will not come to be functioning members of the social group. We propose relationships based on prior research, which differentiated diversity based on separation, variety, and disparity (Harrison & Klein, 2007). Our discussion of the issues faced by newcomers who are different from their coworkers will show that these three forms of diversity have distinct relationships with important socialization processes and outcomes. Additionally, we discuss several variables at the individual and situational levels of analysis that we think will moderate the influence of diversity on individual and interpersonal socialization and adjustment processes.

Key Words: employee socialization, diversity, demography, social identity, adjustment

The Odd One Out: How Newcomers Who Are Different Become Adjusted

Imagine you're just starting a new job and you find that nobody you work with is like you. You're the only woman or man in your workgroup, everyone else is older or younger than you are, people have much more or much less education than you do, or maybe everyone has a very different set of values and priorities than you do. There are certainly drawbacks to being different from your new coworkers. Trying to adjust to a new job is difficult enough as it is, but now you face an additional set of challenges. You not only need to learn how to complete your work tasks, you also have to establish yourself in an environment that is socially unfamiliar. The way your coworkers communicate may be difficult for you to understand, and every encounter could drive home the sense that you are an outsider. At the same time, because your perspective is different from that of your coworkers, you bring new

experiences and insights to bear. You may also have access to resources that they do not. The diversity of the new team could be a source of creative strength and innovation that would not have been recognized in a more homogeneous team. However, for these benefits to be realized, you—the newcomer—have to become successfully integrated into the team.

Now consider the opposite end of the continuum. Your new workplace may be unfamiliar but your coworkers are all about the same age as you are, graduated from the same university you attended, have the same interests, and are just as committed to the job as you are. In this case you find communication easy, your perspective is valued, and you rapidly feel socially accepted. Again, there are drawbacks. Your skills, abilities, and perspective are likely redundant with other members of the group and, as such, you are less likely to offer fresh ideas or produce real change in the way that the group functions, even when change is needed. The advantages of surface similarities might also fade quickly if there are more fundamental differences in the personalities and values of those who make up the team.

These two contrasting examples illustrate the primary argument we make in this chapter: the consequences of diversity for socialization can be profound and complex. Our particular focus is on what happens when there is a discrepancy between a newcomer and his or her workgroup. Because there have been many excellent reviews of the literature on employee diversity in recent years (e.g., Jackson, Joshi, & Erhardt, 2003; van Knippenberg & Schippers, 2007; Williams & O'Reilly, 1998), it will not be our goal here to provide an exhaustive review of this literature. Rather, we wish to focus our attention on those issues and processes that are likely to be especially salient for individuals during the process of socialization and adjustment.

There are numerous reasons for increased attention to the period of initial adjustment in diversity research. For example, top management team demographic effects are stronger for teams made up of more comparative newcomers (Carpenter, 2002). Another study found that race and tenure diversity is especially strongly related to group conflicts in more recently formed groups (Pelled, Eisenhardt, & Xin, 1999). Group norms for lower cooperation among demographically diverse teams are more pronounced among recently formed groups (Chatman & Flynn, 2001). Some forms of diversity are positively related to satisfaction in relatively new groups, whereas the relationship between demographic diversity and satisfaction is much weaker in groups with higher longevity (Schippers, Den Hartog, Koopman, & Wienk, 2003). In sum, although some studies fail to find that time reduces the impact of diversity on attitudes and behavior (e.g., Vecchio & Bullis, 2001), most evidence suggests that diversity is especially salient among individuals who are just getting to know one another.

Figure 7.1 provides a conceptual framework that illustrates our ideas about the impact of diversity on the process of socialization and adjustment for newcomers. Socialization is the process by which the organization and workgroup provide information and resources to newcomers to facilitate adjustment, whereas adjustment is the personal process of establishing oneself as a functioning member of the job, group, and organization. Moving from left to right, we delineate various diversity parameters that might affect a newcomer's perceptions of being different from coworkers. These variables include both demographic or surface characteristics as well as less visible, but potentially more significant, deep characteristics like personality and values (Harrison, Price, & Bell, 1998; Harrison, Price, Gavin, & Florey, 2002). Based on these initial status variables, a series of processes are set in motion that will influence how a newcomer adjusts to the workplace. Adjustment is indicated by a combination of factors, including social acceptance, cohesion, commitment to the organization and workgroup, routine task performance, citizenship behavior, and creative performance. Several important moderators of these processes are also highlighted in the figure. We hope that this figure serves as both a synthesis of various research streams regarding diversity, socialization, and relationships and a starting point for researchers looking to contribute to the literature on diversity and socialization.

Newcomer Diversity and Differences

The construct of diversity is central to our discussion, so we take our starting point from recent theoretical research on the meaning of diversity. Some researchers have noted that diversity can be a "double-edged sword" that can either lead to collaborative learning and development or conflict and exclusion (Williams & O'Reilly, 1998). Theory on diversity as an aggregate construct cannot readily identify which of these tendencies will dominate. Empirically, much research on the topic of diversity has found either mixed results or null results, with various forms of diversity leading to different consequences.

Following from these issues, researchers have begun to ask what it means to say that a group is diverse. Several ways to conceptualize diversity have arisen, including separation (i.e., "differences in position or opinion among group members"), variety (i.e., "differences in kind, source, or category of relevant knowledge or experience among unit members"), and disparity (i.e., "differences in proportion of socially valued assets or resources help among unit members"; Harrison & Klein, 2007, p. 1203). Separation diversity is primarily concerned with differences in underlying values or opinions among group members, and will be at its highest level for a newcomer if he or she has values or opinions that are completely different from other members of the workgroup. Variety diversity is concerned with differences in knowledge, skills, and abilities, and will be highest for a newcomer who has a very different disciplinary or functional background from other members of the new workgroup or has considerably

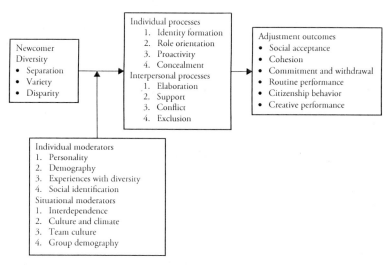

Figure 7.1 A Model of Socialization and Diversity.

less or more experience. Finally, disparity diversity is primarily concerned with differences in hierarchical levels or resources, as might be found by a newcomer who is either higher or lower ranking than his or her new coworkers or who is a member of a stigmatized demographic group.

Diversity of a newcomer vís a vís the remainder of the workgroup can take any of these forms, depending on the newcomer characteristic under consideration. For example, if a newcomer is the only woman in her workgroup she might have distinct opinions from the group (separation diversity), might have knowledge regarding women's issues not possessed by other group members (variety diversity), or might be seen as lower status because of gender stereotypes (disparity diversity). Because of these differences, demography can have subtle and even contradictory influences on newcomer adjustment.

Because each form of diversity has different implications for newcomers, throughout our review we endeavor to specify how each form of diversity will affect outcomes for the newcomer, the workgroup, and the organization.

Diversity and Socialization Processes

We now move to the next portion of Figure 7.1 in an attempt to explain the most significant socialization or adjustment processes that will likely be affected by diversity. The literature is replete with references to a number of processes that explain and characterize the relationships among individuals and coworkers. Drawing from the socialization, relationships and groups, and teams literatures, we have identified and classified those processes we posit to be outcomes of diversity as either *individual* (occurring within the newcomer him/herself) or *interpersonal* (occurring between newcomers and existing employees). In the following section, as a means of stimulating future research in this area, we develop our expectations for the relationships between diversity and newcomer socialization processes. Table 7.1 provides a summary of the relationships we expect to observe among categories of diversity and socialization processes.

Individual Processes

There are many individual processes within the newcomer that may shape adjustment; we identify four that we believe are most important for explaining newcomer socialization and adjustment. These processes include identity formation, the development of a role orientation, proactive socialization efforts, and concealing stigmatized identities.

IDENTITY FORMATION

A social identity is a personal mental construct representing who you consider yourself to be in a specific context (Tajfel & Turner, 1986). People have multiple social identities in any situation, including their definitions of themselves as a newcomer or an insider, a man or a woman, a member of a particular racioethnic group, disabled or not disabled, old or young, college educated or high school graduate, extroverted or introverted, and so on. The key question for social identity theory is: Which social identity will be activated in a given situation, and how will that identity influence behavior?

Table 7.1 Summary of Proposed Relationships between Types of Diversity and Socialization Processes

Socialization Processes	Classification of Diversity			
	Separation	Variety	Higher Status Disparity	Lower Status Disparity
Identity formation: Newcomers must create new identities as part of an organization or workgroup	maintain individual identity	maintain individual identity	maintain individual identity	create group identity
Role innovation: Newcomers enter existing work roles and must decide whether to change those roles or accept them as-is	increased	increased	increased	decreased
Proactivity: Newcomers must decide whether to seek out information about their new positions/jobs actively	decreased	increased	decreased	decreased
Concealment: Newcomers might hide a component of their identity from their new coworkers	concealment	disclosure	concealment	concealment
Elaboration: Newcomers and existing group members must communicate and share information by increasing discussion	low	high	low	low
Support: Existing group members may or may not provide social support to newcomers	decreased	increased	decreased	decreased
Conflict: Newcomers and existing group members might have negative interactions about tasks or personal issues	relational	task	relational	none
Exclusion: Existing group members may seek to exclude newcomers from group activities	exclusion	inclusion	inclusion	exclusion

When newcomers enter organizations they are faced with the task of creating a new identity as a group and organizational member, which must coexist with their existing social identities. Most research on identify formation and diversity has been from the perspective of demographic differences. From this point of view, because newcomers from a distinct demographic category do not share certain social and cultural characteristics with established group members, we propose that they may have more difficulty developing a social identity that includes the new workgroup (Chattopadhyay, George, & Lawrence, 2004; Jackson et al., 1993; McKay & Avery, 2006).

Separation diversity is perhaps the strongest influence on social identification. Newcomers who share the values of their coworkers have higher levels of commitment to the workgroup (Cable & DeRue, 2002; Cable & Edwards, 2004). If a newcomer's separation diversity is based on deep-level differences of opinion, the identity formation process may start off rather smoothly but undergo a disruption once it becomes apparent that the newcomer differs significantly in values and beliefs from the group. On the other hand, it is likely that a demographically dissimilar newcomer who got off to a rocky start might begin to increase identification with the group later in the socialization process as commonalities of perspective are revealed (i.e., when separation diversity is low).

Variety diversity may in some ways facilitate performance while still preventing newcomers from forming an identity as part of the new workgroup.

Theory suggests that an engineer moving into a group primarily made of marketing executives may maintain his or her allegiance to his or her own functional area, and continue to see himself or herself as a comparative outsider. Even if the group is collaborating and cooperating effectively, the differences in language and customs between different functional specializations may prevent the newcomer from identifying with the new workgroup.

Social identity theory is also concerned with the effects of status, which links social identity to the notion of disparity diversity. Those who possess positively distinctive social identities (like being the only member of a workgroup having an advanced degree) will have quite different identity formation experiences relative to those who possess negatively distinctive social identities (like being the only member of the workgroup with a diagnosed mental illness or being the only female in a group otherwise composed of men). We believe disparity diversity is likely to be a strong inhibitor of some forms of social identification. Individuals who come from comparatively higher-status groups will be reluctant to form a social identity that includes members of lower-status groups. As an example, an individual with a very high level of education will take steps to distance himself or herself from a less educated set of new colleagues. It might also be the case that individuals who see themselves as belonging to higher-status demographic groups will be reluctant to associate themselves with colleagues who belong to lower-status demographic groups.

On the other hand, individuals from lower-status groups might be more willing to form identities that include existing members if those members are from comparatively higher status groups. Attempts at upward mobility might facilitate the identity formation process. For instance, an individual from a lower socioeconomic group might find himself or herself a member of a group of coworkers who are all of a higher socioeconomic status. This person might be more eager to create a collective identity with these coworkers than if the situation were reversed.

ROLE INNOVATION

Prior research has emphasized the degree to which a newcomer either accepts a preordained role or innovates and changes the role to shape his or her unique preferences (e.g., Jones, 1983; Van Maanen & Schein, 1979). The ways in which a newcomer differs from his or her coworkers will affect how

innovative he or she becomes. However, research has yet to develop propositions in this regard.

We propose that a newcomer who has higher levels of separation diversity relative to the existing group is likely to engage in greater levels of role innovation than would newcomers with less separation diversity. Those who have different values from the existing workgroup may seek to change the nature of the work role. When one feels separate from one's new coworkers, it is more difficult to accept an assigned role as-is, without change or challenge. As mentioned above, the identity formation process is much more difficult when newcomers experience separation diversity, and the lack of an easily formed collective identity can also hinder the acceptance of an existing role, prompting innovation.

Variety diversity is also likely to increase role innovation, as newcomers who have different skills and abilities will see a need to adjust the work role to fit his or her preestablished work style. For instance, if a group of marketers is joined by a newcomer from a finance background, the newcomer may use his or her unique knowledge of financial statements and valuation of stock offerings as an input into how the group works. Thus, rather than having a role that emphasizes advertising and market share principles, the role (i.e., the core responsibilities and activities of the job) will have to be modified to match a "financial" role. A Hispanic individual brought into a marketing team that has no other Hispanics may innovate in terms of his or her role in a way that reflects his or her unique knowledge of Hispanic culture and the market among Hispanics. The role will need to be changed to accommodate these differences.

Finally, we believe disparity diversity will increase role innovation if the newcomer has a higher level of status, and will decrease role innovation if the newcomer has a lower level of status. Theories of adaptation suggest that when a dominant culture comes into contact with a minority culture, the dominant culture tends to be adopted (Berry, 1997). Newcomers who have more power and authority than the existing workgroup will have greater leverage with which to modify the work role. A graduate from an elite law school may have greater control over adjusting his or her new role if the existing workgroup consists of lawyers who graduated from second-tier schools. Conversely, newcomers who are less esteemed than the existing group members will have less ability to change the work role. If the prior example were flipped (such that the newcomer was from a second-tier school), there may be greater pressure to accept the ordained role. The stigma attached to a group of lower status will make it less likely that a member of such a group will seek to "rock the boat" and draw more attention to his or her difference from the rest of the group. Similarly, those from lower-status demographic groups may also be more likely to capitulate to the existing group's norms in an effort to avoid conflicts with those who have more social power.

NEWCOMER PROACTIVITY

The proactive adjustment literature has demonstrated that newcomers cannot receive all the information they need to do their jobs and become socially adjusted unless they are participants in the process. Proactive newcomers learn to steer clear of social norm violations and increase their social acceptance (Miller & Jablin, 1991). With that said, when newcomers differ from the existing workgroup, proactive socialization may be less likely to occur or may be less effective.

The social relationships literature suggests that because asking for help is a process of disclosing ignorance to others, newcomers may react to separation diversity by being less actively engaged in the socialization process. For those who already have different values from their coworkers, the costs of these proactive behaviors may be too high (e.g., Morrison & Vancouver, 2000). Newcomers may worry about the impression that will be made if they engage in proactive socialization behaviors; asking questions about what behavior is appropriate or how to do your work is an admission of ignorance that might be seen as especially problematic in relationships that are new and/or fraught with uncertainty. Therefore, we think that newcomers who have separation diversity from coworkers will engage in less proactive socialization.

Variety-based diversity in experiences, knowledge, and ability could also affect the level of proactivity required to become socialized. A newcomer's main effort at work involves increasing knowledge of how to do his/her work tasks (Morrison, 1993). The less expertise the newcomer has upon entry into the group, the more proactive effort is needed to learn the requirements of the role. Such effort could involve interaction with other group members and facilitate the development of social relationships and trust; however, the relationships formed might exaggerate status differences between the newcomer and the group members on whose expertise she relies (van der Vegt, Bunderson, & Oosterhoff, 2006). In addition, there is evidence that the less expert a group member appears, the less willing are more expert group members to aid that person, which could frustrate the newcomer's efforts at socialization (van der Vegt, Bunderson, & Oosterhoff, 2006). On the other hand, newcomers with a higher level of expertise than other group members might have less need to be proactive. Rather, existing group members will seek them out for help. This same relationship might be observed when variety diversity exists in terms of functional domain. For instance, when a person whose background is in marketing joins a group of accountants or lawyers, he or she might be more proactive in seeking out information to learn how the job works because of the differences in types of knowledge the newcomer brings to the table.

We also believe disparity diversity may inhibit proactivity. A high-status individual becoming acclimated to a new group of comparatively lower status may be especially reluctant to ask for assistance because of the stigma associated with low-status groups. Proactively seeking to reduce uncertainty by asking others for guidance is less appealing when those who can help are of a lower status. Alternatively, although it may seem that an individual of lower social status might feel more comfortable asking a comparatively high-status group member for assistance, the lack of trust associated with being a newcomer to a disparate group may make lower-status newcomers more wary of signaling their lower status by admitting a lack of knowledge or understanding.

This sense of vulnerability may be heightened if the newcomer is a member of a stigmatized group. Sekaquaptewa et al. (2007) found that African-American women who were the only ones of their race in all-female groups tended to be concerned that their performance would reflect on African Americans as a whole. Anxiety that asking questions could reflect poorly not only on oneself but on one's social group could deter a newcomer from doing so. Thus, for newcomers who are different, proactivity may entail not only the standard set of behaviors assumed to be important for everyone, but also active management of identity cues that could activate strong stereotypes (Roberts, 2005).

CONCEALMENT

The final individual process we propose as a direction for future research in the socialization literature is concealment. In many cases, social identities are not readily observable to outsiders. Researchers call these concealable (Crocker, Major,

& Steele, 1998)—or invisible (Clair, Beatty, & MacLean, 2005)—identities. We expect that those who are different from their coworkers in ways that are not immediately apparent may make affirmative efforts to conceal their status, especially if the status is negatively distinctive. Examples of concealable, potentially stigmatized identities include social class, sexual orientation, membership in religious groups or political movements not supported by coworkers, a history of mental illness, a criminal record, or a history of addiction. In some cases, there are also situationally specific or context-dependent stigmatizing identities, such as one's lack of certain knowledge or experience that is held by other members of the group. Because "stigma" refers to a lower position in a hierarchy of status and resource access, discussion of diversity and concealment necessarily involves disparity diversity.

When a person has an invisible social identity, they face a choice of whether to conceal and "pass" as being part of the majority or to reveal their invisible identity and run the risk of being socially rejected (Clair, Beatty, & MacLean, 2005). If a stigmatized identity is concealed, it can cause internal stress for the newcomer (Pachankis, 2007; Ragins, Singh & Cornwell, 2007), especially if being accepted requires concealment. Those who spend much of their time pretending not to belong to a stigmatized group will begin to live in fear of being discovered (Quinn & Chaudoir, 2009). Individuals who conceal can become disengaged (DeJordy, 2008), negatively affecting adjustment. Furthermore, hiding a stigmatized identity can make one feel inauthentic (Shelton, Richeson & Salvatore, 2005), and authenticity is also important for individuals' adjustment (Erickson, 1995). Even if a person is able to gain social acceptance by concealing an identity, the person will not feel like she has really been accepted. In some cases the decision to pass as part of the majority is not made consciously, but rather arises because everyone assumes the new employee is just like them and the newcomer comes to feel that it would be inopportune, even dangerous, to correct them.

Interpersonal Processes

While individual processes shape the newcomer's experience in powerful ways, because *socialization* is inherently social, interpersonal processes are also likely to explain the relationship between diversity and socialization. Below we describe how different types of diversity can impact how newcomers communicate with existing group members, how they manage conflict and seek out support, and whether they are excluded from social interaction.

ELABORATION

The categorization–elaboration model (CEM) proposes that, in contrast to the largely negative effects of social identity differences on group performance, diverse groups are more likely to engage in information elaboration processes that will improve performance (van Knippenberg, De Dreu, & Homan, 2004). These elaboration processes involve increased discussion and sharing of information that arises from diverse perspectives; however, different types of diversity might affect elaboration and communication in different ways.

The idea that diversity can lead to reduced communication has primarily been assessed in separation-type terms such as *culture* and *personality* (Joshi, 2006). Important precursors to effective relationships, such as perspective-taking and empathy, are likely to be attenuated due to separation diversity (Williams, Parker, & Turner, 2007) because social identities are not shared and trust is not present in the new relationship. In general, people with common backgrounds often have similar reference points, interests, and attitudes (e.g., Joshi, Dencker, Franz, & Martocchio, 2010). Thus, our theoretical model suggests that group members who share an important social identity may develop patterns of informal communication that result in increased elaboration. Discussing issues that are critical to group performance and creativity will not be as likely to occur when newcomers differ from their coworkers in ways that indicate separation diversity.

When the variety of perspectives within a group leads to more discussion and consideration of issues in an attempt to achieve integration, the net result is more thorough and elaborate processing of information. This can help to facilitate problem solving (Tjosvold & Poon, 1998), information gathering from coworkers within an organization (Herek, 1996), and knowledge sharing (Cummings, 2004). If newcomers differ from their coworkers in terms of experiences and background (i.e., there are a variety of different views), they may therefore increase communication and information elaboration in order to learn how to complete their job satisfactorily, allowing them to have more of the sort of interactions that build up relationships over time. Therefore, we anticipate that variety diversity will increase elaboration in the socialization process.

On the other hand, we expect that disparity diversity will reduce elaboration and communication processes because of the status differential between a high-status newcomer and his/her lower-status coworkers (or vice versa). Elaboration will be more likely when there is a shared comfort level among coworkers, and trust will be especially low when the status of the newcomer and existing members are different from one another. High-status newcomers are likely to not feel like they have to discuss various work-related problems with people from lower status, or stigmatized, groups, and low-status newcomers added to higher-status groups are likely to feel increased pressure to not draw attention to their lower or stigmatized status, and thus reduce their efforts to communicate and participate in information elaboration. In this case, the desire to reduce uncertainty about one's job may be trumped by a lack of trust that exists between individuals with stigmatized identities and those without such stigma.

SUPPORT

Social support is a crucial variable in reducing stress, as shown in numerous studies (e.g., Viswesvaran, Sanchez, & Fisher, 1999), so having supportive coworkers is an important part of adjustment for newcomers. Recent research confirms that a low level of social support from established organizational members is associated with lower levels of several adjustment-related variables (Kammeyer-Mueller, Wanberg, Song, & Rubenstein, 2010). Social support can take a variety of forms that are crucial to organizational newcomers, including assistance in performing work tasks, advice on how to perform better, and general social acceptance.

Dissimilar newcomers may face a "double-whammy" regarding social support. Because dissimilarity tends to reduce liking (Tsui & O'Reilly, 1989), and we seek out similar others for our support networks (Ibarra, 1992), they are simultaneously more likely to be disliked by their coworkers (and dislike them in return) and to have weaker social support networks because of the lack of similarity they encounter. This will be most true when there is considerable separation diversity relative to the group, since perception of shared values and goals is especially likely to lead to frequent interactions which provide opportunities for support (Wellman & Wortley, 1990). In sum, we anticipate finding that dissimilarity decreases social support.

Our model proposes that variety diversity is likely to result in increased support for newcomers. When an employee joins a workgroup and has different skills and experiences from his/her new coworkers, the newcomer is more likely to be seen as an asset to the existing workgroup and a sense of interdependence may be fostered. For instance, if a group of individuals with experience in marketing is joined by a newcomer who has copious sales experience, that newcomer will be seen as adding value to the group. Support will be offered to this newcomer in order to foster a greater feeling of interdependence with which the group can solve problems and create solutions. Variety diversity in functional background and experience might also indicate that a newcomer will not have had the same background or experiences as the existing group and will thus need more support in order to integrate well into the workgroup.

Individuals who enter the group in a status disparity may experience less social support, depending on where they fall relative to the rest of the group. We expect that individuals who are low status, like interns, recent labor market entrants, or those from lower-status demographic groups may receive less help and assistance from higher-status coworkers because they will wish to avoid associating and developing ties with individuals who are of low status. At the opposite end of the spectrum, we anticipate that there may not be much help provided to higher-level individuals (e.g., those entering into leadership roles in a group) because they are supposed to be in charge and know how everything works.

CONFLICT

Conflict is a group-level process that has been discussed for many years as an outcome of all forms of diversity. Pelled (1996) first described conflict as resulting from differences, such that diversity would lead to either substantive (also called *task*) or affective (also called *relationship*) conflict. Task-based conflicts involve decisions about how and when to perform certain tasks, which goals should be pursued, and how decisions should be made. Relationship conflicts, on the other hand, are based on anger, distrust, fear, and other negative affective states. Demographic differences are expected to lead to more affective conflict (Pelled, Eisenhardt & Xin, 1999; Mohammed & Angell, 2004), while task-related differences in tenure and experience influence task conflict (Jehn, Northcraft & Neale, 1999). Although socialization researchers have seldom addressed conflicts during the socialization process, the possibility of conflict arising due to diversity seems strong.

Separation diversity can increase relationship conflict for a number of reasons. One stream of thought suggests that because most separation diversity in demographic or value-based characteristics is unrelated to methods of task performance, it is more likely to lead to relationship conflict (Pelled, 1996). Such conflict might arise as either the newcomer or the established group members simply fail to recognize and understand differences in interpersonal characteristics. Newcomers with very different values from the rest of the group, for example, might not question how the tasks of the group are to be done, but rather, feel suspicious of the motives of other group members. Social identity theory also suggests that newcomers who are different will see the established group as a threat, leading to negative affective relationships.

Cognitive diversity, which is a form of variety-based diversity, has been shown to be related to increases in task conflict in a sample of healthcare managers making real decisions, with task conflict operationalized by the number of disagreements regarding the decision-making task (Olson, Parayitam, & Bao, 2007). One interesting illustration of the interaction between deep and surface level diversity found that differences of opinion (deep diversity) were tolerated and given consideration more fully in groups high in surface level diversity relative to groups that showed surface homogeneity (Phillips & Loyd, 2006). For this reason, we expect that variety diversity will increase task conflict in the socialization context as well.

The impact of disparity-based differences between the newcomer and the existing group on conflict are less straightforward, leading us to take an agnostic stance regarding the likely effects. If a newcomer comes from a higher status group than the existing members of the group, conflict might be minimized as the group turns to the new "leader" as a decision maker. At the same time, conflict also might be minimized if the newcomer is from a lower status group, as this individual might be expected to assume a subordinate role that does not invite his or her input into the decision-making processes. In fact, it might well be that the most conflict between newcomers and the existing group will occur when the newcomer is of an equivalent level to the other members of the group.

EXCLUSION

The last interpersonal process we describe is in some ways the opposite of social support: social exclusion. Exclusion of a newcomer infers that coworkers deliberately avoid establishing interactive or dependence relationships with a newcomer.

Unlike social support, which has been addressed in the socialization literature frequently, little work has examined the conditions under which newcomers will be deliberately excluded, and diversity theory may provide some clues as to when exclusion is most likely.

Both social identity and relationship science perspectives suggest that separation diversity can lead to isolation at work (Cox, 1994). When newcomers are different from their group members, they can face exclusion from both formal and information interactions at work (Brewer, 1996; Kramer, 1991). This exclusion can result in poor adjustment for newcomers as they struggle to navigate the complexities of a new workplace. When one is excluded from happy hours, informal conversations, or even formal meetings on process or policy, one is unlikely to feel committed and satisfied, and is also unlikely to experience career success at the level one would desire. Newcomers who are dissimilar from their coworkers in terms of age, education, and lifestyle are less likely to receive challenging assignments, which is a form of excluding them from opportunities for advancement (Kirchmeyer, 1995). Additionally, individuals who deviate from the norms of their existing in-group can experience devaluation and exclusion by their in-group members (Eidelman, Silvia, & Biernat, 2006). This suggests to us that individuals with invisible, stigmatized identities may feel even more pressured to conceal them from their group members, especially if they are otherwise similar to the group. As stated above, concealment can lead to feelings of inauthenticity and stress.

It is our expectation that variety diversity may lead to less exclusion of newcomers because their skills are needed by other members of the workgroup. Dependence between the established workgroup and the newcomer may make it harder to exclude the newcomer. At the same time, if social exclusion is present, variety-based diversity will fail to achieve positive outcomes.

Disparity diversity is likely to lead to exclusion from the existing workgroup of newcomers who are members of lower-status groups. As we noted earlier, lower-status newcomers are more likely to proactively endeavor to become a part of the workgroup, but such efforts may not be very successful if existing members of the workgroup are eager to avoid associating with lower-status individuals. Conversely, high-status newcomers are less likely to be excluded because their presence in the workgroup may enhance the reputation of the group.

Moderators of the Diversity-Adjustment Process

One of the recurring themes in the diversity literature has been the lack of main effects in many studies (e.g., Horwitz & Horwitz, 2007), leading researchers to develop more nuanced theories that take moderating variables into account. In this section we will propose moderators that are both personal and situational. As we will see later in the chapter, understanding these moderators may help in designing effective interventions to maximize the positive and minimize the negative socialization and adjustment consequences for newcomers who differ from members of the existing workgroup.

Personal Moderators

We first consider personal moderators, individual characteristics that we believe are likely to moderate the relationship between newcomer characteristics and adjustment. Five individual-level factors that we consider to be potentially important are (1) personality traits of the newcomer, (2) whether and how the newcomer is demographically different, (3) experience working in diverse groups and/or being in the minority, (4) prior experiences with discrimination, and (5) the newcomer's level of identification with those social categories on which they differ from most or all of the other group members.

PERSONALITY

There has been little research on the role of personality in either diversity or socialization processes, yet personality may affect how people respond to being the "different" newcomer. Of the "Big Five" traits, Wanberg and Kammeyer-Mueller (2000) found that extraversion and openness were the most important predictors of newcomer socialization. Extraversion was positively associated with relationship building, openness with positive framing, and both with feedback seeking. These behaviors predicted newcomers' adjustment and turnover 3 months into their new jobs. Thus, extraversion and openness appear to be assets to new employees in general, but they might be especially beneficial to different newcomers. Being of low status or having a different perspective relative to one's new group members might not be as intimidating for extraverted newcomers, who are more likely to be both assertive and socially skilled. They are also more likely to be motivated to build relationships with their group members in spite of differences.

Those who are higher in openness to experience might actually see having coworkers who are different in some significant way as an opportunity to learn about other people's ways of thinking and living. A highly open newcomer from a different discipline or function than his or her coworkers might be energized by the creative possibilities arising from working with people with expertise in areas unfamiliar to him or her. For him or her, variety disparity would be a strength. Likewise, a highly open recent college graduate assigned to a team of long-tenured individuals might view it as an excellent opportunity to learn from the experience of others and climb the learning curve more quickly (Kammeyer-Mueller, Livingston, & Liao, 2011), thus reaping benefits from disparity diversity.

Self-confidence, or core self-evaluation (Judge, Locke, & Durham, 1997), is another dispositional factor that we believe might influence the ease of socialization for diverse newcomers. Because they believe in their capabilities, newcomers with higher core self-evaluations may feel less threatened by asking questions that might display ignorance. They may also feel confident of being able to make a positive contribution to their new workgroup and of overcoming obstacles to doing so, including differences in status, opinion, or expertise. As a result, self-confident newcomers may be more proactive.

DEMOGRAPHIC DIFFERENCES

Although separation, variety, and disparity serve fairly well for categorizing various types of diversity, they cannot fully capture the ways in which particular forms of demographic differences will moderate the effects of the newcomer socialization process. The effects of each are likely to be influenced by the newcomer's gender or race, two of the most influential dimensions along which newcomers and existing group members may differ (Tsui, Egan, & O'Reilly, 1992; Sacco & Schmitt, 2005).

We cannot expect that simply knowing that a newcomer is demographically different from the rest of the workgroup is sufficient to understand how that person's difference will impact adjustment. We need to know how that person is different, how others interpret that difference, and the impact of that difference on the person's experiences, values, and preferences. The perspectives of members of different racial and gender groups and the stereotypes associated with their groups vary widely. For instance, a lone woman or a lone Chinese-American may diverge in perspective from the workgroup, but the content of their perspectives will likely differ. They are also likely to evoke different stereotypes on the part of existing group members (Fiske,

Cuddy, Glick, & Xu, 2002). Although we cannot explore the implications of the stereotypes unique to every demographic characteristic, stereotypes have in common a tendency to set the newcomer apart from the workgroup. Whether the newcomer is being associated with a positive stereotype (e.g., the Asian American who is expected to be polite, conscientious, and highly intelligent) or a negative one (e.g., the physically disabled individual whose competence is doubted implicitly, even at work that is entirely knowledge-based), the end result is that the individual is seen as an "other," as a member of an out-group distinct from the identity shared by the existing members of the group.

Because of their effects on newcomer perspective and on stereotyping by existing group members, demographic differences might exacerbate the effects of other types of diversity. The difficulties encountered by a newcomer who differs in expertise or status from the rest of the group may be heightened if that individual also differs in surface-level characteristics, particularly if his or her deeper-level diversity seems to confirm or conflict with stereotypes that existing group members hold of the newcomer's demographic group. For instance, a very young newcomer with a higher level of expertise than the other group members might have an even harder time adjusting because of the additional hurdle of establishing credibility, an obstacle that might not be faced by an older worker. On the other hand, a young newcomer who is a relative novice confirms the stereotype of younger people as lacking in useful knowledge and may also, as a result, face impediments to gaining credibility and establishing equitable relationships.

EXPERIENCES WITH DIVERSITY

Adjustment to a new group in which most members differ from the newcomer along one or more dimensions might be reached more quickly by those who have extensive prior experience working in settings where they are in the minority. Newcomers with such experience may be more familiar with the habits and customs of the dominant group. They may also have had more opportunity to reconcile their own social identity with their professional identity, rather than perceiving conflict between the two. Thus, in a new setting, they may expend less energy on managing identity conflicts (Baumeister, Shapiro, & Tice, 1985) and incorporate their role in the group into their identity with relative ease.

Prior experience might also have shaped the expectations a newcomer holds regarding treatment by members of other groups. The belief that she has experienced past discrimination might affect how a newcomer manages her social identities in the workplace. For instance, Kaiser, Vick, and Major (2006) found that women who chronically expected to be the target of sexist behavior were more sensitive to subliminal sexist cues. A woman new to a predominantly male group may be more wary if she has perceived sexism in previous work experiences, potentially inhibiting her willingness to engage in the customs on which the common identity of that group is based. She may also be mistrustful of her new colleagues, hindering relationship-building processes such as self-disclosure and the mutual provision of social support.

Certainly, the influence of perceived discrimination is not limited to women. Anyone who feels they have been discriminated against by members of a certain social group is likely to be more guarded if placed in a situation where they are expected to work closely with members of the offending group. Thus, newcomers' previous experiences with being in the minority can be beneficial to adjustment if they promoted that person's ability to adapt, but they may also be detrimental if they have made the newcomer feel uncertain of being treated equitably by new colleagues.

SOCIAL IDENTIFICATION

Although certain demographic differences, like race and gender, are usually salient to others, social identity is psychological. It is based on the extent to which one's self-concept is tied to a social group and the meaning and emotion attached to membership in that group (Tajfel, 1978). Newcomers who are strongly identified with a social group that is different from their new workgroup (i.e., when there is separation difference between the newcomer and the existing workgroup) may have more difficulty developing an identity in common with their new workgroup, especially when the former seems to conflict with the latter. When the new member belongs to a social category that is of higher status than other workgroup members (i.e., high disparity diversity), the newcomer may be particularly eager to maintain her distinctiveness.

Newcomers may seek ways to sustain their identity by affiliating with like others outside the new workgroup (Mehra, Kilduff, & Brass, 1998). This may take the form of joining an affinity group or reaching out to similar employees in other work units. It may also involve invoking symbols and practices related to one's identity group, a practice which may be comforting to the newcomer but may also signal that individual's outsider status more strongly to existing workgroup members. This signaling could be interpreted as a lack of interest in integrating and could make salient stereotypes of the newcomer's social group that influence the way workgroup members treat her (Kaiser & Pratt-Hyatt, 2009).

It is not clear that newcomers who identify strongly with their cultural group or functional area will necessarily fail to develop an identity in common with their workgroup. While some may take a defensive stance, seeking to protect a valued identity to the point of setting themselves apart from others who do not share that identity, others will seek to balance the goal of integrating with the new workgroup with the need to nurture other valued aspects of their identity. Still others, such as those who identify weakly with a difference that sets them apart from the group, may seek distance from that aspect of their social identity (Ethier & Deaux, 1994; Roberts, 2005), especially if membership in the new workgroup offers rewards (e.g., status, affiliation) that the individual's other social group memberships do not. Yet, distinctiveness may be difficult to erase. A newcomer brought into a group specifically because of his unique knowledge or experience might undermine his very reason for membership by attempting to divorce himself from his distinct identity. For instance, an engineer tasked with bringing technical expertise to a product design team formerly made up solely of marketing professionals may add less value if he attempts to downplay his identity as an engineer, perhaps offering fewer ideas or holding back offers of help. Such attempts to blend in could actually arouse rancor if they seem to weaken the team's effectiveness.

The multifaceted and dynamic nature of social identity makes it difficult to predict how a newcomer's level of social identity will affect socialization. How group members will react to a newcomer's efforts to maintain or minimize an identity likely hinges on several factors such as group members' stereotypes of the newcomer's social group and the extent to which the group's work is linked to the characteristics that make the newcomer unique. In the following section, we consider situational factors that may be relevant to how group members respond to behaviors arising from a newcomer's social identity.

Situational Moderators

It is important to recognize that the impact of any form of diversity is likely to be extremely dependent upon the context. Characteristics of the group's work may influence socialization via the breadth and depth of interaction, communication, knowledge, and creativity required to do the job well. The culture and climate of the group and organization should be influential as well.

INTERDEPENDENCE

Based on research findings that diversity has more salutary effects on teams with highly interdependent tasks and goals (Schippers, Den Hartog, Koopman, & Weink, 2003; Van der Vegt & Janssen, 2003), it seems that high interdependence holds the potential for faster integration of newcomers who are different. Interdependent tasks and goals increase the necessity of communication and make people more motivated to work with others they depend on for success. Working closely with each other may enable the newcomer and existing team members to gain a more accurate picture of and appreciate each other's capabilities and to discover deeper-level characteristics on which they may be more similar. When there is more opportunity for interaction for task performance, there is also less opportunity for the newcomer to be excluded or to distance himself. A shared group goal may create a common focal point, shared by newcomer and incumbents, around which a mutual identity can be constructed. Additionally, interacting as part of the task may also set the stage for nontask-related communication, enabling self-disclosure and breeding the development of affective ties. These processes might help to overcome the initial focus on the newcomer's differences.

CULTURE AND CLIMATE

The climate for diversity in an organization has potentially strong implications for how newcomers who are demographically different will be treated and for how they perceive their new group. *Diversity climate* refers to the degree to which employees collectively feel that their organization is committed to equal opportunity and inclusion (McKay, Avery, & Morris, 2009). Although there is no research on the effect of diversity climate on socialization, there is evidence that diversity climate is linked to racial minorities' and women's organizational attachment (Gonzalez & Denisi, 2009; McKay, Avery, Tonidandel, Hernandez, & Hebl, 2007), and individuals' sense of attachment to the organization likely arises largely from experiences in their proximal workgroup.

The climate for diversity can be signaled directly by the organization in their recruiting materials, policies and procedures regarding discrimination, as well as the presence (or absence) of other individuals who are part of the newcomer's social identity group. Diversity climate can be measured at the level of the group or the organization, but the climate of the former is certainly shaped, at least in part, by the latter. The organization's diversity climate may affect socialization in two ways. First, it may signal to newcomers how they can expect to be treated by their new colleagues. Newcomers who view the organization's climate as inclusive may assume that their new colleagues are unlikely to exclude them on the basis of their differences. In organizations that actively promote the idea of diversity as an asset, newcomers may even believe that the existing group members will view them as a resource. Furthermore, for newcomers wary of being discriminated against, knowing that the organization has adequate policies for handling discrimination and is committed to those policies can alleviate such concerns.

Second, diversity climate may affect how existing group members treat newcomers with deep or surface-level differences. Organizations with positive diversity climates communicate norms of respect, inclusiveness, and fairness. It is likely that there is a higher level of diversity among the leadership and throughout the various functions of such organizations, perhaps counteracting stereotypes and lessening the likelihood that a certain characteristic will automatically be associated with low status in the organization. Thus, existing group members in organizations with positive diversity climates may be primed to embrace new members who are different.

Because of effects on both newcomers' and incumbent group members' perspectives, individual and interpersonal processes are likely to unfold more smoothly in positive climates for diversity. At the level of the individual, the newcomer may feel less reticence about asking for support or information. Those with invisible stigmatized identities may also be less likely to fear that being open will become a basis for rejection or persecution. Thus, the newcomer in a positive diversity climate is likely to be more proactive and to experience greater authenticity and is less likely to perceive conflict between embracing the group's identity and maintaining existing valued identities.

At the interpersonal level, the respect and motivation to understand others engendered by positive diversity climates translates into increases in effortful processing (Brickson, 2000), which should enhance elaboration. Group members, valuing

inclusion, should be more likely to communicate with and offer support to the newcomer. Finally, in an environment where negative stereotypes are counteracted by positive examples and valuing of differences, group members may be less likely to label the newcomer and more likely to trust that person's ability to contribute to the team. In cases of high separation disparity, where the newcomer is of higher status or lower status, a climate of mutual respect should also lessen the divisive effects of status differences. Where the newcomer's arrival introduces higher separation or variety disparity, via divergent values or areas of expertise, a positive climate for diversity should translate into both newcomers' and incumbents' willingness to learn from each other.

TEAM CULTURE

Teams have norms, rituals, and customs that can affect how well a newcomer who is different adjusts. Recall that socialization is a process whereby the group provides information and resources that enable the newcomer to become adjusted. Thus, the norms, rituals, and customs of the team may either promote or inhibit socialization via availability of resources to newcomers. Teams with strong identities are likely to communicate their identity strongly to newcomers, which may or may not help the newcomer adjust. As indicated in the previous section, groups that have positive normative expectations about the potential for diversity to enhance group performance (i.e., those that see diversity from an "integration-and-learning" perspective; Ely & Thomas, 2001) may develop behaviors that facilitate integration of newcomers. Members may share information freely, make frequent offers of help, and attempt to get to know newcomers on a personal level. On the other hand, in team cultures that are ambivalent or hostile toward the idea of diversity, members may doubt that someone who is different from them is even capable of truly being part of the team. A common example is the difficulty that women have integrating into all-male workgroups where, although the work itself may not require it, the identity of the team treats aggressive, "manly" pursuits as integral to the nature of the work which, itself, may be gender-neutral.

Another influential aspect of the group's culture is its openness, which may be informed by the mix of personalities on the team and the team's task. Teams that are highly committed to a certain course of action, either because of heavy prior investment or because most of the team members tend to be conservative and change-averse, might withdraw from a newcomer who increases separation or variety diversity, bringing in divergent opinions or expertise. They may even be threatened by disparity diversity; a new, high-status team member might have the influence to undo practices that the existing team members want to preserve.

Whether the conflicts that diversity can engender are handled in a manner that is constructive depends also on team culture (Ren & Gray, 2009). Collectivists avoid explicit conflicts and try to resolve disputes or disagreements by attributing problems to the situation. Individualists, on the other hand, seek to make conflicts explicit and take personal responsibility for disputes. Supporting this line of thinking, Mohammed and Angell (2004) found that team orientation can reduce the negative effects of surface-level gender diversity and deep-level time urgency diversity on relationship conflict (Mohammed & Angell, 2004). In other words, separation diversity was less likely to lead to relationship conflicts in groups that had higher levels of collective orientation.

GROUP DEMOGRAPHY

For the sake of simplicity, we have primarily conceptualized diversity in terms of a single separation, meaning the difference of the newcomer from all other members of the team. But the extent to which the existing workgroup is diverse will also likely impact the newcomer. Separation, variety, and disparity for a team are highest when there are distinct *faultlines* (Lau & Murnighan, 1998) between two very well defined groups in a team, such as when the team is made up nearly evenly of White and African American members or of members with graduate degrees and those with high school degrees. A newcomer entering such a potentially charged atmosphere will probably be expected to affiliate with one group or another and will likely form an identity based on the subgroup. Even a newcomer who is not interested in joining one group or the other, or who cannot because she does not fall neatly into either group, may have trouble breaking through entrenched patterns of conflict and lack of information sharing that are typical of groups with faultlines (Homan, van Knippenberg, Van Kleef, & De Dreu, 2007; Jehn & Bezrukova, 2010). Indeed, failure to align with either subgroup could leave the newcomer without anyone to turn to for resources needed for effective socialization.

The prospects for newcomer integration seem more optimistic in groups that are relatively diverse but in which there are too few members of any one social category or type for faultlines to have emerged. In such groups, diversity is the norm. The newcomer may differ from all of the existing group members, but the existing group members differ from each other as well. Having worked together for a while, the incumbents may have already accomplished the difficult task of figuring out how to work well together across their differences. They may also have cultivated a more positive climate for diversity. Of course, the converse is also possible. These could be the most fractious groups of all; however, faultlines research seems to suggest that the greatest trouble lies in diverse groups where the categorical divisions are clear.

Outcomes of Socialization Processes with Different Newcomers

Up to this point, we have proposed how newcomer differences from the existing workgroup are likely to produce certain processes at both the individual and interpersonal levels, and we have also discussed individual and situational factors that are likely to moderate these relationships. In this section we will consider the outcomes of these socialization processes, addressing questions of the newcomer's perception of social acceptance, the cohesion of the workgroup, the newcomer's level of commitment to the job and workgroup, routine task performance, and creative performance.

SOCIAL ACCEPTANCE

Socialization researchers have long proposed that social acceptance, or conversely, social isolation, is one of the most important outcomes of the process of newcomer adjustment (e.g., Bauer, Bodner, Erdogan, Truxillo, & Tucker, 2007; Chao, O'Leary-Kelly, Wolf, Klein, & Gardner, 1994; Feldman, 1981). Well-adjusted organizational newcomers are supported by coworkers, are included in social interactions, and are identified as "one of the gang." Individuals who are socially accepted are likely to experience more support, which can be crucial for newcomers. There is ample evidence that feelings of social support for established employees are significantly related to positive moods and productivity at work (Baruch-Feldman, Brondolo, Ben-Dayan, & Schwartz, 2002). Other evidence links social support from supervisors to higher levels among newcomers of role clarity, job satisfaction, and salary growth over time (Jokisaari & Nurmi, 2009). Clearly, social acceptance is one major component of newcomer adjustment.

Although there are some positive features of social identity formation for newcomers, social identities can also serve as a deterrent to the integration of a newcomer. A preference for similarity in social networks has been demonstrated in numerous studies in the past (e.g., Ibarra, 1993; Mollica, Gray & Trevino, 2003). Social identities initiate in-group favoritism, which is a tendency to see members of one's own group as being superior to or more deserving than those who are outsiders. Unfortunately, for newcomers who are already perceived as outsiders, this means that established members of the group will likely see the newcomer in negative terms. Labels like "novice," "rookie" or "newbie" are all used to clearly provide a label for the newcomer's distinct identity as a non-insider (Ashforth & Humphrey, 1997). The power of these labels becomes stronger when demographic identities are linked with outsider status, as shown in derisive, depersonalizing labels like "the rookie woman manager," "that new Black guy," or "the one in the wheelchair who just started working here."

The social relationships literature also highlights the role of trust as part of the process of relationship development. Trust is developed over the course of repeated interactions between individuals. Organizational behavior researchers add to this perspective by noting that the ability, benevolence, and integrity of the actor are likely to be observed as part of the process that generates trust (Colquitt, Scott, & Lepine, 2007). Individuals who are seen as lacking in these characteristics will not be trusted. People are more likely to see those who are in their in-group as having similar values, thereby making them more trustworthy (Leach, Ellemers, & Barreto, 2007). In part, this is because similar individuals are assumed to have similar values and, therefore, are expected to be more benevolent. Because of social identity processes involving in-group bias, those who are seen as in-group members will be seen as being more able as well (Bettencourt, Dorr, Charlton, & Hume, 2001). Thus, initially, dissimilar newcomers are less likely to receive the trust of their fellow group members.

Social relationship scholars have also highlighted interpersonal disclosure as an important component of development of interpersonal bonds. When people know one another better, they tend to discuss issues that are potentially interpersonally sensitive. Many of the most important exchanges that occur between newcomers and established members of the organization require some form of interpersonal disclosure. For example, the literature on proactivity suggests that asking for help is a disclosure of ignorance. The mentoring literature also highlights the importance of disclosing personal feelings and experiences as part of the transmission of knowledge from established and experienced organizational members to individuals who are less knowledgeable (Wanberg, Welsh, & Kammeyer-Mueller, 2007). Again, individuals who do not share values or positions on important social issues may be less likely to participate in high-disclosure relationships with one another. Thus, those who are different from the rest of the workgroup on values or positions are likely to be permanently consigned to a peripheral status and will not develop close interpersonal bonds.

There is much evidence that individuals who are different from their coworkers experience lower levels of social acceptance. Newcomers who are dissimilar to their workgroups in terms of age, education, and lifestyle have been shown to report lower levels of workgroup fit in prior research (Kirchmeyer, 1995). Other research shows that managers who are in the demographic minority have fewer intimate networks at work and had social networks that were quite different from their instrumental networks relative to those in the majority (Ibarra, 1995). It has also been shown that supervisors have lower levels of personal attraction to subordinates who are demographically different from themselves (Tsui & O'Reilly, 1989). Taken from another perspective, research has shown that individuals tend to form friendships with those who are from their own demographic groups more readily than with those who are from different demographic groups (Mollica, Gray & Treviño, 2003).

Several of the processes we have noted might explain why those who are different from their coworkers experience reduced social acceptance. In particular, if newcomers do not develop identification with the workgroup, are concealing important elements of their identities, are not included in support networks, and are excluded from the group, they are unlikely to perceive that they have achieved social acceptance. The resulting social isolation for newcomers who are dissimilar in terms of separation from their coworkers can be severe and, as we will show, may ultimately lead to withdrawal from the job and organization. Individual identity formation may inhibit social acceptance for those who are dissimilar in terms of variety relative to their coworkers, but these forces may be countervailed by increases in disclosure and inclusion.

COHESION

Whereas social acceptance is an individual-level perceptual phenomenon from the perspective of the newcomer, cohesion is a group-level perception (Evans & Jarvis, 1980) that relates to the overall functioning of the group. Cohesion is a group-level characteristic which reflects the degree to which one feels "stuck to" or a part of a certain group (Bollen & Hoyle, 1990). Many researchers have investigated the effects of demographic diversity on cohesion. For example, one study found that gender diversity was negatively related to group cohesiveness for groups that have not been together for long periods of time (Harrison, Price, & Bell, 1998). Likewise, O'Reilly, Caldwell, and Barnett (1989) found that heterogeneity in group tenure was associated with lower levels of group social integration.

Given this literature, the question arises: Can a newcomer who is different from the rest of the workgroup actually reduce the overall cohesiveness of the rest of the group? Our process arguments suggest several reasons why this might be the case. First, if the newcomer does not share a common identity with the remainder of the group, it is likely that the overall sense of group cohesion and identity will also be weakened. Second, a newcomer who decreases group elaboration will reduce cohesion since communication is a vital part of cohesion. In fact, evidence suggests that information sharing is among the most important predictors of cohesiveness in functionally diverse groups (Keller, 2001). Conversely, a newcomer who increases elaboration will enhance cohesion. Third, newcomers who create higher levels of conflict will obviously tend to reduce cohesion in a group, as noted by research showing higher levels of group conflict are inversely related to group cohesion (LePine, Piccolo, Jackson, Mathieu, & Saul, 2008).

COMMITMENT AND WITHDRAWAL

Newcomer commitment is another of the classic "signposts of successful socialization" identified in previous research, whereas withdrawal is a sign that socialization has failed. There is research showing main effects of diversity on commitment that are suggestive of what we might see for newcomers who differ from the established workgroup. Value separation diversity among members of a workgroup has been found to decrease satisfaction, commitment, and intention to remain within the group (Jehn, Northcraft, & Neale, 1999). Several studies have shown that there are lower levels of attachment and higher levels of turnover in groups that have higher levels of heterogeneity (e.g., O'Reilly, Caldwell, & Barnett, 1989; Tsui, Egan, & O'Reilly, 1992). Individuals who are the only representatives

of their demographic groups tend to have especially low levels of job satisfaction (Neimann & Dovidio, 1998). One study examined turnover in workgroups based on similarity-attraction theory and found that demographic dissimilarity resulted in higher levels of turnover risk, especially among organizational newcomers (Sacco & Schmitt, 2005). In particular, sex dissimilarity, racioethnic dissimilarity, and age dissimilarity all increased turnover hazard early in employees' tenure. This fits with our general proposition that separation diversity will have stronger (negative) effects during the process of socialization and adjustment.

Understanding the processes of socialization may help to explain why newcomers who are different from their coworkers are likely to have lower levels of commitment. First, individuals who do not have a strong social identity that includes their current workgroup are unlikely to feel committed to this group, especially given the very strong conceptual and empirical links between identification and commitment (van Knippenberg & Sleebos, 2006). Second, ample research in the area of socialization demonstrates that those who have a more innovative role orientation are likely to be less committed to an organization (e.g., Allen & Meyer, 1990; Ashforth & Saks, 1996). Third, a lack of social support and greater exclusion will lead a newcomer to feel more like a social outsider, which in turn will reduce the extent to which the newcomer feels committed to the group's functioning. Dissimilarity may result in increased organizational deviance behaviors because of lack of perceived support (Liao, Joshi & Chuang, 2004). These processes are likely to produce lower levels of commitment for all forms of differences, whether separation, variety, or disparity.

ROUTINE TASK PERFORMANCE

One of the most important outcomes of successful organizational socialization is how well the newcomer performs his or her new tasks soon after being hired. In the case of newcomer adjustment, the most important issues are both the level and trajectory of newcomer performance over time. As we noted earlier, different types of diversity can lead to either task or relationship conflicts. These types of conflict had been hypothesized to have opposite effects on group performance, but recent meta-analytic evidence suggests that conflict of any type negatively affects group performance (DeDreu & Weingart, 2003). Thus, individuals who are different from their new coworkers may end up experiencing increased conflict with these group members—both due to task-based disagreements stemming from differences in values and experiences and due to relationship-based disagreements stemming from more surface-level differences—which can lead to poor adjustment.

As with other outcomes, we have to partially infer how the presence of newcomers who are different from their coworkers will affect performance based on studies involving intact teams. Research involving top management teams found that among short-tenured top management teams, variety-based diversity in terms of education, function, and tenure were positively associated with performance (Carpenter, 2002). Moreover, evidence across a variety of studies has shown that greater gender diversity in top management teams can be associated with greater firm value, although some studies also find no significant effects (e.g., Campbell & Mínguez-Vera, 2008; Carter, Simkins, & Simpson, 2003). From another perspective, and possibly more relevant to our focus on the individual newcomer, evidence suggests that being demographically different from one's group members is negatively associated with individual performance (e.g., Spangler, Gordon, & Pipkin, 1978; Thompson & Sekaquaptewa, 2002).

What theoretical mechanisms might explain why newcomers who are different from their coworkers might be less or more productive? First, individuals who are less proactive will be less likely to perform well on the job because they will be less likely to have gained the requisite knowledge to perform their work tasks. Second, those who engage in less elaboration with their coworkers will also likely be missing out on information that is relevant for completing work tasks. Additionally, supportive relationships among coworkers can increase performance (Podsakoff, MacKenzie, Paine, & Bacharach, 2000) and the likelihood of career success (Ibarra, 1997). Finally, those who experience frequent conflict regarding their work will be likely to perform worse. It is worth noting that processes associated with separation differences all suggest lower levels of routine task performance, whereas the processes for variety-based differences are more mixed (i.e., more proactivity and elaboration but increased conflict). High status disparity and low status disparity are expected to have potentially contravening effects on task performance as well.

CITIZENSHIP BEHAVIOR

Citizenship behavior involves efforts to improve the social and psychological climate of the workgroup by demonstrating enthusiasm and providing assistance to others with work tasks. Although much of the literature on citizenship behavior has concentrated on the efforts of established group members to provide assistance to one another, or to provide help and assistance to a newcomer (e.g., LePine & Van Dyne, 1998), it is also possible for those who are new to a group to engage in citizenship behavior toward more established group members as well. Newcomers with unique knowledge and skills will have opportunities to provide extraordinary levels of encouragement, information, and assistance to their coworkers.

Evidence showing that separation diversity is negatively related to citizenship has been found in the past. Prior research has shown that individuals who are demographically dissimilar from their coworkers do engage in less citizenship behavior (Chattopadhyay, 1999). Those who are given little support from coworkers will engage in less citizenship behavior based on principles of social exchange—this mirrors results showing that those who are in low-citizenship groups also demonstrate low citizenship themselves (Bommer, Miles, & Grover, 2003).

There are also processes that might increase a newcomers' citizenship behavior. Individuals who form a collective identity will be more likely to see the outcomes for coworkers as being related to their own outcomes, and this shared sense of purpose may increase citizenship. Because some of the process of socialization and adjustment involves reciprocal exchange, people who feel like they aren't supported by their coworkers will be less likely to help them, whereas those who do feel supported are more likely to provide help (Chaiburu & Harrison, 2008). There is also evidence that individuals in more cohesive groups engage in higher levels of citizenship behavior even after taking individual-level work attitudes into account (Kidwell, Mossholder, & Bennett, 1997).

CREATIVE PERFORMANCE

Creativity and role innovation have also been described as important outcomes of highly individualized socialization in prior research (Van Maanen & Schein, 1979). The question here is whether newcomers who are different from their colleagues are likely to have higher or lower levels of subsequent creative performance. Newcomers who have unique and valuable knowledge, skills, and abilities to add to the workgroup will be more productive and innovative in their work roles, whereas those who add little that is new to the workgroup may be less productive and will probably not contribute to creative performance.

The process of elaboration by its very nature should increase creative performance because it increases discussion of diverse points of view. Because variety diversity increases the number of perspectives brought to bear on a problem, researchers typically assume that increases in variety enhance performance on creative tasks. There is evidence that diversity in ethnicity and openness to experience is associated with superior creative performance in short-term computer mediated groups (Giambatista & Bhappu, 2010). At the same time, this study also found that diversity in agreeableness is negatively related to group creative performance. Diverse groups that formed relatively positive, individuated perceptions of one another outperformed more homogeneous groups on a creative task (Swann, Kwan, Polzer, & Milton, 2003). Other evidence shows that in groups where there is high congruence between self-views and the views of others, creative performance increases with greater demographic diversity (Polzer, Milton, & Swann, 2002). It is interesting to note that this sort of congruence effect is likely to be higher when there is ample personal disclosure in groups. In this sense, a positive relationship development experience for newcomers can offset some of the difficulties that arise from a discrepant social identity.

Similarly, role innovation is likely to enhance creative performance for a newcomer. Those who reject the established organizational norms for how a job should be performed will be more likely to generate innovative perspectives on both how work should be performed and what the end product of work will look like. Most forms of diversity are expected to result in increased levels of innovative role orientation.

Implications for Managerial Practice

Organizations can improve the socialization of diverse newcomers by being cognizant of the potential for the dynamics discussed here. In this concluding section, we offer propositions for how organizations might be able to make the process of adjustment for newcomers smoother.

Establish a Positive Diversity Climate

As discussed earlier, a climate that values tolerance and fairness can help alleviate the drawbacks and realize the advantages of introducing newcomers who are different. Organizational practices that communicate a positive diversity climate include the diversity of upper-level management (Herdman & McMillan-Capehart, 2010), fair implementation of policies related to advancement and harassment (Cox, 1994), and the presence of diversity training (Herdman & McMillan-Capehart, 2010). These practices may not only affect individual perceptions, they may also influence the climates of workgroups within the organization.

It is likely, too, that the group leader, if there is one, serves as a conduit for the organization's climate to the group level. The leader's attitude toward organizational policies and behaviors toward subordinates may undermine a strongly positive organizational climate for diversity or create a positive climate for diversity at the group level even when the organizational climate for diversity is weak. Transformational leadership strategies, like emphasizing an idealistic common goal, can lead to superior performance in diverse groups (Shin & Zhou, 2007). Also, performance in diverse groups is enhanced when mean-level leader–member exchange is high and there are not severe disparities in the quality of relationships between leaders and group members (Nishii & Mayer, 2009). Thus, building high-quality relationships across the group contributes to the diversity climate by assuring group members that access to the leader is not contingent on shared characteristics such as race, gender, or educational background.

The leader might establish the climate for socialization of diverse newcomers via the way in which the newcomer enters the group. If the leader is aware, for instance, that the newcomer might be stereotyped as less capable because of membership in a stigmatized group, the leader might emphasize the newcomer's previous accomplishments and experiences in introductions to existing group members. Also, to foster interaction, the leader might assign the newcomer to shadow or work closely with another group member on tasks, emphasizing the importance of those tasks to the group. Finally, establishing that the expression of divergent views and requests for help are acceptable and supported may help minimize the risks of newcomer proactivity and reduce isolation.

Assess and Develop Capabilities

If newcomers' personalities might influence their ability to adjust, then it might be helpful to use assessments of traits like openness and extraversion to gain greater insight into the newcomer's ability to adapt when he or she is different from the rest of the group. Asking questions about the person's previous work experiences in order to assess how proactive the person has been or how well he or she has adapted to such experiences in the past could also be instrumental.

Of course, the entire burden should not fall on the newcomer. Even a highly proactive newcomer will encounter problems adjusting if the incumbent group members are resistant to change or intolerant of differences. Thus, it would also be useful to assess existing members and determine whether, individually, they are capable of adapting to working with someone who is different and whether, collectively, the group's climate is supportive of the integration of newcomers who heighten the group's separation, variety, or disparity diversity.

If either the newcomer or existing group members seem ill-prepared to adjust to an increasingly diverse work environment, diversity training might help to improve their capabilities. The efficacy of various forms of diversity training is still widely contested (Paluck & Green, 2009). Some forms of training have actually been linked to negative consequences for marginalized groups (e.g., Kulik, Perry, & Bourhis, 2000). Nevertheless, there are some recognized best practices. Some of them, such as needs assessment and support from upper management, are necessary components of any effective training program. Others are more particular to diversity training effectiveness. For instance, focusing on the development of competencies for interacting with diverse others is more effective than simply raising awareness of stereotypes and discrimination (King, Gulick, & Avery, 2010). There is also evidence that people are more likely to utilize skills learned in diversity training programs when they perceive that doing so will affect their work outcomes (Roberson, Kulik, & Pepper, 2009). In the current context, this means that it is important for workgroup members to be aware of the potentially negative consequences of group diversity and to recognize the potential for diversity training to overcome those deficits.

Enhance Social Support

Having acknowledged that there are potential issues with diversity in the socialization process, organizations can take an active role in attempting to enhance the outcomes of socialization for those who differ from their workgroups. One technique that has been frequently advocated for individuals who are entering new leadership roles is the development of formal mentoring programs. Research suggests that such programs can indeed be helpful for newcomers, provided that certain principles are

met (Allen, Eby, & Lentz, 2006). Researchers advise that input into the match by both mentors and protégés may facilitate higher-quality relationships. The interpersonal comfort engendered by these more personally selected relationships may enhance both mentor and protégé mutual identification, interpersonal comfort, and liking. Additionally, providing higher-quality training for mentors is also associated with perceptions of higher-quality relationships. Within the context of group socialization, it seems clear that the mentor should be an existing group member.

Promote Collective Identities

Although the traditional advice for managing diverse workgroups is to emphasize the shared identity and common goals of the group, some researchers have proposed that such an approach is less effective than attempting to generate positive intergroup attitudes (e.g., Brickson, 2000; Pittinsky & Simon, 2007; Pittinsky, 2010) or promoting individuation and self-verification (Swann, Kwan, Polzer, & Milton, 2003). There is even the concern that highlighting the unified nature of groups will dilute the positive advantages shown in terms of information elaboration (van Knippenberg, De Dreu, & Homan, 2004). From this perspective, leaders should endeavor to show positive recognition for the diversity of workers and emphasize positive features of different characteristics. Consistent with the Harrison and Klein (2007) framework, the goal is to encourage attention to the positive features of variety in knowledge, skills, abilities, and background experiences. Evidence suggests that compared to emphasizing shared identity, emphasizing relational identities generates more positive attitudes toward out-groups (Brickson, 2008).

Support Unique Identities

A final suggestion for facilitating socialization for newcomers who are different from the existing social group is supporting the newcomers' unique identities and recognizing that they are different. This might seem to run contrary to our previous advice to promote collective identities, but it is possible to simultaneously send a message that "we're all in this together" as well as "we recognize that we aren't all the same." Research in the area of acculturation for minority groups consistently suggests that the highest levels of adaptation are enjoyed by those who are able to simultaneously experience and endorse their own group status, as well as experiencing and endorsing the climate of the majority culture (e.g., Berry, 1997). Theorists from the social identity camp also suggest that it is best for groups to emphasize their joint similarities and make their workgroup membership a more central and salient feature of the workplace than their more divisive demographic identities (e.g., Chatman & Flynn, 2001, Turner, Hogg, Oakes, Reicher, & Wetherell, 1987)

When Problems Arise

The recommendations above are not foolproof, and there is still a lack of evidence regarding what really supports socialization of diverse newcomers. Given this gap in knowledge and the many potential land mines, it is important for organizations to anticipate the possibility that problems will arise when new people enter groups in which they are in the minority in some noticeable or meaningful way. Problems are especially likely early in the newcomer's tenure with the group. Given research that surface-level differences, at least, diminish with time (Harrison et al., 1998), it is likely that newcomers who are demographically different will become more integrated as they and their teammates recognize their underlying commonalties of experience, education, and values. Thus, it might be necessary to give groups in which diverse newcomers have been introduced more time to realize their promise. Furthermore, when there are process or performance problems, it is easy to assume that they are primarily attributable to the newcomer since, after all, he or she appears to be the only element that has changed. But, in reality, introducing any newcomer, and particularly a diverse newcomer, changes the entire dynamic of the group. It may challenge existing group members as much as it does the newcomer. Process or performance problems may, therefore, need to be addressed as a problem of the group, not of a single individual. Finally, organizations need not be blindsided by performance problems in newly diversified groups. Upfront recognition of the complexity of socializing diverse newcomers to groups should suggest the need for ongoing monitoring and assessment. Via formal and informal means, organizations can audit how well the newcomer is adjusting and, therefore, intervene before problems surge.

Conclusion

The development of newcomer social identity as an integrated member of the group can be very beneficial for organizations, and diversity is likely to have strong effects on this process. When a person identifies with a social group, his/her self-esteem becomes intimately linked to the performance of the group (Ashforth & Mael, 1989; Hogg & Terry, 2000). Group success becomes personal success, and group failure becomes personal failure. An employee who truly identifies with the new workgroup will feel elated when the group does well and will put forth considerable effort to ensure that the group is successful. As such, there is a considerable advantage for organizations that can overcome some of the initial problems that arise in social identity formation and progress towards integration of newcomers. Unfortunately, research has not thoroughly considered how newcomer differences from the workgroup can either facilitate or hinder newcomer adjustment. It is our hope that this chapter will stimulate further thinking and research on newcomer socialization and diversity.

We have highlighted a number of future research directions that we think will help to provide better knowledge regarding the antecedents, processes, moderators, and outcomes of the socialization process for those who are different from their coworkers. Future research should pay special attention to the mechanisms that facilitate adjustment for these individuals as a way to help organizations better manage diversity among organizational newcomers.

References

Allen, T. D., Eby, L. T., & Lentz, E. (2006). Mentorship behaviors and mentorship quality associated with formal mentoring programs: Closing the gap between research and practice. *Journal of Applied Psychology, 91*, 567–578.

Allen, N. J., & Meyer, J. P. (1990). Organizational socialization tactics: A longitudinal analysis of links to newcomers' commitment and role orientation. *Academy of Management Journal, 33*, 847–858.

Ashforth, B. E., & Humphrey, R. H. (1997). The ubiquity and potency of labeling in organizations. *Organization Science, 8*, 43–58.

Ashforth, B. E., & Mael, F. (1989). Social Identity Theory and the Organization. *Academy of Management Review, 14*, 20–39.

Ashforth, B. E., & Saks, A. M. (1996). Socialization tactics: Longitudinal effects on newcomer adjustment. *Academy of Management Journal, 39*, 149–178.

Baruch-Feldman, C., Brondolo, E., Ben-Dayan, D., & Schwartz, J. (2002). Sources of social support and burnout, job satisfaction, and productivity. *Journal of Occupational Health Psychology, 7*, 84–93.

Bauer, T. N., Bodner, T., Erdogan, B., Truxillo, D. M., & Tucker, J. S. (2007). Newcomer adjustment during organizational socialization: A meta-analytic review of antecedents, outcomes, and methods. *Journal of Applied Psychology, 92*, 707–721.

Baumeister, R. F., Shapiro, J. P., & Tice, D. M. (1985). Two kinds of identity crisis. *Journal of Personality, 53*, 407–424.

Berry, J. W. (1997). Immigration, acculturation, and adaptation. *Applied Psychology: An International Review, 46*, 5–68.

Bettencourt, B. A., Dorr, N., Charlton, K., & Hume, D. L. (2001). Status differences and in-group bias: A meta-analytic examination of the effects of status stability, status legitimacy, and group permeability. *Psychological Bulletin, 127*, 520–542.

Bollen, K. A., & Hoyle, R. H. (1990). Perceived cohesion: a conceptual and empirical examination. *Social Forces, 69*, 479–50.

Bommer, W. H., Miles, E. W., & Grover, S. L. (2003). Does one good turn deserve another? Coworker influences on employee citizenship. *Journal of Organizational Behavior, 24*, 181–196.

Brewer, M. B. (1996). When contact is not enough: Social identity and intergroup cooperation. *International Journal of Intercultural Relations, 20*, 291–303.

Brickson, S. L. (2000). The impact of identity orientation on individual and organizational outcomes in demographically diverse settings. *Academy of Management Review, 25*, 82–101.

Brickson, S. L. (2008). Reassessing the standard: The positive expansive potential of a relational identity in diverse organizations. *Journal of Positive Psychology. 3*, 40–54.

Cable, D. M. & DeRue, D. S. (2002). The convergent and discriminant validity of subjective fit perceptions, *Journal of Applied Psychology, 87*, 875–884.

Cable, D. M., & Edwards, J. R. (2004). Complementary and supplementary fit: A theoretical and empirical integration. *Journal of Applied Psychology, 89*, 822–834.

Campbell, K., & Mínguez-Vera, A. (2008). Gender diversity in the boardroom and firm financial performance. *Journal of Business Ethics, 83*, 435–451.

Carter, D. A., Simkins, B. J., & Simpson, W. G. (2003). Corporate governance, board diversity, and firm value. *Financial Review, 38*, 33–53.

Carpenter, M. (2002). The implications of strategy and social context for the relationship between top management team heterogeneity and firm performance. *Strategic Management Journal, 23*, 275–284.

Chao, G. T., O'Leary-Kelly, A. M., Wolf, S., Klein, H. J., & Gardner, P. D. (1994). Organizational socialization: Its contents and consequences. *Journal of Applied Psychology, 79*, 730–743.

Chatman, J. A., & Flynn, F. J. (2001). The influence of demographic heterogeneity on the emergence and consequences of cooperative norms in work teams. *Academy of Management Journal, 44*, 956–974.

Chattopadhyay, P. (1999). Beyond direct and symmetrical effects: The influence of demographic dissimilarity on organizational citizenship behavior. *Academy of Management Journal, 42*, 273–287.

Chattopadhyay, P., George, E., & Lawrence, S. 2004. Why does dissimilarity matter? Exploring self-categorization, self-enhancement and uncertainty reduction. *Journal of Applied Psychology, 89*, 892–900.

Chiaburu, D. S. & Harrison, D. A. (2008). Do peers make the place? Conceptual synthesis and meta-analysis of coworker effect on perceptions, attitudes, OCBs, and performance, *Journal of Applied Psychology, 93*, 1082–1103.

Clair, J. A., Beatty, J. E., & MacLean (2005). Out of sight but not out of mind: managing invisible social identities in the workplace. *Academy of management review, 30*, 79–95.

Colquitt, J. A., Scott, B. A., & LePine, J. A. (2007). Trust, trustworthiness, and trust propensity: A meta-analytic test of their unique relationships with risk taking and job performance. *Journal of Applied Psychology, 92*, 902–927.

Cox, T. H. (1994). *Cultural diversity in organizations: Theory, research, and practice*. San Francisco: Berrert-Kohler.

Crocker, J., Major, B., & Steele, C. (1998). Social stigma. In D. T. Gilbert, S. T. Fiske, & G. Lindzey (Eds.), *The handbook of social psychology* (Vol. 2, 4th ed., pp. 504–553). New York: McGraw-Hill.

Cummings, J. N. (2004). Work groups, structural diversity, and knowledge sharing in a global organization. *Management Science, 50*(3), 352–364.

De Dreu, C. K. W., & Weingart, L. R. (2003). Task versus relationship conflict and team effectiveness: A meta-analysis. *Journal of Applied Psychology, 88*, 741–749.

DeJordy, R. (2008). Just passing through: Stigma and identity decoupling in the work place. *Group and Organization Management, 33*, 504.

Eidelman, S., Silvia, P. J., & Biernat, M. (2006). Responding to deviance: Target exclusion and differential devaluation. *Personality and Social Psychology Bulletin, 32*, 1153–1164.

Ely, R. J., & Thomas, D. A. (2001). Cultural Diversity at Work: The Effects of Diversity Perspectives on Work Group Processes and Outcomes. *Administrative Science Quarterly, 46*, 229–273.

Erickson, R.J. (1995). The importance of authenticity for self and society. *Symbolic Interaction, 18*(2), 121–144.

Ethier, K. A.,& Deaux, K. (1994). Negotiating social identity when contexts change: Maintaining identification and responding to threat. *Journal of Personality and Social Psychology, 67*, 243–251.

Evans, N. J., & Jarvis, P. A. (1980). Group cohesion: A review and re-evaluation. *Small Group Behavior, 11*, 359–70

Feldman, D. C. (1981). The multiple socialization of organization members. *Academy of Management Review, 6*, 309–318.

Fiske, S. T., Cuddy, A. J. C., Glick, P., & Xu, J. (2002). A model of (often mixed) stereotype content: Competence and warmth respectively follow from perceived status and competition. *Journal of Personality and Social Psychology, 82*, 878–902.

Giambatista, R. C., & Bhappu, A. D. (2010). Diversity's harvest: Interactions of diversity sources and communication technology on creative group performance. *Organizational Behavior and Human Decision Processes, 111*, 116–126.

Gonzalez, J. A., & DeNisi, A. S. 2009. Cross-level effects of demography and diversity climate on organizational attachment and firm effectiveness. *Journal of Organizational Behavior, 30*, 21–40.

Harrison, D. A. & Klein, K. J. (2007). What's the difference? Diversity constructs as separation, variety, or disparity in organizations. *Academy of Management Review, 32*, 1199–122.

Harrison, D. A., Price, K. H., & Bell, M. P. (1998). Beyond relational demography: Time and the effects of surface- and deep-level diversity on work group cohesion. *Academy of Management Journal, 41*, 96–107.

Harrison, D. A., Price, K. H., Gavin, J. H., & Florey, A. T. (2002). Time, teams, and task performance: Changing effects of surface- and deep-level diversity on group functioning. *Academy of Management Journal, 45*, 1029–1045.

Herdman, A. O., & McMillan-Capehart, A. (2010). Establishing a diversity program is not enough: Exploring the determinants of diversity climate. *Journal of Business and Psychology, 25*, 39–53.

Herek, G. M. (1996). Heterosexism and homophobia. In R. P. Cabaj & T. S. Stein (Eds.), *Textbook of homosexuality and mental health* (pp. 101–113). Washington, DC: American Psychiatric Press.

Hogg, M. A., & Terry, D. J. (2000). Social identity and self-categorization processes in organizational contexts. *Academy of Management Review, 25,* 121–140.

Homan, A. C., van Knippenberg, D., Van Kleef, G. A., & De Dreu, C. K. W. (2007). Interacting dimensions of diversity: Cross-categorization and the functioning of diverse work groups. *Group Dynamics: Theory, Research, and Practice, 11,* 79–94.

Horwitz, S. K., & Horwitz, I. B. (2007). The effects of team diversity on team outcomes: A meta-analytic review of team demography. *Journal of Management, 33,* 987–1015.

Ibarra, H. (1992). Homophily and differential returns: Sex differences in network structure and access in an advertising firm. *Administrative Science Quarterly, 37,* 422–447.

Ibarra, H. (1993). Network centrality, power, and innovation involvement: Determinants of technical and administrative roles. *The Academy of Management Journal, 36,* 471–501.

Ibarra, H. (1995). Race, opportunity, and diversity of social circles in managerial networks. *Academy of Management Journal, 38,* 673–703.

Ibarra, H. (1997). Paving an alternative route: Gender differences in managerial networks. *Social Psychology Quarterly, 60,* 91–102.

Jackson, S. E., Joshi, A., & Erhardt, N. L. (2003). Recent research on team and organizational diversity: SWOT analysis and implications. *Journal of Management, 29,* 801–830.

Jackson, S. E., Stone, V. K., & Alvarez, E. B. (1993). Socialization amidst diversity: The impact of demographics on work team oldtimers and newcomers. *Research in Organizational Behavior, 15,* 45–109.

Jehn, K. & Bezrukova, K. (2010). The faultline activation process and the effects of activated faultlines on coalition formation, conflict, and group outcomes. *Organizational Behavior and Human Decision Processes, 112*(1), 24–42.

Jehn, K. A., Northcraft, G. B., &Neale, M. A. (1999).Why some differences make a difference: A field study of diversity, conflict, and performance in workgroups. *Administrative Science Quarterly, 44,* 741–763.

Jokisaari, M., & Nurmi, J. (2009). Change in newcomers' supervisor support and socialization outcomes after organizational entry. *Academy of Management Journal, 52,* 527–544.

Jones, G. R. (1983). Psychological orientation and the process of organizational socialization: An interactionist perspective. *Academy of Management Review, 8,* 464–474.

Joshi, A. (2006). The influence of organizational demography on the external networking behavior of teams. *Academy of Management Review, 31*(3), 583–595.

Joshi, A., Dencker, J. C., Franz, G., & Martocchio, J. (2010). Unpacking generational identities in organizations. *Academy of Management Review, 35,* 392–414.

Judge, T. A., Locke, E. A., & Durham, C. C. (1997). The dispositional causes of job satisfaction: A core evaluations approach. *Research in Organizational Behavior, 19,* 151–188.

Kaiser, C. R., & Pratt-Hyatt, J. S. (2009). Distributing prejudice unequally: Do whites direct their prejudice toward strongly identified minorities? *Journal of Personality and Social Psychology, 96,* 432–445.

Kaiser, C. R., Vick, S. B., & Major, B. (2006). Prejudice expectations moderate preconscious attention to cues that are threatening to social identity. *Psychological Science, 17,* 332–338.

Kammeyer-Mueller, J. D., Livingston, B. A., & Liao, H. (2011). Perceived similarity, proactive adjustment, and organizational socialization. *Journal of Vocational Behavior, 78,* 225–236.

Kammeyer-Mueller, J. D., Wanberg, C. R., Song, Z., & Rubenstein, A. L. (2010). Support, undermining, affect, and newcomer socialization: Fitting in during the first 100 days. Paper presented at the Academy of Management Meeting in Montréal, Canada.

Keller, R. T. (2001).Cross-functional project groups in research and new product development: Diversity, communications, job stress, and outcomes. *Academy of Management Journal, 44,* 547–555.

Kidwell, R. E., Mossholder, K. W., & Bennett, N. (1997). Cohesiveness and organizational citizenship behavior: A multilevel analysis using work groups and individuals. *Journal of Management, 23,* 775–793.

King, E. B., Gulick, L., & Avery, D. (2010). The divide between diversity training and diversity education: Integrating best practices. *Journal of Management Education, 34,* 891–906.

Kirchmeyer, C. (1995). Demographic similarity to the work group: A longitudinal study of managers at the early career stage. *Journal of Organizational Behavior, 16,* 67–83.

Kramer, R. M. (1991). Intergroup relations and organizational dilemmas: The role of categorization processes. In B. M. Staw and L. L. Cummings, (Eds.), *Research in organizational behavior* (Vol. 13, pp.191–228) . Greenwich, CT: JAI Press.

Kulik, C. T., Perry, E. L., & Bourhis, A. C. (2000). Ironic evaluation processes: Effects of thought suppression on evaluations of older applicants. *Journal of Organizational Behavior, 21,* 689–711.

Lau, D., & Murnighan, K. (1998). Demographic diversity and faultlines: The. compositional dynamics of organizational groups. *Academy of Management Review, 23*(2), 325–340.

Leach, C. W., Ellemers, N., & Barreto, M. (2007). Group virtue: The importance of morality (vs. competence and sociability) in the positive evaluation of in-groups. *Journal of Personality and Social Psychology, 93,* 234–249.

LePine, J. A., Piccolo, R. F., Jackson, C. L., Mathieu, J. E., & Saul, J. R. (2008). A meta-analysis of teamwork processes: Tests of a multidimensional model and relationships with team effectiveness criteria. *Personnel Psychology, 61,* 273–307.

LePine, J. A., & Van Dyne, L. (1998). Predicting voice behavior in work groups. *Journal of Applied Psychology, 83,* 853–868.

Liao, H., Joshi, A., & Chuang, A. (2004). Sticking out like a sore thumb: Employee dissimilarity and deviance at work. *Personnel Psychology, 57,* 969–1000.

McKay, P. F. & Avery, D. R. (2006). What has race got to do with it? Unraveling the role of racioethnicity in job seekers' reactions to site visits. *Personnel Psychology, 59,* 395–429.

McKay, P. F., Avery, D. R., & Morris, M. A. (2009). A tale of two climates: Diversity climate from subordinates' and managers' perspectives and their role in store unit sales performance. *Personnel Psychology, 62,* 767–791.

McKay, P. F., Avery, D. R., Tonidandel, S., Morris, M. A., Hernandez, M., & Hebl, M. R. (2007). Racial differences in employee retention: Are diversity climate perceptions the key? *Personnel Psychology, 60,* 35–62.

Mehra, A., Kilduff, M., & Brass, D. J. (1998). At the margins: A distinctiveness approach to the social identity and social networks of underrepresented groups. *Academy of Management Journal, 41,* 441–452.

Miller, V. D., & Jablin, F. M. (1991). Information seeking during organizational entry: Influences, tactics, and a model of the process. *Academy of Management Review, 16,* 92–120.

Mohammed, S., & Angell, L. C. (2004). Surface- and deep-level diversity in workgroups: Examining the moderating effects of team orientation and team process on relationship conflict. *Journal of Organizational Behavior, 25,* 1015–1039.

Mollica, K., Gray, B., & Treviño, L. (2003). Racial homophily and its persistence in newcomers' social networks. *Organization Science, 14,* 123–136.

Morrison, E. W. (1993). Longitudinal study of the effects of information seeking on newcomer socialization. *Journal of Applied Psychology, 78,* 173–183.

Morrison, E. W., & Vancouver, J. B. (2000). Within-person analysis of information seeking: The effects of perceived costs and benefits. *Journal of Management, 26,* 1–20.

Neimann, Y. F., & Dovidio, J. F. (1998). Relationship of solo status, academic rank, and perceived distinctiveness to job satisfaction of racial/ethnic minorities. *Journal of Applied Psychology, 83,* 55–71.

Nishii, L. H., & Mayer, D. M. (2009). Do inclusive leaders help to reduce turnover in diverse groups? The moderating role of leader-member exchange in the diversity to turnover relationship. *Journal of Applied Psychology, 94,* 1412–1426.

Olson, B. J., Parayitam, S., & Bao, Y. (2007). Strategic decision making: The effects of cognitive diversity, conflict, and trust on decision outcomes. *Journal of Management, 33,* 196–222.

O'Reilly, C. A., Caldwell, D. F., & Barnett, W. P. (1989). Work group demography, social integration, and turnover. *Administrative Science Quarterly, 34,* 21–37.

Pachankis, J. E. (2007). The psychological implications of concealing a stigma: A cognitive- affective-behavioral model. *Psychological Bulletin, 133,* 328–345.

Paluck, E. L. & Green, D. P. (2009). Deference, dissent, and dispute resolution: A field experiment on a mass media intervention in Rwanda. *American Political Science Review, 103*(4), 622–644.

Pelled, L. H. (1996). Demographic diversity, conflict and work group outcomes: An intervening process theory. *Organization Science, 7,* 615–631.

Pelled, L. H., Eisenhardt, K. M., & Xin, K. R. (1999). Exploring the black box: An analysis of work group diversity, conflict, and performance. *Administrative Science Quarterly, 44,* 1–28.

Phillips, K. W., & Loyd, D. L. (2006). When surface and deep-level diversity collide: The effects on dissenting group members. *Organizational Behavior and Human Decision Processes, 99,* 143–160.

Pittinsky, T. L. (2010). A two-dimensional model of intergroup leadership: The case of national diversity. *American Psychologist, 65,* 194–200.

Pittinsky, T. L., & Simon, S. (2007). Intergroup leadership. *Leadership Quarterly, 18,* 586–605.

Podsakoff, P. M., MacKenzie, S. B., Paine, J. B., Bacharach, D. G. (2000). Organizational citizenship behaviors: A critical review of the theoretical and empirical literature and suggestions for future research. *Journal of Management 26,* 513–563.

Polzer, J. T., Milton, L. P., & Swann, W. B. (2002). Capitalizing on diversity: Interpersonal congruence in small work groups. *Administrative Science Quarterly, 47,* 296–324.

Quinn, D. M., & Chaudoir, S. R. (2009). Living with a concealable stigmatized identity: The impact of anticipated stigma, centrality, salience, and cultural stigma on psychological distress and health. *Journal of Personality and Social Psychology, 97,* 634–651.

Ragins, B. R., Singh, R., & Cornwell, J. M. (2007). Making the invisible visible: Fear and disclosure of sexual orientation at work. *Journal of Applied Psychology, 92,* 1103–1118.

Ren, H., & Gray, B. (2009). Repairing relationship conflict: How violation types and culture influence the effectiveness of restoration rituals. *Academy of Management Review, 34,* 105–126.

Roberson, L., Kulik, C. T., & Pepper, M. B. (2009). Individual and environmental factors influencing the use of transfer strategies after diversity training. *Group and Organization Management, 34,* 1, 67–89.

Roberts, L. M. (2005). Changing faces: Professional image construction in diverse organizational settings. *Academy of Management Review, 30,* 685–711.

Sacco, J. M. & Schmitt, N. (2005). A dynamic multilevel model of demographic diversity and misfit effects, *Journal of Applied Psychology, 90,* 203–231.

Schippers, M. C., Den Hartog, D. N., Koopman, P. L., & Wienk, J. A. (2003). Diversity and team outcomes: The moderating effects of outcome interdependence and group longevity and the mediating effect of reflexivity. *Journal of Organizational Behavior, 24,* 779–802.

Sekaquaptewa, D., Waldman, A., & Thompson, M. (2007). Solo status and self-construal: Being distinctive influences racial self-construal and performance apprehension in African-American women. *Cultural Diversity and Ethnic Minority Psychology, 13,* 321–327.

Shelton, J. N., Richeson, J. A., & Salvatore, J. (2005). Expecting to be the target of prejudice: Implications for interethnic interactions. *Personality and Social Psychology Bulletin, 31,* 1189–1202.

Shin, S. J. & Zhou, J. (2007). When is educational specialization heterogeneity related to creativity in research and development teams? Transformational leadership as a moderator. *Journal of Applied Psychology, 92,* 1709–1721.

Spangler, E., Gordon, M., & Pipkin, R. (1978) Token women: An empirical test of Kanter's hypothesis. *American Journal of Sociology, 85,* 160–170.

Swann, W. B., Kwan, V. S. Y., Polzer, J. T., & Milton, L. P. (2003). Fostering group identification and creativity in diverse groups: The role of individuation and self-verification. *Personality and Social Psychology Bulletin, 29,* 1396–1406.

Tajfel, H. (Ed.). (1978). *Differentiation between social groups: Studies in the social psychology of intergroup relations.* London: Academic Press.

Tajfel, H. & Turner, J. C. (1986). The social identity theory of inter-group behavior. In S. Worchel & L. W. Austin (Eds.), *Psychology of intergroup relations*(second edition, pp. 7–24). Chicago: Nelson-Hall.

Thompson, M., & Sekaquaptewa, D. (2002). When being different is detrimental: Solo status and the performance of women and racial minorities. *Analyses of Social Issues and Public Policy, 2,* 183–203.

Tjosvold, D., & Poon, M. (1998). Dealing with scarce resources: Open-minded interaction for resolving budget conflicts. *Group and Organization Management, 23,* 237–255.

Tsui, A. S., Egan, T. D., & O'Reilly, C. A. (1992). Being different: Relational demography and organizational attachment. *Administrative Science Quarterly, 37,* 547–579.

Tsui, A. S., & O'Reilly, C. A. (1989). Beyond simple demographic effects: The importance of relational demography in superior-subordinate dyads. *Academy of Management Journal, 32,* 402–423.

Turner, J. C., Hogg, M. A., Oakes, P. J., Reicher, S. D., & Wetherell, M. (1987). *Rediscovering the social group: A self-categorization theory.* Oxford, UK: Basil Blackwell.

Van der Vegt, G. S., Bunderson, J. S., & Oosterhoff, A. (2006). Expertness diversity and interpersonal helping in teams: Why those who need the most help end up getting the least. *Academy of Management Journal, 49,* 877–893.

Van der Vegt, G. S., & Janssen, O. (2003). Joint impact of interdependency and group diversity on innovation. *Journal of Management, 29,* 729–751.

Van Knippenberg, D., De Dreu, C. K. W. & Homan, A. C. (2004). Work group diversity and group performance: An integrative model and research agenda. *Journal of Applied Psychology, 89,* 1008–22.

van Knippenberg, D., & Schippers, M. C. (2007). Work group diversity. *Annual Review of Psychology, 58,* 515–541.

van Knippenberg, D., & Sleebos, E. (2006). Organizational identification versus organizational commitment: Self-definition, social exchange, and job attitudes. *Journal of Organizational Behavior, 27,* 571–584.

Van Maanen, J. & Schein, E. H. (1979). Toward a theory of organizational socialization. In B. M. Staw (Ed.), *Research in organizational behavior* (Vol. 1, pp. 209–269). Greenwich, CT: JAI Press.

Vecchio, R. P., & Bullis, R. C. (2001). Moderators of the influence of supervisor–subordinate similarity on subordinate outcomes. *Journal of Applied Psychology, 86,* 884–896.

Viswesvaran, C., Sanchez, J. I., & Fisher, J. (1999). The role of social support in the process of work stress: A meta-analysis. *Journal of Vocational Behavior, 54,* 314–334.

Wanberg, C. R., & Kammeyer-Mueller, J. D. (2000). Predictors and outcomes of proactivity in the socialization process. *Journal of Applied Psychology, 85,* 373–385.

Wanberg, C. R., Welsh, E., & Kammeyer-Mueller, J. D. (2007). Protégé and mentor self-disclosure: Levels and outcomes within formal mentoring dyads in a corporate context. *Journal of Vocational Behavior, 70,* 398–412.

Wellman, B., & Wortley, S. (1990). Different strokes from different folks: Community ties and social support. *American Journal of Sociology, 96,* 558–588.

Williams, K. Y., & O'Reilly, C. A., III. (1998). Demography and diversity in organizations: A review of 40 years of research. In B. M. Staw & L. L. Cummings (Eds.), *Research in organizational behavior* (pp. 77–140). Greenwich, CT: JAI.

Williams, H. M., Parker, S. K., & Turner, N. (2007). Perceived dissimilarity and perspective taking within work teams. *Group & Organization Management, 32,* 569–597.

Content and Development of Newcomer Person–Organization Fit: An Agenda for Future Research

Annelies E. M. van Vianen *and* Irene E. De Pater

Abstract

This chapter focuses on the development of person–organization (PO) fit during newcomers' socialization, and their PO fit after this period. We present a review of socialization research that has examined newcomers' PO fit before, during, and after socialization took place. We also discuss the nature of possible changes in PO fit during socialization and the causes of these changes—changes in the organization, the person, or both. We conclude this chapter with an agenda for future research, in which we propose four themes that need further examination: (a) the causes and consequences of poor PO fit, (b) changes over time in newcomers' PO fit perceptions, (c) the sources of these perceptions, and (d) possible interaction effects of different forms of fit.

Key Words: person-organization fit, socialization, organizational entrance, newcomers, socialization tactics, development of person-organization fit perceptions

Introduction

The first few months in a new job are exciting and can be physically and mentally exhausting, as newcomers must process lots of new information about the job, the workgroup, and the organization. Furthermore, in order to arrive at a level of sufficient comfort or fit with the new environment, newcomers have to adapt themselves to their new tasks, roles, and coworkers, which can be emotionally exhausting.

People's adaptive behaviors are driven by a fundamental need to fit with the environment; that is, people have a strong desire that their personal characteristics match with the situational (e.g., Schneider, 2001). A variety of theoretical approaches in the realm of work and organizational psychology support this contention. For example, the *theory of work adjustment* (Dawis & Lofquist, 1984) argues that the relationship between individuals and work is most optimal if there is correspondence between individuals'

needs and environmental supplies, and between individuals' abilities and the requirements of the job. More recent literatures have referred to these correspondences as *need–supplies fit* and *demands–abilities fit* and have labeled them as *complementary* types of fit. Complementary fit has been defined as "the compatibility between people and organizations that occurs when at least one entity provides what the other needs" (Kristof, 1996, p. 4). As an example, complimentary fit exists when an organization needs an individual with very specific skills that other organizational members seem to lack, or when an individual has a strong need for structure that is provided by the instructions he or she receives from the supervisor. Complementary fit is most typically represented by research examining the match between individuals and the work conditions and content of jobs.

However, newcomers in organizations are confronted with other environmental elements than only the features of their job, such as the supervisor, the work team, and the organizational culture. Newcomers wish that their personal characteristics match with these social environments as well. People's fit with the supervisor (person-supervisor fit), work team (person-team fit), and organizational culture (person-organization fit) has been mostly conceptualized as *supplementary* fit, meaning that individuals and environments have similar characteristics (e.g., employees and supervisors have similar personalities and values). Based on Byrne's *similarity-attraction theory* (e.g., Byrne, Clore, & Smeaton, 1986) it has been argued that people are drawn to similar others. Therefore, researchers have mainly focused on supplementary rather than complementary fit when examining person–supervisor and person–team fit. Also, person–organization fit has been typically represented by research examining the similarity between employees' values and those of the organization (e.g., whether an employee and an organization both consider innovation important; Kristof, 1996), because people are looking for consensual validation of their opinions and values (Van Vianen, 2000).

A large amount of person–environment fit studies have evidenced the importance of fit for people's well-being and affective responses, such as job satisfaction, organizational commitment, career-related decisions, and withdrawal cognitions (Cable & DeRue, 2002; Cable & Judge, 1996; Kristof-Brown, Zimmerman, & Johnson, 2005; Lauver & Kristof-Brown, 2001). In addition, research that focused on the relationship between work and health has convincingly shown that mismatches between people and their work settings tend to cause low well-being, stress, and burnout. Mismatches such as those studied in health research typically concern six areas: workload, control, reward, fairness, community, and values (Maslach, Schaufeli, & Leiter, 2001). People experience a mismatch in workload if there is low demands–abilities fit. They experience a mismatch in control, reward, and fairness if there is low need–supplies fit, such as when people's responsibilities are exceeding their authority, when their rewards are inappropriate according to their standards, or when they feel that they deserve more than they get in the workplace. A community mismatch exists when employees do not connect well with their social environment (low person–supervisor or person–team fit), and a mismatch in values exists when they experience a discrepancy between their own values and those of the organization and its members. All in all, different theoretical approaches have addressed the importance of

person–environment fit; newcomer socialization is, thus, the process by which a person acquires fit.

In this chapter we will focus on newcomers' person–organization (PO) fit after socialization and its development during the socialization period. First, research has shown that people's PO fit is one of the strongest predictors of affective outcomes, such as individuals' commitment to the organization (Kristof-Brown et al., 2005). In addition, when entering a new job, newcomers will be particularly concerned with the question of whether the new social environment will match with their personality, preferences, and values. During the stages of job search and selection they may have gained quite accurate impressions of the content of the job and the supplies an organization offers. However, the social context of the new job remains a mystery until one has actually entered the organization.

The purpose of this chapter is twofold. First, we present a review of extant socialization research that has investigated newcomers' PO fit before, during, and after socialization. Despite abundant PO fit research, PO fit has only rarely been studied from a socialization point of view. Rather, most PO fit studies concerned tenured employees. Hence, we focus our attention on issues that are particularly salient during socialization, such as the *development* of newcomers' fit perceptions. We will argue that comparing people's PO fit before, during, and after socialization is problematic because the content of one's PO fit may change over time. For example, people may use other self and environmental features when assessing their fit with a *future* organization (during job search) than when assessing their fit with their *present* organization (when working in the organization).

It is only recently that fit researchers have begun to address the time component of PO fit perceptions. Shipp and Jansen (2011) have argued that individuals craft their current fit perceptions based on past experiences and future expectations. In this chapter, we take a somewhat different stance toward the time component of fit perceptions and reflect on the way in which the content of future PO fit assessments (before organizational entry) may be different from the content of current PO fit assessments (such as during socialization): future PO fit perceptions may include "apples," whereas current PO fit perceptions may include "oranges." In addition, we will elaborate on the nature of possible changes in PO fit *during* socialization and whether these changes are due to changes in the person, the organization, or both. How and which changes occur may depend on newcomers' personalities, organizations' socialization practices, or the interaction of these two factors. We will extensively discuss these individual, situational, and interactionist approaches toward the development of PO fit.

Second, as many questions about the content and development of newcomers' PO fit experiences have thus far remained unanswered, we provide an agenda for future research. We propose four research themes that researchers could address in the future: the causes of and responses to low PO fit, changes in newcomer PO fit perceptions, the sources of these perceptions, and whether and how different fits may interact and influence newcomers' PO fit experiences. We begin by explaining the basic principles of PO fit theory and the ways in which research has treated the PO fit construct.

Person–Organization Fit

PO fit has been conceptualized as the congruence between a person and an organization's culture or, more specifically, as the match between people's own values and those of the organization (Kristof-Brown et al., 2005; Verquer, Beehr, & Wagner, 2003). Values represent conscious desires held by individuals and encompass preferences, interests, motives, and goals, and they are seen as relatively enduring and fundamental to self-identity (Chatman, 1991). It is for this reason that people desire that their values are mirrored by an environment that promotes similar values. Furthermore, people have a biologically anchored need to belong (e.g., Deci & Ryan, 2000). A feeling of belonging is most likely when individuals perceive that they share characteristics with others in their social environment (Brewer & Harasty, 1996; Dasgupta, Banaji, & Abelson, 1999; De Cremer, 2004; Gaertner & Schopler, 1998) and are accepted by other group members (Eisenberger, Lieberman, & Williams, 2003). Similarity in attitudes and values in particular seem to strengthen interpersonal relationships (Byrne et al.,1986; Condon & Crano, 1988; Shaikh & Kanekar, 1994), reduce people's feelings of uncertainty about their social environment (e.g., Hogg, 2000), and preserve the integrity of their self-image (Tajfel, 1969). Hence, the concept of PO fit is strongly linked to similarities between individuals and social environments.

This notion is also the core proposition of Schneider's (1987) Attraction-Selection-Attrition (ASA) framework, which argues that "people make the place." The ASA framework describes that people are attracted to, selected by, and stay in an organization that matches their personal characteristics. This attraction-selection-attrition process will ultimately lead to homogeneity of people in organizations which, in turn, will define organizational structures, processes, and culture. According to this theory, an organization's culture is largely based on the shared values of organizational members. These values are the guiding principles for organizational norms and behaviors (Schwartz, 1992).

People will experience conflict when there is a discrepancy between the behavioral norms of the environment and their own beliefs about what is right and wrong. This is well documented, for example, in regulatory fit research. *Regulatory focus theory* (Higgins, 1997) argues that individuals are either promotion focused (i.e., they pursue goals by focusing on positive outcomes, such as a high performance appraisal) or prevention focused (i.e., they pursue goals by focusing on avoiding negative outcomes, such as avoiding making errors). Organizational cultures can also be framed in terms of either promotion or prevention. For example, employees might be instructed to produce a high quantity (promotion focus) or they might be instructed to take care of the quality of their work and, therefore, avoid making errors (prevention focus). When people experience regulatory fit (both the person and the situational demands are either promotion focused or prevention focused), they will involve themselves more in what they are doing and perform better than when there is regulatory misfit (e.g., Camacho, Higgins, & Luger, 2003). Conversely, people who do not fit may experience ethical conflict: they have to behave in ways that violate their own values and normative standards. This will result in feelings of guilt and depression, and will lower attachment to the organization (Kammeyer-Mueller, Simon, & Rich, in press).

Person–organization fit has been measured by asking individuals directly about their experience of PO fit (e.g., Cable & DeRue, 2002), also referred to as *PO fit perceptions*, or by comparing individuals' cultural preferences or values with those of the organization. This latter operationalization can take two forms. First, person values (P) and organization values (O) are derived from the same person and combined into a fit index that is labeled as *subjective PO fit*. Second, P and O are derived from different sources such that P is based on the person's values and O is based on the aggregated culture perceptions of organizational members; the resulting fit index is labeled as *objective* or *actual PO fit*. These different PO fit measures have been used in research that examined the effects of fit on people's work attitudes, such as their job satisfaction, organizational commitment, and turnover intentions. It was found that PO fit perceptions were more strongly related to these work attitudes than subjective and objective types of PO fit (Kristof-Brown et al., 2005; Kristof-Brown & Guay, 2010).

The distinction in PO fit measures is relevant for research on newcomer socialization. For example, newcomer PO fit *perceptions*, although highly important for successful socialization, are not very informative when examining the processes that underlie the development of PO fit. Subjective and actual fit measures are more useful then. These measures contain information about newcomers' own values, their perception of the organization's values, or the organization's actual values. Any changes in newcomers' PO fit during socialization can then be further disentangled into changes in the person and/or the environment. Also, researchers are then better able to examine the specific reasons for low or high PO fit at organizational entry and whether these were due to people's unrealistic perceptions of an organization's culture. In the next section we will further address people's PO fit assessments before and at organizational entry, since these assessments may have implications for their experiences during socialization.

From Outsider to Insider: Assessing PO Fit

People self-select into organizations based on their PO fit perceptions during the job-seeking (e.g., Cable & Judge, 1996) and selection stages (e.g., Cable & Judge, 1997). These perceptions are, however, rather superficial and vague. Actually, relatively little is yet known about how people's PO fit perceptions arise before, during, and after being selected for a new job. Most likely, the sources from which people derive their PO fit impression as well as its content will dramatically change over time (Van Vianen, Stoelhorst, & De Goede, in press). Moreover, a person's PO fit perception appears not to be based on a rational comparison of commensurate P and O components. It has been shown, for example, that the relationships between different PO fit operationalizations and individual outcomes differ in strength. Furthermore, calculated PO fit indices that result from (objective or subjective) comparisons between individual characteristics and environmental features do not converge with people's reported PO fit experiences (De Goede, Van Vianen, & Klehe, 2009; Kristof-Brown & Guay, 2010). This could be caused by the fact that the content of the P and O components as operationalized by researchers does not reflect the content that people themselves have in mind. Another possibility is that people weigh the P and O components in a different way than PO fit researchers tend to assume: some types of information may have a heavier weight than others.

During job search, individuals have to rely on general, overall impressions of organizations and their cultures that are based on the facts, beliefs, and feelings associated with these organizations. For example, recognizable and familiar organizations (e.g., Fortune 500 companies) have a reputation or image that shapes applicants' evaluations of these organizations (e.g., Allen, Mahto, & Otondo, 2007; Cober, Brown, Levy, Cober, & Keeping, 2003; Slaughter & Greguras, 2009). Most organizations, however, are not yet familiar and may not offer any explicit information about their organizational values. Nowadays, job seekers are most likely to search for this information by browsing an organization's website—but organizational websites are often only designed to present product and service information. Hence, job seekers may base their PO fit perceptions on rather ambiguous indicators of an organization's culture. Recently, De Goede, Van Vianen, and Klehe (2011) showed that job seekers tend to use stereotypic culture perceptions about the branch of industry in which organizations operate. These industry culture stereotypes give individuals a first indication of how well they may fit the culture of a particular organization. The design of an organization's website may further strengthen or weaken this culture stereotype and related fit impressions. De Goede et al. (2011) found that a well-designed (attractive, user-friendly, good content) website reduced job seekers' use of industry culture stereotypes for assessing their PO fit, particularly when the initial industry stereotype did not match well with their culture preferences. Only carefully designed websites apparently stimulate active processing of culture-relevant information and—if this information reflects reality—may attract applicants who fit with the organization. Given that many organizations do not present culture-relevant information, but likely present attractive yet unrealistic information on their websites, job seekers' actual PO fit as established in the attraction stage is far from obvious.

Hence, people's PO fit perceptions before organizational entry are often based on vague culture impressions and may not be very realistic.

Construal level theory proposes that temporal distance changes the way in which people mentally represent events (Liberman, Sagristano, & Trope,

2002; Trope & Liberman, 2003). The greater the distance the more likely it is that events are represented in relatively few dimensions, and in abstract features rather than detailed ones. Hence, job seekers may have rather abstract images of the—distant—organizations they have to choose from. They may think about organizations, for example, in broad categories of values (human orientation, performance and success) or personalities (e.g., Slaughter & Greguras, 2009; Slaughter, Zickar, Highhouse, & Mohr, 2004). After organizational entry, individuals may no longer use these categories for assessing their PO fit.

In addition, recent research (De Goede et al., 2009) suggests that job seekers tend to focus on a limited set of organizational features when assessing their future PO fit. While job seekers should search for organizations that signal the presence of attractive organizational features and the absence of unattractive ones, they seem to base their fit perceptions mainly on the amount of fit with organizational features they find attractive and neglect available fit information about organizational features that they perceive as unattractive. Hence, deliberations about a prospective organization as a good place to work are at a relatively general and abstract level, and likely portrayed in terms of what one wishes to get rather than what one wishes to avoid. It is probably for this reason that newcomers often have optimistic expectations for how they will fit with their new organizational environment (Ostroff & Kozlowski, 1992; Wanous, 1992).

The distance between the job seeker and the organization should decrease during the selection stage when applicants exchange information with recruiters during the selection interview. However, the selection interview seems to have little effect on applicants' initial impressions of the organization. Rather, it has been shown that applicant attraction to the organization is largely determined by their pre-interview attraction to the organization (Chapman & Webster, 2006). Only interviewer friendliness has a modestly positive influence on post-interview organizational attractiveness, which supports the notion that applicants are particularly concerned with the social context of the future job.

All in all, newcomers likely have positive expectations about their fit with the culture and social context of the organization, but these expectations are often built on abstract, fragmented, and tentative pieces of information. When entering the organization newcomers may particularly seek information that supports these expectations, because people strive to confirm rather than disconfirm their decisions (Jonas, Traut-Mattausch, Frey, & Greenberg, 2008). Indeed, the newcomer socialization process tends to start off with positive expectations and attitudes of both newcomers and organizational insiders. However, this so-called "honeymoon" period is followed by a hangover (i.e., a decline in job satisfaction) as soon as newcomers have learned to know their organization (Boswell, Shipp, Payne, & Culbertson, 2009; Jokisaari & Nurmi, 2009).

Changes in Newcomers' PO Fit

The first period of organizational entry is exciting to most newcomers, since they have to seek information, learn the habits of organizational members and organizational rules, make sense of their new environments, and reevaluate their initial impressions and expectations. Although these initial expectations tend to be high, newcomers are aware that they lack solid knowledge about their new environment and face considerable ambiguity upon entry. They will be in a state of heightened attention and the very first experiences after entry are, therefore, powerful signals for answering one of their main questions: "Is this place going to fit me?"

The first 3 to 6 months are critical for newcomer adaptation (e.g., Bauer & Green, 1994; Bauer, Morrison, & Callister, 1998; Chen & Klimoski, 2003). After this period of socialization, no further post-entry changes in newcomer perceptions are to be expected (Lance, Vandenberg, & Self, 2000). As evidenced by Boswell and colleagues (2009) in a study among job changers, the first period after entry most likely ends up with a deterioration rather than improvement of newcomers' initial job satisfaction. This honeymoon/ hangover effect existed irrespective of the reasons that people gave for their job change (voluntary or not), but the effect was stronger when the job change was due to low satisfaction in the prior job. Dissatisfaction with the prior job may have raised individuals' expectations about the new job. Moreover, individuals who were more socialized, in that they had gained more knowledge of the organization, department, and job role, showed a stronger decline in satisfaction with the new job after 6 months, which was due to a higher honeymoon peak in the very first months after entry. The researchers concluded: "... being socialized may certainly help to facilitate a positive reaction toward the job, yet this honeymoon ultimately is accompanied by a hangover as newcomers settle into and are exposed to less attractive aspects of the new job" (p. 852–853).

This hangover effect may not only be caused by initial expectations that were unrealistically high, but also by real changes in newcomers' new environment. Newcomers probably receive much attention and support from others in the work context in the first period after entry, but this support will easily decrease once one has learned the basics of the new job. Jokisaari & Nurmi (2009) indeed found that newcomers experienced decreasing support from their supervisors over time, which negatively influenced their job satisfaction.

Boswell et al.'s (2009) study suggests that newcomers' PO fit experiences change after organizational entry. Little is yet known about how these changes may occur, but there are a few preliminary studies that shed some light on this issue. To begin with, Wang, Zhan, McCune, and Truxillo (2011) found that PO fit perceptions at entry and those several months later were substantially correlated ($r = .61$), which apparently contradicts the idea that newcomers' PO fit experiences change. Yet, this correlation seems to support the hangover effect since newcomers who had positive PO fit perceptions at entry remained relatively positive (although lower than their initial perceptions) over time when compared to those who had lower PO fit perceptions at entry but whose fit perceptions also declined over time. Hence, after the first socialization period newcomers' fit perceptions may have dropped to a similar extent for different levels of initial fit: a general hangover.

Nevertheless, based on the findings of this study one could conclude that newcomers were reasonably able to assess their future PO fit with the organization. Unfortunately, the study provides no indication of how the correlation between pre-entry and post-entry PO fit perceptions was caused. For example, this correlation may have been (partly) caused by specific personality factors such as optimism or positive affectivity. That is, individuals who are optimistic or high on positive affectivity (a dispositional tendency to experience positive emotions) may have positive pre-entry expectations and may remain relatively positive over time despite some post-entry disappointments. If so, PO fit perceptions are the result of stable personality factors rather than the experienced match between person and organizational values.

Alternatively, the pre-entry–post-entry correlation may indeed be due to job seekers' adequate perceptions of an organization's culture. That is, their expectations were rather accurate but generally too optimistic. However, little is yet known about the accuracy and precise content of job seekers' fit perceptions. Furthermore, there is no research evidencing invariance of the content of people's fit perceptions over time. Instead, what we do know is that job seekers' cultural impressions are ambiguous, abstract, and one-sidedly fed by information about organizational features they find attractive (De Goede et al., 2009). Most likely the sources that feed people's PO fit perceptions will shift from abstract categories (pre-entry) to concrete experiences (post-entry), which means that the content of PO fit perceptions changes over time.

Chatman (1991) examined changes in PO fit with a measure of actual PO fit (comparing individuals' culture preferences with the average culture ratings of organizational members) rather than perceived PO fit (as used in Wang et al.'s 2011 study). She also found a substantial correlation between Time 1 and Time 2 (11 months later) fit assessments ($r = .62$). Note, however, that actual PO fit measures are based on commensurate P and O dimensions that are defined by researchers and, thus, do not necessarily reflect the dimensions that people spontaneously have in mind when assessing their PO fit. Therefore, the findings of Chatman's study cannot be easily compared with those of the Wang et al.'s (2011) study, although the similarity of correlations seems to suggest so.

The relatively modest changes in people's actual PO fit in Chatman's study were apparently due to changes in the P component of the PO fit indices, because the O component was the same at Time 1 and Time 2 (the T1 ratings of organizational members). Hence, newcomers had changed their own values. Moreover, newcomers who had spent time with a mentor showed most changes in PO fit; thus, their values may have shifted to those of their mentors. Positive PO fit changes (i.e., personal value changes) also occurred among newcomers who demonstrated endurance and analytical orientations. These newcomers may have been more aware of the need to adjust their values. Indeed, some researchers (e.g., Wang et al., 2011) have argued that it is easier for newcomers to change their own values than to change the situation.

For several reasons we think that this argument is premature and that it is yet undecided whether changes in PO fit are mainly caused by changes in the newcomer, in the organization, or in both. First, it should be noted that people's fit experiences are most likely based on a comparison between their own values and *perceived* (idiosyncratic) rather than *actual* organizational values (the mean ratings of organizational members). Second, when a person moves from being an outsider to becoming an insider, he or she may also change his/her perceptions of the organization, particularly since these perceptions were rather vague in the stages prior to organizational entry. Third, personality traits and values are generally found to be stable over time (e.g., Roberts, O'Donnell, & Robbins, 2004), thus the person (the P component) may be more consistent over time than the (perceived) organization (the O component). Fourth, the small shifts in personal values that some research has shown could have been due to so-called *beta* or *gamma* changes rather than a real (alpha) change in personal values (e.g., Vandenberg & Self, 1993). *Beta change* occurs when the rating scale is interpreted differently at Time 1 (before or at entry) and Time 2 (after the first stage of socialization). For example, newcomers may become more aware of their actual values when experiencing their new work environment and whether these values are supported. This, in turn, alters the use of the rating scale, such that a 4 on a 5-point Likert scale at T1 may become a 5 at T2, whereas this 1-point difference possesses no real meaning. *Gamma change* occurs when newcomers redefine the construct underlying the measures between T1 and T2. For example, if a newcomer had a strong preference for innovativeness at T1, he or she may rate innovativeness differently at T2 because the construct of innovativeness has changed in meaning.

Cooper-Thomas, Van Vianen, and Anderson (2004) have investigated changes in both newcomers' actual PO fit and PO fit perceptions. Actual fit was assessed with the same indirect PO fit measure as used by Chatman (1991), thus comparing newcomers' own values at T1 and T2 with organizational values as rated by organizational members at T1. First, the correlation between Time 1 (at entry) and Time 2 (4 months later) actual PO fit was .74, indicating that newcomers had hardly changed their own values. Second, the correlation between newcomers' Time 1 (at entry) and Time 2 PO fit perceptions (i.e., asking newcomers directly about their fit experience) was lower, namely .42, which indicates that perceptual changes had occurred. Furthermore, no significant correlation was found between actual and perceived PO fit at Time 1 ($r = .03$), whereas there was a significant correlation between these PO fit measures at Time 2 ($r = .36$). These results together led the researchers to conclude that newcomers had primarily changed their perceptions of the organization.

The few studies presented above suggest only small changes in newcomers' own values and larger changes in their organizational perceptions. However, the extent to which newcomers adapt their values or their view on the organization and whether this will affect their PO fit experience may depend on the way in which they are socialized. There are three approaches toward the study of organizational socialization: a situational approach, an individual difference approach, and an interactionist approach. The situational approach focuses on factors in the organization, such as the use of socialization tactics, in shaping newcomers experiences and their fit perceptions. The individual difference approach focuses on the influence of newcomer attributes, such as their personality traits and proactive behaviors. The interactionist approach considers the interaction between situational and individual factors. Below, we will address the influence of socialization tactics, individual attributes and behaviors, and the interaction between both on (shifts in) newcomers' PO fit after socialization.

Socialization Tactics and PO Fit

The primary goals of socialization are to reduce newcomers' ambiguities with regard to their tasks and roles, to promote their social acceptance (coming to feel liked and trusted by peers), and to ensure the continuity of an organization's central values. Successful organizational socialization has typically been understood as the alignment between newcomers' personal values and behaviors and those of the organization (Cooper-Thomas & Anderson, 2006). A common understanding of organizational values and goals will advance effective communications, smooth collaborations, and stability among organizational members.

Organizations use different socialization tactics to initiate newcomers into their basic values and behavioral repertoires. Jones (1986) has distinguished six socialization tactics, which are divided into three categories: context, content, and social (see also Cable & Parsons, 2001). The context dimension concerns the way in which organizations provide information to newcomers, namely collective (as a group) or individual (one-on-one), and formal (occurs outside one's work setting) or informal (on the job). Content socialization tactics relate to the order in which information is given to newcomers: in fixed or variable, and random or sequential ways. The social dimension reflects how newcomers get access to and learn from previous job incumbents (serial socialization) and receive social support from insiders (investiture socialization). Jones (1986) further combined these six socialization tactics into two dimensions: an institutionalized and an individualized dimension. Institutionalized socialization is collective, formal, sequential and fixed; role models for newcomers are present (serial); and newcomers receive support from organization members. In contrast, individualized socialization concerns individual and on-the-job training (informal), and socialization tactics are random and variable.

Two additional types of socialization should be mentioned: divestiture and mentoring. Divestiture socialization, which is collective, formal, and fixed, aims to break down preexisting employee values and attitudes and replace them with those of the organization. Divestiture socialization is, in fact, contrary to investiture socialization that aims to affirm newcomers' attributes and identity through the support of insiders. Finally, mentoring concerns socialization through the support of senior organizational members (Kram, 1983; Louis, Posner, & Powell, 1983; Nelson & Quick, 1991; Ostroff & Kozlowski, 1993).

As noted above, whether newcomers change their own values or (their perceptions of) those of the environment may depend on an organization's prevalent socialization practices. Institutionalized socialization tactics are designed to reduce ambiguity by providing newcomers with explicit information and a fixed set of learning experiences. These tactics are primarily used to sustain the status quo. They, therefore, aim to adapt newcomers' values to those of the environment. Similarly, divestiture tactics that focus on stripping away newcomers' identity and replacing it by a new one try to cause substantial changes in newcomers. Investiture tactics, on the other hand, are not directed toward such personal changes. Studies that measure newcomer experience of investiture tactics typically include items such as "My organization accepts newcomers for who they are," and "The organization does not try to change the values and beliefs of newcomers" (Ashforth & Saks, 1996). Hence, institutionalized and divestiture tactics may be able to cause changes in newcomers' values while individualized and investiture tactics may mainly cause changes in newcomers' direct organizational environment or, more likely, changes in their perceptions of this environment.

Relatively few socialization studies have directly examined this proposition. The divestiture socialization tactic in particular has received relatively little research attention, since this tactic is mainly used in occupations and organizations where a strong uniformity of behavior is required such as in police, military, and medical teams. Note that new entrants in these organizations may have initial cultural expectations that are fairly realistic and are attractive to them. Hence, newcomers' actual PO fit may already be high and divestiture socialization tactics will not change but rather strengthen newcomers' own values. If, however, divestiture socialization tactics force people to change their own values, they may experience ethical conflict (Kammeyer et al., in press), which probably leads to attrition.

Ashforth and Saks (1996) were the first to compare the different effects of institutionalized and more individualized (i.e., investiture) socialization tactics, but they did not specifically examine changes in PO fit (and its constituting entities). They proposed that institutionalized socialization tactics would be positively associated with person change and negatively with role changes, and the investiture tactic would be negatively associated with person change. Person change was assessed by asking study respondents directly whether they had changed with respect to their values and personality when adjusting to their jobs. Their results, first, showed that newcomers' reported person change was on average lower than, for example, their attempts to change roles, at 4 months as well as at 10 months after entry. Second, it was found that person change after 4 months was negatively associated with individualized socialization, and attempts to change roles were negatively associated with institutionalized socialization. The researchers concluded that "socialization practices that endorse a newcomer's incoming identity and attributes are less likely to provoke person change," and that "institutionalized socialization induces newcomers to conform to established goals and methods and thereby maintain the status quo" (p. 169). Yet, institutional socialization practices as a whole barely caused any personal changes; only collective socialization tactics (when considered separately) were slightly associated with personal changes.

Cable and Parsons (2001) examined newcomers' PO fit changes as caused by experienced socialization practices in a period of 2 years after organizational entry. They measured newcomers' own values at entry (T1) and after two years (T3), and newcomers' perceptions of organizational values after one year (T2). Cable and Parsons, therefore, could establish changes in newcomers' values but, unfortunately, they did not compare newcomers' values at T1 with those at T3 directly. Instead, value changes were derived from a comparison between the two subjective PO fit measures at T1 (a congruence index of T1 values and T2 organizational perceptions) and T3 (a congruence index of T3 values and T2 organizational perceptions). The zero-order correlation between the two PO fit indices was .59. The researchers concluded that newcomers' values had shifted toward their perceptions of their organizations' values. This change occurred if newcomers had experienced sequential and fixed (content socialization) and/or serial and investiture socialization (social) tactics, but not when they had experienced collective and formal (context) socialization tactics. Further, after inclusion of control variables, the relationship between the two fit indices raised to .65 (the standardized beta weight), which reaches the standard criterion for a good test-retest reliability over a period of 2 years. Overall, this study provides moderate evidence of personal value changes over time as due to socialization tactics: the more (individualized) time newcomers spend with organizational insiders the more they tend to shift their own values toward their perceptions of the organization. Note, however, that the findings of this study do not resonate with those of Ashforth and Saks' (1996) prior study.

Cooper-Thomas et al. (2004) examined the influence of the two social socialization tactics (serial and investiture) on changes in newcomers' PO fit perceptions, but assessed these tactics separately. They found that the investiture socialization tactic, involving social support from coworkers, was most strongly related to perceptions of PO fit after 4 months. Furthermore, newcomers' initial PO fit perceptions declined less for newcomers who had experienced social support from coworkers. Since socialization tactics did not cause newcomers to change their personal values toward those of the organization, but instead changed their perceptions of the environment, these researchers suggested that newcomers who receive social support may put weight on the positive features of the environment in particular. Social support from insiders helps newcomers to sense a better fit with their new environment. If newcomers develop social ties with other organizational members, they have more access to information and sensemaking, which will promote learning about prevalent values and behaviors. Most importantly, a supportive social environment signals both social inclusion (acceptance of one's identity by others) and the presence of organizational values that people in general tend to prefer (such as cooperativeness and care for others).

To summarize, individualized socialization tactics most likely affect people's perceptions of the organizational environment. Learning about the actual culture of the organization may cause a negative change in newcomers' PO fit perceptions. However, social support from insiders and endorsement of one's identity likely buffer a hangover effect. Socialization tactics that aim to strip away one's identity will strengthen rather than change the values of newcomers who have deliberately chosen an organization's culture. Furthermore, these tactics will also less likely cause personal changes among newcomers who have unrealistic cultural expectations; these newcomers will leave.

Newcomer Characteristics and PO Fit

The extent to which newcomers experience fit with their new organization will not only depend on an organization's socialization efforts but also on newcomers' own characteristics and behaviors. First, dispositional factors may affect newcomer PO fit; that is, some people may inherently match more easily with different environments than others. For example, research on individual differences in job satisfaction has evidenced that individual dispositions matter. Personality constructs such as core self-evaluations (including locus of control, self-esteem, self-efficacy, and emotional stability), positive and negative affectivity (PA and NA), and the Big Five personality factors of conscientiousness and extraversion are all significantly related to job satisfaction (e.g., Judge, Heller, & Klinger, 2008). Stable personality factors that affect people's view on their job may also affect their perceptions of (fit with) the work environment. Therefore, it can be expected that newcomers who are relatively high on core self-evaluations, positive affectivity (PA), conscientiousness, and extraversion, and relatively low on negative affectivity (NA) will not only have higher PO fit expectations before entry but will also experience more PO fit after entry. To our best knowledge there are no studies that have tested this proposition.

In one of our own recent and as yet unpublished studies, we found some preliminary evidence for the relationship between PA, NA, and PO fit in a sample of 71 employees (45% males, mean age = 41 years). PO fit was operationalized both as employees' direct PO fit perceptions (see Cable & DeRue, 2002) and as subjective fit, which was the profile similarity index of employees' values and their perceptions of the organization's values. The P and O components were measured with the *organizational* culture profile (O'Reilly, Chatman, & Caldwell, 1991). We also assessed employees' job satisfaction. Like previous studies, we found significant correlations between PA, NA, and job satisfaction ($r = .30$ and $-.33$, respectively). Moreover, significant correlations were found between PA, NA, and PO fit perceptions ($r = .28$ and $-.43$, respectively), and NA—but not PA—was significantly related to subjective fit ($r = -.27$). Further analyses revealed that affectivity could explain incremental variance in employees' direct PO fit perceptions above and beyond subjective fit. In addition, we found a significant interaction between PA and subjective fit, indicating that low subjective fit was buffered by high PA. Altogether, these results suggest that positive and negative affectivity affected people's spontaneous PO fit perceptions irrespective of their subjective fit (the calculated congruence between person values and perceived organizational values). This corroborates literatures on affect and decision making, which propose that "moods activate mood-congruent material in memory, resulting in mood-congruent judgments" (Clore & Palmer, 2009, p. 22); in other words, mood directs one's attention to the positive or negative features of the environment.

Proactive personality is another trait that may affect newcomer PO fit perceptions. Proactive personality is defined as a dispositional tendency to initiate environmental change in a variety of situations (Bateman & Crant, 1993). Proactive people choose work environments that match their values, and when in the environment they do not accept things as they are but take initiatives in improving current circumstances or creating new ones. More proactive as compared to less proactive individuals are better able to satisfy their needs through pursuing goals that are consistent with their values, interests, and needs. These self-concordant goals, in turn, direct them to persist in goal achievement (Greguras & Diefendorff, 2010). Proactive personality correlates positively with career success (Seibert, Crant, & Kraimer, 1999), performance, job satisfaction, and organizational commitment (Thomas, Whitman, & Viswesvaran, 2010). Further, proactive individuals are involved in social networking (Thomas et al., 2010) and develop high-quality relationships with their supervisors (Li, Liang, & Crant, 2010). The proactive personality construct refers to the initiation of environmental rather than personal changes that could lead to better PO fit.

Extant proactive personality studies were primarily concerned with tenured employees and were correlational in nature. Only a few studies have investigated newcomers' proactive personality at entry and their adjustment to the new job after socialization (Chan & Schmitt, 2000; Kammeyer-Mueller & Wanberg, 2003; Wang et al., 2011). The results of these latter studies are fairly inconclusive. Chan and Schmitt (2000) and Kammeyer-Mueller and Wanberg (2003) found newcomer proactivity to be positively related to task mastery, role clarity, and social integration, which can be conceived of as indicators of demands–abilities fit and PO fit. In contrast, Wang et al. (2011) found nonsignificant and small relationships between newcomer proactivity (as measured at entry) and diverse fit measures several months later.

Wang and colleagues were specifically interested in the role of dispositional adaptability as a possible predictor of changes in newcomers' fit perceptions, and they used both newcomer proactivity and their openness to experience as control variables. They conceptualized adaptability as "an individual's dispositional tendency to make active attempts to adjust him or herself to fit new tasks and new environments" (p. 165). Hence, these researchers argued that adaptability, and thus the adaptation process, is focused on changing the self rather than the environment: newcomers are more likely to reappraise and reframe their values than employ activities that change their environment.

Five dimensions of dispositional adaptability were distinguished: cultural (attempts to adjust the self to fit to different cultures), interpersonal (tendency to be flexible and open-minded when dealing with new people), learning (attempts to adjust the self to learning aspects of the new tasks and new environment), work stress (attempts to adjust the self to fit to a stressful work environment), and uncertainty adaptability (attempts to adjust to the uncertainty existing in new tasks and environments). They examined the relationships between each of the first four adaptability dimensions (thus not uncertainty adaptability) with changes in PO fit, person–group fit, demands–abilities fit, and needs–supplies fit perceptions, respectively. Significant but moderate relationships (path coefficients ranged from .12 to .23) were found between the four adaptability dimensions and the respective fit domains 3 months later. This study showed that people's self-reports about their attempts to adjust themselves to the environment were positively related to their fit perceptions over time. Yet, these findings did not provide robust evidence that people's attempts were exclusively directed toward *personal* changes.

Most of the dispositional factors discussed above seem to affect newcomers' PO fit and adaptation in indirect ways, such as through their influence on newcomers' proactive behaviors. Indeed, personality traits direct people's cognitions and behaviors and influence the choices they make about which activities to engage in (e.g., Mount, Barrick, Scullen, & Rounds, 2005). For example, newcomers differ in the extent to which they cognitively frame their new environment. Newcomers who frame their environment positively (by viewing their situation as a challenge and focusing on the positive side of things) seek information and feedback and attempt to build relationships. They are better adjusted than those who do not show these cognitions and subsequent proactive behaviors (e.g., Ashford & Black, 1996).

Ostensibly, proactive behaviors may be produced mainly by people's proactive personalities. Parker & Collins (2010), however, found that proactive personality was only related to specific types of proactive behaviors, namely proactive *work* behaviors. These behaviors include taking charge, individual innovation, problem prevention, and voice, and are mainly focused on changing the organizational environment. No relationships were found between proactive personality and feedback inquiry and feedback monitoring. These types of proactive behaviors concern the gathering of information about oneself and thus refer to possible personal changes. In other words, proactive personalities show proactive behaviors that change the environment, whereas positive framers show proactive behaviors that could potentially lead to changes in the self and/or the environment—but most likely to changes in perceptions of the environment.

Other personality traits that seem relevant to people's proactive behaviors are openness to experience, intelligence, self-monitoring, and curiosity. People who rate high on openness to experience and intelligence are curious, imaginative and prefer variety (e.g., LePine, Colquitt, & Erez, 2000). They approach new environments with a positive view and are more involved in feedback seeking (Wanberg & Kammeyer-Mueller, 2000). Like the positive framers, they may particularly tend to change their perceptions of the environment.

People high on self-monitoring "typically strive to be the type of person called for by each situation in which they find themselves and thus are particularly sensitive and responsive to interpersonal and situational specifications of behavioral appropriateness; they use this information to monitor and control the images of self that they project to others in social situations" (Snyder, Berscheid, & Matwychuk, 1988, p. 972). High self-monitors actively seek for social cues and adjust themselves to the norms of the situation. Moreover, they are successful in using impression-management techniques, such as ingratiation and self-promotion (e.g., Higgins & Judge, 2004) that facilitate acceptance by other group members. Hence, high self-monitors will experience more PO fit than low self-monitors, who are mainly concerned with keeping the authentic self. Furthermore, high self-monitors will more likely accomplish fit by changing the self toward the environment, whereas low self-monitors will experience fit only if organizational values are congruent with the self.

Curiosity is a narrow trait that reflects the "desire to know" and that energizes people's exploratory behaviors. Harrison, Sluss, and Ashforth (2011) distinguished between *specific* and *diversive* curiosity. The first concerns narrow and direct (e.g., solving specific problems) exploration, whereas the second concerns broader and more indirect forms of exploration (e.g., enjoyment in exploring new ideas). It was found that newcomers' specific curiosity was most strongly associated with information seeking, while diversive curiosity was mainly associated with positive framing. Furthermore, positive framing was positively linked to job performance and taking charge, which points to newcomers' efforts toward changing the environment.

To summarize, extant (although sparse) research suggests that some stable personality traits are predictive of newcomers' (changes in) PO fit, while other personality traits are predictive of newcomers' proactive behaviors, which, in turn, could cause changes in PO fit.

Personality traits that seem to influence newcomer PO fit (perceptions) directly are: core self-evaluations, positive and negative affectivity, conscientiousness, extraversion, and dispositional adaptability. Personality traits that primarily seem to affect newcomers' cognitions and proactive behaviors are: proactive personality, openness to experience, intelligence, self-monitoring, and specific and diversive curiosity.

Note that proactive behaviors such as information seeking do not necessarily result in better PO fit, since this information may inform newcomers that their values are incongruent with those of the organization: familiarity can breed contempt. Hence, whereas progressive learning about the content of the job (the tasks, the skill requirements) may lead to better demands–ability fit, learning with regard to the cultural features of the organization may on average be unrelated to changes in PO fit. However, specific combinations of personality traits and proactive behaviors may relate to better PO fit, due to their potential to change one's environment, perception of the environment, or self. Most personality traits refer to changes in newcomer environmental perceptions, whereas proactive personalities tend to change the actual environment and high self-monitors tend to change the self.

The Interaction of Situational and Individual Factors Affecting PO Fit

Studies that combined organization-driven and individual-driven socialization factors found that both contributed to socialization outcomes such as newcomer learning (Ashforth, Sluss, & Saks, 2007) and fit perceptions (Wang, et al., 2011). Several researchers have examined how organizational socialization tactics and newcomers' personality traits and proactive behaviors interact with each other and predict, among other things, newcomers' PO fit perceptions. Generally, it was found that each of these predictors contributed to newcomers' PO fit perceptions independently. For example, Gruman, Saks, and Zweig (2006) showed that newcomers' PO fit after the first 4 months was significantly related to institutionalized socialization tactics, newcomers' self-efficacy, and proactive behaviors such as general socializing (attending company social gatherings and trying to socialize to get to know coworkers), boss-relationship building, and feedback-seeking. Note that these proactive behaviors were focused on building relationships with the social environment. Information seeking was negatively related to newcomers' PO fit perceptions. The positive relationship between socialization tactics and PO fit perceptions was stronger, however, for newcomers who were low on feedback seeking and information seeking, which suggests that these tactics indeed signal positive organizational features such as care for newcomers and their social inclusion.

Similar results were found in an earlier study from Kim, Cable, and Kim (2005). These researchers also evidenced that institutionalized socialization tactics were positively related to employees' PO fit perceptions. This relationship was stronger for newcomers who had put less effort in building relationships with their supervisors, but also for newcomers who had engaged in general socializing. Apparently, relationship building with the supervisor overrules the effects of socialization practices, whereas general socializing activities harmonize with socialization

practices to create stronger experiences of PO fit. Furthermore, institutionalized socialization tactics had a stronger impact on newcomers' PO fit perceptions for those who rated high on positive framing. These newcomers tend to focus on the positive features of socialization experiences and perceive their organization's socialization efforts as being helpful for their adaptation.

In sum, the few studies that took an interactionist approach to predicting PO fit as an outcome of socialization revealed that organizational socialization tactics together with newcomer dispositions and proactive cognitions and behaviors contribute to newcomer PO fit perceptions. Yet, proactive behaviors, such as seeking feedback and information and building a relationship with one's supervisor, tend to mitigate the influence of institutionalized socialization practices. Information seeking has a negative impact on PO fit perceptions, while seeking feedback from and having a good relationship with one's supervisor impact these perceptions positively. Finally, proactive cognitions such as positive framing and proactive behaviors such as general socializing tend to strengthen the positive effect of socialization tactics. Newcomers' PO fit perceptions seem to thrive when organizations employ socialization activities and when newcomers themselves have a positive mindset, seek to be involved in their social environment, and create good relationships with their supervisors. Institutionalized socialization tactics are probably most effective if they are launched shortly after newcomer entrance, because they open up opportunities for socializing with coworkers. Then, after coworker relationships have been built, newcomers may focus more on creating a good relationship with their supervisors (Chan & Schmitt, 2000), particularly since supervisors tend to lose interest in newcomers over time (Jokisaari & Nurmi, 2009).

Development of PO fit Perceptions: An Agenda for Future Research

Although socialization research has made some progress in determining the factors that influence newcomers' socialization outcomes and PO fit perceptions, the underlying processes of how individuals come to form their PO fit impressions during socialization are yet to be discovered. In this section we will address four central themes for future research. The first theme concerns the specific causes of new entrants' misfits, the affective reactions these may cause, and how newcomers cope with their emotions. A second theme concerns the causes of new entrants' changes in PO fit perceptions and whether these are due to changes in the person or (perceptions of) the environment. Third, we advocate more research with regard to the sources that newcomers use for their PO fit perceptions: Do they derive these perceptions from cultural manifestations at the organizational level, or do they derive them from other sources such as the values and behaviors of organizational members? Finally, we will reflect on the possibility that misfits could be compensated by fits and, if so, how this may affect newcomers' overall fit perceptions.

Causes of and Reactions to New Entrants' Misfits

Above we have argued that most newcomers both form and change their PO fit perceptions during socialization, since their initial perceptions were based on ambiguous sources and types of fit information. These unreliable and overly optimistic PO fit perceptions are the starting point from which they assess their PO fit during socialization. Most likely, their initial PO fit expectations only encompass organizational features they wish to attain (values they find attractive and hope to find in the organization) but not those they want to avoid (values they find aversive and hope not to find in the organization). Therefore, newcomers may also primarily focus on these attractive attributes when entering the organization. Hence, any (negative) change in PO fit perceptions shortly after organizational entry is probably due to disappointment about the absence of organizational attributes they find attractive. For example, a newcomer felt attracted to the new organization because she expected the organization's culture to be innovative, a value she highly appreciates. After entrance the newcomer finds out that the culture is less innovative than expected, which negatively influences her fit perception.

In a next stage, newcomer PO fit perception may further change when experiencing organizational values the newcomer finds unattractive but did not imagine before organizational entry. For example, over time the newcomer finds out that the organization values strong competition among employees, a value she dislikes. The misfit she experiences with regard to competiveness (more competition than preferred) will then negatively influence her overall PO fit perception. These examples illustrate that the content of newcomers' PO fit perceptions may shift during socialization due to the saliency of specific values (from values one finds attractive to those

that are aversive). Future research should examine whether and how the development of newcomers' PO fit perceptions depends on the saliency and content of newcomer and organizational values.

Further research on the specific causes of misfit (i.e., whether they are due to misfit on values that individuals find attractive or aversive) is particularly important for deepening our understanding of newcomer adaptation. That is, adaptation to an organization that lacks the features one finds attractive may entail coping mechanisms that are different from adaptation to an organization that appears to have the features one finds aversive. How do people deal with disappointment as a likely reaction to the lack of attractive features, and how do they deal with anxiety and stress as a likely reaction to experiencing aversive attributes they may not have thought of or expected? Since newcomers will initially be focused on finding attractive organizational attributes, their first affective reaction toward experiencing misfit (the organization does not provide the attractive attributes one wished)—the hangover effect—is disappointment, an emotion that is felt when an outcome is less than expected.

People tend to deal with disappointment by employing a defense tactic called "retroactive pessimism" (e.g., Tykocinski & Steinberg, 2005). That is, they may adjust their ideas about the chance to find another, more fitting organization. They will reason, for example, that their expectations were unrealistically high since most other organizations will not have these attractive attributes either. Furthermore, they may block counterfactual alternatives suggesting that better job alternatives were in their reach. Generally, the use of defense mechanisms when dealing with disappointment depends on the amount of control that people have over their decisions. Due to the complexity of the job choice process, people will often experience less control over their job choice decisions. Moreover, disappointment is naturally associated with feelings of powerlessness (e.g., Zeelenberg, Van Dijk, Manstead, & Van Der Pligt, 1998), which trigger defense mechanisms. Hence, we posit that a drop in PO fit perceptions and associated disappointment will likely lead to reframing or—when possible—changing the situation: an attractive attribute that an environment does not provide could eventually be accomplished by the newcomer himself or herself. Furthermore, socialization tactics may buffer against disappointments by providing newcomers with other experiences that fit, such as the interest and support of the social environment.

Although the first stage of socialization may involve feelings of disappointment due to the lack of preferred organizational attributes, newcomers may also gradually experience misfits with respect to attributes they find aversive: the organization has characteristics one dislikes. These types of discrepancies most likely result in emotions such as threat, fear, and stress. The natural reaction to threat is psychological and/or behavioral escape, avoidance, and protection (e.g., Tykocinski & Steinberg, 2005). For example, if newcomers experience an organizational culture (e.g., highly competitive) that is opposed to their values (e.g., low competition), they may try to reappraise the situation and/or to engage in actual behaviors, such as attempts to change the situation or to withdraw themselves from the situation. However, since organizational cultures tend to be pervasive and stable, aversive organizational attributes will often be difficult to change. It is also doubtful whether socialization tactics will serve as a buffer in this case, since these tactics will strengthen rather than weaken newcomers' negative cultural experiences. Note that socializing with coworkers and efforts to create a good relationship with one's supervisor may not relieve the burden of an aversive environment, because these same organizational members may adhere to the values one desperately seeks to avoid. Hence, a drop in PO fit perceptions that is due to a misfit regarding newcomers' aversive values and that is associated with fear and stress could lead to temporary reframing, but it is more likely to lead to psychological or actual withdrawal. Aversive organizational attributes are difficult to deal with and may not be moderated by socialization practices.

Newcomers' Person and Organization Changes

A second theme for further research concerns the focal entity that instigates changes in PO fit during socialization. *How* do newcomers adapt to their new environment—by changing their own characteristics (P) or those of the organizational environment (O)? A first but provisional answer to this question is that changes in P or O will likely depend on newcomer dispositions, such as their self-monitoring, curiosity, and positive framing. Newcomers high on self-monitoring may focus their adaptive efforts mainly on the self: they produce "a whole new coat of fur or feathers" in order to match the color of their environment. In contrast, newcomers who are curious and/or optimistic may particularly adapt by reframing or changing the organizational

environment: they color the environment in a way that matches their needs.

Based on our own review of extant research as described above, and on theoretical notions about the centrality and stability of human basic values, we argue that, with the exception of some personalities, people in general do not tend to change their initial values during socialization. Furthermore, prior research did not account for the occurrence of beta and gamma changes (i.e., changes in meanings of rating and content of constructs) that could explain the small changes in personal values as due to people's experiences. As an exception, Van Vianen & Prins (1997) measured alpha, beta, and gamma changes in a sample of employees who had remained in their jobs and organizations, or who had changed their jobs and/or organization within a period of 10 months. They found real changes in employee perceptions of organizational culture (O) when newcomers had undergone environmental changes; no real changes occurred in employee culture preferences (P).

Future research should further scrutinize how alpha, beta, and gamma changes in P and O and how these changes affect newcomer PO fit perceptions. If indeed newcomer values remain stable and their organizational perceptions become more realistic over time, newcomer values as measured during selection will be a strong predictor for their future PO fit. In addition, an organization's socialization efforts should then be focused on fostering realism rather than personal changes. If, however, newcomer values appear to be more flexible than assumed, organizations could direct efforts toward influencing newcomers' initial values rather than selecting individuals as based on their prospective PO fit.

The question of whether changes after organizational entry mainly occur in P or O is also of high theoretical importance because two seminal theories about social integration proclaim opposing views: *social identity theory* and *self-verification theory* (see Swann, Polzer, Seyle, & Ko, 2004). Social identity theory emphasizes that individuals tend to see themselves in terms of their membership in a group. Therefore, they may adopt the characteristics of the social environment into their self-views. Self-verification theory, on the other hand, proposes that people have a basic need to preserve continuity in their self-views, especially when they form long-term relationships with others. They want others to see them as they really are, and they want the group to confirm their self-views. Altogether, social identity theory would predict that newcomers will change their own characteristics to those of the group. Conversely, self-verification theory would predict that newcomers would rather change their perceptions of the environment, for example, by paying attention to confirming aspects of the environment or by interpretations of environmental experiences that reinforce their self-view. Altogether, more research is needed that examines whether people convert their adjustment attempts into cognitive and behavioral actions that are focused on changing the self or the environment.

The Sources of PO Fit Perceptions

Changes in P or O may, among others, depend on the sources that people use to establish their PO fit. Both social identity and self-verification theory stress the importance of one's inclusion into the social environment. When entering an organization, newcomers will be mainly focused on the characteristics of the direct social environment rather than on those of the whole organization. Indeed, the socialization period of about 4 months is relatively short to obtain a comprehensive impression of an organization's culture. Therefore, newcomers' PO fit perceptions in this period will presumably not be based on solid cultural information at the organizational level, but may rather be derived from the attributes and behaviors of organizational members with whom they communicate (Van Vianen, Stoelhorst, et al., in press). Newcomers may observe the behaviors of organizational members, and particularly those of successful members who they consider to be role models. The more similarities a newcomer perceives with these role models, the more likely he or she will adopt role models' behaviors (for an extended argumentation see Van Vianen, Stoelhorst et al., in press). Social identity theory refers to these role models as individuals "in good standing" or *prototypical* members (Tyler & Blader, 2002). According to this theory, newcomers will focus on the attributes and behaviors that are distinctive for the prototype and are shared by other prototypes. Newcomers use these attributes to assess their similarities and dissimilarities with the social environment, which are also the bases of their PO fit perceptions. As discussed above, social identity theory suggests that newcomers focus on the attributes of prototypical members and compare these with their own attributes, whereas self-verification theory suggests that newcomers focus on their own most relevant attributes (such as attractive values) and assess whether these

are confirmed by prototypical members. Future research should test these conflicting propositions, since the specific sources that newcomers use for their comparisons could be important for their PO fit perceptions.

The Compensation of Misfits

Our fourth theme for future research relates to the question whether misfits can be compensated by fits. PO fit theory and research assume that PO fit perceptions are equally based on organizational values that support a person's values, that is, attractive values, and values that contradict a person's values, that is, aversive values. As we have discussed above, job seekers' overall PO fit perceptions do not reflect all information equally. Rather, job seekers weigh the presence or absence of attractive values in the organization more heavily than the presence or absence of aversive values (De Goede et al., 2009). Moreover, we have argued that newcomers may also mainly pay attention to fits or misfits on attractive values right after organizational entry, which would imply that the levels of fit with respect to newcomers' aversive and neutral values contribute less to their PO fit perceptions. Hence, also after organizational entry people's PO fit perceptions may not be as comprehensive as has been assumed in the fit literature.

However, newcomers may experience fit on some attractive values but they may experience misfit on other attractive ones. Additionally, the focus of attention may shift over time such that fit on aversive values may become relatively more important. Consequently, because of modifications in the weighing of fits and misfits, newcomers' PO fit perceptions may change accordingly. The steep drop in PO fit perceptions due to disappointments about misfits on attractive values may recover, and the sources of newcomer PO fit perceptions may be more balanced over time. Future research should explore these mechanisms and test whether employees' PO fit perceptions become more comprehensive with tenure.

A related point of discussion is whether different fit domains may interact with each other when influencing individual outcomes such as people's job satisfaction, organizational commitment, and turnover intentions. Could suboptimal PO fit be compensated, for example, by good demands–ability or needs–supplies fit? The few studies that examined possible interactions (for an overview see Van Vianen, Shen, & Huang, 2011) have shown equivocal results. Van Vianen, Shen et al. (2011)

suggest a *theory of multiple fits* that predicts additive effects of similar types of fits and interactive effects of different types of fits. That is, complementary fits (person–job, demands–ability, and needs–supplies fit) all concern the content of jobs, and people may combine these fits into a higher-order construct of overall fit with the job. Similarly, supplementary fits (person–organization, person–group, and person–supervisor fit) concern the social/relational context of jobs, and people may combine these fits into a higher-order construct of fit with the social context. Both these higher-order constructs may interact such that the relationship between overall fit with the job and individual outcomes (e.g., turnover intentions) is moderated by overall fit with the social context of the job, and vice versa. If so, this would further stress the role of socialization tactics since these tactics seem to support newcomers' job fit as well as their fit with the social context.

Conclusion

Newcomer socialization is highly important for the study of PO fit. Yet, most PO fit research has been conducted with samples of tenured employees who were already more or less adapted to their work environments. Newcomers, as opposed to tenured employees, have a fresh view on the work environment and are specifically sensitive to cultural cues. Furthermore, their self-view is relatively detached from environmental influences. Hence, future studies that aim to investigate the processes that underlie the formation of PO fit perceptions should particularly focus on individuals entering new environments. Transitions provide excellent opportunities to obtain a deeper understanding of how people become connected to and integrated into their environment.

In this chapter, we have argued that PO fit is strongly linked to similarities between individuals and social environments. Because cultures are created by people, PO fit can be equated with social connectedness and acceptance. Indeed, newcomer adjustment conceptualized as social acceptance was found to relate to a great variety of outcomes, such as performance, satisfaction, commitment, and stay intentions (Bauer, Bodner, Erdogan, Truxillo, & Tucker, 2007). Moreover, socialization primarily occurs within the context of workgroups. It is through newcomers' interactions with direct coworkers and supervisors that they learn about the values and norms of the group and those of the organization as a whole (e.g., Jokisaari & Nurmi, 2009). We have proposed that newcomers

experience PO fit when their own values and those of salient others in the work environment are aligned. Precisely how they arrive at a state of satisfactory PO fit, by changing (perceptions of) the self, the environment, or both, is a central theme for further research. The focal dependent variable in future research is (the development of) newcomers' PO fit perceptions, because people decide and act in accordance with their perceptions rather than reality (e.g., Ashforth & Saks, 1996; Cable & Judge, 1997).

Both PO fit and socialization researchers (Kammeyer-Mueller, 2007) advocate a dynamic approach to newcomer socialization and PO fit. Recently, a beginning has been made with theorizing about how fit processes may unfold over time. For example, Shipp and Jansen (2011) have argued that individuals craft their fit perceptions. They proposed a temporal model of fit narratives composed of recollections of past fit, perceptions of current fit, and anticipations of future fit. In addition to this excellent initiative to develop a temporal theory of fit, we think that other temporal and more fundamental stances toward the fit concept are necessary. We believe that future PO research should rely more heavily on extant basic theories concerning people's temporal construals, information processing, decision making, and attitude change. In this chapter we have described that newcomers' PO fit perceptions tend to decrease during socialization. However, as newcomers cope with disappointments they mobilize resources (adaptive cognitions and behaviors) to improve their PO fit, which may indeed result in a better fit in the longer run. Future research could pay more attention to the temporal fluctuations in PO fit perceptions as related to people's adaptation capacities and strategies.

The most significant shortcoming of fit research to date is the failure to detect the content of people's fit perceptions and how these perceptions are shaped. If researchers lack knowledge about the fit concept, they also lack the basic information for studying temporal changes. Specifically, by assessing perceptions of fit rather than directly assessing what individuals want versus what the environment provides, we cannot detect what is happening at a specific enough level. Hence, researchers should be careful engaging into the dynamics of fit as long as the fit construct is under debate.

Acknowledgment

Note: This publication was supported by the FMG-UvA Research Priority Grant on Affect Regulation.

References

Allen, D. G., Mahto, R. V., & Otondo, R. F. (2007). Web-based recruitment: Effects of information, organizational brand, and attitudes toward a website on applicant attraction. *Journal of Applied Psychology, 92*(6), 1696–1708.

Ashford, S. J., & Black, J. S. (1996). Proactivity during organizational entry: The role of desire for control. *Journal of Applied Psychology, 81*(2), 199–214.

Ashforth, B. E., & Saks, A. M. (1996). Socialization tactics: Longitudinal effects on newcomer adjustment. *The Academy of Management Journal, 39*(1), 149–178.

Ashforth, B. E., Sluss, D. M., Saks, A. M. (2007). Socialization tactics, proactive behavior, and newcomer learning: Integrating socialization models. *Journal of Vocational Behavior, 70*(3), 447–462

Bateman, T. S., & Crant, M. (1993). The proactive component of organizational behavior: A measure and correlates. *Journal of Organizational Behavior, 14*(2), 103–118.

Bauer, T. N., & Green, S. G. (1994). Effect of newcomer involvement in work-related activities: A longitudinal study of socialization. *Journal of Applied Psychology, 79*(2), 211–223.

Bauer, T. N., Bodner, T., Erdogan, B., Truxillo, D. M., & Tucker, J. S. (2007). Newcomer adjustment during organizational socialization: a meta-analytic review of antecedents, outcomes, and methods, *Journal of Applied Psychology, 92*(3), 707–721.

Bauer, T. N., Morrison, E. W., & Callister, R. R. (1998). Organizational socialization: A review and directions for future research. In: G. R. Ferris, & K. M. Rowland (Eds.), *Research in personnel and human resource management* (Vol. 16, pp. 149–214). Greenwich, CT: JAI Press.

Brewer, M. B., & Harasty, A. S. (1996). Seeing groups as entities: The role of perceiver motivation. In R. M. Sorrentino, & E. T. Higgins (Eds.), *Handbook of motivation and cognition* (Vol. 3, pp. 347–370). New York: Guilford Press.

Boswell, W. R., Shipp, A. J., Payne, S. C., & Culbertson, S. S. (2009). Changes in newcomer job satisfaction over time: Examining the pattern of honeymoons and hangovers. *Journal of Applied Psychology, 94*(4), 844–858.

Byrne, D., Clore, G. L., & Smeaton, G. (1986). The attraction hypothesis: Do similar attitudes affect anything? *Journal of Personality and Social Psychology, 51*(6), 1167–1170.

Cable, D. M., & DeRue, S. D. (2002). The convergent and discriminant validity of subjective fit perceptions. *Journal of Applied Psychology, 87*(5), 875–884.

Cable, D. M., & Judge, T. A. (1996). Person-organization fit, job choice decision and organizational entry. *Organizational Behavior and Human Decision Processes, 67*(3), 294–311.

Cable, D. M., & Judge, T. A. (1997). Interviewers' perceptions of person-organization fit and organizational selection decisions. *Journal of Applied Psychology, 82*(4), 546–561.

Cable, D. M., & Parsons, C. K. (2001). Socialization tactics and person-organization fit. *Personnel Psychology, 54*(1), 1–23.

Camacho, C. J., Higgins, T., & Luger, L. (2003). Moral value transfer from regulatory fit: What feels right is right and what feels wrong is wrong. *Journal of Personality and Social Psychology, 84*(3), 498–510.

Chan, D., & Schmitt, N. (2000). Interindividual differences in intraindividual changes in proactivity during organizational entry: A latent growth modeling approach to understanding newcomer adaptation. *Journal of Applied Psychology, 85*(2), 190–210.

Chapman, D. S., & Webster, J. (2006). Toward and integrated model of applicant reactions and job choice. *International Journal of Human Resource Management, 17*(6), 1032–1057.

Chatman, J. A. (1991). Matching people and organizations: Selection and socialization in public accounting firms. *Administrative Science Quarterly, 36*(3), 459–484.

Chen, G., & Klimoski, R. J. (2003). The impact of expectations on newcomer performance in teams as mediated by work characteristics, social exchanges, and empowerment. *The Academy of Management Journal, 46*(5), 591–607.

Clore, G. L. & Palmer, J. E. (2009). Affective guidance of intelligent agents: How emotion controls cognition. *Cognitive Systems Research, 10*(1), 21–30.

Cober, R. T., Brown, D. J., Levy, P. E., Cober, A. B., & Keeping, L. M. (2003). Organizational web sites: Web site content and style as determinants of organizational attraction. *International Journal of Selection and Assessment, 11*(2–3), 158–169.

Condon, J. W., & Crano, W. D. (1988). Inferred evaluation and the relation between attitude similarity and interpersonal attraction. *Journal of Personality and Social Psychology, 54*(5), 789–797.

Cooper-Thomas, H. D., Anderson, N. (2006). Organizational socialization. A new theoretical model and recommendations for future research and HRM practices in organizations. *Journal of Managerial Psychology, 21*(5), 492–516.

Cooper-Thomas, H. D., Van Vianen, A. E. M., & Anderson, N. (2004). Changes in person-organization fit: The impact of socialization tactics on perceived and actual P-O fit. *European Journal of Work and Organizational Psychology, 13*(1), 52–78.

Dasgupta, N., Banaji, M. R., & Abelson, R. P. (1999). Group entitativity and group perception: Associations between physical features and psychological judgment. *Journal of Personality and Social Psychology, 77*(5), 991–1003.

Dawis, R. V., & Lofquist, L. H. (1984). *A psychological theory of work adjustment*. Minneapolis, MN: University of Minnesota Press.

Deci, E. L., & Ryan, R. M. (2000). The "what" and "why" of goal pursuits: Human needs and the self-determination of behavior. *Psychological Inquiry, 11*(4), 227–268.

De Cremer, D. (2004). The closer we are, the more we are alike: The effect of self-other merging on depersonalized self-perception. *Current Psychology, 22*(4), 316–324.

De Goede, M. E. E., Van Vianen, A. E. M., & Klehe, U.-C. (2009). *Job-seekers perceived person-organization fit: Appetitive, aversive, or holistic fit*. Paper presented at the 24th annual meeting of the Society for Industrial/Organizational Psychology, New Orleans, LA.

De Goede M. E. E., Van Vianen, A. E. M., & Klehe, U.-C. (2011). Attracting applicants on the web: PO fit, industry culture stereotypes, and website design. *International Journal of Selection and Assessment, 19*(1), 51–61.

Eisenberger, N. I., Lieberman, M. D., & Williams K. D. (2003). Does rejection hurt? An fMRI study of social exclusion. *Science, 302*(5643), 290–292.

Gaertner, L., & Schopler, J. (1998). Perceived ingroup entitativity and intergroup bias: An interconnection of self and others. *European Journal of Social Psychology, 28*(6), 963–980.

Greguras, G. J., & Diefendorff, J. M. (2010). Why does proactive personality predict employee life satisfaction and work behaviors? A field investigation of the mediating role of the self-concordance model. *Personnel Psychology, 63*(3), 539–560.

Gruman, J. A., Saks, A. M., & Zweig, D. I. (2006). Organizational socialization tactics and newcomer proactive behaviors: An integrative study. *Journal of Vocational Behavior, 69(1)*, 90–104.

Harrison, S. H., Sluss, D. M., & Ashforth, B. E. (2011). Curiosity adapted the cat: The role of trait curiosity in newcomer adaptation. *Journal of Applied Psychology, 96*(1), 211–220.

Higgins, E. T. (1997). Beyond pleasure and pain. *American Psychologist, 52*(12), 1280–1300.

Higgins, C. A. & Judge, T. A. (2004). The effect of applicant influence tactics on recruiter perceptions of fit and hiring recommendations: A field study. *Journal of Applied Psychology, 89*(4), 622–632.

Hogg, M. A. (2000). Subjective uncertainty reduction through self-categorization: A motivational theory of social identity processes. *European Review of Social Psychology, 11,* 223–255.

Jokisaari M., & Nurmi, J. E. (2009). Change in newcomers' supervisor support and socialization outcomes after organizational entry. *Academy of Management Journal, 52*(3), 527–544.

Jonas, E., Traut-Mattausch, E., Frey, D., & Greenberg, J. (2008). The path or the goal? Decision vs. information focus in biased information seeking after preliminary decisions. *Journal of Experimental Social Psychology, 44*(4), 1180–1186.

Jones, G. R. (1986). Socialization tactics, self-efficacy, and newcomers' adjustments to organizations. *The Academy of Management Journal, 29*(2), 262–279.

Judge, T. A., Heller, D., & Klinger, R. (2008). The dispositional sources of job satisfaction: A comparative test. *Applied Psychology: An International Review, 57*(3), 361–372.

Kammeyer-Mueller, J. D. (2007).The dynamics of newcomer adjustment: Dispositions, context, interaction, and fit. In C. Ostroff & T. Judge (Eds.), *Perspectives on organizational fit,* (pp. 99–122). Greenwich: CT: Information Age Publishing.

Kammeyer-Mueller, J. D., Simon, L. S., & Rich, B. L. (in press). The psychic cost of doing wrong: Ethical conflict, divestiture socialization, and emotional exhaustion. *Journal of Management.* Doi:10.1177/0149206310380249.

Kammeyer-Mueller, J. D., & Wanberg, C. R. (2003). Unwrapping the organizational entry process: Disentangling multiple antecedents and their pathways to adjustment. *Journal of Applied Psychology, 88*(5), 779–794.

Kim, T. Y., Cable, D. M., & Kim, S. P. (2005). Socialization tactics, employee proactivity, and person–organization fit. *Journal of Applied Psychology, 90*(2), 232–241.

Kram, K. E. (1983). Phases of the mentor relationship. *The Academy of Management Journal, 26*(4), 608–625.

Kristof, A. L. (1996). Person-organization fit: An integrative review of its conceptualizations, measurement, and implications. *Personnel Psychology, 49*(1), 1–49.

Kristof-Brown, A. L., & Guay, R. P. (2010). Person-environment fit. In S. Zedeck (Ed.), *APA handbook of industrial and organizational psychology,* (Vol. 3, pp. 3–50). Washington, DC: American Psychological Association.

Kristof-Brown, A. L., Zimmerman, R., & Johnson, E. (2005). Consequences of individuals' fit at work: A meta-analysis of person-job, person-organization, person-group, and person-supervisor fit. *Personnel Psychology, 58*(2), 281–342.

Lance, C. E., Vandenberg, R. J., & Self, R. M. (2000). Latent growth models of individual change: The case of newcomer adjustment. *Organizational Behavior & Human Decision Processes, 83*(1), 107–140.

Lauver, K. J., & Kristof-Brown, A. (2001). Distinguishing between employees' perceptions of person-job and person-organization fit. *Journal of Vocational Behavior, 59*(3), 454–470.

LePine, J. A., Colquitt, J. A., & Erez, A. (2000). Adaptability to changing task contexts: Effects of general cognitive ability, conscientiousness, and openness to experience. *Personnel Psychology, 53*(3), 563–593.

Li, N., Liang, J., & Crant, J. M. (2010). The role of proactive personality in job satisfaction and organizational citizenship behavior: A relational perspective. *Journal of Applied Psychology, 95*(2), 395–404.

Liberman, N., Sagristano, M. D., & Trope, Y. (2002). The effect of temporal distance on level of mental construal. *Journal of Experimental Social Psychology, 38*, 523–534.

Louis, M. R., Posner, B. Z., Powell, G. N. (1983). The availability and helpfulness of socialization practices. *Personnel Psychology, 36*(4), 857–866.

Maslach, C., Schaufeli, W. B., & Leiter, M. P. (2001). Job burnout. In S. T. Fiske, D. L. Schacter, & C. Zahn-Waxler (Eds.), *Annual Review of Psychology* (Vol. 52, pp. 397–422). Palo Alto: Annual Reviews.

Mount, M. K., Barrick, M. R., Scullen, S. M., & Rounds, J. (2005). Higher-order dimensions of the big five personality traits and the big six vocational interest types. *Personnel Psychology, 58*(2), 447–478.

Nelson, D. L., & Quick, J. C. (1991). Social support and newcomer adjustment in organizations: Attachment theory at work? *Journal of Organizational Behavior, 12*(6), 543–554.

O'Reilly, C. A., Chatman, J., & Caldwell, D. F. (1991). People and organizational culture: A profile comparison approach to assessing person-organization fit. *Academy of Management Journal, 34*(3), 487–516.

Ostroff, C. & Kozlowski, S. W. J. (1992). Organizational socialization as a learning process: The role of information acquisition. *Personnel Psychology, 45*(4), 849–874.

Ostroff, C., & Kozlowski, S. W. J. (1993). The role of mentoring in the information gathering processes of newcomers during early organizational socialization. *Journal of Vocational Behavior, 42*(2), 170–183.

Parker, S. K., & Collins, C. G. (2010). Taking stock: Integrating and differentiating multiple proactive behaviors. *Journal of Management, 36*(3), 633–662.

Roberts, B. W., O'Donnell, M. & Robins, R. W. (2004). Goal and personality development. *Journal of Personality and Social Psychology, 87*(4), 541–550.

Schneider, B. (1987). The people make the place. *Personnel Psychology, 40*(3), 437–453.

Schneider, B. (2001). Fits about fit. *Applied Psychology, 50*(1), 141–152.

Schwartz, S. H. 1992. Universals in the content and structure of values: Theoretical advances and empirical tests in 20 countries. In M. P. Zanna (Ed.) *Advances in experimental social psychology* (pp. 1–65). San Diego: Academic Press.

Seibert, S. E., Crant, J. M., & Kraimer, M. L. (1999). Proactive personality and career success. *Journal of Applied Psychology, 84*(3), 416–427.

Shaikh, T., & Kanekar, S. (1994). Attitudinal similarity and affiliation need as determinants of interpersonal attraction. *Journal of Social Psychology, 134*(2), 257–259.

Shipp, A. J., & Jansen, K. J. (2011). Reinterpreting time in fit theory: Crafting and recrafting narratives of fit in medias res. *The Academy of Management Review, 36(1)*, 76–101.

Slaughter, J. E., & Greguras, G. J. (2009). Initial attraction to organizations: The influence of trait inferences. *International Journal of Selection and Assessment, 17*(1), 1–18.

Slaughter, J. E., Zickar, M. J., Highhouse, S., & Mohr, D. C. (2004). Personality trait inferences about organizations: Development of a measure and assessment of construct validity. *Journal of Applied Psychology, 89*(1), 85–103.

Snyder, M., Berscheid, E., & Matwychuk, A. (1988). Orientations toward personnel selection: Differential reliance on appearance and personality. *Journal of Personality and Social Psychology, 54*(6), 972–979.

Swann, W. B., Jr., Polzer, J. T., Seyle, D. C., & Ko, S. J. (2004). Finding value in diversity: Verification of personal and social self-views in diverse groups. *Academy of Management Review, 29,* 9–27.

Tajfel, H. (1969). Cognitive aspects of prejudice. *Journal of Social Issues, 25*(4), 79–97.

Thomas, J., Whitman, D. S., & Viswesvaran, C. (2010). Employee proactivity in organizations: A comparative meta-analysis of emergent proactive constructs. *Journal of Organizational and Occupational Psychology, 83*(2), 275–300.

Trope, Y., & Liberman, N. (2003). Temporal construal. *Psychological Review, 110*(3), 403–421.

Tykocinski O. E., & Steinberg, N. (2005). Coping with disappointing outcomes: Retroactive pessimism and motivated inhibition of counterfactuals. *Journal of Experimental Social Psychology 41*(5), 551–558.

Tyler, T. R., & Blader, S. L. (2002). Autonomous vs. comparative status: Must we be better than others to feel good about ourselves? *Organizational Behavior and Human Decision Processes, 89*(1), 813–838.

Vandenberg, R. J., & Self, R. M. (1993). Assessing newcomers' changing commitments to the organization during the first 6 months of work. *Journal of Applied Psychology, 78*(4), 557–568.

Van Vianen, A. E. M. (2000). Person-organization fit: The match between newcomers' and recruiters' preferences for organizational cultures. *Personnel Psychology,* 53, 113–149.

Van Vianen A. E. M., & Prins, M. G. (1997). Changes in newcomers' person-environment fit following the first stage of socialization. *International Journal of Selection and Assessment, 5*(2), 101–114.

Van Vianen, A. E. M, Shen, C. T., & Chuang, A. (2011). Person-organization and person-supervisor fits: Employee commitments in a Chinese context. *Journal of Organizational Behavior, 32,* 906–926.

Van Vianen, A. E. M, Stoelhorst, J. W., & De Goede M. E. E. (in press). The construal of person-organization fit during the ASA Stages: Content, source, and focus of comparison. In: A. L. Kristof-Brown & J. Billsberry (Eds.), *New directions in organizational fit* (pp....-...). Oxford, UK: Wiley-Blackwell.

Verquer, M. L., Beehr, T. A., & Wagner, S. H. (2003). A meta-analysis of relations between person-organization fit and work attitudes. *Journal of Vocational Behavior, 63*(3), 473–489.

Wanberg C. R., & Kammeyer-Mueller J. D. (2000). Predictors and outcomes of proactivity in the socialization process. *Journal of Applied Psychology, 85*(3), 373–385.

Wang, M., Zhan, Y., McCune, E., & Truxillo, D. (2011). Understanding newcomers' adaptability and work-related outcomes: testing the mediating roles of perceived P-E fit variables. *Personnel Psychology, 64*(1), 163–189.

Wanous, J. P. (1992). *Organizational entry: Recruitment, selection, and socialization of newcomers* (2nd ed.). Reading, MA: Addison-Wesley.

Zeelenberg, M., Van Dijk, W. W., Manstead, A. S. R., & Van Der Pligt, J. (1998). The experience of regret and disappointment. *Cognition and Emotion, 12*(2), 221–230.

PART 4

Socialization Process, Methods, and Measurement

The Role of Time in Socialization Dynamics

Blake E. Ashforth

Abstract

Although socialization is explicitly about preparing newcomers for the future, time plays only a backstage role in most models and studies. To help move time to the front stage, six issues are discussed. First, the distinction between clock time and event time suggests that learning and adjustment are "lumpy" in that they are often prompted by a series of events. Second, the rate of learning and adjustment are strongly influenced by temporally oriented individual differences, the difficulty of transitioning from one's former role to one's current role, and various features of the work context. Third, the rate is also strongly influenced by socialization processes enacted by the organization (socialization tactics) and newcomers (proactivity). Fourth, time lags, the duration of effects, the relative stability of learning and adjustment, and evolving newcomer needs are considered. Fifth, the increasing need for "swift socialization" is recognized, along with how organizations are addressing this need. Finally, prescriptions are offered for when and how often to measure socialization dynamics.

Key Words: learning, adjustment, time, events, role transitions, socialization tactics, proactivity, swift socialization

Introduction

Socialization is explicitly about the future as mediated by the present. The very purpose of socialization, after all, is to prepare the newcomer for an effective role(s) in the organization. From the newcomer's point of view, onboarding activities are explicitly about learning to become a functioning member, and this encourages him or her to think prospectively—to wonder what might be, to anticipate change, and to hope for betterment. This prospective thinking in turn provides the motivation to endure trials of the present—whether from being stretched, digesting minutia, undergoing hazing, being tested, or other hurdles involved in "learning the ropes." Similarly, from the organization's point of view, onboarding activities represent an *investment* in the newcomer, an implicit belief that the longer-term returns will more than compensate for the short-term costs.[1]

George and Jones (2000) wrote, "the role of time must be explicitly incorporated into a theory (and not just treated as a boundary condition) if a theory is to provide an ontologically accurate description of a phenomenon" (p. 658). This is particularly true of socialization, given its inherently dynamic nature. And yet time tends to play only a backstage role in most socialization research, absolutely essential to the process of socialization but largely unheralded (Klein & Heuser, 2008). The purpose of this chapter, then, is to more explicitly consider the role of time in socialization dynamics so that it might better assume the front-stage role that it truly warrants. The discussion is organized under six headings: *(1)* clock time vs. event time; *(2)* rate of socialization: factors affecting the difficulty of learning and adjustment; *(3)* rate of socialization: processes that facilitate or inhibit learning and adjustment; *(4)* learning and adjustment over time; *(5)* swift socialization; and *(6)* putting it all together: when and how often to measure? My central contentions are that socialization research can be enriched considerably by making temporal considerations *explicit* in theoretical models and empirical studies, and that to understand the role of time in socialization—particularly the rate and duration of learning and adjustment—one must understand the role of formative events.

Before beginning, a word about the outcomes of socialization: learning, proximal adjustment, and distal adjustment. Given that socialization entails acquiring knowledge about and settling into one's work context, learning and adjustment are critical outcomes of socialization (Cooper-Thomas & Anderson, 2005; Fisher, 1986; Klein & Heuser, 2008; Ostroff & Kozlowski, 1992; Saks & Ashforth, 1997). Various typologies of "socialization content" suggest that *learning* encompasses the newcomer's job (i.e., bundle of tasks), role (i.e., broader expectations associated with organizational membership), social domain (i.e., interpersonal and group dynamics), and organizational context (e.g., history, culture, politics; see Ashforth, Sluss, & Harrison's, 2007a review; cf. Klein & Heuser, 2008).

Following various scholars, I define *proximal newcomer adjustment* as including role clarity, task mastery, and social integration (Adkins, 1995; Bauer, Bodner, Erdogan, Truxillo, & Tucker, 2007; Bauer & Erdogan, 2012; Chan & Schmitt, 2000; Feldman, 1981; Kammeyer-Mueller & Wanberg, 2003),[2] as well as role crafting (Ashforth, Myers, & Sluss, 2012). While the first three are well known, role crafting is the extent to which one innovates or modifies role-related expectations, ranging from minor tweaks to major changes (Sluss, van Dick, & Thompson, 2010; Wrzesniewski & Dutton, 2001; cf. Van Maanen & Schein, 1979). Very similar concepts include role innovation, role change, role development, role making, and role negotiation (Ashforth, 2001). As the environment becomes increasingly complex and dynamic, role crafting is becoming more common and expected (Evans & Davis, 2005), although the amount of role crafting desired varies widely across contexts. Studies suggest that newcomers may engage in role crafting soon after entry, particularly if they have power and relevant prior experience (Ashford & Taylor, 1990).

Proximal adjustment in turn predicts more distal forms of adjustment, including performance and work-related attitudes such as job satisfaction and organizational commitment (Bauer et al., 2007;

see also Saks et al., 2007). However, I will generally restrict the focus to learning and proximal adjustment (henceforth, "adjustment") because they are most directly affected by socialization processes.

Clock Time versus Event Time

Ancona, Okhuysen, and Perlow (2001; see also Anderson-Gough, Grey, & Robson, 2001) distinguish between "clock time" and "event time."[3] The former views time as linear, "such that the units [of time] are homogeneous, uniform, regular, precise, deterministic" (Ancona et al., 2001, p. 514). Clock time is the default assumption of most socialization research. That is, the typical longitudinal study will administer questionnaires at certain intervals on the implicit assumption that change in the dependent variables has occurred at a more or less steady pace. For example, task mastery would be expected to be less at Time 1 (T1) than at T2, and less at T2 than at T3. It's as if the work context is thought to have exerted a steady and relentless influence on the newcomer, much like a straight piece of wood is gradually shaped into a violin body by the steady and relentless pressure of a press. While this assumption of gradual change is typically workable for cumulative variables, such as learning and proximal adjustment (e.g., Chan & Schmitt, 2000; Cooper-Thomas & Anderson, 2005)—although all these variables are susceptible to disruption—it is more problematic for distal adjustment variables that are subject to fluctuations (as argued later under "Learning and Adjustment Over Time"), such as job satisfaction and organizational commitment. Under the heading, "Putting it All Together: When and How Often to Measure?," I will discuss how repeated measures surveys can be used to more effectively capture clock time (as well as event time).

In contrast to clock time, event time refers to the use of discrete episodes to frame the passage of time. Learning and adjustment are "lumpy" in the sense that they are typically driven by episodes that precipitate new experiences, reflection, and perhaps reinterpretation of previous episodes (Ashforth et al., 2007a). For example, being invited to lunch by one's new coworkers, being entrusted with confidential information, and being treated with compassion during times of stress are events that facilitate and signal social integration (Feldman, 1977). Event time is the use of an episode "as a reference point for things that happen before and after" (Ancona et al., 2001, p. 515). Concepts like surprises (Louis, 1980), turning points (Bullis & Bach, 1989), and critical incidents (Gundry, 1993) speak to the dramatic and discontinuous learning and adjustment that can occur in the wake of an event. It's important to note that such events need not be major in an objective sense. Being invited to lunch may be an ostensibly small gesture on the part of coworkers, but nonetheless conveys an outsized lesson to an anxious newcomer. As Rentsch (1990) put it, "small events [can] carry big messages" (p. 678).

Relatedly, Tesluk and Jacobs (1998) distinguish between the *breadth* and *depth* of work experiences. High breadth experiences introduce the newcomer to a wide variety of tasks, challenges, and role set members (e.g., colleagues, customers); novelty is the watchword. High depth experiences emphasize repetition of a limited variety of tasks and/ or increased complexity within a given task area; consistency is the watchword. The greater the standardization of one's job, the more likely that socialization events will entail depth rather than breadth. Accordingly, Tesluk and Jacobs conclude that quantitative indicators of work experience (i.e., amount, time) predict job performance on standardized tasks more so than on nonstandardized tasks. Because of the eclecticism that characterizes broad work experiences, it is likely that newcomers will initially feel little progress in the conventional sense of task mastery ("Jack of all trades, master of none"). However, as the experiences and their derived lessons mount, newcomers are likely to form relatively dense cognitive schema that facilitate lateral connections among seemingly disparate events, ultimately leading to a sense of versatility and perhaps adaptability. Goodwin and Ziegler (1998), for instance, report that the breadth of one's work experiences (albeit across jobs), but not one's years of experience, was positively associated with the number of unique responses provided for a company-specific problem-solving task.

Event Time and Socialization Research

What does the notion of event time mean for socialization research? A typical longitudinal study *will* implicitly capture the changes that result from an accumulation of broad and deep experiences whose short-term effects can be predicted. That is, although no one may know precisely when a newcomer will encounter a particular episode or learn a particular lesson, the lag between the survey snapshots will capture the (short-term) predictable effects of whatever episodes have occurred in the interim. Much like a topographical snapshot from 30,000 feet, the "lumpiness" of the terrain—the particularized events that punctuate one's time on the job—will appear more as ripples in a more or less seamless expanse (cf. Zaheer, Albert, & Zaheer, 1999).[4]

Conversely, occasional surveys tend to become less useful for capturing event time as the following increase: *(1)* the number of major (i.e., potentially "disruptive") events, *(2)* the unpredictability of the nature and sequencing of both minor and major events, and *(3)* the unpredictability of the effects of the events. Indeed, given the vagaries of event-driven socialization, the associations between variables may be quite erratic over the short term. For example, Vancouver, Tamanini, and Yoder (2010) argue that, although there is generally an inverse relationship between learning (knowledge) and information seeking (i.e., the less one knows, the more one seeks), "disturbances" in socialization may cause the intensity of information seeking and/or the degree of learning to fluctuate wildly such that the association is greatly attenuated or even reversed during a given time frame. The authors conclude: "findings from longitudinal research that arbitrarily cut into the stream of processes might be difficult to interpret" (p. 773).

In short, the greater the number and unpredictability of events (and their consequences), the greater the utility of event time compared to clock time. Event time can be captured especially well by richer methods that are poised not at 30,000 feet but much closer to the ground. Participation, observations, interviews, and diaries—as well as the experience sampling mentioned in Endnote 4—are particularly helpful for providing thick descriptions of events and at least their short-term consequences. Indeed, the literature on occupational and professional socialization includes many excellent ethnographies that illuminate the importance of major and seemingly minor events alike (e.g., Hafferty, 1991; Hill, 1992; Ibarra, 1999; Pratt, 2000; Schleef, 2006).

Event Sequencing

The notion of event time raises the provocative issue of what sequence of particular events is most likely to facilitate learning and adjustment (e.g., Morrison & Hock, 1986; Tesluk & Jacobs, 1998). Although there are certain logical sequences, such as beginning with an organizational orientation and ending with a rite of passage such as a "graduation" ceremony, there remains an untold number of possible sequences given the number of major and minor events that potentially constitute the socialization process and the unpredictability of many of them. Let me offer some initial observations as a spur to further research.

EARLY EVENTS

Early events tend to exert a disproportionate impact "since they influence how *later* experiences will be interpreted" (Katz, 1980, p. 99) and the knowledge gained opens the doors to certain opportunities while shutting the doors to others. First, the less familiar newcomers are with the setting, and the less prior experience they have to fill in the gaps, the more meaning they will read into any particular event. Stohl (1986) found that messages (from insiders) received during the first 2 months of work were generally said by newcomers to be the most memorable. Imagine that a supervisor offers five pointed comments on a newcomer's performance during her first month, four of which are very positive and one very negative. The earlier the negative remark falls in the sequence, the greater its likely impact on her self-confidence precisely because she has experienced fewer positive remarks to help offset the criticism. Second, given individuals' proclivity to seek confirmation—rather than disconfirmation—of their initial impressions (Ashforth & Humphrey, 1995), the meaning newcomers extract from early events can ultimately prove self-fulfilling. A newcomer who interprets the aloofness of a senior coworker as a personal rebuke may behave rudely toward the coworker and thereby *provoke* personal rebukes. Third, and relatedly, research on first impressions indicates that *observers* (in this case, peers, managers, and mentors) are similarly prone to seek confirmation rather than disconfirmation of their initial impressions of a newcomer and to act on the basis of those impressions, thereby triggering a self-fulfilling prophecy (Harris & Garris, 2008). Chappell and Lanza-Kaduce (2010) describe how a police academy recruit was defined as the class "screw-up" (p. 198) and continually treated harshly by instructors. The authors concluded: "Once a recruit earned a negative reputation, it was nearly impossible to change that reputation" (p. 198). Fourth, certain events—notably, the provision of moderately challenging initial work assignments, constructive feedback, and adequate resources—tend to foster newcomers' abilities, self-efficacy, and credibility, thereby increasing the likelihood of further positive events (Hall, 1976; cf. Lindsley, Brass, & Thomas, 1995). The upshot is a success spiral where initial experiences of success increase the likelihood of later experiences of success (Ashforth, 2001; Howard & Bray, 1988; Qureshi & Fang, 2011). Conversely, unchallenging assignments (as when newcomers are required to "pay their dues") or overly challenging assignments, nonconstructive feedback or a lack of feedback, and inadequate resources may trigger a failure spiral. Finally, the specific learning, adjustment, and credentials gained by exposure to certain events makes newcomers eligible for certain other events, thus channeling socialization. For instance, research on careers as "tournaments" indicates the winnowing effect that *not* realizing certain benchmark events (e.g., being promoted within one year) has on individuals' future opportunities (Cooper, Graham, & Dyke, 1993).

STORIES

Shipp and Jansen (2011) argue that "individuals tend to understand temporal phenomena in terms of stories (McAdams, 1993), because stories help individuals generate and sustain meaning (Gabriel, 2000), and make sense of their experiences through integrated and sequenced accounts" (p. 77). Indeed, Van Maanen (1977) likens a newcomer entering an organization to an actor entering a new stage in the sense that he must construct a dramaturgical reading of the set, plot, characters, and his own role—and play that role in front of an audience. Continuing the dramaturgical metaphor, it seems likely that newcomers construct stories partially based on familiar archetypes that suggest certain plotlines and characters such as the respectful apprentice, the ascendant wunderkind, and the short-timer who regards the job as a stepping stone to something better. And, as part of the socialization process itself, the organization is likely to provide institutionalized narratives that explain and legitimate the process.

Stories, like experience itself, are lumpy in the sense that they coalesce around seemingly key events (or sets of related small events). Ibarra and Barbulescu (2010) refer to *emplotment*, "the process by which narratives link temporal events by directing them toward a conclusion" (p. 141). Because socialization pertains to helping the newcomer become a functioning organizational member and perhaps realizing a desired self, stories are typically oriented to these anticipated endpoints (e.g., enduring tedious training as a means to becoming an excellent lawyer). However, Shipp and Jansen (2011) observe that narrators often begin their stories "in the middle," in the sense that they retrospectively construct the past to help make sense of the present and give direction to the future. Similarly, newcomers make sense of socialization experiences in an ongoing way such that "the" meaning of the past may be reconstructed as the present unfolds and the contours of the future take shape, leading to an evolving (and perhaps dramatically changing) storyline (Van Maanen, 1977). As such, stories can provide both a sense of continuity (by reconstructing the past to match the demands of the present and future) and the potential for change (by rewriting the story as warranted by new events and the emerging sense of self; Ibarra & Barbulescu, 2010).[5]

Although constructed and reconstructed, it is important to note that stories are not typically experienced as exercises in writing fiction. Indeed, Ibarra and Barbulescu (2010) define successful stories as those that are not only "deemed valid by their target audience" but "generate feelings of authenticity" in the narrator (p. 136). That said, stories may be constructed and expressed quite self-consciously, and highlight aspirational and idealized features, because major transitions evoke strong needs for sensemaking (regarding the dynamics of the situation and the trajectory of the self) and self-presentation (Ibarra & Barbulescu, 2010; McAdams, 1999).

In sum, to fully understand the role of time in socialization dynamics it is necessary to understand the nature, flow, and impact of events. The meaning that newcomers derive from early events and the stories they construct and reconstruct are particularly likely to affect the trajectory of learning and adjustment.

Rate of Socialization: Factors Affecting the Difficulty of Learning and Adjustment

The rate of socialization refers to the speed at which newcomer learning and adjustment occur (cf. Reichers, 1987). In terms of Figure 9.1, the rate is indicated by the slope of each of the curves. For exposition purposes, it is assumed that learning and adjustment are strongly correlated (although, in practice, learning is likely to foreshadow adjustment; see Ashforth et al.'s 2007a review). Trajectory A appears to be the modal curve for cumulative

outcomes, such as learning, role clarity, and task mastery, where prior learning and adjustment provide a baseline for future learning and adjustment (e.g., proficiency with a technology; Ashforth et al., 2007a), and a certain critical mass of experience is needed before the learning and adjustment begin to crystallize (at which point the slope increases). The other trajectories shown will be discussed later. All else equal, a relatively rapid rate of learning and adjustment is preferred by both newcomers (to shed the unwanted "newbie" label) and the organization (to maximize efficiency; Ashforth et al., 2007a; Reichers, 1987).

Assuming that a given newcomer has a certain amount of learning and adjusting to accomplish in a given time (as indicated in Figure 9.1 by the dotted "maximum" line),[6] the rate of socialization is determined by: (1) how difficult learning and adjustment are for the newcomer in a particular context; and (2) the socialization processes enacted by the organization and newcomer to facilitate that learning and adjustment. This section discusses individual differences and situational factors that affect the difficulty of learning and adjustment. The subsequent section discusses the socialization processes enacted by the organization (i.e., socialization tactics) and newcomer (i.e., proactivity).

Individual Differences

Socialization is inherently interactionist in the sense that: (1) newcomers select and are selected into a particular situation; (2) newcomers actively interpret the situation; (3) newcomers typically have some discretion, coupled with idiosyncratic needs and wants, such they may act on and change the situation; (4) the situation tends to affect different newcomers in different ways (e.g., one individual may be inspired by a group chant whereas another

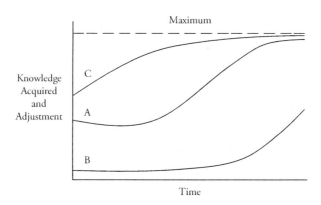

Figure 9.1 Cumulative Learning and Adjustment Trajectories.

may be repulsed); and *(5)* newcomers choose or are chosen to stay or exit, thus reinforcing person–organization fit (Bauer et al., 2007; Frese, 1982; Schneider, 1983). The result is *dynamic interactionism* (Hattrup & Jackson, 1996), where persons and situations reciprocally and continuously "shape" each other over time (Ashforth et al., 2007a). It is important, then, to consider how individual differences may affect learning and adjustment, and thus the rate of socialization.

A myriad of individual differences have been proposed to affect a newcomer's learning and adjustment, from openness to experience (Wanberg & Kammeyer-Mueller, 2000) to conscientiousness (Colquitt & Simmering, 1998), and from self-efficacy (Saks, 1995) to desire for control (Ashford & Black, 1996). Here, I consider four major individual differences that are inherently temporal in the sense that they speak to one's past, present, and future.[7] First, one's *prior experiences*, particularly work-related, are likely to facilitate learning and adjustment to the extent the experiences are relevant and transferable to the new setting[8] and the lag between prior and current experiences is relatively short (Beyer & Hannah, 2002; Carr, Pearson, Vest, & Boyar, 2006; Gibson & Papa, 2000; Morrison & Brantner, 1992; Pinder & Schroeder, 1987). For example, Carr et al. (2006) found that prior occupational experience was associated with lower voluntary turnover, and this association was mediated by pre-entry person–job fit and pre-entry value congruence with the organization. Beyer and Hannah (2002) found that newcomers with longer and more diverse work experience had more diverse latent identities with which to find a connection to their new roles. In short, prior experience gives one a knowledge and skill base for anticipating fit with the new setting, subsequently making sense of one's experiences, and presumably engaging in proactivity (defined below), each of which facilitates learning and adjustment. Indeed, the concept of *anticipatory socialization* (Feldman, 1976; Kramer, 2010; Merton, 1957) speaks to the cumulative impact of pre-entry experiences on one's fit with the new organization and role.

However, there are glimmers in the literature of experience actually *impeding* learning and adjustment (Adkins, 1995; Anakwe & Greenhaus, 2000; Korte, 2009), although the reasons remain unclear. Likely candidates include attitudinal issues (e.g., hubris, false confidence), demographic differences with other employees (e.g., background, age), prior learning that does not fit the current setting (e.g., discrepant values, "bad habits"), and leaving prior jobs for reasons that also impair current learning and adjustment (e.g., poor social skills).

A second major temporally oriented individual difference variable is *temporal focus*, "the allocation of attention to the past, present, and future" (Shipp, Edwards, & Lambert, 2009, p. 2; cf. temporal orientation, Bluedorn & Denhardt, 1988; time perspective, Waller et al., 2001). Individuals can shift their attention among these time periods, although attention tends to be somewhat positively correlated across the three (e.g., individuals who think about the past are also somewhat inclined to think about the future). However, Shipp et al. found that past-focused individuals tend to score higher on neuroticism, negative affectivity, and an external locus of control; experience less optimism and life satisfaction; and are inclined to *contrast* the past with the present such that they see their current job characteristics less positively and have higher intentions to quit. Conversely, current-focused and future-focused individuals experience more optimism, positive affectivity, extraversion, conscientiousness, and life satisfaction; have a higher internal locus of control; and are more inclined to take risks. Also, current-focused individuals view the present more positively, and future-focused individuals are inclined to *assimilate* the (rosy) future with the present such that they see their current job characteristics more positively and have higher job satisfaction and organizational commitment. These findings suggest provocative implications for socialization. In particular, given their greater positive affectivity, optimism, extraversion, and conscientiousness, current-focused and future-focused individuals are likely more willing to embrace and meet the challenges of socialization; indeed, future-focused individuals may be especially willing to invest in rigorous training and endure self-sacrifice in the present because of a forward-thinking goal orientation. Although past-focused individuals may be generally more resistant to socialization, Shipp et al. speculate that such individuals may be more attentive to feedback (since it is inherently retrospective), which would facilitate learning. Indeed, Shipp et al. argue that "individuals who are atemporal (i.e., a weak focus on the past, present, or future) may be the least motivated given their lack of focus on any time period" (p. 18).

Third, Dweck (1986) divides achievement motivation into *learning goals*, "in which individuals seek to increase their competence, to understand or master something new," and *performance goals*, "in which individuals seek to gain favorable judgments of their competence or avoid negative judgments" (p. 1040). A performance goal orientation is associated with perceiving challenging tasks as risky because of the possibility of failure, thereby discouraging individuals from choosing such tasks and persisting in the face of obstacles. In contrast, a learning goal orientation is inherently more future-oriented; it's associated with perceiving challenges as opportunities to learn, thereby encouraging individuals to tackle challenging tasks, seek developmental experiences, be receptive to feedback, and to try new approaches in the face of obstacles (e.g., VandeWalle, Ganesan, Challagalla, & Brown, 2000). Thus, Dragoni, Tesluk, Russell, and Oh (2009) found that junior managers with a greater learning goal orientation were more likely to be in developmental assignments and experience a stronger association between such assignments and actual managerial competencies. It appears, then, that a learning goal orientation would be positively associated with the rate of socialization. Further, Niiya, Crocker, and Bartmess (2004) found that a learning goal orientation can be *primed* (e.g., a manager couching a newcomer's failure as an important learning experience rather than as a test of her ability) such that one becomes better able to cope with failure. This indicates that the orientation is amenable to social influence—including socialization processes—and can therefore be considered a form of adjustment in its own right.

Finally, Cardon (2002) discusses the role of *anticipated organizational tenure*, and Taormina (1997) discusses the role of *future prospects*, in socialization dynamics. Anticipated tenure "reflects the psychological perceptions newcomers have concerning how long they will be affiliated with their new organization" (Cardon, 2002, p. 4), and future prospects is "the extent to which an employee anticipates having a rewarding career within his or her employing organization" (Taormina, 1997, p. 40). In this age of boundaryless careers (Sullivan, 1999), many factors may reduce one's anticipated tenure, including structural barriers to long-term tenure (e.g., contingent work, lack of job security, glass ceiling effects), negative reactions to the job and organization (e.g., reality shock, unmet expectations, psychological contract violations, poor person–job and person–organization fit, lack of growth, poor compensation), ineffective socialization itself (i.e., poor learning and adjustment), external market conditions (i.e., availability and desirability of alternative employment), viewing one's current role as merely a stopgap position or a stepping stone to other external opportunities, and various personal reasons (e.g., continuing education, family responsibilities, dual career concerns). Importantly, all else equal, organizations are more willing to invest resources in the socialization process if they anticipate reasonably lengthy newcomer tenure (Cardon, 2002). For example, Cardon (2002) notes how contingent workers tend to receive relatively casual socialization (Bauer, Morrison, & Callister, 1998). Similarly, because socialization entails a certain amount of organization-specific learning that may not be readily generalizable to other organizations, as well as adjustment to particularized individuals (e.g., to Suzanne and Fred, one's coworkers), a newcomer is more likely to be motivated to learn and adjust the longer is her anticipated tenure. Thus, research suggests that anticipated tenure/future prospects is positively associated with learning about the organization, social integration, job satisfaction, and organizational commitment (Cardon, 2002; Song & Chathoth, 2010; Taormina, 2004). Cardon (2002) did not find a significant association between anticipated tenure and task mastery, likely because even newcomers with low anticipated tenure are required to perform their roles adequately. It's also worth noting that anticipated tenure is likely quite susceptible to change as a function of the socialization process; thus researchers should consider assessing it at multiple time points.

To summarize: relevant, transferable, and recent prior experiences; a current and future oriented temporal focus; a learning goal orientation; and relatively high anticipated organizational tenure are each, generally, likely to facilitate newcomer learning and adjustment.

Situational Factors: Role Transitions

As with individual differences, a variety of situational factors have been proposed to affect the rate of newcomer learning and adjustment. We partition these factors into two sets: *(1)* the role transition; and *(2)* the context of work.

Role transition refers to the process through which individuals psychologically (and if relevant, physically) exit one role and enter another (Ashforth, 2001; Burr, 1972). For our purposes, the exited role refers to the position one formerly held, whereas the entered role refers to the position one is being socialized to occupy. Both the exited and entered roles are inevitably associated with certain context-driven expectations (e.g., one employer may prize innovativeness whereas another prizes conformity). The nature of the prior role, its context, and the exit process may strongly affect entry into the new role and context (Ashforth, 2001; Boswell, Shipp, Payne, & Culbertson, 2009; Louis, 1980). Ashforth (2001) argues that role transitions tend to be more difficult—thereby complicating learning and adjustment in the new role—when the transitions are:

• *Of high magnitude.* The greater the number and extent of core and peripheral features that change between the roles, the more the newcomer has to learn and adjust. Ibarra (2003) discusses transitions of such high magnitude that the individuals essentially "reinvented" themselves, such as one transition from literature professor to stockbroker.

• *Socially undesirable.* The more that others (whether specific individuals, such as one's friends and family, or the generalized "other" of society) regard the change as negative, the more socially undesirable the transition. Although the individual may or may not regard a transition such as a demotion as undesirable, having to cope with the derogation of others can undermine the motivation to learn and adjust.

• *Involuntary.* An involuntary transition, such as a promotion in an up-or-out consulting firm, occurs when the individual has little real choice regarding the transition. Indeed, to forestall the corrosive effects of involuntariness on one's motivation to learn and adjust, organizations often use subtle techniques to create at least an *illusion* of choice (e.g., providing undesirable alternatives) along with a mix of inducements to encourage acceptance (Lewicki, 1981).

• *Unpredictable.* An unpredictable transition occurs when one is unable "to anticipate the date of role exit, the onset and duration of the role entry period, and the nature of the events surrounding the exit and entry" (Ashforth, 2001, p. 99). For instance, Mansfield (1972) discusses the anxiety felt by new recruits who were subjected to a series of training rotations without knowing when and where they would be permanently placed. Unpredictability makes uncertain what and how to learn.

• *Individual rather than collective.* An individual exiting and entering alone, as in an overseas transfer, has fewer opportunities to engage in social learning about the meaning and nature of the transition and to garner social support for mitigating the anxiety of the transition.

• *Of short duration.* Transition duration refers to the length of time between when one seriously contemplates leaving one role and when one is expected to be a functioning occupant in the next role. A short duration, as when one seizes on a desirable job opening, undermines one's ability to prepare for and psychologically come to grips with the change.

• *Irreversible.* An irreversible transition exists when one cannot exit the new role and resume the old role almost as if one had never entered the new role at all; that is, one cannot undo the transition and/or is "marked" by the transition, such as in the adoption of a "public and affectively charged role" (e.g., politician, entertainer; Ashforth, 2001, p. 104). The pressure to adapt to the irreversible role may overtax the individual.

The socialization processes discussed later under the heading, "Rate of Socialization: Processes that Facilitate or Inhibit Learning and Adjustment," can largely mitigate difficult role transitions. For now, recalling our discussion of events, the literature on *rites of passage* indicates that role exit, psychological movement, and role entry are each facilitated by ritualized markers of the process (Ashforth, 2001; van Gennep, 1960). Rites of separation, such as a farewell party (e.g., Jacobson, 1996), facilitate psychological and social disengagement by publicly marking the termination of role occupancy. Rites of transition, such as an organizational orientation and training, facilitate the psychological journey between roles by signaling that one is assuming a new station. And rites of incorporation, such as the successful completion of a probationary period (e.g., Rollag, 2007; Scott & Myers, 2005), signify that the individual has become a legitimate role occupant, thereby facilitating psychological and social acceptance of the change in status. Generally, a succession of ritual markers of development and integration—from the momentous (e.g., passing a final examination; Anderson-Gough et al., 2001) to the momentary (e.g., sharing an inside joke)—signify progress to newcomers and veterans alike and help create a certain social-psychological momentum.

Situational Factors: Context of Work

Another set of situational factors that affect the rate of learning and adjustment among newcomers involves the context of work. Given the absence of a widely accepted theory of organizational context (cf. Johns, 2006), Ashforth et al. (2007a; cf. Mowday

& Sutton, 1993) attempted to articulate *how* the context may affect the socialization process. They proposed the following mechanisms:

• *Proximal (vs. distal) influence.* In adjustment research, proximal/distal refers to time; here, it refers to physical and psychological closeness. Although socialization research typically focuses on the relationship between a newcomer and the organization, most socialization likely occurs at the *local* level—that is, through interactions with one's peers, managers, and mentors during the everyday enactment of one's role (Anderson & Thomas, 1996; Ashforth & Rogers, 2012; Bauer & Green, 1998; Jokisaari & Nurmi, 2009; Korte, 2009; Moreland & Levine, 2001; Nelson & Quick, 1991; Slaughter & Zickar, 2006; cf. Kammeyer-Mueller & Wanberg, 2003). As Katz (1985) put it, "Socialization is a social process" (p. 129), particularly regarding tacit knowledge. The wider organization comes to be known and made salient through the ways that it is enacted in the local context. And much of the information that newcomers strive to learn and find most useful is based locally, such as task behaviors and group norms (Ostroff & Kozlowski, 1992). Indeed, most training tends to occur informally on the job as newcomers look to their more experienced colleagues for guidance, feedback, and support (Chao, 1997; Garrick, 1998). Thus, the rate of learning and adjustment are significantly enhanced by concerted attempts to provide a nurturing local context for the newcomer.

• *Simplifying (vs. complicating) conditions.* The terms *simplifying* and *complicating* are not meant to imply a value judgment, as there are valid reasons for socialization to be relatively short and casual (simple, as in the case of a fast food worker) or long and formalized (complicated, as in the case of an architect). Perhaps the most important condition is job complexity, as hard-to-master knowledge, skills, and abilities require a more protracted and intense socialization process (although job complexity may also enhance the motivation to learn). For instance, Ashforth, Saks, and Lee (1998) found that newcomers' job complexity was positively associated with their organization's use of institutionalized socialization tactics (defined below); conversely, Hsiung and Hsieh (2003) found that job standardization appeared to facilitate the adjustment of new nurses. At the macro level, the more distinctive the organization's identity, culture, structure, and practices, the more

the newcomer needs to learn and adapt. Indeed, distinctive organizations often attempt to actively divest newcomers of their incoming habits and preconceptions so as to render them more amenable to the organization's distinctive ways (Van Maanen & Schein, 1979). A key simplifying condition, particularly for distinctive organizations, is rigorous recruitment and selection, which improves the initial person–organization fit (e.g., Anderson & Ostroff, 1997; Chatman, 1991; Scholarios, Lockyer, & Johnson, 2003).

• *Facilitating (vs. inhibiting) conditions.* If simplifying/complicating conditions indicate the amount of effort required to socialize newcomers, facilitating (vs. inhibiting) conditions indicate ways of expediting this effort. At the local level, role ambiguity, unpredictable change, physical isolation (e.g., telecommuting), conflicting perspectives among socialization agents, demographic dissimilarity, and a politicized workplace may all retard the rate of newcomer learning and adjustment (e.g., Adler & Shuval, 1978; DiSanza, 1995; Kammeyer-Mueller, Livingston, & Liao, 2011; Morrison & Brantner, 1992; Raghuram, Garud, Wiesenfeld, & Gupta, 2001).[9] At the macro level, facilitating conditions include a climate for learning and learning transfer (e.g., openness to inquiry, tolerance of mistakes, constructive feedback), HRM practices that encourage and reward learning and adjustment (e.g., training, skill-based pay), and the provision of adequate resources for socialization practices (e.g., Chen, Tjosvold, Huang, & Xu, 2011; Colquitt, LePine, & Noe, 2000; Noe, Tews, & Dachner, 2010; Salas & Von Glinow, 2008; Sonnentag, Niessen, & Ohly, 2004). A particularly intriguing inhibiting condition is the subjectivity of "newcomer" and "veteran" labels; in rapidly growing organizations with high turnover, a person with only a few months tenure might be labeled a veteran because of her relative seniority, even if her learning and adjustment are woefully deficient (Rollag, 2007; e.g., Haski-Leventhal & Bargal, 2008). Denied the safety of the newcomer label, she may be forced to prematurely assume the veteran role.

To conclude, the rate of learning and adjustment are strongly affected by certain temporally oriented individual differences, the difficulty of exiting from the prior role and entering the current role, and various proximal (vs. distal), simplifying (vs. complicating), and facilitating (vs. inhibiting) contextual factors. The socialization processes discussed next may capitalize on these individual and situational factors to further hasten the rate of learning and adjustment.

Rate of Socialization: Processes that Facilitate or Inhibit Learning and Adjustment

The last section discussed individual differences and situational factors that affect the difficulty of learning and adjustment. The focus here is on how learning and adjustment are facilitated/inhibited by the socialization *processes* enacted by the organization (i.e., socialization tactics) and by the newcomer (i.e., proactivity). For more extensive treatments of socialization tactics and proactivity, see Ashforth et al. (2007a), Bauer et al. (2007), Klein and Heuser (2008), and Saks et al. (2007).

Socialization Tactics

Van Maanen and Schein's (1979) widely cited socialization model includes six bipolar tactics: *(1)* the *collective (vs. individual)* tactic involves having newcomers share common developmental experiences; *(2) formal (vs. informal)* entails separating newcomers from veterans, as in a training class; *(3) sequential (vs. random)* involves a preset series of developmental experiences; *(4) fixed (vs. variable)* involves a preset timetable for developmental experiences; *(5) serial (vs. disjunctive)* entails learning directly from experienced individuals; and *(6) investiture (vs. divestiture)* involves affirming a newcomer's incoming identity and capabilities, rather than "divesting them" in order to reconstruct the newcomer. These rather abstract tactics provide an overarching framework for various specific socialization practices, such as training, apprenticeship, and mentoring. The fixed (vs. variable) tactic is particularly relevant to time: foreknowledge of a fixed ending point helps one to frame the experience of socialization and thereby calibrate one's rate of progress and anticipate the end of "liminality"—the unsettling "betwixt and between" period (Turner, 1969, p. 95; Ashforth, 2001; van Gennep, 1960; cf. prevailing temporal agenda, Blount & Janicik, 2001) where one is neither an outsider nor a true insider.

Five of the tactics—collective, formal, sequential, fixed, and serial—tend to covary (Ashforth, Saks, & Lee, 1997), providing newcomers with relatively structured practices designed to shape the nature and sequence of experiences and the meaning derived from those experiences.[10] Recalling our discussion of the importance of early events, socialization processes that are at least somewhat carefully structured have been found to foster newcomer learning and adjustment (e.g., Ashforth, Sluss, & Saks, 2007b; Cooper-Thomas & Anderson, 2002; Morrison & Hock, 1986; Riordan, Weatherly, Vandenberg, & Self, 2001; Saks et al., 2007; Takeuchi & Takeuchi, 2009). Indeed, because these tactics encourage newcomers to learn and enact "the organization way," Jones (1986) referred to them as *institutionalized socialization*. (It's important to add that this does not necessarily translate into resistance to change: if the organization advocated independence and creativity, then enacting the organization way would imply role crafting.) Conversely, the opposite tactics—individual, informal, random, variable, and disjunctive—represent the *absence* of structure and therefore compel newcomers to learn on their own. Jones (1986) dubbed this approach *individualized socialization*. Learning and adjustment are largely determined by on-the-job events and can therefore be quite haphazard and unpredictable. Hill (1992), for instance, documents the often erratic learning experiences of new frontline supervisors.

The structured events of institutionalized socialization have five features, typically absent in unstructured events, which facilitate learning and adjustment. First, the developmental experiences are designed to be cumulative, such that the learning, role clarity, task mastery, and possibly social integration and role crafting build in a logical progression. In contrast, more haphazard events essentially randomize lessons and make cumulative learning and adjustment more difficult. Indeed, newcomers are forced to respond in real time, whether they are prepared or not. Second, institutionalized socialization includes "instructors," such as occupational veterans and HR professionals, who not only provide constructive feedback but help newcomers make sense of their experiences in a manner consonant with organizational interests. Given the inherent equivocality of meaning (Weick, 1995), unstructured events may instead lead newcomers to construct lessons about the role, organization, and themselves that actually impair adjustment (e.g., superstitious learning; Beck & Forstmeier, 2007). Third, as numerous scholars have remarked, organizational entry is often a very stressful time for newcomers (e.g., Katz, 1985; Nelson, 1987). Structured events have an explicitly developmental focus that may provide a sense of psychological safety whereby newcomers feel less concerned about making mistakes, avoiding risks, and appearing competent (Harris, Simons, & Carden, 2004; Noe et al., 2010). Conversely, in *individualized* socialization, the stress of having to either "sink or swim" undermines psychological safety (Ashforth et al., 2012). Fourth, because the events are planned, the rate of learning and adjustment can be varied by altering the pace or "tempo" (Zerubavel, 1976) of the events. In contrast, unstructured events have an uncontrolled—and likely uneven—tempo. Finally, the presence of a designed sequence of cumulative events symbolizes to newcomers that the organization is concerned with their development and is willing to invest resources in it (Ashforth et al., 2007b; Riordan et al., 2001). In contrast, an absence of structured practices may symbolize indifference.

However, two time-related provisos are in order. First, learning and adjustment can be further facilitated by a judicious blend of structured and unstructured events, assuming newcomers have attained sufficient grounding for interpreting and managing the latter. For example, studies of neophyte firefighters (Scott & Meyers, 2005) and police officers (Harris et al., 2004) describe how individuals were initially exposed to institutionalized socialization in formal training academies, where they were carefully groomed in a broad array of organizationally sanctioned perspectives and behaviors. The firefighters and officers were then assigned to specific fire stations and police departments, where they received more individualized socialization to "fine tune" the transfer of generic academy lessons to the concrete realities of their local situation and personal capabilities.

Second, Ashforth and Saks (1996) found that institutionalized socialization was more strongly related to newcomer adjustment at 4 months than at 10 months. The authors suggested that although the newcomers may have initially welcomed the structured learning environment that such socialization provides, as the newcomers became more comfortable in their new roles they may have started to become indifferent to—or even resent—such structure as intrusive and patronizing. Mitchell and James (2001) define an "entropic period" (p. 539) as occurring when the impact of X on Y (in this case, socialization tactics on adjustment) becomes attenuated over time.

Newcomer Proactivity

Newcomer proactivity is the set of practices through which individuals actively engage with their work environment, primarily to make sense of their role and environment, reduce uncertainty, and possibly shape their role and environment (Crant, 2000; Grant & Ashford, 2008). Various typologies have been proposed. These include: *(1)* behavioral means of information and feedback seeking, including observing, asking questions, scanning secondary sources (e.g., company website), subtly raising issues (e.g., joking about a problematic topic), relationship building, participating in social events, and experimenting (e.g., breaking rules to test limits); and *(2)* cognitive means of self-regulation, including positive framing (viewing events optimistically), goal-setting, monitoring one's own behavior and its causes, and psychological rehearsal (Ashford & Black, 1996; Ashforth et al., 2007a; Manz, 1983; Miller & Jablin, 1991).

Behavioral and cognitive proactivity are complementary, and the greater their joint use the more actively the newcomer probes and processes the environment, thus facilitating learning and adjustment. For example, Ashford and Black (1996) found that both relationship building and positive framing predicted performance. Further, although the structured learning represented by institutionalized socialization may somewhat obviate the need for proactivity (Gruman, Saks, & Zweig, 2006; Kim, Cable, & Kim, 2005), the two are largely complementary in that the tactics legitimate the act of learning and provide opportunities to ask questions, experiment, and so on (Ashforth et al., 2007a; cf. Griffin, Colella, & Goparaju, 2000). Moreover, the relative psychological safety of the structured setting reduces the social costs of asking questions, experimenting, and so forth (Teboul, 1995). Thus, positive associations and interactions have been reported between institutionalized socialization and proactivity (e.g., Ashforth et al., 2007b; Gruman et al., 2006; Kim et al., 2005).

In the discussion of temporally oriented individual differences, it was argued that prior (transferable) experience, a current or future temporal focus, a learning goal orientation, and relatively lengthy anticipated tenure each exert a positive main effect on the rate of learning and adjustment. I would add here that these variables are likely to positively interact with proactivity. First, the future orientation of temporal focus, learning goals, and anticipated tenure should each enhance the motivation to utilize proactive behaviors and cognitions. Second, the pre-existing knowledge basis fostered by prior experiences should provide greater confidence for engaging in proactivity.

Further, because proactivity is driven by the dynamic interaction of the individual and situation, the frequency of each form of proactive behavior and cognition is likely to vary over time. First—as depicted by the three sample trajectories in Figure 9.1—as learning approaches the asymptote (dotted line), there is less need for proactivity (although proactivity aimed at role crafting may well continue). However, the complicating and inhibiting contextual conditions discussed earlier—particularly job complexity and unpredictable change—may extend the time needed and thus continue to motivate high proactivity. For example, Morrison (1993b) found that the frequency with which new accountants engaged in asking questions and monitoring (i.e., observing) was roughly consistent over their first 6 months (although the frequency of monitoring varied over time as a function of the specific information sought), whereas Graen, Orris, and Johnson (1973) found that the involvement of new clerical employees in "assimilation" activities (e.g., "Going to others for help," p. 402) decreased somewhat over 16 weeks. Second, as newcomers gain experience they are likely to shift their behaviors toward less socially costly forms of proactivity. They may, for instance, engage in less overt information and feedback seeking, to avoid appearing naïve and insecure, but continue to quietly observe (e.g., Ashford, Blatt, & VandeWalle, 2003; Jablin, 2000). Third, as Grant and Ashford (2008) argue, learning and adjustment successes and favorable interpersonal reactions are likely to reinforce the tendency to engage in proactivity, whereas failures and negative reactions are likely to punish proactivity. Finally, initial success (failure) experiences are likely to affect a newcomer's self-efficacy regarding proactivity, thereby encouraging (discouraging) future proactivity (Grant & Ashford, 2008). The upshot is that research should include repeated measures of proactive behavior and cognition, and consider disaggregating molar measures of proactivity into specific forms because there may be high variance in the frequencies across forms at given times.

In sum, institutionalized socialization and newcomer proactivity are apt to exert positive main and interactive effects on the rate of newcomer learning and adjustment.

Learning and Adjustment Over Time

This section considers three quite different issues that affect the trajectory of learning and adjustment: (1) time lags and duration of effects; (2) relatively stability vs. instability of learning and adjustment; and (3) stage models and newcomer needs.

Time Lags and Duration of Effects

Mitchell and James (2001) concluded from a review of management research that "most of our research involves causal hypotheses and designs presumed to support causal inferences. Yet, very few papers specifically address, from a theoretical perspective, the time elements involved in X causing Y" (p. 532).[11] This is certainly no less true of socialization research (Klein & Heuser, 2008). However, although management research tends to assume that the impact of X on Y is instantaneous (Mitchell & James, 2001), the common use of longitudinal designs in socialization research suggests that socialization scholars generally do not assume instantaneous effects.

It seems very likely that socialization processes differ in: (1) the *onset* of their impact on learning and adjustment (i.e., time lag); (2) the *magnitude* of their impact over time (as discussed above under rate); and (3) the *duration* of their effects (or, conversely, the extent to which—and rate at which—the impact decays over time). Moreover, as our discussion of events suggests, socialization "causes" differ in whether they are one-time (e.g., providing feedback only in the form of an annual performance review), recurring (e.g., providing feedback after each project), or constant (e.g., providing ongoing feedback).

Regarding onset, the time lag between some socialization processes and their effects is, actually, often instantaneous—but only in a limited sense. For example, a newcomer asking a question is likely to receive an immediate response; however, this data point represents only a grain of sand on a beach. Thus, there is likely to be a discernible lag between proactive behaviors and cognitions—and socialization tactics—and the kind of *aggregated* learning that is typically captured in "socialization content" measures (e.g., "I have learned how things 'really work' on the inside of this organization," Chao, O'Leary-Kelly, Wolf, Klein, & Gardner, 1994, p. 734) as well as the *molar* adjustment that is typically captured in measures of role clarity, task mastery, social integration, and role crafting (e.g., "I know exactly what is expected of me," Rizzo, House, & Lirtzman, 1970, p. 156). Indeed, recalling our discussions of events, broad experiences, and complicating and inhibiting conditions, it may take significant time for the data points to jell into something that is recognizable to the newcomer as actionable knowledge. This would retard measurable learning/adjustment, as depicted by trajectory B of Figure 9.1 (although once the data begin to jell, learning/adjustment may be rapid). Some events may even exercise a "sleeper effect" where the true impact is not realized until later. For instance, Bullis and Bach (1989) found that although new graduate students who participated in social events such as pub runs did not see such events as immediately promoting their organizational identification, the events nonetheless predicted identification 8 months later.

Regarding duration (cf. George & Jones, 2000; Mitchell & James, 2001), a few major socialization events (whether a product of socialization tactics, proactivity, or on-the-job learning), such as hazing or the effusive praise of an important client, are likely to have a long-lasting impact on learning/adjustment. For example, *Fortune* publishes a column, "The Best Advice I Ever Got," where senior executives reminisce about seminal learning experiences. Generally, though, as with the beach analogy, it is the accretion of events conveying similar messages around certain themes (e.g., growing task mastery) that leads to long-lasting learning/adjustment (e.g., Hill, 1992). However, learning and adjustment can decay if they are not "renewed" with some regularity, particularly through ongoing role performance (learning, role clarity, task mastery); engagement with peers, managers, and others (social integration); and continuous improvement (learning, task mastery, role crafting).

Relative Stability versus Instability of Learning and Adjustment

Cooper-Thomas and Anderson (2006) write that:

Research has shown that newcomers adjust rapidly over even short 4-week intervals in the early post-entry period (Chan & Schmitt, 2000; Chen & Klimoski, 2003; Major, Kozlowski, Chao, & Gardner, 1995; Thomas & Anderson, 1998); that early post-entry measures (e.g., attitudes) have stronger or unique effects relative to measures taken later on (Ashforth & Saks, 1996; Bauer & Green, 1994; Liden, Wayne, & Stilwell, 1993); and that early measures of socialization are relatively stable and are important in determining later outcomes (Ostroff & Kozlowski, 1992; Morrison, 1993a, b). (p. 118; see also reviews by Ashforth et al., 2007a; Bauer et al., 1998; Saks & Ashforth, 1997; Tesluk & Jacobs, 1998).

For example, Morrison (1993a) assessed the adjustment of neophyte accountants 2 weeks after they completed an orientation and training program (Time 1) and 6 months after entry (Time 2). Morrison found that T1 task mastery, role clarity,

and social integration were significantly correlated with their T2 counterparts. The rapidity and stability of newcomer learning and adjustment are a testament to the power of early events (including pre-entry events), and their resulting learning and adjustment, to affect later learning and adjustment.

At the same time, based on meta-analytic data from Bauer et al. (2007), Bauer and Erdogan (2011) plotted the mean levels of three adjustment variables over time:

Mean self-efficacy increased over the first few months posthire and then decreased steadily after about 3 months. Mean role clarity dropped in the first few months but then generally increased after the 3rd month. Mean social integration declined more slowly over the first 6 months and then generally increased past that point in time. (p. 59)

In short, these meta-analytic data suggest considerable instability in at least adjustment over the first year. Can we reconcile evidence of stability with evidence of instability?

Earlier, I discussed learning accretion and success spirals, where initial accomplishments pave the way for future accomplishments. These dynamics lead to a "nonlinear increasing trajectory" (Qureshi & Fang, 2011, p. 213), such as the trajectories depicted in Figure 9.1. These trajectories seem most likely for learning, role clarity, and task mastery insofar as these are cumulative variables, as noted, where the attainment of a certain level becomes the foundation for future progress.[12] As long as the tasks and role expectations do not change radically, more learning and greater clarity and mastery can be anticipated—although at some point diminishing returns are apt to set in as one approaches the asymptote for possible attainment. A newcomer who *begins* with relatively high levels of learning, clarity, and mastery (i.e., trajectory C in Figure 9.1) may initially progress at a faster rate as synergies are quickly realized. However, diminishing returns are also likely to set in faster (suggesting the desirability of then enhancing her job complexity). Whether a newcomer enters with low or high levels of learning and mastery, it remains that the initial levels will strongly predict the later levels (e.g., Cooper-Thomas & Anderson, 2005; Qureshi & Fang, 2011), thus accounting for the apparent stability of learning and adjustment over time.

Conversely, various disturbances can cause learning and adjustment—especially the noncumulative, distal attitudinal forms of adjustment—to fluctuate (as depicted in Figure 9.2; e.g., Liu & Lee,

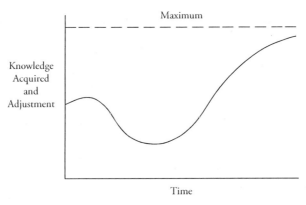

Figure 9.2 A Fluctuating Learning and Adjustment Trajectory.

2008) or even be discontinuous (see Figure 9.3). In particular, the honeymoon-hangover effect may induce newcomers to have a somewhat naïve and rose-colored view of the organization (especially if the individual lacks prior experience and the organization oversells itself during recruitment; Boswell, Boudreau, & Tichy, 2005; Boswell et al., 2009). For example, research involving medical students (Haas & Shaffir, 1984), volunteers for at-risk youth (Haski-Leventhal & Bargal, 2008), and college athletes (Adler & Adler, 1991) indicates a loss of idealism over time (cf. Hicks, 2008). Even rigorous realistic job previews and socialization programs cannot fully insulate a newcomer from the inevitable reality shocks associated with the nuances of any new position and organization (Boswell et al., 2009; Kramer, 1974). Unpredictable changes in role demands (e.g., new technology), contextual factors (e.g., one's manager quits), or personal circumstances (e.g., providing elder care) may also disrupt a newcomer's learning and adjustment. And, as suggested in our earlier discussion of failure spirals, newcomers who are required to "pay their dues" or otherwise wait before engaging in their expected duties are apt to atrophy, begin to question their abilities, and lose their initial fire. Given these potential disturbances it is not surprising that learning and adjustment often suffer setbacks in the early months of entry, perhaps prompting turnover (e.g., Kammeyer-Mueller & Wanberg, 2003), before regaining a roughly upward trajectory among the remaining newcomers.

Methodologically, following the notion of beta change, the standards a newcomer uses to gauge "do I really understand my job?," "am I competent?," and so forth may evolve so that a "4" on a 5-point response scale at one month is seen as a "3" at six months (Golembiewski, Billingsley, & Yeager, 1976). And the notion of gamma change suggests that the very meaning of a construct such as task mastery may evolve from "error free performance" to "creative performance" such that it is seen as an essentially different construct altogether (Golembiewski et al., 1976; e.g., Vandenberg & Self, 1993; cf. longitudinal validity, Ployhart & Vandenberg, 2010). Moreover, periodic surveys are

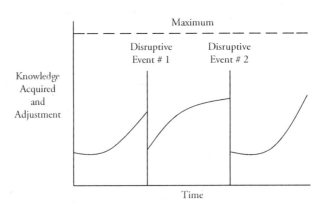

Figure 9.3 A Discontinuous Learning and Adjustment Trajectory.

susceptible to current events, as when a difficult week causes a respondent to be uncharacteristically negative about her learning and adjustment. Indeed, Mitchell, Thompson, Peterson, and Cronk (1997) found that the anticipation and recollection of meaningful life events tend to be more positive than the actual experience of the events themselves.

The upshot is that evidence of stability and instability can indeed coexist in newcomer learning and adjustment trajectories. Ashforth et al. (2007a) described this coexistence "as a classic case of 'the glass is half-full' vs. 'the glass is half-empty'" (p. 47).

Stage Models and Newcomer Needs

Adding to the stability/instability conundrum, various stage models of socialization indicate generalizable phases of newcomer progress (e.g., Feldman, 1976; Porter, Lawler, & Hackman, 1975; see reviews by Ashforth et al., 2007a; Fisher, 1986; Kramer, 2010; Wanous, 1992). Collectively, these models suggest roughly four major phases: anticipation (preparation prior to entry), encounter (confronting the reality upon entry), adjustment (meshing with the new reality), and stabilization (becoming and being a bona fide insider). However, stage models have enjoyed only mixed empirical support (Fisher, 1986; Wanous, 1992). The stages may be fluid (e.g., where adjustment ends and stabilization begins is inherently fuzzy); the stages may be truncated and even skipped (as when an experienced newcomer adjusts rapidly); disruptive events may force a newcomer to recycle through the stages; behaviors and attitudes said to be uniquely associated with certain stages (e.g., role crafting with the adjustment stage) may occur in other stages; and individuals likely proceed through the stages at different rates. That said, the stage models continue to provide a rough heuristic for the challenges that newcomers typically encounter and the activities in which newcomers typically engage as socialization unfolds (Ashforth et al., 2007a; Fisher, 1986; Kramer, 2010; Wanous, 1992).

Consistent with the logic of stage models are arguments that the needs of newcomers tend to evolve over time. Katz (1980), for instance, asserts that newcomers' needs change around the third or fourth month from "an initial emphasis on psychological safety and identity to a concern for achievement and accomplishment" (p. 89). That is, newcomers need to gain a salutary sense of their place in the organization and establish basic task competence and reasonable social integration before they can become truly receptive to the intrinsic motivators in their work. Relatedly, research on newcomer learning indicates that "knowledge in the job and possibly social domain is acquired more quickly than knowledge in the organizational domain (Morrison, 1995; Ostroff & Kozlowski, 1992; Taormina, 1997; cf. Cooper-Thomas & Anderson, 2005)" (Ashforth et al., 2007a, p. 48), suggesting an initial newcomer focus on the local context.

The notions of socialization stages and evolving newcomer needs imply the possibility of *threshold effects* as one fulfills a particular need and/or completes the challenges of a particular stage and prepares for the next need and stage. That is, learning and adjustment may involve not just changes in degree (as implied by the relatively smooth upward trajectories in Figure 9.1), but changes in kind—complete with discontinuities and punctuated equilibria (as depicted in rather extreme form in Figure 9.3). For example, one could imagine how a neophyte IT supervisor—perhaps prompted by a seminal event—might one day "get it" that his job is no longer to be a star troubleshooter but a manager who builds the troubleshooting capabilities of *other* IT personnel (cf. Hill, 1992). Such a reorientation would open the door to new learning and adjustment.

To conclude, the trajectory of learning and adjustment can follow numerous paths (as hinted in Figures 9.1–9.3), depending on the onset, magnitude over time, and duration of the impact of socialization processes, various forces for stability and for instability, and the evolving challenges faced by—and needs of—newcomers as they become socialized.

Swift Socialization

As discussed in Endnote 1, with the decline in the average duration of individual–organization relationships, socialization is becoming more about meeting current job-related needs than longer-term organizational and individual developmental needs. Further, there is a real need to socialize individuals as quickly as possible in: *(1)* organizations with rapid growth in membership and/or rapid turnover (Harrison & Carroll, 1991; Nifadkar, 2009; Rollag, 2004); *(2)* organizations that induct new members in cohorts that are relatively large compared to the number of veterans (e.g., fraternities and sororities); *(3)* temporary groups and organizations such as consulting teams, film crews, and juries (Bechky, 2006; Meyerson, Weick, & Kramer, 1996); and *(4)* contingent work, where individuals are involved with a series of organizations on specific assignments for limited periods (e.g., substitute teacher; Rogers, 2000). Additionally, in virtual teams (Ahuja & Galvin, 2003) and boundary spanning relationships (e.g., with clients, members of other subunits; Gittell, 2006), it is often difficult to utilize traditional socialization processes. The question thus becomes, how can organizations under these and related circumstances foster *swift socialization*, that is, the rapid onboarding of individuals (Nifadkar, 2009)?

At first blush, organizations are probably tempted to use individualized socialization because of its obvious expedience. However, as mentioned, because this practice is actually defined by the *absence* of structured socialization, newcomers are forced to rely solely on their own wits and tend to either "sink or swim." Ashforth et al. (2012) argue that successful onboarding under such circumstances tends to occur *in spite of* the practice rather than *because* of it.

What, then, might structured swift socialization entail? First, as noted earlier, rigorous recruitment and selection may be used to improve the initial fit between the newcomers and the position and organization, thus reducing the need for intense socialization (e.g., Anderson & Ostroff, 1997; Scholarios et al., 2003). Second, given the need for swift socialization, newcomers and veterans alike may be amenable to a certain degree of "time compression" (Ashforth, 2001, p. 229; cf. Blount & Jaricik, 2001) whereby certain socialization processes are telescoped or skipped. For instance, Meyerson et al. (1996) describe the willingness of members of temporary groups to forgo normal means of building trust, such as sharing experiences and engaging in reciprocal disclosure, and extend "swift trust" to one another "*as if* trust were [already] in place" (p. 186).

Third, and perhaps most importantly, the organization may present a "strong situation" to constrain and shape behavior and sensemaking such that change is both accelerated and regulated (Meyer, Dalal, & Hermida, 2010). Examples are legion. Divestiture may be used, as discussed, to encourage newcomers to forsake their incoming identities and be remade in the image of the desired organizational member (Van Maanen & Schein, 1979), and initiation rites may be used to test newcomers' willingness and ability to fit in (Ashforth & Boudwin, 2010). Bourassa and Ashforth (1998) describe how new fishers on an Alaskan trawler were referred to as "new guys" rather than by name, required to do busywork tasks, and were denied pillows and blankets until they had earned the veterans' respect. Certain individuals may serve as role models, providing

templates for emulation. Ibarra (1999) found that new investment bankers and management consultants, despite their inexperience, were required to appear highly professional and competent in front of their clients. The newcomers quickly emulated their more senior colleagues, essentially playing at their roles until they came to feel more natural and self-directed. Rewards and punishments may quickly shape behavior, enabling coordinated activity and providing the impetus for eventual changes in deeper attributes such as values and beliefs. Chappell and Lanza-Kaduce (2010) describe how, despite a police academy's avowed commitment to community policing, instructors used rewards (e.g., putting recruits with military experience in charge) and punishments (e.g., doing push-ups for failing to adhere to the chain of command) to instead reinforce values and behaviors more characteristic of traditional paramilitary policing. Further, communal activities with apparently clear meaning may enable individuals to think of themselves as members of a functional collective. Lennox Terrion and Ashforth (2002) describe how police executives in a 6-week full-time leadership training program engaged in ritualistic putdowns of their shared identities and of each other to help foster a sense of solidarity and clarify normative boundaries. The authors argued that implicit societal rules about how to give and receive putdowns enabled participants to avoid offense and appreciate that the putdowns were "all in good fun."

Fourth, equivocal symbols and practices may be used to paper over differences among individuals and between individuals and the organization, thereby enabling everyone to continue as a seemingly consensual unit. Lennox Terrion and Ashforth (2002) further found that although participants in the leadership training program may have disagreed about the meaning of particular putdowns, the experience of sharing a laugh—facilitated by the implicit societal rules—fostered the *appearance* of consensus. Finally, Bechky's (2006) notion of role-based coordination suggests that individuals may quickly coalesce into a functioning unit if they enter with certain role competencies and reasonably well-understood expectations of one another's roles. Bechky documents how members of newly formed film crews rely on their pre-existing understanding of the general role structure of film production, instantiated on a particular film set through daily shooting schedules and fleshed out by moment-by-moment negotiations of actual roles and emergent issues. This extant and negotiated role-based structure provides a certain relational momentum that carries the participants toward their collective goal—even if they remain quasi-strangers.

It should be emphasized that, while these five practices are likely to facilitate swift socialization, there are potentially major drawbacks to each of them. First, although rigorous recruitment and selection typically improve person–job and person–organization fit, there is inevitably some slippage between what an organization focuses on for recruitment and selection purposes and the full range of capabilities that are actually needed. These slippages can dramatically influence adjustment. For example, a newcomer with otherwise excellent job-related skills may be willing to behave far less ethically than the employer expects. Second, in truncating the socialization process, time compression may lead to certain lessons being only partially learned or skipped entirely. Given the importance of early experiences to later adjustment, discussed earlier, partial learning may ultimately impair the newcomer's ability to function in the organization. More generally, in complex jobs and organizations, long-term immersion is often required to truly "soak up" the necessary tacit knowledge. Third, strong situations can seem overly coercive to newcomers and thus backfire, leading to resistance and poor adjustment. For instance, Yoder and Aniakudo (1996) describe how some African-American female firefighters viewed pranks associated with hazing as outright harassment. Fourth, in papering over differences, equivocal symbols and practices can foster an "illusion of unanimity" (Janis, 1983), which can backfire if the illusion is ever put to the test. It's disturbing to learn that one has badly misread the views of others. Finally, role-based coordination can prove problematic if role occupants need to adapt to complex, dynamic, and ambiguous situations on the fly but lack the interpersonal familiarity and goodwill that typically lubricates such adaptation (Snook, 2000). Bechky (2006) discusses the often ritualistic "effusive thanking, polite admonishing, and role-oriented joking" (p. 11) that were needed on film sets in lieu of the social lubricant of familiarity and goodwill. Clearly, then, future research should assess the nature of the trade-offs inherent in swift socialization and the conditions under which such socialization remains the more desirable path to newcomer learning and adjustment.

Instantaneous Socialization

Socialization is typically discussed as a more or less complex undertaking to facilitate long-term learning and adjustment. The focus is on the future. But what about those situations where one need only adjust to the demands of the moment or the very near future? Examples include one-time customers, employees attending a workshop or off-site event, a manager facing an unusual crisis, and an individual entering the office of a senior executive for the only time.

In many of these one-off situations, individuals typically draw on their stock of experiences, scripts, and social learning (observation, instruction) in similar situations (e.g., Solomon, Surprenant, Czepiel, & Gutman, 1985). Thus, socialization can be achieved almost instantaneously by the judicious arrangement of *cues* to prime participants' expectations (Kesebir, Uttal, & Gardner, 2010; cf. Elsbach & Pratt, 2007). For example, in several lab studies, Kay, Wheeler, Bargh, and Ross (2004) demonstrated how mere pictures of business suits, boardroom tables, and the like primed a business frame such that subjects perceived an ambiguous social relationship as more competitive and behaved more competitively in an ambiguous interpersonal situation. Similarly, a corner office with expensive furnishings may cue deference without the visitor fully realizing it. Indeed, as Kesebir et al. (2010) note, "Once arranged, the environment may be a cost-effective socialization tool" (p. 100). In short, the greater the ambiguity—which can be pervasive in one-time encounters—the greater the nonconscious reliance on situational primes.

In sum, the need for swift and even instantaneous socialization is likely to become more acute as long-term individual–organization relationships erode, suggesting the need for concerted research on the range and efficacy of rapid onboarding practices.

Putting it All Together: When and How Often to Measure?

I argued that the greater the number and unpredictability of socialization events (and their outcomes), the greater the utility of event time (and thus rich qualitative methods that provide thick descriptions) compared to clock time (and its default reliance on periodic surveys)—with experience sampling providing a promising crossover of survey methods to assess event time. My focus in this section is on enhancing the effectiveness of periodic surveys for assessing both clock time and event time, because longitudinal survey research retains tremendous potential for enhancing our understanding of socialization dynamics and such research remains the method of choice for many socialization scholars.

In most organizational research, the mean organizational tenure of participants tends to be at least a few years. This means that, barring some disruption, the participants have likely *already* adjusted to the setting such that the relationships between typical independent (e.g., job design, leader–member exchange) and dependent variables (e.g., job satisfaction, organizational citizenship behaviors) have more or less stabilized. Thus, longitudinal research that shows that Time 1 independent variables predict Time 2 dependent variables is really capturing this stable system of associations. However, the fiction is that the variables at T1 *caused* the observed associations with the variables at T2, when in fact the associations had stabilized some time ago. Conversely, in *socialization* research, newcomer adjustment is still very much in flux such that there is as much instability as stability. What *this* means is that researchers must be very careful about when they measure variables and how often they do so.

Two reviews by Bauer and her colleagues (1998, 2007) indicate that studies of socialization most frequently use 3-month measurement intervals (i.e., entry, 3 months, 6 months, 9 months, and 1 year). However, as numerous scholars have mentioned (e.g., Bauer et al., 1998; Saks & Ashforth, 1997), the literature provides few theoretically grounded benchmarks for when and how often certain processes and outcomes should be assessed. I had intended to conclude with some fairly clear methodological prescriptions but, upon reflection, the best I can offer is that catch-all for most organizational research: "It all depends." That is, the contexts for socialization and the individuals involved are so diverse (as are the interactions between the two), the roles for which individuals are socialized are so variable, the range of potential socialization practices and formative events are so broad, the dynamics of socialization processes are so rich and complex (echoes of chaos theory comes to mind), and the proximal and distal outcomes of socialization are so varied that scholars must think deeply about the likely *contingencies* of socialization for any given study. What is one's research question? What kinds of contexts, roles, and individuals will likely prove most revealing for that question? Is one interested in specific socialization practices (e.g., orientation, mentoring), particular events (e.g., rites of passage), or more holistic and abstract concepts (e.g., socialization tactics)? Is one interested in relatively superficial change such as in behaviors, suggesting relatively swift socialization, or in deeper change such as in values and traits?

In the face of this complexity and dynamism, let me at least offer some general temporal prescriptions for survey research:

• Given the tremendous variety in socialization dynamics across contexts, utilize a pilot study or interviews with key informants in a given context of interest to gain guidance regarding when and how often to measure variables in *that* particular context.

• To truly capture the process of socialization, demonstrate how A (if A is stable over time) or *change* in A (if A is dynamic) predicts *change* in B over some theoretically based time lag. This requires measuring the change-oriented variables at least at two—and preferably three or more (Ployhart & Vandenberg, 2010)—points of time. Methods such as latent growth modeling and random coefficient modeling could then be used to investigate between-individual variability in within-individual change over time (Ployhart & Vandenberg, 2010; Raudenbush, 2001; e.g., Chan & Schmitt, 2000; Jokisaari & Nurmi, 2009). Analogously, to assess change caused by foreseeable discrete events, take pre and post measures of B; the post measure should balance the trade-off between capturing the longer-term effects of the events with the risk of other factors contaminating the causal inference.

• Assess learning and adjustment as soon as possible to establish baseline levels. As the notion of anticipatory socialization indicates, even at the pre-entry stage newcomers typically have some understanding and degree of rapport with the work and work context. After accounting for the possibility of unstable measures due to beta or gamma change (Vandenberg & Self, 1993), these baseline levels can then allow the researcher to model change in learning and adjustment over time (Bauer et al., 1998).

• Most individual differences are viewed as independent or moderating variables in socialization models. In such cases, measure individual differences as soon as possible, that is, before they can be influenced or simply primed by pre-entry and post-entry events. And, obviously, if a researcher is predicting *change* in individual differences such as values and beliefs, an early baseline reading is required.

• If a researcher is relying on self-report measures of socialization processes (as most do), allow sufficient time for the newcomer to experience and become reasonably knowledgeable about the processes.

- Individual differences, contextual factors, and socialization processes were discussed as factors that are likely to affect the *rate* of learning and adjustment. All else equal, the greater the rate the sooner and more frequently the relevant variables should be assessed. In particular, for malleable learning and adjustment variables (e.g., knowledge, behavior), for jobs entailing low complexity and narrow experiences, and for a host of simplifying and facilitating conditions, shorter lags are advisable. For the opposite circumstances (e.g., broad experiences, complicating and inhibiting conditions), longer lags *may* be advisable; I say "may" because the rapidity with which newcomers form initial impressions of— and attitudes toward—their role and organization suggests that short lags may remain advisable at least in the early socialization period.
- Relatedly, measure frequently during the period in which change is anticipated (Cooper-Thomas & Anderson, 2005; Ployhart & Vandenberg, 2010), whether it be positive (cumulative learning and adjustment, as in Figure 9.1), negative (decay), or something more complex (e.g., oscillations, as in Figure 9.2). Frequent measurements also increase the chances of isolating change caused by unforeseeable events. At least three measurements are required to detect curvilinear relationships, four for oscillations, and "perhaps more for rhythms, spirals, and cycles" (Mitchell & James, 2001, p. 538). If the dependent variable is expected to stabilize (e.g., the trajectories in Figure 9.1 as they approach the asymptote) and then possibly decay, measure it during the stable period.
- Once learning and adjustment begin to stabilize, the "default" time lags of 3 (or more) months mentioned by Bauer et al. (1998, 2007) seem serviceable for most socialization research. However, the possibility of decay as well as renewed learning and adjustment in the face of disruptive events (as in Figure 9.3) remain very real and argue against the use of long lags.
- Logically, proximal adjustment precedes distal adjustment. However, although job satisfaction, organizational commitment, performance, and so on are characterized as distal outcomes, newcomers are willing and able to form preliminary impressions and engage in initial task execution that, as noted, are likely to strongly predict later impressions and execution. These outcomes are nonetheless distal in the sense that they are substantially *mediated* by proximal adjustment;

as individuals come to understand, master, and shape their roles and become socially integrated, they are more likely to score well on the indices of distal adjustment. Hence, characterizing certain outcomes as "distal" does *not* mean that they should only be measured late in the socialization process; indeed, as argued above, given the importance of modeling *change* in adjustment, they should be assessed early to obtain a baseline reading.

Finally, a major issue to consider is negative feedback loops where A at Time 1 positively influences B at Time 2, and B then negatively influences A at Time 3 (Saks & Ashforth, 1997). Because the intent of socialization processes is to help newcomers become functioning insiders, such processes should be responsive to the evolving developmental needs of the newcomers. Thus, recursive relationships are likely between socialization activities and newcomers' learning and adjustment. For example, socialization studies are often premised on newcomers' attempts to reduce uncertainty (see reviews by Bauer et al., 2007; Kramer, 2004; Saks & Ashforth, 1997). This suggests that initial uncertainty (operationalized, say, by role ambiguity) will be *positively* associated with proactive behaviors. In turn, as the proactive behaviors foster knowledge gains, proactivity will be *negatively* associated with uncertainty (indeed, studies tend to report a negative association between uncertainty and proactivity; Vancouver et al., 2010). And, complicating the picture further, the *lag* between initial uncertainty and proactivity is apt to be short (faced with ambiguity, the newcomer may immediately start asking questions of coworkers), whereas the lag between proactivity and significantly reduced uncertainty is apt to be much longer (it takes time to develop a true sense of familiarity; e.g., Feldman, 1977). As Vancouver et al. (2010) warn, "collecting single observations of a time-varying variable [like proactive behavior] in a longitudinal study undercuts the value of the longitudinal design and can lead to spurious conclusions" (p. 777).

In sum, because socialization is fundamentally a dynamic process, where learning and adjustment can be justifiably characterized as both stable and unstable, it is imperative that researchers use designs that capture meaningful change over time. And what Ployhart and Vandenberg (2010) wrote of the management literature generally is equally true of the socialization literature specifically: "as theory continues to become more refined, it will often be necessary to hypothesize and test nonlinear and discontinuous forms of change" (p. 117). Cross-sectional designs, and longitudinal designs that do not capture actual change, have served their purpose in getting us to our current state of rich theorizing. However, to progress further, more sophisticated longitudinal designs are warranted.

Conclusion

At its core, socialization is about change over time, and that change is often cued, paced, and facilitated by a succession of formal and informal events from which newcomers and their socialization agents extract meaning. The next generation of socialization scholarship can be significantly enriched by more explicitly incorporating both temporal considerations and formative events in our evolving theoretical models and empirical studies.

Acknowledgment

Author note: I am indebted to Kristie Rogers and Connie Wanberg for their very helpful comments on an earlier draft.

Notes

1. That said, as the duration of the modal relationship between individuals and their organizations continues to decrease, both individuals and organizations are less likely to take a long-run view of their relationship and engage in career-oriented socialization. Accordingly, socialization becomes more oriented to securing person–job fit (developing newcomers' competence to fulfill immediate job demands) than person–organization or person–career fit (developing newcomers' competence to fulfill longer-term organizational and career demands). Gómez (2009), for example, studied administrators overseeing teacher development programs and found that the more administrators perceived that their organization regarded time as scarce and took a present-oriented rather than future-oriented view of time, the less inclined the organizations were to utilize formally structured socialization practices.

2. Although additional proximal adjustment variables have been proposed in the socialization literature (e.g., Saks & Ashforth, 1997; Saks, Uggerslev, & Fassina, 2007), these three appear to be emerging as the most popular.

3. Tesluk and Jacobs (1998; cf. Quiñones, Ford, & Teachout, 1995) draw a similar distinction between work experience that is *quantitative* (i.e., "amount," the number of times a task has been performed, and "length of time on the job") and *qualitative* (i.e., "type," the nature of experience).

4. Of course, the finer the temporal slices and the more open-ended the questions, the closer to the ground the snapshot becomes. Experience sampling methods (e.g., Hektner, Schmidt, & Csikszentmihalyi, 2007) provide a particularly promising way of capturing the "lumpiness" of event time in the context of repeated measures surveys.

5. Ibarra and Barbulescu (2010) note that where stories involve a clear break from the past (e.g., a banker becoming a teacher), the *discontinuity*—the turning point—becomes a central feature of the story. Even so, as a means of demonstrating the narrator's personal agency (a desired feature of stories), the narrator incorporates into the storyline how the "before" animated her choice of the "after."

6. Of course, for a given setting this amount will vary across individuals and, in view of the dynamism of organizations, over time. Indeed, although the assumption of a fixed amount is workable for exposition purposes, it's arguable whether the amount of learning and adjustment is ever truly fixed. In interviewing individuals in the course of several qualitative studies, I often asked, "How long does it take someone in your line of work to become really good at what you do?" Many individuals responded in terms of roughly half their current tenure; that is, a 10-year electrical engineer might say "about 5 years," whereas a 20-year electrical engineer might say "about 10 years." This suggests that individuals continue to discover depths and nuances in their work such that they seldom feel as if they have truly mastered all of its intricacies. Further, as Kristof-Brown and Jansen (2007) wrote, "it is short-sighted to think that once socialized, the individual does not continue to grow and change" (p. 143).

7. Several other particularly promising temporally oriented individual differences include *temporal enactments* (flexibility, linearity, pace, precision, scheduling, separation; Ballard & Seibold, 2003), *time attitude* (e.g., regret, nostalgia, worry, hope; Shipp et al., 2009), and *time urgency* (hurriedness; e.g., Waller, Conte, Gibson, & Carpenter, 2001).

8. Transferability is deceptively tricky because one may have learned the "wrong" lessons (e.g., bad habits, superstitious learning) or the "right" lessons for the "wrong" situation, as when the new organization prefers different approaches than other organizations use. Later, I briefly note how divestiture may be used to facilitate "unlearning."

9. Earlier, role clarity was identified as a form of proximal adjustment. Here, I acknowledge a lack of clarity (role ambiguity) as a contextual constraint on learning.

10. The sixth tactic, investiture, tends to covary with institutionalized socialization (defined later) in most settings. As noted, however, highly distinctive organizations (e.g., armies, trawlers, medical schools, police forces) and industries are inclined to couple *divestiture* with institutionalized socialization in order to divest newcomers of their incoming identities before remaking them in the organization's image (e.g., Bourassa & Ashforth, 1998; Conti, 2009; Hafferty, 1991).

11. Indeed, the authors go on to note: "Nonlinear relationships over time are possible, as are cyclical and oscillating ones. Change can be incremental or discontinuous. Cycles can spiral up or down, and the intensity can change. Various relationships can have rhythms or patterns over time" (p. 532). Although some of these possibilities have been or will be touched on in this chapter, most have not been broached in the socialization literature and remain a provocative direction for future research.

12. Interestingly, Chan and Schmitt (2000) found a linear trajectory for social integration (as well as for role clarity and task mastery) over four 1-month measurement periods for new doctoral students. I suspect, however, that social integration is more susceptible to shocks because of the vagaries of social interaction, the number of individuals with whom a newcomer may regularly interact, and the likelihood of turnover among those individuals.

References

Adkins, C. L. (1995). Previous work experience and organizational socialization: A longitudinal examination. *Academy of Management Journal, 38*, 839–862.

Adler, I., & Shuval, J. T. (1978). Cross pressures during socialization for medicine. *American Sociological Review, 43*, 693–704.

Adler, P. A., & Adler, P. (1991). *Backboards & blackboards: College athletes and role engulfment.* New York: Columbia University Press.

Ahuja, M. K., & Galvin, J. E. (2003). Socialization in virtual groups. *Journal of Management, 29*, 161–185.

Anakwe, U. P., & Greenhaus, J. H. (2000). Prior work experience and socialization experiences of college graduates. *International Journal of Manpower, 21*, 95–111.

Ancona, D. G., Okhuysen, G. A., & Perlow, L. A. (2001). Taking time to integrate temporal research. *Academy of Management Review, 26*, 512–529.

Anderson, N., & Ostroff, C. (1997). Selection as socialization. In N. Anderson & P. Herriot (Eds.), *International handbook of selection and assessment* (pp. 413–440). Chichester, UK: Wiley.

Anderson, N., & Thomas, H. D. C. (1996). Work group socialization. In M. A. West (Ed.), *Handbook of work group psychology* (pp. 423–450). Chichester, UK: Wiley.

Anderson-Gough, F., Grey, C., & Robson, K. (2001). Tests of time: Organizational time-reckoning and the making of accountants in two multi-national accounting firms. *Accounting, Organizations and Society, 26*, 99–122.

Ashford, S. J., & Black, J. S. (1996). Proactivity during organizational entry: The role of desire for control. *Journal of Applied Psychology, 81*, 199–214.

Ashford, S. J., Blatt, R., & VandeWalle, D. (2003). Reflections on the looking glass: A review of research on feedback-seeking behavior in organizations. *Journal of Management, 29*, 773–799.

Ashford, S. J., & Taylor, M. S. (1990). Adaptation to work transitions: An integrative approach. In G. R. Ferris & K. M. Rowland (Eds.), *Research in personnel and human resources management* (Vol. 8, pp. 1–39). Greenwich, CT: JAI Press.

Ashforth, B. E. (2001). *Role transitions in organizational life: An identity-based perspective.* Mahwah, NJ: Erlbaum.

Ashforth, B. E., & Boudwin, K. M. (2010). Initiation rites. In J. M. Levine & M. A. Hogg (Eds.), *Encyclopedia of group processes & intergroup relations* (Vol. 1, pp. 448–451). Los Angeles: Sage.

Ashforth, B. E., & Humphrey, R. H. (1995). Labeling processes in the organization: Constructing the individual. In L. L. Cummings & B. M. Staw (Eds.), *Research in organizational behavior* (Vol. 17, pp. 413–461). Greenwich, CT: JAI Press.

Ashforth, B. E., Myers, K. K., & Sluss, D. M. (2012). Socialization perspectives and positive organizational scholarship. In K. S. Cameron & G. M. Spreitzer (Eds.), *The Oxford handbook of positive organizational scholarship* (pp. 537–548). Oxford, UK: Oxford University Press.

Ashforth, B. E., & Rogers, K. M. (2012). Is the employee-organization relationship misspecified? The centrality of tribes in experiencing the organization. In L. M. Shore, J. A.-M. Coyle-Shapiro, & L. E. Tetrick (Eds.), *The employee-organization relationship: Applications for the 21st century* (pp. 23–53). New York: Routledge.

Ashforth, B. E., & Saks, A.M. (1996). Socialization tactics: Longitudinal effects on newcomer adjustment. *Academy of Management Journal, 39*, 149–178.

Ashforth, B. E., Saks, A. M., & Lee, R. T. (1997). On the dimensionality of Jones' (1986) measures of organizational socialization tactics. *International Journal of Selection and Assessment, 5*, 200–214.

Ashforth, B. E., Saks, A. M., & Lee, R. T. (1998). Socialization and newcomer adjustment: The role of organizational context. *Human Relations, 51*, 897–926.

Ashforth, B. E., Sluss, D. M., & Harrison, S. H. (2007a). Socialization in organizational contexts. In G. P. Hodgkinson & J. K. Ford (Eds.), *International review of industrial and organizational psychology* (Vol. 22, pp. 1–70). Chichester, UK: Wiley.

Ashforth, B. E., Sluss, D. M., & Saks, A. M. (2007b). Socialization tactics, proactive behavior, and newcomer learning: Integrating socialization models. *Journal of Vocational Behavior, 70*, 447–462.

Ballard, D. I., & Seibold, D. R. (2003). Communicating and organizing in time: A meso-level model of organizational temporality. *Management Communication Quarterly, 16*, 380–415.

Bauer, T. N., Bodner, T., Erdogan, B., Truxillo, D. M., & Tucker, J. S. (2007). Newcomer adjustment during organizational socialization: A meta-analytic review of antecedents, outcomes, and methods. *Journal of Applied Psychology, 92*, 707–721.

Bauer, T. N., & Erdogan, B. (2011). Organizational socialization: The effective onboarding of new employees. In S. Zedeck, H. Aguinis, W. Cascio, M. Gelfand, K. Leung, S. Parker, & J. Zhou (Eds.), *APA handbook of industrial and organizational psychology* (Vol. 3: *Maintaining, expanding, and contracting the organization*, pp. 51–64). Washington, DC: American Psychological Association.

Bauer, T. N., & Erdogan, B. (2012). Organizational socialization outcomes: Now and into the future. In C. Wanberg (Ed.), *The Oxford handbook of socialization.* Oxford, UK: Oxford University Press.

Bauer, T. N., & Green, S. G. (1994). Effect of newcomer involvement in work-related activities: A longitudinal study of socialization. *Journal of Applied Psychology, 79*, 211–223.

Bauer, T. N., & Green, S. G. (1998). Testing the combined effects of newcomer information seeking and manager behavior on socialization. *Journal of Applied Psychology, 83*, 72–83.

Bauer, T. N., Morrison, E. W., & Callister, R. R. (1998). Organizational socialization: A review and directions for future research. In G. R. Ferris (Ed.), *Research in personnel and human resources management* (Vol. 16, pp. 149–214). Greenwich, CT: JAI Press.

Bechky, B. A. (2006). Gaffers, gofers, and grips: Role-based coordination in temporary organizations. *Organization Science, 17*, 3–21.

Beck, J., & Forstmeier, W. (2007). Superstition and belief as inevitable by-products of an adaptive learning strategy. *Human Nature, 18*, 35–46.

Beyer, J. M., & Hannah, D. R. (2002). Building on the past: Enacting established personal identities in a new work setting. *Organization Science, 13*, 636–652.

Blount, S., & Janicik, G. A. (2001). When plans change: Examining how people evaluate timing changes in work organizations. *Academy of Management Review, 26*, 566–585.

Bluedorn, A. C., & Denhardt, R. B. (1988). Time and organizations. *Journal of Management, 14*, 299–320.

Boswell, W. R., Boudreau, J. W., & Tichy, J. (2005). The relationship between employee job change and job satisfaction: The honeymoon-hangover effect. *Journal of Applied Psychology, 90*, 882–892.

Boswell, W. R., Shipp, A. J., Payne, S. C., & Culbertson, S. S. (2009). Changes in newcomer job satisfaction over time:

Examining the pattern of honeymoons and hangovers. *Journal of Applied Psychology, 94,* 844–858.

Bourassa, L., & Ashforth, B. E. (1998). You are about to party *Defiant* style: Socialization and identity onboard an Alaskan fishing boat. *Journal of Contemporary Ethnography, 27,* 171–196.

Bullis, C., & Bach, B. W. (1989). Socialization turning points: An examination of change in organizational identification. *Western Journal of Speech Communication, 53,* 273–293.

Burr, W. R. (1972). Role transitions: A reformulation of theory. *Journal of Marriage and the Family, 34,* 407–416.

Cardon, M. S. (2002). *How long is forever? The role of anticipated tenure in organizational socialization.* Paper presented at the annual meeting of the Academy of Management, Denver.

Carr, J. C., Pearson, A. W., Vest, M. J., & Boyar, S. L. (2006). Prior occupational experience, anticipatory socialization, and employee retention. *Journal of Management, 32,* 343–359.

Chan, D., & Schmitt, N. (2000). Interindividual differences in intraindividual changes in proactivity during organizational entry: A latent growth modeling approach to understanding newcomer adaptation. *Journal of Applied Psychology, 85,* 190–210.

Chao, G. T. (1997). Unstructured training and development: The role of organizational socialization. In J. K. Ford, S. W. J. Kozlowski, K. Kraiger, E. Salas, & M. S. Teachout (Eds.), *Improving training effectiveness in work organizations* (pp. 129–151). Mahwah, NJ: Erlbaum.

Chao, G. T., O'Leary-Kelly, A. M., Wolf, S., Klein, H. J., & Gardner, P. D. (1994). Organizational socialization: Its content and consequences. *Journal of Applied Psychology, 79,* 730–743.

Chappell, A. T., & Lanza-Kaduce, L. (2010). Police academy socialization: Understanding the lessons learned in a para-military-bureaucratic organization. *Journal of Contemporary Ethnography, 39,* 187–214.

Chatman, J. A. (1991). Matching people and organizations: Selection and socialization in public accounting firms. *Administrative Science Quarterly, 36,* 459–484.

Chen, G., & Klimoski, R. J. (2003). The impact of expectations on newcomer performance in teams as mediated by work characteristics, social exchanges, and empowerment. *Academy of Management Journal, 46,* 591–607.

Chen, N. Y., Tjosvold, D., Huang, X., & Xu, D. (2011). New manager socialization and conflict management in China: Effects of relationship and open conflict values. *Journal of Applied Social Psychology, 41,* 332–356.

Colquitt, J. A., LePine, J. A., & Noe, R. A. (2000). Toward an integrative theory of training motivation: A meta-analytic path analysis of 20 years of research. *Journal of Applied Psychology, 85,* 678–707.

Colquitt, J. A., & Simmering, M. J. (1998). Conscientiousness, goal orientation, and motivation to learn during the learning process: A longitudinal study. *Journal of Applied Psychology, 83,* 654–665.

Conti, N. (2009). A Visigoth system: Shame, honor, and police socialization. *Journal of Contemporary Ethnography, 38,* 409–432.

Cooper, W. H., Graham, W. J., & Dyke, L. S. (1993). Tournament players. In G. R. Ferris (Ed.), *Research in personnel and human resources management* (Vol. 11, pp. 83–132). Greenwich, CT: JAI Press.

Cooper-Thomas, H., & Anderson, N. (2002). Newcomer adjustment: The relationship between organizational socialization tactics, information acquisition and attitudes. *Journal of Occupational and Organizational Psychology, 75,* 423–437.

Cooper-Thomas, H. D., & Anderson, N. (2005). Organizational socialization: A field study into socialization success and rate. *International Journal of Selection and Assessment, 13,* 116–128.

Cooper-Thomas, H. D., & Anderson, N. (2006). Organizational socialization: A new theoretical model and recommendations for future research and HRM practices in organizations. *Journal of Managerial Psychology, 21,* 492–516.

Crant, J. M. (2000). Proactive behavior in organizations. *Journal of Management, 26,* 435–462.

DiSanza, J. R. (1995). Bank teller organizational assimilation in a system of contradictory practices. *Management Communication Quarterly, 9,* 191–218.

Dragoni, L., Tesluk, P. E., Russell, J. E. A., & Oh, I.-S. (2009). Understanding managerial development: Integrating developmental assignments, learning orientation, and access to developmental opportunities in predicting managerial competencies. *Academy of Management Journal, 52,* 731–743.

Dweck, C. S. (1986). Motivational processes affecting learning. *American Psychologist, 41,* 1040–1048.

Elsbach, K. D., & Pratt, M. G. (2007). The physical environment in organizations. In J. P. Walsh & A. P. Brief (Eds.), *The Academy of Management annals* (Vol. 1, pp. 181–234). New York: Routledge.

Evans, W. R., & Davis, W. D. (2005). High-performance work systems and organizational performance: The mediating role of internal social structures. *Journal of Management, 31,* 758–775.

Feldman, D. C. (1976). A contingency theory of socialization. *Administrative Science Quarterly, 21,* 433–452.

Feldman, D. C. (1977). The role of initiation activities in socialization. *Human Relations, 30,* 977–990.

Feldman, D. C. (1981). The multiple socialization of organization members. *Academy of Management Review, 6,* 309–318.

Fisher, C. D. (1986). Organizational socialization: An integrative review. In K. M. Rowland & G. R. Ferris (Eds.), *Research in personnel and human resources management* (Vol. 4, pp. 101–145). Greenwich, CT: JAI Press.

Frese, M. (1982). Occupational socialization and psychological development: An underemphasized research perspective in industrial psychology. *Journal of Occupational Psychology, 55,* 209–224.

Gabriel, Y. (2000). *Storytelling in organizations: Facts, fictions, and fantasies.* Oxford, UK: Oxford University Press.

Garrick, J. (1998). *Informal learning in the workplace: Unmasking human resource development.* London: Routledge.

George, J. M., & Jones, G. R. (2000). The role of time in theory and theory building. *Journal of Management, 26,* 657–684.

Gibson, M. K., & Papa, M. J. (2000). The mud, the blood, and the beer guys: Organizational osmosis in blue-collar work groups. *Journal of Applied Communication Research, 28,* 68–88.

Gittell, J. H. (2006). Relational coordination: Coordinating work through relationships of shared goals, shared knowledge and mutual respect. In O. Kyriakidou & M. F. Özbilgin (Eds.), *Relational perspectives in organizational studies: A research companion* (pp. 74–94). Cheltenham, UK: Edward Elgar.

Golembiewski, R. T., Billingsley, K., & Yeager, S. (1976). Measuring change and persistence in human affairs: Types of change generated by OD designs. *Journal of Applied Behavioral Science, 12,* 133–157.

Gómez, L. F. (2009). Time to socialize: Organizational socialization structures and temporality. *Journal of Business Communication*, *46*, 179–207.

Goodwin, V. L., & Ziegler, L. (1998). A test of relationships in a model of organizational cognitive complexity. *Journal of Organizational Behavior*, *19*, 371–386.

Graen, G. B., Orris, J. B., & Johnson, T. W. (1973). Role assimilation processes in a complex organization. *Journal of Vocational Behavior*, *3*, 395–420.

Grant, A. M., & Ashford, S. J. (2008). The dynamics of proactivity at work. In A. P. Brief & B. M. Staw (Eds.), *Research in organizational behavior* (Vol. 28, pp. 3–34). Amsterdam: Elsevier.

Griffin, A. E. C., Colella, A., & Goparaju, S. (2000). Newcomer and organizational socialization tactics: An interactionist perspective. *Human Resource Management Review*, *10*, 453–474.

Gruman, J. A., Saks, A. M., & Zweig, D. I. (2006). Organizational socialization tactics and newcomer proactive behaviors: An integrative study. *Journal of Vocational Behavior*, *69*, 90–104.

Gundry, L. K. (1993). Fitting into technical organizations: The socialization of newcomer engineers. *IEEE Transactions on Engineering Management*, *40*, 335–345.

Haas, J., & Shaffir, W. (1984). The "fate of idealism" revisited. *Urban Life*, *13*, 63–81.

Hafferty, F. W. (1991). *Into the valley: Death and the socialization of medical students*. New Haven, CT: Yale University Press.

Hall, D. T. (1976). *Careers in organizations*. Pacific Palisades, CA: Goodyear.

Harris, M. J., & Garris, C. P. (2008). You never get a second chance to make a first impression: Behavioral consequences of first impressions. In N. Ambady & J. J. Skowronski (Eds.), *First impressions* (pp. 147–168). New York: Guilford Press.

Harris, R., Simons, M., & Carden, P. (2004). Peripheral journeys: Learning and acceptance of probationary constables. *Journal of Workplace Learning*, *16*, 205–218.

Harrison, J. R., & Carroll, G. R. (1991). Keeping the faith: A model of cultural transmission in formal organizations. *Administrative Science Quarterly*, *36*, 552–582.

Haski-Leventhal, D., & Bargal, D. (2008). The volunteer stages and transitions model: Organizational socialization of volunteers. *Human Relations*, *61*, 67–102.

Hattrup, K., & Jackson, S. E. (1996). Learning about individual differences by taking situations seriously. In K. R. Murphy (Ed.), *Individual differences and behavior in organizations* (pp. 507–547). San Francisco: Jossey-Bass.

Hektner, J. M., Schmidt, J. A., & Csikszentmihalyi, M. (Eds.). (2007). *Experience sampling method: Measuring the quality of everyday life*. Thousand Oaks, CA: Sage.

Hicks, A. M. (2008). Role fusion: The occupational socialization of prison chaplains. *Symbolic Interaction*, *31*, 400–421.

Hill, L. A. (1992). *Becoming a manager: Mastery of a new identity*. Boston: Harvard Business School Press.

Howard, A., & Bray, D. W. (1988). *Managerial lives in transition: Advancing age and changing times*. New York: Guilford Press.

Hsiung, T. L., & Hsieh, A. T. (2003). Newcomer socialization: The role of job standardization. *Public Personnel Management*, *32*, 579–589.

Ibarra, H. (1999). Provisional selves: Experimenting with image and identity in professional adaptation. *Administrative Science Quarterly*, *44*, 764–791.

Ibarra, H. (2003). *Working identity: Unconventional strategies for reinventing your career*. Boston: Harvard Business School Press.

Ibarra, H., & Barbulescu, R. (2010). Identity as narrative: Prevalence, effectiveness, and consequences of narrative identity work in macro work role transitions. *Academy of Management Review*, *35*, 135–154.

Jablin, F. M. (2000). Organizational entry, assimilation, and disengagement/exit. In F. M. Jablin & L. L. Putnam (Eds.), *The new handbook of organizational communication: Advances in theory, research, and methods* (pp. 732–818). Thousand Oaks, CA: Sage.

Jacobson, D. (1996). Celebrating good-bye: Functional components in farewell parties for retiring employees in Israel. *Journal of Aging Studies*, *10*, 223–235.

Janis, I. L. (1983). *Groupthink: Psychological studies of policy decisions and fiascos* (2nd ed.). Boston: Houghton Mifflin.

Johns, G. (2006). The essential impact of context on organizational behavior. *Academy of Management Review*, *31*, 386–408.

Jokisaari, M., & Nurmi, J.-E. (2009). Change in newcomers' supervisor support and socialization outcomes after organizational entry. *Academy of Management Journal*, *52*, 527–544.

Jones, G. R. (1986). Socialization tactics, self-efficacy, and newcomers' adjustments to organizations. *Academy of Management Journal*, *29*, 262–279.

Kammeyer-Mueller, J. D., Livingston, B. A., & Liao, H. (2011). Perceived similarity, proactive adjustment, and organizational socialization. *Journal of Vocational Behavior*, *78*, 225–236.

Kammeyer-Mueller, J. D., & Wanberg, C. R. (2003). Unwrapping the organizational entry process: Disentangling multiple antecedents and their pathways to adjustment. *Journal of Applied Psychology*, *88*, 779–794.

Katz, R. (1980). Time and work: Toward an integrative perspective. In B. M. Staw & L. L. Cummings (Eds.), *Research in organizational behavior* (Vol. 2, pp. 81–127). Greenwich, CT: JAI Press.

Katz, R. (1985). Organizational stress and early socialization experiences. In T. A. Beehr & R. S. Bhagat (Eds.), *Human stress and cognition in organizations: An integrated perspective* (pp. 117–139). New York: Wiley.

Kay, A. C., Wheeler, S. C., Bargh, J. A., & Ross, L. (2004). Material priming: The influence of mundane physical objects on situational construal and competitive behavioral choice. *Organizational Behavior and Human Decision Processes*, *95*, 83–96.

Kesebir, S., Uttal, D. H., & Gardner, W. (2010). Socialization: Insights from social cognition. *Social and Personality Psychology Compass*, *4*, 93–106.

Kim, T.-Y., Cable, D. M., & Kim, S.-P. (2005). Socialization tactics, employee proactivity, and person-organization fit. *Journal of Applied Psychology*, *90*, 232–241.

Klein, H. J., & Heuser, A. E. (2008). The learning of socialization content: A framework for researching orienting practices. In J. J. Martocchio (Ed.), *Research in personnel and human resources management* (Vol. 27, pp. 279–336). Bradford, UK: Emerald.

Korte, R. F. (2009). How newcomers learn the social norms of an organization: A case study of the socialization of newly hired engineers. *Human Resource Development Quarterly*, *20*, 285–306.

Kramer, M. (1974). *Reality shock: Why nurses leave nursing*. St. Louis: C.V. Mosby.

Kramer, M. W. (2004). *Managing uncertainty in organizational communication*. Mahwah, NJ: Erlbaum.

Kramer, M. W. (2010). *Organizational socialization: Joining and leaving organizations*. Cambridge, UK: Polity Press.

Kristof-Brown, A. L., & Jansen, K. J. (2007). Issues of person-organization fit. In C. Ostroff & T. A. Judge (Eds.), *Perspectives on organizational fit* (pp. 123–153). New York: Erlbaum.

Lennox Terrion, J., & Ashforth, B. E. (2002). From "I" to "we": The role of putdown humor and identity in the development of a temporary group. *Human Relations, 55,* 55–88.

Lewicki, R. J. (1981). Organizational seduction: Building commitment to organizations. *Organizational Dynamics, 10*(2), 5–21.

Liden, R. C., Wayne, S. J., & Stilwell, D. (1993). A longitudinal study of the early development of leader-member exchanges. *Journal of Applied Psychology, 78,* 662–674.

Lindsley, D. H., Brass, D. J., & Thomas, J. B. (1995). Efficacy-performance spirals: A multilevel perspective. *Academy of Management Review, 20,* 645–678.

Liu, C.-H., & Lee, H.-W. (2008). A proposed model of expatriates in multinational corporations. *Cross Cultural Management, 15,* 176–193.

Louis, M. R. (1980). Surprise and sense making: What newcomers experience in entering unfamiliar organizational settings. *Administrative Science Quarterly, 25,* 226–251.

Major, D. A., Kozlowski, S. W. J., Chao, G. T., & Gardner, P. D. (1995). A longitudinal investigation of newcomer expectations, early socialization outcomes, and the moderating effects of role development factors. *Journal of Applied Psychology, 80,* 418–431.

Mansfield, R. (1972). The initiation of graduates in industry: The resolution of identity-stress as a determinant of job satisfaction in the early months at work. *Human Relations, 25,* 77–86.

Manz, C. C. (1983). *The art of self-leadership: Strategies for personal effectiveness in your life and work.* Englewood Cliffs, NJ: Prentice-Hall.

McAdams, D. P. (1993). *The stories we live by: Personal myths and the making of the self.* New York: Guilford Press.

McAdams, D. P. (1999). Personal narratives and the life story. In L. A. Pervin & O. P. John (Eds.), *Handbook of personality: Theory and research* (2nd ed., pp. 478–500). New York: Guilford Press.

Merton, R. K. (1957). *Social theory and social structure* (rev. ed.). Glencoe, IL: Free Press.

Meyer, R. D., Dalal, R. S., & Hermida, R. (2010). A review and synthesis of situational strength in the organizational sciences. *Journal of Management, 36,* 121–140.

Meyerson, D., Weick, K. E., & Kramer, R. M. (1996). Swift trust and temporary groups. In R. M. Kramer & T. R. Tyler (Eds.), *Trust in organizations: Frontiers of theory and research* (pp. 166–195). Thousand Oaks, CA: Sage.

Miller, V. D., & Jablin, F. M. (1991). Information seeking during organizational entry: Influences, tactics, and a model of the process. *Academy of Management Review, 16,* 92–120.

Mitchell, T. R., & James, L. R. (2001). Building better theory: Time and the specification of when things happen. *Academy of Management Review, 26,* 530–547.

Mitchell, T. R., Thompson, L., Peterson, E., & Cronk, R. (1997). Temporal adjustments in the evaluation of events: The "rosy view." *Journal of Experimental Social Psychology, 33,* 421–448.

Moreland, R. L., & Levine, J. M. (2001). Socialization in organizations and work groups. In M. E. Turner (Ed.), *Groups at work: Theory and research* (pp. 69–112). Mahwah, NJ: Erlbaum.

Morrison, E. W. (1993a). Longitudinal study of the effects of information seeking on newcomer socialization. *Journal of Applied Psychology, 78,* 173–183.

Morrison, E. W. (1993b). Newcomer information seeking: Exploring types, modes, sources, and outcomes. *Academy of Management Journal, 36,* 557–589.

Morrison, E. W. (1995). Information usefulness and acquisition during organizational encounter. *Management Communication Quarterly, 9,* 131–155.

Morrison, R. F., & Brantner, T. M. (1992). What enhances or inhibits learning a new job? A basic career issue. *Journal of Applied Psychology, 77,* 926–940.

Morrison, R. F., & Hock, R. R. (1986). Career building: Learning from cumulative work experience. In D. T. Hall & Associates, *Career development in organizations* (pp. 236–273). San Francisco: Jossey-Bass.

Mowday, R. T., & Sutton, R. I. (1993). Organizational behavior: Linking individuals and groups to organizational contexts. In M. R. Rosenzweig & L. W. Porter (Eds.), *Annual review of psychology* (Vol. 44, pp. 195–229). Palo Alto, CA: Annual Reviews.

Nelson, D. L. (1987). Organizational socialization: A stress perspective. *Journal of Occupational Behaviour, 8,* 311–324.

Nelson, D. L., & Quick, J. C. (1991). Social support and newcomer adjustment in organizations: Attachment theory at work? *Journal of Organizational Behavior, 12,* 543–554.

Nifadkar, S. S. (2009). *Newcomer adjustment in a high-speed context: The roles of emotion regulation, organizational socialization tactics, and psychological safety.* Unpublished doctoral dissertation (Paper 2), Tempe, AZ: Arizona State University.

Niiya, Y., Crocker, J., & Bartmess, E. N. (2004). From vulnerability to resilience: Learning orientations buffer contingent self-esteem from failure. *Psychological Science, 15,* 801–805.

Noe, R. A., Tews, M. J., & Dachner, A. M. (2010). Learner engagement: A new perspective for enhancing our understanding of learner motivation and workplace learning. In J. P. Walsh & A. P. Brief (Eds.), *The Academy of Management annals* (Vol. 4, pp. 279–315). New York: Routledge.

Ostroff, C., & Kozlowski, S. W. J. (1992). Organizational socialization as a learning process: The role of information acquisition. *Personnel Psychology, 45,* 849–874.

Pinder, C. C., & Schroeder, K. G. (1987). Time to proficiency following job transfers. *Academy of Management Journal, 30,* 336–353.

Ployhart, R. E., & Vandenberg, R. J. (2010). Longitudinal research: The theory, design, and analysis of change. *Journal of Management, 36,* 94–120.

Porter, L. W., Lawler, E. E., III, & Hackman, J. R. (1975). *Behavior in organizations.* New York: McGraw-Hill.

Pratt, M. G. (2000). The good, the bad, and the ambivalent: Managing identification among Amway distributors. *Administrative Science Quarterly, 45,* 456–493.

Quiñones, M. A., Ford, J. K., & Teachout, M. S. (1995). The relationship between work experience and job performance: A conceptual and meta-analytic review. *Personnel Psychology, 48,* 887–910.

Qureshi, I., & Fang, Y. (2011). Socialization in open source software projects: A growth mixture modeling approach. *Organizational Research Methods, 14,* 208–238.

Raghuram, S., Garud, R., Wiesenfeld, B., & Gupta, V. (2001). Factors contributing to virtual work adjustment. *Journal of Management, 27*, 383–405.

Raudenbush, S. W. (2001). Comparing personal trajectories and drawing causal inferences from longitudinal data. In S. T. Fiske, D. L. Schacter, & C. Zahn-Waxler (Eds.), *Annual review of psychology* (Vol. 52, pp. 501–525). Palo Alto, CA: Annual Reviews.

Reichers, A. E. (1987). An interactionist perspective on newcomer socialization rates. *Academy of Management Review, 12*, 278–287.

Rentsch, J. R. (1990). Climate and culture: Interaction and qualitative differences in organizational meanings. *Journal of Applied Psychology, 75*, 668–681.

Riordan, C. M., Weatherly, E. W., Vandenberg, R. J., & Self, R. M. (2001). The effects of pre-entry experiences and socialization tactics on newcomer attitudes and turnover. *Journal of Managerial Issues, 13*, 159–176.

Rizzo, J. R., House, R. J., & Lirtzman, S. I. (1970). Role conflict and ambiguity in complex organizations. *Administrative Science Quarterly, 15*, 150–163.

Rogers, J. K. (2000). *Temps: The many faces of the changing workplace.* Ithaca, NY: ILR Press.

Rollag, K. (2004). The impact of relative tenure on newcomer socialization dynamics. *Journal of Organizational Behavior, 25*, 853–872.

Rollag, K. (2007). Defining the term "new" in new employee research. *Journal of Occupational and Organizational Psychology, 80*, 63–75.

Saks, A. M. (1995). Longitudinal field investigation of the moderating and mediating effects of self-efficacy on the relationship between training and newcomer adjustment. *Journal of Applied Psychology, 80*, 211–225.

Saks, A. M., & Ashforth, B. E. (1997). Organizational socialization: Making sense of the past and present as a prologue for the future. *Journal of Vocational Behavior, 51*, 234–279.

Saks, A. M., Uggerslev, K. L., & Fassina, N. E. (2007). Socialization tactics and newcomer adjustment: A meta-analytic review and test of a model. *Journal of Vocational Behavior, 70*, 413–446.

Salas, S., & Von Glinow, M. A. (2008). Fostering organizational learning: Creating and maintaining a learning culture. In R. J. Burke & C. L. Cooper (Eds.), *Building more effective organizations: HR management and performance in practice* (pp. 207–227). Cambridge, UK: Cambridge University Press.

Schleef, D. J. (2006). *Managing elites: Professional socialization in law and business schools.* Lanham, MD: Rowman & Littlefield.

Schneider, B. (1983). Interactional psychology and organizational behavior. In L. L. Cummings & B. M. Staw (Eds.), *Research in organizational behavior* (Vol. 5, pp. 1–31). Greenwich, CT: JAI Press.

Scholarios, D., Lockyer, C., & Johnson, H. (2003). Anticipatory socialisation: The effect of recruitment and selection experiences on career expectations. *Career Development International, 8*, 182–197.

Scott, C., & Myers, K. K. (2005). The socialization of emotion: Learning emotion management at the fire station. *Journal of Applied Communication Research, 33*, 67–92.

Shipp, A. J., Edwards, J. R., & Lambert, L. S. (2009). Conceptualization and measurement of temporal focus: The subjective experience of the past, present, and future. *Organizational Behavior and Human Decision Processes, 110*, 1–22.

Shipp, A. J., & Jansen, K. J. (2011). Reinterpreting time in fit theory: Crafting and recrafting narratives of fit in medias res. *Academy of Management Review, 36*, 76–101.

Slaughter, J. E., & Zickar, M. J. (2006). A new look at the role of insiders in the newcomer socialization process. *Group & Organization Management, 31*, 264–290.

Sluss, D. M., van Dick, R., & Thompson, B. S. (2010). Role theory in organizations: A relational perspective. In S. Zedeck (Ed.), *APA handbook of industrial and organizational psychology Vol. 1: Building and helping the organization* (pp. 505–534). Washington, DC: American Psychological Association.

Snook, S. A. (2000). *Friendly fire: The accidental shootdown of U.S. Black Hawks over Northern Iraq.* Princeton, NJ: Princeton University Press.

Solomon, M. R., Surprenant, C., Czepiel, J. A., & Gutman, E. G. (1985). A role theory perspective on dyadic interactions: The service encounter. *Journal of Marketing, 49*(1), 99–111.

Song, Z., & Chathoth, P. K. (2010). An interactional approach to organizations' success in socializing their intern newcomers: The role of general self-efficacy and Organizational Socialization Inventory. *Journal of Hospitality & Tourism Research, 34*, 364–387.

Sonnentag, S., Niessen, C., & Ohly, S. (2004). Learning at work: Training and development. In C. L. Cooper & I. T. Robertson (Eds.), *International review of industrial and organizational psychology* (Vol. 19, pp. 249–289). Chichester, UK: Wiley.

Stohl, C. (1986). The role of memorable messages in the process of organizational socialization. *Communication Quarterly, 34*, 231–249.

Sullivan, S. E. (1999). The changing nature of careers: A review and research agenda. *Journal of Management, 25*, 457–484.

Takeuchi, N., & Takeuchi, T. (2009). A longitudinal investigation on the factors affecting newcomers' adjustment: Evidence from Japanese organizations. *International Journal of Human Resource Management, 20*, 928–952.

Taormina, R. J. (1997). Organizational socialization: A multidomain, continuous process model. *International Journal of Selection and Assessment, 5*, 29–47.

Taormina, R. J. (2004). Convergent validation of two measures of organizational socialization. *International Journal of Human Resource Management, 15*, 76–94.

Teboul, J. C. B. (1995). Determinants of new hire information-seeking during organizational encounter. *Western Journal of Communication, 59*, 305–325.

Tesluk, P. E., & Jacobs, R. R. (1998). Toward an integrated model of work experience. *Personnel Psychology, 51*, 321–355.

Thomas, H. D. C., & Anderson, N. (1998). Changes in newcomers' psychological contracts during organizational socialization: A study of recruits entering the British Army. *Journal of Organizational Behavior, 19*, 745–767.

Turner, V. W. (1969). *The ritual process: Structure and anti-structure.* Chicago: Aldine.

Vancouver, J. B., Tamanini, K. B., & Yoder, R. J. (2010). Using dynamic computational models to reconnect theory and research: Socialization by the proactive newcomer as example. *Journal of Management, 36*, 764–793.

Vandenberg, R. J., & Self, R. M. (1993). Assessing newcomers' changing commitments to the organization during the first 6 months of work. *Journal of Applied Psychology, 78*, 557–568.

VandeWalle, D., Ganesan, S., Challagalla, G. N., & Brown, S. P. (2000). An integrated model of feedback-seeking behavior: Disposition, context, and cognition. *Journal of Applied Psychology, 85,* 996–1003.

van Gennep, A. (1960). *The rites of passage* (M. B. Vizedom & G. L. Caffee, Trans.). Chicago: University of Chicago Press.

Van Maanen, J. (1977). Experiencing organization: Notes on the meaning of careers and socialization. In J. Van Maanen (Ed.), *Organizational careers: Some new perspectives* (pp. 15–45). London: Wiley.

Van Maanen, J., & Schein, E. H. (1979). Toward a theory of organizational socialization. In B. M. Staw (Ed.), *Research in organizational behavior* (Vol. 1, pp. 209–264). Greenwich, CT: JAI Press.

Waller, M. J., Conte, J. M., Gibson, C. B., & Carpenter, M. A. (2001). The effect of individual perceptions of deadlines on team performance. *Academy of Management Review, 26,* 586–600.

Wanberg, C. R., & Kammeyer-Mueller, J. D. (2000). Predictors and outcomes of proactivity in the socialization process. *Journal of Applied Psychology, 85,* 373–385.

Wanous, J. P. (1992). *Organizational entry: Recruitment, selection, orientation, and socialization of newcomers* (2nd ed.). Reading, MA: Addison-Wesley.

Weick, K. E. (1995). *Sensemaking in organizations.* Thousand Oaks, CA: Sage.

Wrzesniewski, A., & Dutton, J. E. (2001). Crafting a job: Revisioning employees as active crafters of their work. *Academy of Management Review, 26,* 179–201.

Yoder, J. D., & Aniakudo, P. (1996). When pranks become harassment: The case of African American women firefighters. *Sex Roles, 35,* 253–270.

Zaheer, S., Albert, S., & Zaheer, A. (1999). Time scales and organizational theory. *Academy of Management Review, 24,* 725–741.

Zerubavel, E. (1976). Timetables and scheduling: On the social organization of time. *Sociological Inquiry, 46,* 87–94.

This Is How We Do Research Around Here: Socializing Methodological and Measurement Issues

Jeffrey B. Vancouver *and* Michael A. Warren

Abstract

Socialization processes involve change in individuals (and organizations) over time. These changes are a function of forces from multiple levels of analysis, including the individual, fellow newcomers, established coworkers, supervisors, the organization, and the larger cultures in which individuals/organizations are nested. The research and measurement methods needed to examine these processes include both classic approaches (e.g., the field experiment) and cutting edge techniques (e.g., computational and longitudinal modeling). This chapter will review these techniques as they apply to socialization research questions that are being asked and need to be asked.

Key Words: socialization, research methods, longitudinal designs, validity, quasi-experimental designs, computational models

Science is about the accumulation and dissemination of knowledge. Dissemination happens through instruction (i.e., teaching) as well as publishing or presenting research. Accumulation happens via the acquisition of new knowledge, which occurs via research or the organization of research (e.g., theoretical development; meta-analyses). A great deal of inference is usually required to interpret research results, often conditioned on the qualities of the design used to collect the observations. Indeed, to facilitate that interpretation and, more importantly, to increase its likely validity (i.e., approximate truth of the interpretation) scientists are systematic about how observations are collected and analyzed. Moreover, from experience and logical analysis, philosophers and scientists have developed a great deal of knowledge regarding how to collect observations systematically, how those observations might be interpreted, and how interpretations can go wrong depending on how the data was collected (i.e., design) or analyzed (Shadish, Cook, & Campbell, 2002). It is the role of chapters on

research methods to disseminate that knowledge so that future research is more likely to generate useful knowledge (i.e., new knowledge that is correct). That is the purpose of this chapter.

Of course, our knowledge of how best to acquire knowledge is vast (by "our knowledge" we mean science's, not the present authors'). Thus, it behooves us (the present authors) to focus on the most relevant issues regarding how to obtain new knowledge in the domain of organizational socialization—the topic of this *Handbook*. To do that we first begin with an overview of the general epistemological issues (i.e., general issues regarding knowledge acquisition) and then use them to address specific issues of relevance to socialization researchers. Although we attempt to be comprehensive regarding relevant methods, we emphasize underutilized and cutting-edge methods because they are most likely to lead to *new* knowledge. In this way we are like an organization that wants to promote certain behaviors or attitudes that might depart from the behaviors and attitudes of its current employees. To do that, a formal intervention is needed because an informal approach will only likely propagate the status quo. This is not to say that current researchers are not to be emulated, but to acknowledge that fields of inquiry grow and the methods applied need to be growing as well.

The structure of our formal "training" program is as follows. We begin with a general description of types of systematic observation and types of validity. This is followed by an overview of threats to validity that can plague interpretations, as well as how one might choose design elements in order to optimize inferences. From there we delve into more specifics about the kinds of questions and methods one might use to further socialization as a field of inquiry. It is in this section that numerous methods and design elements are discussed in detail.

Systematic Observation Methods and the Threats to Valid Inferences

Methods for collecting information are generally classified as *quantitative* or *qualitative*. Quantitative methods invariably involve recording numerical information or translating observations into numerical information. A general advantage of quantitative methods is that they can take advantage of statistical operations, which facilitates the interpretation of large datasets and precise estimations of chance as an alternative explanation to an interpretation. A disadvantage of quantitative methods is that they are limited to the a priori observation-to-numerical assignment. In contrast, qualitative methods may involve direct or translated numerical information (and thus can be subject to statistical analysis), but place greater emphasis on the semantic meaning of symbolic information. A general advantage of qualitative methods is that they can uncover new constructs and processes not expected and allow for the application of humans' considerable pattern recognition prowess via the sematic information. This later advantage might also be considered a disadvantage because it allows for more opportunities for researcher bias to affect the interpretations as well as the degree to which the data collection is systematic in the first place. Indeed, researcher and other biases are very much a concern using either method, so let us turn to what these might be and how we try to minimize, or at least acknowledge, them.

Types of Validity

Validity "refers to the approximate truth of an inference" (Shadish et al., 2002). Since Cook and Campbell (1979), validity has been conceptualized into four somewhat overlapping categories: external, internal, construct, and statistical conclusion.

External validity refers to the degree to which one can generalize an interpretation across or to specific populations, settings, treatments (or procedures), and measurement variables (i.e., outcomes). In addition to this component of external validity, which is called the *structural* component, Vidmar (1979) suggested that external validity also refers to a *functional* component and a *conceptual* component. The functional component is the degree to which the psychological processes operating in a study are similar to the psychological processes one wishes to study. This can be an issue when the exigencies of natural context are difficult to reproduce in an artificial setting (e.g., power differentials among individuals; expected long-term future interactions). The conceptual component is the degree to which the problem studied is important in natural settings (see Campbell, Daft, & Hulin, 1982). Indeed, it seems that applied psychologists, particularly when studying socialization processes, are often most interested in external validity because of these latter two components. That is, the research questions being asked should be interesting (i.e., will provide useful and novel or confirmational information), and the research should involve employees in organizations because the complexities and implications of being in an organization likely matters.

Internal validity refers to the degree to which a cause–effect inference can be made. For many psychologists internal validity is the most important of the validities because science is largely about understanding causal processes (Antonakis, Bendahan, Jacquart, & Lalive, 2010). Indeed, socialization refers to a process of change to individuals (Bauer & Erdogan, 2011), and so researchers of socialization are likely to be concerned about the causes of that change. Unfortunately, the elements of design that most allow for strong internal validity (i.e., experimental control) are the most difficult to implement in settings that maximize external validity (Runkel & McGrath, 1972). This problem makes the design of research not a maximization problem, but an optimization problem (McGrath, Martin, & Kulka, 1982). As we will see later, however, we can use our research question and a thorough understanding of the threats that might invalidate our interpretations to help optimize a study and, perhaps more importantly, a program of research. Moreover, this general concern for optimizing, particularly across external and internal validity, has been the object of epistemological work for over 50 years (e.g., from Campbell, 1957, to Antonakis et al., 2010).

Another, arguably most important, type of validity is construct. **Construct validity** refers to the inferences about the higher-order, latent concepts that any particular measure or treatment (or set of measures or treatments) is purported to represent. Construct validity is critical because without it, internal validity is eviscerated and external validity is non-assessable. That is, if we are not manipulating the cause we think we are with our treatment or procedures, and we are not measuring the effect we think we are measuring, our cause–effect inferences are likely incorrect—at least at the construct level. Likewise, populations and settings can only be identified to the extent their properties are being measured. Invalid measurement (i.e., poor construct validity) makes inferences about generalizability to and across populations, settings, treatments, and outcomes likely incorrect. Fortunately, construct validity is less an issue to the extent that the treatments and variables measured are not latent (i.e., manifest) or are not higher-order (e.g., job performance is the amount of sales, period). On the other hand, few variables of interest to researchers in socialization are manifest, and lower-order constructs are likely to be less general and useful.

Finally, there is statistical conclusion validity. **Statistical conclusion validity** refers to the inferences regarding our estimates of effect sizes. Specifically, effect size estimates should be unbiased, reliable, and stable. A brief review of methods journals would lead one to conclude that statistical conclusion validity is the most important validity concern by far, because nearly all the articles in these journals are devoted to the topic (Aguinis, Pierce, Bosco, & Muslin, 2009). Moreover, graduate programs are likely to offer many more courses in statistics than in research methods. However, these metrics are probably not a very good gauge of importance (i.e., they have poor construct validity). It is just that much progress has been (reflected in number of courses) and can be (reflected in number of articles) made in statistical analysis. Indeed, the volume of material precludes our covering the topic in any depth here. Rather, we will provide references to sources of this information given certain types of questions and designs (e.g., consult Singer & Willett, 2003a, or Klein & Kozlowski, 2000, when designing and analyzing multilevel designs).

Threats to the Validities

As mentioned, several very smart people have been thinking about what might make inferences about observations and study findings go awry. These pitfalls are referred to as *threats to validity* (Cook & Campbell, 1979). Lengthy treatises are available on these threats generally (Shadish et al., 2002), which we do not repeat. However, we do want to hit the main issues. Later we spend more time on specific threats as they relate to specific research issues regarding socialization.

In terms of the structural component of external validity, the primary threat is that what is observed, or inferred, is only locally valid (e.g., would not be observed if collected from different populations, in different settings or times, or using different construct operationalizations). Although this might seem extremely problematic given that the purpose of research is to produce generalizable knowledge (not local knowledge), this threat should probably be our least concern. Empirical evidence reveals that most findings generalize across populations, settings, and time (Anderson, Lindsay, & Bushman, 1999; Locke, 1986). That said, the primary method for mitigating this threat is often misunderstood. That is, the typical advice is to sample across the population, settings, or whatever one wants to generalize across. Although this is good advice, it must be followed up with the appropriate statistical analysis. Assuming that one is concerned about the generalizability of a relationship between two constructs, the appropriate analysis is to determine if the relationship observed *depends* on markers of these populations, settings, and so forth. That is, one must test for interactions (e.g., moderated multiple regression). If the interaction is not significant, only then is collapsing across the settings/populations/ etc. appropriate. If one is concerned about generalizing descriptions, then testing for main effects is sufficient (i.e., do levels of adjustment differ across settings).

Internal validity is likely a very different matter. Here, the primary issue is that covariation (i.e., a relationship), which is a necessary condition for making causal inferences, can result from a number of alternative explanations beyond the one that the researcher wants to advocate. These alternative explanations can include, among others, chance, third variables that are the true cause but are unmeasured or unwittingly confounded with the presumed cause, nonlinearities in the relationships, and reverse causality (James, Muliak, & Brett, 1982). Statistical analysis can usually provide an estimate of the probability that chance can account for a finding. However, to address many of the other concerns, experimental designs (i.e., where a variable is manipulated and a measure of the presumed effect is taken afterward) are advocated when one is trying to make causal inferences, particularly when random assignment to levels of the independent variable (i.e., the presumed cause) is used (Stone-Romero, 2011). Indeed, random assignment helps dramatically reduce the chance that some unmeasured third variable is the true cause of variation in the dependent variable. However, experimental manipulations can still confound constructs (i.e., manipulate more than just the intended construct), making causal inferences from experiments potentially internally invalid (i.e., lacking internal validity).Specifically, Shadish et al. (2002) list 12 threats to validity that could lead to spurious conclusions of a causal effect when interpreting experimental results. Interestingly, most of these are listed in the construct validity section because they are related to confounds with the treatment construct. To be fair, there are about an equal number of threats using experiments (as well as other designs) that lead to a spurious conclusion of no causal effect when in fact there is one (i.e., a Type-II error). Most of these are listed as threats to statistical conclusion validity. All that said, we do not want to discourage the use of experiments for making causal inferences. Their flaws are generally much less problematic than the flaws threatening the internal validity of non-experimental designs. Nonetheless, experiments—particularly experiments with random assignment to conditions—can be difficult to do in field settings or with certain variables (e.g., intelligence), making clean interpretations difficult. We spend considerable space below on this issue.

As just intimated, there are several threats to construct validity. Shadish et al. (2002) list 14 of them. Most of these threats involve either contamination or deficiency. *Contamination* is the problem that the operationalization includes more than the construct of interest (i.e., the measure or operationalization is contaminated). Notice that this is also a source of internal invalidity. *Deficiency* occurs when the operationalization does not measure part of the construct. Moreover, these issues can be asymmetrically distributed across the levels of a construct. For example, a specific threat is *treatment diffusion*. An example of treatment diffusion is when individuals at one level of the independent variable (e.g., members of the control group) receive part of the treatment although they should not have, thus contaminating the control group with the treatment. Treatment diffusion can happen in organizational settings when coworkers communicate about what

they are learning in a training program to colleagues not in the training program. It can be a reason to use preexisting groups, rather than random assignment, to assign individuals to conditions of a field experiment.

Statistical conclusion validity is largely threatened by things that lower the signal-to-noise ratio, making it difficult to detect an effect, or by inappropriate analysis (e.g., violations of assumptions; incorrect level of analysis). For example, low reliability can undermine or bias effects. One of the principle reasons for the popularity of structural equation modeling (SEM) techniques is its ability to provide unbiased estimates because it can take reliability—actually just an estimate of reliability—into account. As a side effect, it motivates better measurement because multiple measures, often using multiple modalities of operation, are needed to use SEM effectively. Thus, SEM not only helps deal with statistical conclusion validity, but also it can motivate better construct validity through design elements. On the other hand, it has little value in increasing internal validity, despite a widespread belief that increasing internal validity is its purpose—a point many authors have made (e.g., Stone-Romero, 2011; Atonakis et al., 2010). Moreover, SEM requires a large number of observations to get stable estimates. Yet, many studies are underpowered, which is another major threat to statistical conclusion validity, warranting the use of power analysis to determine adequate sample sizes for the intended analyses.

Designing to Optimize Validity and Stages of Research

Obviously, the large number of threats to valid interpretations makes designing the optimal study difficult. Fortunately, there are several strategies for addressing the problem. The primary method is triangulation. That is, since no study is perfect we might interpret a constellation of studies, preferably of different designs, to compensate for the flaws endemic to a particular research strategy. This is the primary reason for reviewing the literature, a job that every researcher needs to engage in when designing a study. It sets the stage for the planned study by determining where the validities of interpretations of past work are weak, as well as where knowledge is missing. The literature review should not be an exercise of bashing past research (especially since some might be your own, or ours) but of merely identifying the weakness in the literature as a whole at the given time. Moreover, it can provide information not only about possible findings, but also about possible alternative explanations for findings.

As a result of the literature review, one can identify the research question to be addressed in a given study. The research question then becomes the primary guide for determining the study design (McGrath, Martin & Kukla, 1982). For example, research early in a domain is likely to begin by tackling description. Description involves determining the units, their properties, and the processes that might be responsible for some phenomenon. When beginning research within a domain, descriptive research often involves qualitative methods. Subsequent description research often involves scale development (e.g., exploratory and confirmatory factor analysis). More mature descriptive research involves surveys and other observational methods to catalog variance and covariance among the constructs identified and measured. Circling back to qualitative and scale development is often wise to avoid pluralistic ignorance (e.g., overreliance on one measure or list of constructs can leave alternative but relevant constructs hidden). In general, descriptive research must prioritize external validity, ignore internal validity, and focus on assessing construct validity with the appropriate statistical or qualitative methodology.

After description, the next stage of research typically focuses on *process understanding*. Process understanding involves theorizing about the causal processes, so internal validity becomes a much more central concern. Likewise, construct and statistical conclusion validity remain important. Structural external validity can take a back seat; however, depending on the phenomena under investigation, functional external validity is still an issue. This is arguably the case with socialization, where it is difficult to represent the socialization process in an artificial setting (though exceptions are described below). In terms of methodologies, qualitative research remains a viable approach for understanding, particularly for formulating theory (Strauss & Corbin, 1994). Because of the importance of internal validity, experiments become important—but again, they are very difficult to implement if functional external validity concerns dominate. Indeed, for this reason longitudinal methods are often used as a means to address the shortcomings of non-experimental methods. Longitudinal methods, if done well, can reduce threats to internal validity, but they are also onerous and are often not done well (more on that later). Finally, a hybrid combination

of longitudinal and qualitative research is what we call the *case-intensive* research design. In case-intensive research relatively few participants are used, but there are multiple observations per person over time and variables.

In the final stages of research on a domain, the central issue is control or change. That is, we are interested in developing and assessing treatments to achieve desired ends. The process understandings are critical for developing treatments, though simply rigorously testing colloquial treatments could be productive. Given the causal question, internal validity once again needs to take priority. Given that this is the final stage of research, external validity is also highly relevant; one must know if the treatment works (i.e., causes the desired effect) in the settings in which it will be implemented and on the distal outcomes one cares about. Indeed, within this last stage are three substages that all require internal and external validity, but vary perhaps on construct validity. The first substage is *efficacy research* (Shadish et al., 2002). In efficacy research, treatments are carefully standardized and controlled (i.e., the treatment is the researcher's baby and he/she is going to make sure it is done right), though they are likely to be multifaceted (i.e., include the kitchen sink). The question of efficacy research is, can the treatment be efficacious in the context that one wants to use it? The next substage is *effectiveness research*. Here, construct validity may well suffer because the reality of scaling up a treatment for general use is that treatments lose some integrity (e.g., the treatment is implemented by individuals not involved in its development; it is not their baby). The question for effectiveness studies is whether the treatments will still work in this messier context. The final substage is *efficiency research*. Here, the question is whether some of the facets are active ingredients or unnecessary fluff. Here it is determined if the kitchen sink and bathwater can be jettisoned from the intervention, leaving only the baby.

Because of the priority of causal inferences, the experiment is required for this last stage. That said, the degree of experimenter control—from the nature of condition assignment (e.g., random or not) to the involvement in the treatment—can vary greatly. For example, researchers might take advantage of "natural" experiments, where external sources are providing the manipulation of the levels of the treatment and the researchers' role is merely to observe the results. This is actually good, because in the end it is the organizations, not researchers, who will implement the interventions.

Connecting Methods to Research on Socialization

In this section we discuss the specific kinds of questions researchers might ask regarding organizational socialization and the critical methodological issues given those questions. We organize the section by the stages of research (e.g., description, understanding, and intervention evaluation). Recall, the issue of what are the right questions to ask is called *conceptual external validity*. Above we referred to these kinds of questions at a relatively high (i.e., generic) level. Here we focus more closely on questions of relevance to socialization, though we still only use exemplars and prototypical examples to illustrate the methodological issues that seem most relevant at the current time. For more specific research questions we direct researchers to the other chapters in this *Handbook*.

Let us begin by classifying socialization as a domain within the larger domain of training and development (Ostroff & Kozlowski, 1992). That is, socialization is primarily about the changing knowledges and skills of an individual. Because of this, we can also use the training literature to help us focus our treatise on methods relevant to socialization. Moreover, we can apply the lessons learned from training to socialization research. For example, we discuss how the training literature critiques reaction data, which seems a primary source of information about organizational socialization.

Description

As mentioned above, the first issue for any domain is to describe the phenomena within that domain. This often involves developing taxonomies and measures of constructs. In the case of socialization, the central question is one of adjustment to the organization, group, or role one is entering. Initially, time in the organization (i.e., tenure) was used as a proxy for adjustment (e.g., Gomez-Mejia, 1983). Since then, various lists or taxonomies of the facets of adjustment have been created (e.g., Bauer & Erdongan, 2011; Chao, O'Leary-Kelly, Wolf, Klein, & Gardner, 1994). Typically, these adjustment constructs focus on changes to the individual. For example, most taxonomies include acquiring knowledge of one's role (i.e., role clarity) and how to perform one's job and tasks, as well as knowledge about the organization more generally (e.g., its politics). Some also include changes to the organization or its members (e.g., acceptance of new members by current members).

Although the field has generated these taxonomies, as well as measures to go with them (e.g., Chao et al,

1994; Haueter, Macan, & Winter, 2003; Taormina, 1994), deficiency in terms of the domain as well as the specific constructs is always a concern. In particular, adjustments (or the lack thereof) that can affect newcomers' (a) productivity, broadly defined (Motowidlo, 2003), (b) participation (Hulin, 1991), and (c) quality of life should probably be included within the domain. To the extent that adjustable constructs relevant to these outcomes are not included in current taxonomies, the domain construct is deficient. Qualitative research is most likely the method that might uncover such deficiencies (Lee, Mitchell, & Harman, 2011).

After conceptualizing elements of the adjustment domain, researchers generally develop measures of those elements (e.g., Chao et al., 1994, developed a measure to assess an employee's perception of his/her knowledge of an organization's goals and values, history, language [slang; acronyms], and internal politics, as well as the employee's perception of his or her understanding of the job and connection with coworkers). Usually the measures are self-report questionnaires with multiple items per element. This allows the researcher to apply factor analytic and IRT analyses to the instruments (Reise, Widaman, & Pugh, 1993). In addition, the measures are typically assessed for their relationship to outcomes of relevance to organizations and individuals (see Bauer et al., 2007, for a meta-analysis that includes the assessment of these relationships). As mentioned above, this is done to confirm that the adjustment dimension, and the measure[s] of it, is important (i.e., belongs in the domain). To use the vernacular from the training literature (Kirkpatrick, 1994), this is presumably an assessment of the relationship between *learning criteria* (of a training intervention) and individual-level behavior or *results criteria*.

There are two limitations with the interpretations arising from the above set of methods. First, the self-report methodology likely leads to construct deficiency and contamination. Specifically, we know from the training and other literatures on self-assessment (Dunning, Heath, & Suls, 2004) that these types of self-reports are notoriously inaccurate, usually in the positive direction (i.e., people think they are better than they are). For example, self-report measures of the results of training are operationally similar to the utility component of training reaction data. Unfortunately, a meta-analysis of training criteria (i.e., reactions, learning, and transfer or performance measures) by Alliger, Tennenbaum, Bennett, Traver, and Shotland (1997) found that the utility portion of reaction data only correlated .26 with immediate learning and only .18 with transfer measures. These results imply that these types of self-report measures may be deficient, resulting in downwardly biased effect size estimates when using the measures. That said, Alliger et al. did not find that immediate learning measures to do much better at predicting transfer or on-the-job performance measures.

The second limitation relates to the practice of interpreting correlations between adjustment measures and outcomes as an indication that the adjustment construct/measure is relevant (i.e., belongs in the domain of socialization adjustment). One concern is that common-method bias (Antonakis et al., 2010) associated with using a single source and mode of measurement can inflate correlations between the measures. For example, using both self-report measures of adjustment and self-report measures of outcomes (e.g., performance) are now highly frowned upon. A less recognized issue is that outcomes might affect adjustment measures, especially because they are *perceptions* of adjustment rather than direct measures of adjustment (or learning). Thus, it is easy to imagine people would think they have high role clarity if they were receiving high performance ratings. Yet, performance ratings are often high for reasons other than performance, much less a clear understanding of the job (Murphy & Cleveland, 1995). Thus, this "reversal causality" process could inflate effect size estimates.

Together these limitations raise a potential contamination issue for the adjustment domain. Specifically, the concept of self-efficacy (i.e., the belief in one's capacity to perform specific behaviors or achieve specific ends) is often listed as an adjustment construct (e.g., Bauer & Erdogan, 2011). However, scores from self-efficacy measures likely reflect true levels of capacity (i.e., knowledge, skill, and ability), which might be the reason self-efficacy scores relate to organizationally relevant outcomes. Indeed, Bauer and Erdogan note that "task mastery" is highly related to self-efficacy. Thus, it is unclear if it is actual capacity (i.e., task mastery) and not merely the belief in capacity (i.e., self-efficacy) that is the key adjustment concept. The difference is potentially important in terms of interventions (e.g., training vs. pep talks). Of course, it could be a little bit of both—that is, it may be that both capacity and the difference between capacity and belief in capacity (i.e., overconfidence or underconfidence) is important. This will likely be difficult to determine unless alternatives to self-report measures are used.

Beyond our concerns regarding self-report measures, socialization researchers need to be constantly on guard for measurement deficiency and contamination issues. Whether self-reported or not, important elements of socialization processes or outcomes might be missed if not measured. For example, current measures do not appear to capture relationships between outside stakeholders (e.g., regular suppliers) and job holders. Moreover, assessments of long-term organizational outcomes are largely missing (though understandably difficult to do). Likewise, we do not want to encourage the use of contaminated "objective" measures (e.g., performance indexes affected by contextual variables) due to too much concern for deficient or contaminated self-report measures. Finding the correct mix of measures is likely to be a learning process.

In sum, socialization research has improved in its measurement and description of the constructs in its domain. Moving from using tenure as a proxy for adjustment to specific elements and measures of adjustment was a big step. Nonetheless, the self-report measures of adjustment are essentially reaction-level data (Kirkpatrick, 1994). Although reasonable for certain elements of adjustment, it is likely that less editable measures of learning would increase the construct validity of adjustment measures.

Understanding and Explanation

The bulk of research in a domain focuses on understanding the processes involved and what influences those processes (i.e., antecedents and moderators) so that interventions can be created that optimize outcomes for individuals and organizations. This stage of research will, and we argue should, also include examination of consequences associated with the processes even though those are generally researched when seeking to describe the domain (i.e., descriptive research) and test the interventions (i.e., treatment research). The process of central interest during socialization is essentially learning (Ostroff & Kozlowski, 1992), though other subprocesses are also relevant (e.g., information seeking; Ashford & Cummings, 1983). Therefore, learning curves, like the ones depicted in Figure 10.1, conceptually describe the trajectory of adjustment. The first curve assumes learning starts off quickly and slows to an asymptote over time; the second assumes learning begins slowly, picks up speed, and then slows to an asymptote. In either case, three issues might be of interest to researchers and ultimately to organizations or individuals. First,

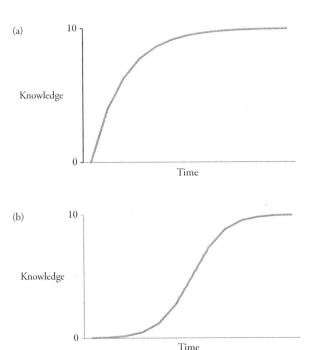

(a)

Knowledge

Time

(b)

Knowledge

Time

Figure 10.1 Learning Curves.

what influences the starting point on the Y axis (i.e., initial level of knowledge)? Second, what influences the rate of change (i.e., rate of adjustment)? Third, what influences the level of the final asymptote (i.e., final level of knowledge)? If one is using the more complex model, one might also ask what influences when the rate begins to increase? These questions all reflect possible points of intervention that might improve socialization, which one might assess in the last stage of research.

As Cronbach (1957) pointed out, psychologists tended to take two approaches to examining influences on variables of interest: the *individual differences* approach and the *situation* (i.e., experimental) approach. In the former case, one might consider the properties of the individual that determine initial level, rate of change, and final level. Armed with that knowledge, organizations might select individuals with the properties that improved the variables, provided there were not negative side effects (e.g., high costs). This approach has not received a lot of attention within the socialization domain, possibly because it is not consistent with the domain (though Cronbach might have argued that it is because few from the individual differences camp study socialization).

The second approach is to identify the properties of the situation (e.g., the organization) that affect the three (or four) elements of adjustment. Labeled *socialization tactics* (Van Maanen and Schein, 1979), this had been the primary approach to studying socialization. Indeed, Van Maanen and Schein had cleverly described many downstream consequences (e.g., organizational creativity) of various tactics given the nature of those tactics. Even organizational tactics that might influence initial level, which seems a difficult parameter for organizations to influence (except on average through selection mechanisms), have been considered and examined (Carr, Pearson, Vest, Boyar, 2006).

Despite the merit and success of the situation approach, a more sophisticated approach to considering psychological phenomena has emerged over the last half century—thanks in large part to Cronbach's observations and urgings—that combines the two approaches. Specifically, the *interactionist* approach is concerned with the interaction among person and situational properties in determining the workings of processes (Jones, 1983). Moreover, and especially because of the inherently dynamic nature of learning phenomena like socialization (as well as motivation), the domain now tends to emphasize the interaction of person, situation, and adjustment over time. The clearest example of this can be found in Reichers' (1987) description of the proactive newcomer who takes charge of his or her own socialization and learning. Indeed, the bulk of current research in socialization focuses on the properties of the individual that most likely lead to proactive socialization processes and the moderating effects of situation properties or interventions. For example, one might ask if certain sources of information work best for certain types of people for certain types of adjustments in certain types of jobs.

The "problem" with the more sophisticated approach to studying phenomena like socialization is that it often requires equally sophisticated research designs and analytic techniques. Fortunately these exist, but unfortunately they are rarely used. We begin this section with a review of what is typically used (i.e., the cross-sectional, passive observational design)[1] and work our way up to more sophisticated designs (i.e., longitudinal; experimental) and methods (qualitative; research simulations; computational models).

PASSIVE OBSERVATIONAL METHODS

Passive observation, often inappropriately called *correlational research* (cf., Stone-Romero, 2011), involves systematically collecting information on variables either at one time (i.e., cross-sectional), or over time (i.e., longitudinal designs). We discuss longitudinal designs in the next section. Here we tackle cross-sectional designs, though we do not have much positive to say about them. They are generally less onerous than the approaches discussed later, and this makes them useful during the descriptive stage, but they are generally so weak on internal validity that they are of little use during the more mature understanding stage of scientific inquiry. Moreover, as Figure 10.1 implies, learning is a process that occurs over time. When one only has information about how things shook out in the end, or on what covariances were among variables at any point in time, one has little information about the processes involved. There are three exceptions we can think of that might make such designs useful during this middle stage of a research domain.

First, passive observational methods might allow for some degree of internal validity if the alternative explanations are well specified and can be modeled (James et al., 1982). This seems unlikely in the case of socialization research because the complexities of learning within the buzzing cacophony of organizational settings are what make the topic interesting. We know a great deal about learning (Weiss, 1990); what we know less about is learning in real life (Snow & Swanson, 1992). Therefore, it is unlikely that researchers have a good enough handle on the alternative explanations that causal interpretations

would be reasonable. Of course, some constructs cannot be manipulated experimentally (e.g., cognitive ability) or done so ethically (e.g., exposure to a toxin), in which case the only choice is passive observational operationalizations. However, this is unlikely to be a valid excuse for socialization researchers. The overarching question is how one might improve socialization within an organization. Even if the primary driver of socialization were some stable individual difference variable (e.g., intelligence or propensity to seek information), one could design a study to determine if an organization (or department) that uses a selection system based on these individual difference variables has better socialization than organizations (or departments) that do not.

The second potential usefulness of passive observational designs stems from the fact that the levels of the variables observed are often continuously distributed. This is in contrast to experimentally manipulated variables, where usually only two levels are operationalized (e.g., the experimental and control groups). With continuously distributed variables the researcher can look for nonlinear relationships. If found, further research might involve manipulating more than two levels of the supposed cause to confirm a causal role. For example, Vancouver, More, and Yoder (2008) found that self-efficacy, manipulated across six levels, both positively and negatively affected resources allocated toward a task. They pointed out that had a two-level manipulation been used, they would have found a positive, negative, or null effect depending on where the two levels fell on the distribution of possible values. Cross-sectional research might have been cited to justify such a sophisticated design. Thus, if one suspects nonlinear effects (e.g., too much of a good thing), a cross-sectional design, where a broad range of observations are made of the suspected cause, might be a reasonable first step.

The final potential use of cross-sectional, passive observational designs is for determining the sources of variance. Where variance exists, one might look for causal agents; where variance does not exist, one can generalize or collapse one's analysis. For example, one might imagine collecting multiple adjustment measures across persons, work units, departments, and organizations. An important question is whether scores differ across measures, persons, units, departments, organizations, and the interactions among these units of analysis. For instance, one might find that mean levels of adjustment vary significantly across work units nested within departments and organizations. This implies that something is going on at the unit level that is influencing adjustment that might merit further investigation. Alternatively, if no variance is found across work units (or in interaction terms), this implies that one can collapse and generalize across work units, and that work unit level variables are likely not involved in influencing adjustment. A caveat regarding this latter interpretation is that it is based on the assumption that potential causal variables are naturally varying within the context. For example, one might miss the effects of artificial drugs, derived from theoretical understandings as opposed to reproducing a naturally occurring ingredient, because those effects could not be observable until the drugs were introduced. What we are talking about is called *variance components analysis*, a cousin of generalizability theory (Cronbach, Gleser, Nanda, & Rajaratnam, 1972). It is likely most useful when a domain is in the middle of its life cycle, when data across lots of studies can be incorporated in the analysis (e.g., Putka, 2002).

One common practice in organization research with passive observation designs is to use multiple regression or structural equation modeling (SEM) to "control for" alternative explanations. Although these techniques can help address specific alternative explanations, there are several limitations associated with them (James et al., 1982). We mention the big three: misspecification, simultaneity (or reverse causality), and construct validity of the dependent variable. Misspecification is the problem that a model does not include all possible third variables that are the true causes of an effect. This should not be a problem in the short run if one has done one's literature review well and has good measures of the possible third variables. That is, some reasonable alternative explanation is not ruled out because a key construct representing the explanation was not included in the model or measured well. If researchers know a priori what alternative explanations are possible, then they should strive to measure them well and include them in their model. Of course, reasonable alternative explanations may appear sometime after a study, so one cannot make causal inferences without caution. But, as we will argue later, that is true with experimental research as well.

For us, simultaneity and reverse causality issues are much more problematic. Simultaneity is similar to reverse causality, except that it is the idea that the causality goes both ways. That is, reverse causality is the notion that the association between X and Y is really because Y causes X. Simultaneity is the idea that X causes Y *and* Y causes X. Statistical modeling methods cannot overcome simultaneity or reversal causality given cross-section and even two-wave panel design (i.e., longitudinal designs). Only the unreasonableness of such effects as an alternative explanation can allow for the possibility of an unbiased causal interpretation. However, simultaneity is likely rampant in socialization. For instance, Vancouver, Tamanini, and Yoder (2010) argued that role clarity affects information seeking which affects role clarity. This has design and analytic implications that cross-sectional designs cannot address.

Finally, Miller and Chapman (2001) argue that a fundamental problem with statistical control methods as a way to make up for non-equivalent groups, whether in an experiment or a passive observational design, is that if the control variables covary with the dependent variable, they eviscerate the meaning of the construct after the controls have been applied. For example, Bandura and Wood (1989) argued that controlling for past performance removes causes on future performance that might have been causes of past performance as well. This will lead to a Type II error (i.e., mistakenly rejecting the hypothesis) when one of these causes is the hypothesized cause of interest.

Before leaving our discussion of cross-sectional designs as they relate to understanding process, we would be remiss if we did not address mediational analysis. Mediation refers to a mechanism responsible for the relationship between an exogenous (X) and endogenous (Y) variable. The concept is inherently causal. That is, the mechanism is considered an explanation of the reason X causes Y. Baron and Kenny (1986) popularized a statistical procedure for assessing mediation using passive observational measures of the mediator (M) and, possibly X. Note that Y is always passively observed. This procedure has become very popular in applied settings because of the frequency with which passive observational methods are used. Recently, a number of authors have questioned the merit of the Baron and Kenny approach (e.g., James Mulaik, & Brett, 2006; Stone-Romero & Rosopa, 2004). We largely concur with the sentiments expressed by these critics. The fundamental problem is that, in principle, many configurations of the three variables can produce effects that are consistent with a mediational interpretation. That is, the potential for alternative explanations abounds. Moreover, failing to pass the various steps needed to support a mediational interpretation does not necessarily mean mediation as hypothesized is *not* occurring. The bottom line is that if mediation is the central question of a study, which it will often be during the understanding stage of research, it is very unlikely a Baron and Kenny type design will be useful. Instead, Spencer, Zanna, and Fong (2005) suggest two alternative designs. The most obvious is called the *causal chain* design, where three experiments are conducted to confirm that X causes Y, X causes M, and M causes Y. Of course this approach is onerous and often not possible, which is what motivated Baron and Kenny's paper.

The second approach, which did not receive a lot of attention even in the Spencer et al. (2005) paper, involves a moderator variable. The moderator is supposed to affect the hypothesized mediating mechanism, thus implicating the mechanism in the process. Spencer et al. argued for manipulating the moderator, but this approach might be used in passive observation studies as well. Consider the following example about the relationship between performance and job satisfaction. Although most thought job satisfaction causes performance, some thought that performance caused job satisfaction through rewards for performance (i.e., a reverse causality process mediated by rewards). To test this idea, Charrington, Reitz, and Scott (1971) measured whether organizations had a merit-based pay system or not and found that the relationship between job satisfaction and performance was only significant in organizations with merit-based reward systems. This finding supported the reverse causality hypothesis as well as its explanation (i.e., via rewards). Of course, the key to this procedure working is (a) a moderator variable that can be measured or manipulated, and (b) little in the way of alternative explanations for positive findings.

In sum, we wish to echo the sentiments of others (Antonakis et al., 2010; James et al., 1982; Stone-Romero, 2011) that passive observational techniques, particularly when used in cross-sectional designs, are of little value when attempting to test causal understandings. Fortunately, methodologists (e.g., Shadish et al., 2002) have described design elements that can help the researcher who feels the need to conduct studies without using random assignment to varying levels of a causal construct. We begin describing these methods by looking at longitudinal designs.

LONGITUDINAL DESIGNS

Longitudinal designs can be both experimental and purely passive observational. In this section we discuss passive observational designs. Longitudinal designs are often considered the cure to what ails cross-sectional designs (i.e., the inability to make causal inferences) because it presumably guarantees time precedence (i.e., the cause occurs before the effect), which is one of the criteria of causation (Shadish et al., 2002). It turns out, however, that much depends on how the study is designed. Most often researchers measure the hypothetical cause(s) at Time 1 and then measure the hypothetical effect(s) at Time 2. There are two good reasons for this design. First, it can reduce common method bias when a single source is used to collect the data (i.e., collecting a self-report measure of self-efficacy at Time 1 and then a self-report measure of performance at Time 2). One can imagine that respondents will match up their self-reported ratings if asked at the same time, but will be less able to do this if measured at different times. Of course, the time lag likely does not eliminate the bias (e.g., respondents may remember more or less what they thought of their capacity when asked way back when). The second advantage is that it might take time for variance to occur on the dependent variable. For example, if one is trying to predict turnover, one needs to let time pass in order for enough individuals in the sample to quit such that covariances can be reasonably assessed.

Unfortunately, measuring one set of variables at Time 1 (i.e., the predictors) and other set at Time 2 (i.e., the criteria) does not often increase internal validity. For example, if one is wondering if self-efficacy at Time 1 causes performance at Time 2, this design is insufficient. It cannot eliminate the possibility that ability or other causes of performance influenced self-efficacy and performance (Vancouver, Thompson, & Williams, 2001). Likewise, when studying the effect of organizational commitment (measured at Time 1) on turnover (measured at Time 2), the researcher cannot eliminate the possibility that those respondents who quit might be denigrating the organization after they decided to leave for a higher-paying job or some other reason that occurs prior to the Time 1 measure. A far better design is to measure all the variables, but at least the hypothetical effect variables, across three waves of data (Ployhart & Vandenberg, 2010). Even better is to have several waves of data collection, not just three. Indeed, to support those efforts, methodologists have described how one might collect just that sort of data from individuals (Beal & Weiss, 2003; Bolger, Davis, & Rafaeli, 2003).

Armed with multiple waves of data one can employ the analytic power of latent growth models (Chan,

2002; Bliese & Ployhart, 2002) and related methods (Schonfeld & Rindskopf, 2007). Conceptually, the critical issue is that one can assess change, not simply covariance across units. To understand the importance of change, consider the evaluation of mentors given quarterly (biannual or annual) performance reviews of their mentees. Suppose one hypothesized that work experience might predict mentoring quality and thus mentee performance. After collecting the data, the researcher finds that experience negatively predicts mentee performance. Before interpreting this as an effect of burnout, diminishing fluid intelligence, or some other cause associated with tenure or age, one might realize that more experienced mentors are given the more problematic mentees—ones that would have performed relatively poorly at the beginning of the mentorship had such a measure been taken. The question is to what degree the mentor can *improve performance*. Only by having a Time 1 as well as a Time 2 measure of mentee performance could such an analysis be done. Of course, several mentors and their mentees need to be in the study in order to assess *relative* change as a function of mentor, department, or organization-level properties. Otherwise, one might just be picking up maturation effects (i.e., natural changes in a variable that are unrelated to the treatment). Finally, with only two measures of mentee performance, one cannot eliminate the possibility of selection-by-maturation effects (i.e., smarter mentees are easier to teach than challenged mentees, thus giving an unfair advantage to the mentors with mentees who were initially performing better).

As the previous example also highlights, measuring change in the presumed effect is not enough to make strong causal inferences about the cause. Experience is confounded with all sorts of variables. For time-varying hypothetical causes—and what is the point if the variable cannot change over time—then using multiple measures allows one to assess change in these variables as well (Schonfeld & Rindskopf, 2007). With only two waves of data, one cannot determine the order of that change (and hence, this is analogous to a cross-sectional study because *change* is a *single* observation made from two observations spread over time). Instead, at least three waves are needed so that change in the hypothetical cause can be assessed between Time 1 and 2 and compared to change in the hypothetical effect between Time 2 and Time 3. This design eliminates reverse causality as an alternative explanation. Unfortunately, a third variable could be causing both changes, so one still needs to be cautious when interpreting these designs. Moreover, a lack of an effect might not be because there is not a causal connection, but because the lags (time it takes causes to have a measureable influence on the effect) is inconsistent with the timing of the waves (e.g., imagine the value of X ebbing and flowing several times within the lag between Time 1 and 2; it would be hard to expect to see any systematic effect on changes in Y between Time 2 and 3). This lag effect is a huge issue in any dynamic phenomenon like socialization (see Ashforth, Chapter 9 of this volume).

If three waves are better than two, is it true that more than three is even better? Yes, particularly if one is interested in examining simultaneity hypotheses (i.e., non-recursive models). Any theory that includes a feedback loop, which is most theories in applied psychology and management including theories in socialization, is a theory of simultaneity. Designs with several waves of data, where all the variables are collected across all the waves, allow one to assess both directions of causality (Schonfeld & Rindskopf, 2007). For example, Jokisaari and Nurmi (2009) used four data collection periods with repeated measures to assess changes in newcomer perceptions of supervisor support and socialization outcomes. Again, these designs suffer from the possibility that missing (unmodeled) time-varying third variables are actually responsible for effects observed, but they (and the 3-wave design described above) eliminate time-invariant and unit-level variables as possible confounds. This greatly reduces the number of possible viable alternative explanations (see, e.g., Vancouver et al., 2001; Yeo & Neal, 2006).

Finally, because change is often nonlinear (e.g., Figure 10.1), more than three waves of data are often necessary to account for these change patterns. Indeed, time series designs, discussed in greater detail in the quasi-experimental section below, generally call for 50–100 observations in order to model the nonlinear and cyclical change often found in these types of studies (Shadish et al., 2002). For information on analyzing the types of longitudinal designs described above, consult Willett and Singer (2003a). Moreover, there are several examples of their use in the socialization literature (e.g., Boswell, Shipp, Culbertson, & Payne, 2009; Buttigieg, Deery, & Iverson, 2007; Chan & Schmitt, 2000; Chen, 2005; Frese, Garst, & Fay, 2007; Jokisaari & Nurmi, 2009; Kammeyer-Mueller & Wanberg, 2003).

EXPERIMENTAL DESIGNS
Experiments are considered the sine qua non of causal inference (Shadish et al., 2002). Although

great fans, we are less enamored than many methodologists for the reasons mentioned earlier (i.e., construct validity threats undermine causal inferences; practicality issues). We discuss our reticence in more detail below, but first some definitions and other points need to be made.

An experiment is a study with a manipulated variable. That is, the researcher operationalizes at least one level of a variable (i.e., the experimental condition) where another level is either manipulated or left at its premanipulation level (e.g., the control condition). This means that at least two levels of the variable (called the *independent variable*) exist, which can be used to assess covariance with one or more dependent variables. The nature of the manipulation can vary on a continuum from lean and clean to mean and messy. Lean and clean manipulations involve only one, simple, operational element. They reduce the chance of contamination of other constructs within the operationalization (i.e., fewer possibilities of confounds), lead to clearer explication of mechanisms, and are likely cheaper interventions in the end (i.e., efficient). Mean and messy manipulations involve multiple elements. They reduce the chance of deficiency and are likely to be stronger than a simple operation. These latter features are important when assessing the efficacy of a possible cause (*can* it cause the effect), or when testing social-technical system interventions where the whole system is presumed to be needed in order to cause a change, not just a part (Trist, 1981). When the mean and messy approach has been used to positive effect, future work can back off elements to determine if some elements are inert as opposed to active ingredients (i.e., efficiency-driven research).

In addition to the manipulation, the second most critical design issue is the method by which individuals are assigned to the levels of the manipulated variable(s). Generally, random assignment, where each individual has an equal chance of assignment to a level, is a very good method because it removes most of the threats to internal validity. Indeed, researchers often think this is a definitional element of the experiment (cf., Shadish et al., 2002). Instead, experiments with random assignment are called *randomized experiments* or *randomized clinical trials*. Unfortunately, Campbell and Stanley (1963) coined the term *quasi-experiment* to describe an experiment where random assignment is not used to determine the level of the independent variable. For us, the problem with the quasi-experimental label is that repeated-measure designs, as well as some other

designs covered under the quasi-experimental label, are sometimes *less* susceptible to validity threats than the randomized experiment—but the modifier "quasi" puts a negative pall on any experiment that is not randomized. Ah, but the cat is out of that bag; thus we will discuss the randomized experiment here and deal with the plethora of non-randomized, quasi-experimental designs in the intervention stage section below.

What is so good about the randomized experiment (and some quasi-experimental designs discussed later) for making causal inferences is that it so closely approximates the counterfactual needed to make a causal inference (Shadish et al., 2002). A *counterfactual* is something that is contrary to fact (i.e., like asking a "what if" question). In this case, one knows the value of a property of the person (or whatever the unit of analysis) on the dependent variable(s) when exposed to the experimental treatment (i.e., the manipulated level of the independent variable). What one wants to know is the value of this property if the same person, over the same time period, with the same initial conditions had not been exposed to the manipulated level of the independent variable. With a randomized experiment one can assume, more or less, that the *average* person (or unit) is the same in both the treatment and control groups at the beginning of the study. Then, when measuring the dependent variable(s) from the entire sample at the same time (at the end of the study), one can expect that the *only* difference between the *groups* is the exposure to the different levels of the independent variable. True, it is not the same person that was exposed to both levels, but by using a lot people who have an equal chance of being in either condition one can assume that the average effect is equivalent to what would have happened if the same persons were exposed to both levels. Note that if one were concerned about the external validity of the effect across different populations, one can use indicators of membership in the population and see if they moderate the effects of the intervention.

One can see how the randomized experiment reduces the possible effects on dependent variables due to selection effects because, probabilistically, the groups are initially equal. Likewise, one can see that whatever effect might occur naturally over time (i.e., maturation) will occur in all the groups, so that effect is accounted for within the design. Indeed, the list of threats to internal validity seems to have been constructed with the randomized experiment as the cure in mind. Only one, attrition (also called *mortality*), which is the loss of participants from the study that is somehow a function of the condition the participant is in, remains as a possible problem for the randomized experiment—at least in the list of threats to internal validity. In lab studies, attrition is generally not an issue because individuals are not likely to withdraw from the study within the short time of the study (though they may withdrawal psychologically). Unfortunately, attrition can be a real problem for socialization research because one should wait awhile before collecting the final waves of the dependent variables. Note, however, it is usually only a threat to internal validity if the attrition is uneven across the conditions. This is unlikely to be the case (i.e., attrition is not systematically related to the independent variable); however, if it is and the attrition is due to leaving the organization, one might consider that to be *the* important outcome variable. That is, when attrition is an outcome variable it is not a mortality threat because the researcher has a final data point for everyone who began the study (i.e., dummy coding as retained or not). Moreover, if multiple waves of data are collected, survival analysis techniques (Singer & Willett, 2003b) can be used for evaluating censored data (i.e., data that cannot be collected because the individual is no longer in the study).

However, as mentioned above, experiments' Achilles heel in terms of threatening the validity of causal inferences can be found in the list of threats to construct validity. Perhaps the most famous instance of this type of problem is the Hawthorne studies carried out at GE in the 1940s (Roethlisberger & Dickson, 1943). The essential problem is that the "special" circumstances represented by the differences in the independent variable, made particularly salient when random assignment is used (unless it seems natural or is not transparent), can cause individuals to act differently than they might otherwise (e.g., when implemented as an intervention). These "individuals" might be the participants, or they might be supervisors or others trying to *compensate* the control condition by providing some of the benefit they see the treatment group getting. This is called *compensatory equalization* (Shadish et al., 2002). A related problem is called *treatment diffusion,* mentioned earlier. In organizational settings, fear of diffusion, compensatory equalization, and other effects (e.g., compensatory rivalry) often motivates researchers to use naturally occurring groups so the members of the different groups are less likely to interact with each other, much less know that they are participating in an experiment. This might

appear unethical because it violates the principle of informed consent, but it often is not because of the numerous exceptions built into the ethics code (consult your local Institutional Review Board). A nice compromise is that if there are several naturally occurring groups, one might be able to randomly assign the groups to conditions. Provided there are a sufficient number of groups, this is nearly equivalent to random assignment of individuals and, indeed, can be more appropriate when groups are the true unit of analysis. Finally, the use of a placebo, particularly when those measuring the dependent variable are blind to the condition, can reduce the construct validity threats associated with experiments. In the case of organizational interventions, this likely means using a training program or treatment that is not expected to effect the dependent variables of interest but that might mitigate treatment effects like diffusion, novelty, or compensatory rivalry.

Besides construct validity problems with the independent variable, there can be construct validity problems with the dependent variable that undermine causal inferences. Above, we discussed issues related to self-report measures of learning. However, even so-called objective measures of learning used at the end of training to evaluate learning validity do not necessarily measure retention (i.e., the degree to which the material is retained in memory and can be recalled when needed), which is more likely to affect transfer validity (i.e., the degree to which the knowledge or skills acquired are used appropriately in a performance context; that is, back on the job). The result is that certain training tactics can look effective because they show better performance on an end-of-training assessment than other tactics. However, when post-training (i.e., near transfer) or on-the-job performance (i.e., far transfer) assessments are taken, these same tactics can then look relatively worse (e.g., Goodman & Wood, 2004). Of course, this issue is relevant no matter what the design. Our point is that one should not be charmed by the results of randomized experimental studies. Skepticism and critical evaluation are still the watchwords of the scientist.

Randomized experiments can occur in the field or the lab and the socialization literature has examples, though few, of both. For instance, Buckley, Mobbs, Mendoza, Novicevic, Carraher, and Beu (2002) described a study where they developed two pre-employment interventions (i.e., a realistic job preview and an expectation-lowering procedure) and then randomly assigned participants into one of the interventions, a combination of the interventions, or neither intervention (i.e., the control group). Six months later they assessed days worked. They found that individuals in the combined intervention group worked more, on average, than individuals in the other conditions. In a lab study of team climate, Chen, Lu, Tjosvold, and Lin (2008) created cooperative, competitive, or independent team climates via instructions and team confederates in a lab setting. They found stronger relationships formed with newcomers socialized in the cooperative climate. Finally, Pinto, Marques, Levine, and Abrams (2010) described three lab studies where they manipulated the treatment of deviant incumbents to assess how new members then react to these types of group members.

QUALITATIVE METHODS

Early on, we noted that qualitative methods are an alternative to quantitative methods. Qualitative methods include case studies, ethnography (e.g., participant observer who enters an organization to examine its socialization tactics; Cunliffe, 2010), in-depth interviews and focus groups, content analysis of open-ended responses or archival material (e.g., examining how organizations present themselves on their websites), and other techniques (see special issue of *Organizational Research Methods, 11*(3)). We conceptualize potential applications of qualitative research methods through three approaches: (a) exploratory purposes, (b) confirmatory purposes, and (c) integration with quantitative methods. Regardless of the approach to qualitative methods, the overall purpose is to identify and understand a complex phenomenon that has not or cannot be studied using traditional quantitative methodology. Additionally, whether one's purpose is exploratory or confirmatory, it is possible to discover intriguing findings that can advance our understanding of organizational and social processes.

The exploratory purpose of qualitative methods is likely the most well-known and respected (Lee et al., 2011). For instance, grounded theory (Glasser & Strauss, 1967) is an inductive approach to qualitative methods that has received considerable attention in organizational and management sciences research. When implementing grounded theory, theory may be formulated from data or, if other grounded theories previously exist, may be borrowed and applied when appropriate (cf. Strauss & Corbin, 1994). This research approach attempts to rigorously match theory against data and make constant comparisons of the data to the developing theories. Using this style of qualitative investigation,

the research questions and tools of investigation are exploratory in nature. For example, Leonardi, Jackson, and Diwan (2009) used semistructured interviews and shadowing to observe engineering student socialization processes. This inductive approach was used to understand why engineers commit to counterproductive behaviors and persist in these practices. Sometimes the exploration can lead to descriptive information, as mentioned above. But it is often useful for finding new explanations or for revisits to an interesting phenomenon to further explicate the underlying processes (Easterby-Smith, Golden-Biddle, & Locke, 2008; Lee et al., 2011).

The second purpose of a qualitative investigation can be for confirmation or theory testing. This type of investigation often uses established and sometimes competing theories to understand peculiar processes in a single unit (i.e., n = 1 organization). One potential approach for qualitative confirmation is the use of a prospective case study (Bitektine, 2008). This approach involves formulating and testing theory-based hypotheses, which often pit two or more theories as explanations for the social processes of interest. In this way the prospective case study approach coincides with traditional prospective quantitative methodology (i.e., hypotheses are formulated, followed by the collection of data). On the other hand, the type of data collected (e.g., open-ended responses or patterns of behavior) and the analytic methodology (e.g., content analysis; Duriau, Reger, & Pfarrer, 2007) is consistent with qualitative approaches.

The third purpose for qualitative methodology we consider to be supplementary. In this approach, we recommend using a qualitative component to provide the "why" behind the numerical quantitative results. The qualitative data may be exploratory (i.e., provide a possible explanation for the quantitative results) or confirmatory (i.e., back up the quantitative results). That is, one can implement qualitative strategies (e.g., open-ended questions) to explore why respondents selected certain options or engaged in various actions that the numbers do not reveal. For example, Poncheri et al. (2008) incorporate open-ended questionnaires into their climate survey.

As with quantitative research, qualitative observations can be biased by the participants editing their responses so as to create a certain impression or based on their lay theories of the processes and mechanisms involved (Strauss & Corbin, 1994; Bitektine, 2008). That said, we believe qualitative techniques are likely to allow disconfirmation of pet theories and the acquisition of new theories to the field of socialization, and we encourage their use.

RESEARCH SIMULATIONS

Research simulations are, by definition, an attempt to reproduce something in the real world in a more controlled artificial world or microworld (DiFonzo, Hantula, & Bordia, 1998). Research simulations are an attempt to obtain the functional external validity provided by field settings (i.e., experimental realism) without sacrificing the control and precision afforded by a laboratory setting (Runkel & McGrath, 1972). Despite this advantage, research simulations are rarely used in applied psychology and organizational behavior (Austin et al., 2002). One reason for this is that they can be difficult and expensive to construct (Sackett & Larson, 1990). Alternatively, one might argue that nearly every laboratory study is a research simulation given that most of the time researchers are attempting to reproduce some element of realism in their protocol (Aronson, Ellsworth, Carlsmith, & Gonzales, 1990), yet few of these studies would be classified as research simulations. Indeed, when we broach the subject of research simulations we are thinking about somewhat sophisticated virtual worlds like one might see in a computer game (e.g., Second Life). Some researchers in other fields (e.g., decision making) have obtained permission to run studies in online gaming worlds where they set up situations with which players (i.e., participants) can interact (Gonzalez, Vanyukov, & Martin, 2005). Participants in these virtual worlds take the experiences seriously, want to fit in, and want to learn the ropes. Some researchers are thinking that player/participants might respond realistically to virtual organizational worlds, where they can introduce interventions and manipulations to test theories and examine processes in detail as the individuals interact in their virtual world (DiFonzo et al., 1998; Griffeth & Vancouver, 2009).

COMPUTATIONAL MODELS

Another rarely used but potentially very useful research tool is the computational model. Computational models are computer programs that represent dynamic theories (Sun, 2008). Because of the platform (i.e., the computer) these models can be simulated, giving the researcher/theoretician the ability to observe the behavior of the simulated unit as it "interacts" with a simulated context over time (e.g., Vancouver, Putka, & Scherbaum, 2005). In this way, the modeler can test the viability of

the hypothesized process (i.e., can the conceptualized "moving parts" work together as expected). Moreover, a working model will make predictions that can either be compared to existing data or serve as the basis of hypotheses in future data collection adventures (Davis, Eisenhardt, & Bingham, 2007; Harrison, Lin, Carroll, & Carley, 2007). For example, Vancouver et al. (2010) recently presented a computational model that represented the uncertainty reduction theory (Berger & Calabrese, 1975) commonly used to explain proactive information seeking in newcomers. They then used this model to account for (i.e., interpret) the relatively weak positive relationship found between information seeking and role clarity (Bauer, Bodner, Erdogan, Truxillo, & Tucker, 2007). An apparent conundrum for the theory is that it states that individuals would seek less information as their role clarity grew, which is a negative relationship. However, the model revealed that conventional (i.e., cross-sectional) and even some of the more recent longitudinal designs did not produce the kind of data that was diagnostic regarding the theory. The authors argued that, given the expense and labor associated with collecting longitudinal field data, it behooves researchers to have a good handle on the patterns of data over time that would be useful for fitting a theoretical model or disconfirming alternative explanations. In this case, Vancouver et al. could explain the findings that existed, but so could a competing theory.

In sum, to develop and test understandings of socialization processes, researchers will generally need to either to conduct experiments or collect multiple waves of data. To facilitate further insights into the process we recommend qualitative data collection strategies. To maximize theory testing we recommend the construction of computational models. To maximize control, we suggest considering research simulations. However, all this work is meant to serve the final stage of a research enterprise, which is the development and testing of interventions. It is to this last stage we now turn.

Interventions and Treatments

Once a field has a reasonable handle on the factors and processes that affect its important outcomes, researchers can turn to developing, testing, and refining interventions designed to affect those processes and outcomes in positive ways. In the case of socialization, that primarily means figuring out ways to (a) select or encourage newcomers to begin with high initial knowledge (see Figure 10.1), (b) compress (i.e., speed up) the growth curves, or

(c) lower the required asymptote (i.e., reduce the knowledge load needed to perform at maximum capacity). Of course, other outcomes would likely be relevant but not obvious, like how the tactics used might affect organizational creativity (Van Maanen & Schein, 1979). Moreover, interventions are not necessarily formal training programs but could also include mentoring programs (Eby, 2011) or open-door policies that might encourage information seeking (Morrison, 2002). At this stage of research there are generally four questions one might ask, all about the interventions under consideration (Baker, McFall, & Shoham, 2008). First, researchers should ask, does the intervention have efficacy. That is, can it work? For this question internal validity is king. Second, researchers should ask if the intervention is effective. That is, does it work when implemented in the types of setting one would want to implement it? For this question internal validity remains central, but external validity is also central. Indeed, a secondary question is whether the intervention can be disseminated effectively (i.e., to an organization's satellites; across organizations). In the training literature this is referred to as *intra-organizational training validity* (Goldstein & Ford, 2002). Third, researchers should ask if the intervention is efficient. That is, how can one maximize the benefit/cost ratio, particularly when considering scaling up the intervention to implement in a population of settings? This might include trimming away unnecessary elements in an attempt to find the "active ingredients" in a messy intervention. Finally, researchers should ask if the intervention is scientifically plausible. That is, are the intervention's mechanisms understood and empirically validated? A strong understanding of the mechanisms can help increase efficiency as well as increase the longevity of the intervention. Indeed, the training field is replete with fads that fade away as more evidence is collected (Goldstein & Ford, 2002).

Because of the need for making causal inferences (i.e., does the intervention cause some set of effects), coupled with the reality that an intervention is a manipulation, experiments will be the method of choice in this stage of research. However, given the external validity concerns, randomized experiments will be less likely than quasi-experimental designs. Hence, we saved discussion of these designs for this last stage, though they can be used during the understanding phase of research. Recall, quasi-experiments are experiments, but they do not use random assignment. For example, Wesson and Gogus (2005) provided a quasi-experimental approach to understanding newcomer orientation. In this study, the researchers used three (nonrandom) newcomer groups to investigate differences in socialization outcomes for a traditional group-based orientation versus a computer-based orientation program. Fortunately, some of these designs can be as powerful and even more powerful than randomized experiments because they might, depending on the specific design, (a) approximate the counterfactual in a way that is better than using an average group value as a proxy for the "same person," (b) allow unique constructs to be measured and incorporated in theory testing (e.g., change), and (c) avoid or allow one to assess the degree to which threats to internal or construct validity are rearing their ugly heads.

Of course, one variation is to use an assignment procedure that, though not random, is unlikely to create a selection threat. For example, the Wesson and Gogus study assigned individuals to groups based on the timing of their entry into the organization. One group was newcomers who entered prior to the creation of the intervention. This might introduce a cohort effect. However, another group was newcomers who were provided the traditional socialization orientation because they joined when such orientation sessions were scheduled. A third group received the computerized orientation rather than wait for the next traditional orientation session. It is difficult for us to think of how this later procedure would introduce any important systematic bias between these last two groups. Indeed, the reasonableness of the process would seem to mitigate some threats that a randomization procedure might introduce because of the seeming arbitrariness of a randomization procedure. Add to this the previous year group and the use of nonequivalent dependent variables (described below), and we are hard pressed to question the causal conclusions Wesson and Gogus drew.

We detail three other variations of quasi-experimental designs below: repeated-measures, interrupted time series, and regression discontinuity designs. More details and other designs can be found in texts (e.g., Shadish et al., 2002) and methods papers (e.g., Antonakis et al., 2010).

REPEATED-MEASURES DESIGNS

The simplest interpretable repeated-measure, quasi-experimental design is the *pre–post only* design (Shadish et al., 2002). In this design only one group is used, but they are measured on the dependent variable both before (pre) and after (post) exposure to the treatment. This case is very close to the counterfactual mentioned above, because it is the same set of individuals that are exposed to both levels of the independent variable and from whom one finds out what has happened. That is, at the beginning of the experiment (at the time of the pre-test), participants are "in" the control condition and at the end of the study they are "in" the experimental condition. What makes it a counterfactual from the ideal is that the exposures were not over the same time period and that the initial conditions were not the same. The differences in time (i.e., when one is exposed to the control vs. the experimental condition) undermines internally valid interpretations because of the possibility of history or maturation effects. History effects occur when something during the time of the treatment, but independent of the treatment, has an effect on the dependent variable. Here a control group helps interpretation because those in the control group *may* be exposed to the same "something," allowing one to assess that something's influence. For example, Klein and Weaver (2000) used a pre/post two-group design to assess the effects of a voluntary 3-hour orientation program. Assignment to the treatment group was via volunteering (or being "volunteered" by their supervisor). The control group simply did not volunteer for the orientation, but completed the Chao et al. (1994) socialization measure twice—just like, and at the same times as, the treatment group. Without a control group one might simply pay attention to other events (e.g., one could consider announcements or rumors of pending mergers to be influential in employee attitudes when investigating the relationship between socialization tactics and job commitment) and/or to ask participants about possible history events in a post-experimental debriefing (see our section on qualitative methods). Finally, and particularly when examining socialization interventions, one might employ a replicates design (or cohort sequential) where subsequent cohorts are exposed to the intervention, provided the history event does not repeat itself (e.g., the intervention coincides with the 6-month probationary review). Indeed, these types of events, which are rare in laboratory research, might not be that rare in organizational settings.

An unlikely threat for studies involving pre-tests is the testing effect (Shadish et al., 2002). *Testing effects* refers to the notion that exposure to a measure affects subsequent scores from that measure. Indeed, pre-tests are also used in randomized experiments to (a) confirm that the groups begin at the same level, and (b) to remove within-group differences in

starting values on the dependent variable. The use of pre-tests essentially allows researchers to establish a baseline in order to assess change, which is the usual intent general of an intervention. Testing effects can threaten causal interpretations from both randomized and nonrandomized experiments if the effect is somehow systematically related to the treatment (e.g., learners who only pay attention to material made salient in a pre-test). To address this possibility the Solomon 4-group design is advocated as a means for assessing it (Solomon, 1949). In a Solomon 4-group, the presence or absence of a pre-test is a factor in a two-factor model. The other factor is the manipulated variable. Thus, the Solomon 4-group involves two control groups; one receiving the pre-test and one not.

Solomon 4-groups studies are rare largely because the concern for testing effects is minimal. However, the addition of one control group, even if not populated via random assignment, is important for handling another, much more critical threat: maturation. Indeed, one might expect to see change in the control group due to proactive information seeking and informal socialization tactics (i.e., maturation), but one might find even greater change in the treatment group. This greater change in the treatment group could allow one to infer an effect due to the intervention, provided one can rule out a maturation-by-selection threat.

Perhaps the most insidious threat with nonrandomized, pre–post experiments with control groups is a maturation-by-selection effect. We already mentioned this when talking about longitudinal research with only two waves of data. The issue is particularly acute with learning processes like socialization because of the nonlinearity typical of learning (see Figure 10.1). That is, if individuals in the different conditions begin, on average, at different places in their learning curves, this difference and not the manipulated variable might account for the differences in the degree of change observed between the pre-test and post-test. Alternatively, something about the nonrandom assignment procedure creates a concern. For example, recall that in the Klein and Weaver (2000) example discussed above, the treatment group was composed of volunteers whereas the control group members did not volunteer for the orientation. One might suppose that the volunteers were a more motivated set of employees, and when left to their own devices they might have been more likely to take advantage of information sources compared to the nonvolunteers (i.e., the greater change in adaptation in the treatment group was due to pretreatment levels of motivation in the group, not the intervention). To deal with that possibility, Klein and Weaver included nonequivalent dependent variables. Nonequivalent dependent variables are variables that should not be affected by the causal variable of interest, but could be affected by historic or treatment threats. In this case, Klein and Weaver's intervention only addressed three of Chao et al.'s (1994) six socialization dimensions but they measured all six. They found slight improvements between the pre-tests and post-tests for nearly all the dimensions for both groups, but they found significantly greater improvements on only three of the dimensions. It did not work out perfectly; one of the significant dimensions (i.e., people) was not in the orientation. Thus, one might conclude the volunteers were on average more people-oriented than the control group, but this is unlikely to account for the treatment effects associated with the history and goals/value dimensions. It also allowed them to conclude that the language portion of the orientation needed more work, given there was no effect for that dimension.

Besides control groups, maturation as a threat to internally valid interpretations can be addressed by adding additional measures to obtain a baseline. That is, a pre-test *prior* to the pre-test allows one to assess change on the dependent variables for the "control condition" period of time so that it can be compared to the "experimental condition" period of time. Preferably the intervals between the first pre-test, second pre-test, and post-test are equal, but by coding time properly, one can fairly compare slopes of change, which is the critical test of the causal effect of the treatment (Willet & Singer, 2003a). Once again, though, more than two pre-tests would be useful if one suspects nonlinear change (see Figure 10.1). However, given that socialization interventions are usually implemented at the beginning of someone's tenure with an organization, obtaining multiple pre-tests is unlikely or perhaps of little meaning (i.e., measuring naturally occurring adjustment changes prior to joining the organization to which one would be adjusting). That said, there might be many instances where organizational entry and some socialization intervention are not hopelessly confounded or where one is looking at an aggregated level of analysis. In those cases, another quasi-experimental design might be feasible.

INTERRUPTED TIME SERIES DESIGNS

A powerful quasi-experimental design that is often used by economists is the interrupted time series design. These designs typically involve archival data of aggregated (e.g., frequency) observations (e.g., crime rates, sales data). The idea behind this design is that several observations occur before and after some change (i.e., intervention) takes place, where the effect of the change on the variables observed is the issue of interest. The multiple waves of observation allow for naturally occurring trends and cyclical effects to be accounted for (i.e., smoothed out) to determine if the change (i.e., the introduction of an intervention) caused a change in the observed variables. The principle threats to this design are history and treatment (i.e., construct validity) threats. Adding a control group can address the history problem, if the control group is also exposed to the historic event. Alternatively, one might collect observations of nonequivalent dependent variables as Klein and Weaver (2000) did.

Interrupted time series designs can be particularly useful for looking at results-level data (e.g., how a training intervention affects organizational performance; Kirkpatrick, 1994). This data is typically only available at the organizational level and thus involves one "case." When multiple cases are available, called *pooled time series*, then multiple-level modeling techniques can often be used as discussed in the longitudinal section (Bliese & Ployhart, 2002). The essence of these designs is to look for discontinuities in level, or change in slopes in the dependent variable, when the intervention is introduced. Low power can threaten short time series, and delays in the onset of effects or the extinction of an effect can adversely affect interpretations if not considered (Shadish et al., 2002).

REGRESSION DISCONTINUITY DESIGNS

A particularly powerful, but non-intuitive quasi-experimental design is the regression discontinuity design (RDD; Shadish et al., 2002). RDDs involve using an assignment variable to determine who gets treatment (or one level of the treatment) and who does not. The assignment variable might be a pre-test, or some other measure of merit or need. Thus, an organization might provide a training program to those most in need or most deserving based on some observable measure (e.g., performance ratings). Using a cutoff on this assignment variable to determine who does and does not get the treatment seems to guarantee a selection effect. However, because the assignment variable is included in the analysis (i.e., it is modeled), the selection threat is completely mitigated. Indeed, what one is interested in testing is whether the relationship between the assignment variable and the dependent variable changes at the cutoff (though sometimes changes in *slope* above and below the cutoff would be expected and tested). In this way, the regression discontinuity design is very similar to the interrupted time series designs, except that the assignment variable is the control variable, not time. Besides construct validity threats associated with introducing an intervention, threats to RDDs are mostly associated with improper implementation or failure to test for nonlinear effects of the assignment variable on the dependent variable. Indeed, RDDs are as powerful as randomized experiments, except that they are slightly more difficult to analyze (Shadish et al., 2002). Mellor and Mark (1998) provide an example of RDD applied in an organizational setting.

Review

Above we described several issues related to the valid interpretations of the results of studies of socialization. Now it is time for a review session. The idea is to hit home the takeaway points. To keep you from getting bored, we interject some of our opinions here as well.

Mind Your Measures

It concerns us that measures of adaptation and learning within the socialization literature are largely self-reports and limited to only a few instruments. This single modality with few operationalizations violates a fundamental principle of the construct validity literature (Shadish et al., 2002). To be sure, this problem is rampant in the organizational behavior literature generally (Sackett & Larson, 1990), but it seems particularly problematic here. Indeed, how could one possibly *know* how ignorant one is? Think about it. Mitigating this concern is the tendency for socialization researchers to measure distal outcome variables, but these are often based on self-report measures as well. To spur some innovation here, consider this: Why not measure employees' mental models (i.e., cognitive representations of relationships or processes)? Mohammed, Klimoski, and Rentsch (2000) reviewed various methods one might use for measuring the mental models of team members, particularly as they relate to other team members. In that paper they describe a study where the mental models of students of statistics regarding statistical information was assessed, indexed, and compared to that of the instructor (Goldsmith, Johnson, & Acton, 1991). They found that similarity predicted performance. If measuring mental

models is too "out there," consider giving a knowledge test.

Careful with Causal Interpretations

Everyone knows that correlation is not causation; witness the absence of the word *cause* in any passive observational study. However, words like *mediation, affect, influence,* or *impact* and phrases like *account for* or *due to* are commonplace. These words imply causation as well. If the design does not warrant a causal conclusion, these words or phrases should not be used, or they should be qualified. Do not get us wrong: qualifying a causal conclusion that has no reasonable alternative explanation is not helpful (at least we do not like it when reviewers make us do it). But if researchers are not thinking of alternative explanations, it is probably because they are not thinking hard enough. Indeed, it is easy to be lulled into complacency by the beauty of one's arguments. However, one needs to play the debate game. That is, one needs to assume the position one is taking (i.e., the conclusion one is drawing) is absolutely wrong; that there *must* be another explanation. We find it helpful to put ourselves in the shoes of our antagonists (if you do not have one now, don't worry, you will). Consider reverse causality or things that might influence the criteria. Did the design control for these?

However, thinking might not be enough. Vancouver et al. (2010) decided they needed external support to think about how the dynamic feedback processes presumed to drive proactive socialization (i.e., information seeking) could affect the variables observed in studies of the process. Thus, they created a computational model to examine the implications of the uncertainty reduction (Berger & Calabrese, 1975), as well as the ego cost theories (Ashford, 1986) of proactive information seeking. Not only did they find that both theories could explain some key findings from existing research, but also that the sign of the relationship between the "cause" and "effect" constructs would depend on the study design choices (e.g., time between data collection waves) due to the simultaneity expected between these constructs. It is possible these effects could have been "thought through" without a computational model, but that had not happened for the more than 20 previous years of research on the topic.

Indeed, the results that can emerge from modeling dynamic, nonlinear processes, like one would expect when feedback processes are involved, imply that experiments or longitudinal designs are not the sole cure for designs that are weak in terms of internal validity. One needs to have a firm grasp of the possible explanations to assess the diagnostic value of a study design. Consider an "intervention" to treat an unconscious diabetic. An injection of insulin could either revive or kill the patient, depending on whether the unconsciousness is the result of too much or not enough glucose in the patient's system. This is because diabetes is a breakdown in a person's ability to regulate glucose, and dysregulation in either direction can lead to a loss of consciousness. However, the treatment depends completely on the direction of the dysregulation. Imagine conducting an experiment investigating the effectiveness of insulin injections on acute diabetic attacks when this key moderator (i.e., the direction of the dysregulation) is not known. Our point is that one needs a clear understanding of what to observe and how those observations should relate to each other, given the theory or theories one is considering, *prior* to designing the study.

Evaluate Interventions

The point of studying socialization is to help individuals, teams, and organizations achieve their goals. This is not going to be accomplished by members of these constituencies reading our literature but via the creation of effective interventions. Socialization interventions might include formal training programs of newcomers or incumbents, policy changes like the development of mentoring programs, and human resource systems modifications (e.g., in performance management or selection systems). However, one cannot assume that the interventions developed actually work as expected or without unintentional side effects. For this reason, one evaluates the interventions.[2] This is called *evidence-based practice* (Briner & Rousseau, 2011). Given this, one might expect to see a lot of intervention studies published in the socialization literature. Looking across 20 years of research, we found the three mentioned above (i.e., Buckley et al., 2002; Klein & Weaver, 2000; and Wesson & Gogus, 2005).

Perhaps one might argue that the lack of published intervention studies is because socialization interventions are inherently local, since they are about improving newcomers' knowledge of the local environment. Indeed, organizations presumably evaluate their own programs (Saari, Johnson, McLaughlin, & Zimmerle, 1988); they just do not publish the results. However, if this argument were true then no socialization research would likely be published, because all that matters is the local content of the training program and that would not be

of any generalizable knowledge interest. Instead, the truth is that the field suspects organizational tactics, policies, and system characteristics *do* matter, and do so generally or in terms of generally important conditionals (i.e., moderating variables). Thus, it would be useful to know if interventions based on these general principles produce positive effects (i.e., efficacy studies), as well as whether the interventions can be scaled up (i.e., effectiveness studies) and trimmed of their unnecessary components (i.e., efficiency studies).

Indeed, the notion that socialization interventions are not evaluated because they are inherently local is also undermined by the observation that the applied psychology literature lacks intervention studies across the board (Briner & Rousseau, 2011).[3] Various reasons for this have been described (e.g., Briner & Rousseau, 2011; Grove & Ostroff, 1991). In those reviews a primary reason given is a lack of training and knowledge of research design. Chapters like the current one are developed to address this specific issue. Another problem is a lack of skepticism regarding the field's practices. Again, chapters like this one attempt to counter that view.

A third issue is inertia and a lack of the social-technical systems that encourage and support intervention evaluation, particularly on a large scale. Consider the medical field, where large-scale, multisite randomized clinical trials are a norm. Even in clinical psychology, intervention evaluation studies dominate their top journals (e.g., *Journal of Consulting and Clinical Psychology*). These efforts are supported by government grants and the prestige that getting and publishing such projects provides the researchers. With some notable exceptions via military funding sources (e.g., Project A; Campbell, 1990), I/O and OB researchers tend to not have access to these kinds of grants, and do not seem to bask in the same scholarly glow, because such studies are often not very theoretically interesting. Indeed, we agree with Hambrick (2007) that one problem with the field's obsession with the theoretical contribution in its top journals is that it largely discourages these important final-stage research projects. Moreover, Briner and Rousseau (2011) argue that the field undercuts its best likely source of funding, organizations, because it does not communicate a proper sense of skepticism for its interventions. This is a tricky position though, because, as Briner and Rousseau also point out (see also, Grove & Ostroff, 1991), identifying a poorly working intervention can lead to the ruin of those organizational insiders who advocated sponsoring the research. Our own view is that one should have enough supporting preliminary evidence and understanding to reasonably expect that the intervention will at least partially work out, particularly in terms of the more proximal outcomes.

Conclusions

We titled this chapter "how we do research around here" to make the obvious connection to socialization. That said, the reader may have noticed that much of the chapter advocated using methods or addressing issues generally ignored by researchers currently in the area. Thus, we really seem to be saying one should not do research the way it is done around here. This impression might not be totally unwarranted. Indeed, when organizations conduct their needs analyses and consider their approaches to socialization (and training), they want to be aware of, and seek to do away with, the bad habits that might have emerged within their ranks over the years (e.g., overreliance on the passive observational, cross-sectional survey study). So, part of our job as we see it is to try to highlight only the good habits and to fill in gaps with new procedures that we hope will become new good habits. However, the bigger issue is that what should be done going forward is somewhat an inverse function of what has been done in the past. Thus, just as organizations in a dynamic environment must constantly innovate to stay competitive, researchers must constantly change what they are looking at or how they are looking at it, because the name of the game is to add *new* knowledge. Thus, we do not mean any disrespect by pointing out the flaws of past research methods or even past research. Even if one were to do the perfect study, one should only do it once; because an exact repeat would add no new knowledge (it would be perfect and therefore perfectly reliable, obviating the need for replication). But we all know there is no such thing as the perfect study. We hope you are now better armed with the information you need to find the flaws in the existing research and design a new study to overcome them. Eventually our field's knowledge level should reach the maximum asymptote. Until then, seek proactively.

Notes

1. Some veterans of the field might be surprised to hear that the cross-sectional design is the modal design in socialization research. Indeed, a little over a decade ago, Bauer, Morrison, and Callister (1998) reported that 70% of socialization research between 1986 and 1997 was longitudinal. However, our own search of the socialization research over the past 12 years put it at 36%, whereas 38% was cross-sectional, passive observational

designs. Nonetheless, there is both good news and bad news in these numbers. One piece of good news is that even at 36%, socialization researchers have a much higher percent of longitudinal studies than typically found in I/O or OB research (Austin, Scherbaum, & Mahlman, 2002; Scandura & Williams, 2000; Stone-Romero, Weaver, & Glenar, 1995). The high percentage is likely due to the recognition that socialization is a process and thus the effect must be measured sometime after the presumed cause. A piece of bad news is that most of the longitudinal studies in the Bauer et al. review merely measured the presumed effect once. This design does not provide much assurance that the construct one assumed was the cause, really was (Ployhart &Vandenberg, 2010). A piece of good news was that most of the longitudinal studies in our sample used repeated measures of the constructs, which substantially improves the conclusions one can draw from the study. Another piece of bad news from the Bauer et al. (1998) review is that they classified only *one* of the 67 studies they reviewed as experimental. We found five (out of 53) were experimental. Better news, but not a strong showing. Overall, it seems fair to say that much progress is needed if the field wants to be able to make confident conclusions regarding the causal processes at play during socialization.

2. Eventually such evaluations might be unnecessary because the effects of the key active ingredients and conditions under which they work best, and with the least amount of adverse side effects, are well known and stable enough that local evaluations only produce redundant information. It is unlikely the field has reached that point. Indeed, innovations and the changing conditions of work likely will make the creation of new interventions and the need for cross-validating old ones always necessary.

3. The possible exception to this is the selection field, where external pressures (e.g., legal) assured that evaluations were conducted.

References

Aguinis, H., Pierce, C. A., Bosco, F. A., & Muslin, I. S. (2009). First decade of organizational research methods: Trends in design, measurement, and data analysis topics. *Organizational Research Methods, 12*, 69–112.

Alliger, G. M., Tannenbaum, S. I., Bennett, W., Traver, H., et al. (1997). A meta-analysis of the relations among training criteria. *Personnel Psychology, 50*, 341–358.

Anderson, C. A., Lindsay, J. J., & Bushman, B. J. (1999). Research in the psychological laboratory: Truth or triviality? *Current Directions in Psychological Science, 8*, 3–9.

Antonakis, J., Bendahan, S., Jacquart, P., & Lalive, R. (2010). On making causal claims: A review and recommendations. *The Leadership Quarterly, 21*, 1086–1120.

Aronson, E., Ellsworth, P. C., Carlsmith, J. M., & Gonzales, M. H. (1990). *Methods of research in social psychology* (2nd ed.). New York: McGraw-Hill.

Ashford, S. J. (1986). The role of feedback seeking in individual adaptation: A resource perspective. *Academy of Management Journal, 29*, 465–487.

Ashford, S. J., & Cummings, L. L. (1983). Feedback as an individual resource: Personal strategies of creating information. *Organizational Behavior & Human Performance, 32*: 370–398.

Austin, J. T., Scherbaum, C. A., & Mahlman, R. A. (2002). History of research methods in industrial and organizational psychology: Measurement, design, analysis. In S. G. Rogelberg (Ed.), *Handbook of research methods in industrial* and organizational psychology. (pp. 3–33) Malden, MA: Blackwell Publishing.

Baker, T. B., McFall, R. M., & Shoham, V. (2008). Current status and future prospects of clinical psychology: Toward a scientifically principled approach to mental and behavioral health care. *Psychological Science in the Public Interest, 9,* 67–103.

Bandura, A., & Wood, R. (1989). Effect of perceived controllability and performance standards on self-regulation of complex decision making. *Journal of Personality and Social Psychology, 56,* 805–814.

Baron, R. M., & Kenny, D. A. (1986). The moderator-mediator variable distinction in social psychological research: Conceptual, strategic, and statistical considerations. *Journal of Personality and Social Psychology, 51,* 1173–1182.

Bauer, T. N., Bodner, T., Erdogan, B., Truxillo, D. M., & Tucker, J. S. (2007). Newcomer adjustment during organizational socialization: A meta-analytic review of antecedents, outcomes, and methods. *Journal of Applied Psychology, 92,* 707–721.

Bauer, T. N., & Erdogan, B. (2011). Organizational socialization: The effective onboarding of new employees. In S. Zedeck (Ed.), *APA handbook of industrial and organizational psychology, Vol. 3: Maintaining, expanding, and contracting the organization* (pp. 51–64). Washington, DC: American Psychological Association.

Bauer, T. N., Morrison, E. W., & Callister, R. R. (1998). Organizational socialization: A review and directions for future research. *Research in Personnel and Human Resource Management, 16,* 149–214.

Beal, D. J., & Weiss, H. M. (2003). Methods of ecological momentary assessment in organizational research. *Organizational Research Methods, 6,* 440–464.

Berger, C. R., & Calabrese, R. J. (1975). Some explorations in initial interaction and beyond: Toward a developmental theory of interpersonal communication. *Human Communication Research, 1,* 99–112.

Bitektine, A. (2008). Prospective case study design: Qualitative method for deductive theory testing. *Organizational Research Methods, 11,* 160–180.

Bliese, P. D., & Ployhart, R. E. (2002). Growth modeling using random coefficient models: Model building, testing, and illustration. *Organizational Research Methods, 5*(4), 362–387.

Bolger, N., Davis, A., & Rafaeli, E. (2003). Diary methods: Capturing life as it is lived. *Annual Review of Psychology, 54,* 579–616.

Boswell, W. R., Shipp, A. J., Culbertson, S. S., & Payne, S. C. (2009). Changes in newcomer job satisfaction over time: Examining the pattern of honeymoons and hangovers. *Journal of Applied Psychology, 94,* 844–858.

Briner, R. B., & Rousseau, D. M. (2011). Evidence-based I-O psychology: Not there yet. *Industrial and Organizational Psychology: Perspectives on Science and Practice, 4,* 3–22.

Buckley, M. R., Mobbs, T. A., Mendoza, J. L., Novicevic, M. M., Carraher, S. M., & Beu, D. S. (2002). Implementing realistic job previews and expectation-lowering procedures: A field experiment. *Journal of Vocational Behavior, 61,* 263–278.

Buttigieg, D. M., Deery, S. J., & Iverson, R. D. (2007). An event history analysis of union joining and leaving. *Journal of Applied Psychology, 92,* 829–839.

Campbell, D. T. (1957). Factors relevant to the validity of experiments in social settings. *Psychological Bulletin, 54,* 297–312.

Campbell, J. P. (1990). An overview of the army selection and classification project (Project A). *Personnel Psychology, 43,* 231–239.

Campbell, J. P., Daft, R. L., & Hulin, C. L. (1982). *What to study: Generating and developing research questions.* Beverly Hills, CA: Sage Publications.

Campbell, D. T., Stanley, J. C., & Gage, N. L. (1963). *Experimental and quasi-experimental designs for research.* Boston, MA: Houghton, Mifflin.

Carr, J. C., Pearson, A. W., Vest, M. J., & Boyar, S. L. (2006). Prior occupational experience, anticipatory socialization, and employee retention. *Journal of Management, 32,* 343–359.

Chao, G. T., O'Leary-Kelly, A. M., Wolf, S., Klein, H. J., & Gardner, P. D. (1994). Organizational socialization: Its content and consequences. *Journal of Applied Psychology, 79,* 730–743.

Chan, D. (2002). Latent growth modeling. In F. Drasgow & N. Schmitt (Eds.), *Measuring and analyzing behavior in organizations: Advances in measurement and data analysis* (pp. 302–349). San Francisco, CA: Jossey-Bass.

Chan, D., & Schmitt, N. (2000). Interindividual differences in intraindividual changes in proactivity during organizational entry: A latent growth modeling approach to understanding newcomer adaptation. *Journal of Applied Psychology, 85,* 190–210.

Charrington, D. J., Reitz, H. J., & Scott, W. E. (1971). Effects of contingent and noncontingent reward on the relationship between satisfaction and task performance. *Journal of Applied Psychology, 55,* 531–536.

Chen, G. (2005). Newcomer adaptation in teams: multilevel antecedents and outcomes. *Academy of Management Journal, 48,* 101–116.

Chen, N. Y., Lu, J., Tjosvold, D., & Lin, C. (2008). Effects of team goal interdependence on newcomer socialization: An experiment in China. *Journal of Applied Social Psychology, 38,* 198–214.

Cook, T. D., & Campbell, D. T. (1979). *Quasi-experimentation: Design and analysis for field settings.* Chicago, IL: Rand McNally.

Cronbach, L. J. (1957). The two disciplines of scientific psychology. *American Psychologist, 12,* 671–684.

Cronbach, L. J., Gleser, G. C., Nanda, H., & Rajaratnam, N. (1972). *The dependability of behavioral measurements: Theory of generalizability for scores and profiles.* New York: Wiley.

Cunliffe, A. L. (2010). Retelling tales of the field: In search of organizational ethnography 20 years on. *Organizational Research Methods, 13,* 224–239.

Davis, J. P., Eisenhardt, K. M., & Bingham, C. B. (2007). Developing theory through simulation methods. *The Academy of Management Review, 32,* 480–499.

DiFonzo, N., Hantula, D. A., & Bordia, P. (1998). Microworlds for experimental research: Having your (control and collections) cake, and realism too. *Behavior Research Methods, Instruments & Computers, 30,* 278–286.

Dunning, D., Heath, C., & Suls, J. M. (2004). Flawed self-assessment: Implications for health, education, and the workplace. *Psychological Science in the Public Interest, 5,* 69–106.

Duriau, V. J., Reger, R. K., & Pfarrer, M. D. (2007). A content analysis of the content analysis literature in organizational studies. *Organizational Research Methods, 10,* 5–34.

Easterby-Smith, M., Golden-Biddle, K., & Locke, K. (2008). Working with pluralism: Determining quality in qualitative research. *Organizational Research Methods, 11,* 419–429.

Eby, L. T. (2011). Mentoring. In S. Zedeck (Ed.), *APA handbook of industrial and organizational psychology Vol. 2: Selecting and developing members for the organization* (pp. 505–525). Washington DC: American Psychological Association.

Frese, M., Garst, H., & Fay, D. (2007). Making things happen: Reciprocal relationships between work characteristics and personal initiative in a four-wave longitudinal structural equation model. *Journal of Applied Psychology, 92*, 1084–1102.

Goldsmith, T. E., Johnson, P. J., & Acton, W. H. (1991). Assessing structural knowledge. *Journal of Educational Psychology, 83*, 88–96.

Goldstein, I. L., & Ford, J. K. (2002). *Training in organizations: Needs assessment, development, and evaluation* (4th ed.). Belmonc, CA: Wadsworth/Thomson Learning.

Glasser, B., & Strauss, A. (1967). *The Discovery of grounded theory*. Hawthorne, NY: Aldine Publishing Company.

Gomez-Mejia, L. R. (1983). Sex differences during occupational socialization. *Academy of Management Journal, 26*, 492–499.

Gonzalez, C., Vanyukov, P., & Martin, M. K. (2005). The use of microworlds to study dynamic decision making. *Computers in Human Behavior, 21*, 273–286.

Goodman, J. S., & Wood, R. E. (2004). Feedback specificity, learning opportunities, and learning. *Journal of Applied Psychology, 89*, 248–262.

Griffeth, R. W., & Vancouver, J. B. (2009, November). *Sim Career: Development of a virtual organizational world (VOW) for studying employee turnover processes*. Presented at the annual Society of Organizational Behavior conference, University of Maryland, College Park, MD.

Grove, D. A. & Ostroff, C. (1991). Program evaluation. In K. Wexley & J. Hinrichs (Eds.), *Developing human resources*. Washington, DC: BNA Books.

Hambrick, D. C. (2007). The field of management's devotion to theory: Too much of a good thing? *Academy of Management Journal, 50*, 1346–1352.

Harrison, J. R., Lin, Z., Carroll, G. R., & Carley, K. M. (2007). Simulation modeling in organizational and management research. *The Academy of Management Review, 32*, 1229–1245.

Haueter, J. A., Macan, T. H., & Winter, J. (2003). Measurement of newcomer socialization: Construct validation of a multidimensional scale. *Journal of Vocational Behavior, 63*, 20–39.

Hulin, C. L. (1991). Adaptation, persistence, and commitment in organizations. In M. D. Dunnette & L. M. Hough (Eds.), *Handbook of industrial and organizational psychology* (2nd ed., pp. 443–505). Palo Alto, CA: Consulting Psychologists Press.

James, L. R., Mulaik, S. A., & Brett, J. M. (1982). *Causal analysis: Assumptions, models, and data*. Beverly Hills, CA: Sage Publications.

James, L. R., Mulaik, S. A., & Brett, J. M. (2006). A tale of two methods. *Organizational Research Methods, 9*, 233–244.

Jokisaari, M., & Nurmi, J.-E. (2009). Change in newcomers' supervisor support and socialization outcomes after organizational entry. *Academy of Management Journal, 52*, 527–544.

Jones, G. R. (1983). Psychological orientation and the process of organizational socialization: An interactionist perspective. *Academy of Management Review, 8*, 464–474.

Kammeyer-Mueller, J. D., & Wanberg, C. R. (2003). Unwrapping the organizational entry process: Disentangling multiple antecedents and their pathways to adjustment. *Journal of Applied Psychology, 88*, 779–794.

Klein, K. J., & Kozlowski, S. W. J. (2000). *Multilevel theory, research, and methods in organizations: Foundations, extensions, and new directions*. San Francisco, CA: Jossey-Bass.

Klein, H. J., & Weaver, N. A. (2000). The effectiveness of an organizational-level orientation training program in the socialization of new hires. *Personnel Psychology, 53*, 47–66.

Kirkpatrick, D. L. (1994). *Evaluating training programs: The four levels*. San Francisco, CA: Berrett-Koehler.

Lee, T. W., Mitchell, T. R., & Harman, W. S. (2011). Qualitative research strategies in industrial and organizational psychology. In S. Zedeck (Ed.), *APA handbook of industrial and organizational psychology, Vol 1: Building and developing the organization* (pp. 73–83). Washington, DC: American Psychological Association.

Leonardi, P. M., Jackson, M. H., & Diwan, A. (2009). The enactment-externalization dialectic: Rationalization and the persistence of counterproductive technology design practices in student engineering. *Academy of Management Journal, 52*, 400–420.

Locke, E. A. (1986). *Generalizing from laboratory to field settings: Research findings from industrial-organizational psychology, organizational behavior, and human resource management*. Lexington, MA: Lexington Books.

McGrath, J. E., Martin, J. M. & Kukla, R. A. (1982). *Judgment calls in research*. Beverly Hills, CA: Sage Publications.

Mohammed, S., Klimoski, R., & Rentsch, J. R. (2000). The measurement of team mental models: We have no shared schema. *Organizational Research Methods, 3*, 123–165.

Morrison, E. W. (2002). Information seeking within organizations. *Human Communication Research, 28*, 229–242.

Motowidlo, S. J. (2003). Job performance. In W. C. Borman, D. R. Ilgen, & R. J. Klimoski (Eds.), *Handbook of psychology: Industrial and organizational psychology* (Vol. 12, Chapter 3, pp. 39–54). Hoboken, NJ: Wiley.

Mellor, S., & Mark, M. M. (1998). A quasi-experimental design for studies on the impact of administrative decisions: Applications and extensions of the regression-discontinuity design. *Organizational Research Methods, 1*, 315–333.

Miller, G. A., & Chapman, J. P. (2001). Misunderstanding analysis of covariance. *Journal of Abnormal Psychology, 110*, 40–48.

Murphy, K. R., & Cleveland, J. N. (1995). *Understanding performance appraisal: Social, organizational, and goal-based perspectives*. Thousand Oaks, CA: Sage.

Ostroff, C., & Kozlowski, S. W. J. (1992). Organizational socialization as a learning process: The role of information acquisition. *Personnel Psychology, 45*, 849–874.

Pinto, I. R., Marques, J. M., Levine, J. M., & Abrams, D. (2010). Membership status and subjective group dynamics: Who triggers the black sheep effect? *Journal of Personality and Social Psychology, 99*, 107–119.

Ployhart, R. E., & Vandenberg, R. J. (2010). Longitudinal research: The theory, design, and analysis of change. *Journal of Management, 36*, 94–120.

Poncheri, R. M., Lindberg, J. T., Thompson, L. F., & Surface, E. A. (2008). A comment on employee surveys: Negativity bias in open-ended responses. *Organizational Research Methods, 11*, 614–630.

Putka, D. J. (2002). The variance architecture approach to the study of constructs in organizational contexts. Ph.D. dissertation, Ohio University, United States — Ohio. Retrieved February 7, 2012, from Dissertations & Theses @ Ohio University.(Publication No. AAT 3062641).

Reise, S. P., Widaman, K. F., & Pugh, R. H. (1993). Confirmatory factor analysis and item response theory: Two approaches for exploring measurement invariance. *Psychological Bulletin, 114*, 552–566.

Reichers, A. E. (1987). An interactionist perspective on newcomer socialization rates. *The Academy of Management Review, 12*, 278–287.

Roethlisberger, F. J., & Dickson, W. J. (1943). *Management and the worker*. Cambridge MA: Harvard University Press.

Runkel, P. J., & McGrath, J. E. (1972). *Research on human behavior: A systematic guide to method*. New York: Holt, Rinehart, & Winston.

Saari, L. M., Johnson, T. R., McLaughlin, S. D., & Zimmerle, D. M. (1988). A survey of management training and education practices in U.S. companies. *Personnel Psychology, 41*, 731–743.

Sackett, P. R. & Larson, J. R. (1990). Research strategies and tactics in industrial and organizational psychology. In M. D. Dunnett & L. M. Hough (Eds.), *Handbook of industrial and organizational psychology* (Vol. 1, pp. 419–489). Palo Alto, CA: Consulting Psychologist Press.

Scandura, T. A., & Williams, E. A. (2000). Research methodology in management: Current practices, trends, and implications for future research. *Academy of Management Journal, 43*, 1248–1264.

Schonfeld, I. S., & Rindskopf, D. (2007). Hierarchical linear modeling in organizational research: Longitudinal data outside the context of growth modeling. *Organizational Research Methods, 10*, 417–429.

Shadish, W. R., Cook, T. D., & Campbell, D. T. (2002). *Experimental and quasi-experimentation designs for generalized causal inference*. Boston, MA: Houghton Mifflin.

Singer, J. D., & Willett, J. B. (2003a). *Applied longitudinal data analysis: Modeling change and event occurrence*. New York: Oxford University Press.

Singer, J. D., & Willett, J. B. (2003b). Survival analysis. *Handbook of psychology: Research methods in psychology* (Vol. 2, pp. 555–580). Hoboken, NJ: John Wiley & Sons.

Spencer, S. J., Zanna, M. P., & Fong, G. T. (2005). Establishing a causal chain: Why experiments are often more effect than meditational analyses in examining psychological processes. *Journal of Personality and Social Psychology, 89*, 846–851.

Snow, R. E. & Swanson, J. (1992). Instructional psychology: Aptitude, adaptation, and assessment. *Annual Review of Psychology, 43*, 583–626.

Solomon, R. L. (1949). An extension of control group design. *Psychological Bulletin, 46*, 137–150.

Stone-Romero, E. (2011). Research strategies in industrial and organizational psychology: Nonexperimental, quasi-experimental, and randomized experimental research in special purpose and nonspecial purpose settings. In S. Zedeck (Ed.), *APA handbook of industrial and organizational psychology, Vol. 1: Building and developing the organization* (pp. 37–72). Washington, DC: American Psychological Association.

Stone-Romero, E. F., & Rosopa, P. J. (2004). Inference problems with hierarchical multiple regression-based tests of mediating effects. *Research in Personnel and Human Resource Management, 23*, 249–290.

Stone-Romero, E., Weaver, A. E., & Glenar, J. L. (1995). Trends in research design and data analytic strategies in organizational research. *Journal of Management, 21*, 141–157.

Strauss, A., & Corbin, J. (1994). Grounded theory methodology: An overview. *Handbook of qualitative research*. (pp. 273–285). Sage Publications, Inc, Thousand Oaks, CA, US.

Sun, R. (2008). Introduction to computational cognitive modeling. *The Cambridge handbook of computational psychology* (pp. 3–19). New York: Cambridge University Press.

Taormina, R. J. (1994). The organizational socialization inventory. *International Journal of Selection and Assessment, 2*, 133–145.

Trist, E. L. (1981). The social-technical perspective. In A. H. Van de Ven & W. R. Joyce (Eds.), *Perspectives on organizational design and behavior* (pp. 19–75). New York: Wiley.

Van Maanen, J., & Schein, E. H. (1979). Toward a theory of organizational socialization. In B. Staw (Ed.), *Research in organizational behavior* (Vol. I, pp. 209–269). Greenwich, CT: JAI Press.

Vancouver, J. B., More, K. M., & Yoder, R. J. (2008). Self-efficacy and resource allocation: Support for a discontinuous model. *Journal of Applied Psychology, 93*, 35–47.

Vancouver J. B., Putka, D. J., & Scherbaum, C. A. (2005). Testing a computational model of the goal-level effect: An example of a neglected methodology. *Organizational Research Methods, 8*, 100–127.

Vancouver, J. B., Tamanini, K. B., & Yoder, R. J. (2010). Using dynamic computational models to reconnect theory and research: Socialization by the proactive newcomer example. *Journal of Management, 36*, 764–793.

Vancouver, J. B., Thompson, C. M., & Williams, A. A. (2001). The changing signs in the relationships between self-efficacy, personal goals and performance. *Journal of Applied Psychology, 86*, 605–620.

Vidmar, N. (1979). The other issues in jury simulation research: A commentary with particular reference to defendant character studies. *Law and Human Behavior, 3*, 95–106.

Weiss, H. M. (1990). Learning theory and industrial and organizational psychology. In M. D. Dunnette & L. M. Hough (Eds.), *The handbook of industrial/organizational psychology* (2nd ed., pp. 171–222). Palo Alto, CA: Consulting Psychologists Press.

Wesson, M. J., & Gogus, C. I. (2005). Shaking hands with a computer: An examination of two methods of organizational newcomer orientation. *Journal of Applied Psychology, 90*, 1018–1026.

Yeo, G. B., & Neal, A. (2006). An examination of the dynamic relationship between self-efficacy and performance across levels of analysis and levels of specificity. *Journal of Applied Psychology, 91*, 1088–1101.

PART 5

Specialized Contexts

The Impact of Socializing
Newcomers on Insiders

Daniel C. Feldman

Abstract

While much of the previous research on organizational socialization has focused on how supervisors and coworkers influence the entry of new entrants into the firm, surprisingly little attention has been given to how the socialization of new employees influences insiders. This paper examines how the entry of newcomers (both new entrants into the workforce and experienced workers changing employers) influences insiders' self-perceptions, how participating in the socialization process influences insiders' attitudes toward their firms, and when insiders will be receptive to change attempts from new hires. The chapter concludes with directions for future research on mutual influence processes during organizational socialization.

Key Words: socialization, organizational socialization, mutual influence, influence, newcomers

From its earliest years, organizational socialization has been seen as a two-way, mutual influence process (Feldman, 1976; Schein, 1968; Van Maanen, 1976; Van Maanen & Schein, 1979). While a firm's "insiders" are certainly likely to have more influence on "newcomers" than vice versa, it is also true that the entry of newcomers can change the groups into which they are being integrated (Bauer, Bodner, Erdogan, Truxillo, & Tucker, 2007; Reichers, 1987). Moreover, newcomers can be a positive influence for constructive change and innovation within organizations (Ashforth, Sluss, & Harrison, 2007; Fisher, 1986). Rather than forcing new entrants to adhere to rigid role demands and group norms, firms can use the entry of newcomers to "unfreeze" the workgroup, that is, as an opportunity to rethink work processes, patterns of social interaction, and even the group's core values and beliefs (Brett, 1984; Nicholson, 1984). In short, the entry of newcomers—whether they are new entrants into the workforce or veteran workers coming in at higher levels of organizations—creates more opportunities for change and greater

impetus to embrace it (Feldman, 1994; Moreland & Levine, 2001; Van Viaanen, 2000).

Perhaps surprisingly, relatively little research has been conducted on the reciprocal influence loop, namely, how insiders respond to the entry and socialization of newcomers (Bauer & Green, 1998). The majority of research in this area has been conducted on the tactics organizations use to socialize young adults making the transition from school to work and the relationships of these tactics to newcomer adjustment (Ashforth & Saks, 1996; Baker & Feldman, 1990; Cable & Parsons, 2001; Gruman, Saks, & Zweig, 2006; Van Maanen, 1978). The socialization of job changers (that is, experienced workers changing firms) has received less attention (Feldman & Brett, 1983), except for two special cases: the relationships between new CEOs and boards of directors (Bennis & Biederman, 1997; Finkelstein, 2003; Gandossy & Sonnenfeld, 2005; Groysberg, 2010; Ward & Feldman, 2008) and the relationships between newly arrived expatriates and repatriates with host nationals and back-home colleagues (e.g., Black, 1992; Feldman & Tompson, 1993).

To be sure, in recent years there has been more research conducted on the level of newcomers' proactivity and how it signifies a successful adjustment to new jobs (Ashford & Black, 1996; Bauer & Green, 1998; Brett, Feldman, & Weingart, 1990; Crant, 2000; Morrison, 1993a, b; Wanberg & Kammeyer-Mueller, 2003). Even here, though, the focus has been on newcomers' willingness to push for change rather than on veteran employees' responsiveness to those requests or how the entry of middle-level and upper-level managers changes the work experiences of insiders. With few exceptions (Feldman, 1994; Slaughter & Zickar, 2006; Sutton & Louis, 1987) there has been little research conducted on how the self-perceptions of "insiders" change as the result of integrating newcomers, how socializing newcomers changes insiders' perceptions of their organizations, and when insiders will be most receptive to change attempts from newcomers. This chapter addresses each of these topics in turn.

Impact of Socializing Newcomers on Insiders' Self-Perceptions

There are a variety of ways in which the socialization of newcomers influences insiders' self-perceptions: how they view their own career success, whether they perceive they are treated equitably, how tied they feel to their current jobs, and how marketable they view themselves to be in the external labor market. As Louis (1980) notes, the socialization process creates uncertainty for newcomers; as a result, their attention is drawn to the surprises, novelties, and contrasts in their environments. A parallel process occurs for insiders. The entry of newcomers focuses insiders' attention on surprising or discrepant information which they discover while recruiting and integrating newcomers (Mignerey, Rubin, & Gorden, 1995). As a result, insiders may be prompted to reflect upon (or change) their perceptions of their own careers, how well they fit into their current positions, and their standing relative to coworkers and new hires. The surprises, novelties, and contrasts insiders perceive when more experienced workers enter their midst can be just as startling as those perceived when recent graduates enter the workplace.

Self-Perceptions of Career Success

Careers researchers usually make a distinction between "objective" career success (e.g., salary and hierarchical level achieved) and "subjective" career success (e.g., feelings of achievement and job satisfaction), although there is certainly some correlation between them (Klein, Fan, & Preacher, 2006; Ng, Eby, Sorensen, & Feldman, 2005). The process of recruiting, selecting, and socializing newcomers impacts how individuals view both types of career success.

The entry of newcomers presents insiders with an impetus to revise self-perceptions of their own objective career success relative to the objective career success of newcomers. During the recruitment and selection process, insiders see a wide variety of candidates and hear a wide variety of views about how candidates stack up against each other. As a result, insiders receive additional feedback regarding how their own credentials would stack up against what is considered desirable in new candidates and which criteria for advancement matter most to their employers (e.g., value placed on international experience vs. value placed on amount of supervisory experience). Jones and Gerard (1967) refer to this phenomenon as *comparative appraisal,* a process in which individuals use their observations of how others are treated to infer where they themselves stand with their employers.

Further, for those who view their career trajectories as linear (Driver, 1979), the entry of newcomers gives insiders the opportunity to recalibrate self-perceptions about how far they have come relative to their competition in the labor market (Klein, Fan, & Preacher, 2006). For example, Rosenbaum's (1979) "tournament model" suggests that there are contests for advancement at various stages of managerial careers and that, once a manager has lost one of those contests, his/her future rate of career advancement is slower. Feldman (1988) suggests that there are norms regarding how far employees should have risen by different ages; moreover, individuals' career advancement (as defined by hierarchical promotions) is disadvantaged when their age and career stage are out of sync. Seeing how far newcomers have come, then, prompts insiders to gauge their own "objective" career success (Ng et al., 2005).

Where the effects of socializing newcomers on insiders' perceptions of objective career success are *direct,* the effects of socializing newcomers on insiders' perceptions of "subjective" career success are *indirect* in nature. While certainly individuals' perceptions of poor objective career success are likely to influence their feelings of subjective career success, there are other factors besides salary and hierarchical promotions that affect feelings of subjective career success. For example, despite not having rapid advancement or a high salary, employees can be highly satisfied with the amount of work–family balance they have achieved or the positive impact they have on the lives of others (Liden, Wayne, & Sparrowe, 2000; Ng et al., 2005; Van Viaanen, 2000). In addition, norms about the "right" career path have become more nebulous over time and vertical mobility is not the only yardstick insiders use to measure either type of career success (Arthur & Rousseau, 1996; Sullivan, 1999).

It is also interesting to note here that being a socialization agent (participating in the recruiting, selection, and socialization process) can enhance employees' perceptions of themselves as helpful and nurturing organizational citizens (Feldman, 1994; Jokisaari & Nurmi, 2009; Sutton & Lewis, 1987). This enhancement of self-image is especially likely to occur for insiders who are actively and constructively involved in the mentoring of newcomers (Hallier & James, 1999; Ostroff & Kozlowski, 1992; Scandura, 1998; Slaughter & Zickar, 2006).

Self-Perceptions of Inequitable Treatment

The socialization of newcomers also opens up questions for insiders about equity and the fairness with which their employers treat them (Feldman, 1994). Although organizations may try to keep salary packages secret, it is frequently possible for insiders to discover how much newcomers are being paid (Schuster & Zingheim, 1992). In assessing the fairness of their rewards, insiders tend to compare themselves to "similar up" referents, that is, colleagues who are doing similar work but are being more highly rewarded than they are (Kulik & Ambrose, 1992). Consequently, insiders are especially likely to be dissatisfied if newcomers in similar jobs receive greater compensation, even if they intellectually understand the issues surrounding pay compression in internal labor markets (Heneman & Schwab, 1985).

While some of the social comparisons insiders make involve salary and compensation, insiders also make comparisons in terms of perceived organizational support (Rhoades, Eisenberg, & Armeli, 2001) and idiosyncratic employment deals ("I-deals") involving flexible schedules and work-from-home arrangements (Rousseau, Ho, & Greenberg, 2006). Relative deprivation theory may be particularly useful in understanding these social comparisons, because it helps explain how individuals deal with discrepancies between what they have, what they want, what they expect, and what they feel entitled to (Crosby, 1976; Feldman,

Leana, & Turnley, 1997; Sweeney, McFarlin, & Inderrieden, 1990).

When insiders view themselves as fairly or even over-rewarded relative to newcomers, their sense of self-worth is enhanced and their identification with the organization is strengthened. However, when insiders perceive that newcomers are getting employment arrangements they perceive as inequitable (e.g., newcomers are given lower workloads, or organizations create jobs for newcomers' spouses), they can respond in a variety of ways that are not in the company's best interest. One way insiders can respond is to lower their level of identification with their employers, thereby distancing themselves psychologically from their organizations (Ng & Feldman, 2008). Another way that insiders can resolve the discrepancy is to raise their sense of entitlement and expectations of what their rewards should be. That is, if newcomers with no experience receive X dollars, experienced insiders might estimate they should receive at least X + 10%. It is also theoretically possible that individuals could lower self-perceptions of their abilities in order to bring their perceived inputs and outcomes into equilibrium. However, that scenario is less likely to occur since individuals generally try to see themselves in as favorable a light as possible (Fine & Nevo, 2008).

Self-Perceptions of Embeddedness and Marketability

One of the goals of many organizational socialization programs is to embed new hires within the firm (Allen, 2006). *Embeddedness* refers to the forces that keep individuals tied to their firms (Mitchell, Holtom, Lee, Sablynski, & Erez, 2001). In the embeddedness literature, high perceived levels of person–job fit, extensive links with coworkers and others in the profession, and high perceived levels of sacrifice associated with leaving all serve to enmesh employees in their current firms (Mitchell et al., 2001).

During the recruitment and selection process, companies try to find applicants who have the kinds of skills and values to fit in and adjust to the organization (Kristof-Brown, Zimmerman, & Johnson, 2005; Pinder & Schroeder, 1987; Van Viaanen, 2000). During the socialization process itself, organizations also try to encourage the development of positive interpersonal relationships with insiders to make sure newcomers feel welcome (Feldman, 1977; Kim, Cable, & Kim, 2005; Saks, Uggerslev, & Fassina, 2007). In addition, by providing desirable financial rewards and challenging work environments to new hires, organizations try to lower newcomers' desires or incentives to leave for other job opportunities (Chatman, 1991; Lewicki, 1981). In short, the socialization process is the first powerful tool organizations can use to embed new employees for long periods of time (Ng & Feldman, 2007).

For instance, there is evidence from the literature on job attitudes that when employees verbalize positive statements about their firms to others, those positive attitudes are reinforced in their own minds (Salancik & Pfeffer, 1978; Sutton & Louis, 1987). From this perspective, then, the act of selling recruits on their organizations makes the positive features of those firms more salient to insiders and raises their attachment to organizations (Berger & Luckman, 1966; Feldman, 1994). Cognitive dissonance research makes much the same prediction (McGuire, 1985). When insiders conform to norms during recruiting to portray reality with a positive spin, insiders are likely to reduce cognitive dissonance by revising their job attitudes in a more positive direction.

It should be noted, though, that socializing newcomers can also inadvertently start a "dislodging" process. As described above, in the process of recruiting and socializing newcomers, insiders may come to perceive that they are undervalued in their present firms, or they may come to believe that any sacrifices associated with leaving are modest compared to the greater rewards they could receive from other firms. Ironically, the act of socializing newcomers can also lead to expanded social networks, as insiders develop new links with people recommending candidates for jobs or scan the environment to benchmark salary offers in competitor firms (Morrison, 2002a; Van Maanen & Barley, 1984). Thus, by exposing insiders to greater information about, and links to, the external labor market, socializing newcomers can also serve to dislodge insiders from their current positions (Ng & Feldman, 2010).

Self-Perceptions of Ethical and Honest Behavior

The final set of self-perceptions addressed here concern insiders' perceptions of themselves as honest and ethical individuals. There is certainly a growing realization in firms that giving recruits more realistic previews of work environments ultimately lowers quick post-entry turnover and inoculates newcomers to inevitable disappointments they will face after they arrive (Wanous & Colella, 1989). At the same time, there is also often a great deal of selling in the recruitment process. Insiders are expected to put on a positive face to the outside world and to present a relatively rosy picture of reality to recruits and newcomers (Carr, Pearson, Vest, & Boyar, 2006; Miller & Jablin, 1991).

During the socialization process, these acts of selling can lower insiders' self-esteem in two ways. First, insiders frequently resort to impression management techniques in selling applicants on accepting job offers and/or in helping newcomers cope with disappointments after they arrive. Just as applicants try to self-promote their successes and personally distance themselves from past failures (Dougherty, Turban, & Callender, 1994; Wayne & Liden, 1995), so, too, do organizations (Fletcher, 1989). Insiders try to minimize the failures and exaggerate the successes of their organizations in order to enhance the firm's reputation in the eyes of potential employees (Gatewood, Gowan, & Lautenschlager, 1993). Second, socializing newcomers often takes a considerable amount of emotional labor (Morris & Feldman, 1996); acting more positively than one feels is emotionally exhausting. Consequently, when insiders have to act in ways that skirt the truth or that deceive newcomers during the socialization process, their perceptions of themselves as honest and ethical individuals may be disconfirmed as well (Jansen & Von Glinow, 1985).

Impact of Socialization Process on Insiders' Attitudes and Perceptions of Organizations

In addition to influencing insiders' self-perceptions, the socialization of newcomers also influences insiders' perceptions of their employers and their attitudes toward them. This section focuses on how the socialization of newcomers can influence insiders' global perceptions of the organization as a place to work, their attitudes toward specific facets of the work environment, and their perceptions of organizational values and priorities.

While one of the main goals of the socialization process is to provide newcomers with the information needed to be effective organizational members (Feldman, 1981; Major, Kozlowski, Chao, & Gardner, 1995; Morrison, 1993a, b), the socialization process also presents an opportunity for insiders to increase their own knowledge about the organization (Sutton & Louis, 1987). In trying to answer questions for newcomers, insiders are prompted to seek out additional information about policies, procedures, and institutional history (Ashford & Cummings, 1983; Ashford & Taylor, 1990). Moreover, just as newcomers try to obtain information during their socialization process, insiders also use participation in the socialization process to reduce uncertainty about their environments. Thus, insiders, too, engage in "sensemaking" as they reconstruct their own schema for explaining how their organization operates (Weick, 1977).

Global Perceptions of the Organization as a Place to Work

Being involved in the recruitment and selection of job applicants creates opportunities for employees to get feedback from the environment about how their organization is perceived by outsiders. If the recruiting process goes well (e.g., the applicant pool is large and talented and most of the applicants chosen accept the job offers), insiders' positive images of their employers are confirmed and their perceptions of the organization become more favorable (LeVine & Campbell, 1972). However, when the recruiting process goes poorly (e.g., the applicant pool is small, good candidates in the external market do not apply, and the best candidates turn down job offers), insiders' impressions of their firm as a good place to work may be disconfirmed. To resolve this cognitive dissonance, insiders are most likely to become less favorably inclined toward their employers because they cannot ignore the hard, objective feedback they receive from the environment. A low "yield rate," then, deflates unrealistically high images of the organization as a place to work (Feldman, 1994).

Specific Job Attitudes

The process of recruiting, selecting, and socializing new employees also increases the amount of time and energy insiders invest in scanning the external environment (Sutton & Louis, 1987). The most obvious part of this scanning involves identifying viable job candidates, but the scanning involves more than this specific task. In addition, it includes benchmarking salary and employment deals with competitor firms and finding out how other organizations entice job applicants to accept job offers and remain committed to their firms.

As a result of this environmental scanning, insiders discover how their employer stacks up against other firms in the industry and geographical region (Chatman & Jehn, 1994). Kulik and Ambrose (1992) note that people tend to make comparisons "similar up"; that is, they tend to compare themselves to others who are basically similar to themselves but in somewhat better circumstances. Consequently, insiders often find that their salaries have fallen below the outside market or that the work demands placed on them are much greater than those placed on colleagues elsewhere. Rousseau (1995) has noted that sometimes new employees change their perceptions of their psychological contracts retrospectively as they discover friends at other firms have better deals than they do. Much the same process can occur for insiders, too. By discovering how their own employment deals stack up against the contracts being offered by competitors, insiders' attitudes toward specific job facets they find lacking (e.g., scheduling flexibility or training opportunities) become more negative as well (Robinson, Kraatz, & Rousseau, 1994; Robinson & Morrison, 2000).

Perceptions of Organization's Values

Top management provides employees with various signals regarding the firm's overall strategy and values (Ouchi & Jaeger, 1982; Pfeffer, 1982). In some cases these signals come from formal communications such as annual reports, news releases, and mission statements. In other cases, though, these signals come from choices management makes when two strongly held values (e.g., supporting diversity and hiring the best available candidate) collide. The decisions senior management makes in these situations reveal their true preferences to others (Goodstein, Gautum, & Boeker, 1994).

Particularly in the recruitment and selection portions of the socialization process, insiders are faced with choices among candidates who have different strengths and weaknesses. The choices ultimately made by insiders reflect where the core priorities and preferences of the work unit reside. In fact, the organization's priorities and value hierarchies become clarified through the socialization process (Van Maanen, 1983, 1984). Thus, the choice of a leader with strong operational experience over a leader with a strong vision sends a signal about which attribute—vision vs. efficiency—is more valued by the firm.

It is also worth noting here that changes in insiders' perceptions of organizational values influence insiders' attitudes toward the firm. When insiders agree with the "revealed preferences" of organizations, attachment to employers (in terms of commitment, involvement, and identification) is strengthened. In contrast, when insiders discover that the organization's actions are not consistent with its espoused values, their levels of attachment to employers are likely to decline (Gatewood et al., 1993; Kristof, 1996; Slaughter & Zickar, 2006).

Furthermore, conflicts over priorities and value hierarchies in these selection decisions often spill over and lower the quality of relationships insiders have with each other, and with the newcomers themselves, at work. Finding out whose values are upheld and whose values are set aside leads employees to reassess the quality of their relationships with others in their firms (Northcraft & Ashford, 1990). For those insiders whose values triumph, the quality of leader–member exchanges, coworker exchanges, and perceived organizational support are likely to increase (Duarte, Goodson, & Klich, 1993; Rhoades, Eisenberger, & Armeli, 2001). However, for those insiders whose values are not supported by recruitment and selection decisions, the level of attachment to supervisors and coworkers is likely to decline (Feldman, 1984). Indeed, disappointed insiders may psychologically withdraw from newcomers and provide them with less mentoring during the socialization process (Scandura, 1998; Scandura & Schriesheim, 1994).

Insiders' Responses to Newcomer Proactivity

Over the past 20 years there has been increased focus on how proactive newcomers are in learning about their new environments and how that proactivity facilitates adjustment to new jobs (Cooper-Thomas & Andersen, 2005; Feldman & Brett, 1983; Finkelstein, Kulas, & Dages, 2003; Kammeyer-Mueller & Wanberg, 2003). In addition, there has been some research on how newcomers try to change their new work environments (Ashford & Black, 1996; Chan & Schmitt, 2000; Chen, 2005; Toffler, 1981; Wanberg & Kammeyer-Mueller, 2000). There has been much less research, though, on how insiders react to newcomers' efforts to change the norms of the work group, the division of labor within the team, organizational policies and procedures, and even the culture of the organization as a whole (Erdogan & Bauer, 2005; Feldman, 1994; Van Viaanen, 2000).

Insiders' responses to newcomer proactivity are important to consider for a variety of reasons. First, insiders exert enormous control over whether proposed changes are viewed as reasonable and feasible (Abrahamson, 1991; Huber, 1991). Second, even if newcomers' ideas are adopted by senior managers, insiders play a major role in whether these changes are implemented successfully or undermined covertly (Haveman, 1992; Marcus, 1988). Third, if insiders perceive they will lose valued resources as a result of proposed changes, organizations may experience increased turnover among some veteran insiders whom they would like to keep (Armenakis,

Harris, & Mossholder, 1993). Thus, as critical as it is to understand when newcomers will become active participants in their own socialization process, it is equally critical to understand when insiders will embrace (or reject) the changes newcomers seek.

Major changes in organizations are inherently political in nature; the "best" or "most rational" idea does not necessarily triumph on its sheer merits (Cobb & Margulies, 1981; Frost & Egri, 1991). Moreover, large bureaucratic organizations are especially slow and resistant to major changes (Daft, 1982). The next section explores when insiders are most likely to be receptive to newcomers' ideas and take them as constructive ways of improving organizations; the section following addresses when insiders are most likely to adopt these changes and implement them conscientiously and/or enthusiastically.

Receptivity to Change
ORGANIZATIONAL PERFORMANCE

There is substantial evidence that firms experiencing declines in growth or declines in profit might be more open to change than firms whose apparent success is continuing (Goodstein, Gautam, & Boeker, 1994; Grosyberg, 2010). For example, in the literature on CEO succession, researchers have found that "outsiders" are more likely to be chosen when the firm's performance has been declining over time (Haveman, 1992; Sonnenfeld & Ward, 2007). The research on "change readiness" also suggests that the "unfreezing" process for change requires some disconfirming, negative event to force individuals to think about their circumstances differently (Lewin, 1951; Marcus, 1988). Indeed, in some cases the hiring of numerous newcomers is itself seen as a mandate for change (Gaertner, Gaertner, & Akinnusi, 1984; Singh, House, & Tucker, 1986).

RELATIONAL DEMOGRAPHY

Another factor that influences insiders' receptivity to change is relational demography (Jackson, Stone, & Alvarez, 1993; Kirchmeyer, 1995). Insiders are more likely to support change when the advocates of that change are similar to themselves in terms of demographic or educational background (Green, Anderson, & Shivers, 1996; O'Reilly, Caldwell, & Barnett, 1989).

Interestingly, though, in his work on "chains of socialization," Van Maanen (1983, 1984) argues that professional organizations try to recruit newcomers from backgrounds similar to their own not only to shorten the socialization process but also to ensure that newcomers will "buy in" to the present culture.

As a result, the greater the demographic similarity between insiders and newcomers the more likely insiders will be receptive to recommendations put forth by newcomers—but the less likely newcomers will be to push for radical or major reforms.

TYPE OF JOB TRANSITION

As Nicholson (1984) notes, the types of job transitions newcomers make can have a major influence on how receptive insiders are to their ideas. Two attributes of job transitions, in particular, have been studied in the context of mutual influence.

First, researchers have made a distinction between the school-to-work transition and work-to-work transitions – that is, between the organizational entry of recent graduates and the entry of employees with more prior work history (Chao, O'Leary-Kelly, Wolf, Klein, & Gardner, 1994; Morrison, 2002b). In general, the research suggests that employees who have greater work experience are more effective in getting their ideas taken seriously (Feldman, 1989a, b). One reason for this finding may be that prior work experience enhances the credibility of newcomers who are recommending changes (Feldman & Brett, 1983; Rollag, 2004). Another reason may be that insiders can characterize the ideas of individuals making the school-to-work transition as naïve or ill-informed and, in so doing, discount the legitimacy of their suggestions (Carr, Pearson, Vest, & Boyar, 2006; Lancaster & Stillman, 2002).

Second, researchers make a distinction between domestic job transitions and cross-national job changes (Black, 1992). Previous research suggests that although expatriates are often sent overseas to transfer knowledge and improve work processes, they are typically far outnumbered by local employees who are suspicious of outsiders' ideas for change. As a result, "host nationals" may be surprisingly unreceptive to recommended changes despite the technical knowledge base and/or hierarchical level of new expatriates (Feldman & Thomas, 1992; Feldman & Tompson, 1992). In contrast, while repatriates do have trouble finding new positions that utilize their overseas experience, their ideas for changing how headquarters deals with overseas subsidiaries and joint ventures tend to gain more traction because repatriates are seen as having rare tacit knowledge about foreign operations (Feldman, 1991; Stroh, 1995).

CONSISTENCY OF FEEDBACK

As noted earlier, insiders engage in sensemaking during the socialization process. The more consistent the feedback received during the recruitment, selection, and socialization process, the more likely insiders will be receptive to the suggestions of newcomers who advocate change. For example, in cases where the feedback from job candidates (both those who accepted job offers and those who rejected them) consistently indicates that the firm is too inflexible regarding telecommuting, insiders may be more receptive to newcomers championing changes in work schedules (Garvin, 1993; Huber, 1991). However, in cases where the feedback from newcomers (and others whom insiders communicated with during recruitment) varies widely, insiders are less likely to conclude that change is needed (Abrahamson, 1991; Martin & Meyerson, 1988; Sanzgiri & Gottlieb, 1992).

COGNITIONS VS. CULTURES

Last here, the socialization literature suggests that insiders are receptive to accepting changes based on additional or different cognitive information provided by newcomers (Ahuja & Galvin, 2003; Nonaka & Takeuchi, 1995). Newcomers feel that actively engaging insiders in discussions regarding new or objectively different information is socially appropriate and less threatening to insiders, particularly when those communications take place via "lean" media such as e-mail (Ahuja et al., 2003; Nonaka et al., 1995).

In contrast, insiders are more resistant to accepting changes in core organizational values, beliefs, and norms (Ouchi & Jaeger, 1982; Pfeffer, 1982). Organizational cultures evolve over time in response to historical or recurring environmental demands (Schein, 1985; Weick, 1985). These cultures then become fairly stable as insiders internalize those cultural beliefs more fully—and transmit them to newcomers—over time (Sheridan, 1992). Organizational cultures can and do change—indeed, shifts in the composition of the workforce can be a major impetus for innovation—but insider resistance to this kind of "deep-level" change is much stronger (Kelman, 1961; O'Reilly, Chatman, & Caldwell, 1991).

Implementing Ideas
IDIOSYNCRASY CREDITS

Previous research suggests that insiders are more likely to implement changes recommended by newcomers who are coming in at higher levels of the organization (Feldman, 1984). According to Hollander (1961), high-level newcomers have more freedom to promote innovation because of the goodwill they have accumulated over the course of their careers. These "idiosyncrasy credits to deviate" come from demonstrated expertise, an objective track record of success, and/or formal power that accrues to the position. Newcomers joining the firm at higher levels, therefore, have more clout in pushing their ideas through to implementation (Wiggins, Dill, & Schwartz, 1965).

SIZE OF INCOMING COHORT

The sheer size of the incoming cohort of newcomers also influences its ability to push innovations through to implementation (Kelman, 1961; Sutton & Louis, 1987). Even in big organizations like IBM or the armed forces, large incoming cohorts whose values and preferences are very different from those of insiders can be influential in changing how organizations operate. As the research on conformity and deviance shows, though, a new lone wolf advocating change is unlikely to be successful (Feldman, 1984).

A related factor is the ratio of newcomers to current employees. In firms of 5,000 employees, the entry of 25 newcomers is unlikely to exert much pressure on insiders to change. However, the influx of 3 new basketball players on a team of 5, or the influx of 80 new congressmen out of 435, creates much more pressure to make concrete changes happen.

AVERAGE JOINT TENURE OF INSIDERS

As the literature on top management teams suggest, some lethargy sets in when boards of directors have high average joint tenure (Groysberg, 2010; Sonnenfeld & Ward, 2007). That is, when board directors have served with each other over a long period of time they develop strong norms about how to behave and which goals to pursue. In cases such as these, it is more difficult for one or two newcomers to succeed in making major innovations (Goodstein, Gautum, & Boeker, 1994; Watson et al., 1993).

There has also been some research conducted in the organizational embeddedness literature on insiders' willingness to innovate (Mitchell, Holtom, Lee, Sablynski, & Erez, 2001). Perhaps surprisingly, this research does not find the same effects of job embeddedness on insiders' willingness to innovate as the top management team (TMT) literature does (Ng & Feldman, 2007). In a longitudinal study with a diverse sample, Ng and Feldman (2010) found that job embeddedness was positively and significantly related to innovation-related behaviors, even after controlling for demographic variables and job attitudes. Ng and Feldman (2010) explain these results by positing that highly embedded workers have greater commitment to helping their organizations succeed in the long run and engage in more innovation-related behaviors to that end.

PERCEIVED PSYCHOLOGICAL CONTRACT BREACHES

In the psychological contracts literature, almost all the research has examined how *newcomers* feel when their expectations of their new employers were unfulfilled (Robinson et al., 1994; Rousseau, 1995). These studies suggest that new hires who feel their psychological contracts have been breached will be less conscientious in the performance of their assigned job duties, less willing to engage in citizenship behavior, and less likely to remain as employees of the firm for a long period of time (De Vos, Buyens, & Schalk, 2003; Turnley & Feldman, 1999). In contrast, virtually no attention has been paid to how *insiders* react when newcomers fail to hold up their end of the bargain. The hypothesis proposed here would be that, to the extent newcomers do not deliver the contributions promised ex ante, insiders will be less willing to implement newcomers' ideas post hoc.

Discussion

In this final section, three overarching directions for future research on mutual influence processes are discussed. The first topic is how initial interactions that occur during the socialization process itself might set the tone for future interactions after the formal socialization process is complete. The second topic is the stress that the socialization process puts on insiders. In addition to forcing insiders to reconsider their assumptions about their organizations and their own careers, being a socialization agent takes considerable time and energy and detracts from other job responsibilities. In turn, higher stress levels can impact how carefully insiders attend to newcomers' ideas and how much effort they put into implementing their suggestions. The third topic discussed below is the "poisoned apple" problem, namely, how insiders respond to newcomers whose counterproductive work behaviors outweigh their constructive contributions to group functioning.

Quality of Interactions between Newcomers and Insiders

In previous research studies, a considerable amount of attention has been paid to socialization tactics (Van Maanen & Schein, 1979). Probably the best known typologies of these socialization tactics have been put forth by Van Maanen (1978) and Jones (1986). In general, these tactics have been characterized as "institutional" (large numbers of newcomers going through a highly structured, formal socialization process) or "individualized" (smaller numbers of newcomers going through a more informal, personalized socialization process). In this research stream, the main focus has been on how newcomers respond to these two sets of socialization tactics (Baker & Feldman, 1990, 1991). By and large, the research suggests that newcomers are more proactive when the socialization process is individualized in nature (Ashforth et al., 2007; Louis, Posner, & Powell, 1983; Wanberg et al., 2000).

However, what has not been studied is how these socialization tactics influence insiders' perceptions of newcomers (Wanous & Collela, 1989). For example, do insiders make different attributions about newcomers' competence, creativity, and potential for new ideas when the socialization process is institutionalized rather than individualized? One could argue, for example, that a socialization process that holds newcomers at arms' length might also make insiders less receptive to newcomers' ideas even after the socialization process has ended—either because insiders make the attribution that newcomers have little to offer or because they define influence attempts by newcomers as socially inappropriate.

A related issue is the relationship between the bases of power insiders use to socialize new hires and the subsequent interaction quality between insiders and newcomers. In the leadership literature, scholars have examined the different sources of power that supervisors use to influence the behaviors of subordinates (Podsakoff & Schriesheim, 1985; Kipnis, Schmidt, Swaffin-Smith, & Wilkinson, 1984). A distinction is usually drawn between "position power," which accrues to individuals by virtue of the titles they hold, and "personal power," which accrues to individuals by virtue of their personality, knowledge, and persuasive ability.

While taxonomies of socialization tactics have dominated much of the research on insiders' approaches to socialization, another way of approaching this topic is considering the bases of power insiders use and how those bases of power impact subsequent relationships with newcomers. When insiders rely on legitimate power and coercive power to bring newcomers into line, initial assumptions about relative expertise and influence are formed and set the norms for future interactions

between them (Feldman, 1984). In these kinds of socialization processes, newcomers learn not to be proactive and insiders learn not to give in to newcomers' demands, if for no other reason than it would be a sign of weakness to do so. In contrast, when insiders rely on personal power to socialize newcomers, a very different set of norms and behavior patterns emerge. In this scenario, engaging in constructive dialogue is encouraged; newcomers feel freer to make suggestions and insiders are less defensive about accepting them (Yukl & Tracey, 1992). Thus, linking specific socialization tactics to insiders' power bases and to subsequent interaction patterns is a fruitful avenue for future research.

Socializing Newcomers as a Stressor

An underexplored topic in the research on organizational socialization has been the time demands and role demands placed upon socialization agents (insiders who are responsible for the recruitment, selection, and socialization of new hires). What has often been ignored in this literature is the fact that recruiting, selecting, and socializing new hires takes a great deal of time if it is to be done properly (Feldman, 1994). With perhaps the exception of human resource professionals, who participate in these activities as a regular part of their jobs, most insiders are having their workload increased by being part of the socialization process. There are two ways in which this increased stress can influence insiders' behaviors toward newcomers.

First, the more frequently insiders are called upon to socialize newcomers and the longer the formal socialization process lasts, the greater the strain being placed on socialization agents (Doby & Caplan, 1995; Nelson & Sutton, 1990). Over time, the demands of being socialization agents, particularly when newcomers are perceived as being entitled prima donnas, increases insiders' frustration levels, impatience, and aggressive behavior. In turn, increased frustration, impatience, and aggression lower the quality of insider–newcomer exchanges.

In recent years there has been increased interest in the topic of mentoring and how mentoring can facilitate a positive socialization experience (Scandura, 1998). In organizational cultures that support devoting time to mentoring and providing organizational support to newcomers, the likelihood that more collaborative relationships will develop between newcomers and insiders is certainly higher (Liden, Wayne, & Sparrowe, 2000).

At the same time, though, there has been increasing attention paid to the notion of "toxic mentoring"

(Eby & McManus, 2004; Feldman, 1999). In part, this research emerged as a counterweight to the notion that negative mentoring experiences are entirely due to the behavior of mentors, who are seen as having insufficient ability, willingness, and emotional warmth to support new hires. In part, this research has also examined the ways in which newcomers engage in behaviors that undermine the quality of the mentoring they receive (Turban & Dougherty, 1994). For example, if new hires are poor performers or poor colleagues, that might be the impetus for insiders to minimize contact with them (Porath & Bateman, 2006; Saks & Ashforth, 1996). The stress perspective presented here suggests yet another explanation for insider withdrawal during the socialization process, namely, role overload. As insiders' responsibilities expand and time demands increase, their psychological resources for providing emotional support and frequent task assistance are simply depleted (Williams & Alliger, 1994).

Second, increased stress on the part of socialization agents decreases their ability to hear and incorporate new information, particularly if that information is inconsistent with what they expect to hear (Miller & Jablin, 1991; Morrison, 1993a, b). When insiders are highly stressed themselves, they are less likely to attend to communication from others, especially those coming "bottom up" (Ginrich & Soli, 1984; Langer & Schank, 1994). This narrowing of the perceptual field is further exacerbated when the information being presented by newcomers is discrepant with insiders' currently-held beliefs (Kahneman & Tversky, 1973; Simon, 1987). Consequently, even when newcomers are behaving appropriately and are making reasonable suggestions, high stress levels make it difficult for insiders to hear those ideas accurately, especially when they fly in the face of widely-accepted perceptions within the organization.

Disruptive Newcomer Behavior

The bulk of the extant literature on insiders' contributions to organizations has a positive bias. That is, most of the research on socialization highlights the many ways in which insiders can help workgroups and organizations grow in positive ways (Schein, 1968; Van Maanen, 1976). However, not all newcomers contribute positively to organizational functioning or to group morale. In some cases, despite efforts to the contrary the "new apple spoils the whole bunch." The socialization literature, to date, has not addressed how the entry of even a small number of disruptive new hires (both

absolutely and percentage-wise) can be dysfunctional for the group as a whole.

There are some related findings in the conformity and deviance literature, however, which might shed light on this issue. For example, insiders might be able to shut down a "bad-behaving" newcomer who has just graduated from school because s/he has no "idiosyncrasy credits" (Hollander, 1958). That is, group members build up goodwill by contributing effectively to the attainment of group goals and by enhancing the group's reputation. When newcomers who are recent graduates engage in counterproductive behavior, insiders are more likely to agree to terminate the newcomers' employment contract at the earliest possible date because there is little to lose. On the other hand, it is harder for insiders to fend off the bad behavior of newcomers who enter the firm at higher levels and those with their professional reputations already firmly established. The opinions of experienced newcomers are likely to be taken more seriously by others in the firm more generally, and the external reputation costs of getting rid of a new senior hire quickly can be considerable (Wiggins, Dill, & Schwartz, 1965).

Another finding from the deviance literature is that insiders will be more tolerant of disruptive newcomers when the group or the organization as a whole is meeting its goals (Feldman, 1984). In such cases, insiders may disapprove of deviant behavior but may be willing to give newcomers more slack. However, when insiders are struggling to meet key performance goals, their tolerance for newcomers' disruptive behavior is both more salient and more threatening (Alvarez, 1968; Sampson & Brandon, 1964).

The intergroup conflict literature also provides some insights into the dysfunctional dynamics that can occur when newcomers enter ongoing workgroups. Newcomers may tip the balance of power within a workgroup, particularly in cases where the group operates largely on a democratic basis; the losing coalition will not experience the contributions of the newcomers quite so positively (Alderfer, 1977). Especially newcomers who enter the firm at higher levels can be strong advocates for changes which politically and/or substantively make life for significant segments of the work unit much more unpleasant (Salancik & Pfeffer, 1974). At the minimum, conflicts over values and work procedures initiated by the entry of newcomers can lead to decreased group cohesiveness and fewer enjoyable experiences at work (Hackman, 1976; Lott & Lott, 1965).

Conclusion

Understanding the impact of socialization on insiders is the next frontier for socialization research. At some point, if organizational socialization is to be taken seriously as a two-way influence process, greater attention simply has to be paid to the effects of socialization on insiders, either as active agents of the socialization process or as passive observers of it. By highlighting how the entry of newcomers can influence insiders' self-perceptions, how participating in the socialization process can influence insiders' attitudes toward their firms, and when insiders will be most receptive to change attempts from new hires, this chapter provides a coherent agenda for future theoretical and empirical research on mutual influence processes.

References

Abrahamson, E. (1991). Managerial fads and fashions: The diffusion and rejection of innovations. *Academy of Management Review, 16,* 588–612.

Ahuja, M. K., & Glavin, J. E. (2003). Socialization in virtual groups. *Journal of Management, 29,* 161–185.

Alderfer, C. P. (1977). Group and intergroup relations. In J. R. Hackman & J. L. Suttle (Eds.), *Improving life at work* (pp. 248–253). Santa Monica, CA: Goodyear.

Allen, D. G. (2006). Do organizational socialization tactics influence newcomer embeddedness and turnover? *Journal of Management, 32,* 237–256.

Alvarez, R. (1968). Informal reactions to deviance in simulated work organizations: A laboratory experiment. *American Sociological Review, 33,* 895–912.

Armenakis, A. A., Harris, S. G., & Mossholder, K. W. (1993). Creating readiness for organizational change. *Human Relations, 46,* 681–703.

Arthur, M. B., & Rousseau, D. M. (1996). *The boundaryless career: A new employment principle for a new organizational era.* New York: Oxford University Press.

Ashford, S. J., & Black, J. S. (1996). Proactivity during organizational entry: The role of desire for control. *Journal of Applied Psychology, 81,* 199–214.

Ashford, S. J., & Cummings, L. L. (1983). Feedback as an individual resource: Personal strategies of creating information. *Organizational Behavior and Human Performance, 32,* 370–398.

Ashford, S. J., & Taylor, M. S. (1990). Adaptation to work transitions: An integrative approach. In G. R. Ferris & K. M. Rowland (Eds.), *Research in personnel and human resources management* (Vol. 8, pp. 1–39). Greenwich, CT: JAI Press.

Ashforth, B. E., & Saks, A. M. (1996). Socialization tactics: Longitudinal effects on newcomer adjustment. *Academy of Management Journal, 39,* 149–178.

Ashforth, B. E., Sluss, D. M., & Harrison, S. H. (2007). Socialization in organizational contexts. In G. P. Hodgkinson & J. K. Ford (Eds.), *International Review of Industrial and Organizational Psychology* (Vol. 22, 1–70). New York: Oxford University Press.

Baker, H. E., & Feldman, D. C. (1990). Strategies of organizational socialization and their impact on newcomer adjustment. *Journal of Managerial Issues, 2,* 198–212.

Baker, H. E., & Feldman, D. C. (1991). Linking organizational socialization tactics with corporate human resource management strategies. *Human Resource Management Review, 1,* 193–202.

Bauer, T. N., Bodner, T., Erdogan, B., Truxillo, D. M., & Tucker, J. S. (2007). Newcomer adjustment during organizational socialization: A meta-analytic review of antecedents, outcomes, and methods. *Journal of Applied Psychology, 92,* 707–721.

Bauer, T. N., & Green, S. G. (1998). Testing the combined effects of newcomer information seeking and manager behavior on socialization. *Journal of Applied Psychology, 83,* 72–83.

Bennis, W., & Biederman, P. W. (1997). *Organizing genius: The secrets of creative collaboration.* Reading, MA: Addison-Wesley.

Berger, P., & Luckman, T. (1966). *The social construction of reality: A treatise in the sociology of knowledge.* New York: Anchor Books.

Black, J. S. (1992). Socializing American expatriate mangers overseas: Tactics, tenure, and role innovation. *Group & Organization Management, 17,* 171–192.

Brett, J. M. (1984). Job transitions and personal and role development. In K. M. Rowland & G. R. Ferris (Eds.), *Research in personnel and human resources management* (Vol. 2, pp. 155–185). Greenwich, CT: JAI Press.

Brett, J. M., Feldman, D. C., & Weingart, L. R. (1990). Feedback-seeking behavior of new hires and job changers. *Journal of Management, 16,* 737–749.

Cable, D. M., & Parsons, C. K. (2001). Socialization tactics and person-organization fit. *Personnel Psychology, 54,* 1–23.

Carr, J. C., Pearson, A. W., Vest, M. J., & Boyar, S. L. (2006). Prior occupational experience, anticipatory socialization, and employee retention. *Journal of Management, 32,* 343–359.

Chan, D., & Schmitt, N. (2000). Interindividual differences in intraindividual changes in proactivity during organizational entry: A latent growth modeling approach to understanding newcomer adaptation. *Journal of Applied Psychology, 85,* 190–210.

Chao, G. T., O'Leary-Kelly, A. M., Wolf, S., Klein, H. J., & Gardner, P. D. (1994). Organizational socialization: Its content and consequences. *Journal of Applied Psychology, 79,* 730–743.

Chatman, J. A. (1991). Matching people and organizations: Selection and socialization in public accounting firms. *Administrative Science Quarterly, 36,* 459–484.

Chatman, J. A., & Jehn, K. A. (1994). Assessing the relationship between industry characteristics and organizational culture: How different can you be? *Academy of Management Journal, 37,* 522–533.

Chen, G. (2005). Newcomer adaptation in teams: Multilevel antecedents and outcomes. *Academy of Management Journal, 48,* 101–116.

Cobb, A. T., & Margulies, N. (1981). Organizational development: A political perspective. *Academy of Management Review, 6,* 49–59.

Cooper-Thomas, H. D., & Andersen, N. (2005). Organizational socialization: A field study into socialization success and rate. *International Journal of Selection and Assessment, 13,* 116–128.

Crant, J. M. (2000). Proactive behavior in organizations. *Journal of Management, 26,* 435–462.

Crosby, F. (1976). A model of egoistical relative deprivation. *Psychological Review, 83,* 85–113.

Daft, R. L. (1982). Bureaucratic versus nonbureaucratic structure and the process of innovation and change. In S. B. Bachrach (Eds.), *Research in the sociology of organizations* (Vol. 1, pp. 56–88). Greenwich, CT: JAI Press.

De Vos, A., Buyens, D., & Schalk, R. (2003). Psychological contract development during organizational socialization: Adaptation to reality and the role of reciprocity. *Journal of Organizational Behavior, 24,* 537–559.

Doby, V. J., & Caplan, R. D. (1995). Organizational stress as a threat to reputation: Effects on anxiety at work and at home. *Academy of Management Journal, 38,* 1105–1123.

Dougherty, T. W., Turban, D. B., & Callender, J. C. (1994). Confirming first impressions in the employment interview: A field study of interviewer behavior. *Journal of Applied Psychology, 79,* 659–665.

Driver, M. (1979). Career concepts and career management in organizations. In C.L. Cooper (Ed.), *Behavioral problems in organizations* (pp. 79–139). Englewood Cliffs, NJ: Prentice-Hall.

Duarte, N. T., Goodson, J. R., & Klich, N. R. (1993). How do I like thee? Let me appraise the ways. *Journal of Organizational Behavior, 14,* 239–249.

Eby, L. T., & McManus, S. E. (2004). The protégé's role in negative mentoring experiences. *Journal of Vocational Behavior, 65,* 255–275.

Erdogan, B., & Bauer, T. N. (2005). Enhancing career benefits of employee proactive personality: The role of fit with jobs and organizations. *Personnel Psychology, 58,* 859–891.

Feldman, D. C. (1976). A contingency theory of socialization. *Administrative Science Quarterly, 21,* 433–452.

Feldman, D. C. (1977). The role of initiation activities in socialization. *Human Relations, 30,* 977–990.

Feldman, D. C. (1981). The multiple socialization of organization members. *Academy of Management Review, 6,* 309–318.

Feldman, D. C. (1984). The development and enforcement of group norms. *Academy of Management Review, 9,* 47–53.

Feldman, D. C. (1988). *Managing careers in organizations.* Glenview, IL: Scott Foresman.

Feldman, D. C. (1989a). Careers in organizations: Recent trends and future directions. *Journal of Management, 15,* 135–156.

Feldman, D. C. (1989b). Socialization, resocialization, and training: Reframing the research agenda. In I. L. Goldstein (Ed.), *Training and development in organizations* (pp. 376–416). San Francisco: Jossey-Bass.

Feldman, D. C. (1991). Repatriate moves as career transitions. *Human Resource Management Review, 1,* 163–177.

Feldman, D. C. (1994). Who's socializing whom? The impact of socializing newcomers on insiders, work groups, and organizations. *Human Resource Management Review, 4,* 213–233.

Feldman, D. C. (1999). Toxic mentors or toxic protégés? A critical re-examination of dysfunctional mentoring. *Human Resource Management Review, 9,* 367–386.

Feldman, D. C., & Brett, J. M. (1983). Coping with new jobs: A comparative study of new hires and job changers. *Academy of Management Journal, 26,* 258–272.

Feldman, D. C., & Thomas, D. C. (1992). Career management issues facing expatriates. *Journal of International Business Studies, 23,* 271–293.

Feldman, D. C., & Tompson, H. B. (1992). Entry shock, culture shock: Socializing the new breed of global managers. *Human Resource Management, 31,* 345–362.

Feldman, D. C., & Tompson, H. B. (1993). Expatriation, repatriation, and domestic geographical relocation: An empirical investigation of adjustment to new job assignments. *Journal of International Business Studies, 24,* 507–530.

Feldman, D. C., Leana, C. R., & Turnley, W. H. (1997). A relative deprivation approach to understanding underemployment. In C. L. Cooper & D. M. Rousseau (Eds.), *Trends in Organizational Behavior* (Vol. 4, pp. 43–60). London: Wiley.

Fine, S., & Nevo, B. (2008). Too smart for their own good? A study of perceived cognitive over-qualification in the workforce. *International Journal of Human Resource Management, 19,* 346–355.

Finkelstein, S. (2003). *Why smart executives fail: And what you can learn about their mistakes.* New York: Penguin Books.

Fletcher, C. (1989). Impression management in the selection interview. In R. A. Giacalone & P. Rosenfeld (Eds.), *Impression management in the organization* (pp. 269–282). Hillsdale, NJ: Lawrence Erlbaum Associates.

Finkelstein, L. M., Kulas, J. T., & Dages, K. D. (2003). Age differences in proactive newcomer socialization strategies in two populations. *Journal of Business and Psychology, 17,* 473–502.

Fisher, C. D. (1986). Organizational socialization: An integrative review. In K. Rowland & G.R. Ferris (Eds.), *Research in Personnel and Human Resources Management* (Vol. 4, pp. 101–145). Greenwich, CT: JAI Press.

Frost, P. J., & Egri, C. P. (1991). The political nature of innovation. In L. L. Cummings & B. M. Staw (Eds.), *Research in organizational behavior* (Vol. 13, pp. 229–295). Greenwich, CT: JAI Press.

Gaertner, G. H., Gaertner, K. N., & Akinnusi, D. M. (1984). Environment, strategy, and implementation of administrative change: The case of civil service reform. *Academy of Management Journal, 27,* 525–543.

Gandossy, R., & Sonnenfeld, J. (2005). *Leadership and governance from the inside out.* New York: Wiley.

Garvin, D. (1993). Building a learning organization. *Harvard Business Review, 71*(4), 78–89.

Gatewood, R. D., Gowan, M. A., & Lautenschlager, G. J. (1993). Corporate image, recruitment image, and initial job choice decisions. *Academy of Management Journal, 36,* 414–427.

Ginrich, G., & Soli, S. D. (1984). Subjective evaluation and allocation of resources in routine decision making. *Organizational Behavior and Human Performance, 33,* 187–203.

Goodstein, J., Gautam, K., & Boeker, W. (1994). The effects of board size and diversity on strategic change. *Strategic Management Journal, 15,* 241–250.

Green, S. G., Anderson, S. E., & Shivers, S. L. (1996). Demographic and organizational influences on leader-member exchange and related work attitudes. *Organizational Behavior and Human Decision Processes, 66,* 203–214.

Groysberg, B. (2010). *Chasing stars: The myth of talent and the portability of performance.* Princeton, NJ: Princeton University Press.

Gruman, J. A., Saks, A. M., & Zweig, D. I. (2006). Organizational socialization tactics and newcomer proactive behaviors: An integrative study. *Journal of Vocational Behavior, 69,* 90–104.

Hackman, J. R. (1976). Groups influences on individuals in organizations. In M. D. Dunnette (Ed.), *Handbook of industrial and organizational psychology* (pp. 1455–1526). Chicago: Rand McNally.

Hallier, J., & James, P. (1999). Group rites and trainer wrongs in employee experiences of job change. *Journal of Management Studies, 36,* 45–67.

Haveman, H. A. (1992). Between a rock and a hard place: Organizational change and performance under conditions of fundamental environmental transformation. *Administrative Science Quarterly, 37,* 48–75.

Heneman, H. G. III, & Schwab, D. P. (1985). Pay satisfaction: Its multidimensional nature and measurement. *International Journal of Psychology, 20,* 129–141.

Hollander, E. P. (1958). Conformity, status, and idiosyncrasy credits. *Psychological Review, 65,* 117–127.

Hollander, E. P. (1961). Some effects of perceived status on responses to innovative behavior. *Journal of Abnormal and Social Psychology, 63,* 247–250.

Huber, G. (1991). Organizational learning: The contributing process and the literatures. *Organizational Science, 2,* 88–115.

Jackson, S. E., Stone, V. K., & Alvarez, E.G. (1993). Socialization amidst diversity: The impact of demographics on work team old-timers and newcomers. In L.L. Cummings & B.M. Staw (Eds.), *Research in Organizational Behavior* (Vol. 15, pp. 45–109). Greenwich, CT: JAI Press.

Jansen, E., & Von Glinow, M. A. (1985). Ethical ambivalence and organizational reward systems. *Academy of Management Review, 10,* 814–822.

Jokisaari, M., & Nurmi, J. E. (2009). Change in newcomers' supervisor support and socialization outcomes after organizational entry. *Academy of Management Journal, 52,* 527–544.

Jones, E. E., & Gerard, H. B. (1967). *Foundations of social psychology.* New York: Wiley.

Jones, G. R. (1986). Socialization tactics, self-efficacy, and newcomers' adjustments to organizations. *Academy of Management Journal, 29,* 262–279.

Kahneman, D., & Tversky, A. (1973). On the psychology of prediction. *Psychological Review, 80,* 251–273.

Kammeyer-Mueller, J. D., & Wanberg, C. R. (2003). Unwrapping the organizational entry process: Disentangling multiple antecedents and their pathways to adjustment. *Journal of Applied Psychology, 88,* 779–794.

Kelman, H. C. (1961). Processes of opinion change. *Public Opinion Quarterly, 25,* 57–78.

Kim, T. Y., Cable, D. M., & Kim, S. P. (2005). Socialization tactics, employee proactivity, and person-organization fit. *Journal of Applied Psychology, 90,* 232–241.

Kipnis, D., Schmidt, S. M., Swaffin-Smith, C., & Wilkinson, I. (1984). Patterns of managerial influence: Shotgun managers, tacticians, and bystanders. *Organizational Dynamics, 13,* 58–67.

Kirchmeyer, C. (1995). Demographic similarity to the work group: A longitudinal study of managers at the early career stage. *Journal of Organizational Behavior, 16,* 67–83.

Klein, H. J., Fan, J., & Preacher, K. J. (2006). The effects of early socialization experiences on content mastery and outcomes: A meditational approach. *Journal of Vocational Behavior, 68,* 96–115.

Kristof, A. L. (1996). Person-organization fit: An integrative review of its conceptualizations, measurement, and implications. *Personnel Psychology, 49,* 1–49.

Kristof-Brown, A. L., Zimmerman, R. D., & Johnson, E. C. (2005). Consequences of individuals' fit at work: A meta-analysis of person-job, person-organization, person-group, and person-supervisor fit. *Personnel Psychology, 58,* 281–342.

Kulik, C. T., & Ambrose, M. L. (1992). Personal and situational determinants of referent choice. *Academy of Management Review, 17,* 212–237.

Lancaster, L. C., & Stillman, D. (2002). *When generations collide.* New York: Harper Business.

Langer, E., & Schank, R. C. (1994). *Belief, reasoning, and decision making.* Hillsdale, NJ: Lawrence Erlbaum Associates.

LeVine, R. A., & Campbell, D. T. (1972). *Ethnocentrism: Theories of conflict, ethnic attitudes, and group behavior.* New York: Wiley.

Lewicki, R. J. (1981). Organizational seduction: Building commitment to organizations. *Organizational Dynamics, 10,* 5–22.

Lewin, K. (1951). *Field theory in social science.* New York: Harper & Row.

Liden, R., Wayne, S., & Sparrowe, R. (2000). An examination of the mediating role of psychological empowerment on the relations between the job, interpersonal relationships, and work outcomes. *Journal of Applied Psychology, 83,* 407–416.

Lott, A. J., & Lott, B. E. (1965). Group cohesiveness as interpersonal attraction: A review of relationships with antecedent and consequent variables. *Psychological Bulletin, 64,* 259–309.

Louis, M. R. (1980). Surprise and sense making: What newcomers experience in unfamiliar organizational settings. *Administrative Science Quarterly, 25,* 226–251.

Louis, M. R., Posner, B. Z., & Powell, G. N. (1983). The availability and helpfulness of socialization practices. *Personnel Psychology, 36,* 857–866.

Major, D. A., Kozlowski, S. W. J., Chao, G. T., & Gardner, P. D. (1995). A longitudinal investigation of newcomer expectations, early socialization outcomes, and the moderating effects of role development factors. *Journal of Applied Psychology, 80,* 418–431.

Marcus, A. A. (1988). Implementing externally induced innovations: A comparison of rule-bound and autonomous approaches. *Academy of Management Journal, 31,* 235–256.

Martin, J., & Meyerson, D. (1988). Organizational cultures and the denial, channeling, and acknowledgement of ambiguity. In L. R. Pondy, R. J. Boland, Jr., & H. Thomas (Eds.), *Managing ambiguity and change* (pp. 93–125). New York: Wiley.

McGuire, W. J. (1985). Attitudes and attitude change. In G. Lindzey & E. Aronson (Eds.), *Handbook of social psychology* (3rd ed., Vol. 2, pp. 233–346). New York: Random House.

Mignerey, J. T., Rubin, R. B., & Gorden, W. I. (1995). Organizational entry: An investigation of newcomer communication behavior and uncertainty. *Communication Research, 22,* 54–85.

Miller, V. D., & Jablin, F. M. (1991). Information seeking during organizational entry: Influences, tactics, and a model of the process. *Academy of Management Review, 16,* 92–120.

Mitchell, T. R., Holtom, B. C., Lee, T. W., Sablynski, C. J., & Erez, M. (2001). Why people stay: Using job embeddedness to predict voluntary turnover. *Academy of Management Journal, 44,* 1102–1121.

Moreland, R. L., & Levine, J. M. (2001). Socialization in organizations and work groups. In M. E. Turner (Ed.), *Groups at work: Theory and research* (69–112). Mahwah, NJ: Erlbaum.

Morris, J. A., & Feldman, D. C. (1996). The dimensions, antecedents, and consequences of emotional labor. *Academy of Management Review, 21,* 986–1010.

Morrison, E. W. (1993a). Longitudinal study of the effects of information seeking on newcomer socialization. *Journal of Applied Psychology, 78,* 173–183.

Morrison, E. W. (1993b). Newcomer information seeking: Exploring types, modes, sources, and outcomes. *Academy of Management Journal, 36,* 557–589.

Morrison, E. W. (2002a). Newcomers' relationships: The role of social network ties during socialization. *Academy of Management Journal, 45,* 1149–1160.

Morrison, E. W. (2002b). The school-to-work transition. In D.C. Feldman (Ed.), *Work careers: A developmental perspective* (pp. 126–158). San Francisco: Jossey-Bass.

Nelson, D. L., & Sutton, C. (1990). Chronic work stress and coping: A longitudinal study and suggested new directions. *Academy of Management Journal, 33,* 659–689.

Ng, T. W. H., Eby, L. T., Sorensen, K. L., & Feldman, D. C. (2005). Predictors of objective and subjective career success: A meta-analysis. *Personnel Psychology, 58,* 367–408.

Ng, T. W. H., & Feldman, D. C. (2007). Organizational embeddedness and occupational embeddedness across career stages. *Journal of Vocational Behavior, 70,* 336–351.

Ng, T. W. H., & Feldman, D. C. (2008). Can you get a better deal elsewhere? The effects of psychological contract replicability on organizational commitment over time. *Journal of Vocational Behavior, 73,* 268–277.

Ng, T. W. H., & Feldman, D. C. (2010). The effects of organizational embeddedness on the development of social capital and human capital. *Journal of Applied Psychology, 95,* 744–751.

Ng, T. W. H., & Feldman, D. C. (2010). The impact of job embeddedness on innovation-related behaviors. *Human Resource Management, 49,* 1067–1091.

Nicholson, N. (1984). A theory of work-role transitions. *Administrative Science Quarterly, 29,* 172–191.

Nonaka, I., & Takeuchi, H. (1995). *The knowledge-creating company.* New York: Oxford University Press.

Northcraft, G. B., & Ashford, S. J. (1990). The preservation of self in everyday life: The effects of performance expectations and feedback context on feedback inquiry. *Organizational Behavior and Human Decision Processes, 47,* 42–64.

O'Reilly, C. A. III, Caldwell, D. R., & Barnett, W. P. (1989). Work group demography, social integration, and turnover. *Administrative Science Quarterly, 34,* 21–37.

O'Reilly, C. A. III, Chatman, J., & Caldwell, D. F. (1991). People and organizational culture: A profile comparison approach to assessing person-organization fit. *Academy of Management Journal, 34,* 487–516.

Ostroff, C., & Kozlowski, S. W. J. (1992). The role of mentoring in the information gathering processes of newcomers during early organizational socialization. *Journal of Vocational Behavior, 42,* 170–183.

Ouchi, W., & Jaeger, A. M. (1982). Type Z organizations: Stability in the midst of mobility. *Academy of Management Review, 3,* 305–314.

Pfeffer, J. (1982). *Organizations and organization theory.* Marshfield, MA: Pittman.

Pinder, C. C., & Schroeder, K. G. (1987). Time to proficiency following job transfers. *Academy of Management Journal, 30,* 336–353.

Podsakoff, P. M., & Schriesheim, C. A. (1985). Field studies of French and Raven's bases of power: Critique, re-analysis, and suggestions for future research. *Psychological Bulletin, 97,* 387–411.

Porath, C. L., & Bateman, T. S. (2006). Self-regulation: From goal orientation to job performance. *Journal of Applied Psychology, 91,* 185–192.

Reichers, A. E. (1987). An interactionist perspective on newcomer socialization rates. *Academy of Management Review, 12,* 278–287.

Rhoades, L., Eisenberger, R., & Armeli, S. (2001). Affective commitment to the organization: The contribution of perceived organizational support. *Journal of Applied Psychology, 86,* 825–836.

Robinson, S. L., Kraatz, M. S., & Rousseau, D. M. (1994). Changing obligations and the psychological contract: A longitudinal study. *Academy of Management Journal, 37,* 137–152.

Robinson, S. L., & Morrison, E. W. (2000). The development of psychological contract breach and violation: A longitudinal study. *Journal of Organizational Behavior, 21,* 525–546.

Rollag, K. (2004). The impact of relative tenure on newcomer socialization dynamics. *Journal of Organizational Behavior, 25,* 853–872.

Rosenbaum, J. E. (1979). Tournament mobility: Career patterns in a corporation. *Administrative Science Quarterly, 24,* 220–241.

Rousseau, D. M. (1995). *Psychological contracts in organizations: Understanding written and unwritten agreements.* Thousand Oaks, CA: Sage.

Rousseau, D. M., Ho, V. T., & Greenberg, J. (2006). I-deals: Idiosyncratic terms in employment relationships. *Academy of Management Review, 31,* 977–994.

Saks, A. M., & Ashforth, B. E. (1996). Proactive socialization and behavioral self-management. *Journal of Vocational Behavior, 48,* 301–323.

Saks, A. M., Uggerslev, K. L., & Fassina, N. E. (2007). Socialization tactics and newcomer adjustment: A meta-analytic review and test of a model. *Journal of Vocational Behavior, 70,* 413–446.

Salancik, G. R., & Pfeffer, J. (1974). The bases and uses of power in organizational decision making. *Administrative Science Quarterly, 19,* 453–473.

Salancik, G. R., & Pfeffer, J. (1978). A social information processing approach to job attitudes and task design. *Administrative Science Quarterly, 19,* 453–473.

Sampson, E. E., & Brandon, A. C. (1964). The effects of role and opinion deviation on small group behavior. *Sociometry, 27,* 261–281.

Sanzgiri, J., & Gottlieb, J. Z. (1992). Philosophic and pragmatic influences on the practice of organization development, 1950–2000. *Organizational Dynamics, 21,* 57–69.

Scandura, T. A. (1998). Dysfunctional mentoring relationships and outcomes. *Journal of Management, 24,* 449–467.

Scandura, T. A., & Schriesheim, C. A. (1994). Leader-member exchange and supervisor career mentoring as complementary constructs in leadership research. *Academy of Management Journal, 37,* 1588–1602.

Schein, E. H. (1968). Organizational socialization and the profession of management. *Industrial Management Review, 9,* 1–16.

Schein, E. H. (1985). *Organizational culture and leadership.* San Francisco: Jossey-Bass.

Schuster, J. R., & Zingheim, P. K. (1992). *The new pay: Linking employee and organizational performance.* New York: Lexington Books.

Sheridan, J. E. (1992). Organizational culture and employee retention. *Academy of Management Journal, 35,* 1036–1056.

Simon, H. A. (1987). Making management decisions: The role of intuition and emotion. *Academy of Management Executive, 1,* 57–64.

Singh, J. V., House, R. J., & Tucker, D. J. (1986). Organizational change and mortality. *Administrative Science Quarterly, 31,* 587–611.

Slaughter, J. E., & Zickar, M. J. (2006). A new look at the role of insiders in the newcomer socialization process. *Group & Organization Management, 31,* 264–290.

Sonnenfeld, J., & Ward, A. (2007). *Firing back: How great leaders rebound after career disasters.* Boston: Harvard Business School Press.

Stroh, L. K. (1995). Predicting turnover among repatriates: Can organizations affect retention rates? *International Journal of Human Resource Management, 6,* 443–456.

Sullivan, S. (1999). The changing nature of careers: A review and research agenda. *Journal of Management, 25,* 457–484.

Sutton, R. I., & Louis, M. R. (1987). How selecting and socializing newcomers influences insiders. *Human Resource Management, 26,* 347–361.

Sweeney, P. D., McFarlin, D. B., & Inderrieden, E. J. (1990). Using relative deprivation theory to explain satisfaction with income and pay level: A multistudy examination. *Academy of Management Journal, 33,* 423–435.

Toffler, B. L. (1981). Occupational role development: The changing determinants of outcomes for the individual. *Administrative Science Quarterly, 26,* 396–418.

Turban, D. B., & Dougherty, T. M. (1994). Role of protégé personality in receipt of mentoring and career success. *Academy of Management Journal, 37,* 688–702.

Turnley, W. H., & Feldman, D. C. (1999). The impact of psychological contract violations on exit, voice, loyalty, and neglect. *Human Relations, 52,* 895–922.

Van Maanen, J. (1976). Breaking in: Socialization to work. In R. Dubin (Ed.), *Handbook of work, organization, and society* (pp. 67–130). Chicago: Rand McNally.

Van Maanen, J. (1978). People processing: Strategies of organizational socialization. *Organizational Dynamics, 7,* 18–36.

Van Maanen, J. (1983). Golden passports: Managerial socialization and graduate education. *The Review of Higher Education, 6,* 435–455.

Van Maanen, J. (1984). Doing new things in old ways: The chains of socialization. In J. L. Bess (Ed.), *College and university organization* (pp. 211–247). New York: NYU Press.

Van Maanen, J., & Barley, S. R. (1984). Occupational communities: Culture and control in organizations. In B. M. Staw (Ed.), *Research in organizational behavior* (Vol. 6, pp. 287–365). Greenwich, CT: JAI Press.

Van Maanen, J., & Schein, E. H. (1979). Toward a theory of organizational socialization. In B. M. Staw (Ed.), *Research in organizational behavior* (Vol. 1, pp. 209–264). Greenwich, CT: JAI Press.

Van Viaanen, A. E. M. (2000). Person-environment fit: The match between newcomers' and recruiters' preferences for organizational culture. *Personnel Psychology, 53,* 113–149.

Wanberg, C. R., & Kammeyer-Mueller, J. D. (2000). Predictors and outcomes of proactivity in the socialization process. *Journal of Applied Psychology, 85,* 373–385.

Wanous, J. P., & Colella, A. (1989). Organizational entry research: Current status and future directions. In G. R. Ferris & K. M. Rowland (Eds.), *Research in Personnel and Human Resources Management* (Vol. 7, pp. 59–120). Greenwich, CT: JAI Press.

Ward, A. J., & Feldman, D. C. (2008). Survival of the embedded: Expelling and embedding forces on the members of the corporate elite. *Corporate Governance: An International Review, 16,* 239–251.

Watson, W. E., Kumar, K., & Michaelsen, L. K. (1993). Cultural diversity's impact on interaction process and performance: Comparing homogeneous and diverse task groups. *Academy of Management Journal, 36,* 590–602.

Wayne, S. J., & Liden, R. C. (1995). Effects of impression management on performance ratings: A longitudinal study. *Academy of Management Journal, 38,* 232–260.

Weick, K. E. (1977). Enactment processes in organizations. In B. M. Staw and G. R. Salancik (Eds.), *New directions in organizational behavior* (pp. 267–300). Chicago: St. Clair Press.

Weick, K. E. (1985). The significance of corporate culture. In P. J. Frost, L. F. Moore, M. R. Louis, C. C. Lundberg, & J. Martin (Eds.), *Organizational culture* (pp. 169–186). Beverly Hills, CA: Sage.

Wiggins, J. A., Dill, F., & Schwartz, R. D. (1965). On status liability. *Sociometry, 28,* 197–209.

Williams, K. J., & Alliger, G. M. (1994). Role stressors, mood spillover, and perceptions of work-family conflict in employed parents. *Academy of Management Journal, 37,* 837–868.

Yukl, G., & Tracey, J. B. (1992). Consequences of influence tactics used with subordinates, peers, and the boss. *Journal of Applied Psychology, 77,* 525–535.

The Perspective of Host Country Nationals in Socializing Expatriates: The Importance of Foreign–Local Relations

Soo Min Toh, Angelo S. DeNisi, *and* Geoffrey J. Leonardelli

Abstract

Failure to adapt is one of the most often cited reasons for the premature return of expatriate assignees. This chapter reviews and builds on research that suggests that the expatriate socialization process involves multiple stakeholders. We review the state of the expatriate socialization literature and introduce recent theoretical developments on the process of expatriate socialization by adopting the host country national's (HCN) perspective, and propose that HCNs have a potentially important role as socializing agents for expatriates. Drawing on social identity and justice theories, we identify relevant social cognitions and organizational practice that influence HCN coworkers' decision to play this role—providing social support and sharing information with expatriates. A broader definition of expatriate success that includes the outcomes of HCNs is also proposed. We conclude by highlighting new theoretical perspectives and research directions for developing our understanding of the expatriate socialization processes.

Key Words: expatriate socialization, information sharing, host country nationals, social identity theory, failure to adapt, procedural justice, multinational corporations, expatriates

As organizations venture into overseas markets, expatriate employees and the local people of the foreign subsidiary—also known as host country nationals (HCN)—are added into the multinational organization's workforce. With the rapid globalization of economies in the past several decades, research on expatriation and the effectiveness of their human resource strategies regarding their success has seen tremendous interest among organizational scientists. Expatriates are individuals who have been assigned to work in a country that is not the country of their birth. They are often utilized by multinational organizations to exert direct control, coordinate subsidiary units for the parent company, and to further the strategic goals of the parent (Harzing, 2001; Martinko & Douglas, 1999). Expatriates may be parent country nationals (i.e., expatriates who originate from the headquarters or parent company country of the multinational

corporation), third country nationals (i.e., expatriates neither of the parent nor the host country), or inpatriates (i.e., foreign nationals who live and work in the parent country; Reiche & Harzing, 2011). Expatriates may be assigned by their employer to be relocated to the foreign location or may initiate the relocation themselves (self-initiated expatriates; Gupta & Govindarajan, 1994; Inkson, Arthur, Pringle, & Barry, 1997; Lee, 2005). In many cases expatriate assignments are time-limited, where expatriates expect or are expected to return back to their home countries after the assignment is completed. The experience from these assignments is often seen by multinational organizations as desirable and increasingly necessary for executive development and promotion (Daily, Certo, & Dalton, 2000).

Expatriation is a specific and unique example of employee socialization. Expatriate assignments constitute a form of work transition, where the expatriate now operates in a different context from before and may be required to perform novel tasks and/or adopt a new role. While expatriates are often not new hires into the organization, they are new to the host country in which they have been assigned to work. Because of the transition that expatriates, like any newcomer to an organization, must face, many parallels can be drawn between the domestic concept of socialization and expatriate socialization.

Organizational newcomers, regardless of whether or not relocation to another country is required, need to learn aspects of the job as well as aspects of the cultural and social situation in order to "fit in." Hence, socialization is a learning and "fitting in" process that requires some kind of change or transition within the newcomer over a period of time. Both the domestic and expatriate definitions imply that some learning about the individual's new role and adaptation are involved in order to become an effective organizational member. In this sense, socialization and expatriate adjustment have been treated as synonymous (Black & Mendenhall, 1990). Like much work on socialization and acculturation, many expatriate adjustment studies have adopted the view that adjustment is multifaceted (Black, 1988; Black & Stephens, 1989; Gregersen & Black, 1990; Kraimer, Wayne, & Jaworski, 2001). Although the specific dimensions differ, both literatures agree that becoming adjusted to the job, to the interaction with other organizational insiders, and to the culture of the work and larger cultural context are key components of expatriate adjustment. In addition, both literatures have been concerned with similar work-related outcomes related to newcomer socialization, including work performance, job satisfaction, organizational commitment, and intentions to quit (e.g., Gregersen, 1992; Gregersen & Black, 1992; Naumann, 1993; Shaffer & Harrison, 1998).

Perhaps most importantly, the process of adjustment that expatriates go through is largely similar to the socialization processes described in domestic studies (Lueke & Svyantek, 2000). In particular, domestic socialization research has established the key role of organizational "insiders" as socializing agents for organizational newcomers (Louis, 1980; Louis, Posner, & Powell, 1983; Major, Kozlowski, Chao, & Gardner, 1995; Slaughter & Zickar, 2006) through the information they provide, as well as the social support offered to newcomers (Nelson & Quick, 1999). Recognizing this, expatriate researchers have been paying more attention to the importance of organizational insiders, and

particularly HCNs, creating a research perspective that is now commonly referred to as the *host country national perspective* of expatriate socialization (e.g., Aycan, 1997). It is this perspective that the present chapter reviews and builds upon further to advance our understanding of the expatriate socialization process. The main goal of the present chapter is to present a different perspective on the problem of expatriate failure, particularly seeing expatriate socialization through the eyes of HCNs, and to suggest important and interesting avenues of research to further advance our understanding and resolution of the problem.

What Constitutes Failure?

Expatriates sometimes fail in their assignments. Although failure is not as common as was once believed (see Harzing, 1995, for a critical review of the misconception) and, although the actual costs of failure are not precisely known (Harrison, Shaffer, & Bhaskar-Shrinivas, 2004), expatriate failure does occur and it *is* costly. The costs of relocation, including predeparture training, relocation incentives, and compensation adjustments, are often high, particularly when a spouse/partner, or family accompanies the expatriate in the relocation (see Harvey, Mayerhofer, Hartman, & Moeller, 2010). Failed assignments mean substantial losses in the investments made to prepare and relocate the expatriate and his/her family. Failed assignments also potentially adversely impact the success of the parent organization and its subsidiaries, various work and career-related plus psychological outcomes of the expatriate (and family), and the morale, commitment, and productivity of HCNs in the subsidiaries. As such, understanding and identifying ways in which multinational organizations can minimize the likelihood of expatriates failing on their assignments, while maximizing the potential for success among expatriate managers, have been significant concerns for both researchers and organizations for the past few decades (Sinangil & Ones, 2001; Takeuchi, 2010 for reviews of the body of research).

The first issue to address is the actual definition of failure—and, by default—success. The most common measure of the failure of an expatriate assignment has been the failure to complete the assignment (Black, Mendenhall, & Oddou, 1991 for a more complete discussion of this criterion measure). That is, an expatriate manager who returns to a home country before the scheduled completion of the assignment is considered to be a failure. This probably makes sense, but typically this is operationalized as the expatriate returning early without any consideration of whether the assigned tasks were actually completed or not. In any event, the mere fact that an expatriate remained in the host country for the assigned time does not determine success.

Success, and thus failure, must be viewed within the context of a firm's international strategy and what it intends to accomplish with expatriate assignments (cf. Connelly, Hitt, DeNisi, & Ireland, 2007). Bartlett and Ghoshal (1998) have proposed four such strategies, which they call *global, international, transnational,* and *multi-domestic*. In each case the exact goal of an expatriate assignment is somewhat different, but the differences really lie in the extent to which knowledge is transferred from the foreign operation to the headquarters. In all cases, though, a critical function of the expatriate assignment is to transfer knowledge and communication to the foreign subsidiary. In fact, several authors have argued that this type of knowledge transfer is the most important goal of any multinational organization (Ghoshal, 1987; Grant, 1996; Gupta & Govindarajan, 1994; Harzing, 2001; Harzing & Noorderhaven, 2006; Jackson, Hitt, & DeNisi, 2003; Teece, 1977).

Therefore, it seems critical that we include this knowledge transfer in any definition of expatriate failure. Regardless of how long an expatriate remains on assignment, the assignment cannot be viewed as successful unless there is some transfer of knowledge from the expatriate to the local operation. However, what we hope to communicate in this chapter is that expatriate success is more likely to occur if there is also some transfer of knowledge from HCNs to expatriates. We make the point that expatriate success is a two-sided coin that also encompasses the outcomes of HCNs. We will return to the broader definition of expatriate failure later in the chapter and we will relate it specifically to the HCNs, who will be a major focus of our discussion. First, though, we turn to the role that adaptation plays in determining the success or failure of any expatriate assignment.

Expatriates' Failure to Adapt

Failure of expatriates to adapt to living and working in the host country is one of the most commonly cited reasons for their premature return and/or ineffectiveness (Sinangil & Ones, 2001; Tung, 1987). The dominant perspective on the reasons for expatriates' failure to adapt is the inability of the

expatriate to overcome the strain of working and living in an unfamiliar environment (Harrison et al., 2004). Culture shock (Oberg, 1960) and its associated strain experienced by expatriates can lead them to be ineffective on their assignments and to the desire to return to their home countries. Expatriates unable to learn the ropes or become fluent in the cultural mores of the organization and the host country have difficulty in adjusting to the demands of the assignment (Black et al., 1991). Unaccustomed changes and new forms of intercultural contact with HCNs create stress and anxiety (Ward, Bochner, & Furnham, 2001). Such interactional difficulties, in turn, adversely affect expatriates' ability to carry out their roles (Shaffer, Harrison, & Gilley, 1999; Toh & DeNisi, 2005).

The difficulties of expatriates noted above suggest that the very expatriates sent to host units to transfer information, knowledge, and values from the parent company to foreign operations and HCNs (Paik & Sohn, 2004) need themselves to be socialized in order to perform effectively (Kraimer et al., 2001; Lee & Larwood, 1983). New to the host unit, expatriates are newcomers to the host organization. The purpose of the expatriate assignment notwithstanding, one of the immediate priorities of new expatriate assignees in the host country organization is to quickly adjust to the unique demands of the new job, diminished social ties, and unfamiliar cultural and organizational circumstances (Black & Mendenhall, 1990; Furnham, 1988; Furnham & Bochner, 1983). Expatriates need to become proficient in managing and interacting with HCNs and thus fulfill the objectives of their assignment (Caligiuri, 2000; Harzing, 2001). Oftentimes expatriates need to learn and adopt local practices to be effective (Maurer & Li, 2006). Adding to the challenge, the informational resources the expatriates relied upon in their home countries are no longer readily available and new networks of support have to be developed (Farh, Bartol, Shapiro, & Shin, 2010). Hence, the socialization of expatriates to the host unit is essential for expatriates to become adjusted to their assignments, particularly for expatriates on assignments that require a great deal of interaction with and cooperation from HCNs (Toh & DeNisi, 2005).

Next, we will elaborate on the focus of expatriate socialization research—expatriate adjustment—and how it has been defined and operationalized. Having reviewed the construct of expatriate adjustment, we briefly discuss the major limitations of extant models of expatriate adjustment, particularly the expatriate-centeredness of much of existing international human resources (HR) management research (Lazarova, 2006) and the narrow focus of expatriate adjustment. We then turn to our focus to the perspective of a key stakeholder in the expatriate adjustment process that has been often neglected—the HCN. We review the state of the literature that adopts the HCN perspective, introduce new developments, and offer innovative directions in this line of research.

Defining Expatriate Adjustment

The goal of socialization in the context of expatriation (Feldman & Bolino, 1999) has most commonly been referred to and studied as *expatriate adjustment*. Expatriate adjustment, as a state, may be conceptually distinguished from other constructs such as acculturation and adaptation (see Harrison et al., 2004 for a review). Black and his colleagues offer the most frequently adopted definition of expatriate adjustment (Black et al., 1991; Black & Stephens, 1989; Gregersen & Black, 1990). Based on a stressor–stress–strain framework, they view expatriate adjustment as the "degree of psychological comfort" the expatriate feels regarding the different aspects of the new situation (1990, p. 463). They also propose expatriate adjustment as tripartite, comprising work, interaction, and general adjustment to the host culture. *Work adjustment* refers to the level of comfort an expatriate feels about the job and responsibilities; *interaction adjustment* refers to the level of comfort the expatriate feels about interacting with local supervisors, peers, and subordinates; and *general adjustment* refers to the level of comfort an individual feels with various aspects of the host country culture including transportation, food, and climate (Black et al., 1991; Lueke & Svyantek, 2000). General adjustment is synonymous to cross-cultural adjustment of the expatriate, which "involves the gradual development of familiarity, comfort, and proficiency regarding expected behavior and the values and assumptions inherent in the new culture" (Black & Mendenhall, 1990, p. 118).

The facets of expatriate adjustment are highly intercorrelated (Aycan, 1997b; Black, 1988), but have been found to be sub-dimensions within the construct of expatriate adjustment and to have different antecedents and consequences (Bhaskar-Shrinivas, Harrison, Shaffer, & Luk, 2005; Parker & McEvoy, 1993; Shaffer et al., 1999). The facets of adjustment may precede others (for instance, general adjustment and interaction adjustment mediate work adjustment: Aycan, 1997b; Newman, Bhatt, &

Gutteridge, 1978), with interaction adjustment suggested as the most fundamental aspect of expatriate adjustment (Bell & Harrison, 1996). Accordingly, the facets also have different value in predicting various outcomes of expatriate adjustment such as job satisfaction, performance, and withdrawal (Harrison et al., 2004; Shaffer et al., 1999).

Expatriate adjustment may also be viewed as process (Harrison et al., 2004). Specifically, research has considered expatriate adjustment as a learning process, competence-gaining (Aycan, 1997b; Furnham & Bochner, 1983; Mendenhall, Kuhlmann, Stahl, & Osland, 2002), or a process of "personal transformation" (Osland, 1995). The process occurs through behavioral modeling, feedback, and reinforcement (Black & Mendenhall, 1990) gained from various sources, such as the expatriate's supervisor, coworkers, and subordinates (Peterson, Rodriguez, & Smith, 2000). In this process, expatriates develop social skills and networks, gain local cultural and work-related knowledge, and master the appropriate behaviors necessary for the performance of the expatriate's new role. The acquisition of key global competences (Caligiuri & Di Santo, 2001) helps expatriates negotiate everyday encounters with members of the host country (Furnham, 1988), facilitate knowledge exchange, gain competence in the new role, and ultimately develop a sense of comfort in the new environment (Gregersen & Black, 1990).

Finally, expatriate adjustment can also be distinguished by stage of adjustment or when adjustment occurs—*before* the expatriate arrives at the host country (anticipatory adjustment) or *after* the expatriate arrives in the host country (in-country adjustment). Depending on the stage of adjustment, different socialization practices may be required and may be more or less effective in facilitating the expatriate adjustment (Black et al., 1991). For example, the content of predeparture training to facilitate anticipatory adjustment should differ from post-arrival training to facilitate in-country adjustment (Black et al., 1991; Harris & Brewster, 1999).

The major models identifying the antecedents of expatriate adjustment have been discussed elsewhere (see Harrison et al., 2004; Mendenhall et al., 2002; Takeuchi, 2010). Hence, we have chosen to focus on the major limitations of the existing literature before introducing the HCN's perspective on expatriate adjustment. In the following section we briefly discuss the limitations in the theoretical perspectives adopted, the neglect of knowledge acquisition, the onus placed mainly on the expatriate to adjust, and the overlooking of the need for HCNs to be socialized and their roles as sources of valuable local and work information.

Limitations of Existing Models of Expatriate Adjustment

Existing models of expatriate adjustment have been criticized for adopting a narrow range of theoretical perspectives (Harrison et al., 2004). A stressor–strain perspective based on the work of Lazarus and Folkman (1984) is most often adopted, where models identify various stressors that lead to stress or maladjustment, which in turn is associated with various forms of strain (Kraimer & Wayne, 2004; Kraimer et al., 2001). This tradition originated 20 years ago with the introduction of Black et al.'s model in 1991. Since then, most studies have adopted this perspective and developed a substantial body of work aimed at refining our understanding of the various stressors that influence an expatriate's adjustment. Nevertheless, adopting additional theoretical perspectives to think about the expatriate management process and breaking away from the tradition of focusing on the expatriate's adjustment is much needed to expand and advance the literature and to explore other issues related to expatriate management that have not yet been fully investigated (Harrison et al., 2004; Takeuchi, 2010).

The literature has also been expatriate-centric in discussing the adjustment process. Typically, the responsibility to adjust successfully to the expatriate assignment belonged primarily to the expatriate and factors associated with him or her, such as the expatriate's individual characteristics and family situation (Vance & Ring, 1994). Other important stakeholders of the multinational organizations have largely been neglected (Harrison et al., 2004; Takeuchi, 2010; Toh & DeNisi, 2003, 2005). Understandably, the resources invested in the expatriate and the cost of expatriate assignment failures are likely significantly greater than those associated with HCNs. Hence, much research in expatriate management has been concerned with identifying the organizational practices, such as socialization and training, selection, and compensation, that would maximize expatriate success and minimize failure (Tung, 1987). This research tended to place the onus of adjustment on the expatriate, while the parent organization's primary role was of selecting, training, and motivating expatriates to the best of its ability (Mendenhall et al., 2002). Consequently, the literature has been somewhat underdeveloped in adopting the perspectives of other members and

stakeholders of the multinational organizations, particularly the HCNs, and their potential roles in the socialization of expatriates (Takeuchi, 2010).

As evinced by the great proportion of expatriate management research focused on expatriate adjustment (Lazarova, 2006), far less attention has been paid to understanding the learning process and the expatriates' ability to transfer and acquire knowledge and know-how from the experience (Vance, Vaiman, & Andersen, 2009). But, before the expatriate can transfer knowledge from the home country he or she must first acquire information about the local environment. According to socialization research, the process of socialization comprises two key dimensions: knowledge acquisition (or learning) and adjustment (Ashforth, Sluss, & Saks, 2007). Knowledge acquisition is a more proximal step in socialization and tends to precede the more distal outcome of adjustment. Yet in expatriate management research, expatriate adjustment is often seen as the outcome of interest, with more proximal processes such as knowledge acquisition not studied (Takeuchi, 2010). This is especially unfortunate given our earlier discussion about the importance of knowledge transfer between the parent organization and its host subsidiaries.

Currently, few studies focus on the knowledge acquisition process of expatriates and the factors that facilitate or impede this process (Bhagat, Kedia, Harveston, & Triandis, 2002; Reiche, Harzing, & Kraimer, 2009a). The focus has traditionally been on the expatriate's ability to transmit knowledge to the HCNs. This focus on the transfer of knowledge from expatriates to HCNs, and not from HCNs to expatriates, reflects again an ethnocentric bias of much expatriate management research. Yet the fact is that expatriates are often also expected to acquire new knowledge that can be applied back in the parent organization or other foreign subsidiaries (Bonache & Brewster, 2001; Downes & Thomas, 2002; Hocking, Brown, & Harzing, 2004; Reiche et al., 2009a; Reiche, Kraimer, & Harzing, 2009b). The knowledge that assignees may acquire during their assignment includes an understanding of the company's global organization, factual knowledge about the assignment culture, knowledge of their specific role in the host organization, and appropriate social behavior (Antal, 2000; Toh & DeNisi, 2007). This knowledge has both practical and strategic value for the expatriate and the multinational organizations, and can often best be obtained from HCNs. Hence, knowledge transfer between members within or across units of a multinational organization is a critical organizational process (Noorderhaven & Harzing, 2009; Zaidman & Brock, 2009), and understanding how expatriates may best acquire the needed knowledge is imperative.

Few studies have actually examined HCNs in the context of expatriate assignments. There has been some work regarding how international HR policies impact HCNs, or how HCNs perceive and react to expatriates and the HR practices that differentiate them from the expatriates (Toh & DeNisi, 2003). But, in general, there has been little attention paid to understanding the role of HCNs in the expatriate adjustment process and how HCNs can more effectively facilitate knowledge flows. As Vance et al. (2009) noted articulately:

> A significant amount of theoretical and empirical research in MNC (multinational corporation) knowledge management renders the impression that the expatriate, in his or her traditional leadership role in a foreign operation on behalf of an MNC, is the exclusive major global player, as if the contributions of the host country workforce were only of minor consequence and not worthy of study in the total picture of MNC knowledge management. (p. 650)

There are, of course, notable exceptions. These include Leung and his colleagues' studies in international joint venture hotels of HCNs' perceptions of pay justice on their job satisfaction (Leung, Smith, Wang, & Sun, 1996; Leung, Wang, & Smith, 2001), as well as Chen, Choi, and Chi's (2002) study, also on the process of making justice evaluations among HCNs in international joint ventures. Others have examined the attitudinal and behavioral reactions of HCNs to expatriates in the context of aiding of hindering the adjustment of expatriates (e.g., Jackson et al., 2003; Thomas & Ravlin, 1995; Toh & DeNisi, 2003; Varma, Toh, & Budhwar, 2006).

Furthermore, the socialization literature has made it abundantly clear that the socialization of newcomers into new roles is highly impacted by other individuals in the work environment (see Jokisaari and Nurmi, Chapter 5 of this volume). The role of organizational mentors, for example, illustrates the potential socialization benefits of insider peers and supervisors. Allen, McManus, and Russell (1999), for example, found that formal group peer mentoring relationships can contribute to the successful socialization of newcomers. They found that newcomers who received psychosocial mentoring (e.g., friendship, confirmation, acceptance) from their peers were better at learning the norms and rules of the organization, as well as better

at performing their jobs. The greater the extent to which newcomers received career-related mentoring (e.g., sponsorship, exposure and visibility, coaching, and protection) from more experienced peers, the more likely the newcomer had established successful and satisfying work relationships. More recently, Slaughter and Zickar (2006) reexamined the role of organizational insiders in the newcomer socialization process and showed that the socialization-related attitudes and behaviors exhibited by insiders have important effects on the development of organizational newcomers. Yet, even within the general area of socialization, a great deal of progress needs to be made with respect to viewing the socialization process from the perspective of coworkers and other stakeholders.

As a result of the relative neglect in these areas, a number of researchers have called for research to adopt a different perspective in understanding the expatriate adjustment process, specifically by encouraging research to adopt the HCN's perspective. The HCN's perspective is also suggested as a means to better understand how expatriates may facilitate knowledge flows in multinational corporations more effectively (Aycan, 1997a; Toh & DeNisi, 2003; Vance & Ring, 1994). It is this perspective to which we now turn our attention.

Host Country National Perspective on Expatriate Socialization

Vance and Ring (1994) were among the first to recognize the neglect of the perspective of HCNs in expatriate socialization practices. They note that much of existing expatriate management research is characterized by an ethnocentric belief that HCNs are not particularly significant in the success of the expatriate or the multinational corporation. With greater awareness of this gap in the literature, more and more researchers are turning their attention to the HCN (Takeuchi, 2010; Vance et al., 2009). The HCN perspective views expatriate management issues from the "other side of the coin," taking into consideration the role of HCNs in the expatriate socialization process (Vance & Ring, 1994). It also examines the impact of expatriation and its associated HR practices on HCNs. It stems from recognizing that expatriate adjustment studies are significantly lacking when they overlook the potential socializing role of HCNs (Toh & DeNisi, 2003, 2005). In fact, very few studies examine the role of HCNs and their outcomes in the context of the expatriate adjustment process, and there have been even fewer theoretical developments in this realm

(Takeuchi, 2010). We take stock of the research on HCNs as potential socializing agents in the socialization process of expatriates next.

The Role of HCNs as Socializing Agents

As early as the 1980s, Black and his colleagues speculated that the support HCNs may provide to expatriates might significantly influence the likelihood of success for the expatriate (Black, 1988; Black & Mendenhall, 1990; Black et al., 1991). Without the cooperation of the HCNs, they theorized that the expatriate is not likely to perform his or her job well (Gregersen & Black, 1992). Toh and DeNisi (2007) drew on domestic socialization research to propose that supportive HCN relationships, including friendships that provide emotional reassurance, information, encouragement, or aid in dealing with stressful situations, can help the newcomer deal with unexpected or unpleasant experiences (Fisher, 1985; Louis et al., 1983; Nelson & Quick, 1999). Organizational newcomers have been shown to feel better adjusted to their environments after being socialized through social support from insiders (Cable & Parsons, 2001; Cooper-Thomas, Van Vianen, & Anderson, 2004). Toh and DeNisi (2005, 2007) argue that HCNs play the role of "insiders," and that the unique information and resources that insiders possess can be a source of support, insight, and assistance to newcomers that secondary sources of information cannot (Morrison, 2002). Access to support from insiders can facilitate learning and decrease the amount of time needed to achieve proficiency in one's task (Pinder & Schroeder, 1987). The researchers further argue, based on research on social support, that even if help is not needed, the mere knowledge that support is available to the expatriate can be (and is often) sufficient to help alleviate the newcomers' stress (Wills, 1991).

A review of the literature reveals that HCNs can assist in the socialization process, and thus the flow of knowledge, in at least two ways: by offering social support or friendship, and by providing unique knowledge (Jackson et al., 2003; Toh & DeNisi, 2005, 2007; Vance et al., 2009). Because expatriates are no longer in a familiar social environment where their networks of friendship are readily available, developing and having available alternative sources of social support can be beneficial to their adjustment. In their meta-analysis of the findings on expatriate adjustment, Bhaskar-Shrinivas et al. (2005) and Hechanova, Behr, and Christiansen (2003) found that HCN coworker support was related to all facets of expatriate adjustment. The friendship that HCNs extend to the expatriates can help expatriates overcome the most stressful periods they face during the adjustment process (Bell & Harrison, 1996; Bjorkman & Schaap, 1994; Black & Mendenhall, 1990; Suutari & Brewster, 1998). In fact, strong social ties (in terms of quantity and quality) with HCNs are found to relate to the different facets of expatriate adjustment (Johnson, Kristof-Brown, Van Vianen, De Pater, & Rigsby, 2002; Liu & Shaffer, 2005). Onsite mentoring from HCNs, whereby expatriates receive task and career assistance as well as psychosocial support, increases the likelihood of expatriates becoming socialized to the new situation more quickly (Feldman & Bolino, 1999). On the other hand, poor relations with HCNs have a negative effect on the work adjustment and commitment of expatriates to the host unit (Florkowski & Fogel, 1999). Hence, consistent with socialization research that suggests insiders may serve as valuable sources of social support (Louis et al., 1983), HCNs in a host unit can also potentially be a source of social support (Toh & DeNisi, 2007).

Next, recent theorizing posits that information sharing from HCN employees to expatriates in the multinational organization can facilitate the prompt and successful adjustment of newcomer expatriates (Farh et al., 2010; Johnson et al., 2002; Liu & Shaffer, 2005; Vance & Paik, 2002). Host country supervisors, coworkers, and subordinates are possible sources of valuable role information (Peterson et al., 2000), knowledge, and feedback (Javidan, Stahl, Brodbeck, & Wilderom, 2005; Osland, 1995). As organizational insiders, HCNs can help expatriates understand the norms of the organization and to learn their work roles. Vance et al. (2009) term the role that HCNs can play as that of *liaison*, potentially being an effective conduit of knowledge to various parties within and across units of the multinational corporation. HCNs have more experience than the newcomer in the organization and if difficulties arise, insiders usually have sufficient knowledge and history to make sense of the situation and resolve it (Louis, 1980). Insiders also have a more established network of other insiders to rely upon, whereas the expatriate newcomer is unlikely to have these.

As cultural insiders, HCNs possess intimate knowledge of the cultural mores and accepted norms that expatriates may not be aware of. Sharing this information with expatriate newcomers can help expatriates become aware of what is socially accepted and avoid committing potentially serious cultural faux pas (Toh & DeNisi, 2005), as well as increase organizational knowledge, organizational knowledge sharing, job performance, and the career development of expatriates (Carraher, Sullivan, & Crocitto, 2008). As such, researchers conclude that the resource networks that HCNs can bring to expatriates is valuable to the expatriate as he/she learns his/her role (Feldman & Bolino, 1999; Toh & DeNisi, 2005, 2007). Some even go as far as to suggest that the knowledge gained from HCNs cannot be substituted by formal training the organization may provide beforehand (Caligiuri & Di Santo, 2001; Oddou, 2002). Relatedly, Vance and his colleagues argue that the design of predeparture and post-arrival training programs for expatriates can benefit from the local knowledge experts, and the input of HCNs should be included even in the planning of the objectives for the expatriate assignment to ensure greater assignment success (Paik, Vance, Gale, & McGrath, 2008; Vance & Ring, 1994; Vance et al., 2009).

Having established the important socializing role that HCNs can and should play, the next question is: How can we ensure that HCNs are willing and able to play this role? Acting as socializing agents for expatriates is often not in the HCNs' job descriptions, and even if it were, HCNs have at least some (if not considerable) degree of latitude in how conscientiously they may engage in this role (Toh & DeNisi, 2007). For example, the work of a secretary does not formally include training his/her incoming expatriate manager. Yet, in addition to assisting the manager with the administrative aspects of her work, the secretary's knowledge is very likely vital to the expatriate manager's ability to perform her job and to successfully integrate into the host environment (Osland, 1995). HCNs may choose not to share information with expatriates, and may even act as saboteurs of expatriates when they intentionally withhold critical information and jeopardize the expatriate's ability to perform his or her job effectively (Florkowski & Fogel, 1999; Toh & DeNisi, 2005).

So why might HCNs choose to withhold information from expatriates—individuals who could most benefit from the unique information that HCNs possess? How can organizations facilitate knowledge sharing? To answer these questions, we review recent theoretical and empirical developments aimed at addressing these issues and propose some ideas for researchers and organizations to consider.

Facilitating HCN–Expatriate Information Sharing: A Social Identity Approach

Recent research has drawn on social identity theory to explain the circumstances under which HCNs might share information with expatriates (Jackson et al., 2003; Toh & DeNisi, 2007). Information sharing from HCNs to their expatriate counterparts does not always occur, it is believed, in part because of the salient intergroup boundaries between HCNs and expatriates in the host unit (Toh & DeNisi, 2007). Salient categories are those that are psychologically and cognitively accessible to the individual's field of perception (Atkinson, 1986; Kahneman, 2003; Turner, Hogg, Oakes, Reicher, & Wetherell, 1987). According to social identity theory (Tajfel, 1978), *salience* refers to a readiness to use a given dimension to categorize oneself as well as others. Categorizations are driven by the perception of clearly identifiable or distinct social dimensions (Cota & Dion, 1986; Lansberg, 1988; McGuire, McGuire, Child, & Fujioka, 1978) that may be based on real or perceived differences, the presence of similar others in close proximity, or the sharing of a common fate with others (Campbell, 1958). Even the mere knowledge of others being in the same social group can be sufficient to elicit a common identity and result in category-consistent perceptions, attitudes, and behaviors (Brewer & Gardner, 1996; Locksley, Ortiz, & Hepburn, 1980).

As organizations recruit more employees from overseas or move them to international assignments, it is clear that local and expatriate categories are becoming increasingly common and increasingly salient within the organization. Toh and DeNisi (2007) identified a number of surface-level and deep-level factors that could increase the salience of HCN–expatriate categories. Organizational factors such as rank and compensation packages that differentiate expatriates from locals also increase the salience of HCN–expatriate categorizations (Chen et al., 2002; Toh & DeNisi, 2003). Expatriates often look and talk differently from the locals and bring with them their national identities, status, and lifestyles, which often ostensibly differentiate them from the locals (Hailey, 1996; Johnson et al., 2002; Van Vianen, De Pater, Kristof-Brown, & Johnson, 2004). These HCN–expatriate categorizations are thus not easily concealed and are often actively maintained for a complex number of macro-level and micro-level reasons (Bettencourt, Dorr, Charlton, & Hume, 2001; Leonardelli, Pickett, & Brewer, 2010; Triandis, Bontempo, Villareal, Asai, & Lucca, 1988). Hence, clear national boundaries within the organization are perpetuated, creating the potential for conflict between expatriate employees and their local counterparts and potentially reducing the likelihood of information sharing.

Because the intergroup relations literature tends to conclude that social categorization leads to intergroup conflict (Dovidio & Gaertner, 2010; see also Tajfel, Billig, Bundy, & Flament, 1971; Yzerbyt & Demoulin, 2010), current expatriate management research has recommended that intergroup boundaries between locals and expatriates should be minimized to facilitate local–expatriate cooperation (Olsen & Martins, 2009; Toh & DeNisi, 2007). For example, Toh and DeNisi (2007) suggested several situational characteristics that influence HCNs' motivation to help expatriates, such as the availability of rewards to HCNs for helping, the perceived supportiveness of the organization, the fairness of HCN–expatriate pay differentials, and the HCNs' desire to be affiliated with the expatriate group. They argue that these characteristics can moderate the negative relationship between HCN–expatriate categorization and HCNs' display of helping toward expatriates. In their model, HCN–expatriate categorization discourages helping from crossing national lines.

However, the most recent evidence suggests the contrary. Universal evidence for out-group discrimination is lacking (e.g., Brewer, 1999; Saucier, Miller, & Doucet, 2005), and a growing body of research challenges the conclusion that intergroup boundaries necessarily lead to conflict (e.g., Brown & Hewstone, 2005; Nadler, 2010; Wright & Richard, 2010). We discuss the implications of this for HCN–expatriate information sharing next. We review recent findings that suggest certain forms of aid, specifically aid that requires some transfer of resources (such as knowledge), is facilitated by clear social categorization under specific conditions.

Social Categorization and Fair Treatment Encourage Information Sharing

Research examining intergroup prosocial behavior finds that salient social group categories need not lead to intergroup conflict (see Stürmer & Snyder, 2010), and work has revealed that social categorization is necessary to generalize positive contact to other moments of contact (see Brown & Hewstone, 2005). Going in this direction, but taking it one step further, Leonardelli and Toh (2011) recently argued that social categorization can lead to *greater* intergroup cooperation, particularly cooperation involving a transfer of resources, because salient social categories can differentiate the group(s) of people in need of aid and the group(s) of people who can give it. Social categories are useful ways of making sense of the social environment, people, and situations, as well as providing direction as to how one might act in various social situations (Tajfel, 1978; Ting-Toomey et al., 2000). Likewise, social categorization could also assist in diagnosing opportunities for helping and prosocial behavior. As applied to expatriate adjustment, categorizing expatriates as an out-group could also serve an important function of making clear to the local employees that expatriate coworkers might benefit from their help.

Leonardelli and Toh (2011) recognized that past research finds that social categorization can also yield intergroup conflict, and proposed that fair treatment or procedural justice could be one moderator of the potential positive and negative consequences that social categorization could bring to facilitating locals' assistance of their expatriate coworkers. According to the group engagement model, procedural justice—particularly when exhibited by organizational authorities—creates identity security and respect (Tyler & Blader, 2003), leading members to become "voluntarily motivated to act in ways that make use of distinctive qualities and abilities" (p. 360). Distinguished from *distributive justice* (i.e., the fair distribution of outcomes), *procedural justice* refers to the fair treatment of individuals. Although it can be exhibited by a wide variety of sources (e.g., peers, subordinates), procedural justice exhibited by authorities has been revealed by research (e.g., Blader & Tyler, 2009; Tyler & Lind, 1992) to be particularly useful, as it increases members' identification with and cooperation within the group.

In the context of intergroup relations, procedural justice can improve cooperation when the groups are nested within a more inclusive superordinate group that includes authority figures. In such a case, procedural justice will lead members of the subgroups to feel secure and respected (Haslam, Eggins, & Reynolds, 2003; Huo & Molina, 2006; Leonardelli & Tormala, 2003), and these feelings will motivate cooperation across group boundaries. Theory and evidence support this notion; for example, White Americans and Black Americans were more likely to support authorities' efforts to maintain intranational justice, including the redistribution of resources between these two groups, when they perceived fair treatment from American authorities (Smith & Tyler, 1996).

Consistent with past research (Smith & Tyler, 1996), Leonardelli and Toh (2011) argued that procedural justice can improve intergroup relations when the groups are nested within a more inclusive "superordinate" group and authorities represent this superordinate group. Next, even though procedural justice may motivate intergroup cooperation it does not help to identify which group of individuals is in need of assistance and which can give aid. Social categorization can do so (Leonardelli & Toh, 2011). Furthermore, it may also motivate group members to perceive social categorization as a "distinctive quality," one where they seek to make use of its cooperative benefits. As a result, Leonardelli and Toh predicted that it is the combination of fair treatment from the multinational organization's authorities and social categorization that together would most successfully increase the degree to which locals gave useful knowledge. Fair treatment motivates locals to cooperate, and social categorization helps them gain insight into the expatriate coworker's needs. Only when fair treatment and social categorization are both high would locals be most likely to report giving expatriates information that would facilitate the expatriate's adjustment to the local culture.

In two studies, Leonardelli and Toh (2011) found just that. Only when locals perceived their organization's authorities as fair, and only when they perceived high social categorization (e.g., by agreeing to statements such as "I consider expatriates as 'one of them' and host country national employees to be 'one of us'"), did HCNs report the highest levels of information sharing with their expatriate coworkers. This novel finding that certain forms of intergroup cooperation require social categorization, where social categories are used to identify a group of people in need of assistance from those who can give aid, suggest new prescriptions for managing expatriate assignments, HCN-expatriate relations in multinational organizations, and in other contexts such as mergers and acquisitions and international joint ventures (Bjorkman & Schaap, 1994). To achieve the positive effects of social categorization, however, one needs to identify the best treatment for encouraging group members to see categorization as an asset. Leonardelli and Toh (2011) argue that procedural justice is better than other intergroup contact treatments (e.g., de-categorization) because it also allows for a "dual identity." A dual identity is one where group members simultaneously identify with a more inclusive superordinate group membership that contains their group and other group(s) (Dovidio, Gaertner, & Saguy, 2009; Leonardelli, Pickett, Joseph, & Hess, 2011). Procedural justice was found to reduce the antagonism that often occurs between a superordinate identity and a subgroup identity. This dual identity is beneficial in multinational organizations because HCNs may reject the organizational identity to protect the identity of their local subgroup to the detriment of the organization's interests. Further, where employee identification with the subgroup and shared superordinate categories are both encouraged, conflict between expatriate and HCN subgroups may potentially be reduced (Hornsey & Hogg, 2000a, 2000b).

Hence, procedurally just organizational authorities can allow HCNs and expatriates to have separate and shared identities. Equally important, procedural justice allows group members to see their category membership as a distinctive asset, one that can be used to assist others. Thus, when HCNs perceive expatriates as a different group and feel that they are fairly treated by the organization's authorities, conditions are conducive for information sharing to occur (Leonardelli & Toh, 2011). This position has not been previously asserted or empirically established and provides a fruitful avenue for further study.

What Should Organizations Do to Facilitate Information Sharing?

It should be clear that the expatriate socialization process cannot do without the input and involvement of HCNs (Paik et al., 2008; Vance et al., 2009). Multinational organizations should be aware that HCNs are vital socializing agents and that HCNs need to be motivated to play this role, as it is often not in their job descriptions nor are they formally rewarded for it (Toh & DeNisi, 2005). So what steps can they take to facilitate the socialization of expatriates and ensure that expatriates gain access to valuable information from HCNs and adjust to the host situation?

First, recognizing that HCNs are valuable sources of knowledge then requires multinational organizations to prepare HCNs for effective interactions with expatriates to increase HCNs' ability to play this role more effectively (Toh & DeNisi, 2005). Like expatriates, HCNs should also be trained in cross-cultural sensitivity, communication, and management (Vance & Ring, 1994; Toh & DeNisi, 2005). The onus is not merely on the expatriate to develop working relationships with HCNS. HCNs too should be equipped with cross-cultural communication and problem-solving skills to aid them in their interactions with expatriates. Key HCNs in the multinational organization can be trained in roles of cultural interpreter, communication facilitator, information resource broker, talent developer, and change partner (cf. Vance et al., 2009). Having the right attitude toward expatriate newcomers is also imperative in building effective working relationships (Florkowski & Fogel, 1999). HCNs should also be involved in the planning of expatriate assignments and in the selection process (Paik et al., 2008). Their input can lead to better-informed decisions on expatriate assignments and objectives. Involvement can also enable key HCNs to be more aware of the knowledge and support that the expatriate assignee needs, and thus be better able to identify the ways in which HCNs and the host unit can support the expatriate in his/her mission.

Second, reward HCNs for socializing expatriates. HCNs may not be fully willing, because the apparent social distance between HCNs and expatriates increases the perceived and real costs of doing so (Javidan et al., 2005; Toh & DeNisi, 2005). Redefining the receiving HCNs' roles to include mentoring or buddying incoming expatriates, and rewarding the fulfillment of this role, will make the socializing behavior more likely to occur. HCNs should see that socializing expatriates could lead to positive outcomes. Rewards may also be informal or personal. HCNs may value the experience of interacting with managers and professionals from other countries, and thus be more willing to interact with expatriates (Toh & DeNisi, 2007).

Socialization research suggests that the socialization process can be a proactive one, where newcomers actively seek feedback and information to fill in the gaps in their knowledge (Wanberg & Kammeyer-Mueller, 2000). Expatriates can and should do the same—proactively seeking out sources of support and information (Farh et al., 2010; Wong, 2001). Learning from HCNs should be encouraged among expatriates. Even if the expatriate's mission is to transfer the parent organization's values and practices to the host unit, expatriates need to understand the values and expectations of the HCN workforce and the unit, and adapt their own ways of managing and interacting with HCNs (Maurer & Li, 2006). Even though simply allowing managers across the units of the multinational corporation to interact can facilitate knowledge flows (Noorderhaven & Harzing, 2009), rather than leaving it to chance, an explicit objective of the expatriate assignment should be learning from HCNs. Expatriates should recognize that HCNs, as local insiders, are reservoirs of unique and valuable information, and be prepared to learn from them. Even expatriates sent as top executives have much to gain if they adopt an attitude of learning and openness toward the different perspectives and insights that HCNs have to offer. Openness to experience is an important characteristic that expatriates should have for adjustment (Caligiuri, 2000). We propose here that it is also a particularly important trait for expatriates for knowledge acquisition and management in multinational organizations. Expatriates who isolate themselves from HCNs, however, will be less likely to tap into the HCN knowledge resource. Ethnocentric expatriates may be less willing to learn from HCNs and thus have greater difficulty in becoming comfortable with their social interactions at work (Shaffer, Harrison, Gregersen, Black, & Ferzandi, 2006; Takeuchi, Yun, & Russell, 2002). Making expatriates aware of the value of learning from HCNs, and putting in place procedures that value learning by expatriates on assignment, could encourage the seeking out of information from HCNs.

Multinational organizations should also provide the right conditions for cooperation between expatriates and HCNs. Pay discrepancies that favor the expatriate may lead to perceptions of injustice and dissatisfaction that get in the way of cooperative relations between expatriates and HCNs (Leung et al., 1996; Leung et al., 2001; Toh & DeNisi, 2003). Furthermore, as demonstrated in Leonardelli and Toh (2011), perceiving the organization's authorities as fair could facilitate information sharing when HCNs see expatriates as different from them. Hence, the fairness perceptions of HCNs are an important area of study (Chen et al., 2002) and can be an important basis to encourage spontaneous cooperation (Tyler & Blader, 2003; for supporting evidence in the expatriate adjustment context, see Leonardelli & Toh, 2011). In addition to the socialization of expatriates and building cooperative relations between HCNs and expatriates, HCNs serve other important strategic roles as well (Harvey, Novicevic, & Speier, 2000). As insiders to other HCNs, HCN liaisons can be particularly credible and thus effective in facilitating the transmission of the parent organization's values and practices to the host unit (Maurer & Li, 2006; Vance et al., 2009). Multinational organizations have much to gain from ensuring that HCNs are satisfied with their jobs and are committed and identified with the organization (Harvey et al., 2000; Leung et al., 1996; Toh & DeNisi, 2007).

But, Returning to the HCNs Themselves...

As noted earlier, the socialization of expatriates is not typically part of the job description of the HCN. We discussed some things an organization can do to facilitate that socialization but, if we consider the broader goal of expatriate assignments to be the transfer of knowledge from the headquarters to the subsidiary, we would argue that the assignment is not really successful unless the HCNs also get something out of the expatriate assignment. That is, the HCNs should be gaining useful knowledge and expertise by working with the expatriate manager if the assignment is to be truly successful. Thus, another implication of widening the scope of consideration to include HCNs is that we include their perspective in determining the success of expatriate assignments. In fact, the process of socializing expatriates can provide HCNs with many opportunities to gain valuable outcomes. Simply stated, the stronger the ties between the expatriate and HCN, the easier should be the flow of information and the better should be the socialization of the expatriate. But, in addition, the stronger the ties, the more opportunities will be generated for the HCN to gain knowledge critical to his or her future career, since information transfer is likely to be facilitated (Reagans & McEvily, 2003; Schaefer & Kornienko, 2009). Furthermore, efforts by the HCN to help socialize the expatriate are likely to be reciprocated by the expatriate in terms of transferring valuable information (cf., Farh et al., 2010).

What exactly can the HCN gain through these interactions? One example is critical information about the norms and values of the parent company which may not be as apparent to the HCN (cf. Black & Gregersen, 1991). But, perhaps the best example of the information that can be gained by the HCN is what DeFillipi and Arthur (1994) refer to as three ways of "knowing" that can constitute real career capital for the HCN (or anyone; e.g., Eby, Butts, & Lockwood, 2003). Specifically, DeFillipi and Arthur (1994) refer to different types of organizational knowledge as "knowing how" (broad competencies such as task-related skills, judgment skills, and the ways to link resources and activities), "knowing whom" (social ties to important and influential individuals inside the organization and outside as well), and "knowing why" (understanding strengths and weaknesses and how they relate to career progression, which leads to increased confidence and motivation). There is evidence that expatriates acquire these types of career capital during their international assignments (e.g., Jokinen, Brewster,

& Suutari, 2008), and it seems reasonable that the HCNs should be acquiring this career capital during their interactions with expatriates as well.

If this were the case, it is clear that our definitions of success and failure of an expatriate assignment would have to be substantially broadened. These definitions would have to include consideration of whether or not HCNs acquired knowledge and career capital during the time spent working with expatriates. It would also require tracking the career progression and development of HCNs. If HCNs are gaining valuable information and career capital, this should translate into better career progression, greater career success, and greater job satisfaction for at least the HCNs who had the opportunity to work directly with the expatriate(s). In other words, if an expatriate assignment is truly successful the expatriate should gain knowledge and experience, the HCN should gain knowledge and career capital, and the organization should benefit, both because of the successful transfer of information that motivated the assignment in the first place and also from the career capital gained by *all* of its employees.

Future Directions

The preceding discussion suggests some new ways to conceptualize success and failure of expatriate assignments, but adopting an HCN perspective also leads to a number of other directions and suggestions for future research.

Expanding Models of Expatriate Socialization

Both organizational socialization and expatriate socialization research have tended to neglect the more proximal outcome of knowledge acquisition relative to adjustment (Ashforth et al., 2007). The bulk of expatriate management research has focused on adjustment as an outcome of interest and as instrumental to expatriate success (e.g., performance, assignment completion, job satisfaction). Both the domestic and expatriate definitions imply that some learning about the individual's new role and adaptation are involved in order to become an effective organizational member (Louis, 1980). Hence, expatriate socialization should be viewed as the degree to which the expatriate learns *and* feels comfortable with various aspects of his or her new organizational role, and operationalized as such (Ward et al., 2001). The time is ripe for embarking on "roads less traveled" in the expatriate management literature (Harrison et al., 2004). We suggest redirecting or at least expanding the focus of research to include the critical step of knowledge acquisition, as has been the key focus of this chapter. In doing so, key concepts such as role clarity, feedback seeking, information seeking, and other proactive behaviors can be drawn from the socialization literature and applied to both HCNs and expatriates.

Much remains to be understood, and the potential is great to draw from various disciplines and paradigms to inform our models. Drawing from the strategic management perspective, expatriate management research could be advanced by drawing on resource-based and knowledge-based views of the firm, and social networks to understand how knowledge flows may occur (Barney, 2001; Liu & Shaffer, 2005; Reiche et al., 2009a). Viewing knowledge management as a means to a sustained competitive advantage is imperative (Argote, McEvily, & Reagans, 2003; Jackson et al., 2003). Drawing from social psychological research, various perspectives such as the social identity theory can yield interesting advancements in our understanding of how knowledge might be acquired and exchanged between social groups (Kane, Argote, & Levine, 2005; Leonardelli & Toh, 2011). Laboratory research in the field of expatriate management is relatively rare (Thomas & Ravlin, 1995; Varma, Pichler, Budhwar, & Biswas, 2009), yet much needed to elucidate the underlying social-psychological mechanisms that are in play in knowledge flows. The expatriate management field could benefit from examining knowledge transfer processes in the laboratory. Research on the psychology of intergroup relations has also seen new developments in understanding the motivations behind the transfer/exchange of resources between social groups (see Stürmer & Snyder, 2010). Integrated with research on cross-cultural psychology, these may be fruitfully applied to understanding the process of information sharing between HCN and expatriate employee groups.

In addition to understanding the individual, social, and organizational factors that encourage knowledge sharing, research is also needed to understand the antecedents of expatriates' willingness to learn and acquire knowledge from HCNs (coworkers, subordinates, leaders). Even if HCNs are willing to share information, expatriates must also be receptive to acquiring and utilizing the new knowledge. Research could determine if the same factors that encourage HCNs to provide aid—namely, social categorization and procedural justice—also create suitable conditions for encouraging expatriates' openness to knowledge seeking, utilization, and exchange. Furthermore, the potential benefits

and downsides for the recipients and providers of knowledge should be explored. Some research in groups suggests that providing knowledge can be a means to exert and maintain one's superior position over another group (Nadler, 2002; Nadler & Halabi, 2006); thus, receiving and utilizing the knowledge may not necessarily be to the best interest of the recipient. Under what circumstances might expatriates (or HCNs) be (un)willing to share/receive knowledge from the other?

Impact of Expatriate Socialization on HCNs

In his review of the expatriate adjustment literature, Takeuchi (2010) noted that there are few studies investigating the impact of expatriates on organizational stakeholders, such as the HCN. Ward and her colleagues note, "When culturally disparate groups come into contact with each other, they tend to have an impact on each other's social structures, institutional arrangements, political processes, and value systems. The nature and extent of these changes will depend on the conditions under which the contact occurs (e.g., whether peaceful or in conquest), the relative power of the interacting groups, and a wide range of other variables. Likewise, the actual accommodation between the groups can take a great variety of forms. In addition, the individuals caught up in the contact also have an impact on each other" (Ward et al., 2001, p. 27). Much of expatriate socialization research has been concerned with how expatriates adapt but not how the presence of expatriates and their socialization processes affect HCNs. Questions remain on the impact expatriates may have on HCNs, and on the adaptation HCNs might go through as a result in terms of their own behavior, values, and attitudes. Perhaps more research is needed to understand how HCNs can be better prepared for working with expatriates and be primed to exchange knowledge with expatriates, such that the individual, social, and organizational consequences of that interaction will be beneficial.

Socialization of Other Types of Expatriates

Thus far, we have discussed the experience and involvement of two groups of stakeholders in the expatriate socialization process—expatriates and HCNs. There are, however, other important groups of stakeholders that need consideration. Inpatriates and repatriates, for example, are groups that are gaining in momentum in research as strategic cross-unit knowledge agents (Reiche, 2011; Reiche et al., 2009a). Inpatriates are foreign nationals who have been transferred from subsidiaries into the multi-national corporation's parent unit; repatriates are expatriates who are now relocated back to the parent unit (Reiche & Harzing, 2011). Other groups of expatriates also needing study include self-initiated expatriates (Lee, 2005; Reiche & Harzing, 2011), expatriates from small firms, and female expatriates (Caligiuri & Cascio, 1998; Napier & Taylor, 2002; Varma et al., 2006). We expect that the socialization experiences of these groups in the parent organization would be somewhat different from those of expatriate assignees, given that the motivations, perceptions, and social dynamics in play are likely to be different (Harvey, Novicevic, Buckley, & Fung, 2005).

Expatriate Socialization in Different Corporate and National Contexts

Research that takes into account various corporate structures, and integrating research examining those structures with expatriate socialization research, is also needed. The literatures on international mergers and acquisitions or international joint ventures have been concerned with ensuring the survival of these structures, and with the integration and cooperation of members of the newly created entity (Bjorkman & Schaap, 1994; Hébert, Very, & Beamish, 2005). Interesting research questions arise in these corporate contexts that relate to socialization of both expatriates and HCNs. For instance, what socialization practices might be useful for expatriates and HCNs in these contexts? Would they vary and would different tactics be needed for the expatriate and HCN subgroups? How should subgroup identities be best managed, and how might positive relations between members of formerly separate organizations be facilitated to enable the successful socialization of both groups to the new culture? Our recent work found that social categorization and procedural justice together are associated with greater information sharing and a dual identity among HCNs (Leonardelli & Toh, 2011). Some laboratory evidence suggests that a dual identity—an "us and them" mindset rather than an "us versus them"—reduces merger resistance (van Leeuwen & van Knippenberg, 2003), and that identity continuity could be key to post-merger identification (van Knippenberg & van Leeuwen, 2001). Much remains to be understood about social categorization processes and identities in the socially complex contexts of mergers and acquisitions and international joint ventures. Future research should explore ways in which the literatures related to these

contexts and the expatriate socialization literature may be integrated and fruitfully inform each other.

Next, the socialization of expatriates to date has also focused on expatriates from the triad countries (United States, Japan, Europe; Reiche et al., 2009b), reflecting a somewhat ethnocentric bias (Paik et al., 2008; Takeuchi, 2010). Research needs to expand its scope to consider expatriates from other regions and countries, and also examine how HCNs of triad countries may react differently to expatriates from other countries. In Napier and Taylor's (2002) study of female expatriates in Japan, China, and Turkey, for example, the expatriates were faced with similar challenges of gaining credibility, and similar frustrations, but varied to some degree in their experiences with harassment in the host country. Selmer's (2002) study of Asian and Western third-country national expatriates in China also came up with findings suggesting that Asian expatriates in China were disadvantaged in becoming adjusted relative to Western expatriates. Clearly, much remains to be understood about the culture-specific influences on the socialization processes of expatriates (Varma, Budhwar, & Pichler, 2009).

Socialization as an Information Exchange Process

Finally, the expatriate socialization research would benefit from more fully understanding the psychological processes that govern knowledge transfer between expatriates and HCNs. There are a substantial number of biases (Kane et al., 2005; Stasser, Stewart, & Wittenbaum, 1995) that can inhibit knowledge transfer, and our theory and research has offered some interesting directions for how to reduce such biases and allow information to be shared. However, for knowledge to be successfully transferred, the recipient of such information must process it and perceive it as valuable. We think that some of our more recent research (Leonardelli & Toh, 2011) helps to facilitate this side of the information exchange process, too. We had previously argued that, when coupled with fair treatment from organizational authorities, social categorization would increase the likelihood that locals will give information to expatriate coworkers. However, these same conditions we think will also make expatriates more receptive to the information they receive from their local colleagues, as social categorization helps to lend confidence to the HCNs' advice; when expatriates perceive their HCN coworkers as locals (and thus different from themselves) they may be more confident in the HCN's advice, as they perceive it to be coming from an expert. Future research will benefit from testing this prediction.

Expatriate socialization research has tended to be steps behind the developments in organizational socialization research (Black et al., 1991). Expatriate socialization has endeavored to draw upon the advancements in the latter to inform research and practice, and should continue to do so for guidance. Research on proactive socialization (Ashford & Black, 1996), social integration (Morrison, 2002), mentoring (Wanberg & Kammeyer-Mueller, 2000; Wanberg, Welsh, & Hezlett, 2003), and fit (Kristof-Brown, Jansen, & Colbert, 2002; Van Vianen et al., 2004) should continue to be drawn upon by expatriate socialization research. As well, models adopting the interactionist approach (Griffin, Colella, & Goparaju, 2000; Reichers, 1987)—examining in tandem the role of the attempts at socialization of newcomers, insiders, and the organization—should be adopted by expatriate researchers. Expatriate researchers should also play a lead role in informing research and practice on maximizing the success of career transitions that involve crossing national boundaries and interacting with people of other cultures—global careers (Thomas, Lazarova, & Inkson, 2005). Another ambitious direction could be the development and testing of more dynamic models of the expatriate socialization process (Farh et al., 2010; Jokisaari & Nurmi, 2009). Little is known about how insiders react to newcomers, or about how developmental relationships evolve and affect the newcomer differently in the course of the socialization process (Slaughter & Zickar, 2006). Like most research, longitudinal expatriate research is acknowledged as imperative, yet is sorely lacking.

In contrast, socialization research might also gain new insights from those gained in the expatriate literature. For example, socialization research has not paid much attention to whether or not coworkers hoard or hide knowledge (Connelly, Zweig, Webster, & Trougakos, 2012) from the newcomer, and the circumstances in which this is more or less likely to take place. Information sharing in the socialization literature has tended to be examined in mentoring relationships (peer or senior mentors; e.g., Allen et al., 1999). Our ideas on how seeing difference can facilitate information sharing in conditions of fair treatment could also be tested in a newcomer–"old-timer" context, and potentially lead researchers to rethink the usefulness of removing the "newcomer" label and assimilating newcomers too quickly. Recent evidence would suggest that if organizational insiders see newcomers as a group

of fellow organizational members in need of help, and themselves as part of a group who are able to help, they are more likely to share information with the newcomers when they feel that the organization's authorities also treat them fairly.

Conclusion

Expatriates face various challenges as they approach their jobs in an unfamiliar cultural environment. They require a great a deal of support from different sources as they navigate different stages of the adjustment process (Farh et al., 2010). To feel accepted by HCNs and interact effectively with them is clearly an integral part of an expatriate's socialization to the host unit (Caligiuri, 2000; Florkowski & Fogel, 1999; Varma et al., 2009). This chapter aimed to take stock of the extant research on expatriate socialization, review recent developments, and to provide new theoretical perspectives on the problem. We feel that the HCN perspective on expatriate socialization has much room for development and that various theoretical perspectives, such as knowledge management, social identity theory, and fairness, may be useful lenses to view the problem of knowledge flows and intergroup relations between HCNs and expatriates. We have also identified several new questions and directions that expatriate management may take. It is hoped that the thoughts reflected in this chapter will spur greater interest and more innovative research in this realm.

References

Allen, T. D., McManus, S. E., & Russell, J. E. A. (1999). Newcomer socialization and stress: Formal peer relationships as a source of support. *Journal of Vocational Behavior, 54*(3), 453–470.

Antal, A. B. (2000). Types of knowledge gained by expatriate managers. *Journal of General Management, 26*(2), 32–51.

Argote, L., McEvily, B., & Reagans, R. (2003). Managing knowledge in organizations: An integrative framework and review of emerging themes. *Management Science, 49*(4), 571–582.

Ashford, S. J., & Black, J. S. (1996). Proactivity during organizational entry: The role of desire for control. *Journal of Applied Psychology, 81*(2), 199–214.

Ashforth, B. E., Sluss, D. M., & Saks, A. M. (2007). Socialization tactics, proactive behavior, and newcomer learning: Integrating socialization models. *Journal of Vocational Behavior, 70*(3), 447–462.

Atkinson, M. L. (1986). The perception of social categories: Implications for the social comparison process. In J. M. Olson, C. P. Herman & M. P. Zanna (Eds.), *Relative deprivation and social comparison: An Ontario symposium* (pp. 181–200). Hillsdale, NJ: L. Erlbaum Associates.

Aycan, Z. (1997a). Acculturation of expatriate managers: A process model of adjustment and performance. In Z. Aycan (Ed.), *New approaches to employee management* (Vol. 4, pp. 1–40). Greenwich, CT: JAI Press Inc.

Aycan, Z. (1997b). Expatriate adjustment as a multifaceted phenomenon: Individual and organizational level predictors. *The International Journal of Human Resource Management, 8*(4), 434–456.

Barney, J. B. (2001). Resource-based theories of competitive advantage: A ten-year retrospective on the resource-based view. *Journal of Management, 27*(6), 643–650.

Bartlett, C. A., & Ghoshal, S. (1998). *Managing across borders: The transnational solution* (2nd ed.). Boston: Harvard Business School Press.

Bell, M. P., & Harrison, D. A. (1996). Using intra-national diversity for international assignments: A model of bicultural competence and expatriate adjustment. *Human Resource Management Review, 6*(1), 41–74.

Bettencourt, B. A., Dorr, N., Charlton, K., & Hume, D. L. (2001). Status differences and in-group bias: A meta-analytic examination of the effects of status stability, status legitimacy, and group permeability. *Psychological Bulletin, 4*, 520–542.

Bhagat, R. S., Kedia, B. L., Harveston, P. D., & Triandis, H. C. (2002). Cultural variations in the cross-border transfer of organizational knowledge: An integrative framework. *Academy of Management Review, 27*(2), 204–221.

Bhaskar-Shrinivas, P., Harrison, D. A., Shaffer, M. A., & Luk, D. M. (2005). Input-based and time-based models of international adjustment: Meta-analytic evidence and theoretical extensions. *Academy of Management Journal, 48*(2), 257.

Bjorkman, I., & Schaap, A. (1994). Outside in the Middle Kingdom: Expatriate managers in Chinese-Western joint ventures. *European Management Journal, 12*(2), 147–153.

Black, J. S. (1988). Work role transitions: A study of American expatriate managers. *Journal of International Business Studies, 19*(2), 277–284.

Black, J. S., & Gregersen, H. B. (1991). Antecedents to cross-cultural adjustment for expatriates in Pacific Rim assignments. *Human Relations, 44*(5), 497–513.

Black, J. S., & Mendenhall, M. (1990). Cross-cultural training effectiveness: A review and a theoretical framework for future research. *Academy of Management Review, 15*(1), 113–136.

Black, J. S., Mendenhall, M., & Oddou, G. (1991). Toward a comprehensive model of international adjustment: An integration of multiple theoretical perspectives. *Academy of Management Review, 16*(2), 291–317.

Black, J. S., & Stephens, G. K. (1989). The influence of the spouse on American expatriate adjustment and intent to stay in Pacific Rim overseas assignments. *Journal of Management, 15*(4), 529–544.

Blader, S. L., & Tyler, T. R. (2003). What constitutes fairness in work settings? A four-component model of procedural justice. *Human Resource Management Review, 13*(1), 107–126.

Blader, S. L., & Tyler, T. R. (2009). Testing and extending the group engagement model: Linkages between social identity, procedural justice, economic outcomes, and extrarole behavior. *Journal of Applied Psychology, 94*(2), 445–464.

Bonache, J., & Brewster, C. (2001). Knowledge transfer and the management of expatriation. *Thunderbird International Business Review, 43*(1), 145–168.

Brewer, M. B. (1999). The psychology of prejudice: Ingroup love or outgroup hate? *Journal of Social Issues, 55*(3), 429–444.

Brewer, M. B., & Gardner, W. (1996). Who is this "We"? Levels of collective identity and self representations. *Journal of Personality & Social Psychology, 71*(1), 83–93.

Brown, R., & Hewstone, M. (2005). An integrative theory of intergroup contact. In M. P. Zanna (Ed.), *Advances in experimental social psychology* (Vol. 37, pp. 255–343). San Diego, CA: Elsevier Academic Press.

Cable, D. M., & Parsons, C. K. (2001). Socialization tactics and person-organization fit. *Personnel Psychology, 54*(1), 1–23.

Caligiuri, P. (2000). Selecting expatriates for personality characteristics: A moderating effect of personality on the relationship between host national contact and cross-cultural adjustment. *Management International Review, 40*(1), 61–80.

Caligiuri, P., & Cascio, W. F. (1998). Can we send her there? Maximizing the success of western women on global assignments. *Journal of World Business, 33*(4), 394–416.

Caligiuri, P., & Di Santo, V. (2001). Global competence: What is it, and can it be developed through global assignments? *Human Resource Planning, 24*(3), 27–35.

Campbell, D. T. (1958). Common fate, similarity, and other indices of the statues of aggregates of persons as social entities. *Behavioral Science, 3*, 1958.

Carraher, S. M., Sullivan, S. E., & Crocitto, M. M. (2008). Mentoring across global boundaries: an empirical examination of home- and host-country mentors on expatriate career outcomes. *Journal of International Business Studies, 39*(8), 1310–1326.

Chen, C. C., Choi, J., & Chi, S.-C. (2002). Making justice sense of local-expatriate compensation disparity: Mitigation by local referents, ideological explanations, and interpersonal sensitivity in China-foreign joint ventures. *Academy of Management Journal, 45*(4), 807.

Connelly, B., Hitt, M. A., DeNisi, A. S., & Ireland, R. D. (2007). Expatriates and corporate-level international strategy: governing with the knowledge contract. *Management Decision, 45*(3), 564–581.

Connelly, C. E., Zweig, D., Webster, J., & Trougakos, J. P. (2012). Knowledge hiding in organizations. *Journal of Organizational Behavior, 33*(1), 64–88.

Cooper-Thomas, H. D., Van Vianen, A., & Anderson, N. (2004). Changes in person—organization fit: The impact of socialization tactics on perceived and actual P-O fit. *European Journal of Work & Organizational Psychology, 13*(1), 52–78.

Cota, A. A., & Dion, K. L. (1986). Salience of gender and sex composition of ad hoc groups: An experimental test of distinctiveness theory. *Journal of Personality & Social Psychology, 50*(4), 770–776.

Daily, C. M., Certo, S. T., & Dalton, D. R. (2000). International experience in the executive suite: The path to prosperity? *Strategic Management Journal, 21*(4), 515.

Defillippi, R. J., & Arthur, M. B. (1994). The boundaryless career: a competency-based perspective. *Journal of Organizational Behavior, 15*(4), 307–324.

Dovidio, J. F., & Gaertner, S. L. (2010). Intergroup bias. In S. Fiske, D. T. Gilbert & G. Lindzey (Eds.), *Handbook of social psychology* (5th ed., Vol. 2, pp. 1084–1121). Hoboken, NJ: John Wiley.

Dovidio, J. F., Gaertner, S. L., & Saguy, T. (2009). Commonality and the complexity of "We": Social attitudes and social change. *Personality & Social Psychology Review 13*(1), 3–20.

Downes, M., & Thomas, A. S. (2002). Knowledge transfer through expatriation: The U-curve approach to overseas staffing. *Journal of Managerial Issues, 12*(2), 131–149.

Eby, L. T., Butts, M., & Lockwood, A. (2003). Predictors of success in the era of the boundaryless career. *Journal of Organizational Behavior, 24*(6), 689–708.

Farh, C. I. C., Bartol, K. M., Shapiro, D. L., & Shin, J. (2010). Networking abroad: A process model of how expatriates form support ties to facilitate adjustment. *Academy of Management Review, 35*(3), 434–454.

Feldman, D. C., & Bolino, M. C. (1999). The impact of on-site mentoring on expatriate socialization: a structural equation modelling approach. *International Journal of Human Resource Management, 10*(1), 54–71.

Fisher, C. D. (1985). Social support and adjustment to work: A longitudinal study. *Journal of Management, 11*(3), 39–53.

Florkowski, G. W., & Fogel, D. S. (1999). Expatriate adjustment and commitment: the role of host-unit treatment. *International Journal of Human Resource Management, 10*(5), 782–807.

Furnham, A. (1988). The adjustment of sojourners. In Y. Y. Kim & W. B. Gudykunst (Eds.), *Cross-cultural adaptation*. Newbury Park, CA: Sage Publications.

Furnham, A., & Bochner, S. (1983). Social difficulty in a foreign culture: An empirical analysis of culture shock. In S. Bochner (Ed.), *Cultures in contact: Studies in cross-cultural interaction*. Elmsford, NY: Pergamon Press.

Ghoshal, S. (1987). Global strategy: An organizing framework. *Strategic Management Journal, 8*(5), 425–440.

Grant, R. M. (1996). Prospering in dynamically-competitive environments: Organizational capability as knowledge integration. *Organization Science, 7*(4), 375–387.

Gregersen, H. B. (1992). Commitments to a parent company and a local work unit during repatriation. *Personnel Psychology, 45*(1), 29–54.

Gregersen, H. B., & Black, J. S. (1992). Antecedents to commitment to a parent company and a foreign operation. *Academy of Management Journal, 35*(1), 65–90.

Gregersen, H. B., & Black, S. J. (1990). A multifaceted approach to expatriate retention. *Group & Organization Studies, 15*(4), 461–485.

Griffin, A. E. C., Colella, A., & Goparaju, S. (2000). Newcomer and organizational socialization tactics: An interactionist perspective. *Human Resource Management Review, 10*(4), 453–474.

Gupta, A. K., & Govindarajan, V. (1994). Alternative value chain configurations for foreign subsidiaries: Implications for coordination and control within MNCs. In H. Thomas, D. O'Neal, & R. White (Eds.), *Building the strategically responsive organization* (pp. 375–392). Chichester, UK: John Wiley.

Hailey, J. (1996). The expatriate myth: Cross-cultural perceptions of expatriate managers. *The International Executive, 38*(2), 255–271.

Harris, H., & Brewster, C. (1999). The coffee-machine system: how international selection really works. *International Journal of Human Resource Management, 10*(3), 488–500.

Harrison, D. A., Shaffer, M. A., & Bhaskar-Shrinivas, P. (2004). Going places: Roads more and less traveled in research on expatriate experiences. In J. J. Martocchio (Ed.), *Research in personnel and human resource management* (Vol. 23, pp. 199–247). Greenwich, CT: JAI Press.

Harvey, M., Mayerhofer, H., Hartman, L., & Moeller, M. (2010). Corralling the "horses" to staff the global organization of 21st century. *Organizational Dynamics, 39*(3), 258–268.

Harvey, M., Novicevic, M. M., Buckley, M. R., & Fung, H. (2005). Reducing inpatriate managers' 'liability of foreignness' by addressing stigmatization and stereotype threats. *Journal of World Business, 40*(3), 267–280.

Harvey, M. G., Novicevic, M. M., & Speier, C. (2000). An innovative global management staffing system: A competency-based perspective. *Human Resource Management, 39*(4), 381.

Harzing, A.-W. (1995). The persistent myth of high expatriate failure rates. *International Journal of Human Resource Management, 6*(2), 457–474.

Harzing, A.-W. (2001). Of bears, bumble-bees, and spiders: The role of expatriates in controlling foreign subsidiaries. *Journal of World Business, 36*(4), 366.

Harzing, A.-W., & Noorderhaven, N. (2006). Geographical distance and the role and management of subsidiaries: The case of subsidiaries down-under. *Asia Pacific Journal of Management, 23*(2), 167–185.

Haslam, S. A., Eggins, R. A., & Reynolds, K. J. (2003). The ASPIRe model: Actualizing social and personal identity resources to enhance organizational outcomes. *Journal of Occupational and Organizational Psychology, 76*(1), 83–113.

Hébert, L., Very, P., & Beamish, P. W. (2005). Expatriation as a bridge over troubled water: A knowledge-based perspective applied to cross-border acquisitions. *Organization Studies, 26*(10), 1455–1476.

Hechanova, R., Beehr, T. A., & Christiansen, N. D. (2003). Antecedents and consequences of employees' adjustment to overseas assignment: A meta-analytic review. *Applied Psychology: An International Review, 52*(2), 213–236.

Hocking, J. B., Brown, M., & Harzing, A. W. (2004). The strategic purposes and path-dependent outcomes of expatriate assignments: A knowledge transfer perspective. *International Journal of Human Resource Management, 15*(3), 565–586.

Hornsey, M. J., & Hogg, M. A. (2000a). Assimilation and diversity: An integrative model of subgroup relations. *Personality & Social Psychology Review, 4*(2), 143–156.

Hornsey, M. J., & Hogg, M. A. (2000b). Intergroup similarity and subgroup relations: Some implications for assimilation. *Personality & Social Psychology Bulletin, 26*(8), 948–958.

Huo, Y. J., & Molina, L. E. (2006). Is pluralism a viable model of diversity? The benefits and limits of subgroup respect. *Group Processes & Intergroup Relations, 9*(3), 359–376.

Inkson, K., Arthur, M. B., Pringle, J., & Barry, S. (1997). Expatriate assignment versus overseas experience: Contrasting models of international human resource development. *Journal of World Business, 32*(4), 351–368.

Jackson, S. E., Hitt, M. A., & DeNisi, A. S. (2003). *Managing knowledge for sustained competitive advantage: Designing strategies for effective human resource management*. San Francisco: Jossey-Bass.

Javidan, M., Stahl, G. K., Brodbeck, F., & Wilderom, C. P. M. (2005). Cross-border transfer of knowledge: Cultural lessons from Project GLOBE. *The Academy of Management Executive, 19*(2), 59.

Johnson, E. C., Kristof-Brown, A. L., Van Vianen, A. E. M., De Pater, I., & Rigsby, M. M. (2002). *Expatriate social ties: The impact of relationships with comparable others and host country nationals*. Paper presented at the Academy of Management, Denver, Colorado.

Jokinen, T., Brewster, C., & Suutari, V. (2008). Career capital during international work experiences: contrasting self-initiated expatriate experiences and assigned expatriation. *International Journal of Human Resource Management, 19*(6), 979–998.

Jokisaari, M., & Nurmi, J.-E. (2009). Change in newcomers' supervisor support and socialization outcomes after organizational entry. *Academy of Management Journal, 52*(3), 527–544.

Kahneman, D. (2003). A perspective on judgment and choice. *American Psychologist, 58*(9), 697–720.

Kane, A. A., Argote, L., & Levine, J. M. (2005). Knowledge transfer between groups via personnel rotation: Effects of social identity and knowledge quality. *Organizational Behavior & Human Decision Processes, 96*(1), 56–71.

Kraimer, M. L., & Wayne, S. J. (2004). An examination of perceived organizational support as a multidimensional construct in the context of an expatriate assignment. *Journal of Management, 30*(2), 209.

Kraimer, M. L., Wayne, S. J., & Jaworski, R. A. (2001). Sources of support and expatriate performance: The mediating role of expatriate adjustment. *Personnel Psychology, 54*(1), 71–99.

Kristof-Brown, A. L., Jansen, K. L., & Colbert, A. E. (2002). A policy-capturing study of the simultaneous effects of fit with jobs, groups, and organizations. *Journal of Applied Psychology, 87*(5), 985–993.

Lansberg, I. (1988). Social categorization, entitlement, and justice in organizations: Contextual determinants and cognitive underpinnings. *Human Relations, 41*(12), 871–849.

Lazarova, M. (2006). International human resource management in a global perspective. In M. J. Morley, N. Heraty, & D. Collings (Eds.), *International human resource management and international assignments* (pp. 24–51). Basingstoke, UK: Palgrave Macmillan.

Lazarus, R. S., & Folkman, S. (1984). *Stress appraisal and coping.* New York: Springer Publication Co.

Lee, C. H. (2005). A study of underemployment among self-initiated expatriates. *Journal of World Business, 40*(2), 172–187.

Lee, Y., & Larwood, L. (1983). The socialization of expatriate managers in multinational firms. *Academy of Management Journal, 26*(4), 657–665.

Leonardelli, G. J., Pickett, C. L., & Brewer, M. B. (2010). Optimal distinctiveness theory: A framework for social identity, social cognition and intergroup relations. In M. Zanna & J. Olson (Eds.), *Advances in experimental social psychology* (Vol. 43, pp. 65–115). New York: Elsevier.

Leonardelli, G. J., Pickett, C. L., Joseph, J. E., & Hess, Y. D. (2011). Optimal distinctiveness theory in nested categorization contexts: Moving from dueling identities to a dual identity. In R. M. Kramer, G. J. Leonardelli & R. W. Livingston (Eds.), *Social cognition, social identity, and intergroup relations: A festschrift in honor of Marilynn Brewer. Psychology Press Festschrift Series* (pp. 103–125). New York: Taylor & Francis.

Leonardelli, G. J., & Toh, S. M. (2011). Perceiving expatriate coworkers as foreigners encourages aid: Social categorization and procedural justice together improve intergroup cooperation and dual identity. *Psychological Science, 22*(1), 110–117.

Leonardelli, G. J., & Tormala, Z. L. (2003). The negative impact of perceiving discrimination on collective well-being: the mediating role of perceived ingroup status. *European Journal of Social Psychology, 33*(4), 507–514.

Leung, K., Smith, P. B., Wang, Z., & Sun, H. (1996). Job satisfaction in joint ventures hotels in China: An organizational justice analysis. *Journal of International Business Studies, 27*(5), 947–962.

Leung, K., Wang, Z., & Smith, P. B. (2001). Job attitudes and organizational justice in joint venture hotels in China: The role of expatriate managers. *International Journal of Human Resource Management, 12*(6), 926–945.

Liu, X., & Shaffer, M. A. (2005). An investigation of expatriate adjustment and performance: A social capital perspective. *International Journal of Cross Cultural Management, 5*(3), 235–254.

Locksley, A., Ortiz, V., & Hepburn, C. (1980). Social categorization and discriminatory behavior: Extinguishing the minimal intergroup discrimination effect. *Journal of Personality & Social Psychology, 39*(5), 773–783.

Louis, M. R. (1980). Surprise and sense making: What newcomers experience in entering unfamiliar organizational settings. *Administrative Science Quarterly, 25*(2), 226–251.

Louis, M. R., Posner, B. Z., & Powell, G. N. (1983). The availability and helpfulness of socialization practices. *Personnel Psychology, 36*(4), 857–866.

Lueke, S. B., & Svyantek, D. J. (2000). Organizational socialization in the host country: The missing link in reducing expatriate turnover. *International Journal of Organizational Analysis, 8*(4), 380–400.

Major, D. A., Kozlowski, S. W. J., Chao, G. T., & Gardner, P. D. (1995). A longitudinal investigation of newcomer expectations, early socialization outcomes, and the moderating effects of role development factors. *Journal of Applied Psychology, 80*(3), 418–431.

Martinko, M. J., & Douglas, S. (1999). Culture and expatriate failure: An attributional explication. *International Journal of Organizational Analysis, 7*(3), 265–263.

Maurer, S. D., & Li, S. (2006). Understanding expatriate manager performance: Effects of governance environments on work relationships in relation-based economies. *Human Resource Management Review, 16*(1), 29–46.

McDonald, M., Sidanius, J., & Navarrete, C. (2011). Developing a theory of gendered prejudice: An evolutionary and social dominance perspective. In R. Kramer, A. Leonardelli, & R. Livingston (Eds.), *Social cognition, social identity, and intergroup relations: A festschrift in honor of Marilynn Brewer. Psychology Press Festschrift Series* (pp. 189–220). New York: Taylor and Francis.

McGuire, W. J., McGuire, C. V., Child, P., & Fujioka, T. (1978). Salience of ethnicity in the spontaneous self-concept as a function of one's ethnic distinctiveness in the social environment. *Journal of Personality & Social Psychology, 36*(5), 511–520.

Mendenhall, M., Kuhlmann, T. M., Stahl, G. K., & Osland, J. S. (2002). Employee development and expatriate assignments. In M. J. Gannon & K. L. Newman (Eds.), *The Blackwell handbook of cross-cultural managment.* Malden, MA: Blackwell Business.

Morrison, E. W. (2002). Newcomers' relationships: The role of social network ties during socialization. *Academy of Management Journal, 45*(6), 1149–1160.

Nadler, A. (2002). Inter-group helping relations as power relations: Helping relations as affirming or challenging inter-group hierarchy. *Journal of Social Issues, 58,* 487–502.

Nadler, A. (2010). Interpersonal and intergroup helping relations as power relations: Implications for real-world helping. In S. Stürmer & M. Snyder (Eds.), *The psychology of prosocial behavior: Group processes, intergroup relations, and helping* (pp. 269–288). Walden, MA: Wiley-Blackwell.

Nadler, A., & Halabi, S. (2006). Inter-group helping as status relations: Effects of status stability, identification and type of help on receptivity to high status group's help. *Journal of Personality and Social Psychology, 91,* 97–110.

Napier, N. K., & Taylor, S. (2002). Experiences of women professionals abroad: Comparisons across Japan, China and Turkey. *International Journal of Human Resource Management, 13*(5), 837–851.

Naumann, E. (1993). Organizational predictors of expatriate job satisfaction. *Journal of International Business Studies, 24*(1), 61–80.

Nelson, D. L., & Quick, J. C. (1999). Social support and newcomer adjustment in organizations: Attachment theory at work? *Journal of Organizational Behavior, 12*(6), 543–564.

Newman, J., Bhatt, B., & Gutteridge, T. (1978). Determinants of expatriate effectiveness: A theoretical and empirical vacuum. *Academy of Management Review, 3*(3), 655–661.

Noorderhaven, N., & Harzing, A.-W. (2009). Knowledge-sharing and social interaction within MNEs. *Journal of International Business Studies, 40*(5), 719–741.

Oberg, K. (1960). Cultural shock: Adjustment to new cultural environments. *Practical Anthropology, 7*, 177–182.

Oddou, G. (2002). *Repatriate assets and firm performance: Toward a model.* Paper presented at the Annual Academy of Management Meeting, Denver, CO.

Olsen, J. E., & Martins, L. L. (2009). The effects of expatriate demographic characteristics on adjustment: A social identity approach. *Human Resource Management, 48*(2), 311–328.

Osland, J. (1995). *The adventure of working abroad: Hero tales from the global frontier* (1st ed.). San Francisco: Jossey-Bass Publishers.

Paik, Y., & Sohn, J. D. (2004). Expatriate managers and MNC's ability to control international subsidiaries: the case of Japanese MNCs. *Journal of World Business, 39*(1), 61–71.

Paik, Y., Vance, C. M., Gale, J., & McGrath, C. A. (2008). Improving global knowledge management through inclusion of host country workforce input. In K. O'Sullivan (Ed.), *Strategic knowledge management in multinational organizations* (pp. 167–182). New York: IGI Global.

Parker, B., & McEvoy, G. M. (1993). Initial examination of a model of intercultural adjustment. *International Journal of Intercultural Relations, 17*(3), 355–379.

Peterson, M. F., Rodriguez, C. L., & Smith, P. B. (2000). Agency theory and event management. In P. C. Earley & H. Singh (Eds.), *Innovations in international and cross-cultural management* (pp. 131–182). Thousand Oaks, CA: Sage Press.

Pinder, C. C., & Schroeder, K. G. (1987). Time to proficiency following job transfers. *Academy of Management Journal, 30*(2), 336–353.

Reagans, R., & McEvily, B. (2003). Network structure and knowledge transfer: The effects of cohesion and range. *Administrative Science Quarterly, 48*(2), 240–267.

Reiche, B. S. (2011). Knowledge transfer in multinationals: The role of inpatriates' boundary spanning. *Human Resource Management, 50*(3), 365–389.

Reiche, B. S., & Harzing, A.-W. (2011). International assignments. In A.-W. Harzing & A. H. Pinnington (Eds.), *International human resource management* (3rd ed., pp. 185–226). London: Sage.

Reiche, B. S., Harzing, A.-W., & Kraimer, M. L. (2009a). The role of international assignees' social capital in creating inter-unit intellectual capital: A cross-level model. *Journal of International Business Studies, 40*(3), 509–526.

Reiche, B. S., Kraimer, M. L., & Harzing, A.-W. (2009b). Inpatriates as agents of cross unit knowledge flows in multinational corporations. In P. R. Sparrow (Ed.), *Handbook of international HR research: Integrating people, process and context.* Chichester, UK: Oxford Blackwell.

Reichers, A. E. (1987). An interactionist perspective on newcomer socialization rates. *Academy of Management Review, 12*(2), 278–287.

Saucier, D. A., Miller, C. T., & Doucet, N. (2005). Differences in helping whites and blacks: A meta-analysis. *Personality & Social Psychology Review, 9*(1), 2–16.

Schaefer, D. A., & Kornienko, O. (2009). Building cohesion in positively connected exchange networks. *Social Psychology Quarterly, 72*(4), 384–402.

Selmer, J. (2002). Adjustment of third country national expatriates in China. *Asia Pacific Business Review, 9*(2), 101–117.

Shaffer, M. A., & Harrison, D. A. (1998). Expatriates' psychological withdrawal from international assignments: Work, nonwork, and family influences. *Personnel Psychology, 51*(1), 87–118.

Shaffer, M. A., Harrison, D. A., & Gilley, K. M. (1999). Dimensions, determinants, and differences in the expatriate adjustment process. *Journal of International Business Studies, 30*(3), 557–581.

Shaffer, M. A., Harrison, D. A., Gregersen, H., Black, J. S., & Ferzandi, L. A. (2006). You can take it with you: Individual differences and expatriate effectiveness. *Journal of Applied Psychology, 91*(1), 109–125.

Sinangil, H. K., & Ones, D. S. (2001). Expatriate management. In N. Anderson, D. S. Ones, H. K. Sinangil & C. Viswesvaran (Eds.), *Handbook of industrial, work and organizational psychology* (Vol. 2, pp. 424–443). Thousand Oaks, CA: Sage.

Slaughter, J. E., & Zickar, M. J. (2006). A new look at the role of insiders in the newcomer socialization process. *Group & Organization Management, 31*(2), 264–290.

Smith, H. J., & Tyler, T. R. (1996). Justice and power: when will justice concerns encourage the advantaged to support policies which redistribute economic resources and the disadvantaged to willingly obey the law? *European Journal of Social Psychology, 26*(2), 171–200.

Stasser, G., Stewart, D. D., & Wittenbaum, G. M. (1995). Expert roles and information exchange during discussion: The importance of knowing who knows what. *Journal of Experimental Social Psychology, 31*(3), 244–265.

Stürmer, S., & Snyder, M. (2010). *The psychology of prosocial behavior: Group processes, intergroup relations, and helping.* Walden, MA: Wiley-Blackwell.

Suutari, V., & Brewster, C. (1998). The adaptation of expatriates in Europe: Evidence from Finnish companies. *Personnel Review, 27*(2), 89.

Tajfel, H. (1978). *Differentiation between social groups: Studies in the social psychology of intergroup relations.* London: Published in cooperation with European Association of Experimental Social Psychology by Academic Press.

Tajfel, H., Billig, M. G., Bundy, R. P., & Flament, C. (1971). Social categorization and intergroup behaviour. *European Journal of Social Psychology, 1*, 149–178.

Takeuchi, R. (2010). A critical review of expatriate adjustment research through a multiple stakeholder view: Progress, emerging trends, and prospects. *Journal of Management, 36*(4), 1040–1064.

Takeuchi, R., Yun, S., & Russell, J. E. A. (2002). Antecedents and consequences of the perceived adjustment of Japanese expatriates in the USA. *International Journal of Human Resource Management, 13*(8), 1224–1244.

Teece, D. J. (1977). Technology transfer by multinational firms: The resource cost of transferring technological know-how. *Economic Journal, 87*(346), 242–261.

Thomas, D. C., Lazarova, M. B., & Inkson, K. (2005). Global careers: New phenomenon or new perspectives? *Journal of World Business, 40*(4), 340–347.

Thomas, D. C., & Ravlin, E. C. (1995). Responses of employees to cultural adaptation by a foreign manager. *Journal of Applied Psychology, 80*(1), 133–146.

Ting-Toomey, S., Yee-Jung, K. K., Shapiro, R. B., Garcia, W., Wright, T. J., & Oetzel, J. G. (2000). Ethnic/cultural identity salience and conflict styles in four US ethnic groups. *International Journal of Intercultural Relations, 24*(1), 47–81.

Toh, S. M., & DeNisi, A. S. (2003). Host country national (HCN) reactions to expatriate pay policies: A proposed model and implications. *Academy of Management Review, 28*(4), 606–621.

Toh, S. M., & DeNisi, A. S. (2005). A local perspective to expatriate success. *Academy of Management Executive, 19*(1), 132.

Toh, S. M., & DeNisi, A. S. (2007). Host country nationals as socializing agents: a social identity approach. *Journal of Organizational Behavior, 28*(3), 281–301.

Triandis, H. C., Bontempo, R., Villareal, M. J., Asai, M., & Lucca, N. (1988). Individualism and collectivism: Cross-cultural perspectives on self-ingroup relationships. *Journal of Personality & Social Psychology, 54*(2), 323–338.

Tung, R. L. (1987). Expatriate assignments: Enhancing success and minimizing failure. *Academy of Management Executive, 1*(2), 117–125.

Turner, J. C., Hogg, M. A., Oakes, P. J., Reicher, S. D., & Wetherell, M. S. (1987). *Rediscovering the social group: Self-categorization theory.* Oxford, UK; New York: B. Blackwell.

Tyler, T. R., & Blader, S. L. (2003). The group engagement model: Procedural justice, social identity, and cooperative behavior. *Personality & Social Psychology Review, 7*(4), 349–361.

Tyler, T. R., & Lind, E. A. (1992). A relational model of authority in groups. In P. Z. Mark (Ed.), *Advances in experimental social psychology, 25,* 115–191.

van Knippenberg, D., & van Leeuwen, E. (2001). Organizational identity after a merger: Sense of continuity as the key to post-merger identification. In M. A. Hogg & D. J. Terry (Eds.), *Social identity processes in organizational contexts* (pp. 249–264). Philadelphia: Psychology Press.

van Leeuwen, E., & van Knippenberg, D. (2003). Organizational identification following a merger: The importance of agreeing to differ. In S. A. Haslam, D. van Knippenberg, M. J. Platow, & N. Ellemers (Eds.), *Social identity at work: Developing theory for organizational practice.* (pp. 205–221): New York: Psychology Press.

Van Vianen, A. E. M., De Pater, I. E., Kristof-Brown, A. L., & Johnson, E. C. (2004). Fitting in: Surface-and deep-level cultural differences and expatriates' adjustment. *Academy of Management Journal, 47*(5), 697–709.

Vance, C. M., & Paik, Y. (2002). One size fits all in expatriate pre-departure training? *Journal of Management Development, 21*(7/8), 557.

Vance, C. M., & Ring, P. S. (1994). Preparing the host country workforce for expatriate managers: The neglected other side of the coin. *Human Resource Development Quarterly, 5*(4), 337–352.

Vance, C. M., Vaiman, V., & Andersen, T. (2009). The vital liaison role of host country nationals in MNC knowledge management. *Human Resource Management, 48*(4), 649–659.

Varma, A., Budhwar, P., & Pichler, S. (2009). Chinese host country nationals' willingness to help expatriates: The role of social categorization. *Thunderbird International Business Review, 53*(5), 353–364.

Varma, A., Pichler, S., Budhwar, P., & Biswas, S. (2009). Chinese host country nationals' willingness to support expatriates: The role of collectivism, interpersonal affect, and guanxi. *International Journal of Cross-Cultural Management, 9*(2), 99–216.

Varma, A., Toh, S. M., & Budhwar, P. S. (2006). A new perspective on the female expatriate experience: The role of host country national categorization. *Journal of World Business, 41*(2), 112–120.

Wanberg, C. R., & Kammeyer-Mueller, J. D. (2000). Predictors and outcomes of proactivity in the socialization process. *Journal of Applied Psychology, 85*(3), 373–385.

Wanberg, C. R., Welsh, E. T., & Hezlett, S. A. (2003). Mentoring research: A review and dynamic process model. In J. J. Martocchio & G. R. Ferris (Eds.), *Research in personnel and human resources management* (Vol. 22, pp. 39–124). Oxford, UK: Elsevier Science.

Ward, C., Bochner, S., & Furnham, A. (2001). *The psychology of culture shock.* London: Routledge.

Wills, T. A. (1991). Social support and interpersonal relationships. In M. S. Clark (Ed.), *Review of personality and social psychology* (Vol. 12, pp. 265–289). Newbury Park, CA: Sage.

Wong, M. M. L. (2001). Internationalizing Japanese expatriate managers: Organizational learning through international assignment. *Management Learning, 32*(2), 237–251.

Wright, S. C., & Richard, N. T. (2010). Cross-group helping: Perspectives on why and why not. In S. Stürmer & M. Snyder (Eds.), *The psychology of prosocial behavior: Group processes, intergroup relations, and helping* (pp. 311–336). Walden, MA: Wiley-Blackwell.

Yzerbyt, V., & Demoulin, S. (2010). Intergroup relations. In S. Fiske, D. T. Gilbert & G. Lindzey (Eds.), *Handbook of social psychology* (5th ed., Vol. 2, pp. 1024–1083). Hoboken, NJ: John Wiley.

Zaidman, N., & Brock, D. M. (2009). Knowledge transfer within multinationals and their foreign subsidiaries: A culture-context approach. *Group & Organization Management, 34*(3), 297–329.

Socializing the "Other" Organizational Newcomers—Customers, Clients, and Guests

Keith Rollag

Abstract

Successful organizations effectively socialize more than their new employees –they also socialize new customers, clients, guests, and others who begin to use their products and services. This chapter extends socialization theory and best practices into the realm of new customers, and explores how some organizations gain a competitive advantage through newcomer socialization by helping new (and especially inexperienced) customers quickly become connected, informed, productive, satisfied, and loyal.

Key Words: customer, client, guest, socialization, newcomer, service provider

Introduction

Successful organizations socialize more than just their new employees—they effectively and efficiently socialize new customers, clients, guests, and others who begin to use their products and services. A thoughtful customer socialization strategy not only can create a positive first impression with new customers, but also help improve overall customer and organizational productivity, leading to increased customer satisfaction, higher customer loyalty and repeat business, and referrals and testimonials that can generate even more customers.

While there has been some research into customer socialization (Evans, Stan, & Murray, 2008; Fonner & Timmerman, 2009; Groth, Mertens, & Murphy, 2005; Kelley, Skinner, & Donnelly, 1992), most socialization research has focused on formal entry into work organizations by new employees. The goal of this chapter is to review and synthesize the existing literature in both customer and organizational socialization and outline a set of socialization design strategies managers might consider in creating an effective customer socialization program. To provide examples of best practice and theory-in-action,

this chapter also describes highly successful socialization strategies at four organizations—Blue Nile, Apple Retail Stores, Harley-Davidson, and Willow Creek Community Church—and concludes with some suggestions for future research.

New Realities and the Importance of Customer Socialization

Several trends are increasing the extent to which organizations must socialize new customers and the impact that customer socialization has on organizational performance. First, a growing percentage of the world economy is based on services, which typically involve frequent interaction with customers including new customers (Reif, Woznick, Thurmond, Kelley, & Ostrea, 1997). Even traditional manufacturing organizations find themselves providing more services to customers, both to generate additional revenue and as a "value-add" to distinguish themselves from competitors (Apte, Karmarkar, & Nath, 2008). While managers might socialize a new employee relatively infrequently, depending on their business context they may interact with new customers or guests on a daily basis.

Second, new technologies allow companies to create more complex products and services, which in turn require more training and support for new users. For example, the simple pushbutton telephone has been replaced by a multimedia communication device with not only telephony but also Internet access, productivity applications, music, and games. The consumer banking experience has changed from interacting with bank tellers to making deposits and withdrawals from ATMs located in malls and convenience stores, as well as paying bills and transferring funds online. Not only do more complex products and services require more customer training and socialization, complexity can potentially intimidate new customers and keep them from trying and adopting new products and services (Kelley, Donnelly, & Skinner, 1990).

Third, in a quest for increased organizational efficiency, many firms have customers assume a greater role in the service process (Fonner & Timmerman, 2009; Halbesleben & Buckley, 2004), which in turn increases the need for effective customer socialization. For example, consumers now can print their own airline boarding passes, bypass movie lines and buy tickets in self-serve kiosks, and use self-checkout lanes in hardware and grocery stores. Customers can also access product support information online instead of interacting with a customer service representative. Marketing researchers often describe this phenomenon as *customer co-production of services* (Bowen, 1986; Lengnick-Hall, 1996; Lovelock & Young, 1979) and note that as customers increasingly take over part of the service process, managers can start to consider them as "partial employees" (Mills & Morris, 1986).

In much the same way as with socialization of employees, effective customer socialization can lead to several important benefits for companies. In service industries, organizational efficiency is partially driven by the performance of customers (Bateson, 2002; Zeithmal, Bitner, & Gremler, 2006). By having customers perform tasks that were traditionally done by paid employees, organizations can often improve organizational productivity through lower labor costs (Lovelock & Young, 1979). Furthermore, properly socialized customers understand the product or service process and their role as customer, and are less disruptive to the service process, not only speeding service flow and productivity, but improving the service experience for other customers. By being more self-reliant, socialized customers also may require fewer organizational resources (Bateson, 2002; Groth et al., 2005).

More importantly, researchers have shown that making an effort to properly socialize customers leads to higher customer satisfaction (Kelley et al., 1992), which can increase customer loyalty and repeat business and decrease customer complaints. Socialized customers are more confident using a product or service, feel more in control of product or service outcomes, and are more capable of customizing the experience to meet their own expectations (Bateson, 2002; Rodie & Kleine, 2000). Having satisfied customers through effective socialization can also increase the probability that customers make positive recommendations to other potential customers, help other customers with product or service queries, and provide constructive feedback on the product or service to the firm (Groth et al., 2005). The more customers understand a product or service, the more they will likely use it, the more innovative they can be in using the product or co-producing the service, and the more willing they will be to share these innovative ideas with the company (Mills & Morris, 1986).

Customer Socialization as a Role-Making Process

Despite the evidence that proactively socializing customers improves organizational productivity and customer satisfaction, research suggests that most organizations do little to socialize new customers (Fonner & Timmerman, 2009). Finding ways to make new customer entry less intimidating and stressful can generate major benefits for the firm. Several researchers have argued that since customers can often be considered "partial employees" who co-produce product and service experiences (Bowen, 1986; Mills & Morris, 1986), we can apply organizational socialization principles to customers (Fonner & Timmerman, 2009; Halbesleben & Buckley, 2004). The following represents a synthesis of organizational and customer socialization literatures.

Similar to organizational socialization of new employees, customer socialization is effectively a role-making process. One can consider a customer's interaction with a product or service as a role performance, and in the case of services, often between two or more social actors (Soloman, Surprenant, Czepiel, & Gutman, 1985). Companies explicitly or implicitly define the role of the customer by how they design a particular product or service, and socialization helps customers learn and master that role over time (Soloman et al., 1985). In terms of role, customers can provide resources into the service process (e.g., soiled clothes to drycleaners, trash to garbage collectors), help co-produce the service outcome (e.g., health clubs, grocery stores), or be the service outcome itself (e.g., college student, hospital patient) (Lengnick-Hall, 1996). Services have varied levels of customer participation ranging from low (e.g., attending a symphony or baseball game) to high (e.g., ski resorts, restaurant buffets;Kelley et al., 1990; Zeithmal et al., 2006). Service customers typically provide both mental inputs (e.g., information, decisions) as well as physical and emotional inputs (Rodie & Kleine, 2000).

Some service situations like Weight Watchers require not only customer interaction with the service provider, but also with other customers (Zeithmal et al., 2006). Customer performance is ultimately a product of role clarity, ability, and motivation (Bowen, 1986; Scott W. Kelley, 1992; Rodie & Kleine, 2000), and customer role is strongly associated with customer identity (Swan, Goodwin, Mayo, & Richardson, 2001). For both employees and customers, entry into a new role can activate needs for meaning, control, identity, and belonging (Ashforth, 2001). Both groups face both social and task adjustments (Moschis, 1985) as they make sense of and master their new roles and seek social acceptance from employees and other customers (Feldman, 1981).

Similar to an employee role, the customer role not only includes expectations for what they should do and what information they should provide, but also the level of courtesy, friendliness, and respect they should display as they perform their role (Kelley et al., 1990; Kelley et al., 1992). Companies also hope that customers engage in citizenship behaviors associated with a particular product or service, such as filling out feedback forms, recommending product or services to others, or providing the firm ideas for improved service (Groth et al., 2005). Companies have some control over how they define the customer role (Halbesleben & Buckley, 2004) and the relative portion of the service performed by the customer (Bowen, 1986), which in turn affects the amount of customer socialization required to create savvy, satisfied customers and efficient, productive service processes.

Inherent in the concept of customer role and socialization are scripts, defined as learned patterns of social behavior (Abelson, 1981). People often process past experience as a series of expected behavioral scripts and then use their set of accumulated scripts to help make sense of and decide what to do in new situations, providing people with a sense of predictability and control (Bateson, 2002). For example, customers use their previous experience at other restaurants to decide how to act and respond in a new restaurant (e.g., how and when to order food, how long to expect to wait for food to arrive, how much to tip, etc.). Scripts can also cross product or service boundaries—for example, a customer taking a cruise for the first time might rely on his or her experience at resort hotels as a script for how to think and act onboard the ship (Rodie & Kleine, 2000).

As children and adolescents, customers are initially socialized with the skills, knowledge, and attitudes associated with buying behavior through parents, school, peers, and mass media (Moschis, 1985; Moschis & Churchill, 1987; Moschis & L., 1979; Ward, 1974). New and novice customers tend to have generalized, concrete scripts with little planning for contingencies, while expert, socialized customers tend to have very detailed, context-specific scripts with a greater ability to handle deviations from the expected experience (Bateson, 2002). New customers that arrive with low levels of role readiness (either through lack of experience, ability, or motivation) may experience role ambiguity, role conflict, decreased performance, and lower satisfaction with the product or service (Mills & Morris, 1986).

The most challenging, stressful situations for new customers (and the greater need for customer socialization) is when their set of accumulated scripts do not prepare them for a new product or service experience, which often occurs when the product or service are relatively complex (e.g., buying a home or insurance), highly customized (e.g., buying a computer), highly infrequent (e.g., funeral or wedding planning), or requires new, specialized skills (e.g., skiing, golf, dancing; Kelley et al., 1990). New customers can be new to the company, new to the product or service, or both, and socialization is probably the most intense and stressful for those customers in situations where they are first-time buyers or users of a product or service (Van Maanen & Schein, 1979). Customer stress and intimidation can also occur when his or her existing scripts and behavioral expectations are initially at odds with the evolving product or service experience (e.g., ordering a specialty coffee for the first time at Starbucks.) The lower stress associated with script familiarity is one of the reasons why some people prefer national restaurant chains, especially when visiting new locales (Bateson, 2002).

Intimidation and stress also occur when the new customer perceives the social cost for role failure to be high, risking dissatisfaction or social rejection from product or service providers or other users and customers. For example, this occurs with young adults trying to look savvy on a first date visit at an unfamiliar, fancy restaurant (Soloman et al., 1985), or a first-time golfer joining a group of more experienced friends and colleagues. The perceived social cost is partly a function of the probability of role failure, coupled with an assessment of how much role failure will be observed and judged negatively by others and the relative desire for social acceptance by others in their immediate reference group. This kind of intimidation and stress can be especially strong when new users or members are attempting to join a strong user community with complex jargon, technologies, rituals, and status hierarchies (e.g., skateboarders, wine enthusiasts, hunters, etc.).

The most efficient service performance occurs when the customer's script (acquired either from past experience or proactive socialization) is aligned with the company's product or service script (Bateson, 2002). The goal is to ensure that new customers quickly gain role clarity, and through successful role enactment and successful performance achieve role validation (i.e. "I can do this!") and thereby reinforce a positive self-concept, leading to increased satisfaction (Soloman et al., 1985). Companies also want new customers to immediately see the reward for successful performance, whether that be increased control over product or service delivery, time savings, or monetary savings (Bowen, 1986).

One particular challenge is deciding whether to design products and services for customer role innovation. On one hand, allowing the customer the freedom to innovate can result in new product uses and new ideas for more efficient service. On the other hand, innovation can risk product failure or major disruption to service flows, which can reduce customer satisfaction or service productivity.

Savvy managers ask themselves the following questions. First, how have I defined the role of my new customer in using my product or service, and what is the desired relationship and interdependencies between new customers and employees? Second, do new customers already understand their role through previous experience, or do they require orientation and training? Third, how can I minimize the perceived social cost of role failure among new customers? Finally, what can I do to either help new customers learn their role quickly and stress-free, or modify the product, service, or customer role to require less socialization?

Attract New Customers that Are Easy to Socialize

One of the simplest ways to effective socialization is to attract new customers that are easy to socialize. As with employees, proper recruitment and selection can simplify socialization requirements (Ashforth, Sluss, & Harrison, 2007)—research has shown that a strong fit between new employees and their organizations can speed entry (Chatman, 1991), something that is likely true with new customers as well. Marketing researchers have suggested that companies preferentially seek customers who are willing to be "good customers" and both help co-produce services (Bowen, 1986; Halbesleben & Buckley, 2004) and improve service quality (Mills & Morris, 1986). There are several kinds of potential fit: customer–role fit, customer–service provider fit, and customer–organization fit (Halbesleben & Buckley, 2004).

Anticipatory Customer Socialization— Before They Arrive

Creating a positive, less intimidating experience for new users and customers can begin before they even hold a product or request a service. Known as *pre-encounter* or *anticipatory socialization*, this typically involves providing new customers information about the product or service so they can feel more informed and confident when they finally use a product or service for the first time (Mills & Morris, 1986). For example, Disney World sends prospective and first-time guests a packet of information about the Disney resort experience (e.g. maps, park attractions, tips for new visitors, etc.) to both pre-socialize customers into the role of Disney guest and set expectations about how their Disney vacation will transpire (Bowers & Martin, 2007; Kelley et al., 1990). Sugarloaf Ski Resort in Maine has an 8-minute "First-Timers Guide" video on their website that shows prospective skiers the entire ski resort experience, from getting picked up in the parking lot by the shuttle bus, to the ski rental shop, ski school, ski lift logistics, and the various dining options (Sugarloaf, 2011). Realtors and mortgage brokers often hold free, no-obligation seminars for prospective home buyers to help demystify the home buying experience, hopefully leading to future customers and sales.

New customers also have incoming expectations about the product or service and the respective roles of customer and employee, and evaluate their initial experience against those expectations (Kelley et al., 1990). Some researchers suggest that realistic service or product previews that aim to lower expectations can help improve the eventual product or service experience (Bowen, 1986; Mills & Morris, 1986; Schneider & Bowen, 1995), while other researchers have found that pre-socializing customers to service expectations can actually reduce satisfaction by priming them to be more informed, critical evaluators (Evans et al., 2008).

Servicescape Design and Customer Socialization

Known by marketing researchers as *servicescape*, another design consideration in customer socialization is the physical environment that new customers encounter when they purchase a new product or attempt to use a new service (M. J. Bitner, 1992). This can include the layout of products and services, as well as signs, symbols and artifacts that provide customers clues about product features or service flow (Bitner, 1992, 2000). The physical environment (or by extension the virtual environment on company websites) can aid or hinder customer socialization by defining the boundaries between customers and employees, and how customers should interact with employees (and each other). For example, many firms use signs, lanes, and ropes to help queue customers, or use counters and windows to provide a barrier between customers and employees. Fast food restaurants use serving trays and strategically placed trash cans to encourage patrons to bus their own tables (Bowen, 1986). The Japanese teppan-yaki-style restaurant chain Benihana designs their cooking and serving areas to encourage social interactions among strangers (Bitner, 1992). "In these ways the servicescape plays a part in conveying the organizational culture and purpose, socializing both customers and employees" (Bitner, 2000, p. 40). Proper store and product design that anticipates new customers' incoming expectations and quickly and efficiently orients the customer to his/her role can reduce the stress and anxiety for new customers (Kelley et al., 1990).

Socialization Tactics and New Customers

Much of the research in organizational socialization has focused on describing and evaluating the various strategies organizations use to assimilate new employees. Van Maanen and Schein (1979) defined six tactical dimensions of socialization, which included group versus individual, formal versus informal, lock-step versus random, fixed versus variable timing, socialization primarily from others versus oneself, and tactics that affirm versus disaffirm the newcomer's incoming identity. Jones (1986) condensed these dimensions into two broad strategies—whether to socialize newcomers in groups in a formalized, planned way through orientations and common learning experiences (institutionalized), or whether to socialize newcomers individually "on the job" in a more informal, newcomer-driven approach. Over time, research with new employees has tended to show that institutionalized tactics have been associated with lower role ambiguity and conflict, higher task mastery and job satisfaction, greater information and feedback seeking by newcomers, and increased organizational commitment, but negatively associated with role innovation (Major, Kozlowski, Chao, & Gardner, 1995; Mignerey, Rubin, & Gorden, 1995; Saks & Ashforth, 1997).

In terms of customer socialization, firms also have a choice in how to socialize new customers, and some limited research suggests that formal, institutionalized socialization is associated with increased customer satisfaction (Fonner & Timmerman, 2009). Formal socialization activities can include orientations, tours, workshops, and demonstrations—in other words, structured, planned activities that not only help orient new customers to both the product or service and their role, but provide psychological and emotional support during the learning process (Bowen, 1986). Formal socialization activities can also be more passive, such as new user guides, maps, orientation pamphlets, and signs, both paper-based and online (Kelley et al., 1990). Even the ubiquitous Directory of Services seen on the desks of most hotel rooms is an example of passive socialization (Bateson, 2002). Customers often appreciate structured, formal socialization activities because not only do they receive information and training to ease entry into the product or service, but also the activity or material itself demonstrates the company's commitment to new customers.

One important decision point is whether to socialize new customers as a group or individually. Socializing new customers as a group through formal orientations or training sessions has several advantages. First, group socialization may be more efficient than trying to orient each new customer or guest separately. Second, new customers can build relationships with each other, quickly generating feelings of social acceptance. Finally, socializing new customers away from more experienced veterans can help reduce the perceived social cost of initial role failure, since their initial reference group will be other newcomers. For example, in order to attract new female customers, Home Depot offers "Do It Herself" small group workshops for women only, which helps orient and socialize women into larger home renovation projects like tiling, installing light fixtures, painting, and other projects that were traditionally the domain of men (Laird, 2010).

Alternately, socializing new customers individually also has advantages. First, individual orientations "on demand" may be more convenient for new customers than scheduled group activities, and socialization efforts can be more effectively tailored to the needs and previous experience of the new customer. New customers may also like the individualized attention and may build a stronger relationship with the product or service provider that can lead to future sales and service use. Some companies utilize both group and individual approaches. For example, most ski resorts offer both group and individual lessons to beginning skiers, allowing their new customers to choose which form of socialization is most appealing.

Whether socialized as groups or individuals, companies need to decide how much they want to identify specific customers as new, both to employees and other customers. For example, most martial arts training companies use a system of colored belts to identify skill level, which quickly identifies new and inexperienced customers. In other environments, new customers may wear special nametags to identify themselves as new. On one hand, identification of newcomers can help service providers target help and orientation to those who most need it and allow new customers to identify with other new customers. Being labeled as new can also help excuse initial performance mistakes, reducing performance anxiety for some new customers. On the other hand, identification of new customers can make them feel "exposed" and subject to special evaluation by more experienced users. The benefits of identifying new customers likely depends on the helping and welcoming orientation of both the company and other customers—if being labeled as a new customer provides the customer more support than scrutiny, it can be a powerful way of customizing socialization to all customers.

New Customer Proactivity and Information-Seeking

New customers often have the greatest need for information but the most reluctance to ask for it. Product and service companies need to develop an information-providing strategy that maximizes efficiency (for both customers and employees) but also minimizes the perceived social cost of asking for help and advice. Both new employees and new customers typically seek information to reduce uncertainty, clarify role expectations, maintain control, and facilitate and improve both decision making and overall role performance (Ashford & Black, 1996; Fonner & Timmerman, 2009; Jablin, 1987; Miller & Jablin, 1991). Among employees, formal organizational efforts to socialize new employees has been shown to help drive newcomer proactivity (Ashforth et al., 2007), which in turn has been associated with increased task mastery, role clarity, and social integration (Morrison, 1993a) as well as higher job satisfaction (Morrison, 1993b; Ostroff & Kozlowski, 1992).

New customers obtain information through a variety of proactive and passive tactics (Fonner & Timmerman, 2009; Kelley et al., 1990). They can proactively approach an employee and ask a question, or in some situations approach and ask another customer (McGrath & Otnes, 1995). They can gain information by observing employees and other customers (Kelley et al., 1990), or listen in as other customers converse or ask questions. Sometimes customers will obtain information about expected product use or service rules by "testing," engaging in specific behaviors and then observing the reaction of employees and other customers (Fonner & Timmerman, 2009). Customers can also proactively send nonverbal signals to employees and other customers that they would like assistance, such as displaying a look of confusion, helplessness, intense concentration, or frustration. New customers also gain information passively when employees proactively approach them to see if they need assistance. In some situations, other customers and guests will proactively provide unsolicited help or advice (McGrath & Otnes, 1995).

Customers often choose a specific information-seeking tactic based on perceived social cost. Fonner and Timmerman (2009) found that customers associated higher social costs with asking questions than with observing or "testing," but found that asking questions was positively associated with role clarity, satisfaction, and intentions for repeat business. They found that "customers who can proactively ask questions or observe others will more likely return for repeat business than those who feel they must resort to more manipulative or clandestine information seeking (p. 264)." In general, customers often desire to ask questions but worry they will appear uninformed, or will annoy the source (Morrison & Bies, 1993).

Customers often decide whether to proactively approach a specific employee for assistance based on three factors—availability, approachability, and helpfulness. Are there employees or service employers nearby? Does their current behavior and demeanor suggest that it is socially appropriate to approach them for help or advice? Will asking my question cause them to think me foolish or incompetent? Finally, do they appear to be someone who could actually help me with my specific information need? All of these elements will factor into a new customer's evaluation of the social cost for proactively asking questions.

Companies can do a variety of things to promote information seeking by new customers, both face to face and online. To improve availability, managers can place or encourage employees to loiter in product or service areas where customers typically have lots of questions. For example, Home Depot stations a cashier near the customer self-checkout lanes to be immediately available to help customers if they encounter problems scanning or paying for product (Bowers & Martin, 2007). Or they can use strategically placed signs, pamphlets, manuals, and self-serve information kiosks to allow customers to obtain the information they need without interacting with employees, actions that often have lower perceived social costs. Online, companies can ensure they have employees ready to answer questions and provide support via a variety of communication technologies (email, chat, etc.). Some companies provide both—insurance company Esurance uses choice as a way to attract new customers with their advertising tagline "People when you want them, technology when you don't" (Ridgeway, 2010).

To improve approachability, managers can train employees to proactively approach customers and ask "May I help you?" or "If you have any questions, please let me know," though too much of this to the same customer by different employees can be annoying. Some firms station "greeters" at the entrance of a store to welcome customers and ask if they need help, which can immediately signal to new customers that employees are approachable. Employees can wear buttons that say "Ask Me a Question" or "How Can I Help?" to signal and legitimize approachability, and be trained to respond in a friendly and enthusiastic way to questions even if they have been asked the same question many times before by other customers. Employees can also be trained to respond to customer eye contact (which is often a signal customers need help). Managers can also create, clearly indicate, and continually staff designated customer service areas—if new customers ascertain that a specific employee's current role is to answer questions, they are more likely to approach them. In some situations, allowing new customers to get help and advice in a location separate from more experienced customers can also reduce the perceived social cost of seeking help or advice.

To improve helpfulness, managers can not only train their employees to be experts on their products and services (or train them to quickly access needed information via databases or online materials), but also empower them with the ability to adjust company policies and procedures (within reason) to help and satisfy customer needs. Many companies also have websites with extensive product information, technical support databases, and other resources they have found useful for customers. One particular challenge with helpfulness is providing feedback to customers on their role performance, especially if the feedback is negative (Halbesleben & Buckley, 2004; Kelley et al., 1990).

Another approach to increase perceptions of availability, approachability, and helpfulness for new customers is to designate an employee (or sometimes another customer) as a mentor or "buddy." Their role is to be the primary socialization agent to the new customer, quickly establishing a close relationship and being available to answer questions and provide advice. Designating someone as mentor or buddy facilitates and provides legitimacy for the new customer to approach the mentor or buddy and ask questions. For example, some nursing homes or preschools will assign an existing resident or student as a "buddy" to a new arrival to provide them with someone they can go for help or advice (Bowers, Martin, & Luker, 1990). Some firms have found success with virtual "socialization agents" to help new customers adjust and function within new online service environments (Kohler, Rohm, Ruyter, & Wetzels, 2010).

Some firms also have harnessed the power of the Internet to build online product and service communities that can also help socialize and orient new customers. Through discussion boards, chat rooms, Twitter, Facebook, and other forums customers can ask questions, share product and service feedback, and build relationships with other customers. Typically questions and conversations are indexed and archived, allowing new customers to search previous conversations for specific information.

Four Examples of Effective New Customer Socialization

To help show how new customer socialization strategies are applied in practice, I've chosen four organizations that have succeeded by proactively attracting and socializing new customers or members. Blue Nile is the largest online retailer for diamond engagement rings, Apple Retail Stores sell and support their entire line of computer products, Harley-Davidson sells high-end motorcycles, and Willow Creek Community Church is a 23,000 + community of worshippers across several campuses in Chicago.

Blue Nile—Success through Socializing New Engagement Ring Buyers

For most men, buying their first engagement ring is a stressful experience. They face enormous pressure to please their fiancé-to-be, but as first-time buyers they lack the knowledge and confidence to shop for and buy a diamond ring. Their previous retail experience does little to prepare them for the role of diamond buyer, and many fear that jewelry stores will take advantage of their ignorance and either sell them an overpriced diamond or pressure them into buying a bigger or higher-quality diamond than they can afford (Greene, 2008).

Blue Nile founder Mark Vadon was also stressed by the engagement ring buying experience. As a new diamond customer he wanted to make an informed, thoughtful decision, but was frustrated by a clerk at Tiffany's who showed him a few rings and told him to buy "what spoke to him" (Acohido, 2003). He ultimately went online and found a basic tutorial about diamond buying at www.internetdiamonds. com, a website by Doug Williams, who owned a small jewelry store in Seattle and was trying to sell diamond rings through the Internet. Mark bought a $5800 ring from Doug that was very similar to the more expensive ones at Tiffany's, and learned through Doug that other men were also willing to spend thousands online to buy diamond rings "sight unseen" if they felt they were making an informed decision (Rivlin, 2007). Seeing a business opportunity, Mark eventually bought Doug's Internet diamond business, raised over $50 million in venture capital, and re-launched the business as Blue Nile in 1999 (Greene, 2008).

Since then Blue Nile has grown to become the third largest diamond retailer behind Zales and Tiffany's (Rivlin, 2007), selling $295 million of jewelry in 2008 (Fowler, 2009). According to CEO Diane Irvine, over 70% of their revenues come from engagement rings (InternetRetailer, 2010), and the average engagement ring sale at Blue Nile is $5500, over twice the industry-wide average of $2700 (Rivlin, 2007).

While part of their success comes from having lower prices than retail jewelry stores through larger inventories and lower overhead (Markels, 2002), much of it can be attributed to their new customer socialization strategy, which emphasizes formal, individualized socialization tactics. The Blue Nile website has a detailed set of tutorials to help teach new engagement ring buyers about the four C's of diamond-buying—cut, color, clarity, and carat weight—and the relative tradeoffs between the four C's in terms of cost. Armed with this knowledge, the new customer can then control four sliding bars (one for each dimension) and dynamically search the Blue Nile database for diamonds that meet their criteria. Buyers can adjust their criteria, for example, trading off diamond size for color or clarity, and see how such tradeoffs affect price. Finally, they can select a specific diamond (or set of diamonds) and see how they will look in a virtual engagement ring setting and then order the engagement ring online, which can arrive within days. They can also call a Blue Nile sales representative (who does not receive sales commissions) to ask questions or complete the purchase over the phone.

Blue Nile succeeds because they provide new customers information and training, and then give them control in the buying process to make their own tradeoffs and design the engagement ring that fits their budget. The typical Blue Nile engagement ring buyer looks over 200 web pages of information and spends more than 3 weeks on the Blue Nile site before buying a ring (Krippendorff, 2010), so the buying process itself helps produce a socialized, confident, savvy customer. New customers also avoid the social awkwardness associated with dealing with a sales representative face to face, and they can make lots of mistakes in the search process without any social penalty. Overall, Blue Nile gets lots of men to buy very expensive diamond rings "sight unseen" over the Internet because they have created a socialization process that helps men become more comfortable and less stressed when buying an engagement ring (Acohido, 2003), which also leads to future jewelry sales for anniversaries, birthdays, and other occasions (InternetRetailer, 2010).

Apple Retail Stores and Orienting New Computer and Phone Users

When Apple Computers opened their first retail store in 2001, there was quite a bit of skepticism about the move. Until then, computer companies had relatively poor success with their own stores, including Gateway, IBM, and Microsoft (Dvorak,

2010). But the Apple Retail Stores have been a resounding success, generating average sales of $4032 per square foot in 2007 compared to $903 at Best Buy or $362 at Saks Fifth Avenue (Useem, 2007). By January 2011 there were over 300 stores worldwide, each attracting an average of 17,400 visitors per week and generating 17.5% of revenues and 21.3% of profits for the company (Allen, 2011). Apple Retail Stores have become such a phenomenon that there is an unaffiliated fan website www.ifoapplestore.com dedicated to the stores (ifo stands for "in front of") that gets over two million hits a month (Allen, 2011).

While much of Apple's overall success is clearly the result of their award-winning, innovative products like MacBooks, iPhones, and iPads, the success of their retail stores is strongly associated with their new customer socialization strategy. Since over half of all Apple Retail computer customers are buying their first Mac (Snell, 2004), attracting and orienting new customers is critical, and Apple has developed a diverse, dynamic mix of formal and informal socialization tactics with both individuals and groups to make buying and learning how to use an Apple product a more comfortable, less stressful experience.

Apple designed their stores to be both cool-looking and inviting. All of their products are displayed in the center of the store, and visitors are encouraged to use and "play with" the computers, phones, and software applications, which suggests a more informal, individualized socialization tactic. However, they also provide several formal, institutionalized tactics to help orient new customers. Every store has a "Genius Bar" toward the back, a counter where Apple representatives are available to answer questions, sell product, and provide setup assistance for new users. While customers can stand in line for the next available representative, they can also make an advance online appointment for the Genius Bar at www.apple.com, which can reduce the reluctance of some customers to seek help by further legitimizing their request (AppleComputers, 2011). Recently Apple has even developed special software that allows iPhone and web-based mobile phone users to automatically notify Apple when they have entered the store so that a representative from the Genius Bar can proactively seek out and meet the customer, further reducing the customer's perceived social cost for seeking information. In terms of anticipatory socialization, the Apple website also contains information about the Genius Bar experience, explaining not only how to make an advance appointment but

what to expect and how to prepare for the appointment (AppleComputers, 2011).

Apple Stores also offer a variety of individual and group-based training, from basic setup and operation for first-time users, to specific training on Apple software, to workshops on project-based themes like how to make a video, create a digital photo album, or design a website. The Apple website has many free tutorials for new users organized under the phrase "Mac 101," and a special set of tutorials entitled "Switch 101" for those migrating from Windows to the Mac operating system. To complement the Genius Bar, the retail stores also include a Studio staffed by "creatives" who offer free small group workshops for customers on Apple software applications.

New Mac purchasers also have the option of purchasing a special assistance package called *One to One* for $99 per year (AppleComputers, 2011). One to One users receive a special "Meet Your New Mac" session in the store, where Apple employees help transition files from the user's old computer to the Mac, and install new software. They can schedule an unlimited number of *Personal Training Sessions* with store representatives to get more specialized instruction on operating systems, applications, and projects. They also have additional access to a special repository of online tutorials for One to One users. CEO Steve Jobs reported that Apple conducts over 80,000 One to One individualized training sessions each week (Allen, 2011). While the One to One service provides additional revenue to Apple, it further reduces the social cost for new customers by legitimizing their requests for information and providing a clear, easy-to-understand conduit for getting help and training. One journalist notes that "Buying a Mac for the first time becomes a lot less scary, especially when Apple Store employees offer to configure your new computer and peripherals for you—for free—before you leave the store" (Snell, 2004, p. 9). Jewelry retailer giant Zales has recently introduced a prototype store modeled on the Apple Retail Store "in an attempt to remove the intimidation factor from jewelry buying" (JCK, 2009, p. 27).

Harley-Davidson—Moving Beyond "Outlaw Nation" to Attract and Socialize New Riders

For Harley-Davidson, the iconic image of the long-haired, leather-clad, rowdy "outlaw" is both a competitive advantage and a socialization challenge. Over the past 100 years, Harley-Davidson has built one of the most powerful brands in the world and a large rider community with a strong culture, deep traditions, and obsessive customer loyalty and passion for Harley's distinctively big, loud motorcycles (Schembri, 2008). Though most modern Harley owners are not "outlaws," they still embrace the free-spirited, nomadic persona and lifestyle depicted in movies like *Easy Rider*, and over 750,000 of them are members of the dealer-sponsored Harley Owners Groups (HOGs), which sponsor local bike rides, rallies and other social events (Bronson & Beaver, 2004). Harley-Davidson has been extremely good at building a brand community, defined as a group of dedicated consumers organized around the "lifestyle, activities and ethos of a brand" (Fournier & Lee, 2009, p. 105).

Though Harley-Davidson has over half of the US market share for large motorcycles, they are facing weakening demand among aging baby boomers (their traditional market), so they are trying to attract younger riders to the brand, especially women (Dale Buss, 2004). By 2001, the average buyer of a new Harley was not the traditional grizzly outlaw but a 46-year-old white male working as a white collar professional (Bronson & Beaver, 2004).

The socialization challenge for Harley-Davidson is how to attract new customers into an extremely strong rider culture and community that can be very stressful for new riders. "People that are new to motorcycling can find us intimidating," admits Jeff Bleustein, Harley's CEO. "They don't know the lingo. They don't know how to get started. We need to lighten our image without losing our edge." (Warner, 2002, p. 32) Overly passionate riders and tight rider communities can scare off new customers who can initially feel inexperienced, intimidated, and unaccepted by the Harley faithful.

To effectively attract and socialize new customers, Harley Davidson has developed a diverse mix of formal socialization strategies, targeting both individuals and groups. To address anticipatory customer socialization, and customize their initial socialization tactics to individual needs, the company designed their website with a "Quick Start Guide" that allows visitors to choose from three categories—Experienced Rider, New Rider, and Never Ridden (Harley-Davidson, 2011). Depending on what they choose, they get targeted information about the company, including rider training events. Interested visitors can also request an "Attainability Program" package (via mail) with information on products, financing, and local dealerships in their area (Buss, 2004). All of these approaches help socialize new customers and make them more knowledgeable and comfortable before they even set foot into a Harley dealership.

To reduce new customer intimidation at the dealership itself, Harley-Davidson uses several approaches. Harleys are typically large bikes that require advanced riding skills to control, so inexperienced riders can't simply test drive new bikes upon arrival. To address this challenge, Harley-Davidson has created the JumpStart Ride Simulator, which consists of a Harley Davidson bike mounted on a frame with the rear wheel on a rotating drum and the exhaust vented to the outside environment. It allows new and inexperienced riders to sit on the bike and rev it through the various gears without the risk of falling over and getting injured. "It's very good for women or people who are intimidated by the size of a Harley." (Dealernews.com, 2011, p. 18)

The most successful socialization strategy to date has been the creation of Rider's Edge, a rider training program targeting new and inexperienced riders. For a modest fee, new riders spend over 25 hours learning how to ride (Bronson & Beaver, 2004), as well as receiving a dealership tour, bike and repair demonstrations, and information on how Harleys are made (Warner, 2002). The objective of this learning experience is to socialize the potential Harley customer to riding and to the brand, reducing the intimidation factor through orientation and training. Lara Lee, director of Rider's Edge, states that "We wanted to take the person who felt like an outsider and turn them into an insider, without insiders feeling as if we were taking away from Harley's image, which is a little bit bad and a little bit separate." (Warner, 2002, p. 33) Over 38% of enrollees have been women (Koons, 2006), and many dealerships offer women-only classes to make the experience less intimidating (Dale Buss, 2004). Rider's Edge has been extremely successful, with over 25% of attendees eventually buying a Harley-Davidson motorcycle (Warner, 2002).

In 2006, Harley-Davidson also launched a series of women-only open house events at local dealerships called "Garage Parties" to attract women to Harley products and lifestyle (Koons, 2006). Designed to help socialize potential customers in a less intimidating environment, the events include basic instruction on riding skills, product and dealership tours, and the chance to connect with other women riders (Bokfi, 2008). Harley-Davidson also introduced the Sportster line of motorcycles with less vibration that appeals more to women (Dale Buss, 2004), who made up 11% of all Harley riders by 2006 (Koons, 2006).

Willow Creek Community Church— Socializing the Unchurched

To demonstrate that the principles of effective customer socialization extend beyond the for-profit world, the final example shows how newcomer socialization can form the basis of a major growth and outreach strategy in churches. In 1975, Pastor Bill Hybels cofounded Willow Creek Community Church in the northwest Chicago suburb of South Barrington, IL (WillowCreek, 2011). To fulfill their evangelical Christian mission, they focused on building their church membership by targeting, inviting and socializing the "unchurched," those who were interested in religion but not regular churchgoing parishioners. Through a diverse mix of customer socialization strategies, they have grown the church to over 23,500 members across six campuses in the Chicago area, becoming one of the first "mega-churches" in America (Van Biema, 2010).

Attending a new church often can be an intimidating, stressful experience. Most church services have a proscribed set of readings, creeds, hymns, communions, and other rituals that can be daunting to the inexperienced, and the deep historical traditions can seem disconnected from modern realities. Most churches also have a closely connected member community, making it hard for newcomers to initially feel welcomed and comfortable.

To transform the newcomer experience, Willow Creek developed a special "seeker" service designed specifically to help attract and socialize the "unchurched," particularly fathers, because if they could attract fathers the rest of the family would likely follow (Mellado & Schlesinger, 1991). They studied the newcomer experience and made a number of changes to the church service to make it more welcoming and less intimidating.

Willow Creek designed their weekend services to appeal to new parishioners, and scheduled the more traditional church service for regular members on Thursdays. They studied their servicescape and optimized it to create a strong first impression, with both clear signage and strategically positioned greeters to help new arrivals smoothly transition from the church parking lot to the church and eventually a seat in the main sanctuary. They trained members to greet new arrivals and answer questions in a way that would not intimidate or overwhelm first-time attendees. The church played soft jazz music before the service because they learned that silence could make newcomers uncomfortable. To make the religious environment less intimidating, they designed the sanctuary with minimal religious symbolism and designed the "seeker" services to reduce religious rituals that might confuse and stress new members. They used upbeat music, dramatic skits, and sermons that were strongly connected to everyday challenges. They also eliminated church activity announcements that could reinforce feelings of being an outsider (Mellado & Schlesinger, 1991).

Unlike most churches, which tend to socialize new members individually as they arrive and "on the job" as they participate in church service rituals, Willow Creek effectively created a group socialization experience where the majority of participants were new, reducing stress by making everyone feel more anonymous, inconspicuous, and less pressured (Mellado & Schlesinger, 1991). Once a "seeker" gained experience and desired a deeper relationship with the church and its membership, they could start to attend the Thursday services, small group workshops, or other church events.

Originally, members invited the "unchurched" to join them at a "seeker" service, but as word spread many arrived on their own. On their website, Willow Creek prominently displays a "I'm New to Willow Creek" link on the home page, which leads to a special web page with a "Discover Willow" video and information about the church such as: What does willow believe? How can willow help me grow? and How can I connect at Willow? (WillowCreek, 2011).

Through these new customer socialization strategies, church attendance grew to over 14,000 per weekend, making Willow Creek one of the most famous mega-churches in the United States. To extend their ministry they have expanded to several other campuses in the Chicago area, and formed the Willow Creek Association with 12,000 other church affiliates to help train other churches on how to invite, welcome, and minister to new members (Van Biema, 2010; Warner, 2006). In 1999 the predominantly white church also initiated a drive to attract more people of color to the church, and by 2009 over 20% of church membership was Hispanic, Asian, African-American, or other nonwhite racial identities. Recently they have adjusted their newcomer socialization strategies to appeal to those who actually want less anonymity and more of a traditional church experience (Buss, 2008), but they continue to be one of the most successful churches in America by optimizing the newcomer experience.

Future Directions

Compared to new employee socialization, new customer socialization is a relatively unexplored phenomenon with only a few studies conducted over the past few decades, mostly in the area of services marketing (cf. Bowers & Martin, 2007; Fonner & Timmerman, 2009; Kelley et al., 1992). There is ample opportunity for researchers to apply theories and insights gained through the study of new employee socialization to the process of orienting and socializing new customers.

For example, while there are dozens of organizational studies that have explored the relationship between new employee socialization tactics and desired outcomes such as performance, satisfaction, and commitment (cf. Ashforth et al., 2007; Bauer, Bodner, Erdogan, Truxillo, & Tucker, 2007), the socialization tactics concept has not been applied extensively to new customers. Are the six socialization tactics identified by Van Maanen and Schein (1979), or the individualized versus institutionalized tactics redefined by Jones (1986), still valid for new customers or should there be a revised set of customer-centric socialization tactics? Which tactics are associated with increased customer performance, satisfaction, and loyalty? Should managers socialize most new customers in groups, or individually? What are the contextual factors (e.g., new customer arrival rate, individual customer characteristics, role complexity, etc.) that moderate the relationship between socialization tactics and outcomes?

While Fonner and Timmerman (2009) have extended the concept of organizational newcomer proactivity and information-seeking tactics to the realm of new customers, there is still much that can be explored and evaluated. What is the comprehensive set of information-seeking tactics available to new customers, and how does this set differ from those tactics used by new employees? Which customer information-seeking tactics are associated with higher performance, satisfaction, and loyalty? How do individual characteristics (e.g., self-efficacy, locus of control, existing role mastery, etc.) affect tactic choice or moderate the relationship between information-seeking tactics and desired outcomes? Given that providing information to customers has associated labor and technology costs, which tactics best balance customer impact and cost effectiveness?

Another area for future research is in the impact of emerging technologies on customer socialization tactics, new customer proactivity, and socialization outcomes. Since customers increasingly seek, compare, buy, and consume products and services via the Internet (and associated technologies), understanding how these technologies affect tactic choice and effectiveness will become more important. How does the availability of online support centers, forums, and knowledge databases affect new customer information-seeking tactics and outcomes? Can and should firms use technology and "virtual socialization agents" to orient new customers (Kohler et al., 2010), and how do they affect the relationship between socialization tactics and outcomes?

Ultimately, researchers can strive to develop conceptual models connecting customer socialization tactics, individual customer characteristics and behaviors, and contextual variables to socialization outcomes like customer satisfaction and loyalty, in much the same way that organizational theorists have done for new employee socialization (cf. Ashforth et al., 2007; Bauer et al., 2007; Saks & Ashforth, 1997). There is much that can be done to provide managers with new insights on how to effectively and efficiently orient new customers.

Conclusion

New customers, guests, and members are the lifeblood of most growing organizations and an efficient, effective new customer socialization strategy can help create knowledgeable, confident, satisfied, competent customers who improve both organizational productivity and profitability. Savvy managers start socializing prospective customers even before they visit or buy through targeted website pages and mailings, and design both the physical layout and the service flow to minimize confusion and intimidation for new customers. They also develop a mix of group and individual socialization activities that help orient, train, and integrate new customers into the user community, and minimize the new customer's perceived social cost for asking questions. The goal is informed, comfortable, accepted customers that not only are loyal to the company but actively refer the firm to other potential customers and provide feedback and ideas on how to make the company's products and services even better.

References

Abelson, R. P. (1981). Psychological status of the script concept. *American Psychologist, 36,* 715–729.

Acohido, B. (2003, October 20). He turned website in the rough into online jewel. *USA Today.* http://www.usatoday.com/tech/techinvestor/2003–10-19-entrepreneur_x.htm

Allen, G. (2011). ifoapplestore.com. Retrieved April 2011, from http://www.ifoapplestore.com/

AppleComputers. (2011). Apple Computer Website Retrieved April 26, 2011, from http://www.apple.com

Apte, U. M., Karmarkar, U. S., & Nath, H. K. (2008). Information services in the U.S. economy: Value, jobs, and management implications. *California Management Review, 50*(3), 12–30.

Ashford, S. J., & Black, J. S. (1996). Proactivity during organizational entry: A role of desire for control. *Journal of Applied Psychology, 81*, 199–214.

Ashforth, B. E. (2001). *Role transitions in organizational life: An identity-based perspective.* Mahwah, NJ: Lawrence Erlbaum Associates.

Ashforth, B. E., Sluss, D. M., & Harrison, S. H. (2007). Socialization in organizational contexts. *International Review of Industrial and Organizational Psychology, 22*, 1–70.

Bateson, J. (2002). Are your customers good enough for your service business? *Academy of Management Executive, 16*(4), 110–121.

Bauer, T. N., Bodner, T., Erdogan, B., Truxillo, D. M., & Tucker, J. S. (2007). Newcomer adjustment during organizational socialization: A meta-analytic review of antecedents, outcomes, and methods. *Journal of Applied Psychology, 92*(3), 707–721.

Bitner, M. J. (1992). Servicescapes: The impact of physical surroundings on customers and employees. *Journal of Marketing, 56*, 57–71.

Bitner, M. J. (2000). The servicescape. In T. A. Swartz & D. Iacobucci (Eds.), *Handbook of services marketing and management* (pp. 37–50). Thousand Oaks, CA: Sage.

Bokfi, E. (2008, Summer). Road Warriors. *Herizons Magazine, 22*(1), 28–33.

Bowen, D. E. (1986). Managing customers as human resources in service organizations. *Human Resource Management 25*(3), 371–383.

Bowers, M. R., & Martin, C. L. (2007). Trading places redux: Employees as customers, customers as employees. *Journal of Services Marketing, 21*(2), 88–98.

Bowers, M. R., Martin, C. L., & Luker, A. (1990). Trading places: Employees as customers, customers as employees. *Journal of Services Marketing, 4*(Spring), 55–69.

Bronson, J. W., & Beaver, G. (2004). Strategic change in the face of success? Harley-Davidson, Inc. *Strategic Change, 13*, 205–217.

Buss, D. (2004, October 25). Can Harley ride the new wave? *Brandweek, 45*, 20–22.

Buss, D. (2008, June 27). Taste—Houses of worship: Less seeking, more thrills. *Wall Street Journal* (p. W11).

Chatman, J. A. (1991). Matching people and organizations: Selection and socialization in public accounting firms. *Administrative Science Quarterly, 36*(3), 459–484.

Dealernews.com (Producer). (2011, May 2). Revving through the winter cold. [Article] (p. 18).

Dvorak, J. C. (2010, October). How Apple stores got it right. *PC Magazine, 29*(10), 1.

Evans, K. R., Stan, S., & Murray, L. (2008). The customer socialization paradox: The mixed effects of communicating customer role expectations. *Journal of Services Marketing, 22*(3), 213–223.

Feldman, D. C. (1981). The multiple socialization of organization members. *Academy of Management Review, 6*(2), 309–318.

Fonner, K. L., & Timmerman, C. E. (2009). Organizational newc(ust)omers: Applying organizational newcomer assimilation concepts to customer information seeking and service outcomes. *Management Communication Quarterly, 21*(2), 244–271.

Fournier, S., & Lee, L. (2009). Getting brand communities right. *Harvard Business Review 87*(April), 105–111.

Fowler, G. A. (2009, September 1). Blue Nile gets makeover to please ladies. *Wall Street Journal*, p. B6.

Greene, J. (2008, June 9). Blue Nile: A guy's best friend. *Business Week,* (4087), 38–40.

Groth, M., Mertens, D. P., & Murphy, R. O. (2005). Customers as good soldiers: Examining citizenship behaviors of internet service deliveries. *Journal of Management, 31*, 7–27.

Halbesleben, J. R. B., & Buckley, M. R. (2004). Managing customers as employees of the firm: New challenges for human resources management. *Personnel Review, 33*, 351–372.

Harley-Davidson. (2011). Harley-Davidson USA. Retrieved May 17, 2011, from http://www.harley-davidson.com.

InternetRetailer. (2010). Blue Nile works to build repeat business. Retrieved April 19, 2011, from http://www.internetretailer.com/2010/09/22/blue-nile-works-build-repeat-business.

Jablin, F. M. (1987). Organizational entry, assimilation, and exit. In F. M. Jablin, K. Putman, H. Robers, & L. W. Porter (Eds.), *Handbook of organizational communication* (pp. 679–740). Beverly Hills, CA: Sage Publications.

JCK. (2009, August 29). Zale unveils modern, "un-intimidating" store. *JCK Magazine, 180*(9), 27.

Jones, G. R. (1986). Socialization tactics, self-efficacy, and newcomers' adjustments to organizations. *Academy of Management Journal, 29*(2), 262–279.

Kelley, S. W. (1992). Developing customer orientation among service employees. *Journal of the Academy of Marketing Science, 20*(1), 27–36.

Kelley, S. W., Donnelly, J. H., & Skinner, S. J. (1990). Customer participation in service production and delivery. *Journal of Retailing, 66*, 315–335.

Kelley, S. W., Skinner, S. J., & Donnelly, J. H. (1992). Organizational socialization of service customers. *Journal of Business Research, 25*, 197–214.

Kohler, C. F., Rohm, A. J., Ruyter, K., & Wetzels, M. G. M. (2010). Return on interactivity: The impact of online agents on newcomer adjustment. *Journal of Marketing, 75*(2), 93–108.

Koons, C. (2006, February 22). Harley-Davidson markets to women. *Wall Street Journal.*1.

Krippendorff, K. (2010, September 1). Selling information, not diamonds. *Fast Company Expert Blog.* Retrieved April 19, 2011, from http://www.fastcompany.com/1686315/selling-information-not-diamonds.

Laird, K. (2010, March 22). Courting the DIY crowd. *Marketing Magazine, 115,* 14–15.

Lengnick-Hall, C. A. (1996). Customer contributions to quality: A different view of the customer-oriented firm. *Academy of Management Review, 21*, 791–825.

Lovelock, C. H., & Young, R. F. (1979). Look to consumers to increase productivity. *Harvard Business Review* (May/June), *57*(3), 168–178.

Major, D. A., Kozlowski, S. W. J., Chao, G. T., & Gardner, P. D. (1995). A longitudinal investigation of newcomer expectations, early socialization outcomes, and the moderating effects of role development factors. *Journal of Applied Psychology, 80*(3), 418–431.

Markels, A. (2002). Baubles and browsers. *U.S. News and World Reports, 133,* 114.

McGrath, M. A., & Otnes, C. (1995). Unacquainted influencers: When strangers interact in the retail setting. *Journal of Business Research, 3*(2), 261–272.

Mellado, J., & Schlesinger, L. A. (1991). *Willow Creek Community Church (A).* Cambridge, MA: Harvard Business School Publishing.

Mignerey, J. T., Rubin, R. B., & Gorden, W. I. (1995). Organizational entry: An investigation of newcomer communication behavior and uncertainty. *Communication Research, 22*(1), 54–85.

Miller, V. D., & Jablin, F. M. (1991). Information seeking during organizational entry: Influences, tactics, and a model of the process. *Academy of Management Review, 16*(1), 92–120.

Mills, P. K., & Morris, J. H. (1986). Clients as 'partial employees' of service organizations: Role development in client participation. *Academy of Management Review, 11*, 726–735.

Morrison, E. W. (1993a). Longitudinal study of the effects of information seeking on newcomer socialization. *Journal of Applied Psychology, 78*(2), 173–183.

Morrison, E. W. (1993b). Newcomer information seeking: Exploring types, modes, sources, and outcomes. *Academy of Management Journal, 36*(3), 557–589.

Morrison, E. W., & Bies, R. J. (1993). Impression management in the feedback seeking process: A literature review and research agenda. *Academy of Management Review*(16), 522–541.

Moschis, G. P. (1985). The role of family communication in consumer socialization of children and adolescents. *Journal of Consumer Research, 11*(4), 898–913.

Moschis, G. P., & Churchill, G. A. J. (1987). Consumer socialization: A theoretical and empirical analysis. *Journal of Marketing Research, 15*, 599–609.

Moschis, G. P., & L., M. R. (1979). Decision making among the young: A socialization perspective. *Journal of Consumer Research, 6*(2), 101–112.

Ostroff, C., & Kozlowski, S. W. J. (1992). Organizational socialization as a learning process: The role of information acquisition. *Personnel Psychology, 45*(4), 849–874.

Reif, J., Woznick, A., Thurmond, M. E., Kelley, J., & Ostrea, R. A. (1997). *Services: The export of the 21st century—A guidebook for U.S. service exporters.* Petaluma, CA: World Trade Press.

Ridgeway, C (2010, July 23). People when you want them, technology when you don't (blog). http://www.theodigital.com/2010/07/people-when-you-want-them-technology-when-you-dont.html

Rivlin, G. (2007, January 7). When buying a diamond starts with a mouse. *New York Times*, p. C1.

Rodie, A. R., & Kleine, S. S. (2000). Customer participation in services production and delivery. In T. A. Swartz & D. Iacobucci (Eds.), *Handbook of services marketing and management* (pp. 111–125). Thousand Oaks, CA: Sage.

Saks, A. M., & Ashforth, B. E. (1997). Organizational socialization: Making sense of the past and present as a prologue for the future. *Journal of Vocational Behavior, 51*, 234–279.

Schembri, S. (2008). Reframing brand experience: The experiential meaning of Harley-Davidson. *Journal of Business Research, 62*, 1299–1310.

Schneider, B., & Bowen, D. E. (1995). *Winning the service game.* Boston, MA: Harvard Press.

Snell, J. (2004, May 2004). Geniuses behind bars. *Macworld, 21*, 9–9.

Soloman, M. R., Surprenant, C., Czepiel, J. A., & Gutman, E. G. (1985). A role theory perspective on dyadic interactions: The service encounter. *Journal of Marketing, 49*, 99–111.

Sugarloaf. (2011). *First timer's guide.* Retrieved May 10, 2011, from http://www.sugarloaf.com/vacationplanning/First_Timers_Guide.html.

Swan, J. E., Goodwin, C., Mayo, M. A., & Richardson, L. D. (2001). Customer identities: Customers as commercial friends, customer coworkers, or business acquaintances. *Journal of Personal Selling and Sales Management, 21*, 29–37.

Useem, J. (2007, March, 19). Simply irresistable. *Fortune, 155*, 107–112.

Van Biema, D. (2010, January 11). The color of faith. *Time Magazine, 175*, 38–41.

Van Maanen, J., & Schein, E. H. (1979). Toward a theory of organizational socialization. *Research in Organizational Behavior, 1*, 209–264.

Ward, S. L. (1974). Consumer socialization. *Journal of Consumer Research, 1*(3), 1–14.

Warner, F. (2002, January). Curb your enthusiasm. *Fast Company*, (54), 32–36.

Warner, F. (2006, October 22). Prepare thee for some serious marketing. *New York Times*, p. B1.

WillowCreek. (2011). Willow Creek Community Church home page. Retrieved May 17, 2011, from http://www.willowcreek.org/.

Zeithmal, V. A., Bitner, M. J., & Gremler, D. D. (2006). *Services marketing: Integrating customer focus across the firm.* Boston: McGraw-Hill Irwin.

PART 6

Socialization in Practice

Are Organizations On Board with Best Practices Onboarding?

Howard J. Klein *and* Beth Polin

Abstract

This chapter reviews what academics are studying and what practitioners are doing with respect to onboarding. The onboarding "best practices" conveyed through practitioner outlets generally do not provide sufficient prescription to implement policies or programs that will achieve desired outcomes. That prescription is also lacking from the academic literature, as there is a paucity of research on specific onboarding practices. Using the Klein and Heuser (2008) Inform-Welcome-Guide framework, we first examine the available insights from the academic literature. We then review the practitioner literature and identify the common recommendations that are made regarding onboarding best practices. We also summarize a recent survey conducted to gain a clearer picture of what organizations are currently doing with respect to onboarding practices. We conclude with a discussion of disconnects observed across these three areas and the identification of future research needs.

Key Words: onboarding, socialization, adjustment, orientation, newcomers, new hires

Introduction

Most organizations offer some type of onboarding to help socialize new employees (Galvin, 2003; Holton, 2001), but the academic literature has not systematically examined the effectiveness of those practices, and the extent to which organizations carefully evaluate those practices is unclear. In short, there is a serious dearth of information about the actual onboarding activities being used in today's organizations and the extent to which those activities are meeting their desired aim of facilitating the organizational socialization of new hires. The objectives of this chapter are to summarize both the academic and practitioner literatures regarding onboarding, share the results of a survey aimed at better understanding current onboarding practices, and identify future research needs to better understand the onboarding process and provide better direction to organizations on how to best design onboarding programs.

It is important to better understand how onboarding practices can facilitate socialization, since socialization has been linked to many valuable outcomes for both the new employee (role clarity, job satisfaction, self-confidence, career involvement, career effectiveness, and personal income) and the organization (productivity, organizational commitment, job involvement, role orientation, and tenure; Bauer, Morrison, & Callister, 1998; Feldman, 1981; Fisher, 1986; Saks & Ashforth, 1997). Furthermore, a confluence of trends including projected skills shortages, as well as greater attention to talent management issues, point to the increased need to effectively and efficiently socialize newcomers (Klein & Heuser, 2008). One of those key trends is the changing employment relationship and increased worker mobility. With a more transient workforce and individuals changing jobs more frequently, it is critical that new organizational members "get up to speed" as quickly as possible (a) so their contributions can be maximized before they leave, and (b) to help form the desired workplace commitments so that they do not leave earlier than expected. Another factor is the role that onboarding practices play in building and maintaining a strong and unique organizational culture, which is increasingly recognized as a key aspect of achieving a competitive advantage through a firm's human capital (e.g., Coff & Kryscynski, 2011).

Onboarding Defined

Some authors have equated onboarding to socialization, implying that *onboarding* is the term managers and Human Resource (HR) practitioners use instead of *socialization*. Bauer and Erdogan (2010), for example, state that "Organizational socialization, or onboarding, is a process through which new employees move from being organizational outsiders to becoming organizational insiders" (p. 51). We, however, believe that onboarding and socialization are distinct concepts that should be more clearly distinguished. We use the term onboarding to refer to *all formal and informal practices, programs, and policies enacted or engaged in by an organization or its agents to facilitate newcomer adjustment.*

Organizational socialization is the process by which employees learn about and adapt to new jobs, roles, and the culture of the workplace (Fisher, 1986; Van Maanen & Schein, 1979). Socialization is a process that occurs within a person, whereas onboarding is the set of practices, polices, and procedures, formal or informal, put in place by managers and HR departments to help structure newcomers' early experiences and thus facilitate the socialization of new employees. Onboarding practices help facilitate newcomer adjustment by both (a) reducing newcomer uncertainty, ambiguity, and anxiety that often accompany a new job (e.g., Allen, 2006; Berger, 1979; Carr, Pearson, Vest, & Boyar, 2006) in order to bring greater clarity and understanding to their new role (Cooper-Thomas & Anderson, 2005; Klein & Weaver, 2000; Saks & Ashforth, 1997), and (b) facilitating the development of social capital (Fang, Duffy, & Shaw, 2011) and relationships (e.g., Rollag, Parise & Cross, 2005).

Another key difference between onboarding and socialization concerns proactivity. Individuals can be proactive (Morrison, 1993a; Reichers, 1987), planning out how they will adapt when entering a new job or organization and taking an active role in their socialization. Organizations can also design onboarding to promote and facilitate proactivity as well as to maximize proactivity effectiveness (e.g., make information and resources easily accessible to employees who seek it out), but newcomers will differ in the extent to which they take advantage of the onboarding opportunities provided by organizations. Yet, proactive behavior on the part of newcomers is outside of the practices, programs, and policies that constitute onboarding (Klein & Heuser, 2008). Onboarding, as we have defined it, concerns what the organization and its agents do, not the actions of newcomers. To provide greater conceptual clarity, we recommend that plans or activities initiated by newcomers to facilitate their own adjustment be referred to in the literature as *transition* activities or plans, to help differentiate those actions from onboarding practices, programs, and policies put in place by organizations or their agents.

A final important difference between socialization and onboarding is that socialization is an ongoing, lifelong process (Feldman, 1989; Van Maanen, 1976) occurring both within and across organizations, whereas onboarding has a set time frame, ranging from hours to months, within a particular organization. Socialization is most intense when starting a new job with a new organization, but socialization occurs whenever there are changes—small or large—to a role, tasks, or job context (Van Maanen & Schein 1979). Such changes may result from changes in team members, supervisors, restructuring, technological innovations, or other organizational changes. In such cases, onboarding practices, programs, and policies are generally not present. Socialization also clearly occurs when changing jobs within organizations or when organizations merge or are acquired. In these events, onboarding may or may not occur, and if it does, such programs are usually directed only at "new" members; socialization, on the other hand, will be occurring for all (Chao, in press).

Just as socialization can be differentiated from onboarding, onboarding can be differentiated from orientation. The term *onboarding* was originally used in organizations to refer to the orientation of managers and executives (e.g., Gordon, 1999), practices that tended to differ from the orientation done for rank and file employees. It has since become a much broader term, extending to the full range of acclimation efforts across all types of employees. Given our aforementioned definition of onboarding, *orientation* should be viewed as a specific type of onboarding program (or possibly a set of programs), typically formal, with a set duration ranging from hours to days.

Onboarding also needs to be differentiated from socialization *tactics*. Those tactics, whether the composite institutional vs. individual, the three broader dimensions, or the original six dimensions as presented by Van Maanen and Schein (1979), are strategies for how new members are socialized. Although valuable, that framework concerns the general approach, not the specific activities that organizations can offer to help socialize newcomers. Onboarding concerns exactly what is done—the practices, programs, and policies, implemented by an organization or its agents and experienced by newcomers. Focusing on specific activities is consistent with Ashforth, Sluss, and Harrison's (2007) recommendation that future research look beyond socialization tactics. It should further be noted that there generally is no concordance between socialization tactics and onboarding practices, as most onboarding activities could be structured and delivered using a variety of socialization tactics (e.g., giving newcomers a tour of the facility could be done collectively or individually, formally or informally, sequentially or randomly, etc.). Furthermore, the different onboarding practices experienced by a newcomer may reflect a mix of different socialization tactics (e.g., some serial activities, others disjunctive; some formal, others informal). Bauer, Bodner, Erdogan, Truxillo, and Tucker (2007) concluded that using composite measures of socialization tactics rather than the original facets may weaken observed relationships and result in the loss of important information. Assessing specific onboarding activities and the manner in which they are delivered should provide even richer and more precise information.

Those specific onboarding practices, programs, and policies can be differentiated along many dimensions, including the nature or type of activity, the purpose of the activity, its scope or content, the organizational level at which it is aimed (e.g., job, workgroup, department, unit, organization), and its timing. For example, in terms of scope or content, Bauer (2010) identified four distinct "C's": compliance, clarification, culture, and connections. Saks and Gruman (2010) presented initial work on an "Organizational Socialization Resources" typology that intermixes activity type, purpose, process, timing, and agents. We believe it is important to keep onboarding activities distinct from when they occur and the agents involved, as most activities could potentially be experienced at any time and delivered in a variety of ways. Klein, Polin, and Sutton (2010) have done initial work on an "Onboarding Activities Checklist" that is based on the typology of specific onboarding practices presented in Klein and Heuser (2008). That framework, which focuses on the primary purpose of the onboarding practice, consists of three major categories: practices that (a) *inform*, (b) *welcome*, and (c) *guide* new hires, with the *inform* category further subdivided into *communication* efforts, providing *resources*, and *training* programs. Specific onboarding activities that fall under each of these categories are shown in Table 14.1. We use this framework to organize our review of the academic socialization literature which follows.

What We Know about Onboarding

We are unaware of any prior comprehensive reviews of the academic literature on onboarding practices and, unlike Van Maanen and Schein's (1979) broad socialization tactics, there is surprisingly little research on specific onboarding practices to summarize. There are only a few studies evaluating orientation programs, despite this being one of the most commonly offered types of training, and the examination of other onboarding activities is even rarer. What can be inferred about onboarding from the academic literature is summarized below.

Inform

The first and largest category of onboarding activities consists of efforts aimed at providing newcomers with information, materials, and experiences to help them learn what they need to know to be successful in their new roles and in the organization. Because so many onboarding activities fall within this category, it is further subdivided into communication efforts, providing resources, and training. Given that socialization is often viewed in terms of the reduction of uncertainty (e.g., Berger, 1979), the *inform* onboarding category serves an important role in addressing that ambiguity. This category also highlights the fact that onboarding can and should begin with recruitment, where the provision of realistic job previews (RJPs; Morse & Popovich, 2009) is an example of providing information. There is considerable research on the general strategy of providing a realistic preview but less research on the specific onboarding practices aimed at doing so.

COMMUNICATION

Inform-communication practices include both one-way messaging (e.g., providing a brochure outlining the employee value proposition during recruitment) and structuring opportunities for

Table 14.1 Inform—Welcome—Guide Categories and Activities

<table>
<tr><td rowspan="20" style="writing-mode:vertical">Inform</td><td colspan="1">

Inform-Communication—Planned efforts to facilitate communication with newcomers. Includes both the provision of one-way messages and opportunities for two-way dialogues.

I went to a question and answer session where new hires were able to ask senior leaders questions.

I was invited to meet with a senior leader.

My manager set aside a block of uninterrupted time to spend with me.

I met with a representative from Human Resources.

Inform-Resources—Making materials or assistance available to new hires. These efforts differ from communication in that the new hire has to take the initiative to access them.

I was shown how to find things on the website the company has for its associates.

I was given an initial plan that outlined opportunities for my development.

I was given a glossary of abbreviations and "buzzwords" used throughout the company.

I was directed to a section of the company website specifically designed for new associates.

I was given a list of names and contact information of important people within the company.

My workspace was ready for me (including all supplies, materials, and equipment).

Inform-Training—Planned efforts to facilitate the systematic acquisition of skills, behaviors, knowledge.

I was shown a new employee video.

I was encouraged to observe a fellow associate for a period of time.

I received on-the-job training on how to perform my job.

I was given a tour of company facilities.

I attended an orientation program with other new hires.

I completed an on-line orientation program.

I attended a session where presentations were given by fellow associates who were expert on certain tasks or procedures.

</td></tr>
</table>

Welcome—Activities that provide opportunities for new hires to meet and socialize with other organizational members and/or celebrate the arrival of the newcomer.

I received a personalized welcome (phone call, email, or letter) to the company from a senior leader.

I received a personalized welcome (phone call, email, or letter) from my manager.

I was given a welcome kit.

I participated in an exercise to get to know my fellow associates.

There was a gathering (meeting, welcome lunch) for me to meet my fellow associates.

A new associate welcome celebration was held.

I was invited to participate in a social event to get to know fellow associates.

My family was invited to attend a social activity held outside of work.

My joining the company was announced in an email, on the company website, or in a company newsletter.

Company t-shirts or other items with the company name/logo were sent to me.

Guide—Activities that provide a personal guide for each new hire.

Someone at a higher level than my manager was assigned to be my mentor.

I had a single point of contact (welcome coordinator) that I could reach out to with any questions.

A fellow associate was assigned as my "buddy" to help answer any questions I might have.

two-way dialogue (e.g., a scheduled call from an HR representative on a newcomer's third day to discuss how things are going). Klein et al. (2010) developed an onboarding practices checklist and assessed both the frequency with which practices were offered across a multi-organizational sample and the helpfulness of those practices as perceived by newcomers. Within the inform-communication category, a common practice that was perceived to be particularly helpful was the manager setting aside a block of uninterrupted time to spend with the newcomer. Beyond this finding, there is little systematic research on the relative effectiveness of specific inform-communication practices. There is, however, research on the (a) type of information to provide (i.e., realistic job previews), (b) information richness of recruitment sources, and (c) role of different information sources.

RJPs have received the most research attention of any aspect relating to the provision of information to newcomers. In addition to studies demonstrating how and the extent to which RJPs work (e.g., Hom, Griffeth, Palich, & Bracker, 1998), there also has been research examining the optimal timing and medium used to convey the RJP (e.g., Wanous, 1989). Based on the Phillips (1998) meta-analysis, RJPs are most effective in terms of improved job attitudes and reduced turnover when given later in the recruitment process, before hiring, and when provided verbally. In terms of impact on job performance, however, providing the RJP after hiring and via videotape were found to be most effective. Given changes in media usage, with many organizations using their websites to convey RJPs to potential applicants, additional research is needed on the optimal media to use. Also relating to recruitment, different recruitment sources are thought to provide differential information to potential new hires, and the manner in which a source is used (e.g., what is put in an ad or what employees are trained to share with potential referrals) can influence how much socialization occurs during talent acquisition (Zottolia & Wanous, 2000). Yet, only a few studies have explicitly looked at the effects of recruitment on socialization outcomes (Breaugh & Mann, 1984; Chatman, 1991; Saks, 1994; Williams, Labig, & Stone, 1993) and none have explicitly examined ways recruitment can be used to begin onboarding efforts.

There has been work identifying socializing agents (e.g., coworkers, supervisors, leaders, mentors) and differentiating those agents in terms of their relative importance at different times or for different types of information (Anakwe & Greenhous, 1999; Bauer & Green, 1998; Moreland & Levine, 2001; Morrison 1993b; Ostroff & Kozlowski, 1992; Riordan, Weatherly, Vandenberg, & Self, 2001). A key but not sole role played by socializing agents is to provide information and feedback. In this role, agents help newcomers make sense of (Louis, 1980) and develop an identity in their new environment (e.g., Sluss & Ashforth, 2007). In addition to providing information, socializing agents serve as role models, providing access to social networks necessary for social validation and integration (Ashforth, 2001; Bauer & Green, 1998; Chan & Schmitt, 2000; Cooper-Thomas & Anderson, 2006; Jablin, 2001; Riordan et al., 2001). Some authors have asserted that adjustment arises primarily through these social interactions (Fang et al., 2011; Moreland & Levine, 2001; Reichers, 1987; Rollag et al., 2005). The literature suggests that a variety of agents should be involved in onboarding, but there is limited research specifically examining the relative effectiveness of involving different agents in different specific onboarding activities.

RESOURCES

Inform-resources practices concern making materials or assistance available to new hires (e.g., having a dedicated section on the company website for newcomers or a newcomer hotline). Klein et al. (2010) found that a common practice in this category that is viewed by newcomers as highly beneficial is having their work space ready for them (including all supplies, materials, and equipment). Again here, there is little other research on the relative effectiveness of specific inform-resources practices. There is, however, a considerable amount of research in the socialization literature on newcomer proactivity (e.g., Gruman, Saks, & Zweig, 2006; Kim, Cable, & Kim, 2005). Although we define newcomer transition activities as being distinct from onboarding, consideration of proactivity is important because making resources available is not sufficient if newcomers do not take advantage of those resources.

Research has demonstrated that proactivity is a function of individual differences such as proactive personality and self-efficacy (e.g., Ashford & Black, 1996; Chan & Schmitt, 2000; DeVos, Buyens, & Schalk, 2003; Finkelstein, Kulas, & Dages, 2003; Kammeyer-Mueller & Wanberg, 2003; Wanberg & Kammeyer-Mueller, 2000), as well as contextual and social variables that provide situational cues (e.g., Gruman et al., 2006; Kammeyer-Mueller, Livingston, & Liao, 2011; Kim et al., 2005;

Morrison & Phelps, 1999). Research further suggests that newcomers vary their use of feedback-seeking tactics and sources depending on the type of information desired (e.g., Chan & Schmitt, 2000). A number of factors have been shown to influence newcomers' decision making regarding the type of information to seek, when to seek it, and how to obtain that information (Morrison, 2002a). Both social costs (e.g., Morrison & Vancouver, 2000) and the perceived difficulty of obtaining the information are considered along with the costs and benefits associated with direct (e.g., loss of face) versus indirect (e.g., proneness to misinterpretation errors) information-seeking tactics when deciding upon the best approach (Miller, 1996). Characteristics of the information source (e.g., accessibility, credibility, supportiveness) and characteristics of the organizational context (e.g., norms, evaluation criteria) are also considerations (Chan & Schmitt, 2000; Gruman et al., 2006; Morrison, 2002a; Morrison & Vancouver, 2000; Wanberg & Kammeyer-Mueller, 2000).

Because of the importance of newcomer proactivity, the need exists to better understand the actions that organizations can take to facilitate and support new hire proactivity (e.g., Gruman et al, 2006; Kim et al., 2005), as well as the specific resources that should be provided, at what times, and using what medium, to best facilitate socialization. Based on the newcomer proactivity research, it would appear that any effort by organizations to make resources available to newcomers must ensure those resources are viewed as helpful, credible, and easy to access with minimal social cost or chance of negative evaluation. Newcomers must be encouraged to focus on learning—not just performance—and explicitly given permission to ask questions (Rollag et al., 2005). It has been demonstrated across many contexts that in novel situations a learning orientation, which can be primed, is more effective than a performance orientation in facilitating both learning and performance (e.g., DeShon & Gillespie, 2005). As such, in addition to providing resources, onboarding programs should seek to prime a learning orientation to facilitate newcomers taking advantage of those resources.

TRAINING

Inform-training practices encompass planned efforts to facilitate newcomer skills and knowledge acquisition. This includes position-specific training and development efforts, as well as orientation training programs. There has been some research on the availability, amount, perceived usefulness, and effectiveness of new employee training and development activities (Holton, 2001; Louis, Posner, & Powell, 1983; Nelson & Quick, 1991; Saks, 1996). Early research examining only the availability of training was mixed, but more recent studies have generally found positive consequences associated with the provision of early training, even for temporary workers (e.g., Slattery, Selvarajan, & Anderson, 2006). Research in this area has coarsely examined all training a newcomer has experienced. Within the inform-training category, Klein et al. (2010) found that both receiving on-the-job training and observing a coworker for a period of time were common practices perceived by newcomers as highly beneficial, whereas watching a new employee video was a common practice that most new hires did not find beneficial. Additional research examining the provision of training and development more granularly is needed to better understand what types of planned learning activities, delivered when, and in what way, are most effective in facilitating adjustment and performance.

Orientation programs are typically formal training programs intended to introduce new employees to the organization and the people that make it up (Klein & Weaver, 2000). These training programs can take many different forms, varying in how they are administered (e.g., formal training programs, informal orienting activities by peers and supervisors, computer-based programs) as well as in the type of information they provide (e.g., Anderson, Cunningham-Snell, & Haigh, 1996). Even for this most ubiquitous of onboarding activities, research is surprisingly sparse. In addition, studies examining orientation training programs have mostly focused on formal, organization-level programs. Such programs are important, but it is also critical to understand the impact of informal programs and activities because there are informal socialization content areas (Chao, O'Leary-Kelly, Wolf, Klein, & Gardner; 1994; Klein & Heuser, 2008) that are unlikely to be mastered through formal means. In addition, onboarding needs to occur relative to several levels (individual, job, workgroup, department, geographic location/business unit; see Ashforth et al., 2007; Klein & Heuser, 2008). Onboarding newcomers to each level can, but need not, involve orientation training, and we located one study examining department-level orientation programs (Holladay, Donnelly, Murray, & Halverson, 2006).

As with research on the provision of early training, more recent research on orientation programs (e.g., Fan & Wanous, 2008; Klein & Weaver, 2000; Wesson & Gogus, 2005) has demonstrated positive effects on learning and socialization. This is contrary to earlier research that raised concerns as to whether formal orientation programs helped foster newcomer adjustment (e.g., Anderson et al., 1996; Louis et al., 1983; Ostroff & Kozlowski, 1992). There were numerous calls in the late 1980s and early 1990s for research on the effects of entry training (Feldman, 1989; Ostroff & Kozlowski, 1992; Tannenbaum, Mathieu, Salas, & Cannon-Bowers, 1991; Wanous, 1993), yet there have been relatively few responses to those calls. Thus, despite the continued prevalent use of orientation programs in practice, relatively little empirical research has examined the optimal content, structure, medium, or timing of orientation programs. Such research is needed because simply providing orientation does not automatically yield benefits, as evidenced by the sometimes negative reactions to such programs if they are not well designed or delivered (Klein et al., 2010; Lundberg & Young, 1997).

Welcome

The second major category of orienting activities consists of practices, programs, and policies aimed at acknowledging and celebrating a newcomer's arrival (e.g., receiving a welcome phone call from an executive) and providing newcomers with opportunities to meet and socialize with their new coworkers (e.g., a welcome lunch). Welcome activities are important for both facilitating relationship building and addressing the emotional needs of newcomers, in contrast to the *inform* activities, which largely focus on informational needs. Lundberg and Young (1997), for example, demonstrate the importance to newcomers of perceiving support, feeling appreciated, being shown concern, and being made to feel welcome. As with most other onboarding practices, research is lacking that evaluates the effectiveness of specific welcome activities. Rollag et al. (2005) did, however, conclude that welcoming activities are more effective when they are planned strategic exchanges, rather than random passing introductions. Those exchanges should be opportunities for interaction with key resources for the newcomer, with a focus on the roles and responsibilities of each person and how they are interconnected, so as to facilitate future interactions. This suggests that newcomers need assistance in establishing relationships with key individuals beyond those in their immediate workgroup. It may be helpful to apply social network analysis, which has been used to study

the development of newcomer relationships (e.g., Morrison, 2002b) in identifying the work and social networks of existing employees for the purpose of identifying those individuals with whom newcomers should have structured welcome activities.

Louis et al. (1983) observed that interactions with others were the most helpful socializing activities, and subsequent research has reinforced those findings. Welcome activities are thought to play an important role in facilitating the development of social as well as work relationships, and research supports the need to establish both types of relationships, as they each have been shown to be differentially critical in facilitating learning, assimilation, and socialization outcomes (e.g., Bravo, Peiro, Rodriguez, & Whitely, 2003; Moreland & Levine, 2001; Morrison, 2002b). The *inform* activities discussed above are necessary, but may not be sufficient for effective socialization because it is not possible to fully anticipate everything a newcomer needs to know or when they need to know it. Helping establish effective relationships allows newcomers to have alternative means for accessing information on an "as needed" basis (Rollag et al., 2005). It further appears from past research that it is important that *welcome* activities facilitate the establishment of relationships with a variety of different current organizational members, because newcomers use different sources for different types of information (e.g., performance feedback versus job-specific knowledge), and obtaining information from different sources is associated with different socialization outcomes (Bravo et al., 2003; Chan & Schmitt, 2000; Gruman et al., 2006; Kammeyer-Mueller & Wanberg, 2003; Riordan et al., 2001; Wanberg & Kammeyer-Mueller, 2000).

Guide

The last category of orienting activities consists of efforts aimed at providing a more "hands-on" personal guide (e.g., assigning a welcome coordinator or coworker "buddy") to help the newcomer navigate the transition. There has been little systematic research on these types of activities, but the aforementioned research on socializing agents and social relationships supports the potential effectiveness of such programs. Four different agents have been suggested as guides in the literature: representatives from HR, coworkers, supervisors, and mentors. We did not locate any research examining the effectiveness of having a guide from HR, nor did we find research on supervisors as guides beyond studies examining them as socializing agents in general (e.g., Anakwe & Greenhous, 1999; Ostroff & Kozlowski, 1992). Neither did we find any studies since Louis et al. (1983) specifically examining "buddy systems" in onboarding. Rollag et al. (2005) suggest that providing a buddy (a) allows easy accesses to resources and a confidant to help facilitate sensemaking, particularly for understanding unwritten rules and learning tacit information; and (b) can further facilitate the development of work and social relationships in ways a supervisor cannot. Klein et al. (2010) found that assigning a coworker as a "buddy" was a common practice that is perceived as highly beneficial.

There has been research on the effectiveness of assigning mentors to new hires. Mentors traditionally have been defined as someone at a level above the supervisor, but the term is now used across these different groups of agents if they are serving in a mentoring role. Research has generally found positive relationships between mentoring and socialization outcomes (e.g., Anakwe & Greenhous, 1999; Chatman, 1991; Lankau & Scandura, 2002; Schrodt, Cawyer & Sanders, 2003), with different forms of mentoring relating differentially to socialization outcomes (Allen, McManus, & Russell, 1999). In the Klein et al. (2010) study, assigning a mentor (defined as being at a higher level than the employee's immediate supervisor), was an uncommon onboarding practice but was viewed as highly beneficial by those newcomers who were given mentors.

It is known from the mentoring literature (e.g., Baugh & Fagenson-Eland, 2007) that assigned mentors often do not replicate informal, emergent mentors. Most guides provided to newcomers as part of onboarding are assigned, and those assignments are typically made without the preparation, training, or structure that is found in many formal mentoring programs. As a result, there is likely great variability in the impact of "guide" activities depending on how those programs are structured and implemented. The onboarding practice of providing coworker buddies, for example, appears to often hope or assume that the buddy will be knowledgeable, trustworthy, and willing to assist the newcomer. Supervisors are similarly assumed to serve a guide role for new hires, but power distance and desire to look competent may limit the effectiveness of such policies if the supervisor is not proactive (or does not have the time or training to be so). Future research thus needs to examine the nature of these interactions and not just the availability of guides. Finally, information-seeking research (e.g., Morrison, 1993b) suggests multiple guides may be needed, as newcomers prefer to get different information from different sources.

Temporality

Temporal issues have been receiving increased attention in the socialization literature, a needed change given that socialization is a process that occurs over time. Ashforth et al. (2007) identified several temporal issues including the changing rate of learning over time, potential time lags before socialization effects are evident (and the possibility that effects may dissipate), and measurement stability issues. The findings by Chan and Schmitt (2000) that newcomers are concerned about different things as tenure increases, and change their information seeking accordingly (in terms of sources and content), highlight the importance of considering temporality. There is also a research methodology question of when to time data collection and the appropriate temporal intervals needed to capture the desired change or variance in variables of interest. Often, survey administration is driven by convenience or what an organization will allow rather than by theoretically based decisions. Given the evidence that socialization begins during recruitment and occurs fairly rapidly after entry (e.g., Bauer, & Green, 1994; Morrison, 1993a), administering a "Time 1" survey after a few weeks of employment may, for example, result in missing much of the onboarding phenomenon.

An experience-sampling study would be informative, with measurements taken daily or even multiple times a day during the crucial days before and during the first week with a new organization. Even if socialization occurs rapidly (e.g., Cooper-Thomas & Anderson, 2005; Lance, Vandenberg, & Self, 2000), all of the learning that needs to occur to facilitate socialization cannot occur within just a few days, which has led to the recommendation that onboarding activities should be spaced out over several weeks or months. Counter to this recommendation, Klein et al. (2010) found that most onboarding practices were occurring on the newcomer's start date. There are limits to how much information individuals can take in at one time, and exceeding those limits may result in misunderstanding, missed information, or frustration (Rollag et al., 2005). Delivering information in timely, smaller doses—on a "just-in-time" basis, for example, when the information is most salient to newcomers (Klein & Heuser, 2008)—should result in more effective learning and understanding. We do not yet have, however, a good understanding of the optimal timing of different onboarding activities or the overall duration of such programs to facilitate that learning.

Summary

The academic literature has identified numerous factors that facilitate socialization, factors that can inform the design of onboarding practices and policies. With a few exceptions, however, researchers have not examined specific organizational onboarding practices. In addition, research has tended to focus on the availability, amount, and helpfulness of onboarding activities (e.g., Klein et al., 2010; Louis et al., 1983), but, given the potential variation in the design and implementation of onboarding practices as well as the resulting variability in both the content and quality of any specific activity or interaction experienced by a newcomer, research needs to examine onboarding at a more detailed level in order to yield better understanding and more accurate prediction of these phenomena. Given the breath of socialization content that newcomers must master (e.g., Klein & Heuser, 2008), no single onboarding activity or practice can suffice.

Some practices may facilitate the learning of more socialization content areas than others, but a range of onboarding activities is likely needed to fully address the needs of newcomers. Klein et al. (2010) asked organizations about numerous different specific onboarding practices and, on average, only nine activities were required by organizations, suggesting that many organizations are not doing as much as they should with regard to the use of formal onboarding to facilitate the socialization of newcomers. In further support of the need for multiple onboarding practices, Kammeyer-Mueller and Wanberg (2003) examined how multiple adjustment antecedents affect proximal and distal socialization outcomes and found that different factors influenced different outcomes. That study, however, assessed the extent to which newcomers had been influenced by each source, not the particular practices, policies, or activities organizations had in place to facilitate influencing new hires. The practitioner literature, summarized next, provides occasional examples of companies thought to do a good job with onboarding, but relatively little empirical research has examined the usefulness, optimal content, structure, or timing of specific onboarding activities.

Practitioner Onboarding Literature

This section explores the messages and advice practitioners are receiving regarding onboarding practices. The insistence by academics that onboarding and socialization are important is reflected in the practitioner literature through the numerous articles relating to onboarding that emphasize the need for and positive consequences of well thought out onboarding programs. The benefits of effective onboarding highlighted in the practitioner literature center on cost savings, retention, improved time to proficiency, and facilitating organizational culture. As an example relating to cost savings, Snell (2006) concluded that a company can achieve an almost $2.3 million return on investment for an optimized onboarding process. That report also identified the costs and benefits of specific actions such as having a work space ready for a new hire (which can cost an organization $1,000 or more a week in lost productivity if not done). Related to the importance of having a newcomer's work space ready, Lavigna (2009) shares the following account: "Two dollars and 85 cents. That's how much change a brand-new government employee found on his desk on his first day on the job. How do we know this? Because this civil servant didn't have a computer at his desk and had nothing better to do than count loose change. Maybe the $2.85 was a hiring bonus?" (p. 65).

The practitioner onboarding literature can be grouped into one of three categories. First, there are white papers by consulting firms presenting descriptive research from across their client organizations. The above-cited report outlining the financial impact of onboarding (Snell, 2006) is an example of this type of resource. Second, there are articles in practitioner periodicals reporting the experiences of companies and providing superficial case studies demonstrating the criticality and benefits of devoting time and resources to the onboarding of new employees (e.g., Wells, 2005). These stories highlight companies that believe they have a successful onboarding program and are eager to share their enthusiasm for the subject. Finally, there are advice columns, both in journals and online, that outline the most critical onboarding issues or present onboarding "best practices" (e.g., Barbazette, n.d.). These lists try to take what has been successful for individual companies and generalize parts of the approach to make it more applicable to a wider audience. It should be noted that many of the "case study" articles also contain such lists.

To summarize the most common messages conveyed in the practitioner literature, we have compiled our own "best practices" list based on our reading of all three types of resources in the practitioner literature. In analyzing the various conclusions and recommendations, we found there was substantial agreement and considerable overlap in what is advocated and presented as best-practices onboarding. Specifically, we identified seven common conclusions that are summarized below.

Onboarding is a Process

The practitioner literature recognizes that onboarding is a process, a "journey" (Jarvis, 2008) and not an "event" (Westwood & Johnson, 2004). Consistent with the academic literature, articles in the practitioner literature assert that it can take "an average of six months for a mid-level manager to get up to speed in a new job" (Moscato, 2005, p. 107). Recommendations consistent with this view include statements that organizations should engage in different onboarding activities at different time periods. For example, one article (Commongood Careers, n.d.) outlines recommendations for what should be done before the first day, on the first day, during the first week, and during the first 3 months and beyond. A specific recommendation prior to the first day is to provide existing employees with information about the newcomer, how their roles interact with the role of the newcomer, and how they might expect to work together in the future. Other resources provide "checklists" for the crucial time periods (before the first day, first day, first week, etc.) to ensure that all activities that should take place during those times are indeed occurring (Government of Saskatchewan, n.d.). Another recommendation along these lines is to have a written onboarding plan outlining—for newcomers and relevant others—the specific timeline, goals, responsibilities, and resources/support available to newcomers (e.g., Vanden Bos, 2010).

Onboarding Should Reinforce Culture

A second theme often highlighted by practitioner articles is how onboarding programs should reflect and reinforce an organization's culture. For example, an article on *trainingmag.com* ("Rock 'n roll," 2009) outlines how the Hard Rock Café uniquely onboards its employees in a way that is consistent with and reinforces their culture while meeting the needs and expectations of their workforce. In the company's School of Hard Rocks—the company's corporate university—the employee handbook is inspired by comic books and the training process is filled with "lots of humor and graphics, limited text, and generous amounts of white space." An onboarding program that embodies an organization's culture obviously cannot be replicated exactly by another organization with a different culture, but the principle of designing onboarding specific to one's organizational culture is generalizable.

One way any organization can use onboarding to convey culture is by communicating success stories (Jarvis, 2008) and conveying to newcomers that they are now a part of something bigger than themselves. Another common practitioner recommendation related to culture and onboarding is the need for onboarding programs to be both true to what newcomers were previously told during recruitment and reflective of what they currently see and experience. First impressions matter, and onboarding is an opportunity to make a good one (Westwood & Johnson, 2004). It is also an opportunity to demonstrate that the organization "walks the talk" and as such, it is important to make an honest impression. As one article puts it, "Top talent in the labor market is educated, connected, discerning, and has access to information that can either validate or refute a company's employment value proposition in a heartbeat" ("Help new hires," 2008).

Onboarding is a Team Effort

Practitioner best practices lists recognize that while onboarding is about acculturating the newcomer, others—including managers, mentors, coaches, senior leaders, trainers, HR staff, and coworkers—have a big part to play (Barbazette, n.d.; Durett, 2006; Jarvis, 2008; Lee, 2006; Weinstein, 2007; Westwood & Johnson, 2004;). It is also often recommended that newcomers be exposed early and in a meaningful way to the CEO or other top leaders (e.g., Stephenson, Smelt, Gerhardt, & Munn, n.d.). Of the various socializing agents, supervisors tend to receive the most attention in the practitioner literature, as they are assumed to be working most closely with newcomers. Bradt (2010), uses a theater analogy to explain how a manager needs to be the producer, director, and stage manager—meaning that supervisors must clarify and align expectations, personalize the onboarding experience for newcomers, and "set the stage" for newcomers by announcing their arrival and introducing them to current employees and their new job.

Take Advantage of Technology

A number of articles in the practitioner literature highlight how technology can be used to help facilitate onboarding in a variety of ways including the coordination and tracking of progress, more efficient processing of paperwork, delivery of training, and social networking. In terms of recordkeeping, applicant tracking and human resource information system programs can help organizations create a seamless transition from recruitment to employment (e.g., Moscato, 2005) and ensure that communications are maintained with newcomers between hiring and the start date. These programs can also have built-in compliance checklists and send e-mail prompts to assist with legal and policy compliance and to verify that onboarding activities are occurring when they should, both before and after the start date. Some programs will even generate reports of newcomers' progress and provide outcome measures after certain periods of time to help an organization track the new employee and his/her contribution to the company.

Technology can also be used to automate completing necessary paperwork, saving the organization time and costs while also saving the newcomer time, hassles, and boring initial experiences (Arnold, 2010; Projections, n.d.). Frequent communication with newcomers and efficient data entry are small parts of the onboarding process but if they go awry, an onboarding experience can be ruined (Snell, 2006). Many articles highlight the value of addressing many of the bureaucratic aspects of onboarding online prior to the start date, allowing newcomers to begin to be involved with the organization as soon as they are hired and to focus on getting them acclimated and feeling welcome on their first day. As one new hire put it, completing paper work online beforehand allows newcomers to get "to the good stuff right away without sitting there signing your name a thousand times" (Arnold, 2010, p. 75).

Using technology to help deliver onboarding and orientation training is becoming increasingly common. Organizations can grant newcomers limited network access via the Internet, and distribute the employee handbook and other materials electronically prior to the start date, to both provide company information and HR self-services for completing administrative details (Boehle, 2008; Moscato, 2005). In addition to using technology to deliver information found in traditional orientation programs, organizations are using technology to create nontraditional orientation programs employing computer games and simulations that help newcomers learn about their new jobs and organizations. These programs have the well-documented advantages of computer-based instruction and are thought to better engage younger generations while ensuring they are learning the skills they need to be effective organizational members (Arnold, 2009). Finally, organizations are beginning to use social networking technology and integrate those tools into their onboarding programs to allow newcomers to interact with and exchange information with current employees (Kranz, 2009).

Give Newcomers a Sense of Purpose

A fifth theme we identified in the practitioner literature is the importance of newcomers (a) clearly seeing the value or benefit of any onboarding activity they are asked to complete (e.g., Barbazette, n.d.) and (b) understanding the significance of their new role and how their presence in the organization makes a difference (e.g., Wells, 2005). Recognizing the value of onboarding helps ensure that newcomers are motivated to learn, are fully engaged with, and get the most out of the onboarding activities. Many practitioners focus on obtaining the support of supervisors and top management for their onboarding program but winning the support, cooperation, and attention of newcomers is also important and, in some cases, more difficult. Some newcomers may believe that they do not need onboarding—that orientation and other activities are a waste of their time. Giving newcomers a sense of purpose in onboarding activities may help provide that perceived value.

That is, organizations should focus on "affirming the new employees' decision to come on board, conveying a sense of the company's culture, and making the new recruit feel a productive part of a team as soon as possible" (Garvey, 2001, p. 111) rather than focusing solely on the information that newcomers need to learn. Gustafson (2005) provides some examples of the programs companies have in place to make sure newcomers understand the importance of their new roles, as well as how those roles influence and are connected to other areas of the organization. In one of those exemplar organizations—Applied Materials—this is done for all newcomers including temporary and contract workers.

Customizing onboarding for each new hire is another way to facilitate a greater sense of value and purpose. Doing so requires obtaining a good understanding of the newcomer through the hiring process so that a more personalized onboarding experience can be designed to meet their unique needs. Wells (2005) describes the approach taken at Bristol-Myers Squibb which involves a "laser-like focus" during the first few weeks of newcomer employment that is aimed at "providing guidelines, clarifying roles, setting up meetings with influential colleagues, and fostering each newcomer's understanding of the company's cultural norms" (p. 56).

Provide Appropriate Orientation Training

Just as the greatest attention in the academic literature has been given to evaluating formal orientation training programs, much of the attention in the practitioner literature focuses on how to design effective orientation programs. Such articles emphasize the need for planning (e.g., Projections, n.d.), discuss the unique opportunity for "teachable moments" during a newcomer's first few days on the job (e.g., Kurtz, 2008), and point out how conventional approaches involving a series of talking heads, filling out a lot of forms, and giving a quick tour are not sufficient (e.g., Walters, 2010). Articles also emphasize principles of effective training needs assessment and design, including understanding who is going through the program and how they best learn, incorporating a variety of mediums and methods to engage learners, applying adult learning theories, and designing the program from the employee's perspective to maximize learning and retention (e.g., Barbazette, n.d.; Kurtz, 2010; Lee, 2006; Westwood & Johnson, 2004). There is no shortage of advice along the lines of admonishments that orientation programs should be kept simple and interesting, and that those providing information to newcomers should be professional, clear, and precise (Edwards, 2008). There are also articles that criticize the practice of waiting until there is a large group of new hires so that they can be onboarded together (e.g., Tyler, 1998), as this results in some newcomers struggling to make sense of things on their own for weeks before they are formally oriented.

Another theme in practitioner articles relating to orientation training is to highlight the unique challenges of particular types of employees. Two examples of this are newcomers entering organizations out of military service (e.g., "Military onboarding," 2009) and executives (Phaneuf, n.d.; Pomeroy, 2006; Stephenson et al., n.d.; "The executive entrance," 2008). Former military personnel are often sought after for their unique skills, but this group often has difficulty making the adjustment to civilian organizations and, as a result, experiences high turnover rates. Organizations can address this by designing programs specifically for such individuals, helping them understand concepts such as "profit vs. mission," and how to operate in a more consensus-based leadership environment rather than the deeply entrenched "command-and-control" leadership style to which they are accustomed ("Military onboarding," 2009). With respect to executives, it is generally recognized that the onboarding of executives needs to be more individualized and flexible (Bauer, 2010) and that the consequences of failing to effectively onboard an executive can be more calamitous than failure for lower level employees (Pomeroy, 2006). Yet, it appears that many organizations do not have any specialized or individualized onboarding program aimed specifically at onboarding executives ("The executive entrance," 2008; Stephenson et al., n.d.). A few other articles recognize the need to onboard members of organizations who move into new supervisory, manager, or other leadership positions, even if they are not new to the organization (e.g., Phaneuf, n.d.).

Provide Feedback Channels

The seventh and final theme we identified in the practitioner literature was the recognition of the value of feedback and the need for there to be feedback in both directions. That is, articles emphasize the importance of newcomers receiving specific feedback as early as possible so that they can adjust behavior to meet company expectations (Stephenson et al., n.d.). There are also articles noting that it is just as important for newcomers to evaluate their onboarding experience so that the company can similarly adjust its program to meet newcomer expectations (e.g., Finn, 2010).

Summary

It is difficult to argue with any of the above prescriptions found in the practitioner literature, but these articles either focus on the desired outcomes of effective onboarding and are rather vague regarding the specific practices, programs, and policies that should be implemented to achieve those outcomes, or provide specifics that are so context-dependent that applying those specific actions in other organizations would unlikely yield similar results. So, socialization is a process... but what exactly needs to occur at the beginning of the process, in the middle, and at the end? Onboarding is a team effort... but who should be involved, when, and in what ways? Similar questions can be asked for the other identified themes. Thus, although many practitioner articles aim to be "how to" guides, they really only hint at idealized results with limited prescription for how to achieve those results. It also appears that designing an effective onboarding system is easier said than done. One survey, for example, found that no employees reported being "very satisfied" with their onboarding experience (Snell, 2006).

There is a disconnect between surveys showing that most organizations do not give much attention to onboarding and the widespread assumption in these articles that onboarding is (a) an important and valuable HR activity, critical to a newcomer's adjustment and ultimate success; and (b) necessary so as not to have wasted the time, money, and effort spent on talent acquisition. One such survey segmented respondents into "Best-in-Class" companies (i.e., the top 20% based on their total score for onboarding effectiveness), "Average" companies (the middle 50%), and "Laggards" (the bottom 30%; see Martin & Lombardi, 2009). The "average" organizations, it was concluded, are not doing what they should to effectively onboard newcomers. In this survey, unlike the average or laggard companies, the majority of "best-in-class" companies have a formal, standardized onboarding process, begin their onboarding program when a job offer is extended or accepted, and enable collaboration between the HR department, recruiters, and hiring managers throughout the onboarding process. Those "best-in-class" companies are also more likely to track and report the progress of new hires through the onboarding process, though this is not yet done by a majority of these companies. Finally, this survey indicates that, compared to previously conducted surveys, onboarding is being taken seriously by more companies (although still not by most) and that those who do have "best-in-class" onboarding are also those companies with better newcomer retention rates, higher engagement scores, and lower time-to-productivity than the other companies.

After reviewing the practitioner literature regarding onboarding, it is clear that although some companies understand the criticality of an effective onboarding program and devote the time and resources to thoroughly onboard newcomers, most organizations do not. One issue preventing organizations from implementing new onboarding programs or revising existing programs may be cost concerns. Such concerns may be shortsighted and result from a focus on costs rather than cost effectiveness or ROI. Clearly there are costs associated with activities that have newcomers off their jobs or require others to take time away from their primary responsibilities to inform, welcome, or guide newcomers. Newcomers are often less productive initially, and coworkers might feel "burdened by picking up the slack" and view newcomers as a liability, which can diminish morale (e.g., Moscato, 2005; Snell, 2006). Morale and that burden will be worse, however, if newcomers quit or take longer to reach proficiency because of poor onboarding. As noted above, there are studies in the practitioner literature emphasizing that newcomers in companies

with "highly-rated" onboarding programs are able to reach performance proficiency sooner and excel on other metrics important to the organization's bottom line (Bilotti, 2008; Martin & Lombardi, 2009). In short, the evidence in both the academic and practitioner literatures is that although best-practice onboarding activities require upfront and ongoing costs, the costs of no or poor onboarding program are far greater.

So what is missing from the evidence in both academic and practitioner onboarding literatures that results in so many organizations not acting on the plethora of articles about effective onboarding? Perhaps practitioner articles are too vague, too idiosyncratic, or present results without clearly outlining the steps to take in order to reach those results, whereas the academic literature has generally not examined specific onboarding activities and thus cannot make predictions regarding the expected consequences of implementing particular practices in given situations.

Current State of Onboarding Practice

Neither the academic nor practitioner literatures reviewed above provide a clear picture of exactly what organizations are currently doing with respect to their onboarding practices. To address this gap, we worked with the Society for Human Resource Management (SHRM) to conduct a descriptive survey of onboarding practices ("Survey findings," 2011). This survey focused on the type, extent, and length of organizations' onboarding programs as well as challenges and changes in the way that organizations are onboarding newcomers. The survey was administered to over 2,500 HR professionals randomly selected from SHRM's membership from November to December, 2010. A total of 482 of those professionals participated in the survey (an 18% response rate), representing a variety of industries and organization sizes. In terms of size, the majority of respondents (78%) were from small or medium organizations. The specific distribution was 21% from companies with fewer than 100 employees, 27% from companies with 100–499 employees, 30% from companies with 500–2,499 employees, 16% with 2,500–24,999 employees, and 5% with over 25,000 employees. Forty-six percent of respondents were with privately owned for-profit organizations, 72% of participants' organizations operate in multiple locations, and for 79% of respondents those operations are only US-based.

The first set of questions centered on the extent to which organizations onboard new hires and the focus of those onboarding programs—the level or areas of the organization targeted by onboarding activities and whether onboarding programs were designed differently for different types of employees. The majority of respondents (81%) reported having some form of onboarding practices or programs in their organization, either formal (i.e., written, documented, standard) or informal. Most respondents (81%) claim that their onboarding program addressed the organization as a whole, as well as the newcomer's specific job (73%), department (64%), and immediate workgroup (56%). The areas least targeted by organization's onboarding programs are the newcomer's business unit (28%) and division (27%). Finally, more than half of respondents reported that they do differentiate their onboarding practices among employees based on three factors: management vs. non-management positions (63%); jobs that require different sets of KSAs, competencies, and/or job requirements (51%); and full-time vs. part-time vs. contingent employees (51%). Far fewer organizations differentiate how they onboard employees along several other potential employee differences including: hourly vs. salaried (30%), geographic location (29%), new-hire personal characteristics (e.g., experience, expectations, potential, learning style) (23%), and union vs. nonunion (14%).

To learn more about the kinds of onboarding programs offered by organizations, we used Klein and Heuser's (2008) Inform-Welcome-Guide framework to ask about the number of activities organizations formally had in place that could be described as (a) inform-resources, (b) inform-communication, (c) inform-training, (d) welcoming, and (e) guiding newcomers. In general, although most organizations have onboarding programs, most are not offering very many formal activities. The majority of organizations are providing no or only one formal activity in each of the welcome (59%) and guide (76%) categories, with one practice being the modal response. For the three inform categories, between 38% and 40% of organizations are providing none or only one activity in each category with a modal response of 2–3 formal practices. Twenty-six percent of respondents provide more than 4 inform-training activities. For the other four categories, between 6% (guide) and 19% (inform-resources) of respondents indicate that their organization provides more than four formal activities.

We also asked respondents about the importance of each of the activity categories for the successful adjustment of newcomers in terms of facilitating their performance, engagement, and retention.

Despite the relatively low numbers of formal activities offered across the different categories, the majority of respondents said that every activity category was "extremely important." The largest majorities were seen in the three inform categories: inform-resources (84%), inform-communication (88%), and inform-training (85%). There were no HR professionals who felt that these categories are "not at all important." The guide category had the most variation in responses, with only 59% saying these activities are "extremely important" and 2% saying that it is "not at all important."

Understanding the types and numbers of activities that are offered is informative, but we were also interested in why onboarding activities are *not* offered. According to the responding HR professionals, the most common reason for not offering more onboarding activities is time constraints—on the part of newcomers and other agents (60%). Second was not having sufficient HR staff to implement more activities (52%). Not surprisingly, financial constraints were also a common reason (33%), followed by a lack of senior management support (30%). On the other end of the spectrum, only 4% of respondents indicated that they do not do more in the way of onboarding because the activities are not valued by newcomers.

The survey also inquired about the timing of onboarding programs and activities. Respondents were asked when their organizations' onboarding programs began and how long they lasted. The modal response was that onboarding programs begin on the newcomers' start date (32%), followed closely by programs starting upon offer acceptance (31%). Fourteen percent reported they their onboarding programs began during the recruitment process and another 15% indicated that they begin onboarding after offer acceptance but prior to the start date. There was even more variation in the reported total cumulative duration of onboarding programs. The modal reported program length was "two to three days" (20%), followed closely by "90 days" (19%), "one day or less" (18%), and "between 8 days and a month" (17%). Only 3% of respondents reported having onboarding programs longer than 6 months in duration, and 6% indicated that the duration of the program depended on several factors. A final timing issue assessed when the different types of activities were thought to be most useful for newcomers. "On the first day" was the modal response for all but the inform-communication category, with between 37% (inform-resources) and 59% (guide) of respondents indicating that the start date was the most useful time to deliver these types of activities. Inform-communication was the most front-loaded activity, with "during recruitment" and "post-hire before start date" each receiving 32% of the responses. Inform-resources was next in terms of the distribution of timing being earlier. Inform-training was the category receiving the most responses after the first day, with 32% indicating that later in the first week was the most useful timing and another 22% suggesting training activities were most useful after the first week.

The survey also asked about the 12 socialization content dimensions outlined by Klein and Heuser (2008). Specifically, respondents were asked to rate both the importance of mastering each content area

for the successful adjustment of newcomers, and the difficulty for newcomers to master each content area on their own if not facilitated by an onboarding activity. Responses to these questions are summarized in Table 14.2. Beginning with importance, for 10 of the 12 dimensions fewer than 15% of respondents rated the dimension as very or somewhat unimportant. The two exceptions, the dimensions with the lowest mean importance ratings, were history and social relationships. The dimensions rated most important were task proficiency and rules and policies, followed by inducements, goals and strategies, and structure.

In terms of the difficulty mastering these dimensions if not covered by an onboarding activity the

Table 14.2 Importance of mastering socialization content areas for newcomer adjustment and the difficulty for newcomers to learn those content areas on their own

Socialization Content Dimension	Mean (SD) Ratings	
	Importance	Difficulty
Culture & Values: the customs, myths, rituals, beliefs, and values—including guiding principles, symbols, and ideology—of the organization.	3.38 (0.85)	2.71 (0.82)
Goals & Strategy: the current product/market mix, competitive position, mission, goals, and strategies of the organization.	3.47 (0.90)	2.51 (0.88)
History: the history, origins, and changes of the organization.	3.11 (0.75)	2.82 (0.88)
Inducements: what is offered in exchange for their contribution, including pay, development opportunities, and intangibles.	3.58 (0.85)	2.85 (0.92)
Language: the unique technical language, acronyms, slang, and jargon used at the organization.	3.41 (0.88)	2.19 (0.77)
Navigation: the implicit rules, norms, and procedures of the workplace.	3.36 (0.76)	2.59 (0.76)
Politics: the informal power structure of the organization, including where actual control of resources, decision making, and influence over decisions resides.	3.27 (0.82)	2.30 (0.79)
Rules and Policies: the formal workplace rules, policies, and procedures.	3.64 (0.85)	2.90 (0.89)
Social Relationships: the necessary information about others in the workplace to develop a network of social relationships, including the extent to which a newcomer has learned personal things about a work colleague (i.e., common interests, family).	2.78 (0.82)	2.83 (0.73)
Structure: the formal structure including the physical layout and where formal responsibility and authority is assigned in the organization.	3.47 (0.80)	2.83 (0.83)
Task Proficiency: the necessary job knowledge and skills needed to successfully perform required "in role" tasks.	3.64 (0.90)	2.35 (0.80)
Working Relationships: the necessary information about others in the organization to establish effective working relationships, including the learning of work colleagues' expectations, needs, and working styles	3.33 (0.89)	2.28 (0.74)

Importance rated on a 1 = Very unimportant to 4 = Very important scale; Difficulty rated on a 1 = Very difficult to 4 = Very easy scale.

ratings were more to the middle of the scale, with most respondents not viewing any dimension as "very difficult" or "very easy" to learn. Language was seen as the most difficult content dimension to master, followed by working relationships, politics, task proficiency, and goals and strategy. In contrast, rules and policies was viewed as the easiest content dimension to master followed by inducements, social relationships, structure, and history. From a training needs assessment perspective, organizations should invest in onboarding practices that will impact those content areas that are both of high importance and difficult for people to master on their own. Using these results, that would point to the content dimensions of task proficiency, language, and goals and strategy. It should be recognized, however, that HR professionals' opinions of the difficulty of mastering these content dimensions may not reflect actual difficulty to learn or the relative newcomers' mastery of these dimensions.

The survey also gathered information on the monitoring of programs, the collection of feedback from participants, and trends in onboarding programs over the past 5 years. In terms of monitoring formal onboarding activities to ensure they are actually happening in the intended manner, many organizations (37%) conduct occasional spot monitoring or frequently monitor their programs (31%), but only 15% conduct extensive monitoring and 17% do little to no monitoring of their onboarding programs. Regarding program evaluation, many organizations (39%) conduct occasional spot evaluations to collect feedback from newcomers or their supervisors for assessing and revising their onboarding activities. However, 28% collect little or no feedback and only 8% extensively evaluate most or all of their onboarding practices.

Finally, respondents were asked about changes in their onboarding practices over the past 5 years. Results indicated that onboarding has become a longer and more intensive process, with more activities offered to help facilitate newcomer adjustment. Organizations are also now using onboarding more strategically, as a key part of their retention efforts. Also, despite advances in technology and its increased use in onboarding activities, a majority of respondents believe that onboarding has become more engaging, interactive, and tailored to individual newcomers, and disagree that the greater use of electronic communications and online delivery of material has made the process less personal. As for the timing of onboarding programs, a slight majority reported that they now begin onboarding newcomers earlier, with more attention being given to the recruitment period. Finally, responses to the question about trends indicated that onboarding programs are occurring for a longer duration now than 5 years ago, with a longer-term focus in that more emphasis is being placed on career paths, development, and advancement opportunities early in the process.

Future Research Needs

As is hopefully evident from this chapter, there is much work to be done to help fill gaps in our understanding of the onboarding process, specific onboarding activities, and the impact of those activities on socialization and socialization outcomes. Research needs to move beyond simply looking at Van Maanen and Schein's (1979) socialization tactics (regardless of how dimensionalized) and instead examine specific onboarding practices. Just as research has examined specific training, recruitment, and selection assessment methods, studies are needed examining specific onboarding practices. In addition, that research must recognize that *what*, *how* (in terms of those socialization tactics), and *when* also matter. As such, future research must take a more holistic view of what activities, what combination of activities, and what circumstances best facilitate the transformation of newcomers into contributing organizational members.

Additional research is also needed that explores *when* onboarding activities should be offered. As noted, little research has explored temporal issues in onboarding (e.g., Ashforth et al., 2007; Chan & Schmitt, 2000) and the research that exists is not necessarily looking at the timing of specific onboarding activities. Most activities are still being offered on a newcomer's start date or within the first few days a newcomer is with an organization, and employees are also reporting that activities are more beneficial the earlier they occur (Klein et al., 2010). Yet, a common theme in both academic and practitioner literatures is that socialization is a process that takes time, possibly up to 2 years. This contradiction begs attention.

Aside from determining what onboarding activities are most impactful and their optimal timing, distinctions must be made in regard to the personalization of these onboarding activities. First, a differentiated focus is needed among levels of onboarding activities (i.e., organization, division, unit, department, workgroup, job). SHRM's survey found that most organizations' onboarding programs welcome the newcomer to the organization and the newcomer's specific job, but not as much attention is given to the department, the workgroup, the geographic location, the business unit, or the division. Organizations may need to alter current activities or add new activities to their onboarding programs such that the newcomer is introduced to all relevant levels of the organization. This will ultimately help the newcomer understand his/her place and contribution in the company.

Second, an increased understanding of the needs of different types of newcomers is required. According to the SHRM survey data, over 50% of organizations do distinguish between non-management and management, job family (e.g., KSAs, competencies, job requirements), and employment status (contingent vs. part-time vs. full-time), but a majority of organizations do not differentiate onboarding programs in regard to other differences such as: entry-level vs. mid-level vs. senior level employees, recruitment source, business unit, geographic location, personal characteristics (e.g., experience, expectations, potential, learning style), or nonunion vs. union employees. While some articles do address the unique needs of executives (e.g., Pomeroy, 2006) or those with prior work experience (e.g., Adkins, 1995), attention to other differences in newcomers is lacking.

Third, key organizational factors also need to be identified. Given the asserted connections between culture and onboarding, for example, research is needed explicitly examining the potential moderating role of culture on the effectiveness of different onboarding practices. According to Klein et al. (2010), many onboarding activities offered by organizations are occurring informally as opposed to formally. Under what conditions—cultural and other factors—are formal or informal activities more impactful on the mastery of various content areas and socialization outcomes? A greater understanding of contingent factors would also be aided by all onboarding studies providing a rich description of the context in which the research was conducted. Stated differently, potential interactions with newcomer characteristics (e.g., prior experience, proactivity, personality) and the organizational context (e.g., culture, type of position) need to be examined.

Numerous practitioner articles delineate the goals organizations should aim to achieve with their onboarding programs, but direction is lacking regarding the specific actions organizations should take to reach those goals. To provide that prescription to organizations regarding what onboarding policies and practices can be used to achieve what

socialization objectives, research needs to focus on the mediating factors through which onboarding practices impact desired outcomes such as retention, engagement, and time to proficiency. Those mediators include but are not limited to the mastery of socialization content (e.g., Klein, Fan, & Preacher, 2006). Examining these important mediators will allow for better theory testing regarding why a particular practice yields desirable outcomes, as well as better prediction.

From a methodological perspective we need more specific tools for capturing organizational onboarding activities. Klein et al. (2010) and the SHRM study ("Survey findings," 2011) demonstrate that the Inform-Welcome-Guide framework can be useful, as it yielded variation in means and patterns across categories of onboarding practices. However, a simple checklist of activities such as that used by Klein et al. (2010) does not effectively capture the degree to which organizations are offering activities in these categories of practices, nor variations in how a particular practice may be implemented. Another methodological issue concerns the most appropriate source for assessing onboarding practices. Addressing most of the above research questions will require examining onboarding from both organizational and newcomer perspectives, and both have their limitations. Different newcomers may have different perspectives of the same event, and an organization's onboarding policies may be differentially implemented in different units. In fact, Klein et al., (2010) found disconnects between what representatives from the HR departments reported in terms of what and how onboarding activities should be occurring and new hire reports of what they experienced.

Summary

We began this chapter with the goal of illustrating the gaps in the academic literature and between the research evidence base and the recommendations found in the practitioner literature. Our review of academic literature demonstrated that while researchers have identified factors that facilitate socialization and which can inform the design of onboarding practices, academics have rarely examined specific onboarding practices, their optimum timing, or their influence on the mastery of socialization content dimensions. A review of the practitioner literature yields a plethora of articles outlining best practices, but those recommendations are not based on research evidence (largely due to the absence of such research). In addition, those recommendations generally lack the specifics needed to implement the ideas, and fail to recognize key moderators or boundary conditions. In sum, practitioners appear to increasingly recognize the importance of onboarding, but do not appear to be fully on board with making the investments needed to implement what are thought to be best practices. Further, until some of the above identified research needs are addressed, those best practices will not be evidence-based recommendations.

References

Adkins, C. L. (1995). Previous work experience and organizational socialization: A longitudinal examination. *Academy of Management Journal, 38,* 839–862.

Allen, D. (2006). Do organizational socialization tactics influence newcomer embeddedness and turnover? *Journal of Management, 32,* 237–256.

Allen, D., McManus, S. E., & Russell, J. E. A. (1999). Newcomer socialization and stress: Formal peer relationships as a source of support. *Journal of Vocational Behavior, 54,* 453–470.

Anakwe, U. P., & Greenhouse, J. H. (1999). Effective socialization of employees: Socialization content perspective. *Journal of Management Issues, 11,* 315–329.

Anderson, N. R., Cunningham-Snell, N. A., & Haigh, J. (1996). Induction training as socialization: Current practice and attitude to evaluation in British organizations. *International Journal of Selection and Assessment, 4,* 169–183.

Arnold, J. T. (2009). Gaming technology used to orient new hires. *HR Trendbook, 53,* 36–38.

Arnold, J. T. (2010). Ramping up onboarding: Effective employee onboarding often begins with a click. *HR Magazine, 55(5),* 75–78.

Ashforth, B. E. (2001). *Role transitions in organizational life: An identity-based perspective.* Mahwah, NJ: Laurence Erlbaum.

Ashforth, B. E., Sluss, D. M., & Harrison, S. H. (2007). Socialization in organizational contexts. In G. P. Hodgkinson & J. K. Ford (Eds.), *International review of industrial and organizational psychology,* (Vol. 22, pp. 1–70). Chichester: John Wiley & Sons, Inc.

Ashford, S. J., & Black, J. S. (1996). Proactivity during organizational entry: A role of desire for control. *Journal of Applied Psychology, 81,* 199–214.

Barbazette, J. (n. d.). Make new employee orientation a success. Retrieved June 24, 2011, from http://www.ideasandtraining.com/New-Employee-Orientation-Article.html.

Bauer, T. N. (2010). Onboarding new employees: Maximizing success. Alexandria VA: SHRM Foundation.

Bauer, T. N., Bodner, T., Erdogan, B., Truxillo, D. M., & Tucker, J. S. (2007). Newcomer adjustment during organizational socialization: A meta-analytic review of antecedents, outcomes, and methods. *Journal of Applied Psychology, 92,* 707–721.

Bauer, T. N., & Erdogan, B. (2010). Organizational socialization: The effective onboarding of new employees. In S. Zedeck, H. Aguinis, W. Cascio, M. Gelfand, K. Leung, S. Parker, & J. Zhou (Eds.), *APA handbook of I/O psychology, Vol. III* (pp. 51–64). Washington, DC: American Psychological Association Press.

Bauer, T. N., & Green, S. G. (1994). Effect of newcomer involvement in work-related activities: A longitudinal study of socialization. *Journal of Applied Psychology, 79,* 211–223.

Bauer, T. N., & Green, S. G. (1998). Testing the combined effects of newcomer information seeking and manager behavior on socialization. *Journal of Applied Psychology, 79,* 211–223.

Bauer, T. N., Morrison, E. W., & Callister, R. R. (1998). Organizational socialization: A review and directions for future research. In G. R. Ferris (Ed.), *Research in personnel and human resource management* (Vol. 16, pp. 149–214). Greenwich, CT: JAI Press.

Baugh, S. G., & Fagenson-Eland, E. A. (2007). Formal mentoring programs: A "poor cousin" to informal relationships? In B. R. Ragins & K. E. Kram (Eds.), *The handbook of mentoring at work: Theory, research, and practice* (pp. 249–271). Los Angeles, CA: Sage Publications.

Berger, C. R. (1979). Beyond initial understanding: Uncertainty, understanding, and the development of interpersonal relationships. In H. Giles, & R. N. St. Clair (Eds.), *Language and social psychology* (pp. 122–144). Oxford: Basil Blackwell.

Bilotti, R. (2008). *The 2008 "Impact of Onboarding" national study results: Executive summary.* Chicago, IL: Novita.

Boehl, S. (2008). True vision. *Training, 45(2),* 32–29.

Bradt, G. (2010). Onboarding: An act of transformational leadership. Retrieved June 22, 2011 fromhttp://www.allbusiness.com/labor-employment/human-resources-personnel-management/14950668–1.html.

Bravo, M. J., Peiro, J. M., Rodriguez, I., & Whitely, W. T. (2003). Social antecedents of the role stress and career-enhancing strategies of newcomers to organizations: A longitudinal study. *Work & Stress, 17,* 195–217.

Breaugh, J. A., & Mann, R. B. (1984). Recruiting source effects: A test of two alternative explanations. *Journal of Occupational Psychology, 57,* 261–267.

Carr, J. C., Pearson, A. W., Vest, M. J., & Boyar, S. L. (2006). Prior occupational experience, anticipatory socialization, and employee retention. *Journal of Management, 32,* 343–359.

Chan, D., & Schmitt, N. (2000). Interindividual differences in intraindividual changes in proactivity during organizational entry: A latent growth modeling approach to understanding newcomer adaptation. *Journal of Applied Psychology, 85,* 190–210.

Chao, G. T. (in press). Organizational socialization: Background, basics, and a blueprint for adjustment at work. In S. W. J. Kozlowski (Ed.), *The Oxford handbook of organizational psychology,* New York: Oxford University Press.

Chao, G. T., O'Leary-Kelly, A. M., Wolf, S., Klein, H. J., & Gardner, P. D. (1994). Organizational socialization: Its content and consequences. *Journal of Applied Psychology, 79,* 730–743.

Chatman, J. (1991). Matching people and organizations: Selection and socialization in public accounting firms. *Administrative Science Quarterly, 36(3),* 459–484.

Coff, R., & Kryscynski, D. (2011). Drilling for micro-foundations of human capital-based competitive advantages. *Journal of Management, 37(5),* 1429–1443.

Commongood Careers. (n.d.) Best practices for employee onboarding. Retrieved June 24, 2011, from http://www.cgcareers.org/articles/detail/best-practices-for-employee-onboarding/.

Cooper-Thomas, H. D., & Anderson, N. (2005). Organizational socialization: A field study into socialization success and rate. *International Journal of Selection and Assessment, 13,* 116–128.

Cooper-Thomas, H. D., & Anderson, N. (2006). Invited manuscript: Organizational socialization: A new theoretical model and recommendations for future research and HRM practices in organizations. *Journal of Managerial Psychology, 21,* 492–516.

DeShon, R. P., & Gillespie, J. Z. (2005). A motivated action theory account of goal oriented behavior. *Journal of Applied Psychology, 90,* 1096–1127.

De Vos, A., Buyens, D., & Schalk, R. (2003). Psychological contract development during organizational socialization: Adaptation to reality and role of reciprocity. *Journal of Organizational Behavior, 24,* 537–559.

Durett, J. (2006). Plug in and perform. *Training, 43(3),* 30–34.

Edwards, J. (2008). A checklist for successful onboarding. Retrieved May 25, 2011, from http://www.hrworld.com/features/onboarding-checklist-73108/.

Fan, J., & Wanous, J. P. (2008). Organizational and cultural entry: A new type of orientation program for multiple boundary crossings. *Journal of Applied Psychology, 93,* 1390–1400.

Fang, R., Duffy, M. K., & Shaw, J. D. (2011). The organizational socialization process: Review and development of a social capital model. *Journal of Management, 37,* 127–152.

Feldman, D. C. (1981). The multiple socialization of organization members. *Academy of Management Review, 6,* 309–318.

Feldman, D. C. (1989). Socialization, resocialization, and training: Reframing the research agenda. In I. L. Goldstein (Ed.), *Training and development in organizations* (pp. 376–416). San Francisco: Jossey-Bass.

Finkelstein, L. M., Kulas, J. T., & Dages, K. D. (2003). Age differences in proactive newcomer socialization strategies in two populations. *Journal of Business and Psychology, 17,* 473–502.

Finn, P. (2010). The importance of being onboarded. Retrieved June 30, 2011, from http://www.nwfpa.org/nwfpa.info/component/content/article/134-organizational-culture/200-the-importance-of-being-onboarded.

Fisher, C. D. (1986). Organizational socialization: An integrative review. In K. M. Rowland & G. R. Ferris (Eds.), *Research in personnel and human resources management* (Vol. 4, pp. 101–145). Greenwich, CT: JAI Press.

Galvin, T. (2003). 2003 industry report. *Training, 40,* 21–45.

Garvey, C. (2001). The whirlwind of a new job. *HR Magazine, 46(6),* 111–118.

Gordon, C. (1999). The next generation: succession planning. *Human Resource Planning, 22,* 16–17.

Government of Saskatchewan. (n.d.). Employee onboarding: A manager's guide to orientation for new employees. Retrieved May 25, 2011 from http://www.psc.gov.sk.ca/Default.aspx?DN=5fa95b25–54d2–4a3b-82de-d4c2bf69587c.

Gruman, J. A., Saks, A. M., & Zweig, D. I. (2006). Organizational socialization tactics and newcomer proactive behaviors: An integrative study. *Journal of Vocational Behavior, 69,* 90–104.

Gustafson, K. (2005). A better welcome mat. *Training, 42(6),* 34–41.

Help new hires succeed: Effective onboarding drives retention, morale, and productivity. (2008). Retrieved June 24, 2011, from http://trainingmag. com/article/help-new-hires-succeed.

Holladay, C. L., Donnelly, T. M., Murray, S., & Halverson, S. K. (2006). *On-boarding employees: A model examining manager behavior, socialization, and commitment.* Paper presented at the Annual Conference of the Society for Industrial and Organizational Psychology, Dallas, TX.

Holton, E. F. III. (2001). New employee development tactics: Perceived availability, helpfulness, and relationship with job attitudes. *Journal of Business and Psychology, 16,* 73–85.

Hom, P. W., Griffeth, R. W., Palich, L. E., & Bracker, J. S. (1998). An exploratory investigation into theoretical mechanisms underlying realistic job previews. *Personnel Psychology, 51,* 421–451.

Jablin, F. M. (2001). Organizational entry, assimilation, and disengagement. *The new handbook of organizational communication: Advances in theory, research, and methods,* (pp. 732–818). Thousand Oaks, CA: Sage Publication.

Jarvis, D. E. (2008). 9 fundamentals of strategic onboarding. Retrieved June 24, 2011, from http://www.danajarvis.org/?p=44.

Kammeyer-Mueller, J. D., Livingston, B. A., & Liao, H. (2011). Perceived similarity, proactive adjustment, and organizational socialization. *Journal of Vocational Behavior, 78,* 225–236.

Kammeyer-Mueller, J. D., & Wanberg, C. R. (2003). Unwrapping the organizational entry process: Disentangling multiple antecedents and their pathways to adjustment. *Journal of Applied Psychology, 88,* 779–794.

Kim, T. Y., Cable, D. M., & Kim, S. P. (2005). Socialization tactics, employee proactivity, and personal-organization fit. *Journal of Applied Psychology, 90,* 232–241.

Klein, H. J., & Heuser, A. E. (2008). The learning of socialization content: A framework for researching orienting practices. *Research in Personnel and Human Resources Management, 27,* 279–336. Emerald Group.

Klein, H. J., Fan, J., & Preacher, K. J. (2006). The effects of early socialization experiences on content mastery and outcomes: A mediational approach. *Journal of Vocational Behavior, 68,* 96–115.

Klein, H. J., Polin, B., & Sutton, K. L. (2010). Effectively Onboarding New Employees. Paper presented at the Annual Meeting of the Academy of Management, Montreal, Quebec.

Klein, H. J., & Weaver, N. A. (2000). The effectiveness of an organizational level orientation training program in the socialization of new hires. *Personnel Psychology, 53,* 47–66.

Kranz, G. (2009). Training that starts before the job begins. Retrieved June 24, 2011, from http://www.workforce.com/section/training-development/feature/training-starts-before-job-begins/.

Kurtz, R. (2008). The importance of new-employee orientation. Retrieved June 24, 2011, from http://www.businessweek.com/smallbiz/tips/archives/2008/05/the_importance_of_new-employee_orientation.html.

Kurtz, R. (2010). A better way to present your company to new employees. Retrived June 23, 2011, from http://www.businessweek.com/smallbiz/tips/archives/2010/01/a_better_way_to_present_your_company_to_new_employees.html.

Lance, C. E., Vandenberg, R. J., & Self, R. M. (2000). Latent growth models of individual change: The case of newcomer adjustment. *Organizational Behavior and Human Decision Processes, 83,* 107–140.

Lankau, M. J., & Scandura, T. A. (2002). An investigation of personal learning in mentoring relationships: Content antecedents, and consequences. *Academy of Management Journal, 45,* 779–790.

Lavigna, B. (2009). Getting onboard: Integrating and engaging new employees. *Government Finance Review, 23(5),* 65–70.

Lee, D. (2006). All aboard! Does your onboarding process lead to employee engagement or buyer's remorse? Retrieved June 24, 2011, from http://www.humannatureatwork.com/articles/employee_retention/all_aboard.htm.

Lundberg, C. C., & Young, C. A. (1997). Newcomer socialization: Critical incidents in hospitality organizations. *Journal of Hospitality & Tourism Research, 21,* 58–74.

Louis, M. R. (1980). Surprise and sense making: What newcomers experience in entering unfamiliar organizational settings. *Administrative Science Quarterly, 25,* 226–251.

Louis, M. R., Posner, B. Z., & Powell, G. N. (1983). The availability and helpfulness of socialization practices. *Personnel Psychology, 36,* 857–866.

Martin, K., & Lombardi, M. (2009). *Fully on-board: Getting the most from your talent in the first year.* Boston: Aberdeen Group.

Military onboarding: The cost of doing nothing. (2009). Retrieved on June 24, 2011, from http://trainingmag.com/article/military-onboarding-cost-doing-nothing.

Miller, V. D. (1996). An experimental study of newcomers' information seeking behaviors during organizational entry. *Communications Studies, 47,* 1–24.

Moreland, R. L., & Levine, J. M. (2001). Socialization in organizations and work groups. In M. E. Turner (Ed.), *Groups at work: Theory and research,* (pp. 69–112). Mahwah, NJ: Lawrence Erlbaum.

Morrison, E. W. (1993a). Longitudinal study of the effects of information seeking on newcomer socialization. *Journal of Applied Psychology, 78,* 173–183.

Morrison, E. W. (1993b). Newcomer information seeking: Exploring types, modes, sources, and outcomes. *Academy of Management Journal, 36,* 557–589.

Morrison, E. W. (2002a). Information seeking within organizations. *Human Communication Research, 28,* 229–242.

Morrison, E. W. (2002b). Newcomers' relationships: The role of social network ties during socialization. *Academy of Management Journal, 45,* 1149–1160.

Morrison, E. W. & Phelps, C. C. (1999). Taking charge at work: Extra-role efforts to initiate the workplace change. *Academy of Management Journal, 42,* 403–419.

Morrison, E. W. & Vancouver, J. B. (2000). Within-person analysis of information seeking: The effects of perceived costs and benefits. *Journal of Management, 26,* 119–137.

Morse, B. J. & Popovich, P. M. (2009). Realistic recruitment practices in organizations: The potential benefits of generalized expectancy calibration. *Human Resource Management Review, 19,* 1–8.

Moscato, D. (2005). Technology can help reduce the time it takes for a new hire to get up to speed. *HR Magazine, 50(4),* 107–109.

Nelson, D. L. & Quick, J. C. (1991). Social support and newcomer adjustment in organizations: Attachment theory at work? *Journal of Organizational Behavior, 12,* 543–554.

Ostroff, C. & Kozlowski, S. W. J. (1992). Organizational socialization as a learning process: The role of information acquisition. *Personnel Psychology, 45,* 849–874.

Phaneuf, W. (n.d.). Leadership and executive onboarding tips. Retrieved June 24, 2011, from http://www.leadingforloyalty.com/executive_onboarding.html.

Phillips. J. M. (1998). Effects of realistic job previews on multiple organizational outcomes: A meta-analysis. *Academy of Management Journal, 41,* 673–690.

Pomeroy, A. (2006). Better executive onboarding processes needed. *HR Magazine, 51(8),* 16.

Projections. (n.d.). Onboarding: Employee orientation beyond "sink or swim." *Author.* Retrieved June 24, 2011, from http://www.attcnetwork.org/explore/priorityareas/wfd/grow/documents/Onboarding.pdf.

Reichers, A. E. (1987). An interactionist perspective on newcomer socialization rates. *Academy of Management Review, 12,* 278–287.

Riordan, C. M., Weatherly, E. W., Vandenberg, R. J., & Self, R. M. (2001). The effects of pre-entry experiences and socialization tactics on newcomer attitudes and turnover. *Journal of Managerial Issues, 13,* 159–176.

Rock 'n roll onboarding. (2009). Retrieved on June 24, 2011, from http://trainingmag.com/article/rock-n-roll-onboarding.

Rollag, K., Parise, S., & Cross, R. (2005). Getting new hires up to speed quickly. *MIT Sloan Management Review, 46,* 35–41.

Saks, A. M. (1994). A psychological process investigation for the effects of recruitment source and organization information on job survival. *Journal of Organizational Behavior, 15,* 225–244.

Saks, A. M. (1996). The relationship between the amount and helpfulness of entry training and work outcomes. *Human Relations, 49,* 429–451.

Saks, A. M., & Ashforth, B. E. (1997). Organizational socialization: Making sense of the past and present as a prologue for the future. *Journal of Vocational Behavior, 51,* 234–279.

Saks, A. M., & Gruman, J. A. (2010). *Getting newcomers onboard: What's an organization to do?* Paper presented at the Annual Meeting of the Academy of Management, Montreal, Quebec.

Schrodt, P., Cawyer, C. S., & Sanders, R. (2003). An examination of academic mentoring behaviors and new faculty members' satisfaction with socialization and tenure promotion processes. *Communication Education, 52,* 17–29.

Slattery, J. P., Selvarajan, T. T., & Anderson, J. E. (2006). Influences of new employee development practices on temporary employee work-related attitudes. *Human Resource Development Quarterly, 17,* 279–303.

Sluss, D. M. & Ashforth, B. E. (2007). Relationship identity and identification: Defining ourselves through work relationships. *Academy of Management Review, 32,* 9–32.

Snell, A. (2006). *Onboarding: Speeding the way to productivity.* Dublin, CA: Taleo Research.

Stephenson, A. R., Smelt, E. H., Gerhardt, T., & Munn, A. (n. d.). Executive on-boarding: How to settle in a new hire. Retrieved June 24, 2011, from http://www.ceoforum.com.au/article-detail.cfm?cid=6266&t=/Ashley-R-Stephenson-and—Edwin-H-Smelt-and-Tilman-Gerhardt-and-Anna-Munn/Executive-Onboarding-how-to-settle-in-a-new-hire.

Survey findings: Onboarding practices. (2011). *SHRM Foundation Publication.* Retrieved June 24, 2011, from http://www.shrm.org/Research/SurveyFindings/Articles/Pages/OnboardingPractices.aspx.

Tannenbaum, S. I., Mathieu, J. E., Salas, E., & Cannon-Bowers, J. A. (1991). Meeting trainees' expectations: The influence of training fulfillment on the development of commitment, self-efficacy, and motivation. *Journal of Applied Psychology, 76,* 759–769.

The executive entrance. (2008). Retrieved June 24, 2011, from http://trainingmag.com/article/executive-entrance.

Tyler, K. (1998). Take new employee orientation off the back burner. *HR Magazine, 43(6),* 49–54.

Vanden Bos, P. (2010). How to build an onboarding plan for a new hire. Retrieved June 24, 2011, from http://www.inc.com/guides/2010/04/building-an-onboarding-plan.html.

Van Maanen, J. (1976). Breaking-in: Socialization to work. In R. Dubin, (Ed.), *Handbook of work, organization, and society*, (pp. 67–130). Chicago: Rand McNally.

Van Maanen, J., & Schein, E. H. (1979). Toward a theory of organizational socialization. *Research in Organizational Behavior, 1*, 209–264.

Walters, C. (2010). Employee onboarding boosts retention, improves productivity. *Rochester Business Journal*. Retrieved June 24, 2011, from http://www.rbj.net/article.asp?aID=184475.

Wanberg, C. R., & Kammeyer-Mueller, J. D. (2000). Predictors and outcomes of proactivity in the socialization process. *Journal of Applied Psychology, 85*, 373–385.

Wanous, J. P. (1989). Installing a realistic job preview: Ten tough choices. *Personnel Psychology, 42*, 117–134.

Wanous, J. P. (1993). Newcomer orientation programs that facilitate organizational entry. In H. Schuler, J. L. Farr, & M. Smith (Eds.), *Personnel selection and assessment: Individual and organizational perspectives,* (pp. 125–139). Hillsdale, NJ: Lawrence Erlbaum.

Weinstein, M. (2007). Balancing act. *Training, 44*(2), 22–28.

Wells, S. J. (2005). Diving in. *HR Magazine, 50(3)*, 54–59.

Wesson, M. J., & Gogus, C. I. (2005). Shaking hands with a computer: An examination of two methods of newcomer orientation. *Journal of Applied Psychology, 90*, 1018–1026.

Westwood, R. L., & Johnson, L. (2004). New employee orientation. *Information Lifeline* (p. 407). ASTD Press.

Williams, C. R., Labig, C. E., & Stone, T. H. (1993). Recruitment sources and posthire outcomes for job applicants and new hires: A test of two hypotheses. *Journal of Applied Psychology, 78*, 163–172.

Zottolia, M. A., & Wanous, J. P. (2000). Recruitment source research: Current status and future directions. *Human Resource Management Review, 10*, 353–382.

The Development of a Comprehensive Onboarding Program at a Big Ten Research University

Stacy Doepner-Hove

Abstract

This chapter deals with the development of a comprehensive onboarding program at a Big Ten research university. It focuses on the program creation process from needs assessment through program development and implementation, including evaluation systems. The chapter includes detailed information on how the development of the University of Minnesota program was (1) driven from the top down; (2) overseen by a full-time onboarding director; (3) branded to leverage the university messaging; (4) created by partnering with other departments; (5) integrated through central, unit, and supervisory level management; and (6) measured to assure its effectiveness. It also discusses specific examples of the onboarding program itself, as well as future directions for employee engagement at the university.

Key Words: program development, onboarding program, comprehensive onboarding, onboarding higher education, employee engagement, employee retention, university onboarding, program branding.

Introduction

Arriving to work on her first day at the University of Minnesota, Nissa felt excited and energized by the campus. Coming from a corporate environment, she was used to hustle and bustle but she looked forward to using her talents to push the boundaries of education and discovery. She interviewed many times, with many different people, and when she got the offer she called everyone she knew to say she was going to work at the University of Minnesota. She even bought a maroon and gold "M" pin to wear on her first day—just to get into the mood. Parking was a problem. No one had really told her what to expect and the first lot next to her building was full by the time she got there. She wasn't from Minnesota, so trudging across a snow-covered campus in her dress clothes was unexpected. No receptionist greeted her, but she knew her office number so she wandered the building until she found her work area. She took a lap around her new department but saw no

one around, so she walked back to her office. Taped to her door she found a key and a note from her supervisor. "I'm in meetings all day. Here is your key. Make yourself at home and hopefully I'll get a chance to meet with you tomorrow." Feeling alone and a bit let down, Nissa let herself into her office, sat down at her desk, and wondered aloud to herself if she had done the right thing in coming to work at the University.

Nearly 66,000 students walk the often snow-covered grasses of the five campuses that hail by the name of University of Minnesota. Over 18,000 full-time employees and another 30,000 or so, if you count the part-time and student workers, work on those same campuses. The Twin Cities campus alone has over 230 buildings and nearly 1000 different academic departments. In stronger economic times the university hired over 1600 new employees every year; in weaker times that number drops, but only to about 1000 a year. With its main location in the middle of a sprawling urban area, and drawn partly by its renowned medical services, over 150,000 members of the general public walk, bike, drive, or bus through the campuses each day of every year. Into this mass of maroon and gold, of teaching and learning, research and discovery, outreach and public service, a single new employee arriving from the neighboring state of Wisconsin or from Bangladesh on the other side of the world can feel stupefied by the infrastructural hierarchy and lost in a search for how his or her work fits into this massive institution.

Laying the Groundwork for a New New Employee Orientation Program
Transforming the U

The story above was told to a team of University of Minnesota employees who were charged with looking at the university's new employee orientation and recommending changes and improvements for the future. This team's project was part of a comprehensive effort to take a look at the academics and administration of the university, also known as "the U." In 2004 the university's president, Robert Bruininks, began an effort called *strategic positioning*, which engaged the work of hundreds of university employees to focus on 39 different areas of interest. These areas ranged across the breadth of the U, from university culture to student graduation to facilities improvements. These 39 task forces took about six months to complete their reports and from the combined efforts came a new vision for the university called "Transforming the U." (University of Minnesota Strategic Positioning Work Group, 2005)

"Transforming the U" has four broad pillars: Outstanding Students, Outstanding Faculty and Staff, Outstanding Organization, and Outstanding Innovation (see Figure 15.1).

The work of the university needs to align with one or more of these four pillars to move toward its aspirational goal of becoming one of the top public research universities in the world. This goal and these pillars help to guide the work of the university.

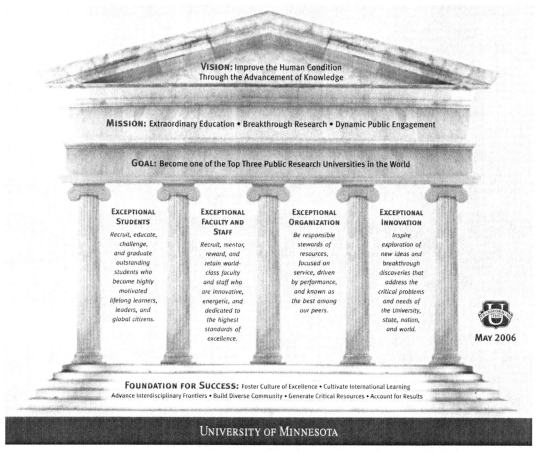

VISION: Improve the Human Condition Through the Advancement of Knowledge

MISSION: Extraordinary Education • Breakthrough Research • Dynamic Public Engagement

GOAL: Become one of the Top Three Public Research Universities in the World

EXCEPTIONAL STUDENTS
Recruit, educate, challenge, and graduate outstanding students who become highly motivated lifelong learners, leaders, and global citizens.

EXCEPTIONAL FACULTY AND STAFF
Recruit, mentor, reward, and retain world-class faculty and staff who are innovative, energetic, and dedicated to the highest standards of excellence.

EXCEPTIONAL ORGANIZATION
Be responsible stewards of resources, focused on service, driven by performance, and known as the best among our peers.

EXCEPTIONAL INNOVATION
Inspire exploration of new ideas and breakthrough discoveries that address the critical problems and needs of the University, state, nation, and world.

MAY 2006

FOUNDATION FOR SUCCESS: Foster Culture of Excellence • Cultivate International Learning
Advance Interdisciplinary Frontiers • Build Diverse Community • Generate Critical Resources • Account for Results

UNIVERSITY OF MINNESOTA

Figure 15.1 Visual Image of the Transforming the U: Commitment to Excellence Plan Created in May 2006.

"Transforming the U" generated teams of employees who would take an in-depth, but time-limited, look at particular subject areas and bring forward recommendations within six months. These efforts were called *Transformational Leadership Projects* (TLP) and one of them was the team tasked with looking at the university's new employee orientation (NEO).

NEW EMPLOYEE ORIENTATION TRANSFORMATIONAL LEADERSHIP PROJECT

From that TLP came a report detailing the state of the university's NEO, as it was in 2006, and 38 recommendations for improving the program to socialize the newest employees. The report focused on the NEO at the Twin Cities campus, the largest of the five University of Minnesota campuses. The NEO program at that time consisted of a 2-hour session for all new employees. The session began with a 1-hour "talking heads" presentation, with person after person coming to the front of the room to go through PowerPoint presentations laying out in detail the benefits and retirement programs for employees, even though many of the employees in the room had already signed up for their benefits before the session. The second hour was a video on the university's code of conduct, an information fair that brought in people from about 15 campus organizations to sit behind tables and answer any questions that might come up, and another presentation from one of the employee group representatives (faculty, professional academic and administrative, civil service, and union/bargaining unit.)

The NEO program as it stood was found lacking. The TLP report emphasized five main areas of opportunity for the university to improve its NEO program:

1. The university could use the program to help achieve its aspirational goals. Becoming one of the top public research universities in the world mandates that the university recruit, retain, engage, and develop the best and brightest talent possible. Its workforce must be informed, committed, and united behind that goal. Creating an NEO that effectively communicates the university's vision, mission, and goals would be one step toward building and maintaining an exceptional workforce.

2. The university could increase its retention rate with an improved NEO. At the time of the report, the 18-month turnover rate was roughly 15%, with some employee groups reaching as high as 22%. The approximate cost for that turnover for all the employees groups totaled in the millions of dollars a year. Any increase in retention could mean significant cost savings for the university.

3. A new NEO program would help employees to be more productive earlier in their careers at the university. By learning about the university's culture and resources, and establishing a clear line of sight between what each new employee is doing in his or her job and the larger university's vision, mission, and goals, employees' chances of success are increased and frustration levels are reduced.

4. An improved NEO program would better meet the needs of the new employees. The time and budget allotted for the 2-hour monthly sessions simply wasn't enough to communicate effectively what needed to be communicated. Specific criticisms of the program were as follows:

a. It was not timely.

b. Insufficient time, resources, and budget were devoted to allow it to be highly effective.

c. It did not provide enough in-depth information on any topic.

d. It was PowerPoint-driven and not interactive.

e. There were no opportunities to network or socialize.

f. The information presented was not audience-specific.

g. The information covered was not sufficiently broad in scope.

h. The "information fair" component was limited in space and time and number of vendors.

5. The university had the opportunity, through a cohesive onboarding program, to reduce redundancies and achieve delivery of timely, consistent, and accurate information to all employees through partnerships with collegiate units, human resources divisions, university relations, and others.

To design recommendations for a 1-year orientation process, the TLP report team drew on input from a number of sources. The team conducted nine focus group sessions with University of Minnesota employees, interviewed staff members responsible for NEO at three local corporations that exhibit best practices (3M, Medtronic, Inc., and Cargill Incorporated), interviewed staff members responsible for NEO at three US universities that exhibit best practices (University of California—Berkeley, University of Wisconsin—Madison, and University of Washington), interviewed staff members responsible for NEO at seven University of Minnesota colleges/administrative units, and conducted brief literary research.

From this research the TLP team came up with 38 recommendations for how to improve the NEO program at the university (see Appendix One for the complete list of recommendations). Not all of these recommendations could be immediately implemented; however, the entire list informed much of the work that was done to create the program. Six of the recommendations formed the foundation for new work that was done to create an entirely new NEO for the Twin Cities campus:

1. NEO should be driven from the top down.
2. A new full-time position should be created to oversee a new, comprehensive NEO at the university.
3. The NEO should be integrated with the University of Minnesota branding.
4. The NEO should partner with existing programs across the university.
5. NEO integration should be implemented at three levels: central human resources, the unit level, and supervisors.
6. Tools to measure the effectiveness of the new program should be put in place (Transformational Leadership Project New Employee Orientation Team, 2006).

The recommendations were given to the vice president for human resources at the university and work was begun to create this innovative and comprehensive program. This chapter will describe in detail how these six recommendations were key to the creation of that program.

Building an Onboarding Program
New Employee Orientation Should be Driven from the Top Down

As with many initiatives in the working world, work done on the front lines is seen as most valuable when those in senior management positions show their appreciation and support for that work. This is especially true with a new initiative. As the TLP team found, central Human Resources at the University of Minnesota had been holding an NEO session monthly for years. Over the years, the budget and staff for the NEO programs had been cut significantly. By the time the TLP report came out, the university was spending less than $5 for each new employee to attend a university-wide training.

Based on the work of the TLP team, senior administrators agreed to put resources behind the important work of socializing the newest employees to the university culture and workplace. The budget for the program was increased significantly and while the program had been deemed "required" for years, now the university president made a special effort to extol the importance of a strong start for employees. In his 2007 report to the Board of Regents, President Bruininks wrote specifically about the new efforts of the NEO program and how "investing in the success of our employees [was] key to achieving the institution's long-term objectives" (Bruininks, 2007). This formal message was followed by a letter from the vice president for human resources to all the deans, directors, and department heads, describing the new NEO initiative and reminding these leaders that the program was mandatory for all new staff members. (New faculty were encouraged to take part but had their own separate new faculty orientation held each August.) This letter to the university leaders included template language that could be used by deans or directors to send a message to all the their unit or department supervisors, reminding them that the new NEO was a required program and all new staff would be expected to attend.

The university affirmatively stated that attendance at the NEO program was to be considered work time and all staff should be given the time and resources to attend. Staff members at the coordinate campuses and outreach centers around the state were encouraged to attend either the sessions held on the Twin Cities campus, or similar sessions that would be created at the coordinate campuses. Consistent language at all levels of university administration gave new importance to the NEO program and reminded supervisors of the importance of bringing new employees into the university culture and work. Supervisors were ready to send their employees to this new program. Now the program just needed to be built.

A New Full-Time Position Should be Created

Under different divisions and with varying budgets, the old NEO suffered from inconsistent leadership. The staff members that ran the program were often pulled in other directions and could never dedicate the time and resources needed to make the program more effective. When the TLP report came out, the vice president for human resources decided that fully implementing such a comprehensive program required a single person whose job would be to create and run a new NEO program. Central HR staff members who had run the logistics of the old

NEO would still help to run the new NEO, but a new HR specialist was needed to focus on program creation and implementation.

In August of 2007, I was hired as the first director of employee onboarding for the University of Minnesota. But as most non-HR people don't know what "onboarding" is, I usually introduce myself as the *new employee orientation director for the U.* For those of us who have created and run the new NEO program at the U, it has been a personal as well as professional journey. When I and the communications program manager who runs communications for the NEO program, Chris Schanus, were hired that August, there was nothing as comprehensive as what we were envisioning anywhere in higher education. Chris and I, along with the person who had handled the logistics for the old NEO program, Myron Guthrie, had a big task ahead of us as we planned to begin the new program in January of 2008. We were joined by another staff member in February of 2008, Caryn Lantz, but Caryn, Chris, and Myron all had other duties assigned to them along with the NEO program. All four of us had to bring both dedication and passion to this project to make such a huge shift in the university culture of decentralized orientation work at the U.

A further challenge was that two days after I began in my new position, my family had a major medical emergency. This put my actual start date at October, after our invitations to the first of the new NEO sessions had already gone out with a start date of the 13th of January. We had about three months to prepare a year-long program for 1600 employees that would be accepted and appreciated by some 45 units around the Twin Cities campus.

The NEO program is housed in the communications division of the university's central Office of Human Resources. Often, this sort of program would be housed within a division like Organizational Effectiveness or Employee Relations. However, this unconventional housing works very well. Our division provides communications for all the work of central HR. This means the NEO team has day-to-day access to what is being communicated by HR to employees around the U, allowing us ready knowledge of what is happening for U employees.

Brand NEO with the University Branding

This recommendation meant more to us than simply making sure we were following all of the color and logo guidelines put forth by University Relations (U Relations), the university's central marketing and communications unit. It meant we needed to do two major things. First, we would work with U Relations to leverage the work they were doing to brand the university in the minds of Minnesotans. Second, we would talk with HR directors around the university to make sure that what we were trying to create would be useful and effective for the people who would be sending their employees to this new program.

The communications division of central HR works very closely with University Relations to ensure that what HR is saying works well with an overall internal communications strategy. As we began to put together a visual identity for the program, we thought about what HR programs try to do for employees. We thought not only about NEO, but about our hopes for employees at the university in general. We wanted new employees to connect with the larger community, understand their part in the aspirational goals of the university, grow in their profession and their work, and thrive as members of our outstanding educational community. We thought of descriptive words and then a visual that would illustrate those words (see Figure 15.2). We included a compass theme, with the hope that the NEO program would help a new employee find his or her way through this large institution.

We also wanted the university branding to be a more integral part of the NEO program. The university Board of Regents had recently adopted a new brand campaign entitled "Driven to Discover." This brand message spanned the five campuses and would soon be as universal as the university colors of maroon and gold. Many of our new employees would have heard about "Driven to Discover" (D2D) from marketing around Minnesota and throughout the higher education community. The campaign focused on the intellectual advancement and practical application of the innovative research being done at the University of Minnesota. In order to capitalize on the visuals and messages associated with the D2D campaign, we worked with U Relations to incorporate their latest videos and branding into the first of our NEO sessions. We do this through an explanation of the campaign, showing the most recent D2D video (a new video is made about every 18 months), using D2D images, and talking about how each of us as an employee of the U is part of that D2D movement. Each of us, no matter what we do as a job, helps to create a university that educates, researches, and changes the world.

In addition to connecting our program with the work of U Relations, we wanted to connect our

Figure 15.2 Descriptive visual for use with all UMN NEO communications

program with the work of the HR professionals in the units and departments around the university. The best way to do that was to talk to them one by one. We created an initial visual of what the program would look like and began holding meetings with HR directors and professionals around the university (see Figure 15.3).

As I met with each person and talked about our vision for the program, I asked what their unit-level orientation was like and how we could help to improve that, if at all. I asked what would be helpful in the central NEO and what would be intrusive. How could our program complement what they were doing, or support them in starting a unit-level orientation, and not be seen as yet another central mandate?

For the university this was a critical step. My meetings were right at the beginning of a series of initiatives from central HR to align more effectively with the unit-level HR work. For many years the decentralized nature of the University meant HR in the units was stronger in some areas and weaker in others. Our program was the first comprehensive program to incorporate what the units were doing into the work of the broader HR role at the University. We needed to be sure that we were seen to be helping the units, not adding to their burden. I met with most of the HR directors in the fall of 2007 and incorporated many of their ideas into the overall plan of the new NEO program. This personal communication helped to build buy-in from the HR professionals. When the letter from the HR vice

president came to the deans, directors, and department heads about the new program, the HR professionals already had the answers they needed to reinforce the importance of the new program with these more senior administrators. In this way we worked both from the top down and the bottom up to build a more unified voice behind the new NEO program.

Partner With Existing Programs

The first session of the new NEO program was held in January 2008. This session in itself was a big improvement on the old NEO events, but it was truly just the beginning of the new program. The program as a whole now consists of three main sessions, several training sessions, social events, online information, and supervisor training. Let me take each portion of the program separately.

THREE MAIN SESSIONS

New employees are invited by their units or supervisors to attend the first of these sessions, usually within the first month of their employment at the university. The employees continue on with the program throughout their first year, with communication about upcoming events coming directly from the NEO team.

Session 1—Discover the U

Conducted: Within first month of employment at the university
Length of time: 3 hours

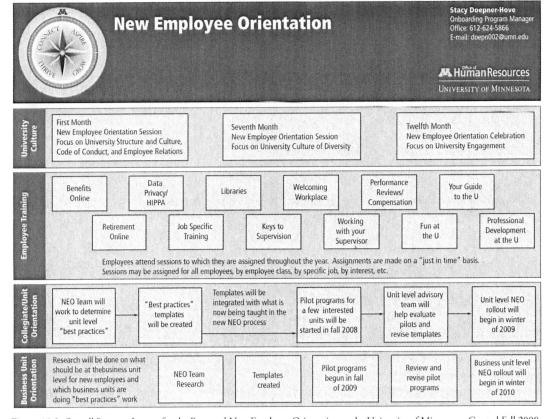

New Employee Orientation

Stacy Doepner-Hove
Onboarding Program Manager
Office: 612-624-5866
E-mail: doepn002@umn.edu

Office of Human Resources
UNIVERSITY OF MINNESOTA

University Culture

First Month	Seventh Month	Twelfth Month
New Employee Orientation Session Focus on University Structure and Culture, Code of Conduct, and Employee Relations	New Employee Orientation Session Focus on University Culture of Diversity	New Employee Orientation Celebration Focus on University Engagement

Employee Training

Benefits Online	Data Privacy/ HIPPA	Libraries	Welcoming Workplace	Performance Reviews/ Compensation	Your Guide to the U
Retirement Online	Job Specific Training	Keys to Supervision	Working with your Supervisor	Fun at the U	Professional Development at the U

Employees attend sessions to which they are assigned throughout the year. Assignments are made on a "just in time" basis. Sessions may be assigned for all employees, by employee class, by specific job, by interest, etc.

Collegiate/Unit Orientation

| NEO Team will work to determine unit level "best practices" | → | "Best practices" templates will be created | → | Templates will be integrated with what is now being taught in the new NEO process | → | Pilot programs for a few interested units will be started in fall 2008 | → | Unit level advisory team will help evaluate pilots and revise templates | → | Unit level NEO rollout will begin in winter of 2009 |

Business Unit Orientation

| Research will be done on what should be at the business unit level for new employees and which business units are doing "best practices" work | NEO Team Research | Templates created | Pilot programs begun in fall of 2009 | Review and revise pilot programs | Business unit level NEO rollout will begin in winter of 2010 |

Figure 15.3 Overall Program Layout for the Proposed New Employee Orientation at the University of Minnesota. Created Fall 2008.

Description: This session provides a quick introduction to the university, giving an overview of the mission and strategic vision of the University of Minnesota as a whole. It also provides a warm-up to the culture and equips new employees with basic university knowledge, which is not typically learned on the job or at the departmental level.

The session consists of the following topics:

- Overview of the U
- History of the University of Minnesota
- Strategic positioning of the U
- Five university campuses and many outreach centers
- Driven to Discover campaign, including the TV ads
- Learning about the four employee groups (union, civil service, professional academic and administrative, faculty)
- Overview of senior leadership
- Featured guest speaker who is one of the senior leaders of the university
- University-based "maroon & gold trivia" (with University of Minnesota branded prizes)

- Some serious topics, some not (e.g., What are the university's "firsts"? How many bike racks are there?)
- Code of Conduct and compliance
- Policy and resource discussion
- Meeting with employee group representatives
- Information Fair
- Tables of different organizations (e.g., Benefits, Student Union, Recycling program, Organizational Development, Employee Assistance Program, On-campus banking, etc.)
- Photo opportunity with Goldy Gopher (University of Minnesota—Twin Cities Mascot)

Session 2—Discover Community
Conducted: After six months of employment at the University
Length of time: 2.5 hours
Description: This session is the second in a 3-part series. The focus of this session is on diversity, equality in the workplace, access to everyone, and inclusiveness. Conducted primarily by the Office of Equity & Diversity, this session discusses the

university's commitment to diversity and provides resources available to employees.

This session is participatory. Employees get an opportunity for self-reflection on their experiences in diverse settings, with a chance to share those experiences. Simulated work-based scenarios are conducted, offering the employees a chance for discussion on different issues of equity in a safe and controlled setting. In session two, employees are also guided through a facilitated discussion on topics of diversity and inclusion. In the end, employees take a self-quiz, which is not reported back to their supervisors but allows for each employee to see how inclusive they are being in their daily work activities. The session consists of the following topics:

- Introduction on "Diversity Drives Discovery"
- Presentation by representatives from the Office of Equity and Diversity
  - Discussion topics:
    - University's commitment to diversity
    - Resources available
- Participation questions (e.g., When was the first time you traveled outside the United States? When was the first time you met someone of a different ethnicity?)
  - Six workplace scenarios dealing with different topics of equity and diversity. Topics include: hierarchy, religion, transgender, hiring, disability, speech patterns.
    - Presentation on becoming an "ally"
    - Inclusive language use
    - Self-quiz (nonreported). Topics include: How inclusive is your work? Is it accessible to all? Do you have presentations available in alternative formats? How in tune are you with diversity topics and issues?

Session 3—Discover You

Conducted: One year after beginning employment at the university
Length of time: 2.5 hours
Description: This is the final session in the series of three sessions, conducted at the end of the first year an employee has been with the university. With a reception flair, this final session focuses on the employee's professional and personal development, as well as providing recognition for the employees who have completed the full training series during their first year of employment at the university.
The session consists of the following topics:

- Presentation videos of real employees and how they have used the university's programs to develop themselves both personally and professionally
- Professional development opportunities available for employees
  - Technology
    - Where to get additional training
    - Technology resources to help in doing work at the U
  - Public Engagement
    - What importance does this have to a land-grant institution
    - What the university does
    - How employees can get involved, both on-campus and off-campus
  - Employee Wellness
    - What is this and why does the university consider it important
    - What programs are available to employees

TRAINING SESSIONS

The general training sessions are split into two groups: job-specific trainings, which are targeted to certain groups of employees, and general trainings for any new employee.

Job-Specific Trainings

Conducted: Ideally, every four months or three times per year. Currently, these modules are held whenever there is a "critical mass" in each job field to do a training session.
Length of time: Varies by training session and position. Two days of training is required for the supervisory session, which includes those who are new to supervising at the university or are new supervisors altogether.
Sessions:

- Human Resources
- Communications
- Research
- Teaching
- Information Technology
- Student Services
- Supervision

Description: The focus of these training modules is job-specific. The New Employee Orientation team creates curriculum in partnership with offices from around the university who are specialists in the field. For example, the New Employee Orientation team works with the University Relations office to develop curriculum and carry out the training for any new employee who does communication work on campus.

General Trainings

The Libraries and U
Conducted: Every month
Length of time: One hour
Description: This training module is a general module that is offered to new employees, but can be taken by anyone at the university. It occurs every month and rotates around to the different libraries that are housed throughout the Twin Cities campus.

The purpose of this module is to foster a working knowledge of the extensive library system, including its resources and search engines, so that employees gain an understanding of resources available to them for their job positions or their own personal edification.

Communicating at the U
Conducted: Twice a year
Length of time: Three 2-hour sessions
Description: This *module series focuses on communication at the university, including the hidden dynamics between communications of different types of employees and different stakeholders. The modules will include the following:

Part I: Communicating Through Differences

The ability to effectively communicate across differences and conflict is critical to working in a large and complex organization like the University. In this sub-module, participants gain a deeper understanding of the nature and value of conflict, increase their awareness and knowledge of how we manage and resolve differences, and learn strategies and skills for effective communication in conflict situations.

Part II: Communicating with Stakeholders

This sub-module covers the basics of stakeholder-service training for all employees. It addresses the vast array of stakeholders that a new employee may come into contact with on a daily basis. Higher education settings not only have customers, colleagues, and vendors, they have students, alumni, and parents to communicate with as well. This session provides tools to identify and work effectively with key stakeholders for any new employee.

Part III: Communication at the U

The university has a unique culture that can pose exceptional communication challenges. This sub-module helps new employees to explore the organizational culture of the university and of its many and varied units. The session provides tools to new employees to work effectively across departments, across unit, and across the hall. It also addresses acronyms and the many other nuances of university culture when communicating for a successful workplace environment.

SOCIAL EVENTS

These events are aimed at helping employees get to know the larger university community and feel pride in the organization as a whole. The events range in size from about 15 to 50 people and allow employees to get to know one another in a social setting, and hopefully learn something interesting about their workplace.

Brown Bag Fun Lunches

Conducted: Twice monthly
Length of time: Over lunch hours
Description: Purely fun lunches, this module is designed to be all about socializing over the lunch hour. Along with the "Brown Bag" theme, this module includes different topics of guided discussion that focuses on different elements of the university. Past topics have included an astronomy lecture by a faculty member, a visit to the university's Raptor Center, a tour of the dairy lab, a lecture on being a "locavore" (eating locally), and a talk and tour of the library archive caverns.

Culture Crawls

Conducted: Monthly during the school year
Length of time: Varies by event
Description: This module is designed to introduce the university's cultural side to our newer employees. Each module includes two different cultural events, usually with an arts theme. Examples might include a tour of the Weisman Art Museum followed by a play performed by the theater department. New employees can bring a guest to promote both networking among the new employees as well as establishing a connection to the university for the new employee's guest.

Gopher Go

Conducted: Monthly during the school year
Length of time: Varies by event
Description: Designed in tandem with the Athletics Department, this module is designed to offer newer employees an opportunity to meet

with the Gophers athletics coaching staff, and to get an opportunity to see different sporting venues, which is a tremendous asset in a Big Ten university. Employees are given discounted rates or free tickets to different sporting events and sit together at those events. They are encouraged to bring family and friends as well.

ONLINE INFORMATION

The NEO team worked to make sure that information about the program would be accessible to new employees online. We created an online social networking site that houses all of the information about upcoming sessions, as well as registration links so new employees can sign up for things directly. The site also allows new employees to start discussion threads with each other, or even begin their own groups that can get together in person or online. This site is housed off the university servers so that really the only people who know about the site are new employees going through the program. Once a new employee has finished the third main sessions they are no longer considered part of the NEO program, and while they still have access to the social networking site they are given secondary priority if they want to attend any of the social events or trainings.

We also created e-newsletters to go out the new employees once a month to update them on trainings and events that are taking place, as well as other things at the university a new employee might want to know about. We send a quarterly newsletter to the new employees' supervisors as well. This newsletter lets the supervisors know about what trainings are available to their employees and gives them onboarding tips for working with their new employees.

SUPERVISOR TRAINING

Training supervisors on onboarding techniques and importance was deemed an essential part of the overall onboarding program, and I explain more about this in the next section of this chapter.

Each of the various parts of the NEO program has the NEO team partnering with departments around campus. We use content experts from around the university to help give new employees information they need to aid them in doing their work as efficiently as possible. Creation of the various program elements is done in conjunction with the content experts, then the NEO team handles all registrations and logistics for each event. It is a win-win situation for all concerned, as the NEO team gets more programming and the other departments get access to new employees to give them the information, support, and resources they need at the beginning of their work instead of when a problem arises.

NEO Integration at Three Levels

Research done by the Corporate Leadership Council, among others, shows that some of the most important and significant work to socialize and engage new employees must be done by the new employee's supervisor (The Corporate Executive Board, 2008). With that understanding, we knew we couldn't simply implement a program through the central HR and expect that levels of engagement and socialization would increase significantly throughout the university. We wanted to face the problem at three levels: through central HR in a system-wide approach, through work and support with the academic and administrative units, and through training of supervisors directly.

Having direct control of the central HR's NEO, we began work with the systemwide approach. The next step connected us directly with university supervisors. The University of Minnesota has a few different supervisory training programs for anyone who manages people at the U. Attendees to these trainings could include anyone from a front-line office manager to a department chair. The NEO team worked with the supervisory trainings coordinator to find places where we could train supervisors directly on the concepts of onboarding and engagement, and why these are important concepts for supervisors to understand.

We built curriculum to target the needs of supervisors. The training includes discussion of return on investment for focusing supervisory work on the areas of engagement and onboarding. Many supervisors at the university aren't familiar with the coming realities of the labor market. They may understand the aging demographics of our population but may never have thought about how that will affect the ability of employers to hire and retain qualified people. We stress in our trainings that supervisors need to be thinking about and planning for these changes and make sure that they are learning to engage their employees now, not only for the sake of the employees and general productivity, but also to help retain these high performers in the future.

The curriculum also gives practical lessons on how to onboard an employee, such as the sorts of things a supervisor should think about when a new employee is set to arrive and how the supervisor can prepare himself or herself, the new employee, the other employees on the team, and the environment and work surrounding for the new employee. All this is within the context of engaging the employee right from the start. Onboarding an employee from the supervisory level, through the unit, and then through a systemwide centralized program helps a new employee to understand where they fit within this large organization and how their work makes a difference in the work of the entire university.

The last piece of this ongoing work to align university onboarding throughout the system was to create tools and templates for unit-level orientations. Many of the academic and administrative units around the university had orientations of some sort for their new employees. Some units had programs that helped to socialize an employee over time, aligned with the central HR NEO, and worked to bring the new employee up to speed and feel engaged with their work. Other units simply gave new employees the requisite forms to fill out and left them to their own devices. Many units were somewhere in between.

Our goal was not to force units to all create an onboarding program that would look like every other unit; rather, we wanted to create tools that unit-level HR professionals could use to easily adapt some best practices to what would work best in their own units. To that end we put together a small taskforce of unit-level HR professionals from around the university to find out what onboarding work was being done in units around the U, and what would be the most helpful tools for HR people to be able to implement new onboarding programs efficiently and effectively.

What we created was an onboarding toolkit for unit-level orientations. This toolkit included the following:

• Information on onboarding and how it provides a high return on investment
• Detailed information on the central onboarding program so units could align their programs to avoid duplication
• Best practices and ideas for building and enhancing unit-level or department-level onboarding
  • An appendix that includes
    • A best practice *New Employee Checklist* to adapt and use with new unit employees

• A best practice template agenda to adapt and use when planning unit or departmental meetings for a group of new employees
• A *Supervisors' Toolkit* for use by HR professionals to go over with the supervisors in the unit or department to explain their critical part in the onboarding process and give them tools they need to do that job well

This toolkit was distributed to the units through a communication campaign that allowed for large group, small group, and individual presentations depending on the needs and requests of the unit. Consulting and training services were also offered to the units so if a particular unit was looking to create a new onboarding program, or improve on an old one, I could be available to offer suggestions or thoughts as a unit went through that process.

This coordinated effort to align the onboarding practices throughout all levels of the university has helped to build a more effective program overall. Aligning the efforts across levels helps to ensure that all the things a new employee needs will come to them at some point, and also helps to avoid redundancy. The efforts are ongoing, as there are always new supervisors and new HR professionals at the U. Some units have embraced this work more readily than others. But overall, this 3-tiered approach has helped to make the program a more integrated part of the socialization of new employees here at the U.

Measure the Effectiveness

Measuring the effectiveness of one particular program within the context of all the other things that can happen to a new employee is difficult, to say the least. Once again, the NEO team partnered with other organizations around the U to use what was already available to enhance the new measurements we wanted to put in place. Logistical challenges and financial realities have made some of this work more difficult than we originally anticipated, but the measurement work is a vital piece of the entire onboarding program.

We began with simple "smile sheets" at the end of each session, training, or event to get a sense of what the employees thought about the session just as it was ending. While these assessments are simple and can be easily tainted by things like room temperature or group attitude, they have been, and continue to be, a good indication of how things are going and what could change. One major change that came from these simple assessments is the shifting of the main Session Three from a session only about public engagement at the university to the current program, where we train on development, technology, engagement, and wellness as discussed above. That change has made a significant difference in both the enjoyment and the usefulness employees say they find from Session Three.

Beyond the simple post-session evaluations, an overall assessment that looks at the interest level in and the usefulness of the program has been implemented. It took time to get the resources in place to make this happen in a comprehensive and easily reportable way. We wanted the survey itself to be as short as possible for a new employee to fill out. We worked with the university's Office of Measurement Services to make sure this survey, given when the employee has been at the university for 14 months, will look at the following:

• The new employee's interest in and enjoyment of each of the sessions and modules they attended
• How useful and effective the new employee found each session or module
• General questions about how things are going for the new employee in his/her new position
• Engagement questions that mirror the university's overall engagement survey (the PULSE survey, introduced below) to help us gauge the engagement level of employees who have been through the new onboarding program and those who have not
• What sessions and modules each employee has attended
• What unit, college, or campus the new employee is from
• Other demographic information

With this information we are able to track how the individual sessions and modules are working for employees, what might be missing from the program, and how the new employees are feeling about their work experience. This information will help us continue to build and refine the overall program.

We have also partnered our survey work with other surveys going on throughout the U. Every two years the university does an overall employee engagement survey called the PULSE for all employees systemwide. The NEO team hopes to use our data on new employees who have been through our program to compare the engagement and retention rates for employees who have been through the program to those who have not, and be able to track that over time.

Central HR has also implemented an exit and entry survey that should help us to understand better why employees come to the U for work, and why they leave. These surveys, taken together, will help give us an elaborate picture of our employees and the rates of engagement found here at the U.

Next Steps—Employee Engagement at the University

With the implementation of the new onboarding program in place, central HR is beginning to look at how to improve engagement throughout the university in general. Much like the onboarding program, this new engagement work began with a study conducted by a group of employees that ended in a report, put out in 2010, on employee rewards, recognition, and appreciation (ERRA). This report looked at the literature on employee engagement, best practices from the private sector and from public and nonprofit entities, and did focus group work with employees from around the university system to hear what employees thought about rewards, recognition, and appreciation at the university.

The ERRA report found room for improvement with employee engagement systemwide. Opportunities identified by the report included:

• Improve our employee rewards, recognition, and appreciation practices.
• Unify practices that are now sporadic and varying.
• Improve employee morale.
• Increase employee productivity.
• Retain talented employees longer.
• Better use our limited rewards, recognition, and appreciation dollars.

The recommendations that came from the report are listed below:

1. Allocate resources to employee rewards, recognition, and appreciation programming including the staff resources needed to build such a program.
2. Garner support from university leadership. If we want employee rewards, recognition, and appreciation to become a part of university culture, we need senior leaders to embrace these ideals and support this work through their words and actions.
3. Involve and train supervisors and managers. Managers and supervisors not only have the most direct responsibility for employee recognition, but the most familiarity with their employees, and are

therefore able to recognize individuals in the most effective, personalized, and thoughtful way.

4. Create a multifaceted program that has several components moving simultaneously to ensure that every employee at every level is included in a way that is meaningful to them.

5. Create an ongoing program. Annual celebrations are effective appreciation tools, but a successful employee rewards, recognition, and appreciation program must include ongoing programming and just-in-time rewards that can be given at any time throughout the year.

6. Ensure that the program aligns with institutional goals.

7. Ensure that the program has a broad reach to include employees throughout the system.

8. Offer meaningful rewards that may be different for different people.

9. Tap into existing university programs and services. Existing programs should be incorporated into a larger program that is multifaceted, ongoing, broad-reaching, and aligned with institutional goals.

10. Develop a communications campaign to promote the ERRA program.

11. Start now. This is a critical time for the university. Employees are very aware that the organization is facing a budget crisis in the midst of major leadership change. As the larger economy improves, university employees will have increasing options and the workforce will continue to decrease. Competition for talent will increase while our dollars continue to decrease. Swift action and innovative programming are necessary to keep employees connected and engaged in this volatile climate (University of Minnesota Employee Rewards, Recognition and Appreciation Work Group, 2010).

The NEO team has been tasked with working with the recommendations from the ERRA report. Building on the work of the NEO program we are creating a new set of initiatives that will span the university at all three levels—central HR, unit-level, and the supervisor. Some of the programs that were created for NEO, such as the social programming and the networking with unit-level HR professionals, will be expanded to reach the rest of the university population. Other things will be new to the ERRA program. However, both the NEO and the ERRA program will reinforce each other as the university continues to look at its employees as its most valuable resource.

Closing the Loop

Employee salaries at the University of Minnesota make up about 60% of the university's budget. As the labor market continues to change and educated, trained, and experienced employees are harder to recruit and retain, the university must look to all levels of human resources and management to help create a truly engaged workforce. The work that we do in the central office of human resources is only part of the whole that makes up both the NEO and the ERRA programs. Working with unit-level HR professionals and providing training and tools to front-line supervisors are key elements to making the programs effective. The process that we went through to create and implement the NEO program is being revisited as we begin to create programming for ERRA as well. As we move forward with both programs, we will be able to build a sustainable workplace environment that provides support and encouragement to recruit, retain, and engage the best workforce possible as we move into an uncertain future.

References

Bruininks, Robert H. (2007). *Transforming the U for the 21st Century, Strategic Positioning Report to the Board of Regents.* Retrieved from University of Minnesota Transforming the U website: http://www1.umn.edu/systemwide/strategic_positioning/pdf/SPReport_FINAL.pdf

The Corporate Executive Board. (2008). *Top Drivers of Employee Engagement.*

Transformational Leadership Project New Employee Orientation Team, University of Minnesota. (2006). *TLP: New Employee Orientation Redesign.*

University of Minnesota Employee Rewards, Recognition, and Appreciation Workgroup. (2010). *Employee Rewards, Recognition, and Appreciation (ERRA) Study Final Report.*

University of Minnesota Strategic Positioning Work Group. (2005). *The University of Minnesota: Advancing the Public Good.* Retrieved from University of Minnesota Transforming the U website: http://www1.umn.edu/systemwide/strategic_positioning/pdf/Strategic_Positioning_Report.pdf.

Appendix One

Transformational Leadership Project on the University of Minnesota's New Employee Orientation. It is recommended that:

1. the strategic goal of New Employee Orientation be to assist in the retention and development of new University employees and faculty members on the Twin Cities campus by providing information necessary to their success, productivity, and sense of community during their first year of employment.

2. new employee orientation be driven from the top down—from the University president, to Office of Human Resources (OHR) leadership and college deans, to supervisors, to employees.

3. a new full-time position be created to manage the new employee orientation program.

4. new employee orientation take place in stages over a one-year period and serve as an onboarding experience for new employees.

5. new employee orientation be an integrated process delivered at three levels—the University level, the college/administrative unit level, and the supervisory level.

6. working in partnership with college deans/directors, a consistently applied, mandated orientation model—or template—be developed for use by collegiate/administrative units, tailored to their needs.

7. HR pros play a key role in delivering orientation and a dotted-line relationship be created between HR pros and the Office of Human Resources.

8. mandatory training be developed for supervisors and HR pros on orienting new employees.

9. partnerships be developed with central OHR divisions to create and efficiently deliver orientation components.

10. the NEO manager partner with University Relations to instill the University identity and a sense of pride in the University's accomplishments and mission.

11. college and administrative units be charged a fee for the mandatory components of University—level NEO programs, regardless of whether or not their employees attend.

12. the new employee orientation program—including information, activities/events, and distribution of information—be developed and tailored to meet the specific needs of the following audiences within the University community: civil service, AFSCME clerical, AFSCME technical, AFSCME health care, Teamsters, P&A, and faculty.

13. the development of the faculty segment of orientation be addressed in FY2008 in conjunction with the Office of the Vice Provost for Faculty and Academic Affairs' new faculty orientation program.

14. orientation of post docs be addressed through the Graduate Assistance Program.

15. orientation of international scholars fall outside the scope of this New Employee Orientation Program.

16. orientation be delivered at various locations and on a schedule to mesh with the work schedules of all University employees.

17. redundant pathways (a minimum of two) be used in the delivery of all orientation-related information.

18. dedicated computers be provided and maintained in all departments for staff members who currently lack computer access and that a computer lab be made available at each campus for employee use.

19. the viability of using the HR Web site vs. One-Stop vs. My U Portal be further examined to determine which is the most viable tool to serve as a key New Employee Orientation device.

20. orientation begin prior to the employee's arrival.

21. new employees be assigned a "buddy" within their department for a given period of time beginning with their first day.

22. a variety of "tours" be created, including physical tours of the campus, including the tunnel system, interactive maps, virtual tours, etc.

23. in-depth information about the University's structure, governance, and policies be provided.

24. the wide variety of activities, opportunities, and materials associated with the following be promoted to increase awareness based on focus group data:

    a. Learning and training opportunities
    b. Career progression and consultation
    c. Performance and expectations
    d. Opportunities on campus

25. the existing Health Benefits Workshop become a "strongly recommended" component of New Employee Orientation.

26. other existing programs, such as the Health & Benefits Fair and all Retirement Planning Seminars and Workshops, be drawn upon for New Employee Orientation.

27. the following components be mandatory and recorded in PeopleSoft Training Administration:
    a. Compliance (policies, University resources, mission, Code of Conduct, etc.)
    b. Sexual harassment training
    c. EEOA—Respectful Workplace and The Power of Respect to Affect Lives

28. after the first month, follow-up be conducted, i.e., via surveys and "checklists."

29. quarterly events for new employees be held during their first year, at least two of which are hosted by University leaders who relay information about new initiatives.

30. information be provided to new employees about opportunities to come together in meaningful ways, i.e., learning, networking, and affinity groups.

31. a quarterly newsletter for new employees be created during their first year.

32. a Web site for new employees be created

33. *Your Guide to the University* be rewritten to include more information and resources with an extensive cross-referenced index for use as a desk-top reference guide and that other vehicles for delivering this same information (i.e., via Web, helpline, CDs, etc.) be determined to ensure effective dissemination and use of this easy-to-navigate reference tool.

34. diversity be incorporated throughout the orientation process as part of the University culture rather than as a specific event, seminar, or component, and that EEOA seminars be offered as part of the orientation process with some being mandatory.

35. a methodology for measuring the effectiveness of the new employee orientation program be developed that includes, in part, the following:
    a. Reduced turnover rate by employee group (see the "Retention & Turnover Cost" section of the "Opportunity Statement" in this report for current baseline to be used for comparative purposes)
    b. Participation in optional and mandatory events and activities drawing on reports from HRMS
    c. Annual focus group sessions
    d. An annual review or survey with supervisors to ascertain factors, such as increased productivity and success
    e. Three, six, and nine-month employee check-ins (perhaps at time of quarterly meetings) to ascertain their sense of belonging and increased awareness of:
        i. key resources
        ii. training and development opportunities
        iii. benefits
        iv. OHR and its function at all levels
        v. Employee e-mail surveys as warranted
        vi. Continued improvement in Pulse Survey results for new employees (provided the data for new employees can be obtained)
        vii. Feedback forms and, where possible, verbal discussion following events/activities

36. outcomes be incorporated from related strategic positioning task forces, such as the Culture, Best Practice Management Tools, People, Single Enterprise, and Administrative Structure Taskforces and the Administrative Services Model of Integrative Services.

37. an Onboarding Advisory Committee be created, comprised of stakeholders from the Office of the President, University Relations, University Services, Office of Service and Continuous Improvement, Office of Institutional Compliance, and one HR pro from a large-sized college to assist in providing feedback and critical analysis in all matters related to the design and implementation of NEO components.

38. a volunteer program, mentor program, recognition program, and supervising at the University training program be created to further assist in accomplishing the University's strategic goals, enhancing the University's culture and employee engagement, and creating a unified sense of community.

Socializing Leadership Talent: Ensuring Successful Transitions Into Senior Management Roles

Jay A. Conger

Abstract

This chapter explores how socialization programs for managers transitioning to senior management roles can play a vital role in both preempting leadership failures and accelerating their relationship building. Managers who are promoted into a senior management level position for the first time in their careers face three daunting challenges. First, they must gain mastery over a complex and demanding role. The learning demands are often the most pronounced in a manager's career. Second, expectations are high. It is assumed that the incoming senior manager already has the depth of experience to lead successfully in the new situation. As a result, there is little developmental feedback or support for those who enter the upper echelons of organizations. These two challenges can conspire to produce a challenge with far greater liabilities—the career derailment of the incoming senior manager. Given the high price associated with leadership failures in senior management ranks, it is essential for organizations to consider sophisticated socialization processes as they onboard individuals into senior management roles. Insights are drawn from an in-depth case analysis of sophisticated socialization programs developed at the Bank of America and at Toyota.

Key Words: socialization, leadership development, onboarding, executive derailment

Any manager promoted into a senior management level position for the first time in his or her career faces three daunting challenges. In a brief period of time, he/she must gain mastery over a complex and demanding role. The learning demands are often the most pronounced in a manager's career. Second, expectations are high. It is assumed that the incoming senior manager already has the depth of experience to lead successfully in the new situation. After all, most of these individuals have already spent years in managerial roles beforehand. As a result, there is little developmental feedback or support for those who enter the upper echelons of organizations. These two challenges can conspire to produce a challenge with far greater liabilities—the career derailment of the incoming manager. Complex new role demands combined with a lack of developmental support can produce a "perfect storm" in terms of failure on the job. Given the high price associated with leadership failures in senior management ranks, it is essential for organizations to consider implementing sophisticated socialization processes as they onboard individuals into senior management roles.

While some organizations have developed formal socialization or onboarding interventions, the typical approach tends to be quite limited in scale and does little to effectively socialize upper echelon leaders to their incoming role demands. Many are simple orientation programs offering an opportunity to network with the CEO and the executive team. They may also provide an overview of the corporate strategy, its financials, and company activities. A handful of organizations, however, have developed more sophisticated socialization programs at the general manager and executive levels

(Fulmer & Conger, 2004), but such programs are very rare in the corporate world. Instead, the standard interventions to preempt leadership derailments tend to be dependent on performance appraisals and talent management practices. The underlying premise is that failures at senior management levels can best be avoided through continuous formal performance feedback to a manager and through the careful selection of jobs and bosses over the *life span* of a manager's career (e.g., McCall, 1988). While this perspective seems reasonable, socialization or "onboarding" interventions are not just an important complement to existing practices but also a necessity. For example, companies renowned for leadership development, such as General Electric and PepsiCo, have long designed their educational programs to facilitate important career transitions especially at executive levels (Conger & Benjamin, 1999). In other words, a comprehensive socialization program has an essential place in any organization's portfolio of development initiatives for senior managers.

This chapter explores the potential of these socialization programs for preempting leadership failures, for accelerating the knowledge and building the relationships necessary to step into senior organizational roles, and for instilling critical perspectives or mindsets into newly appointed leaders. Insights are drawn from an in-depth case analysis of socialization programs developed at the Bank of America and at Toyota.

The Need for Socialization Interventions for Onboarding Senior Management Talent

Senior management roles come with great visibility and accountability. They are extremely demanding and so offer little time for "learning on the job." There may be an executive education program to facilitate the transition, but beyond such interventions there is usually little else. While the promotion to a senior leadership role can be the steepest jump in role demands for a manager in his or her career history, it is paradoxically the one with the least amount of transition support.

The limited transition support is the product of several factors. It is assumed that senior-most talent is "well seasoned" given the many years of managerial experiences required for entry into the top ranks. As a result, the need for developmental feedback and coaching during the transition are perceived to be minimal. Yet, the functional line management roles leading to senior positions are rarely broad enough to provide sufficient preparatory experiences.

Second, the promotion itself and the many years of prior management experience can produce a misplaced self-confidence in newly promoted senior managers that they are "up to the task." This sense of self-assurance may discourage them from seeking out developmental feedback and from being more proactive in self-reflection and learning. There is a natural desire for these leaders to want to appear as "in charge"—in other words, to be seen as effective immediately. Seeking coaching and feedback would dispel this impression, and therefore newly promoted senior managers may be hesitant to seek either. Another contributor is the environment at senior levels which is more politicized. Peers are often competitors jousting for the topmost roles. As a result, developmental support and feedback from colleagues tends to be far more difficult to obtain. In addition, many CEOs do not see coaching their senior managers as an essential part of their role. So the newly appointed leader's superior may provide limited or no developmental guidance.

All of the above factors coalesce to increase the probability of leadership derailments at the upper management levels of organizations. The problem is even more extreme for organizations where outsiders are hired into senior leadership roles. One estimate is that 40% of senior managers hired from the outside fail within their first 18 months in the role (Watkins, 2003). It becomes easy to see why a socialization program designed to help transition managers into senior leadership roles might not only be helpful but essential. But what exactly should be the precise aim of such interventions and how best to design them?

A well-designed socialization intervention for socializing new senior level talent can and should achieve four outcomes. As we have highlighted, the first is to *minimize the possibility of derailment* on the job. By accelerating the new senior manager's understanding of the role demands and by providing support through constructive feedback, coaching, and follow-up, a well-designed program can and should preempt failures. The second outcome is to *accelerate the performance results* of the new leader. For example, research suggests that a senior level manager requires an average of 6.2 months to reach a "break-even point"—the moment at which the new leader's contribution to the organization exceeds the costs of bringing them on board and their acquiring a critical base of insight into the job (Watkins, 2003). Effective socialization interventions should shorten this cycle of learning by accelerating the development of a network of critical relationships, clarifying leadership and performance expectations, and facilitating the formulation of more realistic short and medium term performance objectives. The third outcome is *to socialize higher standards of accountability around core organizational values and operating principles.* In other words, senior leaders must now serve as exemplary models, guardians and promoters of values and principles. A fourth outcome for socialization interventions concerns organizations that are aggressively pursuing acquisitions or experiencing high growth rates. In both cases, they must grapple with socializing an influx of "outsider" senior managers. In these cases, an effective intervention *should facilitate a far smoother integration and socialization experience for "outsider" leaders.* It accomplishes this by helping them to rapidly acquire an understanding of the business environment, socializing them into the organization's culture and politics, building a network of critical relationships, and familiarizing them with the operating dynamics of the executive team. The case studies which follow examine the socialization processes deployed by two organizations to achieve these four outcomes. Using different processes, they both rigorously socialized critical talent for their senior leadership roles.

The Bank of America: A Case Study in Executive Socialization Practices

The Bank of America has one of the most comprehensive approaches to executive socialization in the field today. It has a track record of 11 years with the program that will be described in this chapter. It has shown strong positive results. For example, the Bank of America hired 196 externally recruited executives between 2001 and May 2008 and experienced 24 terminations—a new hire turnover rate of approximately 12%. This compares to estimates as high as 40% turnover in large corporations (Watkins, 2003). The Bank of America has tested its approaches out on a large sample of "onboarded" executives—over 500 internal and external over the last 7 years. Over the last decade, the Bank of America has been actively involved in acquisitions as well as experiencing organic growth. As a result, the organization must annually socialize a significant number of executives—both externally and internally sourced. This demand has created many opportunities to learn about the efficacy of its socialization approaches.

In addition, the Bank of America's socialization program is expressly designed to help new executives learn to be facile at navigating the bank's large and complex organization, as well as building and leveraging networks of relationships for career success and for implementing company initiatives. These same demands are common in most large corporations today. Therefore, this particular case study holds lessons that readers in a wide range of organizations should find useful.

The impetus for the Bank of America's interest in executive socialization is a product of its own corporate history. Over the last two decades, the bank has experienced dramatic growth through acquisitions. It began as a small regional North Carolina bank (North Carolina National Bank) and has grown into one of the largest companies in the world. Today it is the first true national banking brand in the United States. As a result of this history of aggressive acquisitions, it discovered a need to more effectively "onboard" executive leaders from acquired companies and to quickly assimilate them into the Bank of America's standards and expectations for performance. The organization's leadership development group was also familiar with the research on executive derailment that showed high failure rates for executives who were onboarded into acquiring companies. In response, the bank developed sophisticated socialization interventions. Over time, these programs have been expanded to the organization's internal executive promotions to ensure that these individuals will succeed, as well as feel that they are receiving attention equal to that given the outsiders.

It is important to note, however, that executive socialization is only one of several processes that the Bank of America deploys for the development of its senior talent. The range of the bank's executive leadership development activities is extensive and includes selection, onboarding, performance management, processes to upgrade executive talent, developmental experiences, and compensation. The CEO meets every summer with his top executives to review the organizational health and development strategies of each business. In 2 to 3-hour sessions with each executive, the CEO probes the people, financial, and operational issues that will drive growth over the next 24 months, with the majority of time spent discussing the key leaders, critical leadership roles necessary to achieving the company's growth targets, and organizational structure. Business leaders come to the sessions with a concise document (the goal being 3 pages or less to ensure simplicity) that describes strengths and weaknesses in their unit's leadership talent pipeline given business challenges and goals. During these conversations, executives make specific commitments regarding current or potential leaders—identifying the next assignment, special projects, promotions, and the like. There are follow-ups with executives in quarterly business reviews to ensure that they have fulfilled their commitments. As a result, it is a widely held belief that leadership talent directly affects the performance of the bank. This belief sets up a mandate for the organization—to cultivate and retain leadership talent.

Finally, the organizational culture is one that encourages candor, trust, teamwork, and accountability at all levels in the organization, especially at the executive level. The company has a deep comfort with differentiating individual performance (based on what is achieved as well as how these achievements are attained). There is also belief that today's top performers are not necessarily tomorrow's—that even the best leaders can fall behind or derail. As a result, the corporate culture is one where candor is more highly valued than politeness or tolerance for average or poor performance. These beliefs drive what and how the Bank of America builds and measures leadership success, whether it is in programs, performance management, or selection. This overarching environment is critical to the success of the bank's executive socialization program. One cannot understand the executive socialization process without first appreciating the bank's cultural commitment to leadership and high performance.

The Bank of America's Executive Socialization Program: Phases and Interventions

The bank's executive socialization experience spans four core phases—selection of the new executive, initial entry into the executive role, a midpoint phase of 100–130 days on the job, and a final review phase at the end of the first year. Below we will examine each of these phases, their central activities, and their goals.

Selection Phase

The first element of a successful executive socialization process is the selection process itself. While expertise and experience are the overriding criteria, there are additional dimensions when it comes to selection at the Bank of America—leadership ability and cultural fit. If the new executive is lacking leadership and interpersonal skills and cultural sensitivity, he or she has a much higher probability of derailing. To ensure this does not happen, the Human Resources function at the Bank of America devotes a great deal of attention to its partnerships with executive search firms. Recruiters must understand the bank's culture and leadership requirements when hired to conduct an executive-level search. In addition, a leadership development officer from HR (*LD partner* in the bank's terminology) will often interview the candidate to assess cultural fit with bank, value to the team, and leadership approach. This information is meant to complement data from other potential stakeholders who are interviewing the candidate about his or her expertise and experience. The LD partner will solicit responses to the following types of questions from all the interviewers:

1. Would you personally trust your career to this person (the candidate)?
2. Do you see yourself learning from them?
3. Is this person capable of putting enterprise objectives ahead of their own goals and working well across lines of business and constituents?
4. Would this person complement the direct team that he or she would be a part of?
5. Would this person be able to accept, process, and apply candid coaching and feedback in order to continuously improve?
6. Do they have the drive and passion to be part of a winning team?
7. Can you see this person leading from and living the company's core values? Would they fit our culture?
8. Does this person have the potential to assume more responsibility in the future?

Answers to these questions provide insights into the candidate's potential for a fit or misfit with the bank's culture and for their credibility as a leader. If the candidate is hired, the answers to these and other interview questions are then provided to the individual upon their arrival into the job. The sources of feedback, however, remain anonymous.

Job design is another component of the selection process. A clear and calibrated job specification is spelled out and supported by stakeholders before a search begins. Critical stakeholders will be interviewed by the LD and/or HR partners about what is required in the job, as well as other dimensions that are not critical but helpful for the candidate to possess. This selection process is designed so that the hiring executive does not make a blind selection—say, hiring someone with a similar style to their own. The multi-stakeholder involvement also ensures that the hiring executive has a clear sense of the demands of the job from the perspectives of the widest range of stakeholders.

Critical to this phase is the role of the leadership development or LD partner. This individual acts as a "chief talent officer" during the hiring process and onboarding process of each new executive. With usually 10 to 15 years of work experience, LD partners possess a leadership development and/or organizational development background. Most have deep experience in hiring and developing executives. As a result, these LD partners have a strong degree of credibility in the eyes of the new executive and their stakeholders. The LD partner's responsibilities are broad. They essentially "own" the executive's socialization process from beginning to end.

Entry Phase

Following his or her hiring, the new executive's initial few weeks on the job are critical ones. During this time, the individual needs to accomplish four outcomes. They must (1) develop business acumen specific to the new role, (2) learn the organizational culture, (3) master the role's leadership demands, and (4) build critical organizational relationships.

From the standpoint of business acumen, the new executive must be able to efficiently and quickly learn customer and financial information specific to his or her new role. In turn, they must set realistic goals and objectives based on this information. On the cultural dimension, they need to acquire an understanding of the written and unwritten norms of behavior within the organization. From the standpoint of leadership demands, they must be able to rapidly determine the organization's expectations of themselves, as well as establish leadership expectations within their team. Finally, it is imperative that the new executive be able to identify and build relationships with key organizational stakeholders.

To meet these demands, three major categories of socialization interventions are used: (1) tools and processes, (2) orientation forums, and (3) coaching and support. Tools and processes include an onboarding plan and "new leader/team" and "new leader/peer" integration processes. Orientation forums include a general new employee orientation and a New Executive Orientation Program. For coaching and support, there are three primary providers—the hiring executive, an HR generalist, and the LD partner. Each of these interventions is described below.

During the first week on the job, the LD partner prepares the socialization plan for the executive. This early engagement with the LD partner ensures that from the very start he or she will be viewed as a critical resource for the newly appointed executive. The integration plan itself has two primary outcomes. One is to provide new leaders with basic yet critical information about the business they will soon be leading. They are given an overview of their unit's financials, the unit business plan, key initiatives, assessments of their team's leadership talent, and other important background information such as biographies of key managers, customer surveys, and recent presentations on key issues in the unit. The second outcome is to have the executives define successes for their first 90 days on the job. They must identify these along three dimensions—financial, leadership, and organizational. The plan also explores early obstacles the executive is likely to face in terms of people, processes, and technology. The new executive must look at his/her own developmental issues and how he/she can best address these. At this time, the executive is given the names of a peer coach (who is a fellow executive) and senior advisor (typically this individual is at the same level or above). The peer coach is a resource for "insider" information. Peer coaches will have benefited from having their own peer coach in the past, and therefore see the importance of their role. To accelerate the relationship with the peer coach, the LD partner will often try to find some common ground in backgrounds, such as attending the same college or experience in similar industries or companies. Consideration is also given to those who are known internally to be good coaches and who will be candid with the new executive. The senior advisor provides the new executive with mentoring around his or her career. In contrast to the peer coach, the advisor is someone with a broader view of the organization given their seniority. Often this individual is someone with whom the new executive may need to undertake an extensive near-term project. Senior advisors often are chosen from a line of business outside that of the newly hired individual, since projects at the executive level often require cross-company partnerships.

In the first 1 to 3 weeks, further planning is used to identify emerging challenges in the new role, people-related issues, key relationships that must be built, ongoing management processes that need to be established. This planning is captured in the New Leader–Team Integration Session, a critical experience in the entry phase. The objective of this process is to facilitate an effective working relationship between the new leader and his or her team. The process creates an opportunity for both the leader and the team to establish open channels of communication, exchange views, and become more acquainted with their respective operating styles and expectations. When this planning process is done well, it can dramatically shorten the time required for the new executive to become effective on the job.

The New Leader–Team Integration session ideally occurs within the first 30 to 60 days of the new assignment. The process involves three steps—all of which are facilitated by the LD partner (sometimes and often in partnership with an HR partner). In the first step, the LD partner meets with the new executive leader prior to the integration session. The LD partner provides the new executive with an overview of the integration session's objectives and mechanics, identifies the executive's own objectives for the session, and selects the questions that will be used to create a mutually beneficial dialogue between the executive and his or her new team. In addition, the LD partner gauges the new leader's interests and concerns. Questions to solicit this information for the new executive include:

1. What do you need to know about your team?
2. What don't you know about your team?
3. What are your concerns?
4. What things are most important to you as a leader?
5. What does the team need to know about your expectations and operating style?
6. How can the team best support you in your transition into the new role?
7. What key messages would you like to send to the team?

Following this meeting with the executive, the LD partner meets with the new leader's team—either individually or, preferably and more often, as a group—but without the new leader. The purpose of this second step is to develop a preliminary understanding of the group's issues and concerns. Typically, the LD partner will solicit this information using questions such as the following:

1. What do you already know about the new executive?
2. What don't you know, but would like to know?
3. What advice do you have for the new executive that will help him or her be even more effective?
4. What questions do you have for the new executive?
5. What are your concerns about him/her becoming the leader of the team?
6. What major obstacles are you encountering as a team? What opportunities exist?

7. What is going well that you would like to keep? What is not going well that you would like to change?
8. What do you need from the new executive to allow us to be even more effective?

Following these two preliminary meetings for data-gathering, the New Leader–Team Integration session is conducted over a half day period. After describing the meeting objectives and ground rules, the team goes off without the executive to gather responses to their new superior's "questions to the team." In the meantime, the new leader is debriefed on the group's interview responses, and he or she prepares responses to these for the team. The team and the new leader then meet together for two hours of dialogue. The environment is a nonthreatening one. The LD partner begins by reviewing the group's overall messages to the leader. For example, an insight might emerge that direct reports are interpreting certain of their superior's behavior in a negative light. The leader comments on the team's responses as well as communicates his or her key messages to the team and how he/she plans to address the feedback. Facilitated by the LD partner, both the leader and the team establish formal commitments to one another and identify future issues to be addressed. For example, the new executive may commit to a new behavior or set of actions or a clearer vision. She might shift her management practices so that more of her time is spent on addressing future issues.

In addition to the New Leader–Team Integration Session, there is also a New Peer Integration Session, which is also held within the first 30 to 60 days of the new executive's arrival. This session creates an opportunity for the executive to network with his new peers, to seek advice and guidance on onboarding, to learn about norms, and to obtain general support. It also allows the individual's peers to learn about their new colleague's background, operating style, and priorities, and to build an initial working relationship. Similar in design to the New Leader-Team Integration session, it involves three stages. First, the LD partner meets with the new executive to describe the process, select discussion questions, and to explore special issues and concerns. Typical interview questions for the preparation phase include:

1. What would you like your new peers to know about you?
2. What would you like to know about your new peers?

3. Provide a summary of your personal and work history that others might not know.

4. What are you interested in outside of work?

5. How can your new peers support you as you transition into the executive team?

The LD partner then meets with the executive's new peers and solicits responses to the following questions:

1. What advice do you have for your new peer?

2. How would you describe the team's written and unwritten rules?

3. What would you like your new peer to know about the team?

4. The things that make a person successful on this team include?

5. The things that can derail a person on this team include?

6. The things that help a person integrate well into this company include?

7. What can you tell your new peer about each team member's operating style?

In addition to these responses, the LD partner also gathers from each member of the peer team information on their areas of competence where they might serve as a resource to the new executive, their interests outside of work, and the names of spouses and children. This data is recorded on index cards for the new executive.

The integration session is broken into three parts. There is a short overview, setting of objectives, and an introduction of the team and the new peer. This is followed by the peer team and the new peer gathering responses to each other's questions in separate rooms. Each side's responses are recorded on flipcharts. The team and their new peer then gather together in a conference room. Facilitated by the LD partner, there is sharing of the responses and dialogue. Basically the session enables transparency and partnering—both cornerstones of success in the Bank of America's culture. It drives joint ownership for success as well, and like the new team integration session, it facilitates the acceleration of relationships with peers—individually and collectively.

Within the first week on the job, the new leader attends a Welcome orientation (providing an overview of the Bank's business, history, culture, values) that is run on every Monday for all new employees. This is followed by a meeting with the LD partner to discuss the onboarding plan. Within the leader's first few months, he/she is automatically registered to attend the New Executive Orientation Program.

This program is sponsored directly by the CEO. Its purpose is for the executive to network with other new executives as well as the CEO, and with his executive team as well as other executives previously hired into the bank from the outside. On the first day of the program, there is an informal panel with executives who have been hired into the bank within the last 2 years. The panel of executives shares their own onboarding experiences. They explain their experiences, what the new executives can expect, their personal "lessons learned." This is followed by presentations by the CEO and top executives, who cover topics such as the corporate values and culture, leadership philosophies and expectations, company strategy and finances, as well as other key business units' growth strategies and key enterprise initiatives. A social networking event then follows hosted by the CEO and his direct reports. This orientation provides the new executives with insights into the business, the bank's culture, the CEO's expectations for leaders, and how executives can derail at the Bank of America. Beyond the information provided in the orientation, a parallel goal is to create a cohort identity for the new executives. This is important, as they will likely need to work with one another on key projects or business initiatives in the future. The cohort also provides the new executives with a safe haven or resource group to ask questions and to help navigate the complexities of the bank.

Mid-Point Phase (100 to 130 days)

Three to four months into their new assignment, the executive takes part in the Key Stakeholder Check-In session. This intervention involves receiving written and verbal feedback from a select list of their key stakeholders. The experience is designed to accelerate the development of effective working relationships between the new leader and the stakeholders who now share responsibility for the new leader's success. It also aids in helping the newly hired executive understand the feedback and coaching culture that is unique to Bank of America's rich feedback environment. It is essentially a process for the new leader to seek and receive early feedback regarding how stakeholders view the leader's socialization process, operating style, leadership approach, and cultural fit. It can uncover whether there are potential disconnects between others' perceptions and the leader's actual intentions. It can also further clarify the expectations of key stakeholders. Most importantly, it can be used to allow the executive to make early adjustments in approach and in turn avoid potential derailment. Like the earlier integration sessions, it also gives voice to the stakeholders. They can take advantage of a process that permits them to surface potentially sensitive issues or concerns in an anonymous manner. They can share organizational insights that are not readily apparent to the new leader. They can also communicate special needs to the new leader.

In terms of its timing, the bank discovered (using Six Sigma process and tools) that stakeholder reviews held close to the new leader's entry were not effective. The executive did not always have sufficient self-confidence to respond positively to the feedback received from stakeholders. Similarly, staff did not possess well-formed opinions of their superior or peer before the 3-month timeframe. They may not have seen enough of a particular behavior to determine whether it was a pattern or not. On the other hand, within 3 to 4 months, patterns in the executive's behavior become quite clear. Using a timeframe within 130 days, it was harder for new executives to discount feedback that was more critical of their approach. They could not claim that their behavior was simply due to a one-time event. That said, delaying feedback to the executive until the 6-month mark or later created a serious dilemma. By that point, the executive's behavior may become typecast. After 6 months in the job, it was very difficult for the executive to escape the label. For this reason, the feedback occurs ideally by the 130-day milestone.

The process behind the Key Stakeholder Check-In involves an initial planning session with the new leader and the LD partner in which they review and revise the questions that will be used to solicit insights. For example, the LD partner will identify specific areas in which the leader would like to receive feedback and from whom. The LD partner then contacts the leader's key stakeholders to conduct an anonymous 15- to 30-minute interview with each stakeholder. Beyond the questions identified by the new leader, there are additional questions to stakeholders. These often include:

1. What are your initial impressions of your new leader's strengths?

2. What are the potential land mines/obstacles that he or she may come up against?

3. What advice would you give to the new leader to be even more effective and to accelerate performance in the role?

4. What 1–3 things do you specifically need from this individual?

5. To increase effectiveness, what does this individual need to (1) continue doing, (2) stop doing, and (3) start doing?

The LD partner organizes the interview responses, identifies themes, and records specific verbatim comments from specific stakeholders.. They then meet with the new leader and share the interview results. In the review session, the executive constructs an action plan to address specific feedback items and prepares for a discussion with his or her boss. With the superior, they review the action plan and the overall socialization experience overall. The LD partner and the leader hold follow-up meetings to evaluate progress on the action plan and for further coaching. Sometimes these discussions will uncover a problem that even the individual's superior was unaware of. It is worth noting that the superior is not one of the people the LD partner interviews, for this very reason.

This comprehensive check-in process brings great clarity to identifying the new leader's strengths but also highlights development needs and problem areas. For example, a new executive might learn that he possesses strong interpersonal skills and is perceived as highly competent and action-oriented. On the other hand, the same executive might learn that he still needs to build stronger connections with key leaders and learn various business strategies and initiatives at a more granular level. The new executive also may receive feedback that she must spend more time on developing a clearer business vision and communicating to her team. Staff might wish more one-on-one time with the executive. Out of the action planning process, concrete steps will be identified that this executive must undertake over the coming months to build on the identified strengths and address the problem areas.

The Final Phase (One Year to One and a Half Years)

Typically 12 to 18 months after the stakeholder review, the new executive will receive a 360 feedback assessment which provides the leader with feedback on his or her leadership competencies. The timing is designed so that the executive has had an opportunity to make significant progress on the development areas identified in the stakeholder reviews. New executives now also have had a complete performance cycle under their belt. If the executive is successful, his/her improvements will show up in the 360 feedback data. The tool itself is designed around the bank's leadership model as well as common derailing behaviors. When the leader receives 360 feedback, he/she will again sit down with the LD partner to review it, compare it to stakeholder feedback, and use the outputs to further shape development plans and actions. It also triggers another more formal development discussion between the individual executive and his/her boss. The 360 feedback is used along with other data and feedback mechanisms as input into the individual's performance ratings and reviews.

Toyota: A Case Study in Socializing Plant Management Talent

Similar to the origins of the Bank of America's socialization program, Toyota's onboarding initiatives for plant managers are the product of its rapid growth. As the company expanded its operations worldwide, it could no longer rely upon a cadre of internal Japanese managers to lead its manufacturing operations. There were simply not enough "home-grown" plant managers ready to step into such demanding roles. As a result, the company began to recruit more senior talent from the outside. There was a deep concern, however, that outside talent might not fully comprehend the company's sophisticated "continuous improvement" system or TPS (Toyota Production System) and therefore needed to be socialized into its methodology. TPS is built around a philosophy of simple real-time experiments to continuously improve manufacturing operations. Since TPS is seen as central to the company's historic success, the actions of plant managers would have a profound effect on the rigor with which TPS is applied. Toyota developed a rigorous socialization approach to instilling not just the philosophy but also a deep familiarity with TPS methods in the mindsets and behaviors of newly appointed general managers. Below is a description based on an in-depth case study and analysis by Spear (2004), who detailed the onboarding process of a highly accomplished plant manager appointed from the outside to lead one of the company's US-based manufacturing operations.

Beyond a rigorous recruitment and selection phase, the socialization program is built around four phases. The first and second phases comprise two periods of approximately 6 weeks in a manufacturing plant observing and working alongside with front-line workers. The third phase involves approximately 10 days working and making observations on the front lines at Toyota and a supplier plant in Japan. This also includes a period of time where the new plant manager learns how to manage and present improvement projects to the plant staff. In the final phase, the new manager returns to the first plant and works with the production group leader and assistant manager to develop the problem-solving skills of the line workers. Below is a description of each phase.

Phase One—Getting the Right Basics

The new plant manager is first assigned a mentor who is a senior manager from the Toyota Supplier Support Center—the group who are responsible for ensuring that Toyota's supplier plants are highly competent in TPS. This individual will oversee the new manager's progress throughout the entire socialization process. The parallel role at the Bank of America would be the Leadership Development partner. At Toyota, however, the mentor serves to a far greater extent as a hands-on teacher in contrast to the facilitator and feedback broker role at the Bank of America. In many ways, mentors are the central dimension in the socialization process at Toyota.

The mentor's role is multifaceted. First, the mentor assesses the depth of the new manager's technical expertise, his or her ability to work with individuals with different skill levels, aptitudes, and roles, and his or her capability at learning and unlearning. This is done through assignments where the protégé must experiment with improvements on the manufacturing line. Through these, mentors teach the new plant manager how to implement TPS as a set of numerous, simple experiments. This format of learning reinforces in the protégé the importance of structuring all improvements as experiments, testing ideas out quickly and simply, and learning from incremental changes rather than more time consuming and investment heavy system-wide changes. To deepen the protégé's learning, the mentor gradually increases the complexity of the assignments. In addition, there is a critical accountability dimension. At the start of each week, the protégé must propose a set of experiments and the hypotheses supporting them. He or she is then held accountable for presenting experiment outcomes at the end of each week by describing the actual changes that were made and their effect on performance. Gaps have to be explained between predicted and actual results, as well as a set of next steps proposed to remedy the gaps. Through this intensive mentoring, the new manager learns three critical lessons. The first is that TPS is grounded in structuring all changes as experiments. The second is that the role of senior managers is to build the process innovation capabilities of the individuals they lead. In turn, they learn that the role of senior managers is not to be the primary problem solver in the organization but to cultivate a continuous problem-solving capability in the lower levels of management and on the front line. In contrast, plant managers outside the Toyota system often see their roles as problem solvers rather than context shapers. Toyota's socialization process is designed so that outsiders "unlearn" this responsibility. In essence, Toyota is teaching its plant managers its own version of leadership to more directive forms. In contrast to the Bank of America approach that relies upon a distinct set of leadership competencies, the Toyota approach is much more work performance oriented. Feedback is around manufacturing outcomes and the methodologies used to get these outcomes.

The context in which the socialization process takes place is on the manufacturing floor, though not necessarily in the plant where the new manager will be leading. In contrast, the Bank of America socialization experience is in the offices and work environments of the executives themselves. At Toyota, the socialization experience is built around a learning partnership with a small group of line workers and their supervisors. By limiting the scope of the learning experience to a workgroup, the new manager can view the many work cycles of individuals and teams more quickly and learn in greater depth the dynamics of TPS on an actual production line.

This socialization experience with a production team is built around two phases. The first involves observing and working on human factors that influence manufacturing outcomes, while the second phase focuses on the impact of machine factors on production. During the first phase that lasts up to 6 weeks, the new plant manager must help his or her teams of assembly workers improve their operational efficiency, labor productivity, and safety. Under the supervision of the mentor, the plant manager will work with the team to document how various tasks are conducted, who does what, and how materials and information are communicated across the team. Based on these assessments, solutions in the form of simple experiments are implemented and tested for their overall impact on a weekly basis.

What the new leader inevitably discovers is that some of the experiments succeed while others end up compromising important production efficiencies. For example, an experiment may reduce the time required for a production worker to conduct a manufacturing task. The gain on this side, however, creates machinery issues that were inconsequential under the older system but now have magnified effects with the "tighter" improved system. As a result, there are now more machinery bottlenecks. These "setbacks" are meant to be humbling experiences for the new leader and to motivate him or her to more fully comprehend TPS. The setbacks demonstrate powerfully the limited competence that the new plant manager may possess in TPS despite their own years of experience in other manufacturing plants and their exposure to the concepts of TPS elsewhere. The ongoing objective feedback and measurements against targets therefore intensify the learning and socialization experience for the leader. They also are used to reinforce the importance of line workers in the continuous improvement process as problem-solvers, reminding the new leader of his dependence on these individuals.

Once this 6-week phase is completed, a second phase begins of approximately the same duration. This time the focus is on production machinery dynamics. These factors are more difficult to observe because they are often hidden within the machines themselves. They are also more infrequent. Only when the new manager has developed and honed his observation and problem-solving skills from the prior phase is he able to move on to solving these more subtle and complex problems. The mentor will set an operational availability target for the general manager to achieve over the 6-week span. Inevitably, the target is not achieved—again reinforcing the notion that the manager's prior experience is insufficient. The new manager must remain in learning mode. During this phase, he will make changes to the machinery and reconfigure how individuals interact with machinery, all the while learning the rigors of TPS.

During these two phases and those that follow, a fundamental mindset is also instilled in the new manager—direct observation is essential to TPS. At more senior levels such as plant manager, indirect means of observation are often the dominant sources for information—for example, reports, surveys, and statistics. This phase teaches the incoming general manager that such sources are insufficient. In addition, the new plant manager inevitably discovers that she has a strong tendency to assume too much control for making changes herself rather than relying on the production workforce. As a result, the rate at which she is able to make improvements and test them is too slow.

Following this intensive period of 3 months, the new leader will often travel to Japan. There he/she spends time in the Kamigo engine plant where many of the original innovations of TPS were invented. The new manager will work alongside a single production worker. His or her goal will be to make a far greater number of changes than prior targets. This time the goal is to reduce the movements and efforts of the worker that do not add value to the product, or else lengthen cycle times or fatigue the worker or add unnecessary burdens. This experience reinforces the necessity of careful observation, rapid generation of experiments, and implementation with minimal resources. It also powerfully instills the necessity of resolving problems with an eye to the larger context of the production cell as a whole and the effects on production workers' movements. During this time in Japan, the new manager will present his/her findings to the plant managers and the shop's group leaders. Under the guidance of the mentor, he/she will learn how Toyota managers manage and present their improvement projects.

On return to the original US plant, the incoming plant manager will work with the mentor to help the production line managers develop the problem-solving skills of the line workers and team leaders. In essence, this concluding phase of the socialization process is one in which the new manager acts in the same fashion as the mentor, as a teacher and coach. By now, the new manager's perspective on his or her role as a senior leader at Toyota has shifted fundamentally. The aim of the plant manager is to cultivate a cadre of leaders at all levels who learn through continuous improvement. At this point, the new manager can officially assume the full-time leadership responsibility of a plant.

The Design Assumptions That Shape Effective Socialization Interventions for Senior Leaders

In comparing the two case studies, we can see that they share common design assumptions. The baseline assumption is that successful onboarding socialization occurs *over time*. At Toyota, the time span involved is approximately 14 weeks. At Bank of America, the duration was the executive's first 12 to 18 months on the job. This design feature is essential to ensure a virtuous cycle of learning, performing, and feedback. Quite simply, socialization takes time. Both onboarding processes are supported by *multiple interventions* instead of a single event at entry into a senior management role. At Toyota, this involved four distinct phases of learning and application. To be effective, socialization must also be supported by *multiple resources,* especially in terms of *stakeholder* resources. To engage solely the new leader's superior (the hiring executive) is not sufficient to ensure a successful socialization experience. Instead, the fullest possible spectrum of stakeholders must be involved in the new leader's selection, entry and onboarding. The Bank of America engages the new executive's many stakeholders in a simple transparent process with the aim of achieving a broad range of outcomes. At Toyota, the new plant general manager receives feedback from assembly workers, line managers, a senior management mentor, as well as from objective measures of productivity, quality, and ergonomics. Finally, effective socialization interventions are completely dependent upon the quality of the *interaction* between the leader and his or her stakeholders. A purely paperwork-driven or bureaucratic process will not produce optimum results. The approach must therefore focus on the quality of candid *dialogue* and interaction rather than documentation and formal processes. It must also proactively engage the new leader's multiple stakeholders throughout the socialization cycle. In this regard, one of the more important lessons from the Bank of America example is the pivotal role of the LD and HR partner. This individual in essence "owns" the executive's success from the moment of selection to the end of that executive's first year on the job. Their job is to make certain the executive successfully onboards. They play a critical role in engaging the new executive's superior, several peers, and the subordinates in the ownership process. Similarly, the mentor at Toyota "owns" the new plant manager's development. Effective engagement is completely dependent upon the quality of interaction between the new leader and his/her mentor or partner. In the case of the Bank of America, the use of the leadership development partner and the various dialogue and feedback-based integration experiences allow the new executive to obtain rich, candid, and ongoing information on his/her progress over the first year. At Toyota, the mentor provides ongoing feedback along with objective weekly performance feedback. In both cases, the leader receives rich and ongoing performance feedback.

References

Conger, J. A., & Benjamin, B. (1999). *Building leaders: How successful companies develop the next generation.* San Francisco: Jossey-Bass.

Fulmer, R. M., & Conger, J. A. (2004). *Growing your company's leaders: How organizations use succession management to sustain competitive advantage.* New York: AMACOM.

McCall, M., Lombardo, M., & Morrison, A. N. (1988). *Lessons of experience: How successful executives develop on the job.* New York: Free Press.

Spear, S. J. (2004). Learning to lead at Toyota. *Harvard Business Review, 82*(5), 78–86.

Watkins, M., (2003). *The first 90 days: Critical success strategies for new leaders at all levels.* Boston: Harvard Business Publishers.

Socializing Socialization: Everything Is Connected—Especially Recruiting, Hiring, and Accelerating Talent

George B. Bradt

Abstract

This chapter's core premise is that things work better when all efforts point in the same direction, integrated into one Total Onboarding Program (TOP). Onboarding gets new employees up to speed twice as fast as separate efforts to recruit, orient, and manage. The primary requirement is that the hiring manager lead each new employee's onboarding experience all the way through, taking a proactive approach to socializing the new employee into the broader group with a particular focus on the most important relationships by: introducing the new employee to key stakeholders, behind-the-scenes networks, special projects, meetings and events, and connecting tools.

Key Words: socialization, stakeholders, networks, onboarding, PrimeGenesis, culture, BRAVE, relationships

Introduction

In PrimeGenesis' work helping organizations get new leaders up to speed quickly, we have seen repeatedly that a primary cause of misalignment and disengagement of new employees is the way that most organizations split up their recruitment, orientation, training, and management efforts.[1] In many cases, multiple uncoordinated players oversee discrete pieces of the onboarding process and make poor handoffs across those parts. Almost everybody has a story:

• People showing up to interview candidates without a clear picture of the position they're trying to fill, let alone what strengths they're looking for.

• High-pressure interviews that turn off exactly the sort of people the organization is looking to recruit.

• Closing the sale with a candidate who turns out to be wrong for the organizational culture.

• New employees showing up for the first day—and there's no one to greet them, no place for them to sit, no tools for them to work with, and no manager around to point them in the right direction.

• New employees getting off on the wrong foot with exactly the people they need to collaborate most closely with.

• New employees left to their own devices after day one because the organization has a sink-or-swim mentality.

> *"I have witnessed a lack of collaboration, cooperation, and coordination between the recruiting lead, the human resource generalist, and the hiring manager that actually caused a new employee to show up for her first day on the job without anyone knowing it. I reported to the hiring manager, and was asked to take care of "onboarding" this new employee. I was embarrassed for the company, myself, and her."* [2]

A new employee's failure to deliver usually stems from one or more of four things:

1. A *role failure* due to unclear or misaligned expectations and resources (preparation miss). For example, a new global head of customer service

that was hired before division heads had agreed to move customer service from their divisions to a central group.

2. A *personal failure* due to lack of strengths, motivation, or fit (recruiting/selecting miss). For example, a new head of marketing that was hired with direct marketing experience that was woefully out of date.

3. A *relationship failure* due to early missteps (head start/early days miss). For example, a new employee aggressively challenged a colleague before he or she fully understood the situation, making that colleague reluctant to share information with the new employee after that.

4. An *engagement failure* due to early days' experiences (management miss). For example, a new employee's manager who was not around during the employee's first month due to other priorities.

When any person takes on a new role, there is a risk he or she will be misaligned with the organization. When you compound this with the disruption inherent in all organizational transitions, it's no wonder so many new employees fail or decide to leave in the first six months[3] and that as many as 50% of new employees fail to deliver what their organizations expect. (Smart, 1999). Often those failures or decisions aren't apparent early on. But the seeds have sprouted and it's very hard to change the course down the road. A new job is a turbulent event for everyone.

> *"We've found that 40 per cent of executives hired at the senior level are pushed out, fail, or quit within 18 months. It's expensive in terms of lost revenue. It's expensive in terms of the individual's hiring. It's damaging to morale."*— Kevin Kelly, CEO of executive search firm, Heidrick & Struggles, discussing the firm's internal study of 20,000 searches. (Masters, 2009)

Consider this case. A major consumer products company was experiencing high levels of new employee failure. It turned out the organization had three distinct groups each working to improve its own area of responsibility without paying attention to the others. "Talent Acquisition" was focused on cutting expenses by increasing the use of contract recruiters. "Human Resources" was focused on improving the organization's orientation program. "Line Management" was implementing performance-based compensation to keep people more focused on the most important performance-driving activities.

We helped the organization get its hiring managers more involved in recruiting and orienting new employees throughout the process deploying many of the tools of a Total Onboarding Program (Bradt & Bancroft, 2010). The results were immediate and meaningful. Recruiting efforts became more closely aligned with hiring managers' expectations. Selection criteria became clearer. Hiring managers took a personal interest in their new employees' orientations and related activities. Candidates and new employees felt better about the organization at every step of the way, which resulted in increases in their effectiveness over time.

Because so many people have heard (or lived) these or similar stories, many organizations are looking for solutions. Many take recruiting, interviewing, and selecting more seriously. Many have utilized onboarding software or portals to manage hiring paperwork and tasks. Many hold managers accountable for the success of their employees.

All these are good things. Do them. But you don't need this chapter to tell you that.

A complete and well thought through onboarding and socialization process can take your organization to a new level of effectiveness by improving and integrating the disconnected experiences and messages new employees get during the recruiting and on-the-job learning process. This is a powerful, vulnerable time in the life of an employee. It represents the most important *teachable moment* your organization will ever have with its employee. If you can plan and get each new employee and the organization in full alignment so that intelligent onboarding and socialization become part of your culture, you will make a material difference in your business results over time.

We are not reinventing the wheel. Most people understand or can quickly figure out the basics of acquiring, accommodating, assimilating, and accelerating new employees. The core premise is that things work better when all efforts point in the same direction, integrated into one Total Onboarding Program (TOP). Onboarding gets your new employees up to speed twice as fast as separate efforts to recruit, orient, and manage. It enables you to get more done in less time by:

• Compressing recruiting, hiring, and socialization time.
• Reducing hiring mistakes by making everyone, including prospective hires, fully aware

of what the job requires—from the employee and from the organization.

- Reducing new employee *buyer's remorse* and greatly improving retention.
- Aligning new employees with key business strategies.

The primary requirement is that the hiring manager lead each new employee's onboarding experience all the way through. If you are a hiring manager, start by creating the overall onboarding plan. Get people aligned around that plan and its importance. Take primary responsibility for its execution and coordination across people and functions as you recruit. Give your new employee a big head start, and enable and inspire them. If you are the HR manager, or the person in your organization responsible for onboarding, help your hiring managers do those things. Here's a rough chronology:

I. *Prepare for your new employee's success before you start recruiting.* Understand the organization-wide benefits of a Total Onboarding Program. Clarify your destination by crafting your messages to the employee and the organization, and by creating a recruiting brief. Lay out your time line and align stakeholders.

II. *Recruit in a way that reinforces your messages about the position and the organization.* Create a powerful slate of potential candidates. Evaluate candidates against the recruiting brief while pre-selling and pre-boarding. Make the right offer and close the right sale the right way. (Don't kid yourself. Socialization begins here.)

III. *Give your new employee a big head start before day one.* Co-create a personal onboarding plan with your new employee. Manage the announcement to set your new employee up for success. Do what it takes to make your new employee ready, eager, and able to do real work on day one.

IV. *Enable and inspire your new employee to deliver better results faster.* Make positive first impressions both ways. Speed the development of important working relationships. Provide resources, support, and follow-through.

We created this approach out of the best of what we've seen and developed in PrimeGenesis' onboarding work since 2002 with a wide range of organizations around the world like American Express, Cadbury, Johnson & Johnson, MTV, Playtex, RBS, and others. The Total Onboarding Program has delivered breakthroughs in onboarding effectiveness and organizational success for hundreds of managers and client organizations.[4]

> As you are working through the steps of onboarding and socialization, it's helpful to think about your role within the analogy of putting on a theater production in which your new employees are actors and you are the producer, director, and stage manager. The analogy is helpful because it gets you off the new employee's stage. You can't recite their lines for them. You can't hit their marks. Your job is offstage—inspiring and enabling them. In turn, you are:
>
> The **Producer**. While preparing for success and recruiting, think of yourself as the show's producer, assembling resources for the show.
>
> Then, the **Director**. While giving your new employees a big head start before day one, think of yourself as the show's director. You will co-create the plan, make introductions, announce the show and generally get things ready.
>
> Finally, the **Stage Manager**. After your new employees walk out on stage, you will continue to ease the way by managing context and the things happening around them.

With that in mind, let's dig into socialization itself.

> *"Introduce" is a transitive, action verb meaning, among other things, to cause to be acquainted. Just giving someone a list of people to meet and hoping something happens is not enough to cause that person to become acquainted with anyone.*

As referenced before, you can't really expect anyone to work well with others until they are able to do their own work. This requires you and the organization to get aligned around your new employees' roles and to get your new employees the tools they need to do their jobs. Recruiting briefs and onboarding software can help with these.

No one should start recruiting anyone until all the key stakeholders are aligned around what they are looking for, what the new employee will do, and how they will all interact. A recruiting brief is an extremely valuable tool for clarifying that and then guiding efforts to identify and evaluate possible new employees. The format of the brief is far less important than having one. As described by Bradt and Vonnegut (2009), it should address:

- **Mission/responsibilities**: Why the position exists; objectives/goals/outcomes; impact on the rest of the organization; specific responsibilities; organizational relationships and interdependencies

- **Vision** (picture of success)
- **Strengths:** Talents; skills (technical, interpersonal, business); knowledge (education, training, experience, qualifications)
- **Motivation:** How activities fit with person's likes/dislikes/ideal job criteria; how this will help person progress toward long-term goals
- **Fit:** Match between person and organization/group/supervisors behaviors, relationships, attitudes, values, and preferred work environment

There is an ever-growing array of onboarding software and portals designed to help you and your organization do just that. Emerald Software's Chuck Ros (2009) laid out a good list of which tasks can be automated.[5] He defines "transactional onboarding" as "collecting 100% accurate, complete, and relevant new hire forms and data," and "acculturation onboarding" as "getting new employees effective as quickly and efficiently as possible." Specifically, transactional onboarding involves:

- **Paperwork and Forms**: employment application, tax forms, policy forms, benefits forms, special industry forms
- **Data Flow**: recruiting integration, human resource management systems and payroll integration, e-verify integration, document management, IT systems and requisitioning
- **Ensuring Compliance**: complete forms package, accurate forms and data, industry-specific compliance, licensure

In contrast, acculturation onboarding (socialization) involves:

- **Orientation**: welcome messaging, company, team, and job information
- **Adaptation**: personal learning plan, skills remediation, materials, work, and project training, satisfaction surveys
- **Connection**: personal profile, social networking, participations, events, employment resources

Our suggestion is that once you've got the transactional part of onboarding in hand, take the joining in/socialization challenge off the table for your new employee. You didn't hire him or her for his or her strengths in socialization. You hired him or her for what he or she can do and get others to do. However, no one gets anything valuable done without productive working relationships with others. So do anything and everything you can to make your new employee's socialization as easy as possible.

Socialization is a big deal. (Though, if you've read this far in the *Handbook of Socialization*, you're probably sold on that point.) Doing it well makes things far easier for everyone. Getting it wrong triggers relationship risks, which increase delivery risks. There are some basic steps that can help make a huge difference. We suggest you set up meaningful, productive onboarding conversations for your new employees with members of their formal and informal/shadow networks and tap into opportunities and events that can help them strengthen their own networks. We also suggest that you do periodic check-ins with those networks. If issues arise, you want to know about them early so you can help your new employee adjust.

Cirque du Soleil has refined its way of socializing new artists while preserving their "spark." As Lyn Heward describes in *The Spark*, "Our goal is to make the artists comfortable in just about every way possible, so we can make them uncomfortable in their thinking—challenge them, destabilize them. The more we do that, the more they will throw themselves into their roles."[6] This is exactly what you are trying to do with your new employee: make him or her comfortable enough with others to think freely.

Socialization is about Adjusting to the Culture

Culture can be referred to as "the way we do things here." It's the "BRAVE" combination of Behaviors, Relationships, Attitudes, Values and the work Environment (Bradt, Check & Pedraza, 2011). While people generally learn about culture starting with the most superficial (what people say about their culture), culture is rooted in what people really are. A good shorthand we learned from one of our clients is "Be. Do. Say." It works for both people and organizations:

Be: The underpinning of culture (and integrity) is what people really are, their core values and natural moral norms,[7] assumptions, beliefs, and intentions.

Do: These are behavioral, attitudinal, and communication norms that can be seen, felt, or heard, such as signs and symbols like physical layouts, the way people dress, talk to each other, and interact with each other.

Say: What people say about their culture can be found in things like mission statements, creeds, and stories. As Edgar Schein (1985) points out, these articulate the professed culture.

For a culture to be sustainable, *be, do,* and *say* must be in sync. It is relatively easy to see when people's actions don't match their words. It is far more difficult to figure out when their words and actions match, but don't align with underlying assumptions and beliefs.

Yet when that happens, those people's words and actions will change over time. Just as your own *be, do,* and *say* need to line up, the same is true for an organization's.

A strong culture can be a sustainable competitive advantage. Indeed, there are some who argue that it is the only sustainable competitive advantage. Plants can be built. Brands can be bought. People move on. But the culture remains. This is well worth paying attention to.

It's hard for anyone to figure out a new culture alone. But your new employee isn't on his or her own. You're there to help. You are going to share what you know about the culture, going well beyond "the way things are done around here" to *why* they're done that way. You are going to help your new employee adjust to the new culture and help build mutually beneficial relationships with the most important stakeholders. This is what socialization is all about.

Hurdle: Figuring out a new culture
Problem: It is difficult for a new employee to figure out a new culture on his or her own.
Solution: Help your new employee figure out the culture by talking him or her through what you know about what people say, do, and believe fundamentally.

> *"Taking the time to 'culture train' new talent eliminates a great deal of timidity and reduces the time required to develop the person's individual comfort level within the peer group. The basic exchange defines each individual's expertise, limitations, associations, and their hot buttons along with their best line of reproach. It must be a soul bearing exchange to the extent that it provides the new hire with clear insight to the personalities of the individuals on the team as well as the overall group culture."*

Socialization is about Whom You Know vs. What You Know

Patty was clearly the smartest person in the room in almost any meeting. Combining that with her extensive experience in the finance function made her a complete powerhouse. She was self-confident and self-reliant and a real value to any organization to which she belonged.

When Patty joined a company as divisional CFO, she spent a fair amount of time over her first couple of months immersing herself in the numbers so that she could get up to speed quickly and build the knowledge required to make the contributions she knew she could make. She went to all the appropriate meetings, but sat in the back listening until she felt ready to add value; and her manager was fine with that.

Unfortunately, 2 months into her job, the company decided to merge Patty's division with another. The other division's CFO had been in place for a couple of years and was doing a good job and got the new combined job. The company tried to find another role for Patty somewhere else in the company, but few people knew her, fewer had worked closely with her, and no one was ready to stand up for her. She ended up leaving the company.

This is an extreme (but not unique) example of whom you know (or don't know) being more important than what you know.

Contrast that story with Ted, who joined a different company as head of product development. The business had traditionally been run at the regional levels with each region having its own capability to create, manufacture, market, sell, and deliver regionally appropriate products. Ted's predecessor had built a central product development group but had failed to get any of the regional presidents to support its efforts.

Ted started by going out to visit with each regional president one-on-one. He sat down with each and said, "I know we run this business at the regional level. I see the role of the central product development group as supporting the regions. Given that, I'm here to start to understand what you need from us to help you and your team achieve its goals."

He then spent the next 6 months assembling and directing resources to help the regions.

Not surprisingly, the regional presidents were delighted to have their people spend time and share their issues and opportunities with Ted and his team. And when Ted and his team started delivering on their promises of support and innovative new products that helped the regional presidents and their teams build business, the region presidents became fans.

Socialization as a Predictor of Success

A study of IBM interns in 2004 by Chang et al. found that the success of those interns' socialization into the group was directly correlated with their propensity to return to IBM full time after the internship. They found four strong predictors of propensity to return. (Read that as a proxy for onboarding success.) The four predictors were:

- Awareness: How well the knowledge and skills of each person is understood.
- Information access: Extent to which each person was accessible within a sufficient time frame with needed information or advice.
- Information seeking: How often information or advice is sought on projects, work, or operations from other individuals.
- Social closeness: How often each person is met with for nonwork-related activities.

The point is that it's not about the *quantity of interactions*. It's about the *quality of the relationships*. Rob Cross is an Associate Professor of Management in the University of Virginia's McIntire School of Commerce and head of its Research Roundtable. His research (2008) indicates that it's far better to build mutually valuable relationships with a relatively small set of "central connectors" and "brokers" than to build acquaintances with a wide range of "peripheral players."

Central Connectors: Leaders, experts, old-timers, gateway roles, or political players. These people can be assets or liabilities, directly connecting new people with information and resources or standing in the way of new people.

Brokers: Leverage ability to drive change, diffusion, or innovation. These people can also fill liaison or cross-process roles (linking with others who have information or resources).

Peripheral Players: Less well connected or less interested in helping with access to information or resources.

Cross's brokers may be the rising stars. They are the up-and-coming people driving things. They're going to be relatively easy to spot and relatively open to helping. They are well worth connecting with. Steer your new employee toward brokers.

The world is full of peripheral players who want to connect. Many of them will be open to building social closeness. The trouble is that they have neither the knowledge or skills to help, nor strong enough relationships with others who do. They may be seductively distracting. Keep your new employee from wasting time with *peripheral players*.

Too many people ignore the central connectors—often because they've been in position for an extended period of time and are looked down on by people rising

around them. Yet this is where a lot of the institutional knowledge resides. As Rob Cross explains, "Central connectors have a lot of ties. 3–5% of people manage 20–25% of the information flows" (Cross, 2008).

Don't expect your new employee to be able to figure out who are the people with valuable knowledge and skills. Don't wait for him or her to discover the most valuable people themselves. Point out key *brokers* and *central connectors,* and make the connections.

New Employees Need Your Help, Not Just Your Encouragement

There are many things you can do to help your new employee assimilate. We're going to take you through five that are particularly important. Don't leave socialization to chance. You don't want to see if your new employee will sink or swim. That's not the test. The test is whether he or she can deliver the results you need with all the help you can provide. Start with a proactive approach in the five areas we delineate here. Identify the most valuable people for your new employee to work with. Make those connections first.

1. In addition to introducing your new employee to the central connectors and brokers described above, introduce him or her to other important stakeholders. **Stakeholders** may include customers, suppliers, individuals in other functions or regions, and resource controllers.

2. Then, extend your introductions even further! Introduce your new employee to **behind-the-scenes networks** like sports teams, communities of common interest, etc.

3. Assign your new employee to special **projects** that can further his or her socialization.

4. Invite your new employee to **meetings and events** that can further his or her socialization.

5. Introduce your new employee to connecting **tools** (organization face book, mentor, buddy, cohort, touchstone, blogs, wikis).

Stakeholders

Introduce your new employee to stakeholders for meaningful and productive onboarding conversations (up, across, down; internal, external; information providers, resource controllers; suppliers, customers; cross-hierarchy, cross-function, cross-region).

It's a little scary how often people tell us their company has a really good onboarding program that turns out to consist of an orientation followed by giving new employees a list of 20–30 people with whom they should set up "onboarding conversations." Those two things are not bad. They are just woefully inadequate.

"Introduce" is a transitive, action verb meaning, among other things, to cause to be acquainted. Just giving someone a list of people to meet and hoping something happens is not enough to cause that person to become acquainted with anyone. Setting up the meetings, providing brief bios, background, or useful information, and clarifying the specific objective of interactions with both parties should be your minimum standard when you introduce your new employee to stakeholders. Conversations need to be two-way. Each participant should walk away with a deeper understanding of the others' perspective and strengths so they will work together better.

Onboarding Conversations: Signs and Symbols to Consider

Make the call to set up onboarding meetings with stakeholders yourself to signal how much you value the stakeholder and the conversation.

Prepare stakeholders for the onboarding meeting by providing bio or background info on the new employee, along with the recruiting brief and/or your Total Onboarding Plan, to signal how much you value the stakeholder and the conversation.

Prepare the new employee for the onboarding meetings by providing bio or background info on the stakeholders to signal how much you value the new employee, the stakeholder, and the conversation.

Message: We're taking this new position seriously.

Action: Prepare all players for the most productive onboarding conversations possible.

Ideally you and your new employee co-created a comprehensive stakeholder list as part of the new employee's personal onboarding plan. So we won't go into that here. Do take another look at the informal networks toward which you plan to steer your new employee, because they're always evolving. Make sure to "introduce" your new employee to information providers and resource controllers—wherever they sit in the formal organization chart.

For New Employee
Make sure your new employee takes these conversations seriously. The way he or she handles these conversations can make a big impact on what the stakeholders think of your new employee—and of you.

Behind-the-Scenes Networks
We can almost guarantee that you yourself are part of at least one behind-the-scenes network. These don't show up on any organization chart anywhere. Yet, they often explain seemingly unexplainable information flows. Think about people exchanging information in car pools, bowling alleys, on trains, softball fields, golf courses, hunting trips, recruiting trips, at volunteer events, school events, church events....

Almost every employee in almost every organization finds him or herself in some situation outside of normal work hours with someone else from the organization. Inevitably they talk about...their organization. These are the behind-the-scenes networks where relationships build over time.

Chip was a finance guy. Dave was a marketing guy in the same company. They fished together for years. As each of them moved up the ladder or into different roles, they helped each other connect to people who might be helpful. Eventually Chip became CEO and Dave became chief marketing officer. The betting is that a lot of important decisions were really made on the banks of Chip and Dave's trout stream.

We're not saying behind-the-scenes networks are good or bad. They exist. The faster you can get your new employee tapped into some of them, the faster your new employee can start to build relationships and learn. Obviously, you won't be able to inject your new employee into all the behind-the-scenes networks. What you can and should do is connect your new employee with groups or individuals with common interests or hobbies. It's not hard for you to do, and it potentially has a huge impact.

Reality Check
Don't force this one. Making a connection where there's a preexisting common interest is a good thing. Pushing people to accept a newcomer into an area where he or she does not naturally fit can be counterproductive. Look for existing, natural opportunities. Don't manufacture them if they're not there.

Projects
Assigning your new employee to cross-functional projects is a great way for him or her to build a cross-functional network. Looking for special projects that offer opportunities for your new employee to work with people he or she normally would not

work with is particularly important in early assignments, as it is a way to preempt silo behavior.

Diana was named country president for her firm. Her boss assembled a team of people to spend a week with her in her new country to help her think things through. One of the people her boss picked was Jessie, who was relatively new to the region. This was a great opportunity for Jessie to get exposed to some other people from across the region and learn while contributing.

> *"I have always required any new hires in support functions to work in the line of business or field for at least a week prior to filling the support job they were hired for."*

Note to HR
Identifying cross-functional, cross-divisional, cross-geographical projects that can help new employees connect with key players is another way you can help with socialization. Since you are a "broker" yourself, you may have a broader perspective than hiring managers.

Meetings and Events
Meetings and events are great opportunities for new employees to work with and get to know broader groups of people. Have a bias to invite your new employee to as many meetings and events as possible.

If you really want to make an impact, think preparation – delivery – follow-through. If there's someone in a meeting you want your new employee to become acquainted with, let both people know about your objective in advance. Make the introduction during the meeting. Then, make sure your new employee follows through to build on the new acquaintance after the meeting.

Tools
This is one of those sections that will most definitely be out of date by the time you read it. So don't follow our detailed prescription here; follow the principle. The principle is that you should identify and use all of the most important tools at your disposal to help your new employee assimilate into your organization. Let's touch on a couple as examples:

• Organizational **staff directory with pictures**. Most schools have them. They're really useful for matching names and faces. Today they're mostly electronic, relatively easy to put up, and generally

well worth the investment—particularly for assimilating new employees.

• **Mentor**. Assigning a relatively senior person to help your new employee learn the lay of the land generally has a big impact.

• **Buddy**. This is different than a mentor, in that it's someone at the same level as your new employee who can be asked trivial questions without fear of repercussions. Another winning idea.

• **Cohort.** If you are bringing in several people at the same time, you can turn them into a cohort by routing them through the same orientation program and even formally facilitating follow-up cohort meetings so they can share their experiences. Cohort orientation gives participants another set of buddies to talk to.

• **Touchstone.** This one's for more senior people. The idea is to give senior employees a buddy who is at least three levels below them in the organization. This person can tell the senior leader what's really going on and how his or her messages are really being received.

• **Blogs and wikis.** Make sure you tap your new employee into the most important blogs, wikis and new information-sharing tools, both internally and externally, so he or she can start to listen to the chatter and participate in discussions.

Note to HR
You've got three tasks here:
1. Let the new employee know about available tools.
2. Let the hiring manager know about available tools.
3. Create new tools to facilitate even better social networking going forward.

Cherish the Differences
The good news is that if you do the things suggested in this chapter so far, you will be doing a far better job helping your new employee socialize than most managers do. You will be miles ahead of the managers who just give their new employees a list of 20–30 people to talk to and leave them to it.

The bad news is that every new employee is different. Every new employee has his or her own history, perspective, needs, and desires. You are going to need to modify your approach to socializing at least slightly for each new employee. Fortunately, there are some ways to group employees so that you can know what to expect. Look at their socioeconomic background. Look at their cultural background.

Look at their work history. Obviously, your expectations of someone moving into his or her first job are going to be different from your expectations of a new senior employee.

Be alert to differences between generational cohorts. While we're not in any way suggesting anything resembling discrimination by age, we are suggesting that people born in different generations are going to have different perspectives and needs. Being aware of those differences will make you a more effective manager of all of your employees.

Cross-Border Socialization

There are many books on this subject so we won't go into a great deal of depth here. The main point is that people will forgive almost any cross-border socialization mistakes except arrogance. Whether you are bringing your new employee into a new country, region, industry, or organization with its own culture, make sure they know that it is their responsibility to assimilate into the culture and not the organization's responsibility to adapt to them.

During Jean's first year in Japan, he never sat down in a meeting until someone told him where to sit. In some meetings he was the most important person in the room and sat in the seat of honor. In other meetings he was less important. No one minded his asking. They took it as a sign of respect for the cultural differences and a willingness to be coached. On the other hand, people would have been upset and uncomfortable if he'd sat in the wrong place based on the arrogant view that he knew what was right.

You shouldn't worry too much about your new employee sitting in the wrong place or saying the wrong thing or doing the wrong thing. That's going to happen. You should help them adjust their mindset so they seek to understand the new culture instead of merely applying their old way of being, doing, and saying to the new situation.

Technology Can Help

At one level, telephones and videoconferences enable interactions across geographies. Some of the social mapping tools can give new employees insight into the social networks even before they start. Many organizations use electronic onboarding systems and portals to facilitate accommodation.

When it comes to socialization, some technology can supplement face-to-face interactions. Sun Microsystems uses an onboarding game that guides new employees through various stages of learning and interaction with others. A big part of this is learning and accommodation; but it also provides socialization opportunities through the interactions.

The point on technology (at least at the time this is being written) is to use it to help with socialization, not lead it. The lead technology needs to be face-to-face interaction.

Periodic Check-Ins

Adjusting is a big part of a new employee's first 100 days. As they socialize into the new culture, new employees are going to have some missteps. That's OK. Some people will become early supporters of the new employee. Some people will be put off by the new employee. That's par for the course.

It's extremely helpful if you or your HR partner can do some sort of periodic check-in along the way. It doesn't have to be all that formal. It just has to give you some sort of read on what the new employee is doing and saying that's working well and what things he or she could do even better.

The premise here is that the earlier and more frequently you can reinforce the things that are working well and help correct the things that are working less well, the easier the new employee's socialization will be.

> **Master Class**
> Create a newcomers' club with executive sponsors. This will allow newcomers to learn from each other's and the executives' experiences and connections. It will give the executives opportunities to get informal feedback from people with fresh eyes, signal the importance of onboarding and socialization, reinforce their vision and values, and deliberately practice helping people at all levels assimilate into the organization.

Conclusion

Our core premise is that things work better when all efforts point in the same direction, integrated into one Total Onboarding Program (TOP). Onboarding gets your new employees up to speed twice as fast as separate efforts to recruit, orient, and manage.

The primary requirement is that you, the hiring manager, lead each new employee's onboarding experience all the way through, taking a proactive approach to socializing your new employee into the broader group with a particular focus on the most important relationships by:

1. Introducing your new employee to **key stakeholders** for onboarding conversations

(up, across, down; internal, external; information providers, resource controllers; suppliers, customers; cross-hierarchy, cross-function, cross-region)

2. Introducing your new employee to **behind-the-scenes networks** like sports teams, communities of common interest, etc.

3. Assigning your new employee to **special projects** that can further his or her socialization.

4. Inviting your new employee to **meetings and events** that can further his or her socialization (including, but not limited to orientations).

5. Introducing your new employee to **connecting tools** (face book, mentor, buddy, cohort, touchstone, blogs, wikis).

That's the generally applicable piece. At the same time, take into account the socioeconomic, experience, cultural, and generational differences in your new employees. Show "traditionalists" respect, while giving them clarity. Put "boomers" in charge and challenge them. Give "X-ers" interesting and meaningful work choices and opportunities. Stimulate "Y-ers" with fast decisions and continuous, frequent feedback and praise. And mind the cultural differences.

Notes

1. This chapter was adapted from the Introduction and chapter on Assimilation in Bradt and Vonnegut's *Onboarding: How to Get Your New Employees Up to Speed in Half the Time*, with some additional thoughts incorporated from Bradt, Check, and Pedraza's *The New Leader's 100-Day Action Plan*.

2. This is the first of several quotes from managers around the world who agreed to let us use their words just so long as we preserved their confidentiality.

3. Kevin Martin, presentation to the Human Capital Institute, Washington DC, April 16, 2008. Aberdeen group's 2007 study indicated that 86% of employees make a decision to stay or leave the firm in their first 6 months or less.

4. PrimeGenesis has reduced the failure rate for new leaders it's helped from 40% to 10%.

5. Onboarding software and portals that you might consider include Emerald Software, Enwisen, KMS, Silk Road, Taleo among others. The field is ever-expanding.

6. Lyn Heward and John Bacon, *Cirque du Soleil® the Spark: Igniting the Creative Fire that Lives Within Us* (New York: Random House, 2006).

7. from Father Michael Ryan's talk on ethics at the Cornerstone International Group conference, July 9, 2010, Rome, Italy. Fr. Ryan is Professor of Ethics at the Vatican University.

References

Bradt, G. B., & Vonnegut, M. G. (2009). *Onboarding: How to get your new employees up to speed in half the time.* Hoboken, NJ: John Wiley & Sons.

Bradt, G. B., Check, J. A., & Pedraza, J. E. (2011). *The new leader's 100-day action plan.* (3rd ed.) Hoboken, NJ: John Wiley & Sons.

Bradt, G. B., & Bancroft, E. (2010). *The total onboarding program: An integrated approach to recruiting, hiring and accelerating talent.* San Francisco, CA: Pfeiffer, John Wiley & Sons.

Chang, K., Ehrlich, K., & Millen, K. (2004, November). *Getting on board: A social network analysis of the transformation of new hires into full-time employees.* Paper presented at the meeting of Computer-Supported Cooperative Work, Workshop on Social Networks, Chicago, IL.

Cross, R. (2008, June). *The intersection of social networks and talent management.* Paper presented to the Human Capital Institute in Washington DC.

Heward, L., & Bacon, J. (2006) .*Cirque du Soleil® the spark: Igniting the creative fire that lives within us.* New York: Random House.

Martin, K. (2008, April). *Set the Stage for Performance Deliverables through Onboarding.* Webinar presented to the Human Capital Institute, Washington, DC.

Masters, B. (2009, March 30). Rise of a headhunter. *Financial Times (online version) http://www.ft.com/cms/s/0/19975256–1af2–11de-8aa3–0000779fd2ac.html#axzz1lJknqRed*

Ros, C. (2009, April). *Onboarding best practices brief.* Posted on Emerald Software website: http://www.emeraldsoftware-group.com/News/20090317_OnboardingBestPractices.

Schein, E. (1985). *Organizational culture and leadership.* San Francisco: Jossey-Bass.

Smart, B. (1999). *Top grading.* Upper Saddle River, NJ: Prentice Hall.

Developing Organizational Cultural Competence through Mentoring: Onboarding the Menttium Way

Pamela M. Dixon, Lynn P. Sontag, *and* Kimberly Vappie

Abstract

Menttium Corporation integrates structured mentoring experiences into clients' onboarding process in order to assist new employees as they embark on career transitions. Relational onboarding is considered as a preferred approach. Further, the mentoring experience is used to support current employees who are promoted into higher ranks of leadership within the organization. In both instances, the focus of the mentoring experience is on supporting the employee as he or she gains organizational cultural competence. This chapter describes the mentoring system used to facilitate successful onboarding of employees. The system consists of a comprehensive interview and match process, one-to-one and/or group mentoring, direct manager involvement, goal setting and tracking, and measurement. Measurement focuses on progressive developmental outcomes, performance gains, and retention rates, all of which are encompassed in the client organization's Return on Mentoring.™

Key Words: onboarding, relational onboarding, structured mentoring, one-to-one mentoring, group mentoring, organizational cultural competence, career transition

The purpose of this chapter is to give readers insight into the role and efficacy of structured mentoring utilized as part of the onboarding process within US corporations. In particular, the role of structured mentoring is described in terms of supporting an individual's ability to gain organizational cultural competence. That is to say, with the support and guidance of a mentor, newly hired or promoted employees are able to quickly and effectively navigate the superordinate and subordinate cultures within their organizations. Menttium Corporation defines organizational cultural competence as the capacity to be self-aware and the ability to manage the dynamics of difference, acquire cultural knowledge, and adapt to the cultural contexts (and subcultures) within the organization. In addition, we expound on the role of structured mentoring as it pertains to supporting career paths and transitions and accelerating performance. Further, we briefly describe a relational approach to onboarding

and the design components of structured mentoring within the Menttium System used to support onboarding.

Menttium Corporation has partnered with hundreds of organizations across the globe for the past 20 years to design and integrate a structured mentoring process into existing talent management strategies, including onboarding. To set the stage for this chapter, we present two scenarios based on real cases in which structured mentoring programs were utilized as part of onboarding processes in a large automobile manufacturing company located in the Midwest region of the United States. While both scenarios describe the use of structured mentoring in the context of onboarding, each presents two different types of formal mentoring implemented with different purposes and outcomes in mind.

The first mentoring program, Menttor,™ is a one-to-one partnership between mentor and mentee, was integrated into the onboarding process to support career transition and retention within the initial 18 months. The second type of structured mentoring is Circles,™ a group mentoring process between a mentor and a group of mentees, which had a focus on accelerating productivity and performance.

Structured Mentoring as a Part of Onboarding at a US Automotive Manufacturing Company: Two Scenarios

Caleb S. sat at the kitchen table and ate his breakfast anticipating his first day on the job. He felt excited about working at the large automobile company that recruited him, which was based in the Midwestern United States. The company began recruiting Caleb during his first year in graduate school where he was working toward an MBA/Engineering degree. While he attended school, a company recruiter would video chat via Facebook to check in on his progress and talk about long-term career options at the company, as well as near-term opportunities for job shadowing and internship positions over the summer. While he wasn't initially excited about going into the manufacturing industry, Caleb was told that he would be groomed to become a leader and change agent for the company. This, and the fact that a component of the onboarding process was being matched with a mentor, solidified his choice to start his career with this company. Glancing over at the instant messaging (IM) section on his computer monitor he noticed that a few of his new coworkers, also new graduates from his university, were IM'ing in anticipation of their first day on the job.

The automobile company had a comprehensive onboarding process that consisted of an extensive job rotation, supplemental development, and structured mentoring. Job rotation, development, and mentoring were used to accelerate the learning process and get future leadership candidates up to speed on all facets of the company quickly. Caleb and his peers would spend time working in up to five different areas of the company, rotating through different projects and job functions. Some projects would tap their technical knowledge gained in college but the majority would enable them to learn new skills and gain insight into the different market channels and functions.

Once at work, he went to Human Resources where they ran his mobile phone under a scanner in order to verify I-9 status and uploaded all his data to his custom benefits plan. Then he went into a large meeting room to listen to presentations from different areas of the company. As he listened to the presenters, three learning programs, each 5 minutes in length, popped up on his mobile phone, and he completed them on the spot. A friend and now coworker IM'd him about getting together for lunch. He IM'd back confirming plans and then used his mobile phone to update his employee record, verifying completion of the learning programs.

Caleb's supervisor, Susan, greeted him and walked him to an office where he met the production manager and line supervisor from the team he was assigned to work with over the next 6 months. Caleb would start as a 2nd shift assembly line worker on the production line.

After 5 months on the line, Caleb was disillusioned and suffering from culture shock. When he was in school he was at the top of his game and he felt successful. He worked on several projects where his ideas were solicited and implemented and where the team was successful, in large part, due to his leadership. When he worked on the production line he found that his coworkers, many of whom came to work at the automobile company after high school and had worked on the line for 20 or more years, didn't care about his ivy league degree or past academic successes. In fact, some showed animosity and disdain for the young future leader. A long-embedded aspect of the culture on the production line was that you put in your time in order to be seen as a viable leader. Caleb's classmates shared similar experiences; some of them were struggling with the same negative reactions from their supervisors because these supervisors didn't buy into the accelerated career development and job rotation aspects of the onboarding process.

Prior to coming on board with the automobile company, the group from the university had been told they were hired because the senior leadership at the company knew that in order to remain competitive they needed to implement large-scale changes and needed leaders who were able to make it happen. In reality these young recruits found a large, complex system that would be slow to change. They had to learn to navigate politics very quickly and learn to manage themselves in a culture they never anticipated. They learned a lot about management theory and operations while at the university; however, their new reality was very different. For example, when Caleb was on the production line he experienced a unionized environment where the union rep and workers could stop the line at any time when they weren't happy about something. Caleb found it to be a waste of time and highly unproductive. Yet, he couldn't change it. When he objected to what he perceived as time-wasting practices, he was shunned. He realized quickly that he wouldn't be able to influence the kind of change he thought was needed.

Early on Caleb met with his mentor regularly. His mentor had been with the company for 15 years. During one meeting over the course of a dinner, Caleb openly disclosed his frustrations and challenges on the production line. Because he and his mentor had built trust, he felt comfortable talking about a loss of hope and confidence that he could actually make the changes necessary to keep the automobile company competitive and sustainable in the future. His mentor listened and asked Caleb questions about his experiences and his reactions to the environment. He talked about his own experiences, successful and not, and the lessons learned from each. He talked about strategies—operational, interpersonal, and personal—that Caleb could test back on the job. At the end of the conversations with his mentor, Caleb always felt better about his situation and had an action plan to execute.

During his 14th month working at the automobile company, Caleb was on a project team with a group of engineers. He was enjoying the work and the collegial atmosphere. During this time, Caleb was asked to present a proposal to a group of executives and board members. He turned to his mentor as he prepared the presentation. The mentor coached Caleb on what the executives and board members would want to hear in the proposal. He also gave Caleb insight into the dynamics of the group and the key players—those he needed to influence the most to ensure the proposal was considered.

Eighteen months into the onboarding program, Caleb and his cohort of university graduates were still with the automobile company. When asked what contributed to their willingness to stay, even though the obstacles and challenges they faced within the culture seemed insurmountable, they attributed their tenure, as well as their ability to keep from derailing early on, to the fact that they had a trusted mentor who guided, coached, listened, empathized, and supported their professional and personal growth.

In the same automotive company a second type of structured mentoring was implemented as part of an onboarding process in the sales area. In this case, the purpose of formal mentoring was focused on accelerating productivity and performance outcomes and utilized a group approach, called Circles.™ Each Circles group consisted of one mentor who had no more than 2 years tenure in the organization and worked in the same sales region as the mentees. The mentees consisted of a group of 10–19 newly hired sales people. After 18 months on the job, some of the new sales team members had achieved and in some cases exceeded expected performance results. For example, one group that worked in the East Coast region was able to deliver a successful sales campaign that focused on the benefits of a particular car. The mentor in this group put the mentees through an exercise whereby each mentee drove a competitor's car and then drove the company's car. After driving the cars the mentees came together, discussed the differences, and identified key benefits of their company's car over the competitor. These benefits were the spotlight in a presentation to the senior vice president of sales and all distributors in the region. The newly hired sales members learned how to sell by knowing the vehicle, knowing the competitor's vehicle, and educating others on the benefits.

Feedback from the mentees indicated that the support they received from their mentors was a primary reason for their success. The mentors in this case were close to the mentees in terms of age and experience. Mentors had no more than 2 years' experience in the sales region, reported to the same vice president of sales, and focused on guiding the mentees as they navigated a rigid hierarchy and internal hurdles found in the sales culture. Further, mentors took time upfront to establish rapport and create tight bonds with mentees. Group mentoring accelerated mentees' understanding of how to be effective in the culture. A theme that emerged from follow-up conversations with mentees in the program was that support from the group and mentor enabled them to communicate ideas to the right people in the right way, which enabled them to accelerate their ability to effectively execute those ideas.

In the groups that were successful the mentors provided direct input to the content to be learned and were more directive about keeping the mentees on track, as compared to groups that were not as successful. Proactivity on the mentor's part has been shown to be associated with more career and psychosocial mentoring (Wanberg, Kammeyer-Mueller, & Marchese, 2006). Circles groups in sales regions that were not as successful consisted of mentors who were older and had more years of experience (more than 5 years). In these cases, feedback suggested that the mentor was more hands-off and waited for the mentees to approach them for help, which was more in line with the traditional sales culture that prevailed for so long. They provided less guidance in terms of how to get their ideas across and how to navigate the culture. When the mentors had entered the company more than a decade earlier, the mentality was that you forged your own path and didn't seek out help from peers. In fact, peers treated each other as competition.

The scenarios presented above represent structured mentoring in a very large company with a long history and deeply engrained norms within the superordinate and subordinate cultures. In the first case, the senior leadership espoused the need for change; however, occupational subcultures (i.e., the production line) were steadfast in their beliefs regarding how one's career should progress and work should be done. Organizational culture does not exist independent of employees. Rather, culture is constructed by employees. In addition there are multiple subcultures that are separate and overlapping with employees maintaining and/or challenging the status quo (Schein, 2009). This has major implications for establishing career paths and transitions on the part of new organizational members.

Career Paths and Transitions

Today, there are fundamental shifts occurring within U.S. corporations that change the traditional notion of career paths and have implications for making career transitions. These shifts are driven by changes in corporate structure and shifts in the workforce in terms of capabilities, demographics, and mobility.

Due to flattened hierarchies and matrix structures, no longer is the focus solely on climbing a corporate ladder to achieve career aspirations. Rather, the focus is on moving within a corporate lattice where career moves are multidimensional—up, down, lateral, and diagonal (moving across functions or industries; Deloitte Development, 2011). Careers unfold based on individuals' actions to reinvent themselves (Hall & Chandler, 2007). Identity, in the context of the organization, does not occur by internalizing values and norms of the company; rather, individuals identify with a group category and begin to think and relate accordingly (Alvesson, 2000). In essence, as new employees engage with others—be it through face-to-face communication or social media—they adapt to the new environment and begin to alter their identity (Ibarra, 1999; Ibarra & Barbulescu, 2010).

The "protean" career has emerged as a way to understand the role of building capability and career transition. The word *protean* is derived from

the Greek god, Proteus, who could change shape at will (Kakabadse, Bank, & Vinnicombe, 2004). The protean career is based on characteristics first elucidated by Douglas Hall (1996). Hall proposed that development is ongoing, relational, and driven by workplace challenges. Further, he contended that careers are the responsibility of the person, not the organization, and that they evolve based on experiences, learning, and changes to individual identity. Given these characteristics, *protean* is an apt label for workers today given the trend toward a highly adaptable and mobile workforce.

Current demographic shifts have altered the makeup of the workforce, including an increased number of educated women in the workforce (US Department of Education, 2007), as well as heightened ethnic, cultural, and generational diversity. For example, Millennials, the up-and-coming leadership, will represent 47% of the workforce by 2014 (Meister & Willyerd, 2010).

Mostly enabled by technology, today's workforce is highly mobile. Employees are not staying with one organization for their entire career span. There are estimations that the average US-based employee will change jobs 10.2 times over 20-year time span (Bauer, Bodner, Erdogan, Truxillo, & Tucker, 2007) and by the Society for Human Resource Management (Bauer, 2010), which indicates that more than 25% of the US population experiences some type of career transition each year.

The convergence of the changes noted above has implications for individuals' career paths, as well as organizations. The implication for an individual is that he/she will experience the process of socialization several times over their career span (Chao, 2007). Specifically, they will need to build relationships, learn the power structures, and navigate the politics within the organization (Chao, 2007). The primary implication for organizations consists of designing and executing effective talent management strategies focused on attracting, engaging, developing, and retaining key talent.

There are indications that current strategies to retain key employees may not be effective. For example, a study by the Corporate Executive Board (Corporate Leadership Council, 2003) cited data from the Center for Creative Leadership indicating that 40% of external hires fail within 18 months. At the executive level, the primary reason has been suggested to be a failure to build the key relationships with peers and staff (Elbin, 2006).

A study conducted by Stahl & Voigt (2008) provides evidence that new hires leave because of lack of perceived organizational culture fit. Making the transition to a new professional identity and engaging with new colleagues while navigating the culture can be a formidable task, especially when the journey is made with little structure or support from others. A great deal of effort and investment go into recruiting and selection. Once hired, unless an effective onboarding process is in place the new member is left to figure it out on his/her own, which equates to a higher risk of voluntary turnover.

Onboarding

According to a study by the Wynhurst Group (2007), organizational members that went through a structured onboarding process were 58% more likely to still be with the organization up to 3 years later. Given the context of workforce trends today, a robust onboarding process necessarily takes a relational approach (Fishel, 2009) and includes a structured mentoring component.

Relational onboarding places emphasis on supporting new hires to become connected with internal networks for the purpose of building productive relationships, finding sources and sharing expertise, and improving organizational socialization. Structured mentoring has been associated with improved organizational socialization (Chao et al., 1992), which has been shown to result in the solidification of the employee's choice to take the job and become an effective and influential member of the organization (Schrodt, Cawyer, & Sanders, 2003).

Onboarding has been defined in a broad sense as assimilating new members who are placed from inside or outside the organization, and supporting acceleration of their learning and productivity (Stimpson, 2009). Stimpson identifies multiple transactional functions within the onboarding process, but expounds on the need for an approach to onboarding that accelerates productivity and retains the current workforce.

Initially, new employees are a net loss in terms of productivity. The company pays the new employee a salary, incurs training costs, and allocates coworkers' time with limited immediate returns. According to a study by Williams (2003), lost productivity resulting from the learning curve for new employees is between 1% and 2% of total revenues. In terms of transactional functions, much is being left to technology today. Rapidly changing social media and information technologies are a consideration as they relate to creating efficiencies with transactional requirements. For example, as described in the first case, the federal government now has an online system for I-9 verification that can be accessed through a mobile phone (Arnold, 2010). In addition, social media are being used as tools to facilitate two-way communication, information sharing, building networks, and as a way to shape organizational culture (Canfield, 2010).

While productivity is limited initially, new employees represent an opportune source of creativity and new perspectives. Yet new employees, both college recruits and senior leaders, are initially confronted with obstacles to getting their ideas heard and accepted. This is particularly true in companies with a long history and strong culture, as was demonstrated in the scenarios used at the beginning of this chapter.

It has been estimated that the probability of a new employee voluntarily leaving the company reaches a peak at 1.5 years and declines after that (Dickter, Roznowski & Harrison, 1996). When onboarding takes a relational approach it addresses the need to quickly enable the new employee to build strong relationships within a network. In this way, organizations have a better chance of leveraging insights from new employees before they give up trying to create change.

Mentors are conduits for new employees in terms of building strong internal networks. The use of internal mentors helps the new hire to gain clarity around alignment between their role and the big picture and corporate perspective, as well as assisting the new hire in engaging with internal (and external) networks, involvement in projects, and other development experiences. Further, new employees are more apt to align their expectations with the realities of the job and a given culture when they have mentors. When new employees don't have the guidance of mentors and strong positive relationships within their networks, they are more apt to run up against obstacles and constraints that could have otherwise been avoided. Conversely, there is evidence to suggest that when organizational members leverage diverse connections that are rich in experience and expertise, they will perform at higher level (Cross, Davenport, & Cantrell, 2003).

Other considerations driving the need for a relational approach to onboarding include the new generation of workers (Levin, 2008). The new generation of workers will deliver results and stay with an organization for as long as they perceive they are appreciated, valued, and can be productive (Sujansky & Ferri-Reed, 2010). Millenials expect that their ideas will be heard and their skills will be leveraged on important projects. Further, they expect that the company will support their professional development. Deliberately making strong connections to others, including a mentor, is a critical component of their career development and their enthusiasm to stay with the organization.

In summary, onboarding is intended to support a new employee as he or she learns work processes and procedures, and to provide new employees with the psychosocial support needed via new internal networks. It is through these networks that new employees are able to gain insight into expected behaviors and underlying values that are part of the culture and in turn begin to alter their professional identify (Ibarra, 1999, 2004).

Organizational Cultural Competence

Culture has been defined as "a historically determined set of denotative (what is), normative (what should be), and stylistic (how done) beliefs shared by a group of individuals who have undergone a common historical experience and participate in an interrelated set of social structures" (Kitayama & Cohen, 2007, p. 847). In the context of culture, social structures can be viewed as making up the organization's identity. Organizational identity has been defined as a process of "continuous interaction between the actors involved in a company and its social-cognitive context" (Peverelli, 2004, p. 4). Peverelli posits a theory of organizational identity as a social-cognitive structure, produced and reproduced due to ongoing social interaction (Peverelli, 2004). In other words, organizational identity can be viewed as "who we are and how we think collectively."

Together, Kitayama and Cohen, and Peverelli's research informs the complex dynamics involved in effectively interacting with organizational members, navigating power dynamics, and successfully executing functional activities within an organization's culture. Further, it supports a shift regarding culture that has moved away from a single, static cultural perspective whereby corporate leaders were the main shapers of culture in organizations (Schein, 1985), to a theory of organizational culture that is constructed and shaped by employees, not just leadership, as a result of interactions between the different social or occupational groups existing within the company (Hofstede, Hofstede & Minkov, 2010; Goldsmith, 2009; Schein, 2009). In effect, organizational culture includes both superordinate (overall corporate culture) and subordinate (occupational or functional subcultures) levels that are created based on interactions between groups that are dynamic and ongoing.

Two primary aspects of an organization's identity and culture have been noted to be social and cognitive (Peverelli, 2004). The social aspect is described as employees making connections with one another, and the cognitive aspect as the ideas, perceptions, and ways of doing things that are shared by employees within an organization. Each aspect applies to the superordinate and occupational subcultures within an organization (Schein, 2009).

As new employees are onboarded into a company, making connections with others and understanding how to be effective requires a high degree of organizational cultural competence. Martin and Vaughn (2007) define cultural competence as the ability to interact effectively with people of different cultures. Menttium Corporation has operationalized the term at the organizational level. For an individual entering a new organization or new ranks within an organization, organizational cultural competence can be defined as the capacity to be self-aware, manage the dynamics of difference, acquire and institutionalize cultural knowledge, and adapt to the cultural contexts (superordinate and subcultures) within the organization. As a consequence, they are able to influence the status quo as members of interdependent groups within an organization (Ulrich & Brockbank, 2005). Menttium designs structured mentoring programs as part of an onboarding process that places emphasis on building organizational cultural competence and successfully impacting change within organizations.

Structured Mentoring and Onboarding

Structured mentoring provides a fourfold path to onboarding newly hired or promoted employees. It provides a formal structure that enables a new employee to build organizational cultural competence, transition into a new professional identity, establish a career path, and accelerate performance.

Mentors help the new employee address the mixture of personal and organizational forces that can either undermine or ensure success in his or her new position. As was noted in the one-to-one mentoring scenario earlier in this chapter, the mentee openly disclosed his fears and lack of confidence to his mentor. By his doing so, the mentor was able to manage the source of the mentee's personal obstacle and counsel the mentee appropriately. The high level of disclosure on the part of the mentee has been shown to positively impact outcomes of mentoring (Wanberg, Welsh, & Kammeyer-Mueller, 2007). Also, the components of mentoring enable the mentee to gain a clear understanding of the organization's superordinate and subordinate cultures, including political dynamics; how the dynamics impact the individual in the new position; and how to apply this understanding to create personal and organizational strategies that support success in the new position.

Early on, new hires need to know how their roles as well as their careers fit within the organization. Having a mentor during a time of career transition is particularly impactful. Mentors help a new employee quickly absorb the organization's social norms, navigate the learning curve inherent in the new role, and begin the process of identity transformation (Chao, 2007). Specifically, mentors have an impact on confidence (through self-awareness) and the development and enhancement of emotional intelligence (Waters, McCabe, Kiellerup, & Kiellerup, 2002; Betts & Pepe, 2006), both of which have an impact on an individual's identity transformation.

Relationships with mentors can be leveraged as a continual source of coaching, feedback, positive role modeling, and influence. Continual application of learning is enriched when reinforced and supported through this key relationship. Further, leveraging the relationship of a mentor has been shown to increase career and job satisfaction (Kammeyer-Mueller & Judge, 2008) and ensure readiness for career progression (Allen, Eby, Poteet, Lentz, & Lima, 2004).

Finally, the mentor facilitates dialogue and coaches the mentee in order accelerate learning (Ehrich, Hansford & Tennent, 2004) and to ensure a high level of productivity and effective performance on the job (Chao, 2007).

Menttium System—Components to Structured Mentoring

The Menttium System provides a structure for mentoring as part of onboarding that follows four primary steps:

- Identify the business objectives that will best measure the Return on Mentoring™
- Choose a structure that best matches the organization's needs (one-to-one and/or group mentoring)
  - Implement the interview and match process
  - Measure progress and outcomes

Business Objectives

There are three primary business objectives that are a focus of structured mentoring as part of onboarding. They consist of support for career transitions, accelerated productivity and performance, and retention beyond the initial 18 months of employment.

TRANSITIONAL SUPPORT

Mentoring partnerships that are utilized as part of onboarding are scheduled to begin between 20 to 30 days into employment. Doing so provides time for the newly hired or promoted employee to begin acclimating to his/her new environment. During this time, the employee will learn about team/unit goals, essential functions of the job and associated work processes, and the new employee will have an opportunity to interact with his/her new boss, coworkers, and direct reports (if applicable).

After the mentoring partnership has been initiated, the mentee has an opportunity to discuss his/her early impressions of the work environment, ask questions and/or talk about how to address concerns. The mentoring relationship is confidential and time is spent up front to build trust. The mentor's primary role at this stage is to provide transitional support. The mentor is a sounding board, confidant, guide, and an important part of the newly hired or promoted employee's support system.

ACCELERATED PRODUCTIVITY AND PERFORMANCE

The mentor helps the newly hired or promoted employee to gain clarity around alignment between their role and the big-picture corporate perspective. In addition, the mentor provides access to connections within the organization for the purpose of building productive relationships, finding sources of information, and sharing expertise. These connections enable the mentee to access and leverage knowledge and ideas from diverse connections, resulting in higher performance on the part of the mentee (Cross, Davenport, & Cantrell, 2003). Finally, newly hired or promoted employees represent an opportune source of creativity and new perspectives. In their role, mentors share strategies and coach their mentees on how to navigate the organizational culture in order to gain visibility and get their ideas heard.

RETENTION

Mentors and mentees dedicate between 2 and 3 hours per month to their partnership. Best practices for utilizing this time together consist of two-way communication and feedback, and ongoing coaching and positive role modeling on the part of the mentor. Given this continual source of support, the mentee has a greater sense of organizational fit and increased job satisfaction—which, in turn increases the mentee's level of commitment and intent to stay with their organization.

In order to ensure successful achievement of business objectives, goal setting and action planning are integrated into the process. Working with the mentor, the mentee sets goals based on his/her own personal transition and career goals, as well as the needs of the organization. Goals tend to vary temporally and in terms of organizational impact. Goals may be short-term or long-term, and outcomes may be tactical or strategic in terms of impact. An example of a short-term goal typical of a newly hired or promoted employee is to establish good relationships with coworkers, bosses, and/or direct reports. More specifically, a mentee may be challenged by interacting with a particular personality within his or her team/unit. The mentee's goal may be to apply strategies for building rapport and adapting his/her communication style. An example of a long-term goal is the design and implementation of a new cross-functional work process, or execution of a strategy to support greater market penetration for a new product line.

Structured mentoring partnerships used as part of onboarding typically last between 12 and 18 months. During this time, mentees' progress toward goal achievement, as well as obstacles and enablers, are tracked and an aggregate report is provided to the organization.

Choose a Structure

The Menttium System utilizes two primary modes of structured mentoring for onboarding new organizational members: one-to-one and group mentoring. For the purpose of onboarding, regardless of the mode, mentoring is typically conducted as an internal program whereby both the mentees and mentors come from within one organization (versus cross-company).

ONE-TO-ONE MENTORING

Menttium's one-to-one internal mentoring process is called, Menttor™ Utilized as part of a company's onboarding process, companies can leverage the expertise and experience of their own senior leaders. As part of the onboarding process, employees who are new to the organization or new to a higher-level position are matched with mentors from other business units or functions who are typically at a higher level and have much more experience within the organization. Mentees set professional goals that typically revolve around their careers and commit to a monthly meeting agenda to focus on their goals and continuously monitor their progress throughout the program.

GROUP MENTORING

Circles™ was created to provide a group mentoring model that matches a senior leader with multiple mentees within the organization. The structure of Circles creates a learning environment that is driven by the participants and intended to accelerate learning, productivity, and performance. Mentees and their mentor collectively identify and design their learning activities, and throughout the year-long program they develop and implement action plans and provide feedback to each other. Learning activities are closely aligned with business needs and include gaining a better understanding of the organization's culture in order to effectively execute and leverage learning activities.

Mentors contribute to the learning process by guiding activities, sharing their experiences, organizational perspectives, and expertise. A supplemental benefit of group mentoring is the opportunity for peer-to-peer mentoring. Similar to the mentor, mentees are able to share perspectives and experiences, which makes for a richer mentoring experience and outcomes.

Interview and Match

Over the past 20 years, Menttium has honed a proprietary match process that begins by collecting profile information via technology. Then, we take it a step further by utilizing a human resource intensive process that consists of conducting interviews with both mentees and mentors in order to match against critical pre-established match criteria. In the end, our interview and match process ensures that new organizational members are matched with a mentor who has the experience, expertise, and critical mentoring capabilities (e.g., asking probing questions) to guide and support the mentee(s) as they embark on their career transitions, build key internal networks, and navigate the organizational culture.

Measurement

In order to determine the Return on Mentoring™ for our clients, we incorporate assessments and checkpoint questionnaires that support the mentee as he or she establishes goals, monitors progress toward goal achievement, and measures outcomes aligned with the organization's business objectives. The framework used to evaluate overall effectiveness and impact of the mentoring experience consists identifying business impact measures, determining the most appropriate methods of data collection, isolating the effects of the program, and determining the return on investment, as well as intangibles (Phillips & Phillips, 2007).

Data is collected from mentees, mentees' managers, and their mentors regarding the mentee's application of learning to the job and organization, as well as observed outcomes related to performance, career progression readiness, relationships with coworkers, engagement, and retention (mentee's intent to stay with the organization). This comprehensive measurement system informs decisions made about mentor training and general program-related process and content. Further, it provides client organizations with information that supports their decision to utilize mentoring as a component of the onboarding process.

Conclusion

In this chapter we have described structured mentoring and its role in the onboarding process. In particular, we described the impact that structured mentoring has on new employees' ability to gain and leverage organizational cultural competence. In the next section, we provide some thoughts on future directions for research on structured mentoring and onboarding.

Future Directions

In 2007 we contributed to the *Handbook of Mentoring at Work* (Ragins & Kram, Eds.) where we outlined future directions and recommendations for research on formal mentoring. Two recommendations were made for more research in the areas of virtual mentoring and global mentoring. As we reviewed the literature published since that time, we found important new contributions to the topic of formal mentoring in the context of virtual mentoring (Bennett, 2009; Leppisaari & Tehnhunen, 2009; Loureiro-Koechlin & Allan, 2009; McWhorter, 2010).

Bennett (2009) and McWhorter (2010) discuss virtual mentoring as part of a discourse on the integration of technology into human resource development practice and research overall. Leppisaari and Tehnhunen (2009) provide a Finnish case with a focus on virtual mentoring for entrepreneurs. Comparisons were made between virtual one-to-one and peer mentoring. Virtual mentoring in general was viewed as supportive of practical professional development, and peer mentoring in particular is preferred over one-to-one mentoring. Further, Loureiro-Koechlin and Allan (2009) studied virtual mentoring as part

of an online learning community used as a means of encouraging women to progress into management positions in the logistics and supply chain industries. Virtual mentoring was analyzed in the context of social theory that concentrated on the relationships between human agency and social structures.

In the context of global mentoring we found studies with a focus on expatriate mentees (Harvey et al., 2010), whereby social learning theory was used as a foundation for the development of a mentoring program. In addition, a study by Lather & Sharma (2010), conducted within an Indian firm, argued that mentoring is a culturally sensitive process and that organizations often neglect broader national and organizational cultural issues. Further, Casado-Lumbereras et al. (2011) studied the influence of culture on mentoring relationships within the software engineering industry. Findings suggested that cultural differences affected both formal and informal mentoring, and that mentors who take into account the cultural differences and were sensitive to culture expectations created a positive experience for the mentee. Further, the authors concluded that mentoring positively impacted the transfer of corporate culture knowledge and how to navigate the subtleties of the informal political system; however, technical competencies were not improved.

Given the proliferation of technology (in particular social media), the emerging strata of generations in the workforce, and the impact of globalization on most US organizations today, more research is needed on onboarding and mentoring in the context of cross-generational and cross-cultural partnerships, focused on ethnicity and national cultural differences along with the utilization of social media as tools to support communication within those partnerships. Specifically, questions we have include: What are the critical success factors for mentoring partnerships that consist of cross-cultural and/ or cross-generational mentors and mentees? In the scenario provided at the beginning of this chapter, some mentees who were partnered with mentors closer in age and experience were more successful in terms of outcomes produced. What are the underlying generational factors that support a partnership's success? In addition, what are the major challenges or obstacles that mentoring partnerships face due to differences in cultural backgrounds of the mentee and mentor?

Further, we found a dearth of empirical studies related to structured mentoring as part of onboarding and business performance. Having a firm understanding of the value contributed by structured mentoring and onboarding to an organization's strategic goals is critical for talent development research in general, and structured mentoring in particular.

Mentoring has been found to contribute to organization-level performance within public sector agencies (Allen, et al., 2009); however, studies in the context of corporate performance are limited. Specific questions we have include: What are the organization-level outcomes for publicly traded and/or privately held corporations? How much of an impact does structured mentoring used as part of onboarding have on organizational-level performance? For example, is there a correlation between individual (mentee) results achieved during mentoring as part of onboarding, and business outcomes such as top line revenue, deceases in costs, or levels of customer satisfaction?

Finally, we note that utilization and outcomes of executive mentoring has received attention from some researchers; however, it is limited. While there are a large number of executive education programs being implemented in major universities, Harvard and Wharton Business School being two prominent examples, in a survey of executive teams (de Haan, et al., 2010) it was revealed that very little development occurring at the executive level is planned or viewed as a priority within executive teams. Clutterbuck and Megginson (1999) indicate that the topic of executive mentoring has focused primarily on sponsorship rather than development. Questions we have include: What are the outcomes of newly promoted or hired executive mentoring as it pertains to business results? What are the motivating factors that would drive executives to utilize mentoring? Would mentors prefer to be paid, as is the case with executive coaching? If so, how would this change the mentoring dynamics? When comparing one-to-one or group (peer) mentoring, what are the outcomes achieved for the executives, as well as for their respective organizations?

Mentoring has been shown to be effective in terms of positive impacts on the onboarding process for both the individuals and organizations involved. In the future, there is an opportunity to expand the research stream on these two important topics to include processes that are virtual and global, outcomes that are at the organizational level, and a focus on executive-level mentees.

References

Allen, T., Eby, L., Poteet, M., Lentz, E., & Lima L. (2004). Career benefits associated with mentoring for protégés: A meta-analysis. *Journal of Applied Psychology, 89*(1), 127–136.

Allen, T. D., Smith, M. A., Mael, F. A., O'Shea, P. G., & Eby, L. T. (2009). Organization-level mentoring and organizational performance within substance abuse centers. *Journal of Management, 35*(5), 1113–1128.

Alvesson, M. (2000). Social identity and the problem of loyalty in knowledge-intensive companies. *Journal of Management Studies, 37*(8), 1101–1123.

Arnold, J. T. (2010). Ramping up onboarding. *HR Magazine, 55*(5), 75–78.

Bauer, T. (2010). Onboarding new employees: Maximizing success. *Society for Human Resource* Management. Retrieved from http://www.shrm.org.

Bauer, T., Bodner, T., Erdogan, B., Truxillo, D., & Tucker, J. (2007). Newcomer adjustment during organizational socialization: A meta-analytic review of antecedents, outcomes, and methods. *Journal of Applied Psychology, 92*, 707–721.

Bennett, E. E. (2009). Virtual HRD: The intersection of knowledge management, culture and intranets. *Advances in Developing Human Resources, 11*(3), 362–374.

Betts, S. C., & Pepe, L. J. (2006). The perceived value of mentoring: Empirical development of a five-factor framework. *Journal of Organizational Culture, Communications and Conflict, 10*(2), 105–115.

Birenbaum, I. (2007, April). Onboarding. Conference Proceedings, Washington DC: Society for Human Resource Management.

Canfield, J. (2010). Social media & corporate culture: Strategic tools for change management. *Social Media Today.* Retrieved from http://socialmediatoday.com/index.php?q=SMC/190846.

Casado-Lumbreras, C., Colomo-Palacios, R., Soto-Acosta, P., and Misra, S. (2011). Culture dimensions in software development industry: The effects of mentoring. *Scientific Research and Essays, 6*(11), 2403–2412.

Chao, G. T. (2007). Mentoring and organizational socialization. In B. R. Ragins & K. E. Kram (Eds.), *The handbook of mentoring at work: Theory, research and practice* (pp. 179–196). Thousand Oaks, CA: Sage Publishing.

Chao, G. T., Walz, P. M., & Gardner, P. D. (1992). Formal and informal mentorships: A comparison of mentoring functions and contrast with non-mentored counterparts. *Personnel Psychology, 45*, 619–636.

Clutterbuck, D. & Megginson, D. (1999). *Executive mentoring and coaching.* MA: Butterworth-Heinemann.

Corporate Executive Board. (2003). Linking employee satisfaction with productivity, performance, and customer satisfaction. *Corporate Leadership Council.* Retrieved from www.corporateleadershipcouncil.com.

Cross, R., Davenport, T., & Cantrell, S. (2003). The social side of performance. *MIT Sloan Management Review, 45*(1), 20–22.

de Haan, E., Wels, I., Lucas, B., Winter, J., & Clutterbuck, D. (2010). Development at the top: Who really cares? Ashridge Research Report. Retrieved from www.ashridge.org/uk.

Deloitte Development Consulting. (2011). *2011 human capital trends.* Alexandria, VA: Author.

Dickter, D. N., Roznowski, M., & Harrison, D. A. (1996). Temporal tempering: An event history analysis of the process of voluntary turnover. *Journal of Applied Psychology, 81*, 705–716.

Ehrich, L.C., Hansford, B., & Tennent, L. (2004). Formal mentoring programs in education and other professions: A review of the literature. *Educational Administration Quarterly, 40*(4), 518–540.

Elbin, S. (2006). *What insiders know about executive success*. CA: Davies-Black Publishing.

Fishel, B. (2009). *Accelerated leadership performance at the top: Onboarding process that leads to employee engagement and retention*. Proceedings from Onboarding Talent Summit, Atlanta, GA.

Goldsmith, M. (2009, May 4). Evaluate how you fit your company culture. Retrieved from www.blogs.hbr.org/goldsmith/2009/05/evaluate_how_you_fit_your_comp.html.

Hall, D. T. (1996). Protean careers of the 21st century. *Academy of Management Executive, 10*(4), 8–16.

Hall, D. T., & Chandler, D. E. (2007). Career cycles and mentoring. In B. R. Ragins & K. E. Kram (Eds.), *The handbook of mentoring at work: Theory, research and practice*. Thousand Oaks, CA: Sage Publishing.

Harvey, M., Napier, N. K., Moeller, M., & Williams, L. A. (2010). Mentoring global dual-career couples: A social learning perspective. *Journal of Applied Social Psychology, 40*(1), 212–240.

Hofstede, G., Hofstede, G. J., & Minkov, M. (2010). *Cultures and organizations: software of the mind* (3rd ed.). NY: McGraw-Hill.

Ibarra, H. (1999). Provisional selves: Experimenting with image and identity in professional adaptation. *Administrative Science Quarterly, 44*, 764–791.

Ibarra, H. (2004). Men and women of the corporation and the change masters: Practical theories for changing times. *Academy of Management Executive, 18*(2), 108–111.

Ibarra, H., & Barbulescu, R. (2010). Identity as narrative: A process model of narrative identity work in macro work role transition. *Academy of Management Review, 35*(1), 135–154.

Kakabadse, A., Bank, J., & Vinnicombe, S. (2004). *Working in organizations* (2nd ed.). Burlington, VT: Gower Publishing Company.

Kammeyer-Mueller, J. D., & Judge, T. A. (2008). A quantitative review of mentoring research: Test of a model. *Journal of Vocational Behavior, 73*, 269–283.

Kitayama, S., & Cohen, D. (Eds.). (2007). *Handbook of cultural psychology*. NY: Guilford Press.

Lather, A. S., & Sharma, H. (2010). Impact of national and organizational culture on mentoring environment in Indian context. *International Journal of Indian Culture and Business Management, 3*(4), 434–448.

Leppisaari, I., & Tenhunen, M. L. (2009). Searching for e-mentoring practices for SME staff development. *Service Business, 3*(2), 189–207.

Levin, B. (2008). On-demand workforce-communications technologies help organizations meet critical business goals. *Employment Relations Today, 35*(2), 43–50.

Loureiro-Koechlin, C., & Allan, B. (2009, June). Time, space and structure in an e-learning and e-mentoring project. *British Journal of Educational Technology, 41*(5), 721–735.

Martin, M., & Vaughn, B. (2007). Cultural Competence. *Strategic Diversity & Inclusion Management Magazine*. San Francisco, CA: DTUI Publications

McWhorter, R. R. (2010). Exploring the emergence of virtual human resource development. *Advances in Developing Human Resources, 12*(6), 623–631.

Meister, J. C., & Willyerd, K. (2010). *The 2020 Workplace: How innovative companies attract, develop, and keep tomorrow's employees today*. NY: HarperCollins.

Peverelli, P. (2004, August) *Creating corporate space: In search of Chinese corporate identity*. Retrieved from http://personal.vu.nl/p.j.peverelli/page3.html.

Phillips, J. J., & Pulliam Phillips, P. (2007). *The value of learning: How organizations capture value and ROI*. San Francisco, CA: John Wiley & Sons, Inc.

Schein, E. H. (1985). *Organizational culture and leadership*. San Francisco: Jossey-Bass.

Schein, E. H. (2009). *Corporate culture survival guide*. San Francisco: Jossey-Bass.

Schrodt, P., Cawyer, C. S., & Sanders, R. (2003). An examination of academic mentoring behaviors and new faculty members' satisfaction with socialization and tenure and promotion processes. *Communication Education, 52*, 17–29.

Stahl, G. K., & Voigt, A. (2008). Do cultural differences matter in mergers and acquisitions? A tentative model and examination. *Organization Science, 19*(1), 160–176.

Stimpson, J. 2009. On boarding new staff. *Practical Accountant, 42*(4), 18–28.

Sujansky, J. G., & Ferri-Reed, J. (2010). Motivating Millennials: They have different expectations. *Sales and Service Excellence, 10*(1), 6.

Ulrich, D., & Brockbank, W. (2005). *The HR value proposition*. Boston, MA: Harvard Business School Press.

US Department of Education, National Center for Education Statistics. (2007). *Digest of education statistics,* Table 258. Washington, DC: US Department of Education. Retrieved from http://nces.ed.gov/Programs/digest/d07/tables/xls/tabn258.xls.

Wanberg, C. R., Kammeyer-Mueller, J., & Marchese, M. (2006). Mentor and protégé predictors and outcomes of mentoring in a formal mentoring program. *Journal of Vocational Behavior, 69*(3), 410–423.

Wanberg, C. R., Welsh, E. T., & Kammeyer-Mueller, J. (2007). Protégé and mentor self-disclosure: Levels and outcomes within formal mentoring dyads in a corporate context. *Journal of Vocational Behavior, 70*(2), 398–412.

Waters, L. M., McCabe, M., Kiellerup, D., & Kiellerup S. (2002). The role of formal mentoring on business success and self-esteem in participants of a new business start-up program. *Journal of Business and Psychology, 17*(1), 107.

Williams, R. (2003). *Mellon learning curve research study*. New York: Mellon Corp.

PART 7

Conclusions

Moving Forward: Next Steps for Advancing the Research and Practice of Employee Socialization

Connie R. Wanberg *and* Yongjun Choi

Abstract

This chapter briefly describes the advances in the area of organizational socialization and highlights a number of important future research directions outlined by the preceding chapters within this handbook. Next directions for research include new antecedents and outcomes of newcomer socialization, how to explore socialization process and dynamics in conjunction with time issues, and how to expand the lessons from newcomer socialization to individuals experiencing different types of newness, such as expatriates. In addition, the authors provide four suggestions for socialization researchers: tie research to socialization, draw upon nonsocialization areas of research, connect different areas of socialization research, and be ambitious. Implications for socialization practitioners and organizations are discussed.

Key Words: socialization, adjustment, onboarding, new employees, newcomers, future research

This handbook offered an overview of the current research and practice of employee socialization into new roles. A great deal of territory was covered. The socialization experience was portrayed as variously challenging, uncomfortable, exciting, stressful, and full of opportunity for the newcomer. New employees may feel welcome or they may feel insecure, lonely, and left out. They may quickly gain an understanding of their role within the organization and how it fits in with other roles, or they may flounder, uncertain about priorities, how they are doing, and whether or not their work is appreciated.

Chapters portrayed individual, organizational, and situational factors that facilitate versus hamper employee socialization, and the types of outcomes organizations can expect if employees adapt more quickly and easily to new roles. We now draw a close to the discussion with remarks about progress and future work in this area. First, we describe the thought leadership provided by these chapters and the associated implications for new research. Second, we provide some general thoughts and observations

for researchers to consider as they aim to continue the momentum and progress of this literature. Finally, we discuss the implications of this volume for socialization practice within organizations.

Research: Progress and Next Directions

It is heartening to see the progress this literature has made in the last 20 years. A solid understanding is emerging of the socialization process and how companies, peers and supervisors, and new employees themselves can facilitate this process. Yet, there is still work to be done with respect to solidifying our understanding of the antecedents and outcomes of successful socialization, the process and mechanisms through which socialization occurs, the dynamics of the process, and how this process applies to new role experiences beyond new hires.

Antecedents of Newcomer Adjustment

Newcomer adjustment involves the extent to which new employees understand, master, and feel confident about their job and task demands. The newcomer should also feel comfortable and socially accepted by the members of the work group and perceive a good fit between his/her skills and values and that of the job and organization (Bauer, Bodner, Erdogan, Truxillo, & Tucker, 2007; Klein & Heuser, 2008). Three main classes of variables have been studied as antecedents of newcomer adjustment: organizational practices or tactics, characteristics and behaviors of the newcomer, and the role of other parties such as coworkers and supervisors. There is significant opportunity to move the research ahead in each of these antecedent categories.

Let's start with organizational practices and tactics. Although socialization tactics undertaken by the organization have received a great deal of attention from socialization researchers (e.g., Jones, 1986; Van Maanen & Schein, 1979), this volume provides a reconceptualization and refinement of these tactics. In Chapter 3, Saks and Gruman argue that the literature on socialization tactics is highly fragmented, leaving many questions unanswered about which organizational practices are best for specific desired outcomes, and how long newcomers need help with their socialization. The authors introduce 17 socialization resources that organizations can provide to enhance the newcomer experience and suggest that the delineation of these resources will make it easier to move research ahead on issues such as what different types of newcomers need when they enter an organization. Klein and Polin (Chapter 14) suggest that research can look beyond Van Maanen and Schein's (1979) socialization tactics by delineating specific socialization practices. According to Klein and Polin, research must drill down to provide a detailed understanding of what *specific activities* and what *combinations of activities* are most effective, as well as *when* and *from whom* they should be offered to organizational newcomers.

Many chapters within the handbook delineate ways in which newcomer characteristics and behaviors are important to the socialization experience. Cooper-Thomas and Burke (Chapter 4) provide a valuable overview of the research to date on employee proactivity in the socialization process. During the course of this review, the authors suggest several provoking questions about proactive behavior among newcomers, such as: How do established employees within the organization (e.g., coworkers) react to newcomer proactive behavior? Do they continue to proactively offer help to the newcomer, or do they begin to sit back and wait for the newcomer to come to them? When are proactive behaviors beneficial to the individual and organization, and

when might they backfire or produce negative consequences? Feldman (Chapter 11) similarly argues it will be useful for research to examine the impact of newcomer proactivity on insiders, suggesting there is a need to understand when insiders may accept versus reject newcomer initiative.

In reality, newcomers do not always take initiative. Why do some individuals proactively seek information and feedback, solicit advice when needed, and work to build their networks, while others don't? Chapters in this handbook provide insight into individual differences and organizational factors that may be related to newcomers being less proactive. Drawing from the impression management literature, Ashford and Nurmohamed (Chapter 2) suggest that organizational values can play significant roles in determining newcomer's proactive behaviors. In other words, since newcomers choose behaviors consistent with organizational values, it is very likely that newcomer proactivity is determined by whether organizations or newcomers' supervisors value initiative on the part of newcomers. Hurst, Kammeyer-Mueller, and Livingston (Chapter 7) suggest that newcomers may worry about the impressions they give others when they ask for help (i.e., disclosing ignorance can be difficult). These authors also propose that newcomers who have high disparity (e.g., pay, income, and status) and/or separation diversity (e.g., opinions, beliefs, and values) may be especially reluctant to be proactive. The framework presented by Hurst et al. raises additional questions to be explored in future research regarding the role of diversity in the socialization process, such as: To what extent and under what conditions does newcomer diversity create increased workgroup conflict or exclusion and lack of support for the newcomer? How do certain moderators, such as organizational culture or newcomer personality, facilitate or hurt the successful integration of a diverse newcomer?

Finally, multiple authors in this handbook argue that we need to pay more attention to how coworkers, supervisors, and broader social networks play a role in the socialization process. Jokisaari and Nurmi (Chapter 5) introduce a theoretical framework for understanding how newcomer networks are related to learning, sensemaking, and success in the organization. These authors raise several questions that can be explored in future research, including: How do social networks change for organizational newcomers over time? What factors explain why some individuals grow networks more successfully than others? How long does it take newcomers to become a valuable social tie for organizational veterans? What are the predictors and outcomes of supervisory support of newcomer network development? Ashford and Nurmohamed (Chapter 2) suggest it is important to more concretely explore coworkers' and supervisors' roles as sources of socialization. Saks and Gruman (Chapter 3) note that in addition to paying attention to the role of coworkers and supervisors, attention should be paid to the socializing forces of other socialization agents such as members in other departments, subordinates, customers, and clients. Expatriate research has similarly ignored how and through what processes peers (i.e., host country nationals; HCNs) help expatriates adjust to their new work roles. Focusing especially on knowledge acquisition, Toh, DeNisi, and Leonardelli (Chapter 12) suggest that expatriate research should better explicate how knowledge flows occur between HCNs and expatriates. When are expatriates more willing to learn from HCNs?

Socialization Outcomes

How does socialization affect important individual and organizational outcomes? A wide array of proximal (e.g., role clarity, self-efficacy, and social acceptance) and distal (e.g., job performance, job satisfaction, organizational commitment, intentions to leave the organization, and actual turnover) outcomes have been studied in this literature (Bauer et al., 2007). The chapters in this handbook make apparent that socialization matters to these outcomes, and explicate the need to dig deeper into questions of how and under what conditions socialization facilitates versus hinders these outcomes.

A few chapters suggest that future research will benefit from examining a broader scope of individual and organizational outcomes. For example, Bauer and Erdogan (Chapter 6) note that work–life balance can be affected during the first several months of a newcomer's adjustment to a new role. Individuals beginning a new job may spend more time away from home as they try to learn their new roles and get to know new coworkers. In addition, the authors note that having newcomers in the workplace may affect supervisor levels of stress and well-being. During newcomer socialization, supervisors have extra work on their plates as they have to clarify the roles of the newcomer, make introductions, and coordinate new work teams. Bauer and Erdogan also suggest it is important for researchers to explore how newcomers affect established social relationships within the organization. For instance,

when and under what conditions do newcomers change the dynamics of an existing work group?

The primary focus of Feldman (Chapter 11) is on this latter point, the impact of newcomer socialization on individuals already working within the organization. Feldman suggests that we have not sufficiently studied how socialization tactics influence insiders' perceptions about the newcomer. For example, we know that individualized socialization is associated with higher newcomer proactivity. Do the practices that organizations use also have implications for how organizational veterans view the newcomer? Feldman also suggests that future research should consider the time and energy it takes organizational veterans to socialize newcomers, and how this may affect their behavior toward newcomers. For example, he suggests that especially when newcomers get treated as "prima donnas," organizational veterans may react with frustration, impatience, and even aggressive behavior. Finally, he calls for more research on how the entry of one or a small number of disruptive new hires may have dysfunctional consequences for a workgroup.

van Vianen and De Pater (Chapter 8) address newcomer perceptions of person–organizational (PO) fit, suggesting that there is opportunity for a better understanding of the antecedents and outcome of perceptions of fit. They argue there are many rich questions to explore, such as how, when, and why newcomers' PO fit perceptions change over time, and how newcomers react and adapt to low perceived fit. Do individuals change their own characteristics or values, and if so under what conditions, or do they primarily reframe or modify their new environment? What processes are involved in the formation of PO fit perceptions? Because PO fit is fundamentally important to outcomes such as job satisfaction, commitment, and retention, such avenues of research are worth pursuing.

It is likely that social integration, as an outcome, matters more than we have explicated in the literature. Social integration of newcomers has been emphasized in the socialization literature less than job performance factors such as role clarity and task mastery. Although learning the ropes is critical for newcomers, relying solely or heavily on learning aspects of socialization might be limiting, since organizations consist of many social and personal interactions among members. Chapters in this handbook provide ideas about when the social integration of newcomers may be particularly important. Hurst et al. (Chapter 7) note that newcomers who are different from insiders (i.e., who have high diversity) are less likely to be socially accepted, which leads them to be excluded from support networks in their groups. The extent to which newcomers are socially accepted by insiders may also influence whether newcomers can be change agents (Bauer & Erdogan, Chapter 6). In a similar vein, newcomers' PO fit after entry can be conceptualized as social acceptance, since organizational cultures or values are constructed and held by organizational members (i.e., insiders; van Vianen & De Pater, Chapter 8). Future research should look more closely at newcomer social integration as a key outcome of PO fit. Beyond social integration, organizational socialization research should examine how quickly newcomers earn coworkers' and supervisors' respect and trust. To the extent that a predecessor has been irresponsible, difficult, or not very good at his or her job, this may be easier. To the extent that a predecessor was beloved or to the extent the newcomer is not introduced properly to the work group, this may be more challenging.

Process, Time, and Dynamics

The socialization literature has proposed several process models, explicating *how* and *through what mechanisms* individuals adapt to and learn a new job. For example, the early socialization literature proposed process models from both organizational (e.g., Feldman, 1981) and newcomer perspectives (e.g., Miller & Jablin, 1991). More recently, Bauer et al. (2007) found that role clarity, self-efficacy, and social acceptance mediated the relationship between newcomer information seeking and socialization tactics and more distal outcomes (e.g., job performance and job satisfaction). Saks, Uggerslev, and Fassina (2007) demonstrated that proximal outcomes (e.g., role ambiguity, role conflict, and fit perceptions) partially mediate the relationships between socialization tactics and distal outcomes (e.g., role orientation, job satisfaction, organizational commitment, intentions to quit, and job performance).

Yet, the chapters in this handbook suggest we have a lot more to learn about the socialization process. Toh et al. (Chapter 12) suggest we need to know more about the psychological processes involved in knowledge transfers between expatriates and HCNs. In addition, underlying mechanisms in the socialization process are less known. For example, what are the processes through which diversity influences the development of interpersonal relationships between newcomers and their coworkers (e.g., information elaboration process, interpersonal conflict, and social exclusion; Hurst et al., Chapter 7)?

There is also a call for research about the two-way processes between newcomers and insiders. Whereas most socialization literature focuses on the roles of insiders for helping newcomer socialization, Feldman (Chapter 11) emphasizes socialization as mutual influence process. That is, the authors argue that future research should pay special attention to the process of how newcomers influence insiders.

In another discussion of the process of socialization, Ashford and Nurmohamed (Chapter 2) suggest that future research should elucidate the role of newcomer cognitive and affective experiences during the first months in a new job. Over time, the socialization literature has incorporated affective outcomes such as job satisfaction and organizational commitment, but has not sufficiently examined how newcomers feel and display emotions (for a review of emotions in socialization, see Ashforth & Saks, 2002). Ashford and Nurmohamed point out emotions such as excitement, disappointment, doubt, alienation, anxiety, and stress play a substantial role in the newcomer experience. Understanding the extent to which individuals experience these emotions and how they manage them may be valuable to the socialization literature. While cognitive processes have been emphasized more than affective processes, Ashford and Nurmohamed suggest that there is still ample opportunity to develop a deeper understanding of newcomers' cognitive experiences. They suggest, for example, that the extensive literature on cognitive heuristics should be applied to the experience of socialization. For example, newcomers may allow prominent early experiences to create inaccurate beliefs or premature impressions.

Tied closely to the topic of process is dynamics. Socialization is a fundamentally dynamic process, and there are many important questions to be answered about how learning, role clarity, self-efficacy, social integration, and adjustment evolve over time as individuals start a new job. Ashforth (Chapter 9) stimulates a myriad of time and process related questions, such as: What individual and situational factors facilitate faster learning among newcomers? What factors might disrupt the learning trajectory of a newcomer? How can we better understand the importance and consequences of discrete, episodic events (such as a lunch invitation, or being forgiven for making a major error) that occur during the first few months of a newcomer's tenure? Even more complex, how can we learn more about event sequencing and how certain events and occurrences foster self-efficacy and credibility on the part of the newcomer, thereby increasing the likelihood of further success within the organization?

The need to more fully explicate how socialization plays out over time was also stressed by other authors in this handbook. For example, Toh et al. (Chapter 12) note a need to delineate how relationships between HCNs and expatriates develop and grow after the expatriate's organizational entry. Jokisaari and Nurmi (Chapter 5) note a need to explore the reciprocal exchange between newcomers' socialization (e.g., learning) and their social networks, as well as how newcomers' positions in social networks develop over time. Other questions about the evolution of the socialization process that can be explored include: How are newcomers' fit perceptions shaped over time (van Vianen & De Pater, Chapter 8) and how can disruptive newcomers influence a work group (Feldman, Chapter 11)?

In order to correctly study process, time, and dynamics issues, it is imperative to carefully consider research design and analysis issues (e.g., Ashford & Nurmohamed, Chapter 2; Ashforth, Chapter 9; Vancouver & Warren, Chapter 10). Vancouver and Warren offer an excellent overview of methodological issues pertaining to doing research in the socialization area. The chapter covers the way we should understand the socialization phenomena and links that to methodological approaches in socialization research, such as experimental or longitudinal designs, computational models, and qualitative methods. Specifically, experience sampling methods or ethnographic methods may be fruitful avenues for future research to explore socialization dynamics (Ashford & Nurmohamed, Chapter 2).

Socialization Beyond the Newcomer

The socialization literature, due to its focus on beginning new roles, can be applied to other types of newcomer experiences such as being an expatriate, being promoted into a higher level job, and being a new customer. For example, similar to organizational newcomers, expatriates are beginning a new role. It may be with the same organization but it is within a new (and international) location. In the expatriate adjustment process, Toh et al. (Chapter 12) argue that, whereas expatriate literature has mainly focused on how expatriates transfer their knowledge to HCNs, it is equally critical to understand the roles of HCNs, as socializing agents, in facilitating the information sharing between HCNs and expatriates. For this, it is forward-looking to explore the roles of organizations, such as how organizations

establish procedural justice with respect to expatriate work. In addition, it seems desirable to incorporate contextual (corporate or national) factors in expatriate adjustment research. For instance, do expatriates in recently merged companies go through different adjustment processes? What are the most effective socialization tactics for expatriates in those new situations? Or, do we need different tactics for them? Beyond commonly known expatriates, the authors note that future research should pay more attention to other types of expatriates such as inpatriates, repatriates, self-initiated expatriates, expatriates from small firms, and female expatriates who are likely to have different motivations to expatriate assignments from normal expatriates. Do these other types of expatriates go through the same or different socialization process?

The socialization literature can also be applied to the experience of individuals newly promoted into *higher level jobs*. Do newly promoted executives experience the same socialization process as entry-level new hires? Many chapters in this handbook imply that the socialization process for those higher level newcomers can be somewhat different from the entry-level newcomer socialization process. Conger (Chapter 16) argues that socializing newly promoted individuals into their new roles is not very common. Due to disparity diversity, Hurst et al. (Chapter 7) note that higher level newcomers are especially less likely to get much help from others, since they are supposed to be in charge and know how everything works. Collectively, it seems quite useful to explore the newcomer socialization process involved when individuals move into higher level positions.

Rollag (Chapter 13) provides several ideas about how socialization theory can be applied to the new customer experience. Are the socialization tactics and practices outlined for new employees generalizable to new customers? Which practices are associated with new customer satisfaction and loyalty? When should companies socialize new customers individually versus in groups? Rollag notes that researchers should aim to develop conceptual models that outline factors (i.e., socialization tactics, customer characteristics, and contextual variables) associated with important new customer outcomes.

General Remarks about Research on Socialization

There are many ideas in this handbook for future research. At a much more general level, we have some additional thoughts and suggestions for researchers to consider as they design and write up research on this topic. Specifically, we propose four suggestions for socialization researchers: tie research to socialization, draw upon nonsocialization areas of research, connect different areas of socialization research, and be ambitious.

Tie Research to Socialization

To some extent, it is difficult to ensure that socialization research is truly tied to the context of an individual *starting a new job*. This is a strange statement to make! What do we mean by this? We mean that investigators should take care to think about why what they are studying is particularly important to *newcomers,* and not just for *any employee* (i.e., regardless of how long they have been with an organization). For example, perhaps you are studying the relationship between coworker social support and newcomer job satisfaction. You find a positive relationship. Because social support is important for *all* employees, it is important to demonstrate that social support is related to an outcome unique to newcomers, such as how quickly they adjust or learn the ropes at their new job. Job satisfaction would be an appropriate outcome in this hypothetical study, but something in the study should tie the hypotheses uniquely to the newcomer experience. Most studies do make this distinction, yet from time to time there are examples of researchers examining relationships within the socialization context without a unique argument for why it is of particular importance in the newcomer context.

Connect Different Areas of Socialization Research

While tying research explicitly to the socialization context, researchers must also comprehensively build upon previous research efforts within the socialization literature. This, too, seems obvious. Yet, there is some useful insight in the statement. Saks and Gruman (Chapter 3) stress this point with respect to socialization practices, suggesting that each of the socialization practices they review (orientation programs, training programs, socialization tactics, job characteristics, and socialization agents) have been independently studied in the socialization literature. They note that the socialization literature is less integrated within itself than is desirable, noting *"In fact, the only integration across topics in the socialization literature seems to have been a handful of studies that investigated newcomer proactive behaviors in combination with socialization tactics."* As an example, these authors make the argument

that we do not really know much with respect to what training content for newcomers is important. Training content should draw directly upon what we know is important about the socialization process. Researchers studying socialization should know the socialization literature well, not just a small pocket of previous research related to the specific question they are asking.

Draw Upon Nonsocialization Areas of Research

While researchers should know the socialization literature well and draw upon it carefully, there are many studies and theories related to work, emotions, social support, learning, diversity, careers, and other areas that may help develop insight about socialization. We encourage socialization researchers to make ample use of other literatures. Drawing upon other literatures can help researchers to ask new questions, develop the socialization literature more fully, and avoid recreating concepts that have been described in other literatures. For example, we agree with Saks and Gruman (Chapter 3) when they suggest that the literature needs a comprehensive model or framework that portrays how different socialization agents contribute to successful new employee adjustment. Such a framework could draw upon the social support literature (e.g., Lakey & Cohen, 2000; Sarason, Sarason, & Pierce, 1990; Viswesvaran, Sanchez, & Fisher, 1999), the burgeoning literature on work relationships (Dutton & Ragins, 2007), and research on the development of relationships in other new contexts, such as starting college (Brissette, Scheier, & Carver, 2002; Hays, 1985). It is possible that there is something unique about relationships and support of newcomers, something that has not been uncovered in other areas in which interpersonal relationships and social support has been studied, yet these literatures offer a solid base from which to begin.

Most recently, synergies between the socialization literature and the following literatures have been recognized: PO fit (van Vianen & De Pater, Chapter 8), expatriation (Toh et al., Chapter 12), mentoring (Dixon, Sontag, & Vappie, Chapter 18), social networks (Jokisaari & Nurmi, Chapter 5), and diversity (Hurst et al., Chapter 7). The cross-fertilization of information across these related literatures is valuable and helps to create new research directions and insights.

Be Ambitious

A lot goes into designing a good study. The contribution that a study brings to the literature, as well as its constructs, mediators, moderators, and theoretical arguments, must be thought through carefully. The design of the study must be rigorous. Authors must think carefully about the appropriateness of the sample and defend the content, source, and timing of the measurements they use. The body of literature that must be consulted to create and form sound hypotheses is growing exponentially. Studies can suffer if authors tackle too much (i.e., too many hypotheses, too many constructs, or too many paths). Yet, they can also suffer if authors present hypotheses that are too obvious or simplistic, or if the associated literature review and argumentation are not sufficiently rich.

This, however, all adds up to a constructive and exciting challenge. Although significant progress has been made in the socialization literature in the last 20 years, there are still many opportunities. A wealth of ideas was provided within the chapters in this handbook for continued research in the socialization area. As researchers implement these and other new directions, they can consider the suggestions and advice outlined by Colquitt and George (2011). Specifically, they urge researchers to consider the following issues when launching a research study: *(1)* significance (is the focus of the study in some way bold, unconventional, or on an unresolved issue?); *(2)* novelty (am I presenting any new ideas, insights, or new directions?); *(3)* curiosity (is the study interesting, does it go beyond the obvious?); *(4)* scope (are you being too narrow or slicing your data too thin?); and *(5)* actionability (will your study offer insights for practice?). At times, good research ideas can be developed by drawing upon real life experience and examining where there are gaps within the literature in knowledge.

Practice Implications

Chapters in this handbook provide a number of practical implications for managers and organizations. It is particularly important to highlight Klein and Polin's chapter (Chapter 14), which portrays a wealth of information about the current use of onboarding practices in organizations. While most organizations are aware of the importance of onboarding programs, most do not develop their programs sufficiently. Here, we highlight other useful practice-based information and suggestions presented in this handbook.

First, several chapters offer a *broad picture* of how to develop, implement, and evaluate onboarding programs with real examples and cases, such as Pricewaterhouse Coopers (PwC; Saks and Gruman,

Chapter 3), a Big Ten university (the University of Minnesota; Doepner-Hove, Chapter 15), and the Bank of America and Toyota (Conger, Chapter 16). Doepner-Hove (Chapter 15) offers a comprehensive onboarding program development history, from the beginning to how well each onboarding practice worked out in a Big Ten university. Dixon et al. (Chapter 18) provide information on how to design mentoring programs for the purpose of newcomer socialization, especially for those in higher rank positions. Socialization Resources Theory (SRT) by Saks and Gruman (Chapter 3) offers a nice framework to develop, monitor, and evaluate onboarding programs. Managers can audit their organizational socialization porgrams with the sample questions they provide. Lastly, Conger (Chapter 16) provides two valuable cases explicating the socialization process for senior level newcomers such as executives and plant managers. Given the importance of leadership in organizations, the two cases suggest a number of factors to consider when designing socialization programs for upper echelon leaders, such as the importance of quality interaction between newcomers (i.e., new leaders) and their stakeholders. These comprehensive frameworks would be helpful for organizations that are either starting new onboarding programs or refining them.

Second, it is important for organizations to be *well prepared* for developing and implementing onboarding programs. Doepner-Hove (Chapter 15) suggests that in order to deliver onboarding programs efficiently and effectively, it is critical to have quality partnerships with key organizational units (e.g., HR department) and existing programs. In addition, to build an onboarding program it may be important to hire a person into a full-time position for onboarding program development. Hiring a manager to lead onboarding programs is also emphasized in Bradt (Chapter 17).

Third, chapters provide insightful practical implications for *enhancing onboarding program effectiveness* and *facilitating newcomer socialization*. Bradt (Chapter 17) suggests that organizations should align their efforts in recruitment, orientation, training, and management efforts in one direction, integrated to into one "Total Onboarding Program." Given that those activities are mostly disconnected in organizations, positive synergy effects are expected. It is also critical for organizations to build up a positive diversity climate and enhance social support so that minority newcomers can successfully adjust to workplace (Hurst et al., Chapter 7). For expatriates, Toh et al. (Chapter 12) suggest that, in order to promote expatriate adjustment, colleagues in the host country should be encouraged to share information with expatriates. Organizations should be cognizant of host country nationals as important sources of knowledge and help expatriates to have effective interactions with these individuals by emphasizing a cooperative atmosphere for both expatriates and HCNs. Formal or informal reward systems might also be established to encourage host country nationals to assist with expatriate socialization.

References

Ashforth, B. E., & Saks, A. M. (2002). Feeling your way: Emotion and organizational entry. In R. G. Lord, R. J. Klimoski, & R. Kanfer (Eds.), *Emotions in the workplace* (pp. 331–369). San Francisco, CA: Jossey-Bass.

Bauer, T. N., Bodner, T., Erdogan, B., Truxillo, D. M., & Tucker, J. S. (2007). Newcomer adjustment during organizational socialization: A meta-analytic review of antecedents, outcomes, and methods. *Journal of Applied Psychology, 92,* 707–721.

Brissette, I., Scheier, M. F., & Carver, C. S. (2002). The role of optimism in social network development, coping, and psychological adjustment during a life transition. *Journal of Personality and Social Psychology, 82,* 102–111.

Colquitt, J. A., & George, G. (2011). From the editors: Publishing in AMJ part 1 topic choice. *Academy of Management Journal, 54,* 432–435.

Dutton, J. E., & Ragins, B. R. (2007). *Exploring positive relationships at work: Building a theoretical and research foundation.* Mahwah, NJ: Lawrence Erlbaum Associates.

Feldman, D. C. (1981). The multiple socialization of organization members. *Academy of Management Review, 6,* 309–318.

Hays, R. B. (1985). A longitudinal study of friendship development. *Journal of Personality and Social Psychology, 48,* 909–924.

Jones, G. R. (1986). Socialization tactics, self-efficacy, and newcomers' adjustments to organizations. *Academy of Management Journal, 29,* 262–279.

Klein, H. J., & Heuser, A. E. (2008). The learning of socialization content: A framework for researching orientating practices. In J. J. Martocchio (Ed.), *Research in Personnel and Human Resources Management* (Vol. 27, pp. 279–336). Bradford, UK: Emerald.

Lakey, B., & Cohen, S. (2000). Social support theory and measurement. In S. Cohen, L. G. Underwood, & B. H. Gottlieb (Eds.), *Social support measurement and interventions: A guide for health and social scientists* (pp. 29–52). New York, NY: Oxford University Press.

Miller, V. D., & Jablin, F. M. (1991). Information seeking during organizational entry: Influences, tactics, and a model of the process. *Academy of Management Review, 16,* 92–120.

Saks, A. M., Uggerslev, K. L., & Fassina, N. E. (2007). Socialization tactics and newcomer adjustment: A meta-analytic review and test of a model. *Journal of Vocational Behavior, 70,* 413–446.

Sarason, B. R., Sarason, I. G., & Pierce, G. R. (1990*). Social support: An interactional view.* New York, NY: Wiley.

Van Maanen, J., & Schein, E. H. (1979). Toward a theory of organizational socialization, In B. M. Staw (Ed.), *Research in Organizational Behavior,* (Vol. 1, pp. 209–264). Greenwich, CT: JAI Press.

Visweswaran, C., Sanchez, J. I., & Fisher, J. (1999). The role of social support in the process of work stress: A meta-analysis. *Journal of Vocational Behavior, 54,* 314–334.

INDEX

A

acceptance by insiders, 100
  organizational change and, by
    newcomers, 106
acculturation onboarding, 318
accumulation, in scientific process, 187
Adams, Douglas, 8, 20
adaptability. *See* dispositional adaptability
adjustment, of expatriates, 233–235
  general, 233
  HCN role in, 235
  interaction, 233
  knowledge transfers through, 234–235
  as learning process, 233
  with mentors, 235
  models for, 233–235
  socialization literature on, 234
  stage of, 233
  stressor-stress-strain framework for,
    233, 234
  work, 233
adjustment, socialization and, 13.
    See also adjustment, of expatriates;
    diversity, adjustment processes
    with
  acceptance by insiders in, 100
  antecedents of, 339–341
  emotions during, 17
  hangover effect with, 174
  during honeymoon period, 174
  individual/organizational facilitation
    in, 12–13
  job turnover during, 86–87
  needs of newcomers as influence on,
    175
  newcomer adjustment model for,
    12, 35–36
  for newcomers, to work environment,
    80
  organizational commitment level
    during, 86
  perceived overqualification during, 107
  perception of social integration during,
    86

performance self-efficacy during, 101
  proximal newcomer, 162
  proximal outcomes for, 100–101
  Pygmalion effect in, 16
  role clarity in, 100–101
  socialization tactics and, 35–36
  social networking and, 86–87
  stability *versus* instability and, as
    influence on, 173–175
  stage models for, 175
  theory of work adjustment and, 139
  over time, 172–175
  unpredictable role demands and, 174
  voluntary turnover during, 86–87
affective experiences, of newcomers,
  17–18
  alternative methodologies for, 18
  learning processes and, 17–18
  positive framing for, 17
  self-regulatory tactics after, 17
African American women, diversity
  anxiety for, 120
age, newcomer proactive behavior and, 67
American Society for Training and
  Development, 3
anticipated organizational tenure, 167
anticipatory customer socialization,
  253–254
  expectations of customers in, 253–254
anticipatory socialization, 9, 13, 47
  socialization over time and, 166
anxiety
  for African American women, diversity
    and, 120
  during training programs, 33–34
  in uncertainty reduction theory, 28
Apple Retail Stores, 257–258
  customer training programs, 258
  product design, 258
  store design, 258
appraisal, of newcomers. *See* comparative
  appraisal
appreciation. *See* recognition and
  appreciation, in SRT

approachability improvement strategies,
  256
articulation-based theory, for
  socialization, 9
ASA framework. *See* Attraction-Selection-
  Attrition framework
Asia, expatriates from, 243
assignments. *See* job assignments
attitudes of insiders, towards organization,
  218–220
  of cultural values, 219–220
  through external comparisons, 219
  global perceptions, 219
  during recruitment process, 219
  through scanning, 219
  through sensemaking of organization,
    218–219
  specific perceptions, 219
Attraction-Selection-Attrition (ASA)
  framework
  conflict in, 141
  in PO fit, 141
autonomy, as job characteristic, 38, 38
availability improvement strategies, 256

B

Bank of America, executive socialization
  practices, 305–311
  challenge identification in,
    307–308
  check-in process for, 309–310
  design focus of, 305
  development history of, 305
  entry phase, 307–309
  final phase of, 310–311
  integration sessions in, 309
  midpoint phase of, 309–310
  organizational culture for, 306
  orientation forums in, 307
  peer coaches, 307
  selection phase of, 306–307
  tools and processes in, 307
  turnover rates, 305
behavioral proactive behaviors, 171

Behaviors, Relationships, Attitudes, Values and work Environment (BRAVE), 318–319
behind-the-scenes networking, 321
bias
    in cognitive experiences, 17
    in qualitative method research, 201–202
Bleustein, Jeff, 259
blogs, for newcomers, 322
Blue Nile, 257
borrowed social capital, 90
boss relationship building, 61
branding, for comprehensive onboarding program, 292–293
BRAVE. *See* Behaviors, Relationships, Attitudes, Values and work Environment
brokers, 320
Bruininks, Robert, 289
buddy systems
    for newcomers, 322
    in onboarding guide activities, 274

C

career paths, structured mentoring and, 328–329
categorization-elaboration (CEM) model, 121
central connectors, 320
chain of socialization, 220–221
Chao et al. socialization scale, 101–102
check-in systems
    for Bank of America, 309–310
    for newcomers, 323
checklists, in onboarding literature, 276
Circles mentoring program, 326, 327–328, 332
citizenship behaviors
    in customer role, 252
    after diversity adjustment processes, 131
    separation diversity and, 131
Clarke, Arthur C., 20
classification scheme, for socialization tactics, 35–37
clock time
    definition of, 162
    event time compared to, 162–165
cognitive diversity, 123
cognitive experiences, of newcomers, 17–18
    alternative methodologies for, 18
    heuristics and biases in, 17
    learning processes and, 17–18
cognitive proactive behaviors, 171
cohesion. *See* group cohesion
cohort effects, 203
cohorts, for newcomers, 322
collective identity, manager strategies for, 133
collective role transitions, 168
collective socialization tactics, 35
commitment, to organizations
    after diversity adjustment processes, 130

after socialization adjustment, 86
common method bias reduction, 197
comparative appraisal, 216
complementary fit, 139
computation models, for research, 202
computer-based orientation programs, 32
concealment, of social identity, 120–121
    passing as part of majority, 121
    social stigma as cause of, 121
confidence, uncertainty reduction theory and, 28
conflict. *See also* work-life conflict
    in ASA framework, 141
    from cognitive diversity, 123
    from disparity diversity, 123
    from diversity, socialization and, 122–123
    from relationships, 122
    from separation diversity, 122–123
    task-based, 122
consensus. *See* symbolic consensus
Construal Level Theory, 142–143
construct validity, 189
    contamination in, 190
    deficiency in, 190
    for experimental research design, 200
    threats to, 190
    treatment diffusion in, 190
contamination
    in construct validity, 190
    of research descriptions, 193
content dimension, of socialization tactics, 35, 145
    learning in, 162
    onboarding and, 281
context dimension, of socialization tactics, 35, 145
control, in socialization literature, 11–12
conversation. *See* disguising conversation
cooptation, of newcomers, 15
creativity, after diversity adjustment processes, 131–132
Cross, Rob, 320
cross-border socialization, 323
cross-functional projects, for newcomers, 321–322
cross-national job transitions, 221
cross-sectional designs. *See* passive observation methods
cultural climate, for diversity, 126–127. *See also* values, of organization
    with expatriates, 240
    at interpersonal level, 127
    managerial strategies for, 132
    positive, 127
    signal indicators for, 126–127
cultural values. *See* values, of organization
curiosity, as personality trait, 149
current-focused individuals, 166
customer co-production of services, 251
    levels of, 251–252
customer role
    citizenship behaviors as part of, 252

customer identity in, 252
    in customer socialization, 251–253
    scripts in, 252
    in service process and, 251
customer satisfaction, 251
customer socialization. *See also* new customers, socialization of
    anticipatory, 253–254
    benefits of, 251
    customer satisfaction from, 251
    product design and, 253
    recruitment requirements for, 253
    role in service process and, 251
    as role-making process, 251–253
    scripts in, 252–253
    service economies as influence on, 250
    servicescape design and, 254
    technology and, 251
    trends in, 250–251

D

deficiency, in construct validity, 190
demographic differences, adjustment to
    diversity and, 124–125
    as situational moderator, 128
    stereotyping and, 124–125
derailment minimization, for senior management, 304
description, in research, 192–193
    contamination issues in, 193
    limitations in, 192–193
    measurement methodology for, 192–193
    self-reports in, 192–193
    taxonomy development for, 192
discrimination, perceived experiences with, 125
disguising conversation, 14
disjunctive socialization tactics, 35
disparity diversity, 116–117
    conflict from, 123
    elaboration processes for, 121–122
    exclusion with, 123
    newcomer proactivity and, 120
    role innovation and, 119–120
    social identification and, 119
    social support for, 122
dispositional adaptability, 148
disruptive behavior, of newcomers, 224
    hierarchical influences on, 224
    idiosyncrasy credits and, 221–222
    through intergroup power shifts, 224
    performance goals and, 224
dissemination, in scientific process, 187
distal outcomes
    for ethical behavior, 105
    for job attitudes, 103
    for job performance, 103–104
    for job turnover, 104
    for newcomers in organizations, 15, 102–105
    for newcomer stress, 105
    for organizational socialization practices, 30

for person-job fit, 104
for PO fit, 104
in socialization over time, 169
diversity. *See also* disparity diversity;
separation diversity; variety
diversity
through disparity, 117, 119
gender, task performance and, 131
through separation, 116, 118
as social construct, 116–117
through variety, 116–119
diversity, adjustment processes with,
115–116, 118–139
citizenship behaviors after, 131
commitment to organization after, 130
creativity after, 131–132
cultural climate as influence on,
126–127, 132
demographic differences influences on,
124–125
extraversion and, 124
group cohesion from, 129–130
group demography and, 128
interdependence as influence on, 126
openness to experience and, 124
perceived discrimination experiences
and, 125
personality variables for, 124
personal moderators for, 124–126
prior experience with diversity, 125
role innovation as result of, 132
routine task performance after,
130–131
self-confidence and, 124
signaling of outsiders, 125–126
similarity-attraction theory and, 130
situational moderators for, 128,
126–128
social acceptance as result of, 128–129
social identification and, 125–126
social isolation as result of, 129
socialization outcomes from, 128–132
stereotyping and, 124–125
team culture within organization,
127–128
trust through, 129
withdrawal from organization after, 130
diversity, socialization and, 117–123.
See also disparity diversity;
elaboration processes, for diversity;
separation diversity; variety diversity
adjustment strategies with, 115–116
African American women and, 120
capability assessment for, by managers,
132–133
collective identity promotion and, by
managers, 133
concealment and, 120–121
conflict from, 122–123
cultural climate as influence on,
126–127, 132
exclusion with, 123
identity formation and, 117–119

individual processes for, 117–121
interpersonal processes for, 121–123
managerial strategies for, 132–134
newcomer proactivity and, 120
problem solving for, by managers,
134
role innovation and, 119–120
social support for, 122, 133
stigma and, 121
unique identity support and, by
managers, 133–134
divestiture socialization tactics, 35
for PO fit, 146
domestic job transitions, 221
dynamic interactionism, 166

E
early events, 164
failure spirals from, 164
initial impression confirmation from,
164
negative feedback as, 164
as self-fulfilling prophecies, 164
specific learning in, 164
success spirals from, 164
effectiveness research, 191
efficacy research, 191
efficiency research, 191
ego networks, 81. *See also* personal
networks
elaboration processes, for diversity,
121–122
CEM model, 121
disparity diversity and, 121–122
information-sharing with, 121
separation diversity and, 121
variety diversity and, 121
embeddedness, self-perceptions of,
217–218. *See also* environmental
embeddedness, of social networks;
relational embeddedness, of
social networks; structural
embeddedness, of social networks
emotions. *See also* affective experiences, of
newcomers
positive framing and, 17
social adjustment influenced by, 17
emotional labor, of insiders, 218
emplotment, 164–165
employee rewards, recognition, and
appreciation (ERRA) report,
299–300
encounter stage, of socialization, 13
learning during, 14
engagement failure, 316
entry-socialization experience, 28
uncertainty reduction theory in, 28
environmental embeddedness, of social
networks, 80–81
ERRA report. *See* employee rewards,
recognition, and appreciation report
ethical behavior, 105
self-perception of insiders and, 218

social learning theory and, 105
event time. *See also* early events
clock time compared to, 162–165
definition of, 162–163
reference points in, 162–163
sequencing for, 163–165
socialization research and, 163
stories and, 164–165
survey methodology for, 163
evidence-based practice, 207
exclusion
with disparity diversity, 123
with diversity, socialization and, 123
with separation diversity, 123
with variety diversity, 123
executive management. *See* senior
management, socialization for
expatriates, socialization of, 343.
See also adjustment, of expatriates;
adjustment, socialization and;
failure, of expatriates; social
categorization
alternative types of, 242–243
from Asia, 243
assignments for, as time-limited, 230
corporate context as influence on, 243
costs of, 231
cultural climate for, 240
definition of, 230
employment of, globalization as
influence on, 230
expanding models of, 241–242
failure of, 231–232
future research for, 241–244
general adjustment for, 233
HCN perspectives on socialization of,
235–236
in host units, 232
as information exchange process,
243–244
information sharing with, by HCNs,
236–240
as inpatriates, 230, 242–243
interaction adjustment for, 233
knowledge transfers from, to HCNs,
241
knowledge transfers to, by HCNs,
234–235
mentoring for, 235
as parent country nationals, 230
proactive behaviors by, towards HCNs,
240
procedural justice and, 238–239
as repatriates, 242–243
social identity theory and,
237–238
socialization of, 230–231
social support for, by HCNs, 236
social tie strength for, 241
strategic management perspectives on,
242
as third country nationals, 230
work adjustment for, 233

internal validity and, 188–189
statistical conclusion validity and, 189
informal socialization tactics, 35
information activities, with onboarding, 269–273. *See also* inform-resources practices
inform-communication practices for, 269–271
inform-training practices for, 272–273
information-seeking, by newcomers. *See also* learning, for newcomers
patterns of change for, over time, 69
as proactive behavior, 12–13, 59–60, 99–100
for self-change, 59–60
in uncertainty reduction theory, 28
information-seeking, by new customers, 255–256
approachability improvement strategies, 256
availability improvement strategies, 256
company strategies for, 256
factors for, 255–256
helpfulness improvement strategies, 256
through media sources, 256
through mentors, 256
social costs of, 255
information sharing, trust and, 72
through adjustments to diversity, 129
elaboration processes for diversity and, 121
facilitation of, by organizations, 239–240
by HCNs, to expatriates, 236–239
with interpersonal disclosures, 129
procedural justice and, 238–239
social categorization as influence on, 238–239
social identity theory for, 237–238
inform-communication practices, 269–271
RJPs in, 271
with socialization agents, 271
inform-resources practices, 271–272
feedback in, 272
information source characteristics and, 272
organizational context for, 272
personality variables for, 271–272
proactivity and, 272
social costs of, 272
inform-training practices, 272–273
orientation programs and, 272–273
inpatriates, 230
socialization of, 242–243
inquiry, learning for newcomers through, 14
social costs, 14
insiders, socialization and. *See also* attitudes of insiders, towards

organization; disruptive behavior, of newcomers; receptivity to change, for insiders; self-perceptions, of insiders
acceptance by, in newcomer adjustment, 100
attributes of, newcomer similarity, 66
dislodging process for, 218
emotional labor of, 218
HCNs as, 236
implementation of newcomer ideas by, 221–222
impression management by, 218
newcomer proactive behaviors and, reaction to, 65–67, 220–222
position power of, 223
quality of newcomer interactions for, 222–223
reciprocal influence loop for, 215
research history for, 216
self-esteem of, 218
socialization as stressor for, 223–224
socialization tactics for, 222–223
instantaneous socialization, 177
institutionalized socialization, 35
of new customers, 254
PO fit and, 146
over time, 170–171
integration. *See* social integration
interaction adjustment, for expatriates, 233
interactional zone, in social networking, 80
interactionist approach, to research, 194–195
interdependence, adjustment to diversity influenced by, 126
internal validity, 188–189
of interventions, 203
for longitudinal design, 197
passive observation methods and, 195
threats to, 189–190
interrupted time series design, 205
RDDs and, 206
interventions, in socialization research, 202–206
academic inertia towards, 207–208
cohort effects in, 203
evaluation of, 207
evidence-based practice and, 207
internal validity of, 203
as manipulation, 203
mentoring programs, 203
open-door policies as, 203
for senior management, 304–305
intimidation, in new customer socialization, 252–253
investiture socialization tactics, 35
PO fit and, 147
involuntary role transitions, 168

irreversible role transitions, 168
Irvine, Diane, 257

J

JD-R Model. *See* Job Demands-Resource Model
job assignments
social networking and, 87–88
in SRT, 50
job attitudes, 103
job change negotiation, 62
job characteristics, 37–39
autonomy and, 38
feedback on, 37–38
MPS and, 38
research study for, 38–39
task significance and, 38
job demands, 46
Job Demands-Resource (JD-R) Model, 46
job demands under, 46
job resources under, 46
outcome prediction in, 46
principles of, 46
job performance
disruptive newcomer behavior and, 224
distal outcomes for, 103–104
organizational socialization's influence on, 4
self-efficacy with, during adjustment stage, 101
for senior management, acceleration of, 304–305
social networking and, 82–83
with structured mentoring, 331
job resources, 46, 49–50
Jobs, Steve, 258
job-seeking period, perceptions of PO fit during, 142–144
job transitions, 221
cross-national, 221
domestic, 221
school-to-work, 221
work-to-work, 221
job turnover
during adjustment stage, 86–87
at Bank of America, 305
distal outcomes for, 104
organizational socialization's influence on, 4
under similarity-attraction theory, 130
social networking and, 86–87

K

knowledge sources. *See also* inquiry, learning for newcomers through
information-seeking by newcomers, as proactive behavior, 12–13
socialization agents as, 40
in SRT, 50
uncertainty reduction theory and, 28
knowledge transfers
through expatriate adjustment, 234–235

knowledge transfers (*Cont.*)
    failure of expatriates through, 232
    by HCNs, to expatriates, 234–235
    to HCNs, from expatriate socialization, 241

L

Lantz, Caryn, 292
leader-member exchanges (LMXs), 40
learning, for newcomers, 14
    as affective experience, 17–18
    as cognitive experience, 17–18
    through disguising conversation, 14
    duration of effects, over time, 172–173
    during encounter stage, 14
    as goal orientation, 166–167
    hangover effect with, 174
    during honeymoon period, 174
    through inquiry, 13–14
    needs of newcomers as influence on, 175
    through network-building, 14
    through proactive behaviors, 14
    through self-monitoring, 14
    sensemaking compared to, 84
    through social networking, 14, 82–83, 88
    sources of, 14
    specific, in early events, 164
    stability *versus* instability and, as influence on, 173–175
    stage models for, 175
    success spirals for, 173
    over time, 172–175
    time lags for, 172–173
    unpredictable role demands and, 174
learning goal orientation, priming of, 166–167
liability of newness, 89
life satisfaction, 107
LMXs. *See* leader-member exchanges
longitudinal design, for research, 197–198
    common method bias reduction with, 197
    internal validity for, 197
    multiple data waves in, 197–198
    temporal elements of, 197, 198
low reliability, in statistical conclusion validity, 190

M

males, newcomer proactive behavior by, 67
managers. *See also* senior management, socialization for
    capability assessment by, 132–133
    collective identity promotion by, 133
    cultural climate influenced by, 132
    problem solving by, 134
    socialization with diversity, strategies for, 132–134
    social networking with, 84

social support strategies by, 133
    unique identity support by, 133–134
marketability, self-perceptions of, 217–218
maturation-by-selection effects, 205
meditational analysis, 196–197
    limitations of, 196–197
mentors. *See also* Menttium Corporation, mentoring practices; Menttor program; role models; structured mentoring
    assignment of, 322
    Circles mentoring program, 326–328, 332
    for expatriates, 235
    in guide activities, for onboarding, 274
    for information-seeking, by new customers, 256
    in intervention programs, 203
    newcomer proactive behaviors and, 66–67
    in organizational socialization practices, 29
    PO fit and, 146
    as socialization agents, 41
    toxic, 223–224
    in Toyota management socialization practices, 311–312
Menttium Corporation, mentoring practices, 331–334
    accelerated job performance and, 331
    for business objectives, 331–332
    with Circles program, 332
    cultural competence for, 325
    in groups, 332
    information retention with, 331–332
    through interviews, 332
    through match criteria, 332
    measurement methodology for, 332–333
    one-to-one, 332
    transitional support with, 331
Menttor program, 325–326
monitoring. *See* self-monitoring
morale, of organization, 279
motivating potential score (MPS), 38
multinational organizations.
    See expatriates; host country nationals

N

narratives, in social identity theory, 12
needs, of newcomers
    socialization influenced by, 175
    threshold effects with, 175
negative feedback
    from early events, 164
    socialization over time and, 179
NEO program. *See* New Employee Orientation program
networking. *See* social networking

newcomers, to organizations.
    See also adjustment, socialization and; disruptive behavior, of newcomers; diversity, adjustment processes with; diversity, socialization and; expatriates, socialization of; implementation of newcomer ideas, insider response to; information-seeking, by newcomers; insiders, socialization and; learning, for newcomers; mentors; organizational socialization practices; person-organization fit; proactive behaviors, of newcomers; receptivity to change, for insiders; role models; self-perceptions, of insiders; socialization resources theory; social networking
acceptance by insiders, 100, 106
access to resources for, through socialization, 80
adjustment facilitation, 12–13
adjustment to work for, 80
affective experiences of, 17–18
anticipatory socialization for, 9, 13, 47
assimilation factors for, 320–322
autonomy for, 38, 38
behind-the-scenes networking for, 321
blogs for, 322
borrowed social capital for, 90
buddy system for, 322
check-in system for, 323
cognitive experiences of, 17–18
cohorts for, 322
comparative appraisal of, 216
cooptation of, socialization as, 15
cross-functional projects or, 321–322
distal outcomes for, 15, 102–105
during encounter stage, 14
encounter stage for, 14
ethical behavior by, 105
goal differences between, 18
honeymoon period for, 17
identity formation for, 118
idiosyncrasy credits for, 224
impression management of, 218
individualization of, 18–19, 322–323
insiders and, attribute similarities to, 66
involvement within socialization process, in literature, 10
job skill learning for, 79
knowledge for, 14
as liability, 89
in meetings, invitations to, 322
needs of, 175
newcomer socialization questionnaire, 102
onboarding literature for, 277

organizational socialization.
See also adjustment, socialization
and; diversity, adjustment
processes with; diversity,
socialization and; expatriates,
socialization of; insiders,
socialization and; newcomers, to
organizations; person-environment
fit theory; person-organization fit;
proactive behaviors, of newcomers;
research on socialization, methods
of; social identity theory;
socialization agents; socialization
tactics; social networking; swift
socialization; time, socialization
over; veterans, in organizations
access to resources through, 80
adjustment to work and, 80
anticipatory, 9, 12, 47, 166
brokers for, 320
central connectors for, 320
as chain, 220–221
Chao et al. scale, 101–102
content scales for, 102
contexts for, 20
as cooptation, 15
cross-border, 323
as cultural adjustment, 318–319
definition of, 3–4
distal outcomes for, 15, 102–105
duration of, 9–10
dynamic interactionism and, 166
dynamics of, 342–343
encounter stage of, 13–14
engagement failure in, 316
of expatriates, 230–231
feedback and, 79–80
honeymoon period in, 16–17
importance of, 4
individualized, 146, 170, 278
by individual organization, 19
of inpatriates, 242–243
instantaneous, 177
institutionalized, 35, 146,
170–171, 254
job performance influenced by, 4
job turnover influenced by, 4
leader stress as influence on, 108
leader well-being as influence on,
108
learning processes for, 14
life satisfaction and, 107
local factors for, 16–17
newcomer knowledge in, 14
from newcomer perspective, 4
newcomer socialization questionnaire,
102
new forms of, 19–20
onboarding compared to, 3, 268
organizational changes and, newcomer
influence on, 105–106
organizational socialization inventory
for, 102

outcomes of, 9–10, 341–342
parameters of, 4
patterns for, 10
perceived overqualification and, 107
peripheral players for, 320
personal failure in, 316
person-job fit and, 104
practice implications for, 345–346
as predictor of success, 319–320
as process, 342–343
proximal outcomes for, 15, 100–101
reciprocal influence loop and, 215
relational aspects of, 319
relationship changes and, 108
relationship failure in, 316
of repatriates, 242–243
role failure in, 315–316
role modeling in, 16
role of networks in, 82–87
sensemaking and, 79
social networking and, 79–80, 87–91
stabilization stage of, 13
as stressor, for insiders, 223–224
success in, parameters for, 15–16
tacit knowledge, for newcomers, 14
theory development for, 52
over time, 161–162, 165–172
timing issues in, 15–16
as two-way process, 215–216
unemployment duration and, 107
work-life conflict and, 106–107
organizational socialization inventory, 102
organizational socialization practices.
See also job characteristics;
orientation programs; socialization
agents; socialization tactics;
training programs
availability and helpfulness of, 29
for critical incidents, 29
daily peer interaction in, 29
definition of, 28–29
distal outcomes for, 30
effectiveness criteria for, 30
to guide, 43
to inform, 43
mentor helpfulness in, 29
proximal outcomes for, 30
within PwC, 43–45
research on, 42–43
supervisor helpfulness in, 29
to welcome, 43
orientation programs, 30–33
for Bank of America, 307
computer-based, 32
design issues with, 33
formats for, 30–31
inform-training practices and, 272–273
for new customer socialization,
254–255
onboarding compared to, 268
onboarding in, 99
in onboarding literature, analysis of,
278

purpose of, 30
research studies on, 31–32
ROPES, 32–33
socialization compared to, 30
outgroup discrimination, 238
overqualification for job. *See* perceived
overqualification

P

parent country nationals, 230
passing, as part of social majority, 121
passive behaviors, by new customers,
255
passive observation methods, 195–197
analysis with, 195–196
internal validity and, 195
meditational analysis and, 196–197
moderator variables in, 197
reverse causality issues with, 196
with SEM techniques, 196
simultaneity issues with, 196
variable distribution in, 195
past-focused individuals, 166
P-E behaviors. *See* person-environment
behaviors
peer coaches, 307
people processing techniques.
See socialization tactics
perceived organizational support (POS),
217
perceived overqualification, 107
during adjustment stage, 107
perceived psychological contract breaches,
222
performance. *See* job performance
performance goal orientation, 166–167
peripheral players, 320
personal failure, 316
personality
adjustment to diversity and, 124
curiosity as trait, 149
dispositional adaptability and, 148
extraversion and, 124
inform-resources practices and,
271–272
newcomer proactive behavior and,
67–68, 99
PO fit and, 145, 147–148
proactive, 148
self-confidence, 124
social integration influenced by, 88–89
personal networks, 81
density of, 81–82
personal planning, in SRT, 50
person-environment (P-E) behaviors, 57
person-environment fit theory
in socialization literature, 11
stress factors in, 11
person-job fit, 104
person-organization (PO) fit, 104
ASA framework for, 141
assessment of, 142–143
causes of misfit, 151–152

treatment diffusion, in construct validity, 190

trust, information sharing and, 72
    through adjustments to diversity, 129
    elaboration processes for diversity and, 121
    facilitation of, by organizations, 239–240
    by HCNs, to expatriates, 236–239
    with interpersonal disclosures, 129
    procedural justice and, 238–239
    social categorization as influence on, 238–239
    social identity theory for, 237–238
turnover. *See* job turnover
2001, A Space Odyssey (Clarke), 20

U

uncertainty reduction theory, 28
    anxiety strategies in, 28
    confidence and, 28
    in entry-socialization experience, 28
    feedback in, 28
    information access in, 28
    social support and, 28
unemployment, duration of, 107
University of Minnesota. *See* onboarding, comprehensive program development for
unpredictable role transitions, 168

V

Vadon, Mark, 257
validity, in research, 188–191
    construct, 189–190, 200
    control issues in, 191
    definition of, 188
    effectiveness research for, 191
    efficacy research for, 191
    efficiency research for, 191
    external, 188–189
    internal, 188–190, 195, 197, 203
    literature review for, 190–191
    optimization of, 190–191
    process understanding in, 191
    research question description for, 191
    by research stage, 190–191
    statistical conclusion, 189–190
    threats to, 189–190
    triangulation design for, 190–191
    types of, 188–189
values, of organization
    conflicts over, 219–220
    insider attitudes toward, 219–221
    onboarding influenced by, 283
    in onboarding literature, 276
    PO fit and, 141, 145
Van Maanen, John, 19
variable socialization tactics, 35
variety diversity, 116–117
    cognitive diversity and, 123
    elaboration processes for, 121

    exclusion with, 123
    newcomer proactivity and, 120
    role innovation and, 119
    social identification and, 118–119
    social support for, 122
veterans, in organizations
    as role models, for newcomers, 16
    as social construct, 16

W

welcome activities, for onboarding, 270, 273
    social interactions in, 273
well-being, of leaders, 108
whole networks, 81
    centrality in, 81
Williams, Doug, 257
Willow Creek Community Church, 260
    servicescape design for, 260
withdrawal, from organizations, 130. *See also* job turnover
    under similarity-attraction theory, 130
work adjustment, for expatriates, 233
work experiences, 163
    high breadth, 163
    high depth, 163
work groups, social networking within, 90
work-life conflict, 106–107
work-to-work transition, 221